Sport and Recreation: An Economic Analysis

Chris Gratton
Manchester Polytechnic
and
Peter Taylor
North Staffordshire Polytechnic

London   New York
E. and F.N. Spon

First published in 1985 by
E. and F.N. Spon Ltd
11 New Fetter Lane, London EC4P 4EE
Distributed in North America by
Venture Publishing, Inc.
1640 Oxford Circle
State College, Pa 16803

Reprinted 1988

Printed in Great Britain by
J.W. Arrowsmith Ltd, Bristol

ISBN 0 419 13140 X

British Library Cataloguing in Publication Data

Gratton, Chris
    Sport and recreation : an economic analysis.
    1. Recreation—Economic aspects
    I. Title   II. Taylor, Peter, 1949–
    338.4'779   GV174

    ISBN 0-419-13140-X

Contents

Preface

The purpose of this book is to apply economic analysis to the field of sport and recreation. It originated when we were faced with teaching this subject in October 1982 and quickly realised there was little or no material to which students could be referred.

Ideally, this book requires an introductory knowledge of economics. However, we are confident that readers without such knowledge will get something out of reading it. So the primary market is students on sport and recreation degrees – including sports science, recreation management and more general leisure studies. We also feel the material is suitable for a second or third year option, or simply as an applied microeconomics topic, on economics degrees. The second market comprises recreation management practitioners and those engaged in recreation management courses. We believe this book provides a core discipline for the training of such managers and coincides happily with the initiatives started by the Yates Report (1984) in the UK.

We gratefully acknowledge the help of a number of diverse people, without whom the production of this book would have suffered. Kath Gannon, Belinda Orme and Henrietta Scott typed innumerable drafts of chapters and tables. Pat Eachus and Hilda Francis also contributed to the typing of later chapters. Our respective Heads of Department, George Zis and John Bridge, made the extra workload much less of a burden than it could have been. Three cohorts of second year students on the Sport and Recreation Studies degree at North Staffordshire Polytechnic have suffered the labour-pains of this book admirably and sharpened our minds to the task. Chris Gratton received help from many people involved in leisure and recreation in the United States and Canada when he was in North America researching this book; Barry Tindall of the National Recreation and Park Association was particularly helpful. Last, but not least, we thank Christine and Alexandra for the domestic support necessary for this effort.

Finally, a word of warning to any other prospective authors in this field. Although we did receive recreation benefits in the writing of this book, from a week in the Lake District struggling over yet another draft, the net effect on our recreation participation and fitness has been very damaging!

Section One

Introduction

_____

1 Sport, recreation and economics

1.1 Introduction

The 1960s and 1970s saw a rapid growth in Britain of participant sport and recreation of all kinds. This growth was paralleled by greater government involvement in the provision of facilities for sport and recreation, in particular the creation of a new type of public recreation facility, the indoor leisure centre. This growth in both public and private expenditure has raised various economic issues within this area, not least questions relating to the role of government in recreation and the cost-effectiveness of public expenditure. However economics offers a comprehensive framework for analysing all aspects of the sport and recreation market and we attempt in this book to develop such a framework. To set the scene for this analysis it is appropriate, in this introductory Chapter, to look at the main trends in the recreation market over the recent past in a little more detail.

Sport in the Community . . . The Next Ten Years (The Sports Council, 1982) outlines the recreation explosion in the UK. Outdoor sports showed a fairly steady rise throughout the 1960s and 1970s, although certain outdoor activities grew at a very rapid rate. This was particularly the case with 'adventure' sports such as water skiing, hang-gliding and more recently windsurfing. In indoor sports, however, increases in participation have been quite dramatic. Evidence from social surveys indicated that participation in indoor sport doubled between 1973 and 1977. Accompanying this increase in the numbers of people participating was an increase in the frequency of participation. One very important factor related to this increase was the rapid increase in the provision of indoor facilities over the same four year period. The number of indoor public swimming pools increased by 70% and the number of indoor sports halls increased by over 300%.

Probably the best indicator of this growth in participation and of the rising interest in sport is the staggering rise in the popularity of marathon running in the late 1970s and early 1980s. Following on the success of the New York mass marathon, the first London marathon was run in March 1981. Eighteen thousand entry applications were received for that first mass marathon in this country although only seven thousand runners were accepted. Within a few years the number of runners in the London marathon had risen to 18 000 with more than four times that number applying to run. Following the first London marathon, similar events were arranged in virtually every major UK city. Within a relatively short time period, an activity that had previously only been the domain of a few dedicated, highly experienced and physically conditioned athletes suddenly became a national mass participation sport.

As trends in participation have exhibited this, sometimes startling, upward rise, other aspects of the recreation market have reflected it. Statistics on expenditure on recreation-related goods show that the recreation boom is a feature of most western industrialized economies. Edwards (1981) analysed all aspects of leisure spending in the European community and found that expenditure related to participant sports had been one of the fastest growing areas of leisure expenditure throughout the EEC. The US News and World Report (1981) estimated total leisure spending in the United States at $244 billion in 1981, up 321% from its 1965 level. Their definition of leisure spending is a wide one, but individual active recreation expenditure is a significant portion of this total. According to their estimates, jogging alone had 36 million participants in 1981 in the US; and they spent $328 million for 13.5 million pairs of jogging shoes. Martin and Mason (1979) looked at broad categories of leisure expenditure in the UK from 1970-77, and compared to a total increase of leisure spending of 3.6% per annum over this period, expenditure on sport and active recreation was increasing by 8.1% per annum.

This explosion of demand in the 1970s shows no sign of abating in the 1980s. In fact, we are likely to see a further expansion of demand, if we are to believe the popular speculation concerning the dawning of a 'leisure age', stimulated hopefully not so much by the mass unemployment of recessions but rather by technological change (for example, microelectronics, biotechnology). There have been widely differing forecasts of the effects of microelectronics on the demand for labour but one probable outcome of the new technology is that there is likely to be an acceleration in the rate at which the average working week declines over time. Working hours are also likely to be much more flexible. The average worker at the end of the 1980s will be faced with more leisure time than he has today and the demand for sport and recreation is particularly dependent on the total amount of leisure time available.

1.2 Leisure, recreation and sport

The title of this book indicates that our interest is in sport and recreation. It would be convenient at this stage to give a neat, short definition of sport and recreation and then move on to apply economic analysis within the boundaries of that definition. Unfortunately, defining subject areas is never quite so easy.

There is general agreement that a leisure activity is something different from work and in particular takes place in non-work time. But even at this basic starting point there are problems. The person that goes jogging every night after work is certainly pursuing a leisure activity in non-work time, but are the athletes in an Olympic final also similarly participating in leisure? Many leisure researchers would argue that it is impossible to have an objective definition of a leisure activity since it depends crucially on the perceptions of the individual participant. The argument is that the same activity can be leisure to one person, and non-leisure to another. In fact, it would be quite possible to write a whole book on the question of the definitions of leisure, recreation and sport; but we do not intend to do that here.

Our interest in this book is sport. If leisure refers to activities that take place in non-work time, then most sport is certainly leisure but all leisure activities are not sport. Some researchers regard recreation as another word for leisure; others understand recreation to be a broad definition of sport. We subscribe to the latter view.

The main question to be answered here is how do we distinguish between active sport and recreation and other, more general, leisure activities. Obviously certain activities fall easily into one category or the other: squash, badminton and marathon running are sport and recreation whereas going to the cinema, visiting a stately home, or going out for a meal are 'pure leisure activities'. It is at the margin that problems arise. Are darts and snooker sports or leisure pursuits? In some ways they are clearly a sport. They receive wide-ranging media coverage in the sports section of newspapers and the sports programmes on radio and television. They are certainly highly competitive. On the other hand, there is clearly no health connection with these activities since no physical exertion is involved. In fact a quick look at world-class darts professionals would indicate a negative health relationship in that overweight, drinking, smoking competitors seem to be the order of the day.

The *European Sport For All Charter* (Council of Europe, 1980) possibly gives a classification of activities that might solve the problem:

A great range and variety of activities is covered by the term sport; they subdivide into four broad categories:
   1. Competitive games and sports which are characterised by the acceptance of

rules and response to opposing challenge.

2. Outdoor pursuits in which participants seek to negotiate some particular 'terrain' (signifying in this context an area of open country, forest, mountain, stretch of water or sky). The challenges derive from the manner of negotiation adopted and are modified by the particular terrain selected and the conditions of wind and weather prevailing.

3. Aesthetic movement which includes activities in the performance of which the individual is not so much looking beyond himself and responding to man-made or natural challenges as looking inward and responding to the sensuous pleasure of patterned bodily movement, for example dance, figure-skating, forms of rhythmic gymnastics and recreational swimming.

4. Conditioning activity, i.e. forms of exercise or movement undertaken less for any immediate sense of kinaesthetic pleasure than from long-term effects the exercise may have in improving or maintaining physical working capacity and rendering subsequently a feeling of general well-being.'

From these general characteristics of sport, Rodgers (1978) developed a case list of activities that would be clearly agreed to be sports. He adds:

'Ideally all the four following elements are present in a sport, and the first two are always present. Any sport involves physical activity, it is practised for a recreational purpose, there is an element of competition and a framework of institutional organisation. Activities which place the muscular and cardiorespiratory system under only slight stress, but which demand precise physical coordination are accepted, for example, shooting. Certain 'mechanical sports' like motor racing may be included on the same principle.'

Normally our analysis is concerned with sport and physical recreation as defined above. However we do not adhere strictly to this definition since leisure activities do not always fit into tight categories and there will always be some activities regarded as sport by some and 'pure leisure activity' by others. In general we try to include such marginal activities in our analysis. Our central interest though is with those activities that possess the particular economic characteristics we now discuss.

1.3 The economic characteristics of sport and recreation

Sport provides both psychic and physical benefits to participants. Psychic benefits arise from the sense of well-being derived from being physically fit and healthy, the mental stimulation and satisfaction obtained from active recreation and the greater status achieved in peer groups. Physical benefits relate directly to the health relationship with active recreation. Exercise is a direct, positive input into the health production function. A person who engages in regular physical exercise is likely to live longer, have higher productivity over his working life, and have greater life satisfaction and improved quality of life than a non-participant, by being physically capable of carrying out more activities. Quality of life experiments have shown a clear relationship between low life satisfaction and lack of recreational opportunity.

Let us look at these benefits in greater detail and attempt to classify them into an economic framework. Active sport and recreation generates several types of benefit for the individual who participates (here we use an appropriate categorization used by Cullis and West (1979) when looking at the benefits of health).

1. The participant is physically in better shape. Demanding sports have a particular beneficial effect on the cardiovascular system. This is a *durable consumption good* since its benefits accrue over several periods but it depreciates without regular participation. The essential point is that there is a time dimension to the utility stream: the activity gives utility in the future as well as in the present.

2. Participation also has aspects of a *non-durable consumption good* since the non-health utility aspects only relate to the time of consumption. Thus the aesthetic appreciation and enjoyment of gymnastics or ice-skating, and the tension and excitement of competitive team sports are forms of enjoyment, and hence utility, that are specifically generated only at the time of the activity. This non-durable benefit is likely to be the sole basis of the decision to participate in the very young; and even older participants, although aware of the other benefits to be derived, still hold the immediate benefit as crucial. Not all active sports generate this immediate enjoyment though, for example, jogging on a cold, wet night . . .

3. A third benefit is similar to the first since it relates directly to the health benefits of exercise, but is a different type of benefit. In periods following increased exercise and hence higher health status there is a benefit in the form of a *capital good* being one that yields a return as part of a *market production process*. This capital good aspect can be quantified, being a monetary 'pay-off' measured by increased production (and hence income) consequent on improved health status of the individual concerned.

Thus a fitter, healthier, person compared with one with a lower health status may have less time off work through illness, may have greater productivity while at work, and therefore supposedly would receive higher earnings as a result. Whether or not this occurs is an empirical matter and the importance of this investment benefit from active recreation is essentially a matter of measurement since days off sick, productivity, and earnings, are all easily measurable and can be related to people's levels of active recreation participation.

To regard benefits of recreation in this way is not a new concept. It is purely an extension of Becker's human capital theory (1964). In the same way that machines can be of different qualities, so can people. A person can 'invest' in himself in order to increase his productivity. The obvious way to do this is through education and it is in this area that human capital theory has been exploited. However, health status is also an investment in these terms and since exercise contributes to health status, it becomes an investment good.

There is another aspect to pecuniary investment, that is investment that yields a rate of return in the market, that does not relate to the health connection referred to above. This is the investment of time and effort in training that increases skill and performance to the point that a pecuniary return results from the sporting activity itself. The obvious examples of this are the elite sportsmen and sportswomen who earn their living through participation in sport. This is the classic case of human capital theory. The individual invests time and effort in himself in order to become a capital good in the production process of producing a saleable market good. For example, the professional footballer is an integral part of the production process of producing a football match. Although his returns depend to a large extent on his innate ability, the harder he trains and acquires new skills then the greater his reward. The increased reward is the return to his investment.

4. Finally there is another capital good benefit. The investment benefit in Point 3, above, looks at the return measured as part of the market production process. However, Becker (1965) has shown that we can regard consumers as producers combining their time with market purchased inputs to produce 'consumption activities', essentially activities carried on for their own sake in non-work time. Examples include going to the cinema, taking the family out for a picnic, or preparing a meal for a dinner party with friends. In Becker's view, both non-work time and the goods purchased on the market should be regarded as necessary inputs for the activities.

If, through participating in active sport and recreation, itself a 'consumption activity' in Becker's terms, the participants become more active in other consumption activities, either because they feel more healthy or because they generally tend to develop a more 'active' disposition, then the sport and recreation activities are a *capital good* that yields a return in the *non-market production* process.

Different sports will confer a different mix of benefits on participants. This mix of benefits is also likely to change with age and with experience in the activity. At one extreme, darts is likely to generate non-durable benefits, but not much, if any, durable health benefits – in fact, negative health benefits are likely if the pot-bellied, beer-swilling image of the average darts player is to be believed. At the other extreme, jogging is not always an activity from which one derives immediate pleasure yet the durable health benefits are well-known. Young participants are likely to be unaware of durable health benefits or non-pecuniary and pecuniary investment aspects: they are more interested in pure pleasure. As they grow older, however, it is likely that awareness of the other three types of benefits increase with a possible change in participation to take advantage of them.

Some of the benefits mentioned in the classification above relate directly to the connection between participation in sport and recreation and health. Fentem and Bassey (1978, 81) have indicated that there are numerous physical and psychological benefits that follow from increased exercise. The benefits are wide-ranging, and they indicated that exercise was particularly beneficial to the elderly and the chronically sick. On the other side of the coin we have health disbenefits from sport and recreation. Sports injuries, and deaths from dangerous sports such as mountaineering and hang gliding, are negative health aspects associated with sport. We really need some quantitative research into the relative size of these positive and negative aspects of the exercise-health connection.

To sum up, what we have described in this section is a series of benefits that accrue from sport and recreation. This means that the participation decision may be more complicated than the consumption decision for other commodities.

The private demand curve of an individual is not a simple affair. The question is not simply: is the satisfaction I will get from taking part greater than the price I have to pay? Other factors complicate the issue. Some part of the satisfaction does not accrue immediately. The decision to participate depends to some extent on how we value today satisfaction that will be obtained in the future, i.e. the consumers time discount rate. Also a person may participate now even though there is no present or future satisfaction from the activity itself. He participates purely as an investment that will yield a return. His decision depends again on his discount rate, but also on the time paths of future returns. In general, for any one individual, participation will give aspects of all four benefits discussed above, but the relative weight of each category of benefits is likely to vary substantially from one individual to another.

All the above assumes that it is only the private demand of the individual that we need to consider. However, sport and recreation is a commodity that has associated with it characteristics that suggest there will be a social demand over and above the private demand.

1.4 Market failure in sport and recreation

One important feature of sport and recreation in many countries is the extent to which governments are involved in subsidizing and encouraging recreation participation. This would suggest that the market mechanism is somehow inadequate in allocating resources to the recreation market. There are several reasons that have been suggested for market failure in sport and recreation.

1.4.1 Externalities

There are at least three external benefits associated with recreation participation. There is an externality element to some of the health benefits discussed earlier. Bassey and Fentem's evidence suggests that the main beneficiaries from participation would be those more dependent on health care services. Such services, provided in the main by the government in the UK, are therefore released from dealing with preventable health problems, and are more able to concentrate on inevitable health problems, to the extent that the sport and recreation prevents the former. Although we generally assume that sport participation will have a positive effect on health we must not forget that sports injuries increase as participation increases, therefore increasing the pressure on health services. The general view is that there is still a net benefit to health status as a result of exercise, despite the fact that there has been little research on the participation-injury relationship.

If exercise contributes to health, and a healthier workforce means an increase in productivity and less days lost in industry due to illness, some of this benefit accrues to the employing firm and the nation as a whole, and is therefore external. The external benefits of relieving stress and boredom by participation in physical activity have perhaps been best demonstrated by industrial psychology studies. The result of exercise facilities in some Japanese factories has been to improve the productivity of the workforce and the stability of their individual and collective temperament. There is evidence that American companies are rapidly becoming aware of the benefits of providing exercise facilities for the workforce in worktime. Thus this health externality may be a benefit that is external to the worker but internal to the firm.

A second type of externality is based on the argument that participation in sport and recreation will 'improve life for many who would otherwise be attracted to delinquency and vandalism' (Department of the Environment, 1977). 'Hard' evidence in support of this argument is difficult to come by but patchy evidence that it does exist suggests that the scope for this external benefit could be very large. A quote from the *Guardian* (July 1982) over a Youth Opportunities Programme project in dance at the Crawford Arts Centre in Liverpool, illustrates the possible benefits in motivating the largely disillusioned, unemployed trainees who had joined the scheme:–

'Clearly the discipline inherent in such a dance training must be highly regarded, while the demanding physical training requirements ensure that all change physically for the better. Apparently the trainees also begin to take a greater interest in their appearance and self-esteem rises too. But perhaps the most significant factor to emerge is that for many, the dance programme is obviously one of the few educational experiences which has made any impact on them. It seems that active involvement in this art form, both as participant and observer, has given these people degrees of knowledge and understanding which is meaningful to them.'

A third type of externality occurs when people have an 'option demand' for facilities they are not certain to use. In a free market the owner of sports facilities does not get any payment for the option benefit to the consumer. On a purely commercial basis the sports facility could close due to a lack of demand when in fact it is providing benefits that are not paid for.

It is possible to internalize this externality by selling options, club membership, where the consumer buys the right to use the facility in the future. Greenley, Walsh and Young (1981) have attempted to empirically measure, amongst other things, the 'option value of assured choice of recreation use in the future' of water resources under threat of pollution, and they found the size of this externality to be quite significant.

These three groups of externalities together are important enough to indicate that market allocation will underprovide resources to sport and recreation. There is however another externality argument that is different enough from the others to require special treatment.

1.4.2 Sport and recreation as a merit good

Mishan (1982) argues that the term merit good has been used rather loosely by economists to 'indicate a good that is socially desirable independently of the valuation placed on it by beneficiaries'. Mishan prefers to look at the concept of a merit good as an externality, one arising from the dependence of a person's welfare on the particular sorts of goods consumed by others. It is different from option value in that the increase in the person's welfare has nothing at all to do with his own consumption either now, or possibly at some future date.

Thus market intervention on grounds of merit goods are based on the value judgement that consumers are not the best judges of their own welfare. The basis of government interference for merit good reasons is usually perference distortion due to consumer ignorance or irrationality. The Health Education Council's *Look After Yourself* campaign is an example of an attempt to overcome such consumer failings. Inherent in the merit good concept is a belief that social welfare may be maximized by overriding, in certain circumstances, the individual's view of the merits of a particular good. Private preferences are viewed as 'distorted' as compared with some socially determined norm. However government interference on these grounds is controversial. It is deemed by some to be paternalistic and offends the idea of the all powerful consumer free to allocate money where he likes.

1.4.3 Public goods

The third type of market failure in the area of sport and recreation is that of public goods. When external benefits become so large that consumers cannot be excluded from obtaining the benefits, then a public good results. This is another market failure in the sense that once one person consumes the product, many others derive the same benefits. The commodity is not only non-excludable in this way but also non-rival in consumption: one person's consumption does not prevent another from consuming the product. In such circumstances the 'free' market will underprovide the commodity, because demand will be characterized by the 'free-rider' problem, that is the consumer who waits until someone else pays for the good, and then reaps the utility benefits.

Many goods in sport and recreation have aspects of public goods, but are neither purely private nor public. National, countryside and urban parks are all facilities which are non-rival, until congestion becomes a problem and difficult or expensive to exclude non-payers from. The facilities of large lakes and the sea for water sports have similar characteristics.

One aspect of sport is close to a pure public good, international sporting success. A quote from the 1975 White Paper *Sport and Recreation* indicates the point:

'Success in international sport has great value for the community not only in terms of raising morale but also by inspiring young people to take an active part in sport.'

We have seen many examples of the importance of this effect. England's 1966 World Cup success created a sense of national pride rarely seen since. Many commentators attribute Harold Wilson's electoral success in the autumn following the World Cup more to England's football success than any political factors. A similar sense of national pride followed from the Olympic success of Sebastian Coe, Steve Ovett, Alan Wells and Daley Thompson in 1980. Later Jayne Torvill and Christopher Dean generated a similar effect through their success in ice-dancing in the early 1980s.

These three categories of market failure are the major reasons why the private benefits of recreation participation outlined in Section 1.3 above are not a true reflection of society's benefit from consumption of this 'good'. The appropriate type of government intervention to correct for this market failure is obviously an important issue in recreation economics, which we discuss in Chapter 10.

1.5 The role of the economist

Stewart (1979) in his discussion of the job of the applied economist comments that:

'. . . most economists would agree that it is not their job to choose economic goals, nor to take the action by which these goals are to be attained. These things are up to politicians, managers, consumers and all other actors on the economic scene. What the economist does instead is to give *advice*: advice on the economic consequences of aiming for one goal rather than another, or on the alternative means of reaching a given goal.

The adviser is a specialist, in that he accumulates the knowledge, skill, and experience that are most relevant to the kind of advice he is called upon to give. In calling for advice, we do so in the expectation that the expert adviser will be able to save us time and effort in problem-solving, and this will more than outweigh the payment we have to make to him for his services.'

The basis of the economist's specialist knowledge and skill is economic theory. In this book we use the 'tool-kit' of microeconomic theory to analyse the sport and recreation market. Economics is concerned with resource allocation and the essential question to be answered is what quantity and quality of resources should be devoted to sport and recreation, and how are these resources allocated within the recreation market. This requires an understanding of the demand-side and supply-side influences on the recreation market.

In Section 2, we look at the factors that determine the demand for sport and recreation. Chapter 2 analyses the prior question of the demand for leisure time. There is a large literature in economics on different aspects of the work-leisure choice. We attempt to select from this literature those areas with the most specific relevance to active recreation.

When we look at the demand for activities themselves we follow the structure of approach suggested by Vickerman (1975a). He perceives a hierarchy of demand, with the basic demand for a recreation activity sitting at the top. The first stage is the construction of a demand model for sport and recreation activities. Various approaches to this are discussed in Chapter 3. The main factors accounting for variation in demand for any activity have already been identified from social surveys carried out in the 1960s and 1970s. A person is more likely to participate the higher his income, his socioeconomic group and educational achievement; males are much more likely to participate than females; and participation is inversely related to age. This information though is only a starting point in the search for an appropriate demand model for recreational activities.

In the hierarchy of demand the participation decision is the parent demand function. From this are derived demands for equipment, facilities, and travel. These derived demands are considered in Chapter 4. Although there are similarities in the factors that determine each derived demand, there are also important differences, and in one case in particular, demand for facilities, there is a serious question as to whether we can genuinely consider it as a derived demand.

The fourth part of the demand section considers the issue of demand forecasting. Adequate planning for leisure and recreation requires accurate forecasting. There is no shortage of choice of techniques, and the alternatives are reviewed in Chapter 5. There is a problem though in that no technique has proved its accuracy within the short time-period that leisure forecasting has been practised.

Section 3 looks at the supply-side of the market. The 'production' side of the sport and recreation market is a complicated mixture of the public and private sectors. In fact we can identify three categories of recreation provider: the public sector, the private/voluntary (not-for-profit) sector, and the commercial (for-profit) sector. Each has different objectives and different means of satisfying them. In Chapter 6, we try to identify these objectives and indicate the structure of supply of sport and recreation in the UK.

Chapter 7 analyses the economic theory of supply. The starting point in the conventional theory of the firm but we have to develop this to examine the divergences in organization and behaviour of sports provision from the accepted theoretical paradigm. Clearly the behaviour of suppliers will depend on their objectives, but whatever the objectives, fulfilment of them depends crucially on the relationship of cost to output, and Chapter 7 is mainly concerned with establishing this relationship. However, prior to this, the chapter discusses the fundamental problem of how to define output in recreation supply.

Chapter 8 moves on to the related issue of pricing and marketing recreation resources. Again different objectives are reflected in differing pricing criteria adopted, and although we consider conventional pricing behaviour (e.g. cost plus pricing), and ideals suggested by economic theory (e.g. marginal-cost pricing), it is necessary to explore the rationality of other prices found in practice.

The final section of the book, Section 4, deals with contemporary issues in the economics of sport and recreation. We focus on three specific areas, the role of government (Chapter 10), sports sponsorship (Chapter 11) and professional team sports (Chapter 12). These issues are chosen since at the time of writing there is considerable debate in the sporting press in all three areas. The debate is not normally structured along economic lines, and these three chapters concentrate on the economist's perspective. Emphasis is placed on using the analysis of earlier chapters to suggest appropriate policy solutions in these three areas.

The aim throughout the book is to develop a comprehensive economic framework for the study of sport and recreation. We use the tools that have already been applied to health, education, housing and other areas of applied economics. Because we are attempting to establish a framework, the basis of every chapter is theoretical. The theory gives us a set of testable hypotheses. In many cases we provide evidence that gives some support to these hypotheses. Where possible this evidence comes from the UK. However in many cases appropriate UK data does not exist and we have drawn on North American data to fill these gaps. The power of economics lies in its ability to yield testable hypotheses and through empirical verification gain a greater understanding of the process of economic decision-making. We hope that the methodology we have employed in this book helps sport and recreation researchers to more fully understand decisions of consumers and suppliers in the sport and recreation market.

SECTION TWO

Demand

2   The demand for leisure time

2.1 Introduction

Many researchers have indicated that we are moving slowly but surely into a leisure age. Despite some contrasting evidence, the amount of time we spend at work is generally falling, and the mirror image of this picture is increasing leisure time. In this chapter we examine such evidence and analyse the factors that are causing and constraining this change in the allocation of time. Does it reflect the claims of workers who demand more leisure time? Alternatively, is it enforced leisure because of reduced demand for labour brought about, for example, by technological development such as microelectronics? Consequently is the non-work time actually 'leisure' or is it 'unemployment' in the worst social sense? Economic analysis has a long tradition of looking at the former questions, whilst sociological work has devoted some attention to the latter, particularly in view of the rising unemployment of the 1970s and early 1980s.

2.2. The income/leisure trade-off

To the extent that the increasing leisure time available reflects greater demand for it, the economic analysis of income/leisure choices is relevant. In the analysis at its simplest, an individual derives utility from the income gained at work and from leisure, but is constrained in the achievement of ever higher utility by the rate of pay per hour (or year) and by the finite amount of time available. The analysis shown in Fig. 2.1 represents a daily choice of income and leisure.

The position of the indifference curves reflects the preference pattern of the individual, each one representing a single level of utility

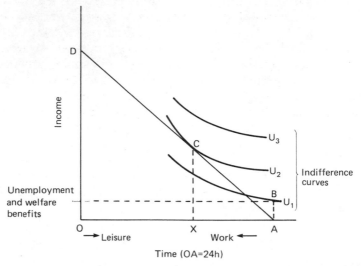

Fig. 2.1 The income/leisure trade-off.

(satisfaction) derived from alternative combinations of income and leisure. Indifference curves further from the origin represent higher levels of utility. if no work is done, unemployment or other welfare benefits will be received. Such income is represented by AB. Any work moves the person to the budget or income constraint, AD which has a slope equal to the wage rate, since

$$\text{the slope of AD} = \frac{\text{CX}}{\text{AX}} = \frac{\text{daily earned income}}{\text{number of hours worked in the day}}$$

$$= \text{hourly wage rate}$$

How will a rational individual behave in this situation? If he or she is intent on maximizing utility, which we normally assume of consumers, then position C is the optimum since, given the budget constraint, U_2 is the highest utility attainable, at C. This gives CX earned income per day from AX hours of work, and also gives the consumer OX hours of leisure. Any other feasible choice, e.g. no work at B, gives lower utility – U_1 in the case of point B. At the optimum consumer choice between income and leisure the formal condition for utility maximization is that the slope of the indifference curve is equal to the slope of the budget constraint. The former is the marginal rate of subjective substitution (MRSS) between, in this case, income and leisure; the latter is the wage rate. Thus the optimum is where the MRSS equals the wage rate.

Any change in this choice is occasioned by either a change in the tastes of the individual or by a change in the budget constraint. Taking an increase in the hourly wage rate, for example, in Fig. 2.2, the budget constraint moves from AD to AG. A rise in the wage rate triggers off two effects:

1. It increases the price of leisure, which is the income foregone. This causes a rational individual to switch his or her choice to consuming more work and less leisure because the opportunity cost of leisure is more expensive. This is known as the substitution effect.
2. It increases the real income to such an extent that more income and leisure time can be achieved, if desired. Which of these is actually increased depends on the preference pattern of the individual, who may choose to exploit all the potential advantage in the form of increased income, but who more typically is likely to exploit some of the potential advantage in the form of increased leisure. This effect is known as the income effect.

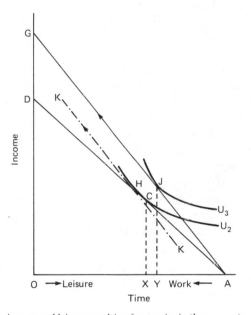

Fig. 2.2 *The change in income and leisure resulting from a rise in the wage rate.*

So the substitution effect means that a change in the relative prices causes a switch away from the more expensive commodity (in this case leisure), towards the relatively cheaper commodity (work and income). The income effect means that the individual's real income changes, which can affect consumption of both commodities. If leisure is a normal good then a rise in real income, caused by a higher wage rate, will lead to a rise in demand for leisure.

Formally the substitution and income effects are shown in Fig. 2.2 by employing an artificial budget constraint KK. This is drawn parallel to the new constraint and thus reflects the new wage rate, but is at the old utility maximum U_2. By doing this the income effect is eliminated, leaving a pure substitution effect from C to H. Restoring the actual new budget constraint gives the income effect from H to J, which does in fact show leisure to be a normal good, since the increase in income from KK to G causes leisure consumption to rise. In Fig. 2.2 the income effect outweighs the substitution effect so that the net result of the rise in the wage rate is an increase in leisure and a fall in work time – a move from X to Y in the allocation of time.

This analysis is possible only with the support of some important assumptions about consumer behaviour. Before examining leisure time indicators it is worth critically reviewing these assumptions, which affect the way we interpret the evidence and also lead on to other analysis later in the chapter:

1. The consumer is rational and interested in maximizing utility. If this is not the case, then sub-optimal choices will result. We take up this point in Section 2.4.
2. The allocation of time is an individual decision. It is more likely that such decisions are household ones; this modification is developed in Sections 2.4 and 2.5.
3. Time is divided into paid work and leisure. More realistically, time is spent in a variety of ways, some of which are neither paid work nor leisure, e.g. housework, eating, travelling. Section 2.5 also caters for this sophistication.
4. Work generates disutility, for which compensation is necessary in the form of income. This simplistic assumption ignores the utility that work generates aside from income. It also ignores other rewards for work, e.g. regularity of employment, probability of success, responsibility and skill acquisition.
5. Allocation of time is a continuous choice. Despite the flexibility afforded by part-time work and overtime, most workers are faced with a choice of a 40 hour week, or nothing. This is a discrete choice, rather than a continuous one.
6. The process of change can be taken for granted. The analysis gives no insight into the adjustment processes that individuals or households go through to reach a new optimum. Such changes may be very slow and will themselves be constrained by adjustment costs.

2.3 Leisure time demand indicators

Whether leisure time increases or decreases as wage rates rise is an empirical question. Some indicators show increasing leisure time, but others do not. The picture is confused further by complications in the interpretation of the data. In support of a dominant income effect, we present evidence of declining male and female hours of work, falling male labour force activity and increasing holiday entitlements, all against a background of rising real wage rates. This evidence is shown in Figs. 2.3 and 2.4 and Table 2.1.

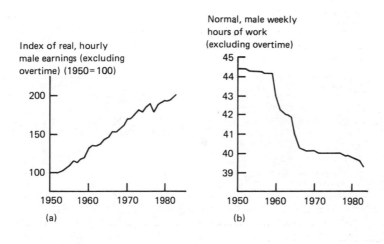

Fig. 2.3 Changes in male manual earnings, hours of work and labour force activity, 1950-83, UK: (a) earnings, manufacturing industry; (b) hours of work, manufacturing; (c) activity rate. From: British Labour Statistics 1886-1968; Department of Employment Gazette; Social Trends.

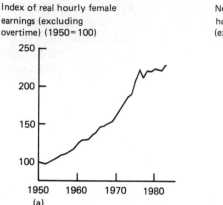
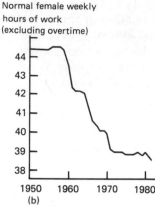

Fig. 2.4 *Changes in female manual earnings and hours of work, 1950-83, UK manufacturing industry: (a) earnings; (b) hours of work. From: British Labour Statistics 1886-1968; New Earnings Survey.*

Table 2.1. *Basic holiday entitlements, Britain, 1951-83.*

	Percentage of workers having basic holiday (weeks) of:–								
	1	1-2	2	2-3	3	3-4	4	4-5	Over 5
1951	28.0	3.0	66.0	2.0	–	1.0	–	–	–
1960	–	–	97.0	1.0	–	2.0	⇁	–	–
1971	–	–	28.0	5.0	63.0	4.0	–	–	–
1980	–	–	–	–	2.0	24.0	19.0	55.0	–
1983	–	–	–	–	–	5.0	17.0	60.0	18.0

From: British Labour Statistics, *Department of Employment Gazette.*

However, some words of warning are needed, since superficial interpretations of such data are not enough. Much of the decrease in the male activity rate has been due to the increase in demand for further and higher education and to earlier retirement. Whereas early retirement in some circumstances is a leisure choice, education is not. The labour force activity of 'prime' age males is as high as it was 30 years ago. Holiday entitlement is not an individual choice, but still involves a trade-off in collective bargaining. It may also partly derive from employers' attempts to diversify their wage costs, for example to avoid the constraint imposed by incomes policies on their powers to reward workers. More recently the increase in holiday entitlement may be stimulated by employers because financially it may make sense in a period of recession to close down a plant completely for longer periods, rather than attempting to operate in a three or four day week.

Some evidence in direct contradiction with the dominant income effect, and its associated growth of leisure time, is represented in Figs. 2.5 and 2.6; i.e. the proportion of male manual workers who work overtime and female labour force activity. Both of these show long run increases as real pay rates have risen.

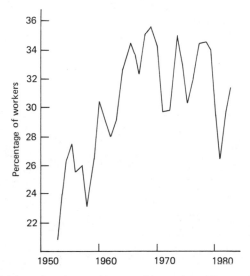

Fig. 2.5 Proportions of manual workers working overtime, 1953-83, UK manufacturing industry. From: British Labour Statistics, 1886-1968; Department of Employment Gazette.

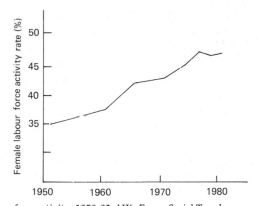

Fig. 2.6 Female labour force activity, 1950-83, UK. From: Social Trends.

Again, the immediate conclusions drawn from such evidence must be tempered by other considerations. The very existence of overtime premia and opportunities is bound to cause a dominant substitution effect, with its longer working hours and reduced leisure time. It is enticed by a premium rate of pay that only applies to overtime hours. In other words, as Fig. 2.7 demonstrates, the overtime premium, CG, allows only one choice for change i.e. to work more. Some workers will always have preferences such that a move to a new optimum is rational as at point J in Fig. 2.7a. Other workers can only choose to stay at the old optimum point C, as in Fig. 2.7b. Hence the net effect is always to decrease aggregate hours of leisure.

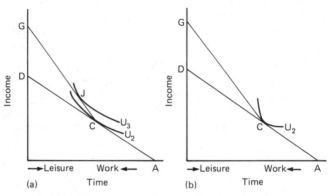

Fig. 2.7 *The effects of overtime premia on income/leisure choices.*

That this one-way 'choice' is presented to the worker by the employer demonstrates that overtime is partly the result of employer choice. Overtime may be an official or unofficial part of some job specifications and analyses of the fixed costs of employment have pointed to the rationality of employers using more overtime. Fishwick (1979) suggested that these fixed costs, including paid annual and public holidays and employers' social security contributions, were 26% of total wage payments in 1975 but had risen to over 30% by 1979, due to increased National Insurance contributions and the growth of pension schemes and welfare arrangements. The evidence of rising holiday entitlement also contributes to the argument that the fixed costs of labour are rising, and thus it is more profitable to make existing workers work more hours, rather than taking on more workers.

Married women's increasing labour force activity is not a simple substitution for 'leisure time'. In order to fully understand it we need to sophisticate the notion of leisure time, at least into 'housework' and more 'pure leisure activities'. Because of technological, time-saving developments in housework, and also because of relaxed social attitudes to women and work, the substitution that has occurred is mainly one of market work for housework (which includes child-rearing). Whereas the labour force activity of women has risen, so has participation by women in leisure activities like sport, as shown in Table 2.2.

There are other anti-leisure choices for which less reliable data is available, including overtime by non-manual workers and second or multiple job-holding, called 'moonlighting'. Alden (1978) suggests that moonlighting in Great Britain lies between 3% and 8% of the labour force, depending on the data used. In the USA the Department of Commerce (1980) reports it to be around 5% of labour force since the mid 1960s. The main problem with such data is that moonlighting is likely to be informal, part of the 'black economy' and so official records are probably underestimates.

Overtime and moonlighting choices may reflect preference maps for the individuals concerned that treat leisure time as something of a disutility – presumably because it is boring and unproductive. However, the hypothesis underlying the approach of Scitovsky (1976) would suggest that such individuals have far from perfect information – they are largely ignorant, in fact, of the potential for stimulus and enjoyment to be found in leisure activities. It is this challenge to the rationality of leisure–averse choices, that we turn to in the next section.

Finally, evidence on overall changes in leisure time is provided by time budget studies (see, for example, BBC 1965, 1978 and Szalai 1972), which investigate the daily use of time by a sample of the population. Gershuny and Thomas (1980) summarize such work in the UK and USA and Table 2.2 presents some of the findings.

Table 2.2. *Per cent change in daily time allocation: (a) 1961-74/5, UK and (b) 1965-75, USA.*
(a) UK

	All persons	Male	Female	Age (years) 25-44	45-64
Paid work	−6.4	−12.1	+ 6.4	− 3.4	− 7.4
Unpaid work	−12.1	− 3.5	−14.0	−16.3	− 8.9
Sport	+39.7	+27.9	+57.0	+42.7	+42.9
All leisure*	+13.7	+14.5	+67.0	+17.7	+11.5

(b) USA

	All persons	Male	Female
Paid work	−4.4	−11.3	+ 3.1
Unpaid work	−16.9	+ 8.0	−17.8
Other leisure†	+ 1.0	+14.4	− 7.1
All leisure*	+10.6	+13.5	+ 8.5

* 'All leisure' excludes paid and unpaid work, personal care and sleeping.
† 'Other leisure' includes sport, eating and drinking 'out',
civic activities, reading and hobbies at home.
Adapted from Gershuny and Thomas, (1980)

It is clear that during the late 1960s and early 1970s, British and American women reduced their unpaid work time in order to increase both paid work time and leisure time. Men, on the other hand reduced paid work time and expanded leisure time, whilst their unpaid work time rose in the USA and fell in the UK.

2.4 The use of leisure time and consumption skills

The title of Scitovsky's book *The Joyless Economy* reflects a misdirection he feels that USA consumers have taken because of their own ignorance, together with a lack of government incentive to overcome such ignorance. The misdirection concerns the materialistic aspirations which form the cliched image of middle-class America. Individuals need comfort and pleasure, and Scitovsky draws on psychological evidence to demonstrate that optimum arousal contributes to such feelings. This optimum can be achieved by want satisfaction, which reduces arousal from too high a level, for example, discomfort from hunger. It can also be achieved by stimulation, which increases arousal from too low a level, for example, boredom. In the USA, materialistic aspirations have, for many people, exhausted the arousal from want satisfaction, or at least run into heavily diminishing returns (each additional acquisition adding proportionately less utility). The other source of arousal, stimulation, has been underexploited – hence the overall picture of an affluent but bored, joyless society. (Chapter 3 examines further the effects of stimulation on demand for sporting activities.)

The salvation for such a society lies in acquiring the consumption skills necessary to enjoy leisure time. Otherwise leisure is boring and society remains leisure-averse, causing such phenomena as institutional overtime and moonlighting. One major problem is that just as with production skills, consumption skills take time and a good deal of learning and experience to acquire. Only after such skills have been learnt can sophisticated leisure pursuits be exploited for the stimulation and pleasure they are capable of providing. Without such skills these sophisticated pursuits are too stimulating and hence do not afford much pleasure.

It is possible to provide examples of Scitovsky's hypothesis in the field of sport. If, for instance, a person goes on to a squash court, or even a football field for the first time, in the company of relatively expert participants, the experience is unlikely to be pleasurable. It is too new, perhaps frightening or bewildering; the stimulation is too great. There would be little incentive to continue in the sport without careful guidance. It is possible, however, to derive a certain amount of stimulation from sports of a lower skill level such as walking and jogging, but these do not have the potential stimulation that higher skill sports have. Even swimming, one of the most popular, widespread sporting activities in the UK, has a skill threshold to overcome before the stimulation is reduced to manageable proportions and it becomes pleasurable.

Given the consumption skill requirements necessary for effective use of leisure time, education has an important role to play in imparting such skills to as wide a range of consumers as possible. However, Scitovsky claims that in the USA the education system has exacerbated the problem of the bored society, not eased it. This is because it has concentrated largely on material production skills, not consumption skills. Education for leisure has a very minor role to play. This bias in education derives from economic necessity but it is outdated in a society that has significantly reduced want from many parts of the population. The value of consumption skills to individuals and to society as a whole is more difficult to estimate and less obvious than the value of production skills, but that does not mean that this value is negligible, as the later section on unemployment demonstrates. Scitovsky (1981) points out the dangers to society from not channelling the desire for excitement into acceptable areas like sport. He produces statistics to show that in the face of less stimulation from insecurity at work, in the post-war period, so other forms of self induced danger increased, for example, gambling, crime and violence. Participation in competitive and dangerous sports has also risen, but clearly the potential for diverting demand for excitement into harmless, yet fulfilling activities has not been fully realized.

With respect to the main theme of this chapter, therefore, the demand for leisure time is constrained by consumer ignorance of the skills necessary to fully enjoy it, according to the hypothesis of Scitovsky. The main recommendation resulting from this analysis is that more resources should be devoted to education for leisure, thus channelling man's natural desire for excitement into acceptable and less costly outlets.

2.5 Household production functions and the importance of time allocation

Individuals making decisions about the allocation of their time are not faced with a simple choice between work and leisure. Time can be more realistically split into a spectrum of allocations ranging from pure market work, through on-the-job leisure, paid holidays, time travelling to and from work, necessary allocations to eating, sleeping and housework, to more or less pure active and passive leisure pursuits, for example, sport, watching television. Becker's approach to this complication (1965) is to use a household production function, which demonstrates that any activity (Q) by an individual or household, even a pure leisure activity, involves inputs of market goods (M) and time (T), as in the following equation:

$$Q = f(M, T)$$

Becker terms these activities 'composite commodities'. Each composite commodity involves different inputs of market goods and time, so that when the price of time or market goods alters, the effect on consumption of different activities will be varied.

In the long run, as real wage rates increase, the price of time rises relative to the price of market goods. Time is a finite input to household production, whereas market goods can be continually expanded. The change in relative prices causes consumption patterns to alter. Once again substitution and income effects operate to give a change in the optimum consumption pattern. In Fig. 2.8 a rising wage rate and the consequent change in the relative prices of time and goods causes the budget constraint to move from AB to CD.

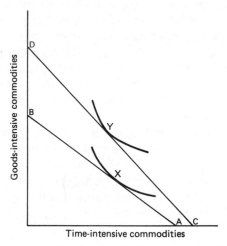

Fig. 2.8 *Wage changes and consumption of goods-intensive and time-intensive commodities.*

The new solution, Y, involves household production and consumption of a different package of time-intensive and goods-intensive commodities. In this example the substitution effect dominates, since the end result is falling consumption of time-intensive commodities. In practice the household and individual face not just the two-dimensional choice represented in Fig. 2.8, but a multi-dimensional choice between composite commodities of varying degrees of time-intensity and goods-intensity. Where the individual ends up on the new budget constraint depends on the relative strengths of the substitution and income effects, as in the conventional analysis.

The sophistication of this approach is to show that the demand for leisure time is, in fact, composed of many demands for different types of commodities with differing degrees of time-intensity and goods-intensity. As time becomes relatively scarcer and more expensive, household production and consumption of goods-intensive activities will increase relative to more time-intensive activities. It is still possible for consumption of time-intensive activities to rise, however, since the conventional income effect may ensure that it does. However the dominant pressure is for goods-intensive activities to increase, i.e. the substitution effect. This can be seen in the increasing goods inputs and reduced time input in many so-called 'leisure' activities which may be seen as inferior, for example, cooking, shopping, washing and cleaning contrasted with the maintained, and often increased, time input in more enjoyable leisure activities, like sport. Table 2.2 confirms this for the UK, with large increases in time devoted to sport and reductions in unpaid work time.

Even in such areas as sport it has been noted by Vickerman (1980) that:

'Pure leisure activities are also becoming more capital-intensive, ranging from passive activities such as air travel based holidays in the sun to the main growth sports, e.g., squash, all water sports and the UK television-induced boom in snooker.'

Whereas Vickerman sees this greater capital (or goods in our terms) intensity as being:

'at odds with a society in which leisure time is likely to become a cheaper and cheaper commodity'

the household production function approach suggests that the greater goods-intensity in activities is a rational household decision, because rising wage rates make time more expensive relative to market goods. Vickerman is making the assumption that the growth in leisure time is going to have a bigger influence than the effects of increasing wages on the relative scarcity of time. According to the indicators in Section 2.3, leisure time is not expanding rapidly, but later evidence and analysis of unemployment lends support to Vickerman's assumption when it is applied to the unemployed.

The time-intensity of sporting activities is often not reducable, for example, soccer and squash. So marginal changes in time allocation to sport may be difficult. In addition, evidence suggests that sport is a superior activity, i.e. as incomes rise, participation rises more than proportionately (see Table 3.4). It seems logical to suggest, therefore, that the income effect will continue to outweigh the substitution effect.

In other words, participation in sport, even time-intensive sport, will continue to increase despite the rising relative scarcity and relative value of time.

Linder (1970) also explores the changing value of time and concludes that leisure is becoming less self-determined and less 'leisurely'. The dominant tendency of increased affluence causes increased consumption of goods-intensive activities and this traps the consumer into maintenance of this increased goods input in the household production process. Furthermore, the same affluence encourages an increased array of leisure time activity choices. These pressures result in time becoming even more scarce and this brings about the 'harried leisure class'. Other writers (for example, Godbey, 1975) bemoan the decreasing leisureliness of leisure time – in particular the emergence of an 'anti-leisure' attitude, filling non-work time with greater amounts of compulsive activities, complete with such work-related traits as anxiety, externally imposed conditions and time consciousness.

Sport obviously falls into such 'anti-leisure' as defined, although in terms of Scitovsky's analysis that is not anti-leisure but a more fulfilling, stimulating way of utilizing non-work time. Regarding this choice of activities in practice, Roberts (1978), using evidence from a survey in Liverpool, suggests that as hours of work fall, activities increase significantly only for white collar workers. Blue collar workers, given more leisure time, tend to use it for other purposes, such as watching television. Again, this evidence could be interpreted as showing that the blue collar sector is more ignorant of leisure opportunities than the white collar sector; the latter having had better education in leisure time use.

2.6 Time-dating and leisure activities

So far, the analysis of demand for leisure time has dealt mainly with quantitative choices, such as how many hours to work in a week. The purpose of this section is to examine *qualitative* considerations. Shiftwork, in principle, provides workers with an opportunity for a qualitative choice over hours of work. However, in practice, it is not so much a choice as a requirement to work anti-social hours. It is probably damaging to participation in recreation activities, particularly those of a more social nature, such as team sports.

Another qualitative way in which workers can influence leisure time is to bargain for different types of leisure time. Young and Willmott (1973) asked workers in two factories what type of leisure time they preferred. The responses indicated that given a choice workers can improve the value of their leisure time by having it organized in a flexible manner. In one factory, for example, just over half the workers preferred extra annual holiday to other forms of leisure time, a third of the workers preferred extra half days off at the weekend and 16% preferred shorter working days.

Such qualitative considerations as shiftwork and choices of different types of leisure time point to a major qualitative choice constraint, i.e the fixed time of day, week and year that many activities are limited to. This is called time-dating. The cliched nine-to-five job is the most obvious example of this time-dating, but other activities, eating and sleeping in particular, are just as inflexible. Many leisure activities are similarly undertaken by the majority of people at certain specific times of the day, week and year: football, rugby, darts, even country walks, all display peak activities at certain times. Toyne (1974) cites examples of peaking leisure activities, and then concludes:

'The effect of introducing workshifts would be to distribute demand more evenly over the whole day and whole week whereas the effect of reducing the length of the working week would be to extend the daily and weekly peak over a slightly longer period of time.'

Our brief considerations of shift-working do not support the beneficial role attributed to it by Toyne, but the general principle of evening out the peaks in activities, in order to make leisure time more productive on average, is a sound one.

In sport much time-dating is heavily influenced by fixed hours of work for participants, although light and weather conditions combine with this to narrow the appropriate times for many activities. Such time-dating as this presents an additional consideration for the household production function analysis. It means that time will have different marginal values at different points in the day, week and year, because of the varying degrees of compulsion in the time-dating of activities. The relative scarcity of time varies according to the time-date considered. Time-intensity in certain activities prohibits consumption in normal working hours, but is of little consequence on holiday, for example, sailing. For less time-intensive activities like squash, however, participation is possible during lunch-breaks and before or after work. For leisure activities in general, time at off-peak parts of the day, week and year is much more productive, because not only may the facilities be cheaper at such times, but also there is likely to be less congestion of facilities and fewer travel problems in reaching the facility.

Time-dating is obviously one of the principal reasons for peak-load problems in the use of leisure facilities, just as it is for similar problems in transport, energy and communications. The consequences of peak-loads for pricing, investment and capacity utilization of suppliers will be considered in Chapters 7, 8 and 9. In the meantime it should be stressed that peak-load problems would be eased to the extent that time-dating can be broken down.

Evidence of the strength and consistency of time-dating is provided in studies by Szalai (1972), for twelve countries, and the BBC (for example, 1965, 1978) for the UK. Figure 2.9 presents some of the evidence from the first of the BBC surveys.

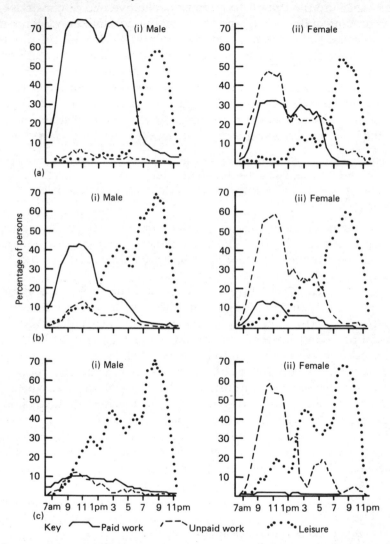

Fig. 2.9 Daily time-dating of paid and unpaid work and leisure, UK, 1961: (a) weekdays; (b) saturdays; (c) sundays. From: BBC, 1965.

Not surprisingly Fig. 2.9 shows that 5% or less males engaged in core leisure up to 5.00 pm on weekdays. Peak leisure time for males (58%) is from 8.00 pm to 9.30 pm. The female time-dating pattern is only slightly more flexible, 4% or less participating in core leisure up to 1.00 pm, 15% or less up to 6.00 pm and a peak of leisure activity from 7.30 pm to 8.30 pm. The fact that female time-dating of leisure is very similar to males during the week may, of course, reflect the high female participation rate at work – 33% in 1961. However, Szalai's evidence distinguishes between working women and housewives and he found that housewives follow a very similar time-dating pattern to working men, although not so extreme. Although this evidence does not include the UK, it is not generalizing too much to say that it supports one of the assumptions underlying Becker's analysis, that allocation of time decisions are commonly household ones. At weekends, Fig. 2.9b and c show a very similar profile for participation in 'core leisure' for males and females.

The inference of such evidence is that because the allocation of leisure time is a household one, the potential for family sporting and recreational facilities is something that could be exploited by suppliers. Contrary to initiatives in this direction in the USA, where, for instance, attendance at football and baseball matches is very much a family affair, the picture in the UK is more family-splitting than anything else. The cliched 'golf-widow' and Saturday 'soccer-widow' are testimony to the image of an individual in an isolated sports participation or spectating position, that is, 'individual' and 'isolated' in a family sense.

Can time-dating of activities be broken down, to reduce the pressures caused by peak demand and off-peak slack? To a certain extent it may be that it is not only self-imposed but also necessary to preserve mental and physical stability. Regular eating, sleeping and even work patterns are not just a convenience, but are conditioned by circadian and other rhythms. Evidence of the same biological time-dating for exercise is not forthcoming, but the withdrawal symptons of an injured soccer player on a Saturday afternoon in mid season suggest a similar effect. However, by and large there appears to be no essential reason for time-dating of sports activity other than the major time-dating constraint posed by work.

There is one growing example of a reduction in this constraint, which therefore has consequences for sports and other leisure activities. This is flexitime, which allows choice by the individual about which hours are worked, it allows 'credits' to be built up and taken as extra days off, and it normally specifies a minimum 'core-time' which people are expected to work in the day. Young and Willmott (1973) asked in their main survey whether or not people would like to start and finish work earlier or later and 30% said that they would. Such evidence again indicates that for many workers time has different values in different activities at different times of the day, week and year. As Owen (1979) states, in connection with flexitime:

'Perhaps the most common use is to improve the quality and productivity of household production time.'

A relaxed time-dating constraint would thus allow greater utility to be gained from leisure activities.

2.7 Unemployment and leisure time

Arguably the most dominant statistic of the late 1970s and early 1980s has been unemployment, which has taken a depressingly sharp upward turn not only in the UK, but worldwide. Most forecasts of unemployment from those brave enough to estimate actual numbers project this pessimism, and one of the principal causal influences is said to be technological development, especially microelectronic technology. Despite the fact that these forecasts are very speculative, however, there is a remarkable consensus on the likelihood of unemployment remaining at a level unprecedentedly high by post-war standards.

In so much as unemployment consists of those people who are willing and able to work but unable to find a suitable job, then they are suffering from an enforced excess of leisure time. To the extent that their idleness is enforced there is no choice involved in their income-leisure trade-off. Traditional analysis has concentrated on issues of geographical and occupational mismatch of workers and jobs, or the causes of deficient aggregate demand which results in less jobs than workers. More modern analysis has brought another dimension to unemployment theory, i.e. that unemployment does reflect a certain amount of worker choice. This choice may be a rational one to extend search-time for a job and hence lengthen the duration of what is called friction unemployment – the usual space of time between jobs of a few weeks. Alternatively the choice of unemployment may not be such an explicit one, and the theory of implicit contracts suggests that workers, by their own collective decisions, are implicitly contracting for more precarious employment security by defending or increasing their real wages, particularly at a time of recession.

Here is not really the place to consider this debate about whether or not unemployment is partly the choice of the unemployed. The implications for the use of time by the unemployed are, however, of consequence. Unemployment gives greater time opportunities and less income opportunities for all leisure activities. With reference to sport, the *General Household Survey*, 1973 and 1977 (Office of Population Censuses and Surveys, 1976, 1979) provides evidence of participation of the unemployed in indoor and outdoor activities. The participation rates for 1977 are given in Table 2.3.

Table 2.3 *Participation in sport by the unemployed compared with those working full-time, UK, 1977.*

Activity	Percentage participating in last four weeks	
	Unemployed	Working full-time
Golf	1.6	3.5
Walking	21.8	17.8
Football	5.2	4.7
Cricket	1.3	1.2
Tennis	1.8	1.5
Bowls	0.4	1.0
Fishing	4.8	3.5
Swimming (outdoor)	2.5	2.7
Total active outdoors	**35.0**	**33.8**
Badmington	1.6	2.9
Squash	0.1	3.1
Swimming (indoor)	4.5	6.1
Table tennis	1.7	3.4
Billiards, snooker, etc.	11.4	9.9
Darts	15.3	14.9
Total active indoors	**26.7**	**31.6**

From: General Household Survey, 1977.

There are substantial differences between participation of the unemployed and those in full-time employment. The activities in which the unemployed participation rate is significantly greater than that of the employed are walking, football, tennis, fishing, billiards and snooker etc. and darts. Such activities, not surprisingly, are more time-intensive and/or less goods-intensive than other activities in which the unemployed participation rate is lower (for example golf and squash). It would appear from Table 2.3 that overall participation of the unemployed is not substantially lowered by their status, rather that it features a few activities more prominently, as a result presumably of the combination of excess leisure time and inadequate income.

Another important consideration, the prime focus of attention of such studies as Smith and Simpkins (1980), is the extent to which unemployment is not really identifiable with leisure, because of the social and psychological effects of not having a job. The unemployed tend to isolate themselves in a way that adds a further constraint to conventional sporting participation, besides the lack of income. Vickerman (1980) notes that:

'unemployed people have typically lower rates of participation in organised or outside-the-home leisure activities – even when allowance is made for the two obvious constraints of low incomes and a higher incidence of living in areas of recreational deprivation.'

Smith and Simpkins suggest that a complex variety of social and psychological variables cause this reduction in participation. Firstly work has a place of centrality to an ordinary life-style. This makes organization of non-work existence very difficult. Consequently the unemployed develop an anomic, low income, socially isolated life style and, without the centrality of work, leisure becomes less meaningful because it has not been 'earned'.

Furthermore formal and informal social pressures reinforce the isolation of the unemployed. In particular a system of State benefits that financially penalises the unemployed, and as Smith and Simpkins (1980) put it:

'an almost total lack of education for unemployment in terms of the development of leisure and recreation opportunities.'

Because of this stigmatization, and also stereotyping of the unemployed as 'idle scroungers', their leisure choices become more home orientated, for example, watching television, listening to the radio and sleeping, and their normal social activities decline. Only when unemployment becomes the norm does normal social activity appear to resume. In Liverpool where one in five were unemployed in 1982, and in other English cities, experimental soccer leagues for the unemployed play at weekends. However, such organized sporting activity for the unemployed remains an exception to the normal effect of unemployment on participation.

Smith and Simpkins conclude that:

'in terms of life style and the use of free time, the experience of unemployment is not leisure (and furthermore) given the almost certain rise in unemployment ... what is needed is some awareness of the advantages of education for unemployment – and that, by the best definitions of leisure in terms of creative self development, means leisure education.'

Such a policy need coincides with the cry for such education emanating from Scitovsky's analysis of consumers ignorant of the benefits of skilled leisure consumption. The parallel is strengthened by the worst problem of unemployment, according to many studies, i.e. sheer boredom. With education and organization, unemployment would lose some of its stigma and move a little closer to the conventional idea of leisure.

Such potential is particularly relevant to the young unemployed, on whom attention has been drawn by their disproportionately high unemployment rate and by the social unrest of 1981 in the UK. *The Scarman Report* (1981) on this unrest identified unemployment as a contributory factor and one that is likely to become a persistent structural feature:

'Unemployment remains . . . an evil that touches all of the community. There
can be no doubt that it was a major factor in the complex pattern of conditions
which lies at the root of the disorders in Brixton and elsewhere.'

(Scarman, p. 107)

The boredom arising from such unemployment is a logical cause of
rioting in terms of the analysis put forward by Scitovsky (1981). A riot is
much more stimulating than hanging around street corners. This is
exacerbated by the lack of alternative stimulation.

'One other important aspect of the physical environment is the relative lack of
leisure and recreation facilities in Lambeth, and in Brixton in particular . . . It is
clear that the exuberance of youth requires in Brixton (and other similar inner
city areas) imaginative and socially acceptable opportunities for release if it is not
to become frustrated or be directed to criminal ends.'

(Scarman, p. 7)

With respect to the lack of alternative stimulation, Scarman noted the
importance of local authority facilities such as the new Brixton
Recreation Centre. Other relevant initiatives include the Sports Council's urban deprivation programme for helping participation in areas of
special need, and widespread price discrimination in favour of the
unemployed at leisure facilities.

2.8 Conclusions

One aspect of leisure time not explicitly covered in the preceding
discussions is the forecasting of future developments. This subject has
been the focus of much attention recently, particularly with respect to
the impact of microelectronic technology on unemployment. Whilst we
do not intend to join the speculative ranks of such leisure forecasters, it
seems opportune to conclude this chapter by looking in this direction. In
particular, since most forecasting is based on relationships that exist
now and existed in the recent past, our analysis of demands for leisure
time does have implications for forecasting. It also demonstrates a broad
and complicated set of relationships that go far beyond the technology-
unemployment one.

Although aggregate trends in unemployment are a key feature in
forecasts of leisure time, our observations of economic and sociological
work in the area suggest that this is not entirely appropriate.
Unemployment may be seen as largely involuntary, non-work time.
Qualitatively, therefore, it may not be a suitable dimension to 'leisure
time i.e. the income-leisure trade-off. However, the household
qualitative considerations we have highlighted are the form and place of
leisure time i.e. in what sized periods and at what time of the day, week,
year, or even working life, it appears. The 'form' and 'place' of leisure

time affects the productivity of its use, and hence the nature of demand for it. Purely quantitative forecasts are therefore deficient.

Despite many criticisms, we still believe some value attaches to the relationship between changing real wages and the demand for leisure time i.e. the income-leisure trade-off. However, the household production function sophisticates the simple analysis by demonstrating the interdependence between demand for leisure time and the use to which this time is put, i.e. demand for leisure activities. The prediction of future demand patterns is not easy when the 'mixture' of time-intensity and goods-intensity is itself variable between activities and, possibly, within activities over time.

This interdependence between the demands for leisure time and leisure activities is also an implication of Scitovsky's work. The leisure boredom factor is difficult to quantify but is important to the productivity of leisure time use and hence leisure time choices. If through experience or formal education the general level of leisure skills increases, then leisure-time demands may intensify. The next chapter demonstrates clearly that such skills in sport i.e. sport literacy, are almost certainly increasing, with important implications for forecasting.

3 The demand for sport and recreation activities

3.1 Introduction

Although the economics of the work-leisure choice is the essential context in which we study the demand for recreation, the central core of the demand analysis is the participation decision. We are interested in analysing the factors that result in participation or non-participation in active recreation activities.

The neo-classical economic approach is to start the analysis at the most micro level, the individual consumer's demand for the most disaggregated type of activity. All other aspects of demand can then be deduced once we have analysed this consumer choice situation. This will be our starting point. However there are several good reasons why the neo-classical consumer choice model is only likely to give, at best, a partial insight into the demand for sport and recreation. In this chapter we present a variety of alternative demand models.

3.2 Evidence on recreation participation

We will not only examine various economic approaches to demand but also the available evidence, and it is useful initially to outline the sort of evidence that exists on recreation participation and some of the difficulties that arise in using it. The evidence we use typically comes from large nationwide surveys of people's recreational activities and their attitudes to recreation. In Great Britain the best source of information is the General Household Survey, which, although carried out annually, only collects information on leisure activities every three years. At the time of writing, three data sets are available 1973, 1977 and 1980 (Office of Population Censuses and Surveys, 1976, 79, 82). The USA has a similar survey but confined solely to recreation. Again it is carried out periodically but we will use evidence from the 1977 survey reported in the *Third Nationwide Outdoor Recreation Plan* (US Department of the Interior, 1979). Finally a slightly different type of survey is carried out in Canada. This is much broader than the other two and concentrates not only on people's activities but also on fitness levels and attitudes to active recreation. The data we use comes from the 1981 Survey (Canada Fitness Survey, 1983).

At the outset we should be aware of the problems of using this type of information. This survey data is cross-section data taken from a sample of households at a particular point in time. It seems that one of the most important aspects of demand, the relationship of quantity demanded to price (the demand curve) is excluded from analysis on the basis of this data as price is not a variable over the cross-section. However in recreation, price is a composite variable and some aspects of price (for instance, travel-cost) do vary from household to household at a particular point in time. Unfortunately though these national surveys do not usually collect this type of information.

A second problem that arises with this type of data relates to attempts to use successive surveys, taken at different times, to establish time trends. The most serious problem arises when one attempts to compare surveys carried out by different organizations. Veal (1976) indicates the problem by comparing the results of the *General Household Survey* (1973) with those of the *Pilot National Recreation Survey* (British Travel Association/ University of Keele, 1967) and *Planning for Leisure* (Sillitoe, 1969)*, two earlier surveys carried out in 1965 (see Table 3.1). We would have expected participation to have increased over this eight-year period and yet the 1965 results clearly suggest much higher participation.

There are several reasons for these differences. Firstly the questions asked in the surveys were relating to behaviour over different time periods. The *General Household Survey* asks respondents what activities they participated in four weeks prior to interview. The 1965 surveys asked for activities participated in over the last twelve months. The latter question will yield a higher participation rate than the former since it picks up infrequent participation. It is also much more affected by poor memory and exaggeration. Also the sampling frames were different for the surveys with the major difference being between the General Household Survey, where only persons of 16 years of age and

---

* The Pilot National Recreation Survey (PNRS) was carried out by the University of Keele for the British Travel Association. Planning For Leisure (PFL) was carried out by the Government Social Survey. The figures in the PNRS/PFL column in Table 3.1 for summer sports are the average of PNRS and PFL and for winter sports are the PFL figure since PNRS did not cover winter sports.

Table 3.1 *General Household Survey (GHS, 1973) compared with Pilot National Recreation Survey (PNRS, 1965) and Planning for Leisure (PFL, 1965).*

Sport	GHS (1973) Percentage participating 4 weeks prior to interview	PNRS/PFL (1965) Percentage participating in year prior to interview
Golf	2.7	3.5
Long distance walking	3.3	5.0
Football	3.0	5.0
Cricket	1.4	4.0
Tennis	2.4	4.5
Bowls	1.0	3.0
Fishing	3.2	5.0
Badminton/squash	1.8	3.0
Table Tennis	0.9	6.0
Swimming (indoor)	3.7	} 11.5
Swimming (outdoor)	4.6	

From: Veal (1976).

over were sampled, and the *Pilot National Recreation Survey*, where persons aged 12 and over were sampled. As we shall see, age is a major influence on participation.

Some of these problems should be solved by having results from the same survey over different time periods. For instance we have *General Household Survey* results every three or four years. However, there have been problems in comparing *General Household Survey* results from one survey to another because of differences in the questions asked and, in particular, because of changes in the prompt card shown to respondents. Changes in the prompt card made substantial differences to recorded participation rates in some activities between 1973 and 1977.

Perhaps a better source of time-series information for the UK is the *Family Expenditure Survey*. This Survey records household's expenditure on various categories of goods and services, some of which are directly related to recreation participation (for example, admission charges for participant sports and sports equipment expenditure). The problem with the data is that no participation information is recorded. However certain indirect information on overall demand for recreation can be obtained from the number of households in the survey recording expenditure on recreation items. Table 3.2 records this from 1967 to 1977. Despite substantial year to year variations the data clearly shows a steady rise in the number of households recording expenditure on participation-related items. Although this is the only information that relates to participation, we will use the data again in Chapter 4 when we consider expenditure on facilities and equipment.

Table 3.2. *Households recording expenditure on recreation in the family expenditure surveys, 1967-77.*

	Year										
	1967	1968	1969	1970	1971	1972	1973	1974	1975	1976	1977
Total number of households in survey	7356	7184	7008	6393	7239	7017	7126	6695	7203	7203	7198
Percentage of households recording expenditure on ad-hoc admission charges (participant sports)	10.7	10.7	11.1	10.5	10.8	11.7	12.2	11.9	14.3	13.4	15.9
Percentage of households recording expenditure on sports goods (excluding clothing)	4.3	4.6	4.3	4.1	4.7	4.8	4.5	5.3	5.4	5.5	5.4

Estimates from unpublished Department of Employment (Family Expenditure Survey) data.

In addition to the problems concerning the basic source data on recreation participation there are several statistical problems that arise when these data are used to estimate economic demand models. However before we consider these problems we move on to describe a simple model of the demand for recreation.

3.3 A simple model of consumer demand for recreation

Consumer choice theory gives us a demand function where the quantity demanded of Good A (Q_{DA}) by a consumer is a function of the price of the good (P_A), the prices of other goods (P_1, P_2, . . . P_n) and the consumer's income (Y):

$$Q_{DA} = f (P_A, P_1, P_2, . . . P_n, Y)$$

This simple framework provides a starting point for our investigation of the demand for sport and recreation activities, but we must adapt this general framework to the specific market we are studying.

3.3.1 The dependent variable: the quantity demanded

The first question that arises is how we measure a consumer's demand for a recreation activity. Veal (1976) suggests two ways of measuring participation using General Household Survey data. The most common measure is the 'participation rate', the proportion of the population that participates in a given time period. This is easy enough to calculate as the total number recording participation in the activity over the total number of adults responding to the question. Veal, however, prefers the alternative, the engagements per 1000 adult population per annum. In the case of squash, an engagement is a 'game'; in the case of a country pursuit, it is a 'visit' to a particular site. The engagements measure takes into account frequency of participation. Respondents not only record whether or not they engaged in an activity in the four weeks prior to interview in the General Household Survey, but also on how many days they participated in the previous four weeks. Thus the engagements measure is a better indicator of quantity demanded since it combines both aspects of demand, participation and its frequency.*

---

* Veal (1976) outlines the details of the calculation for the engagements measure: 'Multiplying numbers of people by numbers of engagements gives total engagements for the sample for an average four week period in each quarter. Multiplication of this by 3.25 (the number of four week periods in a quarter) and division by the sample size divided by one thousand gives the number of engagements per thousand adult population for that quarter. Adding these figures for each quarter gives total engagements per thousand adult population per annum'.

Veal's measures provide a summary measure of quantity demanded for a specific activity but American studies (for example, Cicchetti, Seneca and Davidson, 1969) have used regression analysis, using dependent variables similar to Veal's, to obtain statistical estimates of the demand model above. Cicchetti, Seneca and Davidson use a two-step procedure in their regression analysis. In the first step, the dependent variable is one if the individual participates and zero if he, or she, does not. This equation then allows the estimation of the conditional probability of participation. The second step is an equation where the dependent variable is the number of days of participation (i.e. the frequency) for those who did participate.* To complete such a regression model though, we need to establish which explanatory variables to include on the right-hand side.

3.3.2 The determinants of demand
(a) The price of the activity

For most goods, identifying the price presents no problems. For a recreational activity data on price is not obtainable easily since the cost of participation is a composite item involving entrance charges, the rental value of any equipment used, travel costs, and time costs. Much of recreational demand analysis has concerned itself with recreational activities with zero entrance charges and the underlying assumption has been that travel costs, or a combination of travel and time costs (which are normally closely related anyway), are the major elements of cost. This again is often the case for resource-based outdoor recreation activities but is certainly not the case for indoor activities where entrance charges and equipment costs are often dominant. Also for outdoor activities such as skiing, equipment and entry charges are by no means negligible.

The price factor affects the quantity demanded in two different ways. The average cost of participation, taking into account all aspects of cost (equipment, entrance charges, travel and time costs) is the major influence on the participation decision. The higher the average cost, other things being equal, the lower the participation rate. However, for some activities, a large element of cost is fixed cost. The golf enthusiast,

---

*The regression analysis used in these studies encounters serious econometric problems. In the first place, the participation data for individual consumers is a dichotomous variable taking on a value one if the consumer participates and zero if he or she does not. Simple regression analysis results in a model where the predicted dependent variable represents the probability of participation but gives predictions outside the range 0 to 1 (i.e. a prediction that cannot be interpreted as a probability). The logit or probit transformation can be used to remedy this problem but this solution leads to a further problem, heteroscedastic disturbances.

once he has purchased his clubs and paid his membership to a golf club, faces very low marginal costs of participation (depending on how far he lives from the golf club). It is this marginal cost of participation that is the major determinant of *frequency* of participation, as opposed to the participation rate. In general, other things being equal, the lower the marginal cost of participation then the greater the frequency of participation. Having said this, it must be remembered that there are little or no degrees of freedom attached to the frequency decision for some recreational activities. This is particularly the case with team sports where fairly rigid time-dating is the norm.

Overall estimates of the price elasticity of demand for specific activities are not available, mainly because of the problems of estimating the true composite price. There is evidence of the price elasticity of demand for components of the overall price, such as travel cost, or entry charges for specific facilities but we will discuss this in the next Chapter.

(b) Income

Most commentators on recreation demand make the implicit, or explicit, assumption that recreation is a luxury good: that is, the income elasticity for most recreation is greater than one. One quote from *The Third Nationwide Outdoor Recreation Plan* (US Department of the Interior, 1979) illustrates the point:

'Another important factor that has produced increased recreation participation is the Nation's rising real income. As disposable income increases, the proportion of money available to spend on recreation pursuits increases. While income must first be applied to meet basic needs, after a point its uses are discretionary, and a rise in real income implies a rise in discretionary income . . . Most people are using more of their available discretionary income on recreation than ever before. A recent study indicates that expenditures for recreation and leisure activities are rising faster than consumer spending as a whole.'

National recreation surveys indicate a strong positive relationship between participation rates and income levels for virtually every recreation activity. Table 3.3 reflects this pattern for the 1977 British Data. The table shows a steady rise in the participation rate as income rises. The relationship between participation and income is most striking for indoor sports.

Survey cross-tabulations of income against participation allow us to obtain preliminary estimates of the income elasticities for participation in different sporting activities. One of the authors (Gratton, 1979) has estimated the elasticities for the 1977 data and these are presented in Table 3.4. For some activities, horse-riding and sailing, the income elasticities are very high indicating that participation in these activities is

Table 3.3. *Sport participation rates by total household income, 1977.*

	Percentage engaging in activity in the 4 weeks prior to interview by gross weekly household income (£)						
	Up to 40	40.01 to 60	60.01 to 80	80.01 to 100	100.01 to 150	150.01	Total
Total outdoor sports	14	22	26	31	33	41	27
Total indoor sports	5	15	24	26	29	32	22

From: General Household Survey, 1977.

Table 3.4. *Great Britain income elasticities, 1977.*

Sport	Income elasticity
Outdoor	
Horse riding	3.64
Sailing	3.13
Cricket	2.51
Rugby	2.27
Tennis	2.14
Golf	1.86
Athletics	1.45
Football	1.43
Fishing	0.80
Bowls	0.54
Long distance walking	0.32
Indoor	
Squash	2.82
Self-defence	2.20
Badminton	1.42
Keep-fit	1.17
Swimming	0.99
Billiards/snooker	0.84

From: Gratton (1979)*.

clearly a 'luxury good'. On the other hand sports which have the highest numbers participating, walking, swimming and fishing, have income elasticities less than unity, indicating that participation grows less than proportionately with income. The striking feature of Table 3.4 is the variability in income elasticity from one activity to another. However we must have serious reservations about such estimates. Income is correlated with a whole series of variables known to be important in

* These income elasticities are estimated from a double-log regression of participation on income. The data is obtained from detailed, unpublished, cross-tabulations of income and participation from the *General Household Survey*, 1977, provided by the Office of Population Censuses and Surveys. The estimates are not only subject to the problems outlined in the text but also to the problems discussed in the footnote on Page 46.

tastes and preferences for active recreation. Thus simple statistical relationships between participation and income are not revealing the income elasticity of demand. To find this we really need to analyse changes in participation in relation to income change, for a population with identical preferences. Alternatively we should statistically include in the relationship variables that are known to be correlated with different preferences. As we indicate below educational background, age, sex and occupation are all important indicators of different recreational preferences. However since all these variables are closely correlated with income this causes a serious statistical problem (i.e. multicollinearity) in regression analysis that prevents precise estimates of the effect of each separate variable being obtained. Thus although Table 3.4 gives us a hierarchy of income elasticities that fits our prior expectations closely we must be sceptical of their numerical accuracy.

(c) Prices of other goods

Probably the most interesting question when looking at the demand for a particular sport is which activity would be a substitute, and which complementary, to the given sport. Unfortunately we have virtually no information on the cross-price elasticities of demand for recreation activities which would allow us to answer such a question. Skjei (1977) suggests that the most serious problem in recreational demand analysis is the bias that arises from the inability to include information on the prices of substitute and complementary activities in the specification of the demand function. This specification problem arises because of the difficulties, discussed above, in constructing a price variable for an activity. Cicchetti, Seneca and Davidson (1969) tried to identify substitutes and complements by including participation terms for other activities on the right-hand side of their regression equation for participation in a given activity. The results of this exercise though proved difficult to interpret.

There are approaches though that might enable substitutes and complements to be identified. Lancaster (1966) views the consumer as maximizing a utility function which has, as its arguments, commodity attributes rather than the quantities of the goods consumed. If we find 'product characteristics' for recreation activities we may be able to find substitute and complement relationships between activities on the basis of these characteristics. For instance we would identify level of physical activity or degree of competitiveness as specific characteristics of sports. For those sports possessing a similar collection of characteristics we would expect to have substitute relationships. The problem with Lancaster's approach is first of all identifying the relevant attributes of recreation activities and, secondly, obtaining objective measurements of such attributes for any given activity. These problems have tended to discourage any empirical work within Lancaster's framework and recreation researchers have instead looked to various multivariate techniques as a means of identifying activities that 'go together'.

Proctor (1962) was probably the first to use factor analysis in recreation studies and Burton (1971) used both factor analysis and cluster analysis to identify 'recreation types'. The basis of this analysis is to identify groups of activities such that individuals participate in several activities within a given group, but do not participate in activities outside the group. The choice of groups is based on the correlation coefficient between participation rates for different activities. As Burton explains:-

'If every respondent who took part in, say, soccer also took part in cricket, then the correlation between the two activities will have a value of 1. If none of the respondents who participated in soccer participated in cricket, then the value of the coefficient will be zero. Finally, if all of the respondents who did not participate in soccer did participate in cricket, then the value of the coefficient would be –1 . . . Obviously these extreme values do not occur very often . . . Most of the coefficients will have values lying somewhere between +1 and –1. Both cluster analysis and factor analysis use those correlation coefficient to group activities together.'

Table 3.5. *Burton's relatively stable recreation groups.*

Group I	*Group II*
Soccer	Roller skating
Cricket	Ice skating
Table tennis	Youth club
Tennis	Horse riding
Group III	*Group IV*
Rugby	Picnicking
Athletics	Driving in the countryside
Basketball	Gardening
Keep fit	Dining out
Badminton	
Cycling	

From: Burton (1971).

On this basis Burton identified four relatively stable groups; stable, that is, in that they always tended to be in the same groups whatever type of analysis was employed. These groups are shown in Table 3.5. Thus we see that people who play soccer are also likely to play cricket and tennis, but are not very likely to play rugby or go horse riding. On the other hand, people who play rugby are also likely to play basketball and badminton. The technique gives us an indication then of complementary relationships between activities. For a given activity, complements will be the activities within the same group. These methods though do not allow us to identify substitute relationships.

Alternative techniques to factor and cluster analysis have been used to represent patterns of association among leisure activities. Holbrook (1980) suggests that multidimensionally scaled correlation analysis is an appropriate technique for identifying grouping of activities. His analysis suggests that inter-activity correlations are explained mainly by two key dimensions: the solitary/social scale and the indoor/outdoor scale. The advantage of this method is that it identifies objective measurements on the chosen scales with the activity groupings. In some ways it approximates the Lancaster attributes approach and therefore, with further development, could be a fruitful technique for identifying both substitutes and complements.

(d) Tastes and preferences

The simple consumer demand model analysed so far assumes that all consumers have the same preferences and only differ in levels of income. In fact the most variable factor in the study of consumer demand for recreation is the tastes of the consumers. Early studies of participation patterns identified certain key socioeconomic variables that were important in determining peoples preferences for active recreation. These were age, sex, educational background and occupation. The most significant relationship is between participation and age and sex.

Numerous studies have shown a consistent negative correlation between age and participation in virtually every sporting activity. Tables 3.6 and 3.7* provide evidence from both the UK and the US. Age is probably the most important variable in explaining variation in those sports that require physical contact and strength. But even in many less strenuous sports, participation normally drops off steadily with age (golf is a notable exception to this rule).

---

* The US participation rates are much higher than those for the UK, but note that the questions asked were substantially different. The US Survey asked for participation over a 12 month period, the UK Survey asked for details of participation over the four weeks prior to interview. As we commented earlier the latter question always yields lower rates of participation. These tables again reveal the difficulties of comparing one survey with another. These difficulties are further compounded when different countries are involved (see Rodgers (1978)).

Table 3.6. *Percentage of respondents who participated in selected recreation activities more than 4 times during the previous 12 months (1977, USA).*

Activity	Age						
	12-17	18-24	25-34	35-44	45-54	55-64	65+
Sailing	9	7	5	4	3	2	1
Waterskiing	9	17	10	8	4	1	0
Fishing	51	40	36	38	36	34	21
Outdoor pool swimming	75	67	62	57	37	27	11
Backpacking	19	23	23	21	11	10	6
Horse back riding	17	13	10	7	4	2	0
Golf	10	11	11	12	12	15	5
Tennis	46	38	34	25	13	4	1
Downhill skiing	9	10	5	3	1	0	0

From: Nationwide Outdoor Recreation Survey, 1977.

Table 3.7. *Percentage of respondents who participated at least once in the 4 weeks before interview (1977, Great Britain).*

Activity	Age						
	16-19	20-24	25-29	30-44	45-59	60-69	70+
Outdoor							
Golf	2	2	3	3	3	2	1
Football	12	9	5	2	0	0	0
Tennis	5	3	2	1	1	0	0
Fishing	4	3	3	3	2	1	0
Total outdoor	**43**	**39**	**35**	**33**	**24**	**22**	**11**
Indoor							
Badminton	6	3	4	3	1	0	0
Squash	3	5	5	3	0	0	0
Swimming	10	8	8	7	2	1	0
Total indoor	**48**	**41**	**36**	**28**	**13**	**6**	**2**

From: General Household Survey, 1977.

Rodgers (1977a) offers an interesting hypothesis concerning the relationship between age and sports participation. Rather than accepting the conventional view that people 'drop out' of active participation as they get older, he suggests that many people in the older age categories were never participants, even when young. He introduces the concept of 'sports literacy', the extent to which sections of the population are exposed and conditioned to active recreation. The older generation, he suggests, reveals a much higher proportion of 'illiteracy' than the younger generation. He presents some evidence to support this view. His 'index of sports penetration' measures the number of adults who have ever played at least one sport as a proportion of all adults. Figure 3.1 shows how this declines steadily with age. This view of the causes of lower participation of older people has important implications for forecasting, which will be discussed in Chapter 5. But it also has

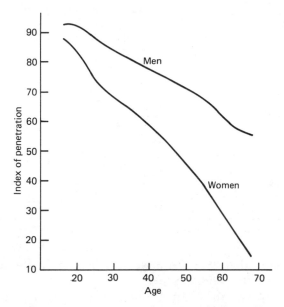

Fig. 3.1 The relationship between 'sports literacy' and age. From: Rodgers, 1977a.

implications for sports policy. If the aim of the government is to increase participation, then for many older people, this means taking up an activity for the first time and not re-adopting one they have given up.

A similar argument also relates to sex differences in recreation participation. Many surveys have shown that men have higher participation rates than women. Studies documenting the lower participation rates in many activities among girls explained these differences as due to the fact that, during childhood and adolescence, females are more constrained in exposure to, and opportunities for, active sport: in Rodgers' terms they are more 'sports illiterate' than boys. However recent evidence shows that these sex related differences are diminishing rapidly. The 1977 *Nationwide Outdoor Recreation Survey* (US Department of the Interior, 1979) found that females were just as likely to begin participation in an outdoor recreation activity during the last year as were males. Figure 3.2 illustrates this. More women than men are beginning tennis, water skiing and 'other outdoor sports'. Gershuny and Thomas (1980) also found that between 1961 and 1975 there had been a 57% increase in time allocation to sport by females compared with an increase of 28% by males.

Again this changing pattern of 'sports literacy' among women has important implications for forecasting and sports policy. Rodgers (1977a) noticed that it was only the level of participation that was

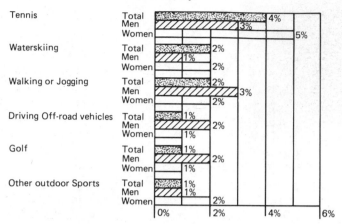

Fig. 3.2 Sex differences in new recreation participation. From: Nationwide Recreation Survey, 1977.

different between the sexes. Women who did participate, were likely to participate just as frequently as men.

Thus although age and sex may have been good proxies for tastes in the past the problem is that tastes are rapidly changing and established differences between the activities of different age groups and sexes may not continue into the future. This only serves to make the analysis of demand that much more complicated.

3.4 Further demand considerations

Although the above analysis is a conventional approach to consumer demand, it ignores certain special features of the product we are studying, sport and recreation. Consequently further consideration is necessary of those factors that are specific to this market. We have already met Becker's household production approach in Chapter 2, where we considered the time-input into leisure activities. This view provides an alternative model of consumer demand for recreation activities. It is a more useful framework than the classical utility-maximizing model since it not only gives us demand functions for the activities but the model also generates derived demands for facilities, travel and recreation goods. It is a hierarchical demand model with the demand for activity playing the role of the parent demand function. Vickerman (1975a) uses this approach as the basis of his demand model for leisure. But perhaps the most novel application of the household production approach is that by Grossman (1972) whose demand for health model has direct implications for the demand for sport.

3.4.1 Sport as a means to health: the investment demand

There is no doubt that a large proportion of sport participants, particularly those over 30, use sport as a means to maintain or increase health status. This makes sporting activity not purely a consumption good yielding utility, either now or in the future, but also an investment good, where people sacrifice present satisfaction in order to reap future returns. The returns will be of the form of higher health status in future years, which is really an investment in human capital, which will yield a return in higher incomes.

Grossman characterises the 'health production function' as being dependent on several inputs, one of which is exercise (the others being diet, housing conditions, work conditions and the health services of doctors and hospitals). The amount of exercise demanded will be related to the rate of return on health capital. This depends on two variables: the wage rate and the number of healthy days generated by increased exercise.

The effect of wage rates is a result of two conflicting elements. The higher the level of the consumer's income, then the higher the marginal product of health capital; on the other hand, the higher the level of income, the more valuable is the consumer's time, and so the cost of generating health capital through exercise is higher. The relationship of investment demand for exercise and income is therefore not unambiguous. We might expect higher income individuals to have a greater investment demand (because of the high rate of return) but to economize on the time input by choosing that form of exercise that yields the highest health benefits per unit time interval. It would be useful to be able to test this prediction and examine the importance of this aspect of demand for recreation. The sort of data we would need would first of all clearly distinguish the motivation for recreation. From those who specified a pure health motive we would want to compare recreational activities with income. The Canada Fitness Survey (1983) does have data on motivations for participation. Table 3.8 reports the reasons for being active. The Table shows clearly that the investment demand aspect is important in motivating people to exercise. 'To feel better' is obviously a rather non-specific reason but there are connotations of improved health status. Those regarding 'to control weight', 'to relax', 'to reduce stress' and 'doctors orders' as important reasons are obviously concerned about the health benefits of exercise. Most reasons remain stable in comparison with earlier surveys but it is significant that the only one to increase in importance is 'doctors orders'. It seems that in practice, a larger proportion of people are taking this route to improved health status through the health production function. However this data does not really test the predictions of Grossman's theory. To do this we need to have these responses cross-classified by income, and by type of activity engaged in.

Table 3.8. *Reasons for being active in persons aged 10 years or over, Canada 1981.*

Reasons	Percentage rating it as 'very important'				
	Total	Male	Female	Active	Sedentary
1. To feel better	60	58	62	65	44
2. For fun or excitement	44	44	43	49	26
3. To control weight	42	33	51	45	30
4. To improve flexibility	40	37	43	44	30
5. To relax, reduce stress	34	31	36	36	25
6. For companionship	24	21	27	25	21
7. Doctors orders	23	20	25	22	19
8. Challenge abilities	21	23	19	24	14
9. To learn	19	18	21	21	15
10. Fitness leaders advice	19	17	21	20	16

From: Canada Fitness Survey, 1983.

The second major influence on investment demand is age. This works through two channels. First of all, as a person gets older the rate of depreciation of health capital increases and so more investment is required each year to maintain a given stock of health capital. That is, the costs of producing health capital increase. At the same time the rate of return on health capital is lower since with advancing years and an assumed fixed age of retirement there are fewer and fewer years to reap the benefit of health capital in the labour market. If we define the total product of health capital as the discounted sum of future earnings then with each year of age the number of years we add together is decreased by one. Thus Grossman's model leads to the rather surprising result that an individual will choose a lower health state in each successive year. This will eventually lead him to choose his length of life as the optimal health stock will ultimately decline below some necessary life-supporting minimum.

Although Grossman's model is a general model of the demand for health, the importance of exercise in the health production function, allows us to use the model to add another dimension to the overall demand function for recreation. The analysis of the investment aspect of demand is useful for three reasons.

First of all it gives us an insight into why income is an important determinant of demand. Classical demand theory regards income as a constraint on consumer choice, but the implication of this is that the constraint would be binding for some expensive activities such as skiing or sailing, but not binding for, say, walking or jogging. Yet even for inexpensive recreation pursuits we still find a strong positive correlation of participation with income. We can explain this by saying that tastes are correlated with income, but this is untestable. Grossman's analysis offers a more analytical treatment of why rational economic behaviour would require higher participation by higher income groups.

Secondly, the analysis allows some insight into which activities will be substitutes for one another, and which will be complements. If the prime motivation of the participation decision is the investment one, then a close substitute to a particular sport will be another activity that produced a similar quantity of health capital for a similar input of time and money. Thus a person who takes up jogging for health reasons may regard aerobic fitness classes or cycling, as a good substitute, and snooker and motor sports as a poor substitute. Complementary activities are likely to be outside the recreation field and include such behaviour as a high fibre diet, adequate sleep and non-smoking. Table 3.9 provides evidence from the Canada Fitness Survey that this is exactly the case.

Table 3.9. *Activity and health habits for persons aged 20 years or over, Canada 1981.*

Of those who are:	What percentage also . . .		
	Smoke?	Get 7-8 hours sleep?	Have a good breakfast?*
Active	37	70	51
Moderate	44	70	45
Sedentary	42	63	43
Total	**40**	**69**	**48**

* One that contains protein in the form of meat, milk or cheese.
From: Canada Fitness Survey, 1983.

Finally Grossman's analysis indicates that people will respond differently to changes in certain variables depending on whether their motivation for participation is consumption rather than investment. For instance, let us take two joggers, one (Jogger A) participates primarily for the utility aspects, the other (Jogger B) primarily for health reasons. Both are promoted to higher-paid, but more demanding jobs involving greater time commitment and more stress and anxiety. We would expect Jogger A to respond by reducing the hours spent jogging since these changes are unlikely to change the marginal utility of an hours jogging, but the time costs have increased considerably. On the other hand, Jogger B is likely to maintain or increase exercise activity since the extra stress will accelerate the rate of depreciation of health capital and at the same time the increased income has increased the marginal product of health capital.

However there are problems in applying Grossman's model to the demand for sport and recreation. The model assumes that the individual has perfect knowledge of the health production function and the rate of return on health capital. In reality, people are uncertain of the impact of exercise on their health capital, but even more uncertain as to the rate of return on health capital. But probably the biggest weakness of applying Grossman's theory to recreation relates to the categorization of sport and recreation as an economic good in Chapter 1. There we specified that sport had aspects of an investment good, but also of a consumer durable. Grossman assumes that the only benefit to increased health status is in income returns in the labour market. The consumer durable aspect of exercise relates to the feature that many participants report that increased exercise gives them the energy and motivation to take part in many more 'household production' activities, outside the labour market. That is, the exercise yields a future utility stream by raising the level of consumption activities. These returns are likely to be greater the older the individual, and therefore demand from this source may be positively related to age. The general point is that Grossman has been too restrictive by limiting returns to health capital purely to those realized in the labour market.

The application of Grossman's model to the demand for sport and recreation has led us to the discussion of motivation for participation. That is, aspects of psychology are intertwined with the economic analysis. Another economist has taken the integration of psychology into economics much further, and his ideas, although discussed earlier in relation to the time aspects in Chapter 2, are also relevant to the participation decision.

3.4.2 Sport as a source of stimulation

Scitovsky (1976) uses psychological theory to criticise the classical theory of consumer demand. He investigates the relationship between pleasure and consumption activities, and shows that this relationship is crucially dependent on arousal levels. If a consumer is below the optimum level of stimulation and arousal he will experience boredom; if he is above it, he will experience stress and anxiety. These feelings will induce him to activity which will bring arousal to its optimal level.

The classical economist's view of demand is consistent with this view to some extent. At its most basic we may consider the demand for an essential item such as food. If an individual is deprived of food, he experiences discomfort and a heightened level of arousal. Consumption of food relieves the discomfort and lowers the arousal level back towards its optimum. Thus consumer demand theory can be classed as want satisfaction, where ability or pleasure flows from the reduction in arousal level.

However this is not the only source of pleasure. Pleasure flows from the change in arousal level rather than the state of being at a particular level. Pleasure will also follow from moving from a low level to a high one: the relieving of boredom. Some activities are so stimulating that they raise arousal levels too high, causing anxiety and tension, but pleasure still follows when the activity finishes and arousal levels fall. The important point is that pleasure is related to changes in arousal level and not the level itself.

Scitovsky criticises economists for only considering the want satisfaction (lowering too high arousal) aspects of demand and completely ignoring stimulation-seeking behaviour (raising too low arousal). This point becomes increasingly important to his more general thesis which is that in different societies there is less and less opportunity for pleasure through want satisfaction since most of the basic demands (food, clothing and shelter) have already been satisfied. In such societies want satisfaction can be more or less equated with comfort, and the main alternative to comfort is stimulation.

It is this aspect that concerns us here. Scitovsky states:

'The simplist remedy for too low arousal is bodily exercise. Not only is bodily exercise a good weapon against boredom it is also pleasant. It seems most pleasant when it fully engages our skill and powers . . . Competitive sports and games are popular because the pleasantness of exercise is maximised by the full exertion of our strength and skills called forth by competition. Higher animals also engage in playful combat and other forms of competitive behaviour.'

The basic source of stimulation is experience that is new, unexpected, or surprising. New and surprising experience is always stimulating, but if it is completely outside the bounds of our previous experience it can be so stimulating as to be disturbing. As Scitovsky indicates:

'What is not new enough and surprising enough is boring: what is too new is bewildering. An intermediate degree of newness seems the most pleasing.'

What an individual considers 'new' obviously depends on his previous experience. What is stimulating to one person, may be boring to another; not because of differences in tastes, but because of differences of experience. The nursery slope can be terrifying to the person on skis for the first time, and yet boring to the expert.

From this we get Scitovsky's theory of skilled consumption, or skilled learning, as outlined in Chapter 2. To enjoy a stimulating activity it has to relate enough to previous experience not to be too disturbing. But the important point is that Scitovsky has created a new aspect in the demand for sport: stimulation seeking behaviour. People demand certain risk activities because the stimulation gives pleasure. This aspect is different from the consumption and investment aspects referred to so far.

There is some patchy evidence to suggest that this aspect of demand may not only be important, but is becoming increasingly important. We saw in Table 3.8 that 'for fun and excitement' was the second most important reason given by active people for participation. Perhaps the most interesting feature of the table is that it is on this reason that there is most difference between the opinions of active people and sedentary people.

The *Third Nationwide Recreation Plan* in the USA noted 'the soaring popularity of high-risk recreational activities' amongst the 25 to 34 years age group. The plan indicated that:

'along with increasing risk comes greater numbers of fatalities, particularly in such pursuits as hang-gliding, rock-climbing, off-road and recreation vehicle use, scuba-diving, flying and snow mobiling. The Metropolitan Life Insurance Company estimates that 10,000 Americans die each year as the result of some planned risk taken for fun or adventure.'

In trying to explain the increasing popularity of high-risk sports the plan suggests it is due to:

'psychological benefits for individuals participating in high-risk activities such as experiencing natural beauty; testing and challenging oneself; relief of stress and boredom and feelings of self-confidence and accomplishment derived from exposure to unpredictable or unknown situations.'

But perhaps the strongest evidence of the importance of stimulation-seeking through sport is provided by Rosenthal (1980). He presents evidence that 'risk exercise' (as he calls physical activity that involves risk):

'invigorates one physically and mentally and produces a state of well-being and elation, ofttimes bordering on euphoria. All this adds up to a sense of joy and happiness, a renewing of one's courage and vigor, a peace of mind'.

He argues that his work adds:

'a new dimension to the concept of physical fitness; namely a mental adjunct. This is accomplished by the addition of well-calculated risks to the exercise programs.'

Rosenthal's evidence also adds weight to Scitovsky's concept of skilled learning. Rosenthal looked at 890 individuals who participated in risk exercise sports. 99.7% of those who participated enjoyed them, 63.6% were elated and 19.7% were euphoric. Rosenthal found that:

'For each person the degree of the physical and mental reactions were directly related to his proficiency in the RE sport . . . it was found that among those who felt invigorated physically and elated-to-euphoria mentally, approximately 75% were in the good-to-expert category.'

He presented evidence relating to the time of occurrence of the feeling of well-being, indicating that it was more normal to experience this after participation had finished. This evidence fits closely with Scitovsky's explanation of pleasure arising from changes in arousal level, and particularly from 'coming down' from heightened arousal. Scitovsky (1981) extended his theory to explain that rising crime rates and increasing civil disturbance and riots were symptoms of the same stimulation seeking. Rosenthal (1981) again provides supporting evidence by looking at 100 university students who either demonstrated or spectated at violent and non-violent demonstrations. The mental reactions of the students were similar to the individuals engaged in risk exercise reported above. The question arises of whether the socially acceptable 'risk exercise' was a substitute for the socially unacceptable, violent demonstrations. One further study suggests that it is. Rosenthal (1982) reports a study where 120 juvenile offenders were split into two samples of 60. One set were sent to outward bound schools, the other to conventional training schools.

'The results showed positive changes in regard to altruism, alienation, socialisation, manifest aggression, social maladjustment and value orientation for Outward Bound graduates. Significant positive changes also occurred by creating an increased level of aspiration and maturity. A one-year follow-up indicated only 20% of the wilderness – adventure group had later lapsed while 42% of the boys in traditional institutions lapsed.'

How does Scitovsky's theory change our analysis of the demand for sport? Basically it creates another category of demand. So far we have talked of consumption demand, that relates to utility maximization, and investment demand, that relates to improvements in health capital. The third category of demand relates to stimulation seeking. It is completely different from the other two in that this form of behaviour cannot be explained by conventional demand theory. People consciously seek danger, pain, tension, discomfort and anxiety in order to feel excitement and euphoria, although the latter is normally only after the danger has ceased. The other difference is that to experience this pleasure, one has to have a certain skill level: it is skilled consumption. If government wishes to positively encourage such activity, as a means of reducing its socially unacceptable substitutes (vandalism and delinquency), then there is an education role in helping individuals to acquire the necessary skills. In other words, unlike conventional demand theory, where tastes and preferences are taken as given, Scitovsky's analysis suggests that government has a role in changing peoples tastes, teaching them to gain pleasure from certain types of consumption. In effect, this is another form of market failure in the sport and recreation market.

3.4.3 Constraint models

An alternative view of consumer demand for recreation is that classical consumer demand analysis fails to take account of the full range of constraints operating on the individual. In its simplest form conventional theory sees the consumer faced by only one constraint, the budget constraint. Household production theory extends this by including the time constraint. But in the recreation area, this may not be enough.

Rodgers (1977a) suggests that, although we can see that sports participation is related to age, sex, education, social class and income, these factors are only 'background influences, working at the aggregate level; a social environment within which sport flourishes or fails'. His point is that none of these social factors is:

'causal at the level of the individual: no-one is directly disqualified from the chance to participate simply because they belong to what is, in general, a disadvantaged group. Participation is not determined by these social relationships: they work, rather, in probability terms to define the groups most likely or least likely to participate in active recreation. The decision of the individual to take part or remain passive is determined by different factors – by a set of stimuli and constraints that are, to a such greater degree, within the power of the sports administrator to influence, within the framework of his policies.'

He views sports participation as a system, a system that may be viewed from two perspectives: the aggregate and the individual. A system has 'input', 'throughput' and 'output'. For sport, the participation system output is wastage. This view allows a more specific definition of policy objectives: to maximize 'input', to prolong 'throughput' and minimize 'wastage'.

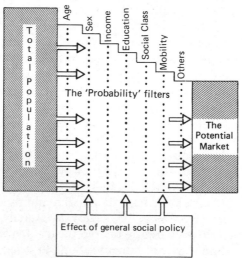

Fig. 3.3 Participation – the social filters. From: Rodgers, 1977a.

At the aggregate level he views the 'constraints' on behaviour as filters (Fig. 3.3). From the total population age, sex and the other socioeconomic factors associated with participation 'filter out' the non-participants and leave us with the potential market for sport. Rodgers' argument is that though such a process will lead to an aggregate relationship between participation and the socioeconomic variables we have outlined earlier, it does not describe the individuals decision to participate. Such general social factors, which change slowly in response to national social policy, only determine the size of the potential market for sport.

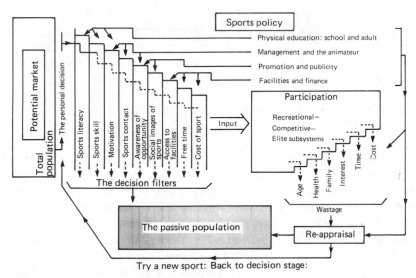

Fig. 3.4 The participation system. From: Rodgers, 1977a.

The personal decision of whether or not to participate is affected by a much more complex series of contraints, or filters, as indicated in Fig. 3.4. These include aspects such as sports skill, motivation and free time, thus taking account of the influences we have discussed earlier in this section. Rodgers indicates how the system operates:

'If even a single 'filter' produces an adverse result the individual may drain away into passive population. Those who successfully pass through the filter-system become 'input' into the participation system. They may join one of three sub-systems, the 'recreational', the 'competitive', or the 'elite' (or progress from one to another). They may stay long or only briefly in the participation system: ultimately they are 'filtered' out of participation by such factors as age and health, family commitments and free time. There is some process of re-appraisal, by which they either become passive or go back to the decision stage and take up a new sport that fits their changed circumstances.'

The systems approach is a dynamic model compared to the static neo-classical demand model. The problem lies in the movement from a conceptual framework to an empirical model. The only evidence quoted in support of the model relates to social survey evidence on the importance of the various constraints. Rodgers cites a study of the North West region of Britain (North West Sports Council, 1972) which revealed that one-third of non-participants blamed lack of time for their inactivity, 31% blamed a lack of local facilities, and 18% attributed it to the high cost of sport. This evidence conflicts with that from a more recent study (Romsa and Hoffman, 1980). Their evidence suggested that non-participation by lower income people was due to lack of interest, rather than lack of opportunity. It was only active participants that identified price, time, and lack of facilities as barriers to their pursuit of certain activities. They identified lack of facilities as the most important constraint, then lack of time and finally costs. Romsa and Hoffman's study casts doubt on the constraint model because it suggests the constraints are not objective barriers to participation. Rather each individual has different perceptions of recreational opportunity even when faced with a similar set of constraints.

Rodgers' model in some ways adds very little to our understanding of the forces that determine participation. Most of the factors he mentions we have already discussed. The novelty is the way the factors are described within the two-tier 'system' framework. It focusses attention on policy objectives and also the means of achieving these objectives. It shows the role of central government in reducing the force of the aggregate constraints, and hence expanding the size of the potential market. It also allows inter-regional comparisons to assess the extent to which the actual participation is below the potential. When this situation arises, the model suggests action at the local level may be required to reduce individual constraint barriers.

His approach has little connection with the utility-maximizing framework we began with, but is probably the most comprehensive in that all the other influences we have mentioned (for example, those outlined by Grossman and Scitovsky) can be easily integrated into the system approach. His model also leads us to a serious problem with the standard utility-maximizing model. One of Rodgers' individual filters is 'access to facilities'. As we will see in the next section, if this factor proves to be an important influence, the standard economic treatment may be totally inappropriate.

3.5 Problems in demand analysis

Even if we manage to obtain a consensus on the most appropriate economic model for the analysis of demand, we would still be faced with serious problems in obtaining a meaningful empirical model. We have mentioned specific statistical problems in relation to each of the approaches reviewed. However there are some general problems that apply to all models.

3.5.1 Supply-created demand: the identification problem

The standard economic approach to demand analysis assumes supply changes are independent of changes in demand, and vice-versa. There are certain strong indications that, in the sport and recreation market, creation of new supply directly influences demand. There seems little doubt that building a new sports centre in an area will result in people taking up an activity for the first time. Veal (1975) found that the proportion of users taking up an activity for the first time at a newly built centre could be as high as 60%. This sort of supply-created demand creates serious problems in obtaining a statistically estimated demand curve. The problem is indicated in Fig. 3.5. When new facilities are built the supply curve shifts from S to S_1. This shift in supply would normally create a new point of equilibrium at point B, and observed points such as A and B can be used to estimate the demand curve. However, if the provision of new facilities itself generates new demand then the demand curve shifts to a new position D_1. In these circumstances, every shift in supply causes a shift in demand, and points such as A and C will be observed. Using regression analysis to fit a curve to such points would give neither a demand curve, nor a supply curve. The demand curve is not identified.

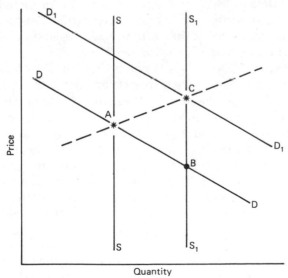

Fig. 3.5 *The identification problem.*

There has been a lively debate in the literature on this problem, which we can only summarize here. Cicchetti *et al.* (1972) discussed the problems of obtaining an empirical demand function from National Recreation Survey data. The survey collects data on individual participation in various activities but does not collect information on the supply opportunities available to each individual. As they indicate:–

'the identification of the individual's demand for recreation of a particular type requires each individual to enumerate the sites and/or his travel cost to reach them for every subset of his total annual participation. In the absense of such information, we do not have sufficient restrictions to account for the diversity of opportunity available to individuals.'

The solution they propose is one employed by Cicchetti, Seneca and Davidson (1969), which is to estimate a 'reduced-form' of the demand-supply model where participation data is regressed on the demand determinants we have mentioned earlier *and* aggregate measures of supply available at county, state, census division and region. The problem with this solution is that the estimated parameters cannot then be interpreted as demand elasticities, therefore such estimates are of little use for the analysis of the participation decision, although they are useful for forecasting purposes.

Other researchers have suggested that it is possible to identify the individual's demand function. Kalter and Gosse (1970), took the position that within any region the supply of recreational facilities was perfectly inelastic. Regional variation in supply can therefore be used to identify the demand function. Their solution will work as long as the participation data is also at the regional level. Unfortunately Kalter and Gosse used the participation data from the National Recreation Survey, and lack of information on the within-region variation of the supply of facilities leaves the demand function under-identified.

An alternative solution is suggested by Skjei (1977). He argues that in the short period over which recreation data are collected, each individual faces a given supply position. However an individual's supply curve for a recreational opportunity is perfectly elastic since he may visit the facility as many times as he likes at the same cost. He then points out that if we assume all facilities are homogeneous, any rational consumer will maximize his utility by participating in the activity at the closest (cheapest) site. Under this assumption, the demand function is identified by variation in the supply curve over different individuals. The crucial assumption here is that of homogeneity of facilities. Whereas this could be the case for an indoor facility, such as a squash court, it is likely to be unrealistic for outdoor facilities, such as National Parks.

The obvious solution to the identification problem in recreation demand analysis is to collect information on the supply opportunities facing each individual at the same time as demand (participation) data is collected. The problems with Kalter and Gosse's solution then disappears. At the moment social surveys are still proceeding with the collection of demand variables without taking account of the fact that such information cannot be used to its greatest advantage, the complete analysis of the participation decision, without further information on supply.

3.5.2 Need versus demand

This chapter has concentrated on the economist's concept of effective demand. As in other areas of social policy there is a debate by recreation researchers as to whether or not this is the appropriate focus of study. One of the main reasons for analysing demand is to assist planners in assessing the type and scale of facilities required both now, and in the future. Because of the nature of the externalities associated with recreation participation, it could be a serious mistake to direct resources to areas where the effective demand is greatest. It has been suggested that the concept of 'need' is more important than demand, when making decisions about resource allocation. Culyer (1980) points out the difference between need and demand:

'Whichever view one takes of need, one should note that they each involve a judgement being made independently of the receiving individual's preferences. It is this that makes a need based on caring preferences different from demand, for a demand is a want for some good or service backed by a willingness to sacrifice resources for it. Where demand and need come together is when one individual wants something for someone else and is prepared to sacrifice resources for it. Need is thus an external demand. It represents one party's view of what another should have.'

This view of need is directly related to the concept of merit goods which we discussed in Chapter 1. Another view of need was suggested by Bradshaw (1972). He suggested four types of need.

1. Normative need, which represents the views of an expert (in our case a recreation professional).
2. Felt need, which relates to the perceptions of the individual consumer.
3. Expressed need, which is felt need converted into effective demand.
4. Comparative need, which assesses need as existing when one group with given characteristics does not have a given facility or service whereas other groups with identical characteristics are provided with facilities or services.

Bradshaw's definitions are different from Culyer's but they do provide practical suggestions to the solution of the problem of how to assess recreational need. The analysis we have reviewed in this chapter allows us to analyse expressed need for recreation. Dower *et al.* (1981) point out that public provision of recreation facilities on the basis of expressed need can involve serious dangers in meeting policy objectives. Demand-based assessments of required provision, they argue, tend to lead to policies which over represent the preferences of current user groups. There is a danger of creating an elite or favoured group of participants. Dower *et al.* suggest that we should seek to understand the 'felt needs' of the community and then fit the structure of provision into this. The focus of attention should be the constraints and inhibitions that prevent people from taking advantage of activity opportunities. Their approach is consistent with Rodgers' constraint model above. The difference is their emphasis on need rather than demand.

The introduction of the concept of need raises many questions relating to such matters as the measurement of community needs and what policy action is required to cater for these needs. We will return to these questions in Chapter 10.

3.6 Conclusion

We see then that there is no simple, unique, approach to the analysis of the demand for sport and recreation activities. Some of the approaches we have presented in this chapter go outside the boundaries of conventional economic analysis into a wider social science framework, drawing particularly on psychology. The question arises then, of which of these approaches is the 'right' approach. The answer, unfortunately is at the moment unknown. The hypotheses put forward have been supported with patchy empirical evidence but none of the hypotheses has been subject to rigorous empirical testing. The Rodgers framework presents a model that allows most of the other approaches to be incorporated within it. The problem with the 'system' approach is the difficulty of moving from the theoretical model to an empirical one. All the approaches are difficult to test empirically because of the problem of the identification of the demand function in addition to the other statistical problems mentioned above.

The aim of this chapter has been to present a series of ideas and approaches that help us to understand the consumer's decision on whether or not to take part in active recreation. Further research is needed, and more detailed data will have to be collected, before we can be confident that these ideas have empirical validity.

4 The derived demand for recreational facilities, travel and equipment

4.1 Introduction

All the issues raised in the previous chapter relate to the primary demand for sport and recreation activities. Participation in these activities involves inputs of, and therefore demands for, various factors in the household production process. One of these, time, has already been examined in Chapter 2. This chapter concentrates on three other major inputs to the recreation experience, i.e. facilities, travel and equipment. Because the demands for these inputs are only created by the parent demand for activities, they are called 'derived demands'. For some activities the importance of one or more of these derived demands may be small, for example, playing table tennis at home does not require a formal facility nor any travelling; but on aggregate the extent of these derived demands is substantial. Sport and active recreation are only a small part of this total leisure spending, but they grew at well above the average rate for the 1970s in the UK, as Table 4.1 shows.

Leisure spending can be subdivided according to goods and services as Martin and Mason's (1980) pioneering estimates have done for the UK sports market. Their evidence is reproduced in Table 4.2.

One possible influence on the balance between goods and services and on their combined growth in the UK, is any changes in facility provision. In the UK, for instance, consumer expenditure on local authority sports services grew from a negligible amount in 1970 to some £84 million in 1979, as a result of the expansion in indoor facility provision.

Having described the size and growth of these markets we must now structure our analysis and focus on important economic issues concerning them. These issues can be divided into two sets. The first concerns the inter-relationships between the various demands, whilst the second concentrates on each derived demand in turn.

Table 4.1. *Percentage shares and percentage increases in leisure spending items 1971-80, UK.*

Item	Percentage share (1980)	Percentage change (1971-80)
Beer	18.9	16
Wine	6.1	75
Spirits	9.1	74
All Alcohol	**34.1**	
Television rental, licences	4.7	117
Television, audio purchase	3.4	86
Records and tapes	1.3	84
All television etc.	**9.4**	
Tourism overseas	11.8	22
Holiday accommodation (overseas tourists)	1.2	39
Holiday accommodation (UK tourists)	2.7	−10
All holidays	**15.7**	
Sports goods	2.5	67
Sports services	1.5	43
All sport	**4.0**	
Books	1.4	32
Magazines	1.2	−14
Newspapers	3.7	−10
All reading	**6.3**	
DIY	6.4	16
Hobbies	3.9	8
Gardening	2.4	6
Creative home production	**12.7**	
Eating out	5.7	10
Entertainment	2.0	8
Cinema	0.5	−44
Gambling	4.7	− 2
Entertaining outside home	**12.9**	
Toys and games	2.0	− 4
Pets and pet food	3.0	−12
Unweighted average, all items		26

From: Sports Council, 1982.

Table 4.2. *Sports expenditure: goods and services, 1973-81, UK.*

	Sports goods			Sports services			
	Current Prices (£m)	1975* Prices (£m)	Percentage of Total	Current Prices (£m)	1975* Prices (£m)	Percentage of Total	Total
1974	255	311	64	142	165	36	397
1975	310	310	64	178	178	36	488
1976	392	334	65	213	191	35	605
1977	480	359	65	257	188	35	737
1978	582	393	65	310	201	35	892
1979	681	414	65	362	219	35	1043
1980	761	417	63	442	229	37	1203
1981	794	411	62	493	228	38	1287

* Deflated by Retail Price Index, 1975 = 100
From: Leisure Consultants (1980 and 1983).

4.2 Inter-relationships in demands for sport and recreation

The conventional relationships assumed are those expressed so far, i.e. that demand for activities is the parent demand, and demands for facilities, travel, equipment, etc. are derived demands. This hierarchy, represented as (a) in Fig. 4.1, is only one possibility, however. Most of the other permutations involve the ranking of travel demand, whose position can vary from primary demand to second stage derived demand depending on the type of recreational activity studied. For urban recreation, travel is probably just a means to an end, a disutility. As such it is derived from demands as in hierarchy (b). Vickerman (1975b), however, stresses from the outset in his analysis of recreation and travel demand that:

'To regard it (travel demand) strictly as a derived demand is inadequate, it is more correctly a joint demand.'

The main reason for this is that travel is not always a disutility. In rural recreation, it is often the major part of the experience and is utility-giving, pleasure driving being the most obvious example. It is plausible to suggest that even when a specific sport or recreation activity is engaged in, travel may in many cases be an integral, joint demand, as in (c), (d) and (e) in Fig. 4.1. The final two relationships, (d) and (e), also speculate on the relative standing of facility demand. It could be argued that the 1970s expansion of indoor facilities in the UK created demand for the facilities as much as for the activities that could be done in them – i.e. joint demands. Consumers with leisure choices to make are as likely to ask 'Where shall we go?' as 'What shall we do?'

	Parent demands	Derived demands		
		Stage 1	Stage 2	Stage 3
(a)	Activity	Facility Equipment Time Travel	Travel mode	
(b)	Activity	Equipment Facility Time	Travel	Travel mode
(c)	Activity travel	Equipment Facility Travel mode Time		
(d)	Facility travel	Time Activity Travel mode	Equipment	
(e)	Activity facility travel	Equipment Time Travel mode		

Fig. 4.1 Hierarchies of recreation demand.

Another inter-relationship of importance is the substitutability between recreational travel, equipment, facilities and time inputs. One measure of this is the elasticity of substitution, i.e. the proportionate change in the use of the different inputs in response to a given change in their relative prices. We have already implicitly analysed this concept in the context of time and goods inputs to leisure activities in Section 2.5. However, in that analysis 'goods' included facilities, travel and equipment and here we try to separate out these three demands. The analysis of Chapter 2 is rather speculative regarding the substitution of recreation time inputs by goods inputs, especially when it attempts to forecast likely developments in the future as the price of time rises relative to the price of goods. It does, however, show precisely why such predictions are speculative – since income and substitution effects are operating at the same time and they probably pull in opposite directions.

The same problems occur in this chapter when looking at the elasticity of substitution between the various inputs. There is little evidence which relates specifically to the recreational derived demands that we are investigating, so we can only form *a priori* expectations about the relationships between them. Facilities and travel are likely to be complements. Only a small proportion of indoor facility users incur no travel costs (i.e. by walking or cycling) and since the average distance travelled is fairly low the rest are not burdened with high travel costs. Nevertheless, increased frequency of visits raises travel expenses and this will be a much more important relationship for those countryside trips that are to specific, managed sites, which were 25% of all such trips in one UK survey (Countryside Commission, 1982). Facilities and equipment may be complements or substitutes. Most participation in formal facilities requires an input of equipment. However, if the equipment is suitable for the production of recreation activities at home, such production may substitute for use of formal facilities. The relationships between time on the one hand, and facilities and equipment on the other, may be complements or substitution effects, depending on the strength of income and substitutes, (see Chapter 2). Time and travel demands are most likely to be complements since any increase in travel requires more time.

Evidence concerning such relationships is available at a much more aggregate level than just recreation. Changing relative prices and consumption patterns from a recent UK Treasury report (1983) are presented in Table 4.3. One implication of this evidence is that demand for services including, for instance, sports facilities is income elastic, since higher than average price increases have not prevented a growth in relative demand.

Table 4.3. *Changing relative prices and consumption patterns 1963-83, UK.*

	Changing relative prices* +1963-83 (%)	Changing consumption† shares 1963-83 (%)
Services	+12.4	+5.2
Transport	+2.8	+65.9
Durable household goods	−36.7	+4.9
Clothing	−45.1	−25.0
Leisure time	+51‡	+125.0 (holidays) +7.7 ('leisure' time)§

* Relative to changes in retail price index.
†Percentage changes in share of household expenditure.
‡ Price of leisure taken, arbitrarily, as equal to real average earnings.
§ 'leisure' time = non-work hours per five day working week.
From: Treasury Economic Progress Report, 1983.

Similarly transport demand appears to be income elastic, since relative demand has increased substantially whilst relative prices have remained fairly stable. Durable goods have only slightly increased their relative demand and clothing has suffered a considerable reduction, despite substantial falls in both sets of relative prices. There are no signs in Table 4.3 of the four types of commodity being strong substitutes for each other. Gershuny (1978, 1979) stresses not only the complementary relationship between services and goods inputs in the consumption process, but also a parallel process, which suggests that informal production at home, with household capital equipment, is being substituted for formal use of market services. As the role of household capital is critical to both effects, we will return to this when dealing with the derived demand for equipment. Recreation-specific evidence of changing consumption patterns is provided in the UK by Martin and Mason (1980) and is reproduced in Table 4.4.

Table 4.4. *Recreational goods and services expenditure 1973 and 1979, UK.*

	1973		1979	
	£m	Percentage of total	£m	Percentage of total
Equipment	145	49	412	41
Clothing, footwear	68	23	294	30
Services	84	28	284	29
Total	**297**	–	**990**	–

From: Martin and Mason, 1980.

Whilst we have no recreation-specific relative prices information, we can nevertheless make some observations on this evidence. The major difference with aggregate figures is that clothing and footwear have increased their share of recreational expenditure, and equipment has a steadily falling share. Whilst it is possible to attribute this to the sharp relative fall in prices of the former, this would only be valid if the price of sports equipment had not also fallen relative to average prices. In any case this discussion highlights one weakness of the elasticity of substitution. This is that other influences may be more important than price. In the case of Table 4.4 it is quite likely that the expansion of public sector facilities is responsible for the increasing share of expenditure going to services. Also different sports use different proportions of equipment, clothing and services, so that differences in the growth rates of different sports will alter the aggregate balance in demand for these

Table 4.5. *The largest expenditure sports, UK, 1979.*

	Goods (i.e. equipment, clothing and footwear)		Services			
	£m	Percentage of total	£m	Percentage of total	Total	Fast growing sports
Boating	224	92	20	8	244	
Golf	73	57	54	43	127	X†
Swimming	50	63	29	37	79	
Billiards, snooker	1	2	48	98	49	X*
Soccer	35	76	11	24	46	
Squash	19	41	27	59	46	X* X†
Tennis	36	80	9	20	45	X†
Horse riding	14	31	31	69	45	X*
Fishing	34	77	10	23	44	
Athletics	21	75	7	25	28	

* In 10 fastest growing by either members of clubs or numbers of clubs (see Duffield, Best and Collins, 1983).
† At least 10% faster than the average growth for all sports in terms of participation.
From: Martin and Mason, 1980.

inputs. Table 4.5 reproduces the ten largest sports in terms of expenditure, from Martin and Mason (1980). The fast growing sports identified by two sources are, as a group, not biased towards goods-intensity or services-intensity.

Other considerations first pointed out by Marshall (1885), arise from the inter-relationships between recreation demands. These concern the way each derived demand responds to its own price changes, i.e. own-price elasticity of demand. Now known as Marshall's laws, they state that this elasticity will be lower under the following circumstances: (NB we apply the laws directly to recreation demands).

1. The lower the elasticity of demand for the parent recreational activity. For example, if increases in the overall cost of playing tennis have very little effect on the amount of tennis played, then a rise in the price of tennis rackets is unlikely to substantially affect the demand for rackets.

2. The lower the elasticity of substitution between the derived demands. For example, there is no substitute for a tennis racket in a game of tennis! Even if the price of rackets increased dramatically, there will be little substitution by other inputs and so less effect on the demand for rackets than if such substitution had been possible.

3. The smaller the input's share of the total cost of participation. For example, if the cost of buying a tennis racket is a very minor part of the total cost of playing tennis, then even a large increase in racket prices will not have much effect on the demand for rackets, or games of tennis.

4. The lower the elasticity of supply of co-operating inputs (either substitutes or complements). If, for example, the price of one make of tennis racket increased relative to another, the switch in demand to the cheaper racket may be constrained by a slow supply response. On the other hand, if the price of all makes of tennis rackets fell substantially, the potential increase in demand may be stifled by a lack of tennis courts. Such supply constraints are most likely in the short run. Over time they are more easily overcome.

Since evidence suggests, if anything, complementarity between the derived demands for sport and recreation, then the second of Marshall's laws would seem to suggest that elasticity of demand for these inputs will be lower than otherwise expected. We examine evidence concerning own-price elasticities in the context of each individual derived demand later in this chapter.

As already indicated, the inter-relationships between the three major derived demands will partly depend on the type of recreation activity studied. For the sake of convenience, we will concentrate on indoor facilities when analysing the demand for facilities and on countryside recreation when dealing with demand for travel. Travel demands are obviously present in the demand for indoor facilities, but they are likely to be minor compared with their importance for outdoor recreation trips. Duffield (1975) reviews evidence which suggests that distance (and hence travel costs) does not 'explain' local trips of less than about fifteen miles. Since the typical catchment area of an indoor facility is well within this distance, we make only passing reference to travel costs and demands in relation to facility demand. On the other hand Mansfield (1969) in a study of trips to the Lake District, suggested that distance 'explained' 85.6% of the variation in day trips and 92% of the variation in half-day trips. Accordingly, countryside trips are suitable as evidence for a study of travel demand, even though a substantial minority of such trips are to managed facilities.

4.3 The demand for recreational facilities

Many studies now exist in the UK concerning the users of sport and recreation facilities – for a full list see Veal (1985). They yield consistent information of a kind which is not readily available for similar facilities in the USA, so the UK evidence will form the backbone to this part of the chapter. This evidence is mostly confined to the effects of 'social' filters in Rodgers' (1977a) terms, i.e. age, sex, etc. Little evidence relates to individual filters such as motivation, skills and costs.

The demand function for facilities is likely to be a reflection of the demand for parent recreation activities, although other more facility-specific variables are likely to be important, for example, facility management attitudes. Before examining such causal variables separately, two words of warning are appropriate. In all the facility demand studies referred to, and implicit in our approach, no systematic attempt is made to distinguish the independent effect of each variable from the interdependencies between the variables. Because of this weakness it is important to identify the likely associations between the so-called 'independent' variables. The second warning concerns the nature of the evidence. Although some follow-up studies have been done, the bulk of the evidence is cross-sectional, and so any responsiveness of facility demand to changes in the independent variables is not necessarily capable of being transcribed into developments over time.

4.3.1 Price

Surprisingly, the first causal variable in most economists' demand functions receives little attention in user studies. One might expect a normal inverse relationship between price and quantity demanded, but what really counts for management purposes is the elasticity of that demand in response to price changes. Only by accurate assessment of this elasticity can we comment objectively on the attitude frequently expressed in the UK and typified by Coopers and Lybrand (1981b) in one report to the British Government:

'there was significant scope for increasing charges, with operating costs being far higher than operating revenues in the majority of centres examined.'

Even if time series evidence could be reliably gathered, it would suffer from the fact that other causal variables are never constant, so that, for example, when prices rise even in real terms, changing incomes, fashion or access in favour of a facility may boost demand. Similarly, cross sectional evidence is not reliable, since comparison of demand in different facilities which have different prices needs standardization of all the other variables that influence demand. This is the identification problem again.

Another related problem encountered in the context of UK local authority centres is that the entrance price is so low because of government subsidies that it is not a major causal variable, and little relationship is detected. This was reported, for instance, in the Scottish Sports Council's study (1979) where price increases were accompanied by a fall in use in some centres and an increase in use of others; the conclusion being that entrance fees were of little importance in the decision making of consumers. It is perhaps, therefore, only in very poor socioeconomic areas that a heavily subsidized price will still have an impact on demand. In one such area in Manchester, Moss Side, a report (North West Sports Council, 1978) concluded:

'it is probably no coincidence that the rank order of sports according to use by local residents is inverse to that according to price per person.'

For more conventionally commercial facilities, price may be expected to assume greater importance in the demand function. However, we have no recreation-specific examples of such elasticity of demand. Another type of 'facility' of great importance to recreation demand is the outdoor and countryside outlet. For many of these there is no direct entry price, for example, National Parks, urban parks and open spaces. However, economists have a technique – the Clawson method (1959) – which identifies what prices people would be willing to pay for such 'facilities', but this is more relevant to the forecasting of demand which we deal with in the next chapter. One consideration that the Clawson method highlights is relevant here though, and that is the importance of travel costs to some facility visits.

4.3.2 Travel cost

This influence is really composed of two costs – transport and travel time. Many user studies of indoor facilities ask questions relating to the distance travelled and the time taken – the former clearly being a proxy for transport costs – together with information on transport mode. The average picture from Veal's study (1981), see Fig. 4.2, is that since 77% of users travel five miles or less to the centre, then:

'for the majority of users of sports centres travel costs are probably insignificant, whichever mode of transport is used.'

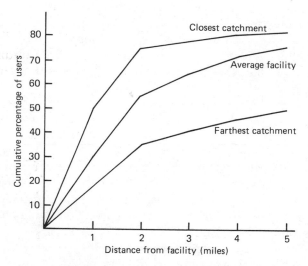

Fig. 4.2 Distance decay functions: UK public sector facilities. From: Veal, 1985.

However, this is not to say that such costs are not influential on facility demand decisions. Veal notes the rapid decline in user numbers per square mile and per 1000 population as distance from the centre increases. For the average UK sports centre he finds that out of every hundred users, 8.7 per square mile come from less than one mile away, but from four to five miles distance the rate has fallen to just 0.1 user per square mile. The visit rates per thousand population were between nine and forty users within one mile of the centre, but only one to twelve users for two or more miles from the centre. Even for larger facilities, which according to Hillman and Whalley (1977) have wider catchment areas, the visit rates decline rapidly with distance, causing access problems:

'such is the extent of the fall off of demand that it could be argued that large facilities create areas of deficiency within the intended catchment area in respect of people whose travel potential, or mobility, is low.'

The problem is made worse by evidence that frequency of participation is lower for larger facilities. Whilst we do not suggest that such declining visit rates are due only or mainly to travel cost differences, it may be a contributory factor. Of the other possible causes, convenience and familiarity with the centre have been less systematically examined in relation to distance, whilst the influence of competing facilities is considered next.

4.3.3 Competing facilities

It might be expected that the existence of other facilities nearby, and their pricing and programming policies, would have an influence on demand for a facility, especially as distance from the facility increases. However, it is not always the case that the facilities are substitutes. In tourist areas, a pattern of different facilities may well be complementary in attracting visitors. In urban areas, an array of similar facilities may be seen as a network of provision not only designed to minimize travel distance for users, but also to provide facilities that complement each other in terms of activities offered, coaching and training opportunities, types of user catered for, and/or opening and closing times.

The limited evidence available on the use of competing facilities suggests a great deal of cross-use. In a study of one South Wales area, Torfaen, the proportion of users who visited other centres ranged from 53 to 75%, (Whaley, 1980). This is in one of the most well-provided recreation areas in the UK in terms of indoor facilities. Whaley's conclusion is that far from spreading a limited clientele more thinly, the provision of more competing facilities has in fact boosted local participation rates by an equivalent proportion, as well as promoting multiple-centre use by participants. Thus the demand for each individual facility in Torfaen is equal to that of other centres in less well-endowed areas. As Veal (1985) says:

'There can be little doubt that sports centres are introducing people to new activities and generating a great deal of sports activity which would otherwise not have taken place.'

4.3.4 Income, occupation and socioeconomic group

It is impractical to ask about income in user surveys, so the proxy variables normally identified are occupation and employment (or economic) status. The bulk of evidence about facility users is, as has already been noted, for UK public sector indoor facilities. One would therefore expect a user profile which at least reflected the population as a whole, and one might even hope for a profile biased in favour of lower

Occupation

income groups. In fact, as Veal (1985) confirms, it is the professional and managerial classes that are over-represented in the use of these UK public sector indoor facilities, whilst the semi-skilled and unskilled manual groups are under-represented. The former groups make up 24% of users, yet are only 14% of the population of England and Wales. The latter, lower income groups, make up only 13% of users, but are 27% of the population. Veal offers two reasons for the under-representation of the lower skilled occupations – the physically demanding nature of manual work and their lower car ownership levels. However, there is no evidence concerning the impact of such deterrents and it remains a worry that public sector facilities are biased in favour of the higher income groups. The equity problems inherent in this concern are more fully considered in Chapter 10. Whaley's study of Torfaen offers one possible solution to this problem – the provision of more neighbourhood facilities. Such provision has occurred in Torfaen with the result that use by the lower socioeconomic groups is proportionately higher than for the average UK sports centre. Semi-skilled and unskilled manual groups account for about 29% of the population of Torfaen, and 22% of the facility users in Whaley's sample – a considerable reduction in their under-representation compared with the UK average. Such evidence suggests that the travel cost/access constraint is important for poorer users.

Regarding economic status, two user groups are consistently under-represented compared with their numbers in the whole population, these are full-time housewives and retired people. Is this under-representation a problem? If it is caused by constraints the answer is likely to be 'yes'. However, if it is the result of differing preferences by these groups, then there is no problem.

4.3.5 Sex

Creche

The evidence on use of public sector indoor facilities is very conclusive on this issue – women are under-represented. This problem is a lot worse for mothers with young children, a fact that is widely recognized but rarely countered with meaningful measures, such as a creche. Not only is there under-representation, but female demand is also confined to a few activities. The public sector facility manager thus faces a dilemma. Either the imbalance in use by the sexes can be accepted as a proper reflection of recreation demands, or it can be seen as symptomatic of a social problem which government is obliged to try and correct. If the latter approach is taken, then positive discrimination in favour of female users can take the obvious forms of programming 'female' activities and/or giving preferential access at certain times.

programming for women.

4.3.6 Age

Logically we can expect a similar dilemma here as with sex differences above, i.e. that use of facilities for physical activities in particular is likely to be biased in favour of those more capable of such activities, and with more social drive to participate – younger groups. Veal's evidence (1985) confirms our expectation. All age groups below 45 years are over-represented in facility use compared with their importance in the population as a whole, by 10% to 20%. This leaves the 45 years plus age band with tremendous under-representation. They comprise only 8% of users but 47% of the population. It is possible that this result overstates the bias in participation. Older people are more likely to go on informal recreation trips or use other local authority facilities, for example, community centres and village halls. In North America, facilities for the elderly, senior centres, are growing rapidly and a more balanced picture is evident.

Any under-representation may be seen, rather paradoxically, as a source of both social and commercial concern. On the one hand the spectre of older people 'cut-off' from public sector facilities because of inappropriate programming and marketing is embarrassing. The UK Sports Council's campaign *50+, all to play for* is clearly a response to such a feeling. On the other hand, an ageing population means a shift in purchasing power which certain commercial interests have been quick to respond to, for example, tourism, but which the average leisure centre has not.

4.3.7 Car ownership

Despite its close association with travel cost and distance, this variable is worth singling out as representative of ease of access. User surveys show the importance of the car for access to facilities on short and long recreation trips. In Veal's study an average of 67% of users travelled by car to get to the facility, although the range around this average is wide – 26–88%. Obviously, dependency on cars will vary according to the geographical location of the facility and associated factors like socioeconomic make-up, population density and public transport provision. The fact that the majority of facility users are dependent on cars for access does highlight the cause of the minority who have no private transport. Hillman and Whalley (1977) are particularly concerned about this problem. It is worth remembering that although on average 60% of UK households have access to at least one car, in some deprived areas this can fall to as little as 10%. This can distort the effective catchment area of a facility.

4.3.8 Management Policy

Even if two facilities were sited in identical areas with respect to the variables above, their demand characteristics could differ markedly because of facility management decisions. Most local authority facilities in the UK have such a diverse range of objectives that choices have to be made trading off one type of demand with another. This results in important variations in activities offered and users attracted by different facilities. For example, management attitudes vary on the 'correct balance' of club use and casual use, and on the degree of positive discrimination to be used in favour of such groups as the unemployed. Some managers offer a comprehensive free package of opportunities and guidance for the unemployed, whilst others offer nothing because they feel this would be unfair to the employed on low incomes (see Glyptis and Riddington, 1983).

4.3.9 Facility location

Even though the spatial context is implicit in some of the above variables, it is important to be explicitly aware of its importance. The exact physical location of a facility in relation to housing areas, town centre, principal transport routes, etc., will be a fundamental influence on user demands. We have already noted Veal's findings concerning the rapid fall-off in visit rates in relation to distance from a facility. It is also

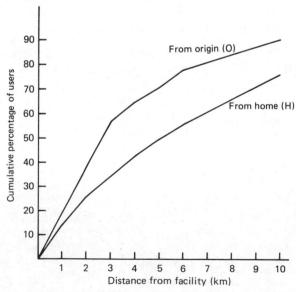

Fig. 4.3 Distance decay functions: squash at Moss Side. From: North West Sports Council, 1978.

important to make a distinction between those users who travel from home and those who travel from work. This can be very important for some city or town centre facilities, where a substantial minority of users may travel from work. The study of Moss Side leisure centre (North West Sports Council, 1978) revealed just this problem, as the distance decay function for squash at the centre shows; see Fig. 4.3.

Forty-one per cent of squash players in the weekday sample came direct from work. This caused the large difference between the distance decay functions recorded by actual distance travelled (O) and by distance from home (H) in Fig. 4.3. Similar differences existed for other sports at the centre, leading to questions about who the priority users were supposed to be in such a deprived inner city area.

4.4 The demand for recreational travel

Most of the evidence used in this section is from countryside recreation, since it has such a major travel input. Furthermore, much of this type of recreation does not accord strictly with our terms of reference i.e. physical activities. According to the 1972/3 National Travel Survey, 6% of all travel trips are for informal recreation, and only 1% for sport, although some informal recreation will involve physical activity, for example, long walks, sea swimming, horse riding. Unfortunately, much of the evidence does not disaggregate into physical and non-physical activities.

The variable normally used to represent recreation travel is the number of trips, although the number of passenger-miles is often used in transport studies. As most of the countryside recreation literature relates to the former, we shall assume this is the quantity of demand referred to for the rest of this section. The causal variables investigated include those common to other derived demands, such as price, income and some that are particularly important to travel demand, such as distance.

4.4.1 Distance

Travel demand has commonly been expressed in 'gravity models' as having a consistent inverse relationship with distance travelled. The further away from a destination, the lower the visit numbers (and the lower the visit rate, although this is rarely identified except in Clawson demand curve exercises). Distance decay functions such as those in Fig. 4.2 show this relationship. However whereas evidence of distance decay for facilities is well-documented, when recreation travel demand across all facilities is studied the results are not quite so clear cut. Duffield (1975) provides evidence which suggests that the volume of recreation trips does not consistently fall with distance, but that the effect of distance varies depending upon the length of the journeys. It would appear that distance is a less reliable predictor of numbers of trips for shorter distances (less than 15 miles) and for long duration trips (where the total trip exceeds 7 hours). One of the principal reasons for this lack of consistent 'explanatory' power is that travel yields positive utility in many trips. In any case the simple gravity model does not explicitly consider the possible reasons for any relationship between travel demand and distance, and it is to such reasons that we now turn.

4.4.2 Travel costs

For countryside recreation, generally, travel costs are likely to be a significant proportion of total costs, especially for day trips and half-day trips. However, in examining the relationship between travel demand and travel costs we must be aware of the difficulties of separating the influence of travel costs from that of other variables. The Countryside Commission (1982) in their 1977 and 1980 surveys also encountered this problem:

'The overall picture that emerges is confusing. Increases in income, holiday entitlement and car ownership point to increased visitor use, while increased unemployment, higher travel costs and a strong pound all suggest reduced recreation travel in England and Wales. On top of this one must consider the prevailing economic climate and mood of the population.'

Nevertheless the initial conclusion in this report was that higher travel costs had caused a substitution of shorter recreation trips for longer ones as well as an overall fall in all trips. By comparison a recent *USA Economic Review of Travel* (US Travel Data Center, 1983) suggested the inverse because of falling travel prices:

'Lower travel price inflation . . . reduces the attractiveness of . . . alternatives to pleasure travel, such as local recreation.'

Shucksmith (1980) warned of very elastic travel demand curves associated with countryside recreation activities and predicted the substitution of shorter for longer trips, in response to rising real petrol prices. Further Countryside Commission evidence seemed to partially support this prediction. In response to an 11% rise in real petrol prices from 1977 to 1980, day trips fell by 5% whilst holiday trips fell by 46% in the average summer month; the superficial interpretation being that day trip demand is inelastic and holiday trip demand is elastic for the price changes covered. However this is not necessarily the case, since other influences almost certainly contributed to the different rates of decline in trip making, in particular the recession and a strong pound.

In common with the UK, rising travel costs in the USA have combined with other factors to depress travel demand. 1982 saw an 11% fall in vacation person trips and a rise of 5.5% in the USA travel price index. Figure 4.4 shows the change in USA real travel sales and travel prices in the period 1973 to 1982.

Fig. 4.4 Real travel sales and travel prices, annual percentage changes 1973-82, USA. From: US Travel Data Center, 1983.

Whereas there are some signs of an inverse relationship, it would be wrong to draw inferences from such data about the price elasticity of travel demand, because of changes in other influential variables. Another complication is that any change in relative real prices causes both a substitution effect and an income effect on consumption, as shown in Chapter 2. The *Third Nationwide Recreation Survey* for the USA (1977) gives evidence which suggests that the income effect varies as travel prices rise. The upper income groups maintained their recreation levels, whereas lower income groups made substantial cutbacks.

The future relationship between travel costs and demand for travel promises to be as unpredictable as in the past. It is highly likely that a normal inverse relationship exists, but the price elasticity of travel demand has not been clearly identified. Real petrol prices may well fall in the short-run because of world oil gluts, but this is only one effect on travel demand, and it is, possibly, only short-term.

Returning to UK evidence, it does appear that price elasticity of demand for travel varies according to which activities or groups are considered. Table 4.6 shows that the growth activities at a time of rising real petrol prices are all sport related, whereas the more passive pursuits declined.

Table 4.6. *Changing patterns of countryside activities 1977-80, UK.*

	Activity days per 1000 people (Summer Month)		
	1977	1980	Percentage change
Drives, outings	1000	680	–32
Long walks	800	850	+6
Visits to undeveloped coast	700	430	–39
Visits to historic buildings	200	180	–10
Watching sport	130	200	+54
Visits to zoos	60	50	–17
Fishing	130	100	–23
Other sport	150	270	+80
Horse riding	50	60	+20

From: Countryside Commission, 1982.

There is also evidence from the same source that higher income and socioeconomic groups have a less elastic demand in response to travel price increases, as in the USA.

One final problem in relating travel demand to travel prices is stressed by Elson (1979). This is that a growing proportion of recreation trips by car are subsidized i.e. using company cars. In 1977 this proportion was 20% overall, but is likely to be higher for certain occupational groups.

4.4.3 Age

Given the relationships between age on the one hand and activities and facility demands on the other, one might expect travel demand to be similarly biased towards younger age groups. However, as regards countryside recreation trips, available evidence suggests much less bias. The Countryside Commission surveys show the relationship between age and trip making, as shown in Table 4.7. The deterioration in trips with age does occur but far less noticeably than demand for activities and facilities. Vickerman (1975b) also found age to be an insignificant influence on numbers of trips. This is no doubt due to the less physically demanding nature of most countryside recreation pursuits and the importance of travel in its own right.

If evidence were to single out countryside travel demand associated with sporting activities, we would still expect the same age bias as the parent demand function displays.

Table 4.7. _Age and countryside recreation trips, 1977-80, UK._

Age range	Percentage participating in last four weeks	
	1977	1980
16-19	59	49
20-24	56	48
25-29	57	45
30-34	61	50
35-39	60	47
40-44	59	42
45-49	53	39
50-54	49	41
55-59	51	35
60-64	49	33
65-69	44	32

From: Countryside Commission, 1982.

4.4.4 Income, occupation and socioeconomic group

These are considered together, as before, because of their inter-dependency. An _a priori_ expectation would be that travel demand rises as income or status group increases and evidence tends to confirm this (see Table 4.8 and Fig. 4.5). One curiosity is that although real disposable income rose on average by 18% from 1977 to 1980, participation in all income groups fell by a significant proportion. However, this apparent contradiction between cross section and time series evidence is explained by the other downward pressures which outweighed the influence of rising incomes – notably economic recession and rising transport costs. Vickerman (1975b) qualifies such findings with evidence that income does not have an independent effect on travel demand but that:

'the inter-relationship of income with occupational, age and other social indices means that a classification of the population by income can provide a good indicator of likely leisure trip generation.'

This once again demonstrates the difficulties and importance of identifying both the independent and joint influences of the causal variables.
Fitton (1979) raises a question about Fig. 4.5 that we have posed before, i.e. is the under-representation and over-representation a reflection of constraints to participation, or preferences? He presents evidence of different strengths of preferences for countryside recreation trips, which to some extent lends support to the preference hypothesis. Some 31% of

Table 4.8. *Income, socioeconomic group and countryside recreation trips, 1977 and 1980, UK.*

	Percentage participating in last four weeks	
	1977	1980
Income		
Low	43	32
Middle	58	42
High	63	54
Socioeconomic group		
A,B	67	58
C1	55	50
C2	55	39
D,E	38	29

From: Countryside Commission, 1982.

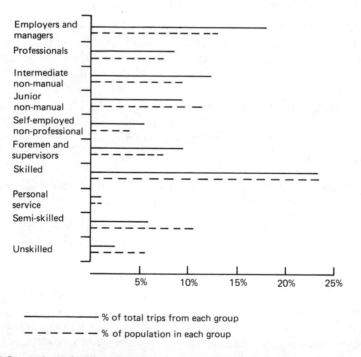

———————— % of total trips from each group

— — — — — — % of population in each group

Fig. 4.5 Occupation and countryside recreation trips, 1977, UK. From: Fitton, 1979.

unskilled workers preferring urban to countryside leisure, 25% of semi-skilled workers, 21% of skilled workers and only 10% of employers, managers and professional occupations.

4.4.5 Travel mode

Nearly every study of demand for recreational travel, be it for sport or informal recreation, stresses the importance of car ownership. In 1978, three quarters of UK holiday destinations were reached by car, and four-fifths of countryside day trips (Countryside Commission, 1982). Sixty-three per cent of car owners made trips, but only 32% of non-car owners. Even 64% of these non-car owners who made trips used a car. However, Hillman and Whalley (1977) and Duffield (1975) point out that each type of recreation trip and activity demonstrates a different pattern of travel mode use, and hence distances travelled. The evidence cited by Hillman and Whalley (1977) is reproduced in Table 4.9.

Table 4.9. *Travel modes for different recreation purposes.*

Recreational activity	Walk	Car	Public transport	Other
Sport	33	50	12	5
Informal recreation	64	27	5	4
London parks	78	8	11	3
Urban parks (Tyne and Wear)	71	14	12	2
Rural/coast (Tyne and Wear)	22	48	20	10
Country parks	16	80	2	2
Rural (Clwyd)	3	95	1	1

From: Hillman and Whalley, 1977.

Clearly, informal recreation in this table is dominated by short, urban trips. For rural recreation the importance of the car is self-evident. Hillman and Whalley criticize the bias in recreation planning in favour of the car user, since this bias discriminates against the recreationally disadvantaged, i.e. the elderly, the poor etc.

4.4.6 Other causal variables

Evidence presented by Vickerman (1975b) suggests unemployment, household size and head of household status to be consistent negative influences on recreational trip demand. Hillman and Whalley (1977) suggest that facility size and quality have positive effects. Another set of possible influences examined by a number of researchers, is the extent of individual and collective information on, and perceptions of, recreation opportunities. These are influenced by not only the demographic and socioeconomic factors considered above, but also by such considerations as life-styles, life-cycles, social situations and family obligation. Fitton's evidence (1979) that 75% of countryside recreation trips are made to places that the people have visited before, often many times, is indicative of the limits of recreational information and the constrained perceptions of recreation opportunities that participants suffer from.

Finally, we should never forget the weather! According to Duffell (1975) this can alter demand for recreation travel by anything up to 80% on a single day.

4.5 The demand for sport and recreation equipment

The demand for equipment has one different characteristic to the other derived demands studied – it is demand for a durable consumer good, whereas facility and travel demands are non-durable. So, just as there is an investment aspect to the parent demand, as seen in the last chapter, there is also an investment aspect here. In analysing the causes of changes in the demand for sports equipment therefore, it is not enough to look at the variables examined in both the previous sections – price, income, age, sex etc. We also need to represent the investment aspect, and this is done by reference to a long-established theory of investment in economics, the accelerator, with implications for forecasting and integration in equipment markets.

Before taking up this theme, we will examine the evidence from both sides of the Atlantic on the sports equipment market, in order to specify any aspects of importance to the subsequent analysis.

4.5.1 Dimensions of the sports equipment market

One important distinction to be made within the sports equipment market is that between expenditure on equipment and expenditure on sports clothing and footwear. They appear to display different medium term trends, as Table 4.4 shows. The relative consumption of equipment and clothing/footwear will differ for different sports, so care must be taken to bear this in mind when investigating the 'equipment' market.

Contrary to what might be expected, it is not the mass participation sports that dominate sports equipment expenditure. Table 4.10 lists the top ten sports by expenditure on sports equipment, including clothing and footwear, for the UK and the USA. Top of both expenditure lists is boating, and whereas it is the sixth largest sport by participant numbers in the USA, it is only the 16th largest in the UK. It accounts for a massive 25% of the total equipment expenditure market and a very high expenditure per head. Three high ranking participant sports in the UK are not represented in the expenditure top ten. These are darts, billiards/snooker and table tennis. In the USA the inconsistency between participant numbers and expenditure is greater by this indicator, since five high ranking participant sports are not in the expenditure top ten – swimming, walking, bowling, jogging and pool/billiards.

Table 4.10. *Top ten sports, UK 1979 (by expenditure on sports goods) and USA 1979 (by expenditure).*

Sport	Goods expenditure (£m, UK; $m, USA)	Number of participants* (Millions)	Goods expenditure per participant* (£, UK; $, USA)	High growth expectations†
UK‡				
1. Boating	224	0.6	373	
2. Golf	73	1.9	38	X
3. Swimming	50	12.8	4	X
4. Tennis	36	1.7	21	X
5. Soccer	35	3.2	11	
6. Fishing	34	2.0	17	
7. Cricket	23	1.6	14	
8. Walking	22	9.9	2	
9. Athletics	21	1.6§	13	
10. Badminton	19	1.2	16	X
Squash	19	1.1	17	X
USA				
1. Pleasure boats etc	3630	37.9	96	X
2. Firearms etc.	1357	19.7	69	
3. Bicycles etc.	1290	69.8	18	X
4. Athletics (team sales)	1225	3.0	408	
5. Tennis	661	32.2	21	X
6. Snow skiing	606	12.9	47	X
7. Golf	537	15.9	34	X
8. Fishing	515	59.2	9	
9. Camping	488	40.3	12	X
10. Snowmobiles	254	8.6	30	

* UK participant figures for adults only.
† Above average growth expectations, 1973-91, UK, Veal. In ten fastest growing sports, 1973-6, USA, Department of Commerce.
‡ Recreation vehicles, exercise equipment excluded – not sport specific.
§ Athletics participants include outdoor and indoor – some possible duplication.
From: Martin and Mason, 1980; US News and World Report 1981; US Department of Commerce, 1979.

The sports with high growth potential appear to be the more goods-intensive sports, according to evidence presented earlier in Table 4.5. The only one with a greater services input is squash, but even here the goods input is not low. One logical hypothesis concerning the growth in goods-intensive sports is that their relative prices are lower. Certainly sports goods in the UK are becoming no cheaper than UK goods generally as Fig. 4.6 demonstrates, although this only relates to domestic prices. The most important comparison with respect to our earlier analysis, however, is between sports goods prices and sports services prices, and unfortunately no consistent long-run information on the latter is available.

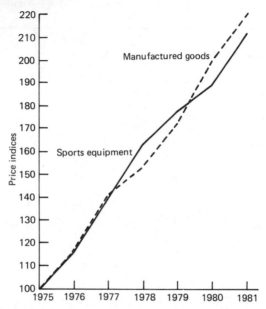

Fig. 4.6 Changes in prices of sports equipment and manufactured goods, 1975-81, UK. From: Business Monitor PQ 494.3, Economic Trends.

Sports goods and services may be complements or substitutes, as argued in Section 4.2. Where home production is technically possible for the majority of users, a substitution of goods for services is likely. Where this is not technically possible, for example, in squash and team activities, a complementary relationship is more probable. Some activities, like darts, have very little input of services anyway and for others the inputs of both equipment and services are very low, since clothing and footwear are the only major expenditure items, for example, walking, jogging and marathon running.

Another important influence on the changes in sports equipment prices relative to other goods and to sports services prices is the extent to which the market is penetrated by imports. In the UK, this position changed dramatically in the sports equipment market in the 1970s as Fig. 4.7 demonstrates. It shows high and rising import penetration.

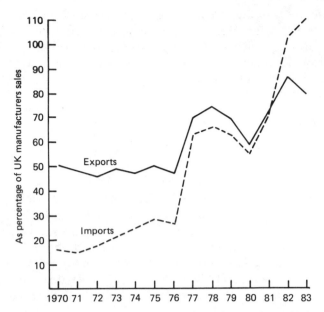

Fig. 4.7 Sports equipment exports and imports, 1970-83, UK. From: Business Monitor PQ 494.3 and PQ 494.2.

In the USA, in 1978, imports were a lower proportion of total sales (about 30%), so import prices will have had less of an impact on average equipment prices than in the UK. The UK picture is complicated by the change in 1976 when imports as a percentage of UK manufacturers' sales doubled, but when exports also rose. We can find no particular reasons for this shift in the balance of trade. Other information of particular relevance regarding imports would be their sources and unit prices, since if they are predominantly at the cheaper end of the market, then they would have a dampening effect on average equipment prices, and encourage the substitution of goods for other inputs.

Having distinguished various types of sports 'equipment', we now revert to looking at this type of good as a single entity. The purpose of this is to investigate possible determinants of changes in equipment demand.

4.5.2 Price and income

Unlike facility demand, which is highly subsidized, the sports equipment market is a more-or-less normal commercial market. The influences of price and income on demand are therefore expected to be important. Estimation of both price and income elasticities are possible.

The estimated equation below (from Gratton, 1979) uses sales of equipment from the *Business Monitor Series* (Government Statistical Service, HMSO) price indices from the same source, and national income data. The coefficients attached to the price and income variables are direct measures of elasticity because the regression is estimated in the conventional double log form for demand equations. The implications are that sports equipment is both price and income elastic, with price elasticity being particularly high.

Production = 11.565 –2.91 price + 1.119 income

(t=6.01)   (t=2.81)

R2 = 0.951

The income elasticity coefficient is consistent with estimates for the parent demand generated from cross sectional data in Table 3.4. The price elasticity estimates must be qualified by a reminder about the complications of elasticity of derived demand as discussed earlier. High price elasticity for equipment demand may reflect a high elasticity of demand for the parent activities and/or a high elasticity of substitution between, for example, equipment and facilities, travel or time.

4.5.3 Changes in parent demand: the accelerator

As well as parent demand influencing the price elasticity of derived demand such as sports equipment, it may also influence absolute changes in this derived demand. The accelerator theory of investment at its simplest level is represented by the following equation

$$\triangle K = a \triangle O$$

where $\triangle K$ = changes in capital stock (i.e. investment)

$\triangle O$ = change in output (i.e. parent demand)

a = accelerator coefficient (= capital/output ratio)

$$\text{since } a = \frac{\triangle K}{\triangle O} = \frac{K}{O}$$

For our purposes capital is sports equipment for an activity and output is the number of participants in an activity. 'a' is the ratio of equipment to participants, i.e. the average value of equipment per participant. We can estimate such average prices by dividing the domestic market's equipment expenditure (i.e. domestic production minus exports plus imports) by the number of participants for any sport. A certain amount of investment in sports equipment is necessary to cover depreciation, so we have to make an assumption about the average length of life of sports equipment in any activity investigated.

To illustrate the accelerator effect, Table 4.11 takes three sports – squash, fishing and table tennis. We assume the following:-

1. Squash and fishing have the same annual equipment costs to participants (£20), whilst table tennis costs only £5.
2. Fishing and table tennis equipment depreciates constantly over a ten year period, after which it is replaced. Squash equipment depreciates faster and needs to be replaced after five years.
3. Each sport has four successive annual changes in participant numbers of 10, 0, 5, 10%.

Table 4.11. *The accelerator effect on sports equippment demand: an illustration.*

	(1) Participants		(2) Equipment stock	(3) Desired equipment stock	(4) Depreciation	(5)=(4)+(3)-(2) Annual equipment demand	
	Millions	%change	£M	£M	£M	£M	%change
Squash							
Year 1	1		20	20	4	4	
Year 2	1.1	10	20	22	4	6	50
Year 3	1.1	0	22	22	4.4	4.4	-27
Year 4	1.155	5	22	23.1	4.4	5.5	25
Year 5	1.2655	10	23.1	25.31	4.62	6.83	24
Fishing							
Year 1	1		20	20	2	2	
Year 2	1.1	10	20	22	2	4	100
Year 3	1.1	0	22	22	2.2	2.2	-45
Year 4	1.155	5	22	23.1	2.2	3.3	50
Year 5	1.2655	10	23.1	25.31	2.31	4.52	37
Table Tennis							
Year 1	1		5	5	0.5	0.5	
Year 2	1.1	10	5	5.5	0.5	1	100
Year 3	1.1	0	5.5	5.5	0.55	0.55	-45
Year 4	1.155	5	5.5	5.78	0.55	0.83	51
Year 5	1.2655	10	5.78	6.33	0.578	1.13	36

The accelerating effect of changes in participation on changes in equipment demand is clear to see. What appears to be the significant factor is not the price of equipment – Fig. 4.8b and c have different prices – but the rate of depreciation of equipment. Where this depreciation differs, as in Fig. 4.8a and b, a different accelerator effect emerges. The longer the depreciation period (i.e. the slower the depreciation) the larger will be the accelerator effect.

So far we have talked in terms of depreciation as wear and tear of equipment. In sports equipment demand there will also be an element of 'relative depreciation' regardless of the physical state of the existing stock of equipment. This relative depreciation will be brought about by technological changes in equipment construction, or by fashion changes in design which encourage sports participants to replace equipment

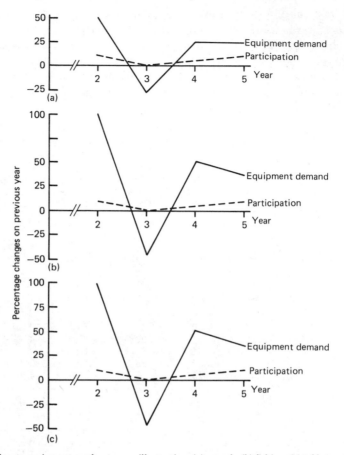

Fig. 4.8 Sports equipment accelerator: an illustration: (a) squash; (b) fishing; (c) table tennis.

before it is physically necessary to do so. It is in the interests of sports equipment manufacturers to encourage such relative depreciation when their products have long depreciation periods. In fishing, for example, fibreglass rods would often last a lifetime, but were superceded technically or in fashion terms, first by carbon fibre rods, and then by boron rods, so that the fibreglass rods are replaced sooner than is necessary. Similarly, but more emphatically, ski equipment undergoes annual changes in design largely stimulated by fashion consciousness. Such demand behaviour will reduce the 'depreciation' period for equipment and therefore reduce the volatility of equipment demand changes in response to changes in the numbers participating. It means that replacement demand rises as a proportion of total demand; otherwise too much dependence on new participants' demand would increase the accelerator effect.

Thus we see that there are two ways for an equipment manufacturer to expand, and to reduce the volatility of his market: either by action to shorten the perceived length of life of sports equipment or by encouraging new participants.

4.6 Conclusions

Many of the issues covered by this chapter are relevant to the decisions of planners, administrators and managers in recreation. Since we are examining planning and supply efficiency in subsequent chapters, it seems appropriate to direct these conclusions towards such issues.

Planning has very strict information requirements and this chapter has shown the lack of specific information on certain inter-relationships between recreational demands. In particular the demands for travel and facilities have been examined mainly under a strict *ceteris paribus* assumption. There remains uncertainty about the joint influence of the so called independent variables and therefore their separate effects are also subject to bias. This identification problem increases the error margins likely in any forecasting exercise to predict such demands. There is also a dovetailing of planning interests with respect to transport networks, land use and recreation provision, and the relationships between these different demands in a recreation context need to be identified. Otherwise problems of access and unsatisfied potential demand may arise.

Managers and administrators also have an information requirement, much of which relates to recreation demand. Price elasticity of demand, for instance, is an important economic concept which many commercial managers have an intuitive feel for, even if they never calculate it. There is evidence that managers and administrators of UK public sector indoor facilities are slow to experiment in such a way as to reveal this elasticity (Coopers and Lybrand, 1981b). We have demonstrated the complicated nature of the elasticity of derived demand, and in Chapter 8 we consider elasticity and revenue consequences in a rational approach to pricing in facilities.

Much of the facility information covered picks out the existence of under-represented groups. Is it equitable that this under-representation should occur? Whilst we raise the possibility that it may be the result of preferences, it is clear that in the UK at least, the bias in indoor facility usage is a cause for concern.

Another planning issue arises in analysing travel demands. The importance of the car to recreation participants cannot be denied, but nor can the existence of poor access groups without cars, and possibly without an efficient public transport network too. If planning criteria are based on the average user, then poor access groups will continue to have problems. Again the information requirement is important; some consistent measure of access problems is necessary for efficient siting of facilities.

In the sports equipment market, our application of the accelerator principle infers two rational management strategies. The first is built-in obsolescence, if not in the physical sense, then according to fashion. This would impart more stability to their markets. The second is vertical integration into 'grass roots' participation. This, if successful, might encourage a consistent rise in participant numbers which would guarantee growth in the equipment market. This is one aspect of market segmentation that manufacturers have largely ignored. The more noticeable participant involvement has been at the elite end, in sponsorship deals. We will investigate this in Chapter 11.

Finally we return to one of the principal questions posed at the beginning of this chapter. Would it be sufficient, for planning purposes, to assess recreation derived demands on the basis of the parent demand functions? In other words could planners use the type of analysis in Chapter 3 to proxy changes in demands for facilities, recreational travel and sporting goods? By and large the answer is 'yes' although it is heavily qualified by additional considerations. Each derived demand has influences that are specific to it, for example, management policy in facilities, distance for travel demand and the accelerator investment effect in sports equipment demand. It must also be said that at the level of individual sports the characteristics of the derived demand functions vary enormously from the average, but that is also true of the parent activities.

5 Demand forecasting and recreation planning

5.1 Introduction

This is very much a pivotal chapter. Not only does it look back to the recreation demands of the last three chapters, these being the quantities to be identified and forecasted, but it also looks forward to the supply decisions to be examined in subsequent chapters. Pricing, marketing and investment appraisal all rely, to a considerable extent, on accurate demand forecasting.

The main purpose of this chapter is to review the available methods of demand forecasting, with the help of recreation examples, and then to set them in a planning context. We first examine demand forecasting for a specific site, the main emphasis being on the Clawson method (1959). The following section examines forecasting in wider fields – single and multi-sport markets in regions or nations.

By examining these techniques we hope to offer suggestions for the role and scope of such exercises in recreation planning. The scope is particularly important, since recreation forecasts can range from a study of one sport over the next year or so in one locality, to predictions of demand for whole fields of leisure activities until the end of the century for a whole country. Different considerations emerge from experience with various empirical methods which have implications for the geographical scope, the choice of time period and the choice of activities and/or facilities to be investigated.

Before examining the relevant methods of investigation, it is necessary to clarify the different types of demand that forecasting attempts to uncover (see Burton, 1971).

1. Existing demand or revealed preference. This may be comparatively straightforward for a formal, indoor facility with entry prices and

automatic monitoring of user numbers, but it is not so easy for unconfined activities occurring in natural recreation resources, for which no entry price is charged and visit monitoring is only possible in small samples. The Clawson method attempts to deal with the latter case.

2. Latent demand – i.e. demand unrealized because of an access or facility supply constraint. Such demand will obviously be revealed by building a new, nearby facility.

3. 'Induced' or 'generated' demand (cf generated traffic in transport studies). This is demand over and above latent demand, created by a new facility. The convention is to value this less than other demands, since it only occurs because costs have fallen to such an extent that participation has become attractive, whereas other forms of demand, for example, latent or diverted, would have existed even at higher costs to participants, and would only have needed facility provision to have been realized.

4. Diverted demand, i.e. diverted to a new facility from an older competing facility, for at least the short-run.

5. Substitute demand, i.e. demand that is diverted from one activity to another as a result of a new facility or recreation opportunity. This is termed substitute demand to distinguish it from diverted demand.

5.2 Forecasting demand for a specific site or facility

In this section we review two forecasting methods, each with obvious weaknesses. The question that emerges, therefore, is whether or not such exercises are worthwhile in practice. It is important to consider this question since the little evidence available suggests that not much demand forecasting takes place at the facility or site level (see Chapter 8, Sections 8.7.4 and 8.7.6). Cowell, 1979, suggests that a major reason for this lack of forecasting may be distrust of the techniques:

'It was felt (by managers) that such assessments had rarely given accurate forecasts.'

5.2.1 The Clawson method*

Despite the fact that its use has been almost entirely restricted to a narrow range of large, resource based, recreation outlets, and studies using it have been largely academic as opposed to practical planning exercises, the most common forecasting technique for a specific site is still the Clawson demand curve – also known as the Clawson-Knetsch or

* For two recent, comprehensive reviews of the Clawson method, see Baxter (1979) and Gibson (1978).

Clawson-Knetsch-Hotelling method. It is a technique commonly associated with benefit estimation in recreation cost-benefit analysis, but we introduce it here, since it is primarily a method which identifies present demand and forecasts future demand, usually where little or no direct price is paid by participants. It has been used in the USA and the UK to identify demand for such existing sites as national parks, reservoirs, game reserves and fishing in a river. It has also been used to forecast demand for proposed projects; we examine one such study, by Mansfield (1971), in Chapter 9, Section 9.2.2.

The Clawson method uses information on travel costs to generate a final demand curve for a recreation outlet. Hence it is most appropriate for those outlets where travel cost is a major component of total visit costs – typically, free countryside outlets. It can best be demonstrated by reference to a simplified example. Suppose a survey reveals the information in Table 5.1 concerning visitors to a large countryside site which is used primarily for recreational purposes. The only information required is, in fact, the number of visitors attending a site in a specific time period and the distance they travel, which can be collected by a survey. Distance is assumed to be closely related to the cost of travel. Having identified the distances travelled, this information is grouped into distance zones around the site; the nearer the zone is to the site, the cheaper the travel cost. The total population of each zone will be known from, for example, census data, and hence for each zone a visit rate may be calculated, for example, one visit per year per 1000 population in Zone B in Table 5.1.

Table 5.1. *Clawson demand curve example: Stage 1.*

Zones	Average distance travelled by users (Miles)	Visit rate per 1000 population	Zone population	Total visits
A	10	2	500 000	1000
B	30	1	1 500 000	1500
C	50	0.5	10 000 000	5000
D	70	0.2	3 000 000	600
Total				**8100**

So, for each zone a visit rate is associated with an average distance travelled. This distance can be converted to a visit cost by multiplying by the average travel cost per mile. Hence we arrive at a relationship for each zone between the visit rate and the visit cost; the full set of these relationships is represented in Fig. 5.1. In this figure, the average travel cost is assumed to be 10p a mile and for the sake of simplification it is also assumed that only cars are used to reach the site and that the average car occupancy rate is two people. Therefore the travel cost per person equals half the travel cost per car. In this first instance travel cost is assumed to be the total visit cost.

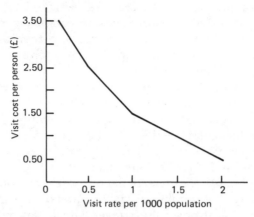

Fig. 5.1 Clawson demand example, stage 2: visit cost and visit rates.

It is now possible with the help of Fig. 5.1 to add to travel costs any nominal entry price and work out the effect on total demand. An entry price of £1, for instance, increases Zone A's visit cost to £1.50 per person. Applying the appropriate visit rate (1 per 1000) to Zone A's population gives the number of visits from this zone at the new visit cost, i.e. 500 visits. Repeating this procedure for the other zones gives total visits at the new visit cost. Table 5.2 has this information, plus similar calculations for higher entry prices. Each successive round of calculations indicates one point on the final demand curve. The initial

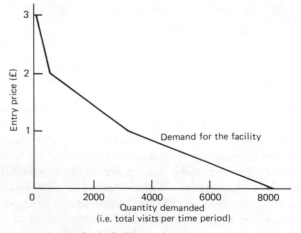

Fig. 5.2 Clawson demand example: the final demand curve.

stage in Table 5.1, gave us the total number of visits at zero entry price: 8100 visits. Table 5.2 adds the number of visits at prices of £1, £2 and £3. The complete final demand curve is portrayed in Fig. 5.2.

Table 5.2. *Clawson demand curve example: Stage 3.*

Zone	Users' average total visit cost*	Visit rate (per 1000 population)	Zone population (1000's)	Total visits
Entry price of £1				
A	1.50	1	500	500
B	2.50	0.5	1 500	750
C	3.50	0.2	10 000	2000
D	4.50	0	3 000	0
Total				**3250**
Entry price of £2				
A	2.50	0.5	500	250
B	3.50	0.2	1 500	300
C	4.50	0	10 000	0
D	5.50	0	3 000	0
Total				**550**
Entry price of £3				
A	3.50	0.2	500	100
B	4.50	0	1 500	0
C	5.50	0	10 000	0
D	6.50	0	3 000	0
Total				**100**

* Any visit cost exceeding £3.50 is assumed to reduce the visit rate to zero.

This simplified example serves to illustrate some of the problems with the technique – in particular the assumptions necessary to generate the demand curve.

The first set of problems is caused by the transferring of visit rates from the zones in which they applied in the original data, to other zones when arbitary prices are added to the visit cost. To do this requires the implicit assumption that all possible influences on visit rates other than visit cost are the same for all zones. This is unrealistic since a number of key variables are likely to vary between zones. Any visit, particularly to countryside sites, has a time input that has a value. The further the distance, the greater the cost of travel time; this is not accounted for in the example above. It is, however, allowed for in many of the Clawson studies, although there are problems in doing so. Travel time costs are very closely related to travel costs, so accounting for both separately causes a statistical problem – multicollinearity. Also, as indicated in the last chapter, travel time is not necessarily a disutility, particularly in respect of countryside sites. This has led at least one study (Flegg, 1976) to give a zero value to the cost of travel time. A related problem is actually choosing which travel time costs to use, if it is decided that they are finite. This is no new problem to economists – in transport economics the major benefits to road schemes are usually time savings, and the costs of time chosen, especially leisure time, are arbitrary choices based on some proportion of average hourly wage rates.

Other variables likely to vary between the zones and hence influence visit rates are income, age, education, and the urban/rural balance of zones' populations. All of these have been employed in Clawson studies, but only income seems to come out with any kind of universal support. Also, it is likely that the visit rates from some parts of some zones will be affected by the existence of competing facilities, i.e. diverted demand exists in these zones, possibly unevenly. The example used above is typical of most Clawson studies in its assumption that any competing outlets have a negligible influence on visit rates to the site. If this is not the case, as for instance with large countryside recreation resources or with urban facilities, then it may be more appropriate to build a multiple equation system to represent an inter-dependent set of competing outlets.

A second set of problems arises from the method of zoning visits to a site. Choosing the zones is an arbitrary selection procedure, probably influenced as much by statistical performance as by rational distance or population dimensions. This choice would be even harder for urban facilities where populations are more evenly spread in the catchment areas. Zoning also aggregates the data for each zone, so that individual variables representing different zones' tastes – for example, age and education – do not perform well statistically. When they are aggregated and averaged for each zone, one zone ends up looking very much like another. A possible answer is to use disaggregated data – either by having many more zones identified, or even by using individual or household data. However, this then makes the whole method much less simple and, according to Baxter (1979):

'there is no overwhelming evidence that wholly disaggregated models produce significantly different estimates . . . from aggregate models with a reasonable number of zones.'

Most examples of the use of the Clawson method concern existing facilities, and this being the case the only type of demand that is forecasted is revealed demand. The other categories are neither explicitly nor implicitly considered. A final criticism of the method is that by adding arbitrary entry prices we are assuming people's visit rates will be affected in the same manner by these prices as by travel costs. In fact, entry prices are far more conspicuous and so might generate more demand sensitivity. If the Clawson exercise is to identify demand at different prices, as we have used it here, then any entry price and revenue implications will depend critically on different reactions to travel costs and entry prices.

5.2.2 Time series extrapolation

If evidence is available on actual demand for recreational activities and inputs over time, then time series analysis can establish, by simple least squares correlation, the trend that is apparent in such data and extrapolate it into the future. The basic relationship used is one where the dependent variable, for example, the number of visits (V) is a function of time, for example, years (Y), as in the following equation.

$$V = a + bY \qquad\qquad 5.1$$

Having established the coefficients 'a' and 'b' from past data, any future year can be taken and V forecasted. A more sophisticated relationship, useful for short-run forecasts especially, identifies detailed aspects of the basic relationship between visits and time, as in Equation 5.2.

$$V = a + b_1 T + b_2 C + b_3 S + b_4 R \qquad\qquad 5.2$$

where T = time trend; C – cyclical variations; S = seasonal variations; R = random variations.

The existence of data suitable for time series extrapolation at the individual facility level depends largely on the efficiency with which visits are monitored. It is likely that most recreation organizations keep annual records of aggregate numbers of visits made, at least for sport and recreation activities. Such information is not usually published but it does serve as a basis for informal, short-run forecasting in practice. For instance, in the UK, local authorities' budget preparation is conventionally for one year ahead and annual visits data is one common input into the bid for funds. A 'base budget' is likely to be formulated according to the status quo – i.e. broadly the same visit numbers as in the previous year. Indeed, it is a common practice to project last years' visit numbers into next year, even regardless of such factors as changing prices; revenues for alternative prices may even be worked out using the same visit numbers! This indicates a very crude, informal time series approach, using a very small period of time as the basis for a forecast. A kinder interpretation of this practice is that there is some rationality in relying more heavily on the most recent visit numbers for forecasting than on numbers in the not-so-recent past. However, a more formal time series approach can deal with this, by such methods as exponential smoothing.

If annual data for visits exists in an organization, it can be used in time series extrapolations to yield forecasts for any time period ahead, but most reliably the short and medium terms. Better still, of course, would be the monitoring of disaggregated visit data and therefore separate forecasting for different activities, user types and times of day (i.e. peak and off-peak). Moreover, the data could easily be recorded weekly or monthly, rather than just annually. Such detailed forecasts will enhance the quality of management decision making, especially in the field of marketing, as we point out in Chapter 8. For outdoor recreation resources this forecasting is particularly important in order to anticipate the need to control demand in line with the carrying capacities of the resources, and thus prevent costly damage.

Time series does, however, only extrapolate past trends of revealed demand. It will not 'forecast' changing supply conditions and their effects on, for example, latent and induced demand, nor will it cater for changes in other causal variables. In fact, it does not explain any trends at all, it merely describes them. Furthermore, time series can only be used to forecast demand for existing facilities, because it is based entirely on past demand data. It also requires the demand data to have been accurately recorded. It is therefore, in a sense, complementary to the Clawson method, which has neither of the last two requirements. Time series does not suffer from the same degree of conceptual problems as the Clawson method and it has one important advantage – it is relatively simple to calculate. For these reasons it is more feasible for single site forecasting than the Clawson method. It is also likely to be more appropriate at this disaggregate level than regression analysis, which although superior at explaining changing demand patterns, is too complicated for most site management. We confine our discussion of regression analysis, therefore, to the wider context of the next section.

5.3 Forecasting demand for whole sports and markets

At regional and national levels there is surprisingly patchy potential for generating data over time. The quality of information on such variables as participation, membership and numbers of clubs for individual sports is very much dependent on the responsible governing bodies and associations, as Duffield, Best and Collins (1983) found out. The only other major source is national, cross-section surveys that are repeated at regular time intervals, for example, the *General Household Survey* and *Family Expenditure Survey* in the UK. Other suitable time series data includes the *Business Monitor* series, with information on production, imports and exports of sports equipment, and also such regularly published indicators of leisure time as hours of work, holidays and unemployment.

5.3.1 Time series

At a more aggregate level, extrapolations are prone to becoming more ambitious. However the longer the time period over which such extrapolations are made, the greater the likely error margin. In the USA the federal government's *Nationwide Outdoor Recreation Survey* of 1965 attempted to extrapolate participation trends through to the year 2000, but by only 1977 the projections proved to be generally far too conservative (up to 300% so). Not that this kind of mistake deters forecasters! The same survey, repeated in 1977, was used as a base for extrapolations to the year 2030 by the United States Forest Service (see American Recreation Coalition, 1983). This time a more cautious set of high, medium and low estimates was calculated for a range of outdoor activities. Although the use of ranges of estimates is more realistic, it is also tacit admission that error margins are probably too great for any such long-run forecasting to be worthwhile. The US Forest Service forecasts also included consideration of the effects of twenty social and economic factors but:

'the major conclusion of this analysis is that uncertainty is certain, given the considerable lack of predictability for both the social-economic factors and their relationships to recreation supply and demand.'

Unfortunately, time series forecasts for participation in indoor activities and in European countries are not available, because of the inadequate quantity and quality of data. Expenditure data, on the other hand, is available. Edwards (1981), for example, produced forecasts for leisure expenditure in eight European countries up to 1990, regressing the rate of increase in leisure spending on the rates of increase of household expenditure and leisure time. He too acknowledged the uncertainty of forecasting by using high, low and medium alternative values for the projected independent variables, resulting in a range of possible outcomes.

For reasonable forecasts of participation in sport and recreation activities at an aggregate level, therefore, one of two developments is needed. The first is the production of more and better quality time series information on participation; this obviously takes time before it becomes usable for forecasting purposes. The alternative is a workable link between expenditure and participation. The expenditure time series data might then be a reasonable proxy for participation in forecasting.

In the absence of such developments, forecasters are still faced with the uncertainty of their forecasts to an undesirable degree. Next we consider two techniques which attempt to reduce this problem. One, which we examine shortly, is disenchanted with the poor predictive power of time series models and is based on the premise that 'the future will be nothing like the past' (Moeller, 1975). This is the Delphi technique. The other method seeks to explain the reasons for time series participation patterns by regression analysis. Time series extrapolations assume implicitly that any causal relationships will remain stable for the forecast period. This is unlikely, and this is a probable source of high error margins. Hopefully, analysis which accounts for changes in causal relationships, such as regression, will yield better predictions.

5.3.2 Regression analysis

Probably the forecasting technique with the most statistical sophistication is the regression method. American studies using National Recreation Survey data have made long-range forecasts using this method and the best documented study is that of Cicchetti, Seneca and Davidson (1969). The forecasting aspects of their work are discussed in Cicchetti (1973). As we saw in Chapter 3, the major problem with such analysis is the identification of the demand function. Cicchetti *et al.* (1969) respond to this problem by including supply variables on facility provision at the state, county and regional level in a reduced-form framework. As we pointed out earlier, this solution leads to problems in the interpretation of the regression coefficients. However, it does give us a model that is particularly suited to forecasting, since the reduced-form is the appropriate form of a simultaneous equation model to use to obtain forecasts.

Cicchetti, Seneca and Davidson's model adopts a two stage procedure. The first step is an equation where the dependent variable (P) represents the probability of an individual participating. This probability depends on that individual's demand characteristics (represented by variables $D_1...D_n$) and the supply of facilities available to the individual (S). Thus we have the equation below.

$$P = a_1 + b_1 D_1 + b_2 D_2 \ldots + b_n D_n + c_1 S \qquad\qquad 5.3$$

The demand variables are the ones outlined in Chapter 3 as the determinants of demand (such as, age, income and sex). These demand characteristics identify 'recreation types'. They can be used to obtain the total number of participants by multiplying the probability of a given 'type' participating by the number of individuals of that type in the population.

The second step has the intensity of participation as the dependent variable, that is the days of recreation per participant in any given time period. The explanatory variables in this regression are the same as in Equation 5.3. Again, the total number of recreation days is obtained by multiplying the days per participant of a particular 'type', as defined by the demand characteristics, by the number of participants of the given type in the population.

The model above is first estimated for a given cross-section of survey data to give us the estimated values of a, b_1, ... b_n, c_1. In order to forecast the total number of participants for some future period, we first of all have to forecast how the demand characteristics D_1, to D_n and the supply of facilities will change. To do this we have to employ a large degree of judgement. Normally there are forecasts available for changes in the socioeconomic characteristics of the population but these are notably inaccurate, and become more inaccurate for longer-term forecasts. There is even more difficulty in obtaining accurate information on the future availability of recreation facilities. The solution normally adopted is to present a range of forecasts offering different scenarios regarding recreation policy. It is assumed that policy will influence the level of participation mainly through this supply variable.

Although this forecasting method is statistically the most sophisticated, there are a whole series of problems in obtaining accurate forecasts in this way. In Chapter 3, we discussed some of the statistical problems in obtaining accurate estimates of the regression parameters from cross-section survey data such as the General Household Survey and the National Recreation Survey. These problems are compounded when the models are then used to forecast over time. One source of inaccuracy lies in the inevitable errors that arise in forecasting future levels for the explanatory variables. But there is a more general problem that casts serious doubt on the appropriateness of this forecasting technique.

The problem relates to the use of a cross-section regression model to forecast time-series relationships. We have seen in earlier chapters that there have been dramatic changes in all aspects of recreation demand over the last decade. These changes cannot be adequately explained by any of the variables in Equation 5.3 because the dominant factor is a steady trend increase in demand for recreation. This trend can only be represented statistically with time-series data and will be completely omitted if we use a cross-section model to predict the future. A similar problem arises in using a cross-section regression estimate of the effect of a variable to predict what effect changes in that variable will have over time. Meyer and Kuh (1957), in a classic article, indicate the pitfalls that can arise with this procedure. Essentially, cross-section variation is of a completely different type than time-series variation. Take the relationship between participation and income for example. The cross-section model measures how an individual with an income of £10 000 per annum has a different participation demand than an individual with £20 000. As indicated in Chapter 3, much of this difference is a reflection of differences in taste. Over time we are measuring how the aggregate demand for participation changes as all individuals receive higher incomes. Here tastes are assumed static and so is the income distribution. If, over a ten year period, all individuals on £10 000 a year double their income, they are unlikely to behave in the same way as the £20 000 per annum man did initially. For this to happen there would have to be a substantial change in preferences. The main point we are making here is that cross-sectional models measure different types of variation than time-series ones, and therefore are not appropriate for forecasting over a long period.

Of course, this problem could be solved by having a time-series of participation data and then estimating the model over time. There is nothing essentially wrong with the regression method of forecasting. There is something wrong with the data-base that has been used with this method. If the aim is to forecast over time then time-series data must be used in the estimation of the regression model.

5.3.3 The Delphi technique

This is really a specialized survey technique designed to overcome the speculative and isolated nature of expert opinions. A sufficiently large sample of experts are presented individually with a list of events on which to attach probabilities and to which other events, with probabilities, may be added.

Round two involves the experts being told what the distributions of probabilities are for each event. They are given the chance to change their probabilities and justify any decisions to remain outside an emerging consensus. Further rounds of information exchange and revised probabilities should lead to an emerging consensus in the form of median dates for the occurrence of events, scales of agreement and other information such as the impact and desirability of each event. Such a system avoids the psychological pressures of open discussion and produces forecasts for the future that are not simply based on projections of what is happening now and what happened in the past.

Some recent Delphi exercises have been recreation-specific (see, for example, Moeller, 1975), but testing the accuracy of their forecasts is not yet possible, especially since the predictions are only meant to be general perspectives. To some extent the technique's value is unknown in the field since it has been primarily used in the forecasting of technological events in space and medicine. It does seem from such exercises that the technique is more appropriate at the national scale of forecasting recreation, since a large enough sample of experts is required (i.e. hundreds) for the duration of the exercise.

5.3.4 Cohort analysis

Although multiple regression is the most commonly used method in demand forecasting models, there are similar yet simpler alternatives. Veal (1980) commends the simplicity of cohort analysis, whereby a population is divided according to certain key variables – age, income etc – and the average participation rates calculated for each cohort. Then, forecasting participant numbers simply involves predicting the population of each cohort for some date in the future and multiplying it by the appropriate participation rate. In Fig. 5.3 for example the participation rates P_1 to P_{15} would be calculated from, for example, the General Household Survey in the UK. Then, if a forecast was required for 1990), P_1 would be multiplied by the predicted number of 0 to 19 year old men in Socioeconomic Group 1 in 1990. After similar calculations for the other cohorts in the matrix, a forecast of aggregate male participation in this sport in 1990 would be built up.

	Socioeconomic groups				
	1	2	3	4	5
Men Age					
0–19 years	P_1	P_2	P_3	P_4	P_5
20–39 years	P_6	P_7	P_8	P_9	P_{10}
40+ years	P_{11}	P_{12}	P_{13}	P_{14}	P_{15}

Fig. 5.3 Cohort analysis: a schematic example for a particular sport.

In a sense this method is committing no worse an act of simplification than multiple regression or simple time-series extrapolation. In each case the relationship between dependent and independent variables is assumed to be constant into the future. In the case of cohort analysis the weakness can be seen in terms of assuming that changes in participation can only be caused by changes in the population's structure by age, income etc. It ignores any changing preferences that may occur within these age cohorts, income cohorts etc. If therefore suffers from the same weaknesses as regression analysis, using cross-sectional data for forecasting over time. At any moment in time, as Chapter 3 demonstrates, as much as 70% of explained variation in participation is accounted for by age and sex. Rodgers (1977a) shows that if sports literacy increases over time, the influences of age and sex may diminish, since preferences of all age and sex groups may change in favour of sports participation. In such circumstances, cohort analysis will underestimate future numbers of participants. As with time series analysis, this method also ignores changing supply factors and so effectively ignores latent and induced demand.

5.4 The planning implications of forecasting

We started this chapter by justifying the place of forecasting in the context of recreation management and planning decisions, and it is appropriate now to return to this context. Given the range of methods and their drawbacks, how useful is forecasting to planning? Ideally the two processes should be closely linked, but in practice it appears they are not.

Elson (1977) expresses the problem thus:

'It is surely . . . of some concern to recreation researchers that planners, in both urban and rural situations, and at national and local levels, have gone ahead to provide whole new patterns of recreation opportunities on the most meagre evidence of likely demands.'

It is apparent, however, that this concern is not universal amongst recreation researchers. There is a belief that, as yet, forecasting is not accurate enough to be useful. Furthermore, in reference to the more sophisticated, statistical forecasting techniques, Rodgers (1977b) stated:

'work of this kind is wholly empirical: it lacks any theoretical foundation. It is philosophically blind.'

Clearly, we need to be realistic rather than idealistic about the relationship between forecasting and planning. The attitude expressed by Rodgers leads to a plea for better models of consumer decisions in recreation; the criticism of the implicit models underlying most of the methods reviewed above is that they assume individuals are always prevented by one or more factors from increasing participation. What is missing is a proper model of consumer awareness, motivations and reasons for choices. Such a model, however, is likely to be micro, i.e. highly individual, and will not be immediately capable of transposition into a forecasting or planning exercise, even at the local level. It may well be that the broader constraints approach is the only viable forecasting one, despite its weaknesses.

The accuracy hurdle is an equally difficult one for forecasting to overcome. To be of use in planning a forecast must be of acceptable accuracy, and recreational demand forecasting does not have a good track record on this criterion. Even the most statistically sophisticated and accurate forecasting, such as Settle (1977) will require 'informed' estimates to be made about key variables such as the rates of growth of income, activity participation and certain population sub-groups. In fact Settle admits:

'there is no element of projection in the present study, the multiple regression analysis being merely the first stage in a two-stage process.'

It should also be stressed again that if the first stage is successfully negotiated, i.e. identifying the present or past relationships between recreation demand and its major causal variables, the second stage has to assume that future relationships will be the same, and nearly all researchers point out that this is very unlikely. Furthermore, the sophistication of such forecasting exercises limits their applicability to regional and national planning contexts – it is unlikely that they would be employed in planning at the facility and local area levels.

Accuracy will deteriorate, the longer the forecast, so it would appear that any recreation forecasting exercise has no justification in going beyond five years or so, if it is statistically based. The only method that lends itself to longer period forecasting is the Delphi technique, since this is based on expert opinion. Accuracy over different time periods is critically dependent on the changing supply situation, as we have noted. Much attention is now being given to the proper representation of supply in demand forecasting – i.e. both quantity and quality of recreation facilities. Supply is also central to one of Veal's major criticisms of the way recreation forecasting normally takes place (Veal, 1980). This criticism rounds on the sequence of assessing demand as if it is totally exogenous to the planning system and only then using it to devise plans to meet the estimated demand. Veal suggests a more practical partnership whereby, for facility-confined activities, supply is anticipated in the first place, together with important policy decisions such as pricing and programming. Then forecasting would follow as an estimation of the likely response of demand to planning decisions. Such an approach is most appropriate at the local and facility levels. For those activities that are not confined to specific facilities, Veal suggests that the conventional 'exogenous demand' approach is suitable, since planning decisions will have less impact on the demand for these. However, as we have already noted, in the case of regression analysis this confines the relevance of forecasting to regional and national plans. Only simple time-series extrapolation, survey methods and basic statistical man-ipulations such as frequency distributions and cross-tabulations are likely to be adopted at the local level, and of these only the first represents proper forecasting.

If demand forecasting becomes predominantly an exercise to validate or choose between planning decisions, its role would be closer to a deterministic exercise rather than an objective, unconstrained, predic-tion exercise. Instead of predicting what will happen as a basis for plans, it would predict what will happen as a *result* of plans. However, since such activities are constrained by facility provision in any case, this change in direction is not quite the threat to consumer sovereignty that it appears to be – the supply of facilities is an all important variable either way. The major benefit of the deterministic role is that forecasting would hopefully not be so divorced from actual planning decisions as it appears to have been in the past. A further step towards such 'deterministic' forecasting can be seen in the implementation of standards for sports provision as planning criteria. It is to such planning criteria that we now turn.

5.5 Planning criteria

Is demand forecasting a mere adjunct to recreational planning, or is it a pre-requisite? In order to answer this question we briefly examine criteria either used, or potentially useful, in recreational planning. All planning has implicit or explicit demand forecasting, so it is also instructive to look at the implied forecasting method in planning criteria. The task is made easier by the predominant use on both sides of the Atlantic of one type of criterion – planning standards. Examples of these standards are given in Table 5.3.

Table 5.3. *Standards for recreation provision, some examples.*

Facility	Standard
UK	
Playing fields	Six acres per 1000 population.
District indoor sports centres	One per population of 40 000 – 90 000 plus one for each additional 50 000 population, (17 m² per 1000 population).
Local indoor sports centres	23 m² per 1000 population approximately.
Indoor swimming pools	5 m² per 1000 population approximately.
Golf courses	One 9-hole course per 18 000 population.
Children's play areas	One and a half acres per 1000 population.
USA	
Baseball diamonds	One per 6000 population
Softball diamonds (and/or youth diamonds)	One per 3000 population
Tennis courts	One per 2000 population
Basketball courts	One per 500 population
Swimming pools (25 metre)	One per 10 000 population
Swimming pools (50 metre)	One per 20 000 population
Playlots	One per 500 – 2500 population
Vest pocket parks	One per 500 – 2500 population
Neighborhood parks	One per 2000 – 10 000 population
District parks	One per 10 000 – 50 000 population
Large urban parks	One per 50 000 population

From: Veal (1982), National Park, Recreation and Open Space Standards National Recreation and Park Association, Washington, DC (1970).

Such standards are basically derived from a set of assumptions about the participation rates of different populations. The implicit forecasting model suffers from a familiar problem in this chapter – that is, it assumes that what people did at the time of the setting of the standard is a reliable indicator of what they will do for the whole of the period the standard is used. In a comprehensive critique of this approach, Veal (1982) points out, by way of an example, that the UK playing fields standard originated in 1925, with many simplistic assumptions about, for instance, the age structure, sports participation rates and use of school facilities. By using the same standard now, the implied forecasting model has assumed constancy of all these variables for sixty years! Clearly this has not been the case – the population generally has aged, the use of school facilities has expanded with joint provision and dual use, and participation rates will have altered in response to higher levels of provision, changes in preferences and many other influences. Because such standards are based partly on actual participation rates they are influenced by the state of supply of facilities at the time they were set up. Instead of just identifying and using revealed demand at one point in time, any forecasting or planning device should attempt to assess other demand types such as latent and induced demand, as well as changes in the revealed demand.

Another aspect of the changing supply situation and its effects on demand, which is also ignored by most standards, is pointed out by Gibson (1978). Using the UK standard for swimming pool provision as an example, Gibson reveals that no account is taken of the diverted demand that may result from implementing the UK standard. Figure 5.4 illustrates the point.

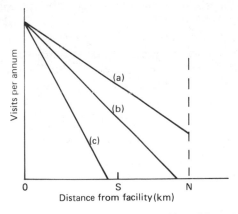

Fig. 5.4 Standards of provision and diverted demand. Adapted from Gibson, 1978.

ON is the distance within which the facility is the nearest available. If implementation of a standard by building new facilities reduces this distance to *OS*, the effect on demand will vary according to which distance decay function is appropriate. If it is (a) then substantial diverted demand will occur from this facility to new ones. If it is (b) somewhat less diverted demand will occur, whilst distance decay function (c) implies no diverted demand. The standard actually implies a constant visit rate throughout the catchment area, but as both Gibson and Veal point out, this rate will diminish rapidly with distance (see Section 4.3.2). So any increase in facility supply is likely to stimulate diverted demand, as well as latent and induced demand.

It should be clear by now that the use of planning standards of the type shown in Table 5.3 only picks up demand very imperfectly. The implied demand forecasting is more 'deterministic' than 'exogenous' in spirit. In marketing terms the standards indicate product-orientated planning rather than consumer-orientated planning (see Chapter 8, Section 8.7). Veal (1982) reviews several alternatives to the use of standards in recreation planning. We consider below how each of these approaches relates to formal demand forecasting:

1. *Gross demand approach.* This converts the future participant numbers, derived from cohort or regression analysis, into facility requirements. For example, a regional forecast of the total weekly hours of squash demanded in, say, ten years time could be divided by the number of hours of squash sustainable by one squash court. This would give the number of squash courts needed to satisfy the forecasted regional demand. This planning is directly based on exogenous demand forecasts, but it suffers from the weaknesses associated with these forecasts, as reviewed in Sections 5.3.3 and 5.3.4.

2. A *spatial approach* would focus on locational differences of access. Visit rates could be estimated for all areas around a facility, which would identify not only its actual catchment area, but also any areas of recreational deprivation as indicated by their low visit rates. However, whilst this method may be good for identifying spatial dimensions of revealed demand, it still does not forecast the likely changes in latent, induced and diverted demands arising from new facility building.

Facilities	Client group numbers using the facilities (in a representative month)		
	Over 50 years	Single parents	Unemployed
Pools	50	30	130
Indoor sports centre 1	30	20	25
2	30	0	40
3	40	0	5
Total using facilities	150	50	200
Total in local area	10 000	300	2000
Percentage of residents using facilities	1.5%	16.7%	10%

Fig. 5.5 The grid approach to recreational planning: a simplified example.

3. A *grid approach* attempts to identify weaknesses in the links between facilities and target client groups. A very simplified example is given in Fig. 5.5.

The choice of target groups will depend on the objectives of the supplier organization, and the exercise may be done for any part of the service. For example in Fig. 5.5 user numbers for three types of clients are compared with the total population of these client groups in a reasonable local area, to give 'penetration rates' for indoor sports facilities – the percentage in the final row. These penetration rates will be assessed in the light of objectives and if they are deficient, as the 1.5% penetration for the over 50s may be in Fig. 5.5, this leads on to the planning of new programmes or even new facilities to improve the appropriate penetration rates.

This type of planning could exist without the aid of demand forecasting; the process would be a repetitive one of monitoring penetration and changing policy. However, it could also be accompanied by formal demand forecasting. This would identify either the exogenous demands of target groups and/or their responses to policy changes.

4. *Facility hierarchies*. Instead of treating one type of facility as a homogeneous entity, this approach establishes a hierarchy, the levels of which are identified by different uses and catchment areas. For example, 'leisure centres' could be broken down into regional centres, area centres, neighbourhood centres and further divided into 'dry' and 'wet' centres. This establishes a specific planning framework, within which demand forecasting may take the conventional forms.

5. An *'organic approach'* illustrates that it is not necessary to organize planning in one direction, as the previous methods do – i.e. by facility types, or activities, or location. This approach involves parallel planning of two or more of these types. It, too, is a planning framework, within which formal forecasting techniques may be employed.

6. An *'issues approach'* also concentrates on setting the boundaries of a planning exercise. By identifying 'key issues', any forecasting can be confined to these areas, rather than being diffused too widely. The Third Nationwide Outdoor Recreation Plan in the USA (US Department of the Interior 1979) is based on sixteen key issues, although, as Veal points out, the criteria by which these issues were chosen are not identified in the plan itself. The main question mark against this technique is the rationality of the initial choice of key issues, since this decision preceeds any detailed forecasting exercise.

7. A *'community development approach'* is more of an expression of ideology than an actual planning method. The main objective of this approach is to encourage community organization, decision-making and motivation. This can be done by encouraging voluntary neighbourhood

associations, clubs, societies and opinion leaders. Formal demand forecasting would most probably be replaced by more direct, short-run expressions of demand.

Many planning approaches, therefore, are compatible with the use of formal demand forecasting techniques. It is important to stress, however, that even those approaches that preclude such forecasting have assumptions about the future state of recreation demand implicit in their operation.

5.6 Conclusions

In the two chapters previous to this one, analysis concentrated on explaining past and current patterns of demand for recreational activities and their derived demands. This chapter has demonstrated that to move into forecasting requires additional techniques and specific data needs. Where time series data is not available, nearly all forecasting techniques put themselves in danger of greater error margins by adopting cross-sectional evidence. A common planning criteria, standards, also falls into this trap, since it is based on participation patterns at a moment in time.

The most obvious need that arises from these considerations is for time-series participation data at all levels of provision and planning. This is relatively easy to satisfy at the site-specific level, but as the level of aggregation increases, encompassing a variety of providers and informal as well as formal recreation, so the task becomes more difficult. The only attempt to collect such data at the moment is by private consultancies, using surveys with fairly small sample sizes.

Our analysis of forecasting has implications for the remaining sections of this book. Improvements in forecasting and its accuracy should better enable managers and administrators to set prices appropriate to market demand, to improve capacity utilization, and to plan for increases in capacity. Such issues are central to the next section on the supply of recreation opportunities. Forecasting at an aggregate level is a necessary forerunner to any government initiatives to promote or respond to recreation demands in an efficient and equitable manner.

This chapter has been fairly critical of a number of aspects of forecasting, both in principle and in practice. However, this is not to be mistaken for a sympathetic nod in the direction of the attitude that forecasting is not worthwhile. Only through valid criticisms will data and methods improve. In any case, without the employment of forecasting techniques the future becomes much more uncertain and the whole idea of forward planning becomes more speculative. Forecasting and planning techniques may have their weaknesses, but without them there is an information gap that has serious repurcussions for efficient management and policy. Any systematic planning initiatives, therefore, are to be applauded.

Section Three

Supply

6   Supplier objectives and the structure of supply

6.1 Introduction

The supply-side of the sport and recreation market is a peculiar mixture of three types of provider: the public sector, the voluntary (or private non-profit sector), and the commercial (or private for-profit sector). The picture is similar, in some ways, to the situation in the Arts, as described by Peacock and Godfrey (1973):

'The private producers may be subsidized, although they operate on commercial lines, whereas the public producers although not profit-making, may charge for services . . . Both private and public producers may receive support from non-profit-making private institutions, such as cultural foundations, gifts from individuals, and even subsidies from private firms in other lines of production.'

Each sector has different objectives and differing means of satisfying them. In this chapter we try to analyse the relationship between the three sectors and their basic objectives. We are hindered in this task by the availability of the empirical data on the various sectors. Some aspects of provision are well-documented, whereas information on other aspects is virtually non-existent.

6.2 The public sector

We saw in Chapter 1 that there were specific arguments likely to lead to market failure in the supply of sport and recreation and therefore lead to an under-provision of such services. As in education, health, transport, and the arts, we expect the public sector to respond to this under-provision either by directly supplying facilities and services or by subsidizing the supply of other agencies. In all modern industrial economies, the government fulfills this role in the sport and recreation market. The specific type of government intervention will vary from one economy to another, but we should be able to identify specific objectives and features of this type of government activity.

One area of government supply that follows automatically from the welfare arguments of Chapter 1, is the provision of collective consumption goods. In the recreation area, this involves the conservation, management and development of natural resource-based recreation resources: forests, lakes and reservoirs, mountains, rivers and coastlines. We can split these resources into three, not necessarily mutually exclusive, categories. Firstly, we have National Parks, areas of natural beauty that attract recreation participants from all parts of the country and abroad. The National Park Service in the United States administers nearly 300 areas covering 31 million acres. Canada and the UK also have substantial government involvement in the provision and management of National Parks. Table 6.1 shows government expenditure on National Parks in England and Wales in 1979-80, and the importance of recreation expenditure in this total. Secondly there are water-based recreation resources. This is an area of joint-production since reservoirs, rivers, canals, and coastlines, which provide recreational opportunities, also serve purposes such as water supply, transport, flood control and power generation. Thirdly, we have local parks and countryside parks providing recreation from local natural resources.

Table 6.1. *National Park Expenditure 1979-80.*

	Expenditure (£1000s)	Percentage
Management, administration and planning	3196	36.6
Recreation	2744	31.5
Information and publicity	1608	18.4
Conservation and estate maintenance	680	7.8
Land acquisition	235	2.7
Debt charges	28	0.3
Other expenditure	240	2.8
Total	**8731**	**100.0**

From: National Park Statistics, County Council Gazette (1980).

All these natural resource-based recreation facilities have aspects of collective consumption. The consumption benefits of such resources are to some extent non-rival and non-excludable and for this reason economic theory would expect government involvement on the supply-side. Objectives of government for these facilities are not confined to recreation, since conservation or preservation may be the prime objective, and sometimes recreational use may conflict with this objective. However, the main recreational objective in this area is clearly non-financial and is rather the promotion of outdoor recreational activity. In fact for this class of resources we would specify an objective of maximizing participation subject to the constraint of minimum environmental damage.

These resource-based recreational facilities are not the only aspects, though, of collective consumption in recreation. We saw earlier that international sporting success is a public good. In fact, the benefits of such success are perhaps closer to the 'pure public good' concept than resource-based recreational consumption. For this reason most governments are involved in the promotion of excellence of sporting achievement and the financial support of elite sportsmen and sportswomen.

In Britain the government promotes national sporting success by funding the Sports Council. Table 6.2 indicates the level of government grant-in-aid to the Sports Council since it received executive status in 1972. The Sports Council has, for a major objective, the promotion of sporting excellence, which, if achieved, should produce returns in international competition. It tries to achieve this objective by funding the training and coaching of elite performers, and by the subsidizing of international events through its grants to governing bodies of sports. It also finances several National Centres which are specifically aimed at the elite performer. A major part of the Sports Council's budget goes in 'Sports development expenditure' which is concerned to a large extent with the programmes above, that is with the elite sector of sports participation. However, the Council has another important objective, the general promotion of sports participation at all levels ('Sport for all') and therefore the largest single item in the budget is grants towards capital expenditure on sports facilities, in order to widen sporting opportunities.

Table 6.2. *Grant-in-aid to the Sports Council.*

Year	Grant-in-aid (£ million)
1972/73	3.6
1973/74	5.0
1974/75	6.6
1975/76	8.3
1976/77	10.2
1977/78	11.5
1978/79	15.2
1979/80	15.6
1980/81	19.3
1981/82	21.0
1982/83	22.8
1983/84	27.0
1984/85	29.4

From: Sports Council (Annual Reports).

Like Britain, Canada has a specific agency for the promotion of sport and recreation called Fitness and Amateur Sport. This agency has moved around from one Ministry to another but its role and objectives have stayed basically the same: to promote excellence and generate national success in international competition (the Amateur Sport branch) and to promote participation in physical activity of all kinds (the Fitness branch). Financially though the former objective is more important. Of the $37 million budget in 1981/82, $31 million went to Sports Canada, and only $6 million to Fitness Canada. As in the UK, most of Sports Canada expenditure goes to the governing bodies of sport, as well as contributing to the staging of national and international events.

The USA, on the other hand, does not have similar government involvement in promoting national sporting success. The President's Commission on Olympic Sports (1977) indicated that:

'America's weakness in sport is not lack of talent for it has awesome talent which has kept the country's Olympic performance respectable.'

The Commission pointed to lack of organization as the major problem:

'US sports organisations are fragmented, not bound by common purpose or any effective co-ordinating system. No clear policy or direction in amateur sports, physical education or physical fitness can be or has been maintained.'

The solution suggested was the formation of a new institution, a Central Sports Organization (CSO), not unlike the Sports Council in Britain and Fitness and Amateur Sport in Canada. But despite their recommendations, little has changed, mainly because of the lack of a tradition in the United States of government funding for sport. Despite this, in most countries, we do see government financial involvement at the elite level, where the objective is to generate international sporting success and to promote sporting excellence.

However, much government involvement in sport and recreation is concerned with services or activities that on the surface seem to be private activities: they are rival and excludable. A typical example is an indoor gymnasium. What is also confusing is that often we see both the public and private sectors providing similar types of facility, in apparent competition with each other. Though these services are clearly excludable and rival, there are collective consumption aspects in the positive externalities associated with such activities. As with national parks, or national sporting success, the private market is likely to under-provide these services. Consequently the government supplies these services at below cost in order to encourage participation in various recreation activities.

In the UK, these types of activities are the ones that command the major share of government financial support for sport and recreation. Historically local authorities have been responsible for the provision of parks and swimming pools and, more recently, with the encouragement of the Sports Council, they have expanded into the provision of indoor sports facilities. Although capital expenditure on such facilities reached a peak in the mid 1970s in real terms, it was still £83 million in 1978/79, and current expenditure continues to expand because of the operating loss such facilities make. Table 6.3 shows how current expenditure by local authorities in sport and recreation has risen in the 1970s and 1980s. One of the main reasons for this increase in expenditure (other than inflation) was the increase in provision of indoor facilities, particularly multi-purpose sports centres, and swimming pools.

Table 6.3. *Current net revenue expenditure on sport and recreation by local authorities in England and Wales (current prices).*

Year	Expenditure (£1000s)
1969/70	69 368
1970/71	78 861
1971/72	91 193
1972/73	107 278
1973/74	135 728
1974/75	202 708
1975/76	275 487
1976/77	314 316
1977/78	347 895
1978/79	395 825
1979/80	494 367
1980/81	544 157

From: Local Government Financial Statistics: England and Wales.

Table 6.4 looks in detail at the 1981/82 estimates for local authority expenditure on sport and recreation.

Table 6.4. *Local authority expenditure on sport and recreation in England and Wales. (Estimates 1981/82).*

	Gross expenditure (£ million)		Net expenditure (£ million)		Percentage gross spending covered by receipts
Indoor swimming pools	107.58	(19.73%)	89.95	(19.15%)	19.6
Sports halls/ leisure centres	109.06	(23.19%)	84.22	(17.93%)	29.5
Community centres	35.70	(6.93%)	30.67	(6.53%)	16.4
Outdoor sports	25.00	(4.22%)	21.42	(4.56%)	16.7
Golf	3.73	(1.81%)	2.16	(0.46%)	72.5
Urban parks and open spaces	252.16	(44.13%)	241.30	(51.37%)	4.5
Total	553.23		469.73		

From: (CIPFA, 1981).

We see that the conventional local authority function of providing urban parks and open spaces still accounts for over half of the net expenditure on sport and recreation (although less than half of gross expenditure, since income from this source is negligible). We can see the large area of growth in the 1970s by the 43% of gross expenditure that now goes on indoor swimming pools and sports halls/leisure centres. The 23% of gross expenditure that goes to the latter is a rise from virtually zero in 1970. Table 6.4 shows how subsidies are allocated from one facility to another. Golf retrieves the highest proportion of gross expenditure in charges, and some local authorities (37 out of a total of 456 in 1981/82) report a surplus on the running of golf courses. Sports halls recover about 30% of gross expenditure and swimming pools about 20%.

The objective behind the provision of these facilities at subsidized prices is the promotion of sport and recreation participation. The goods and services provided are essentially private, and so the reasons for government involvement are different from the 'public good' provision above. The aim is to increase consumption of these private goods above the market-determined level, because of the external benefits associated with consumption.

Thus we see that the public sector basically follows social welfare objectives of promoting participation and promoting excellence in order to maximize the collective consumption benefits identified in Chapter 1. However these objectives are rather 'global' in nature and when we get down to the level of the individual facility then more specific objectives may become obvious. One such objective may be to encourage variety in sports provision. This concern with minority activities follows from the 'global' objectives in that a public service, in promoting participation, might aim to cater for all interests and there might be an increased chance of sporting success in minority sports. This objective must have some importance because most public sector multi-purpose indoor facilities in the UK could operate to capacity with just three or four activities – badminton, squash, indoor soccer and popmobiity or aerobics – and yet all these centres offer many more activities which are less popular. But this is just one example of a host of specific objectives to be found at the level of the individual facility. Another objective relates to who uses the facility, when an underlying aim is to attract participants across the whole social spectrum of the community. Some objectives may be consistent with the 'global' ones, but some may be in conflict. We leave further discussion of these more specific objectives to a later chapter.

In the 1980s, with governments committed to reducing public expenditure in the UK and North America, these social objectives of public recreation programmes are increasingly overshadowed by the financial constraint. Despite the increasing importance of financial problems, in no circumstances are we likely to find public sector agencies aiming to make a profit from recreation provision. Rather than financial returns being an objective, it is purely a constraint which acts as a restriction on the pursuance of other objectives.

6.3 The voluntary (private not-for-profit) sector

In the last section we saw that government traditionally acts to overcome the free-rider problem and correct for private market allocative failure. The question then arises as to what role is there for a voluntary sector, that is neither government, nor commercial. If the government corrects for commercial under-provision, then how is it that there is a sector sandwiched inbetween. Weisbrod (1978) criticises the conventional economic welfare split between government and commercial suppliers:

'The problem with this perspective on collective goods is that it views the economy as having only two sectors. All goods, collective and private, are seen implicitly as being provided either in a private-for-profit sector or in a public sector. From this perspective it follows that if the private-for-profit market fails to allocate resources efficiently to collective goods, then there is only one potential collective agent, government.'

Weisbrod sees the voluntary sector as essentially fulfilling the same role as government, providing collective goods. There is a need for this sector since government fails to correct for all private market failures. This is due to two reasons: government itself lacks adequate information on consumer demands and also government officials often follow their own personal objectives rather than acting on the basis of abstract concepts of allocative efficiency and distributional objectives. The voluntary sector therefore corrects for a specific type of resource allocation inefficiency. Weisbrod states:

'Just as there are theoretic reasons to believe that private, profit-orientated institutions will fail to allocate resources efficiently (or equitably) under specified conditions, so too, there are reasons to believe that government institutions 'fail' under certain conditions. The concept and sources of 'government failure' have not been studied at the conceptual level to the degree that the sources of private market failures have been, but there are clearly limits to what government institutions can accomplish.'

Weisbrod also picks out an important characteristic of voluntary non-profit organizations that is particularly relevant to sport and recreation. He recognizes that:

'when a collective good is collective for only some persons – in the sense that the good enters positively the utility functions of only those persons – the potential for organising collective good activity outside of government, in voluntary non-profit organisations, appears more likely.'

In effect, Weisbrod is saying that there has to be a wide degree of consensus on the collective nature of a good before government enters the market. We have seen in Chapter 3, that any individual sport involves a small minority of the adult (voting) population. Even 'mass participation' sports such as football, athletics or golf have adult participation rates of less than 4%. The formation of football clubs, athletic clubs, or golf clubs is therefore likely to be voluntary sector activity.

Buchanan (1965) and Olson (1965) investigated the economic motivations for the formation of clubs. Sandler and Tschirhart (1980) in their survey of club theory comment:

'Olson recognised that clubs would form to exploit the economies of scale and to share public goods. He also distinguished between inclusive and exclusive clubs. Inclusive clubs share pure public goods and require no membership size restrictions, while exclusive clubs share impure public goods and require size restrictions owing to crowding and congestion. Impure public goods are those characterised by either partial rivalry or some excludability of benefits. In Buchanan's attempt to bridge the Samuelsonian gap between private and public goods, the first analytical statement of the provision and membership conditions was derived for clubs sharing impure public goods. Moreover, Buchanan demonstrated how these decisions interact . . . diverse definitions for clubs have been stated, depending upon what was being shared. In an attempt to provide a unifying definition, we define a club as a voluntary group deriving mutual benefit from sharing one or more characteristics, or a good characterised by excludable benefits.'

The economic theory of clubs gives us an insight into the objectives of the voluntary sector. Buchanan saw the objective of the club as the maximization of the net benefit of the typical member. The voluntary sector club differs from the public sector in that it may aim to exclude the benefits to its own members. This is certainly true for most voluntary sports clubs such as squash clubs or golf clubs. Another major difference between the public and voluntary sectors is that voluntary bodies do not have the ability to raise tax revenue and therefore are affected by basic commercial constraints. Whatever the overall social objectives, in the long-run revenues must at least cover costs, otherwise the organization will cease to exist.

When we come to assess the importance of the voluntary sector in the sport and recreation market we are hindered by a lack of comprehensive data. There are two problems here. Firstly we have to identify whether or not an organization providing recreation, outside government, is in the voluntary sector or the commercial sector. As we have indicated, there is a financial objective (at least to break-even) underlying voluntary sector activity that will often cause the organization to behave like a commercial provider. Weisbrod suggests a solution to this problem in the form of a 'collectiveness index'. This is the percentage of the organization's revenue that comes in the form of gifts and grants. The argument is that an organization providing purely private goods will have all its revenue from sales, whereas an organization providing collective goods will have to augment its revenue, presumably from gifts and grants, since free-rider behaviour and exclusion costs will limit sales revenue.

If this collectiveness index enables us to identify voluntary sector organizations, it does not solve our data problems. By the very nature of voluntary sector activity, assessment of its economic importance is virtually impossible. Many of the inputs into the organizations' activities go unrecorded. This is particularly the case with the labour input since much labour is normally provided free. Equally the output of such organizations is rarely measured, mainly because many voluntary organizations are small and records of their activities are not available, except to the organizations' members. We can get some impression though, of the economic characteristics of the voluntary sector by looking at probably the most important voluntary body concerned with recreation in the UK, the National Trust, and also by reference to Butson (1983), who looked at a sample of governing bodies of sport.

Although created by an Act of Parliament, the National Trust is independent of the state and exists without specific subsidy from public funds. The main aims of the Trust are to preserve Britain's national heritage and to provide recreational opportunities on the lands and properties it owns. Much of the land in England's National Parks is owned by the National Trust. The size of the National Trust's activities is illustrated by the number of visits to sites where an entrance fee is charged. In 1980, there were 6 602 446 visits to such sites. In addition there were millions of unrecorded visits to Trust-owned open country-side and coastal properties where no entrance charge is levied. Given the prominence of walking in the recreation participation statistics, it is probably true to say that the National Trust is the single largest provider of recreational opportunity in Britain. Figure 6.1 gives a breakdown of the income and expenditure of the National Trust for 1982.

If we take subscriptions, gifts and legacies, and grants as falling under Weisbrod's 'gifts and grants' category, then the National Trust's collectiveness index is 56%. Gifts and legacies alone account for 18% of total revenue. It is interesting to note that although no specific subsidy is given from government, of the £4.1 million given in grants, 41% came from the Manpower Services Commission, a government agency concerned with job creation schemes. This has proved an important source of revenue in the early 1980s.

INCOME (total)   EXPENDITURE (total)

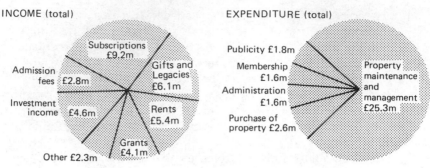

Fig. 6.1 *National Trust income and expenditure. From: National Trust Accounts, 1982.*

Butson (1983) also provides data on voluntary organizations in sport and recreation. She obtained data on 242 governing bodies of sport (108 in England, 69 in Wales and 65 in Scotland). Aggregating these 242 organizations together, their total income amounted to nearly £20 million, and their total expenditure was about £19 million. Table 6.5 shows how this income and expenditure breaks down into various categories.

Table 6.5. *Income and expenditure of a sample of 242 governing bodies of sport.*

Income		Expenditure	
Subsidy			
Sports Council Subsidy	18%	Administration	41%
Other Subsidies	2%		
Total subsidy	**20%**	Events	33%
Own income		Coaching development	13%
Membership	12%		
Investment income	4%	Facilities/equipment	7%
Coaching	4%		
Events	39%	Grants to other bodies	3%
Other	10%		
Total own income	**69%**	Other expenditure	3%
External income			
Sponsorship	3%		
Donations	8%		
Total external income	**11%**		
Total income £20 million	**(100%)**	**Total expenditure £19 million**	**(100%)**

From: Butson (1983).

We see here that there is an overt government subsidy, mainly in the form of Sports Council grants. If we adopt a wide definition of 'gifts and grants' the collectiveness index rises to 43% (subsidy, membership and external income). On a narrow definition (subsidy plus donations) the index is 28%. In total, although these organizations have higher income than expenditure, they are clearly within the voluntary sector in Weisbrod's terms.

This breakdown of the revenue figures illustrates the interconnections between the voluntary sector and the other two sectors in recreation supply. As well as the government's substantial support, the commercial sector also makes a contribution to the voluntary organizations' income, through sponsorship. There are also links with the commercial sector in that staging events accounts for over a third of both income and expenditure and there is a tendency in some sports to make profits out of such semi-commercial activities.

Table 6.5 gives the total figures for all Butson's sample. The percentage figures for the various categories of income and expenditure might therefore represent a 'typical' governing body. The variation, though, from organization to organization is quite substantial. For instance, 76 bodies received more than 40% of their income from Sports Council grants. On the expenditure side, 46 bodies spent more than 70% of their total expenditure on administration, whereas for another 48 bodies administration accounted for less than 25% of total expenditure.

The above data on voluntary bodies gives us some insight into the diversity of organizations making up the voluntary sector. This diversity is probably the major characteristic of this sector. Another characteristic is the tendency of voluntary bodies to either receive some funding from the public sector or to have close links with the public sector in other ways, such as using public sector facilities for events and competitions. Finally, voluntary bodies also have commercial aspects in that they often offer a product (for example, an international sporting event) for which the consumer (i.e. spectator) pays a price. The increasing search for sponsorship money provides another link between the voluntary sector and the commercial sector.

6.4 The commercial (private-for-profit) sector

The commercial sector of sport and recreation is a rapidly growing area of supply. It is also the sector that most conventional economic theory relates to: the provision of private goods for the purpose of profit. Actions and decisions of commercial suppliers are conditioned by the rate of return on capital invested, and that action yielding the greatest difference between revenue and cost will be the one taken. The commercial operator is not interested in sport and recreation because it is a merit good, or because society is likely to be a better place because people are active in recreation. Rather he is a supplier of recreation because he is likely to be richer as a result.

It would be easy to characterize commercial organizations by the nature of the good supplied. That is, we could split the market into those goods having aspects of collective consumption and those that are purely private. The voluntary and government sectors would provide the former, the commercial sector the latter. In some ways this typology does work, since the manufacture and supply of sports and recreation equipment is easily the most important aspect of commercial supply. However we also see commercial operators providing exactly the same types of service as we see in the voluntary and government sectors and therefore we cannot simply characterize the supplier by the nature of the output.

Butson divides the commercial sector in sport into three broad categories:
1. The provision of sports facilities and/or the manufacture of sports goods (for example, equipment, clothing, footwear) with a profitable return on investment as the basic motivation.
2. Sponsorship of sport (events, teams/individuals, etc.) as a means of promoting products or services.
3. Provision of sports facilities for employees as a fringe benefit.

The first category is clearly for profit and we have dealt with this area in Chapter 4. It should be noted, though, that in the provision of sports facilities the commercial sector is often in direct competition with the public sector and the voluntary sector. The second category, sponsorship, is less overtly directly for profit; but the overall objective is to increase sales, and, if successful, this should boost profits. We will leave a full discussion of the important area of sports sponsorship until Chapter 11.

Sports facilities at the workplace provided by firms for their employees is an under-researched area in the UK. Out of the three categories it seems to be the least related to profit; in fact it can involve the firm in substantial expenditure. Roberts (1983) looked at the costs of one particular company-provided facility and indicated that the firm paid out about £65 per employee per year to run the facility. The other main sources of income to the sports facility were bar, food and fruit machine profits. Roberts outlined a fairly depressing picture of industrial recreation in Britain. There was little evidence of any benefits accruing to the company from its expenditure and the main interest from employees seemed to be for drinking and other social activities, rather than for active sport and recreation. He suggested that many workplace facilities were severely under-utilized and that some firms were keen to close the facility and sell off the buildings and land. However, we must remember that his conclusions were based on very limited evidence.

In the US, the picture could not be more different. The President's Council on Physical Fitness and Sports estimates that 50 000 business organizations in the US have some sort of organized recreational programs. The American Association of Fitness Directors in Business and Industry (AAFDBI) was formed in 1974 with an initial membership of 36 individuals connected with fitness programmes in business. By 1983, membership had risen to 3000. United States companies are well-known for their profit-consciousness and yet the most striking trend over the last decade has been the tremendous growth in the provision of fitness programmes at the workplace. The implication is that there are benefits to the firm from this type of provision.

There are several benefits that might result from improving employee's fitness. The obvious one is a productivity benefit from having a healthier workforce. Also we may expect a reduction in absenteeism, sickness, industrial accidents, premature retirement and death. Another argument is that the morale of the workforce is increased and there is a closer identification of the worker with the company. Perhaps one of the important reasons for the growth in company-provided recreation facilities, though, is the fact that top executives have come to expect these facilities to be provided. Companies without sports facilities find it more and more difficult to recruit the executives they desire.

Both the USA and Japan, two of the strongest industrial economies, have recognized the importance of industrial recreation facilities in developing company identification, loyalty and productivity. It can be justified in terms of a long-run profit-maximization objective, but the more immediate objective of the firm is probably likely to be the generation of the benefits we have outlined above.

6.5 The inter-relationships between government, voluntary and commercial sectors

Having analysed the nature and role of the various types of recreation supplier, the question arises as to what are the factors that determine which goods and services will be provided by the government, which by commercial suppliers, and which by voluntary bodies? Weisbrod (1978) develops a model in which certain behavioural and organizational constraints limit public sector and for-profit sector activities whilst they stimulate the voluntary sector.

Government is unlikely to satisfy demand for collective goods, given the heterogeneity in demand for such goods (normally related to differences in the socioeconomic background of the consumers). Weisbrod perceives a production set including collective consumption goods, private good substitutes and ordinary private goods. For instance, a public park (provided free of charge) has a private good substitute in the grounds of a stately home (where a charge is levied). They are not the same goods, but there is a private good substitute to the public good. From the consumer's point of view there is likely to be an important disadvantage with the collective good compared with the private good substitute: the consumer will have a lower degree of individual control over its form, type of availability and (particularly with sports facilities) times of availability. The private market substitute will cater more to specific consumer demands. Since the degree of individual control desired by consumers is likely to be positively related to income, the private supplier will 'skim' the market and cater for the demands of the higher income consumer (Weisbrod calls this his 'income hypothesis').

The consumer who turns to the private market option will expect to pay a higher charge and in return he will get a product closer to his individual demands. He is also likely to choose a form of the good that maximizes his personal benefits, and probably minimises external benefits.

Where does the voluntary sector fit into this model? The rationale for the voluntary sector is as 'extra-government providers of collective consumption goods'. The more collective the good then the more difficult it is for the private market to provide it, due to the free-rider problem. The more heterogeneous the demand for collective goods then the more difficult it is for government to cater to this demand. The voluntary sector fills the gap. It follows that the size of the voluntary sector in the supply of a good is directly related to the collective nature of the good and the heterogeneity of consumer demands for that good.

How can we apply Weisbrod's ideas to the sport and recreation market? We have seen that sport and recreation exhibits many characteristics of collective goods. We have identified facilities like National Parks, coastlines and local and countryside parks as having characteristics of public goods. Weisbrod's theory predicts that these facilities will be supplied by public and voluntary agencies, with the latter being more important the higher the variance of demand. This is exactly the pattern of supply we have in Britain and North America. Even in the USA, where government support for sport is not traditional, the government is highly involved in the provision of these outdoor recreation areas.

Other outdoor facilities, such as football pitches and golf courses, are rival and excludable to a greater extent, though there are collective consumption aspects. Here we are likely to see all three sectors involved in provision. The economic theory of clubs indicates that the voluntary sector will be particularly important since clubs will form to maximize benefits for members. However, these clubs will often use public sector facilities. Where activities attract high income consumers, we would expect to see some 'skimming' of the market by the commercial sector. Thus we see some commercial provision of golf-courses, and golf-driving ranges, due to the high income elasticity of golf.

Indoor sports facilities show least aspects of collectiveness. A squash court is completely rival and excludable. The only collective good characteristics associated with squash relate to the positive externalities generated by any involvement in physical exercise (see Chapter 1). With indoor facilities, we do see the commercial sector involved, and often at the top end of the market. The commercial squash club provides a similar facility to the public squash court but the surroundings are plusher, the bar more attractive, and booking problems less severe. The major feature though of the supply of indoor sports facilities over the last fifteen years in the UK has been the rapid growth in public provision. Is this lack of correspondence of indoor facility provision with Weisbrod's hypothesis an indication that Weisbrod is wrong? Or are we missing some essential collective good characteristics of indoor sports facility provision? We will tackle these questions in Chapter 10.

7 Production efficiency and costs

7.1 Introduction

Despite the wide range of suppliers of sport and recreation services discussed in the previous chapter, and the consequent diversity of objectives and behaviour, it is likely that they are all interested in getting the most out of the inputs they employ. In this chapter our main purpose is to examine this 'technical' efficiency. We also examine the nature of costs in recreation, which takes us into allocative efficiency considerations.

First, we need to make clear the distinction between three types of efficiency relevant to this supply section.

1. *Technical efficiency* concerns the physical relationships between inputs and outputs. Many managers of recreational facilities are faced with regular decisions about what combinations of inputs to use in order to produce the right mix of outputs and also what the best level of output is. Such decisions about 'best' use of inputs, often aiming at maximum output, are concerned with a quest for technical efficiency.

2. *X-efficiency*. Even when all the right technical ingredients for successful production are present, it is possible that output is not maximized or is of an unsatisfactory quality. This can occur because of a lack of motivation, or 'human error' and it is termed X-inefficiency. According to Leibenstein (1966) it is in competitive environments that managerial incentives are most likely to keep this problem to a minimum, and produce X-efficiency. The implication is, therefore, that in public sector services and in uncompetitive private markets this X-efficiency is least likely to be achieved, even if the right technical decisions have been made.

3. *Allocative efficiency*. In recreation services this requires efficient

allocation of factors of production between firms, and efficient distribution of services among consumers. Clearly for such efficiency to be achieved, it is necessary to make 'correct' decisions about the prices to pay factors of production and the prices to charge consumers. It also involves the effectiveness with which the services are marketed to consumers. We deal with pricing and marketing in the next chapter.

Sport and recreation facility owners and managers need to be aware of the relationships between inputs and output; we employ one technique – linear programming – to illustrate the principles of this technical efficiency. We also look at available evidence of costs in sport and recreation facilities to see if this conforms with economists' theories of how costs behave in the short-run and long-run. Such theory and evidence is likely to yield implications for pricing, investment and other managerial decisions. As well as the costing of facilities, recreation managers also require information on the costs of different activities, and we consider attempts to provide such information. Before all this, however, we need to look a little more closely at what supply means in sport and recreation, in other words what exactly is being produced, for without clarity on this point the concepts of technical efficiency, productivity, etc., lose operational meaning. It is also necessary to measure output when monitoring performance of a facility, as we shall see in Chapter 9.

7.2 Sport and recreation supply

When seeking a measure of sport and recreation supply, it is tempting to draw on readily available indicators such as the number of visits to a facility or participant hours. After all, the people who visit are the tangible result of opening a facility and of great importance to management. Unfortunately, this easy way out of the problem is a mistaken one, since these are measures of demand rather than supply. So, in the same way as a producer of cabbages supplies a certain quantity, not all of which may be sold, a producer of sport and recreation services must be producing a certain output, not all of which will be taken up by demand. The output that is supplied is therefore the capacity of the facility. Combining this supply concept with the demand indicators will yield one measure of performance – capacity utilization.

For many types of sports facility neither the concept of capacity nor the measurement of it is straightforward. This is particularly the case for outdoor facilities such as national parks where the potential problem of 'over-use' has led to consistent attempts to identify carrying capacities. In principle, the following types can be identified.

Biophysical

1. Physical – defined by damage to, for example, soil and geomorphology.
2. Ecological – defined by damage to, for example, vegetation and wildlife.

Behavioural

1. Perceptual – defined by damage to participants' perception of satisfaction from a facility.
2. Economic – this can be narrowly defined by the level of use at which financial costs exceed financial benefits. A wider economic definition would be the point at which all costs exceed all benefits i.e. including external costs and benefits that are not part of financial accounts.

The biophysical approach is the more tangible, although even with this, the term 'capacity' depends on what is deemed a 'critical' threshold, which types of users and activities are considered and what inputs of maintenance and repair work are envisaged.

The behavioural carrying capacity is less easy to identify in practice. For instance, at what level of use does a participant's satisfaction from a recreation experience start to diminish and at what rate does dissatisfaction set in, as congestion increases? Clearly these considerations will vary from person to person and once again the manager or administrator of the facility has to decide which level is the critical threshold or capacity above which congestion is unacceptable. Similarly the wider economic carrying capacity is difficult to measure, since it involves valuation of externalities which are often intangible, for example, noise, congestion.

So, capacity for outdoor facilities, whether biophysical or behavioural, is essentially a value judgement. The USA National Park service classifies land into six categories, (Stottlemeyer, 1975).

1. High density use.
2. Moderate density use.
3. Natural areas.
4. Outstanding natural or scientific features.
5. Primitive/wilderness.
6. Historical sites.

This categorization is largely based on value judgement. Carrying capacities are implicit in the increasing severity of development and activity controls as one goes through the list. Actual carrying capacities are not identified, however. This pragmatic, if arbitrary, solution to the problem highlights both the conceptual problems and the practical difficulties of measuring capacities for every site.

Capacity in indoor facilities can be straightforward when an area is activity-specific and the activity requires a fixed number of participants, for example, three squash courts. If, for example, a centre has three courts, open for half-hour sessions from 9.00 am until 9.00 pm for seven days a week, then the weekly capacity is simply:

7 (days) $\times$ 12 (hours) $\times$ 3 (courts) $\times$ 2 (sessions per hour) $\times$ 2 (participants)

$$= \quad 1008 \text{ participant sessions}$$

or $\dfrac{1008}{2 \text{ (sessions per hour)}}$ $\quad = \quad 504 \text{ participant hours}$

However, most indoor facilities are not activity-specific and many activities do not have a fixed number of participants in any session. Even those activities with fixed participant requirements often use different amounts of space in a multi-purpose hall. In such cases the concept and measurement of capacity is almost as elusive as for outdoor facilities, since it depends on the activity programming of managers and value judgements concerning congestion thresholds for different activities. Birch (1972) and Peacock (1979) both retreat from the measurement of indoor capacity in the face of such problems and instead concentrate on a standard, 'yardstick' measure by which to judge capacity utilization. In Birch's case this yardstick is the average number of actual users per badminton court hour (multi-purpose areas being divided into badminton courts for convenience). However, this yardstick is more a reflection of demand than supply and it is influenced by the programming of the facility, making comparisons between facilities difficult. Peacock uses the same space-time standard, the badminton court hour, but her yardstick for use is doubles play, i.e. four activity man hours per badminton court hour. The weekly capacity yardstick thus becomes:

4 nw man hours
i.e. 4 players
n badminton court hours available in the facility in any hour
w weekly hours of opening for the facility

This measure has the advantage of being independent of demand, but it must be stressed that it is only a yardstick; it is not an actual capacity measure. Assessment of capacity utilization based on this measure may well exceed 100%, if space-intensive activity programming has been adopted, for example, popmobility, discos, gymnastics.

A simpler capacity measure could ignore the number of users and just measure the total space-time available, for example, badminton court hours, as shown on most booking sheets. However this pre-supposes that so long as a space is booked it does not matter how many users are involved. This might be reasonable for pure supply considerations, but it is inadequate when used in capacity-utilization measurement as part of performance assessment. Indeed, some facilities have a policy of withdrawing booking rights to clubs who provide too few users for their regular booking time. Another problem may be the accuracy of booking records – especially for those occasions when bookings are not taken up, and when casual users participate.

To sum up, therefore, in answer to the question 'what is sport and recreation supplying?' we can answer with one word – capacity. However, for most indoor facilities and all outdoor recreation resources, the concept of capacity is a malleable one and its measurement is equally problematic. Furthermore, our notion of output as capacity is not the one commonly used in the field of sport and recreation as a basis for cost calculations. These estimates do not even use a yardstick measure of the type reviewed above. Instead most cost calculations are made per visit or per visit hour, so the implicit output measure is demand-based, not supply-based. To return to our previous analogy it is equivalent to calculating the cost per cabbage sold instead of the cost per cabbage produced. Our preferred basis for cost calculations however, would seem to be mostly unattainable in view of the difficulties reviewed above.

7.3 Output choice, technical efficiency and linear programming

Technical efficiency requires the efficient combination of factors of production to produce maximum output. The major constraint to this objective is that in the short-run some important inputs are fixed. In a sports centre, such fixed factors are the building, equipment and such overheads as administrative and management staff, full-time employees, rates and debt charges; most of these are normally varied over a time span measured in years. Notice that even labour is included in this category, since there are many fixed costs to labour, for example, insurance and training, which inhibit a classic hiring/firing policy when, for example, demand fluctuates.

It is quite normal, therefore, for a facility manager to have fixed inputs and to have to make the most of these. A theoretical parallel to this situation is linear programming, which is a method of choosing technically efficient production under conditions of fixed input combinations (or coefficients). The best way to demonstrate linear programming and the principles it indicates, is by reference to an example. We shall use the case of a sports centre producing two sports, badminton and gymnastics, and using three inputs to do so : fuel, labour and equipment (which includes building space).

In the short-run the inputs are fixed at the following quantities per month: fuel, 18 000 units; labour, 2000 units; equipment, 4 500 units. The minimum amounts of each input required to produce one participant hour of each sport is shown in Table 7.1.

Table 7.1. *Minimum input required to produce one particular hour.*

	Badminton	Gymnastics
Fuel	18	18
Labour	1	2.5
Equipment	5	2.5

Therefore in each month, if all the fuel allowance was used to provide badminton, the maximum participant hours produced would be 18 000 / 18 = 1000 (since 18 000 units is the allowance, and each participant hour uses 18 units). Alternatively if all the fuel allowance was spent producing gymnastics, the maximum participant hours produced would also be 1000, i.e. 18 000 / 18. This gives the two extremes of the production limits imposed by fuel availability, plotted and joined in Fig. 7.1 as the fuel constraint.

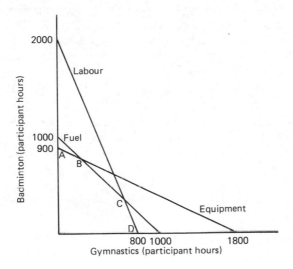

Fig. 7.1 *Sport centre constrained production – a linear programming example.*

The same reasoning also applies to the two other constraints, labour and equipment. The three constraints together impose a capacity on the attainable monthly participant hours of each sport. This capacity is represented by the production possibility frontier, ABCD in Fig. 7.1. Beyond this frontier production is not possible. Any production on this frontier is technically efficient. Just which combination of the two sports is selected is determined by the facility's objectives. Two examples of objectives illustrate the point in Fig. 7.2.

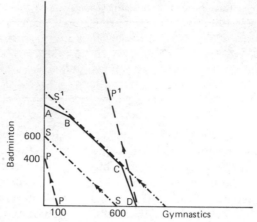

Fig. 7.2 Production choice under alternative objectives.

If the centre's objective was to maximize profits, and if the profit from each participant hour of badminton was 10p and gymnastics 40p, then a profit of, for example, £40 can be achieved by either 400 participant hours of badminton, or 100 participant hours of gymnastics.

Plotting these two extremes and joining them up gives a profit function PP in Fig. 7.2. If we move this profit function out until it is tangential to the production possibility frontier (i.e. P_1) we identify the output combination that maximizes profit. In our example the centre would produce no badminton and would concentrate all its resources on producing gymnastics, i.e. at Point D, if profit maximization was its objective. Alternatively if the centre's objective was to maximize social welfare, treating both sports as of equal social value, then SS is a function which represents such relative value, since its co-ordinates are at the same value on each axis. S_1 is the maximum social welfare attainable as it is tangential to the production possibility frontier. Any combination of outputs between B and C on this frontier will satisfy the objective of maximizing social welfare whilst assuming both sports are of equal social value.

It must be remembered that linear programming is a technique that only operates under certain restrictive conditions. The main ones are that there are fixed coefficients in production and that there are constant returns to scale. We will examine the question of economies of scale in sports provision later in this chapter. Despite the restrictive conditions underlying the analysis above, it does illustrate the principle of constrained maximization of output, and the choice of output combinations according to facility objectives. It is not efficient to be producing less than the production possibility frontier allows – to do so would be either technically or X-inefficient. Another implication is that different objectives will possibly lead to different programming solutions. The variety of objectives to be found in a typical public sector facility is quite likely to be internally inconsistent in terms of activity programming. In the long-run the production frontier may be shifted by technological change, by changes in the amount of inputs available and by changes in the input combinations needed to produce a sporting service*. We leave until Chapter 9 perhaps the most important long-run decision, i.e. whether or not to invest in new capital. One of the considerations relevant to this decision is the behaviour of unit costs as output gets larger and in the remaining parts of this chapter we explore the behaviour of costs.

7.4 Cost categories

Information on the behaviour of costs in relation to production is essential for three basic reasons. Firstly, it is necessary to monitor costs in the short-run to help assess efficiency. Secondly, more long-run information on costs is important when deciding on the scale of future production, its output mix, etc. Thirdly, accounts have to be presented to justify operations to shareholders, or members, or the government and the general public. Before considering these aspects, however, it is necessary to briefly categorize the types of costs encountered in economics. The categories that follow are not mutually exclusive.

1. Marginal costs : the addition to total costs which results from production of one extra unit of output, for example, the cost of one more badminton court hour. This is a very important theoretical concept, especially for pricing decisions and for determining the profit-maximizing output level. However, in practice it is often very difficult to measure, for example, when many sports are being produced by one centre and they share the use of inputs. Also one extra unit of output is too small to have any operational significance. As a result of such problems, a more generalized and practical form of marginal cost is incremental cost or avoidable cost. This measures the costs incurred by, for example, starting a new activity in a centre, or opening a new area of parkland. Such increases in costs could then be compared with estimated revenue to see if the new development is worthwhile. A similar concept to this is attributable cost, which is the cost per unit of output that could be avoided if, for example, an activity or space were closed or sold off, without changing the supporting managerial or administrative structure.

*Linear programming is not, of course, a technique confined to two outputs and three inputs as in our example. It can handle any number of outputs and inputs.

2. Average cost : the total cost divided by the number of units of production gives the average or unit cost, for example, the average cost of each badminton court hour. This is much easier to calculate than marginal cost and therefore more likely to be important to decision making for those who run sport and recreation facilities.

3. Variable cost : those costs that vary with the amount of output produced, for example, fuel for lighting. Such variation can be proportional to output changes, or more or less than proportional. In accountancy the approximate equivalent is direct costs, and they are also termed primary costs since so long as they are covered it is worth continuing production in the short-run.

4. Fixed cost : costs that occur whatever the level of output, i.e. they are inescapable, especially in the short-run, for example, rates. Some costs are only fixed for small changes in output, and vary for substantial changes in output, for example, labour. The accounting term for fixed costs is indirect cost, whilst other terms for the same concept are overheads, and secondary costs. Capital costs are often a major component of fixed costs.

5. Joint costs : where provision for one service necessarily provides another and one output cannot be ceased without stopping the other, then the costs are joint ones for both services.

6. Common costs : where services share costs, but are not inter-dependent, as in the case of joint costs, these are common costs. This is typically the case in a multi-purpose sports area where the costs are common to a variety of activities and user types. The main problem with common costs, as with joint costs, is allocating them between the various services, for pricing and performance monitoring.

7. Potential costs : the costs that occur at capacity output level, for example, cost per visit at peak load capacity-utilization.

8. Actual costs : the costs that occur at the actual capacity-utilization, for example, the average cost per visit. This will fluctuate according to the load factor – i.e. the percentage utilization that a facility achieves.

9. Private costs : production costs incurred by the actual supplier of the commodity.

10. Social or external costs : costs imposed by the production process on parties other than the actual supplier. These may be borne by other producers, by consumers, or by society as a whole.

11. Controllable costs : those costs that are under direct control of line managers. This is important for technical and X-efficiency. All too often in the UK public sector, sports facility managers have too few controllable costs and therefore cannot 'manage' properly, since much decision-making is done by a committee process which is divorced from the day-to-day running of the centre.

7.5 Short-run costs

One example of the dimensions of such costs is in the Scottish Sports Council's study, *A Question of Balance* (1979), where operating expenditure is broken down for different types of sports facilities as shown in Table 7.2.

Table 7.2. *Operating costs for different sports facilities.*

	Staff	Fuel	Local tax and insurance	Repairs	Others
Sports centres	57%	15%	16%	4%	8%
Pools	58%	19%	11%	6%	6%
Wet and dry centres	62%	18%	12%	2%	6%

From: Scottish Sports Council 1979. Figures are averages.

Of these costs staff, local taxes and insurance are, in practice, largely fixed in the short-run, whilst fuel and repairs are more likely to vary with output (and with other factors, for example, weather). So over 70% of these short-run costs are fixed.

The usual way in which short-run costs are represented in economics is shown in Fig. 7.3, with fixed costs becoming, on average, of little importance at the optimum production level of minimum average total costs, Q_1.

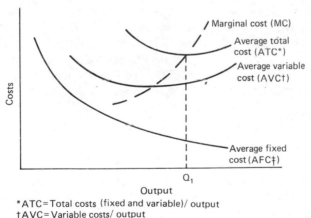

*ATC=Total costs (fixed and variable)/ output
†AVC=Variable costs/ output
‡AFC=Total fixed costs/ output

Fig. 7.3 Short run costs: conventional representation.

In fact, given the figures above, which seem to be typical of UK and USA cost structures, the more accurate representation may well be Fig. 7.4. In this figure, the relatively insignificant costs at the optimum production level would be variable costs and the average total cost is most heavily influenced by a falling average fixed cost curve.

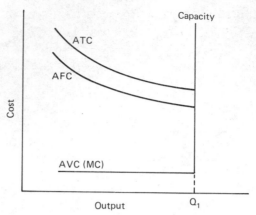

Fig. 7.4 Short run costs in sports centres.

The optimum production level is, in fact, at a recognized capacity level, which coincides with the simple output maximization assumption earlier in the chapter. Figure 7.3 has no such distinction of capacity output and, given our earlier discussion, is thus inappropriate to recreational facilities in the short-run, especially at peak times. We suggest that Fig. 7.4 is a preferable representation for these facilities. The facility may cut its capacity, or output, below this level by, for instance, opening for less hours, or opening less of its space. It is the relationship between such changes in output and costs that gives the conventional economist's cost curves. This will have important implications for pricing and capacity-utilization, as we shall see in the next chapter. For the moment it would appear that 100% capacity utilization is a reasonable technical efficiency objective. The other major implication of Fig. 7.4 is that marginal costs are both low and constant over a wide range of output.

7.6 Long-run costs

7.6.1 Economies of scale

In the long-run, managers and administrators of sport and recreation are not only interested in the efficiency with which existing facilities are run, but also in the possibilities of expansion and creating new facilities. Essential to such decision-making is some knowledge about the size of facility that is most efficient technically. If there are increasing returns to scale, i.e. economies of scale, this implies that technically it is best to build large facilities. Of course there may be other reasons why this may not be desirable, for example, community access, but this technical consideration of long-run costs is important. It is also an area within which economic analysis is well developed.

It is possible to suggest economies of scale that may be present in sport and recreation facilities. They are likely to be internal ones and possibly more applicable to indoor facilities. As such places are basically boxes, or a series of boxes, then the capital scale economy of increased dimensions applies, whereby the building cost per unit of space diminishes as the size of the facility increases.

Regarding operating costs, as the size of the facility increases so division of labour increases and specialization is possible in management responsibilities, for example, finance and marketing, and on the activity side, for example, coaching and sports leadership. This may cause both unit cost savings and quality improvements in output. Also some indivisible inputs are likely to be under-utilized in smaller facilities and will be better utilized in larger centres, for example, a receptionist is necessary for ten customers in a day, but is more productive when dealing with a hundred.

Much of the general empirical work on economies of scale in manufacturing industry has reached a consensus on the shape of long-run cost curves, and this is shown in Fig. 7.5, with economies of scale up to the point of minimum efficient scale (MES), constant returns thereafter, keeping unit costs constant, and possible diseconomies of scale at a very high output level.

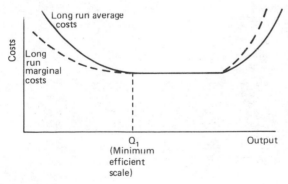

Fig. 7.5 Typical long run cost curves.

In relation to sport and recreation facilities, therefore, we need to investigate whether economies of scale exist, and if they do at what size of facility MES is reached. Before examining empirical evidence however, we need to establish the main conditions necessary for an objective appraisal of economies of scale.

Firstly, it must be assumed that all facilities examined are technically efficient, i.e. operating at, or near, capacity output level, or at the very least that they all work at the same level of capacity-utilization. Secondly, all facilities should face a given state of technology which might be proxied by all facilities being of a similar vintage. Thirdly, each facility should be faced with the same input prices, i.e. unit costs of factors of production are the same. Fourthly each facility should be producing similar products in terms of sports offered.

One study with sufficient information on size, costs and participant numbers is *A Question of Balance* (Scottish Sports Council, 1979) where 21 centres were investigated. Whereas it is impossible to generalize from this small case study sample, it does illustrate the pitfalls in an economic analysis of economies of scale in sports provision. The study examines the capital cost (expressed as annual loan charges), operating cost and total costs of each centre, and all these are expressed as average costs per visit. However, although we have already criticized this basis for cost estimation, it is an adequate measure relating to capacity output so long as the first of our conditions above holds. Table 7.3 summarizes the results pertinent to our question about evidence of economies of scale.

Table 7.3. *Costs of different sized sports facilities.*

	Loan charge per visit (£)	Operating costs per visit (£)	Average total costs per visit (£)
Large dry sports centres	0.59	0.52	1.11
Small dry sports centres	0.53	0.63	1.16
Large city pools	0.56	0.58	1.14
Small town pools	0.34	0.52	0.86
Large wet and dry centres	0.36	0.50	0.86
Small wet and dry centres	0.33	0.51	0.84

From: Scottish Sports Council, 1979.

There is, in fact, substantially more variance in the capital and operating costs per visit across dry sports centres than for swimming pools or wet and dry centres. This large variance is not, according to the study, due to vastly different capacity-utilizations, since all the centres operated at or near capacity levels. The Scottish Sports Council (1979) therefore suggest that:

'the main reason for wide variations between individual sports centres would appear to lie in either programming policies (some centres perhaps favouring high space/low number sports) or the relative building costs.'

The implication is that the dry sports centre data is not consistent enough in terms of the third and fourth of our earlier conditions for comparisons.

This leaves us with pools, and wet and dry centres. The pools are relatively homogeneous in terms of their product and the initial interpretation of the evidence in Table 7.3 is that there are no economies of scale; quite the opposite in fact since both loan charges and operating costs per visit are higher for large, city pools than for small, town ones. However, there is no indication that capacity-utilization in the two types of pool are similar. It could also be argued that the two sizes of pool do in fact provide different products. At the larger complexes there will be a main pool, other pools for training, diving etc., and a range of subsidiary facilities. The smaller ones are likely to have just one pool and vending machines. Therefore the higher average costs of larger pools may be justified by a better quality product. It could be argued, though, that the better quality product is not attracting sufficient extra participants, thus making it expensive in terms of average cost per visit. This interpretation leads to the conclusion that smaller pools are better value. Even the 'better quality in larger pools' argument lends no support to any idea of economies of scale. So, little support for larger pools emerges from this study.

The figures for wet and dry centres are inconclusive, although such centres are larger scale facilities, in general, and they have the lowest costs per visit in Table 7.3. Apart from this, however, there is little evidence in these figures to suggest economies of scale in indoor sporting facilities. However, it is necessary to reinforce the words of warning issued earlier about such interpretations, again using the Scottish case study as an example, i.e.

1. If capacity-utilization is lower in larger facilities than in smaller ones then an interpretation that there are no economies of scale may be wrong. Such a mistake is represented in Fig. 7.6, whereby the larger facility appears more expensive according to costs per visit (B compared with A) but the reason is low participant numbers rather than diseconomies of scale. The larger facility has the potential to lower costs to C.

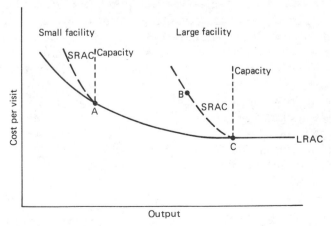

Fig. 7.6 Economies of scale: misinterpretation of evidence.

2. It is difficult to say whether or not facilities are of the same technology. The opening dates in the Scottish sample range from 1963 to 1974 for pools, 1968 to 1975 for dry sports centres, and 1971 to 1975 for wet and dry centres. Whilst these seem reasonable clusters, we do not know how rapidly technological advance took place in design and materials, etc., during this period.

3. Input costs are unlikely to be the same for all facilities – for example, larger centres in large towns often face higher land costs and local taxes per unit of space. Also building costs vary for centres of essentially similar size.

4. The offered products are unlikely to be the same qualitatively within any category of facility, because of different programming policies.

The most serious problem in assessing economies of scale by the cross-section, 'statistical' method of comparing costs of different sized facilities, as above, is the first of those covered, sometimes called the load factor problem. The Scottish study looks at costs related to actual numbers of participants (visits). Ideally, as we have stressed, costs should be considered at the offered capacity number of participants. If the larger facilities have the potential advantage represented by Point C in Fig. 7.6, but do not realize this potential because of a short-fall in demand, then two policy alternatives present themselves. Firstly, as the short-fall is likely to be at off-peak times, policy should concentrate on improving use at such times, perhaps even by very low or zero prices or by increasing schools use. Secondly it may be more allocatively efficient to build smaller facilities, where off-peak slack is not so expensive, nor so difficult to counter. There would be problems with peak time excess demand, but if the concern is with average cost per visit as an indicator of performance, this policy would improve that indicator, judging by the available evidence. Such a policy is supported by examples of neighbourhood provision in the UK, such as Torfaen in South Wales where, according to one study (Whaley, 1980), the provision of many smaller facilities with dual use has raised participant numbers to aggregate levels that would have been unlikely if all the capital expenditure had gone on one or two large centres.

One other result from the Scottish study is worthy of mention, and it demonstrates another benefit arising from larger scale. Wet and dry centres have the lowest costs per visit, and also the smallest variation in these costs. This would suggest that an additional facility can increase participant numbers proportionately more than costs. The Scottish Sports Council (1979) specifically refer to:

'evidence to show that the throughput of a swimming pool is apparently substantially increased by the fact of it being part of a large wet and dry complex' and 'evidence too which shows that the cost effectiveness of main halls is also increased by their being included as part of wet and dry centres.'

Whilst this is not an economy of scale, since costs per unit of output are not reduced, it is an aspect of allocative efficiency since it is the joint nature of the facility that encourages greater visits.

7.6.2 Cost differences for profit and non-profit suppliers

Long run differences in costs are likely to exist between different types of suppliers. In general we suggest that capital costs are likely to be effectively lower in the public and voluntary sectors, than in the commercial sector. Labour costs are likely to be lower in the commercial sector than in the public sector, but lowest in the voluntary sector. The capital cost differences derive mainly from the sources of finance for investment, which in the non-profit sectors are likely to include major contributions from grants, cheap loans and charitable donations. Also, private commercial entrepreneurs are likely to invest in higher quality capital for a given service. Labour cost differences may emerge because public sector bargaining is likely to establish rigid pay scales, whereas commercial rates of pay are more downwardly flexible and in the voluntary sector labour is, of course, much cheaper!

To simplify analysis of the consequences of such long-run cost differences, we will use an example of a public sector facility and a commercial facility, both assumed to have the same annual budgets, and both producing two sports services, one of which is capital intensive and the other labour intensive. We assume constant returns to scale for both suppliers. The situation is represented in Fig. 7.7. This analysis is adapted from similar work in health economics by Cullis and West (1979).

The main implication of Fig. 7.7 is that the public non-profit facility will produce more of the capital intensive sport and less of the labour intensive sport than the commercial profit making facility. Normally the lowest cost supplier should dominate market supply sooner or later if the cost difference persists. In the case of both the sports considered in our example, however, this simple interpretation is inadequate. It is unlikely that the low capital cost facility in the public sector will be interested in a monopoly position for the capital intensive sport, since it is not interested in maximizing profits. So despite the capital cost difference there is room for commercial, profit-maximizing supply to exist. To offset its capital cost disadvantage, this commercial facility will typically offer exclusivity in the form of better quality and lower congestion. This will enable it to 'skim off' those participants who are willing and able to pay for exclusivity (see $0Q_1$ in Fig. 7.7b (i) compared

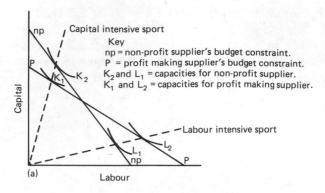

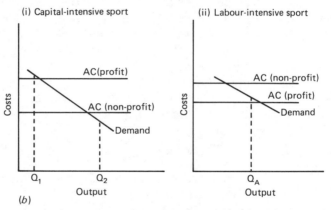

Fig. 7.7 A comparison of profit making and non-profit making suppliers with differing costs: (a) production; (b) costs and demand.

with Q_1Q_2 for the public facility, which is assumed to make a loss).

The lower labour cost should enable the commercial facility to supply any amount of the labour intensive sports market, but if the public sector considers this sport to be of value socially then it may provide a certain capacity at a subsidized price which will ensure it retains a certain market share (see 0QA in Fig. 7.7b (ii). Unless the labour cost differential is substantial, there is not much a private commercial supplier can do in the face of such a subsidy, except market the sport by its quality or exclusivity again, rather than its price.

Such analysis as this gives some indication of the market shares potential in a situation where a profit-maximizer competes with a public non-profit supplier. However, any conclusions are heavily qualified by reference to the pricing strategies of both types of supplier, and in the next chapter we examine pricing decisions more closely. Meanwhile the analysis also presumes that information is available on the costs of different types of sporting activity, and it is to this costing that we now turn.

7.7 The costing of activities

The function of a sports centre is to provide facilities for sporting activities. Specific measures of output may include the number of activity man hours offered by a facility. The activity is thus an important concept. It seems logical, therefore, to organize cost information in such a way that each activity or event can be costed. This would provide one rational basis for pricing activities. It would also facilitate financial performance monitoring, for example comparing cost recovery of different activities over time, possibly in different facilities. Such disaggregated performance indicators would provide a valuable input to planning, programming, budgeting sytems, which we investigate in Chapter 9, Section 4.

The costing of activities can also be termed cost centering – i.e. centering costs on a particular activity or event, or at least on a certain area within a facility – or functional costing, since it is attributing costs to primary functions within the facility. In principle such cost information is very important for managers. In practice it is very rarely achieved, especially in the public sector – the commercial sector has more incentive to work out such costs accurately. Activity costing is certainly more difficult than calculating average costs for the facility as a whole, but it is not impossible.

The main problem in activity costing within a sports facility is common costs. Different areas within a facility will share costs such as labour, fuel and rates. Also within each area most inputs are likely to be helping to produce a number of activities. So activity costing is a two stage process of allocating common costs. The first stage involves calculating the percentage of each common cost attributable to a particular area – which may be done via the proportion of time an input spends in that area (for example, for labour) or the proportion of total space the area represents (for example, for fuel). The second stage then divides the area-specific costs into the activities that are held in the area. This is most easily done according to the average percentage of time the area is in use for different activities, although adjustments may be necessary to account for the extra costs imposed by non-standard or closely supervised activities, for example, shows and discos. These total activity costs for a given time period may then be divided by the number of hours each activity has been held, to give the activity costs per hour. Alternatively they may be divided by the number of participants (either capacity or actual), to give the activity costs per participant.

Unfortunately, as we have noted, such an exercise is rarely under-taken in sport and recreation facilities, even on a piece-meal basis. In the face of this lack of potentially useful management and planning information, Stabler (1982) has shown how such costings may be calculated from available information, at least for local authority sports centres in the UK. Three approaches are suggested by Stabler.

1. The income method : whereby operating costs are allocated between activities in the same proportions as the shares of income derived from the activities.
2. The area method : allocating costs according to the proportion of the total area of the facility used by each activity.
3. A combined approach : dividing costs into (a) fixed, to be allocated by the area method, and (b) variable, to be allocated according to the number of participants an activity attracts, which is similar to the income method.

The first of these methods makes the implicit assumption that as participants in an activity increase, so costs will increase, and in direct proportion to the visits. Given our earlier observations about the likely balance between fixed and variable costs in sports facilities, this assumption is unrealistic. The area method is more of a reflection of fixed costs. However, compared with the income method it will show a higher unit cost for activities which use a lot of space but without many participants, for example, five-a-side soccer. It will also give a lower unit cost for low space activities, which is not necessarily accurate. The third approach, therefore, with an appropriate mixture of fixed and variable cost estimates, would seem a suitable compromise. Unfortunately, sports centres rarely distinguish between fixed and variable costs in the economist's sense of the terms, and so the third approach is not feasible. Stabler (1982) presents evidence for twelve types of indoor activities in two UK sports centres using the income and area methods. As expected the income method biases upwards the attributed costs of any popular activity, whilst the area method imparts a similar upward bias on any space intensive activity.

As a purely pragmatic exercise, it would be worth taking a straight average of the two methods' results as a basis for comparing different activities, or the same activities over time or between centres. This average may be weighted by an estimated ratio of fixed to variable costs for each activity. As an aid to decision-making in such fields as programming, facility expansion and pricing of activities, the informa-tion would be better than nothing.

7.8 Conclusions

In this chapter we have not only specified the dimensions of technical efficiency, but also revealed implications for a number of issues dealt with in other chapters. We therefore conclude by making these implications more explicit.

Even though we started out attempting to abstract the analysis as far as possible from different supplier objectives, on the grounds that all suppliers should be interested in technical and allocative efficiency, the objectives still emerged as fundamentally important. The fact that different suppliers are likely to have long-run cost differences has implications for pricing and market shares that are impossible to be accurate about without precise specification of suppliers' objectives. Technical efficiency itself, as identified by linear programming, is not a single solution, but an array of possible output mixes. Only explicit recognition of the objectives of the supplier will reveal one output target. This target, and indeed the whole array of technically efficient production choices are all at the production frontier, i.e. at capacity for a facility. This coincides with the minimum cost position, as defined by our presentation of short-run costs in Fig. 7.4.

In the long-run, capacity can be changed, and the choice of optimum capacity is one of investment. We have examined the difficulties of investigating economies of scale in the provision of sport and recreation services, and we cannot be conclusive about the evidence. Quite simply, there is not enough reliable evidence to make this judgement yet, so the question of optimum capacity is an open one.

The sections on short-run costs and the costing of activities are both important to the pricing decision. If minimum costs are at capacity, and marginal costs are low and, perhaps, constant, then the opportunities for an allocatively efficient but subsidized price at marginal cost exist. This may be particularly relevant for certain user groups and at certain times of the day, and we examine such price discrimination in the next chapter. As prices are usually based on activities, the costing of these activities is an important exercise for rational pricing. Whereas this costing may involve quite high error margins, we nevertheless consider it to be too useful to ignore.

Finally, two of the concepts in this chapter – output and costs – are fundamental to performance measurement in sport and recreation services. Output we have defined as capacity, and capacity-utilization is the obvious performance indicator. The most commonly used cost-effectiveness indicators in sport and recreation, as we show in Chapter 9, are actually indirect capacity-utilization measures. Any attempt, therefore, to improve the measurement of capacity in sports facilities can only help performance monitoring. Another dimension to performance is the financial one, and accurate cost information is essential to its measurement. Most indicators tend to be at aggregate levels – i.e. for a whole facility or a number of facilities of the same type. Activity costing enables a more disaggregated financial monitoring to be achieved within facilities. This would help not only programming decisions, but also any critical review of objectives in comparison with other facilities, and over time.

8 Pricing and marketing recreational services

8.1 Introduction

Pricing behaviour in recreational economics is a bit like Pandora's box - take the lid off and a bewildering array of options present themselves, not all of which, thankfully, are ill-conceived. Some are rational, some pragmatic and some, whilst in principle seeming to be logical, turn out to be impractical. The main part of this chapter presents a critical guide to these options, with reference to both theoretical analysis and recreational pricing in practice. The last part of the chapter widens the scope beyond pricing to its parent discipline, marketing. Economists are too inclined to overplay the importance of price in attracting customers and to decry the influence of marketing. However, we recognize from the outset that marketing may often be more important than price. The two influences are clearly inter-dependent, although for convenience we separate their analyses.

Much of the variety in recreation pricing decisions is caused by the diversity of supplier types and their objectives. Prices can be set to maximize profits at one extreme whilst at the other the service may be free. In many parts of public sector recreation provision there is a tradition of zero pricing, for example, outdoor resources, for reasons that have been reviewed in Chapter 1. Recent financial pressure has called to question the extent to which this practice is tenable in both the USA and the UK. Is the 'need' element of recreation provision sufficiently great to warrant free use? Should the poor and elderly pay taxes to provide facilities that they are unlikely to use? Does not free use incite disrespect and vandalism? We examine such questions later. Above this level of zero pricing, a variety of pricing objectives present themselves – for example, maximizing or improving revenue, market share or participation opportunity; equitable pricing; rationing to avoid congestion; reducing dependence on other revenue sources. Clearly many of these objectives are inconsistent with each other and it is unfortunately the case that recreational organizations often have a multiplicity of inconsistent objectives concerning the pricing of their services. This is particularly the case in the public sector. However, we begin in the private sector, since this should not be confused by social objectives.

8.2 Private sector pricing

A convenient starting point for an examination of pricing behaviour is conventional economic theory of private markets, which assumes profit-maximization where marginal cost equals marginal revenue, and a price derived from this point, as in Fig. 8.1.

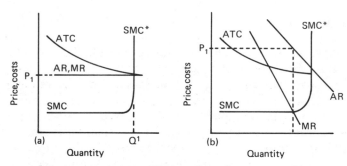

*Short-run marginal costs SMC become vertical at capacity Q^1;
any greater quantity would need a new facility.

Fig. 8.1 Firms' pricing in perfect and imperfect private markets: (a) perfect competition; (b) imperfect competition.

In each of the cases the price (P_1) is determined by both the costs of production on the supply side, and revenue on the demand side. Furthermore if costs or demand conditions alter, this will cause prices to change – i.e. marginal adjustments.

In practice it would appear that actual pricing of goods and services does not conform to this conventional theory. The evidence is that firms are more likely to base prices on costs alone and virtually ignore the demand side. Such pricing behaviour has been given various names, including full cost pricing, cost-plus pricing and mark-up pricing, but basically the idea is that price equals total unit cost, i.e. average variable cost plus average fixed cost, plus a profit margin. There is certainly not sufficient information in practice to work out the economist's marginal cost equals marginal revenue solution; average costs are more readily available for calculating prices, as indicated in the previous chapter.

Whether suppliers ignore demand considerations when deciding prices is open to a continuous debate in economics literature, since, for instance, demand conditions are often reflected in the behaviour of costs themselves. In Chapter 6 we noted the complexity and possible unreliability of demand forecasting, which may make the exercise impractical for sports services suppliers. However, we also pointed out that ignorance is not always rational and knowledge of demand can only improve decisions such as programming, pricing and investment. Subsequent developments in pricing in this chapter also attach a greater importance to demand than full-cost pricing suggests. Howard and Crompton (1980) indicate another pricing strategy that begins with a consideration of demand. This involves estimation of consumers willingness to pay for a service, followed by provision of services appropriately costed to fit this willingness to pay. However, there is little evidence in favour of or against such pricing and service delivery behaviour in recreation.

Regarding marginal pricing adjustments in response to changes in costs or demand conditions, this also seems unrealistic in practice. Frequent price changes are costly to administer and they annoy customers and management alike because of the uncertainty they cause. So the emerging picture is that in practice private sector pricing does not conform to the strict profit-maximization objective. This may mean that profit-maximization is not the only objective, as we have seen already, or simply that the information on marginal values necessary to pursue this objective is not obtainable. In practice 'bounded rationality' is the norm, but how much of the boundary is avoidable is the moot point. Much of it may be self-imposed for no more rational a reason than defending the status quo.

8.3 Public sector pricing

In the public sector, pricing is complicated by social considerations. Ideally, in this sector, price should equal marginal cost, thus simulating pricing in a perfectly competitive market (see Fig. 8.1a). In addition there are externalities and income distribution effects to consider, from which marginal social cost emerges as the pricing criterion. The public sector facility's position is summarized in Fig. 8.2.

D_p is the conventional demand curve, representing people's private responses to changes in price. We assume that public sector facilities are unable to make profit or break even, so the best financial position attainable is loss minimizing at P_1 where $MC = MR$. However, such an objective is rarely found in this sector, at least in the UK, and a more fitting price would appear to be P_2, i.e. marginal cost pricing where $MC = D_p$. This maximizes social welfare since at any higher price

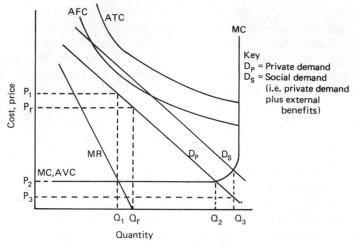

Fig. 8.2 Public sector pricing options.

willingness to pay, as reflected by the demand curve D_p, is greater than the cost of provision, MC. Thus there is unexploited consumer surplus. At a lower price quantities above Q_2 will be sold under conditions where MC exceeds willingness to pay, thus reducing social welfare. If there are external benefits arising from the service, then a social demand curve, D_s , can be drawn above D_p, the distance between the two representing the value of these benefits. To maximize social welfare it is necessary to encourage sufficient consumption by individuals, Q_3, so that MC = D_s, by similar reasoning as given above for MC = D_p; this time it is the relative values of MC and social welfare, as represented in D_s, that decide the optimum quantity Q_3. To achieve this consumption level, it will be necessary to further subsidize the price, bringing it down to P_3 – at this price consumers of their own accord will consume Q_3, as D_p shows. A further subsidy may be justified on distributional grounds to encourage use by the poor, although the evidence of previous Chapters (3 and 4) suggests that even heavily subsidized facilities may be shunned by lower income groups.

Unfortunately, the theoretical ideals embodied in P_2 and P_3 appear to be unworkable in practice. Marginal private costs are rarely calculable, and social costs and benefits arising from recreation provision remain almost totally unquantified – i.e. the position of D_s is unknown. So if the ideals are not achievable, how are public sector recreation prices decided? One recent opinion, from the Audit Inspectorate, 1983, is not very complimentary:

'Most leisure centres make primary reference to prices at other centres or local facilities; . . . No centre visited set prices in relation to the cost of providing facilities.'

It would appear that public sector prices bear little relation to demand or costs, although for outdoor facilities, USA local authorities claim costs to be the primary basis for pricing decisions, as Table 8.1 shows.

Table 8.1. *Major considerations in pricing outdoor recreation in the USA public sector.*

	Ranking		
	City	County	State
Operating and maintenance costs	1	1	1
Estimated public benefits	2	2	5
Comparable public sector prices	4	3	2
Price administration costs	3	4	6
Investment needs	5	5	7
Controlling access	8	6	8
Comparable private sector prices	8	7	3
Avoid restrictions in use	7	8	9
Measure visitation	6	9	4
Reduce demand	10	10	10

From: Bureau of Outdoor Recreation (1976).

Even in these rankings, however, 'going rate' or 'copy-cat' pricing rates highly. Both Howard and Crompton (1980) and Coopers and Lybrand (1981b) confirm the impression that comparable prices elsewhere are used as a common decision criterion. The main advantages of this are that it is non-controversial and convenient. If reference is made to comparable private sector prices, there may well be resource allocation benefits, since private facilities will not be priced out of the market by heavily subsidized public facilities. However there is little logic in this tactic, since price is supposed to be a signal to and from demand and supply. With 'copy-cat' pricing there is little chance of prices accurately reflecting either the strength of demand or the costs of provision.

All the references cited above suggest more appropriate, rational methods of pricing recreation in the public sector. Coopers and Lybrand recommend the setting of explicit financial targets, commercial pricing in appropriate parts of the service (for example, bars, shops, catering) and premium pricing to exploit excess demand where it occurs. They suggest that 'sports centres can be moved much closer to a self-financing position' and also stress the need for more effective marketing and programming. The Audit Inspectorate concur on all these recommendations. According to Howard and Crompton, pricing to cover average variable costs is very common in the USA. They also recommend partial overhead pricing, which requires a contribution to fixed costs and is equivalent to premium pricing. However, such prices once again require a rationale for a particular level of subsidy, and this is unlikely to be quantifiable.

In outdoor facilities pricing to cover operating costs is unrealistic, even in the USA. According to the Bureau of Outdoor Recreation (1976), operating cost recovery from direct prices for outdoor facilities averaged 19% in cities, 28% in counties, 32% in states and 6 to 10% in federal facilities. In the UK the equivalent figures are much lower. Table 6.3 shows operating cost recovery from direct prices to be only 4.5% for UK public sector urban parks and open spaces and 16.7% for outdoor sports facilities. Even indoor facilities in the UK public sector only achieve 30% operating cost recovery.

Another criticism common on both sides of the Atlantic is that responsibility for pricing decisions in the public sector is all too often divorced from the actual facility management. In such circumstances there is less likelihood of prices being consistent with either costs or demand at an individual centre. In a survey of over 250 public sector authorities in the USA, pricing decisions were taken at a central agency level rather than the facility level in the case of 20% of cities, 31% of counties and 85% of states (Bureau of Outdoor Recreation, 1976). In the UK the Audit Inspectorate concluded that:

'at only very few leisure centres is the management given any scope to display entrepreneurial skills in the area of pricing'

whilst Coopers and Lybrand pleaded that:

'sports centre managers should be allowed to develop their own pricing policies within overall targets set for them . . . subject to guidelines on social aims.'

At this point a word of warning is necessary. It may be that in order to relieve financial pressure, public sector facilities are seeking to increase revenue from direct prices. However, it is important to stress the role of elasticity of demand in securing greater revenue. A House of Lords Committee (1973) suggested 'high charges will increase revenue.' The Bureau of Outdoor Recreation also implied inelastic demand in response to price increases:

'the majority of evidence indicates that instituting fees initially or raising fees has no net impact on visitation levels.'

However, at least one authority in England has discovered an elastic response to price reductions, with consequent financial improvements. As reported in the *Sunday Times*, February 20, 1983:

'faced with a massive dent in their income this year, with fewer and fewer people using their six sports centres, Salford City Council took the radical step two months ago of slashing prices by 50%. The result is a 100% increase in attendance and a 30% increase in income.'

Moreover, this was no 'novelty' effect. In the subsequent eighteen months these sports centres maintained the improvement in income and utilization, at least partly as a result of freezing prices at their low (1979) levels.

Whether revenue could be increased by raising or lowering price takes the discussion away from a fundamental issue in public sector recreation provision and pricing. This is that revenue is not the major consideration in this sector; an explicit or implicit decision is made to provide such services with a permanent subsidy. If, to increase revenue, it is necessary to increase price, the 'social' cost of doing so is that demand may fall substantially. In Fig. 8.2, for example, if price is initially at marginal cost (i.e. P_2), it would have to be raised to P_r to maximize revenue. This would mean the number of visits would fall from Q_2 to Q_r, which may not be acceptable with respect to the social objectives of the suppliers. If, on the other hand, it is necessary to reduce price to raise revenue, then the two objectives are happily coincidental. Only test marketing can establish which situation exists for an activity and/or facility at any time.

8.4 Price discrimination

Rather than a blanket subsidy, vaguely justified on distributional or external benefit criteria, another pricing strategy commonly adopted in recreation is price discrimination. Such discrimination can favour particular times, activities, facilities, user groups and/or frequency of use. It relies on being able to split a market into segments which have different demand characteristics. Then, despite the fact that the marginal costs of provision are approximately the same for each segment, different prices are charged to take advantage of the separate demand characteristics. So, for example, a popular activity in a facility located in a high income area at peak time can be 'exploited' by a high price, whilst a minority activity, programmed in a low income area in off-peak time will probably need a very low price to attract a reasonable demand level. The marginal costs of provision of these two activities may be exactly the same, but a purely cost-based price such as those reviewed earlier would miss important opportunities. Three types of opportunity or objective may be associated with price discrimination – social, cost-recovery and capacity-utilization. These three objectives may be consistent with each other if, for instance, higher capacity-utilization causes higher revenue which is used to cross-subsidize the participation of socially deserving groups. However, this pattern of events need not and indeed does not always happen in practice.

The social objective is implicit in many discounts offered by local authority recreation facilities. The Bureau of Outdoor Recreation Survey (1976) revealed a substantial minority of authorities offering reduced rates for different types of user and use, as Table 8.2 shows.

Table 8.2. *USA public sector price discounts in recreation.*

Favoured groups	Percentage with reduced prices		
	City	County	State
Children	55.1	30.7	38.5
Young adults	13.5	11.3	10.3
Elderly people	50.6	21.0	46.2
Low income	24.7	8.1	2.3
Annual use (season tickets)	14.6	11.3	49.0
Authority residents	9.7	24.7	18.5

From: Bureau of Outdoor Recreation (1976).

In the UK, Glyptis and Riddington (1983) identified 42% of English and Welsh local authorities as having concessionary prices for the unemployed, with another 5% having more comprehensive concessionary schemes. It is also very common, if not universal in UK local authorities, to have lower prices (usually about half-price) for children. This raises interesting issues, since if anything children incur higher marginal costs than adults, for example, supervision and damage, whilst the social, merit good advantages of encouraging children's participation in recreation is unquantified and largely unquestioned.

The cost recovery objective in price discrimination is achieved by exploiting the different elasticities of demand of market segments, as shown in Fig. 8.3. Two sports, judo and table tennis, share the same cost function. If either sport is produced on its own, average costs could not be covered – the demand (average revenue) curves are both below the average cost curve. If the two sports were produced together, then their

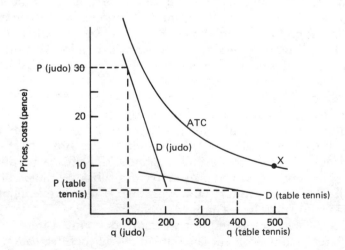

Fig. 8.3 Price discrimination: an example.

combined average revenues would make a break-even position possible at X, but only if they were priced discriminately according to their separate demand curves. In Fig. 8.3 judo, with a high price (30p) yields £30 revenue, whilst table tennis, with a low price (5p) realises £20 revenue. The combined revenue equals the total cost of £50 (10p average cost multiplied by 500 visits).

Evidence from the Scottish Sports Council (1979) lends some support to this analysis, and is summarized in Table 8.3.

Table 8.3. *Costs and subsidies per visit by functional area, Scotland, 1976.*

	Operating cost per visit (£)	Operating subsidy per visit (£)	Total cost per visit (£)	Total subsidy per visit (£)
Swimming	0.46	0.33	0.65	0.54
Squash	0.59	0.22	0.86	0.49

From: Scottish Sports Council (1979).

Although swimming has the lower cost per visit, squash has the lower subsidy per visit. The most likely explanation for this is that squash is more highly priced and has fewer users, so costs per visit are high, but cost recovery is good; whilst on the other hand swimming has prices held down because of its elastic demand, thus attracting many users which brings costs per visit down. However, elasticity of demand for swimming is not high enough to reduce the subsidy per visit to that of squash. This example also demonstrates that a commonly used cost effectiveness, performance measure, i.e. cost per visit, is critically affected by pricing policy and its effects on visit numbers, a point we take up in Chapter 9.

One interesting rider to this revenue objective in price discrimination emerges from the survey of willingness to pay for outdoor recreation in the USA by the Bureau of Outdoor Recreation (1976). Seventy-six per cent of users preferred to pay for entrance rather than for particular activities, whilst only 30-40% of public sector adminstrators had the same preference. Clearly, if entrance fees were dominant the opportunity to discriminate in price by activity would be lost, with consequent revenue implications.

The third objective for price discrimination is maximum capacity-utilization. Discrimination by time of day is one answer to a very serious under-utilization problem facing most sports facilities on weekday mornings and afternoons, and excess demand that often occurs on weekday evenings and parts of the weekend. This is the peak-load problem, already encountered in Chapter 2, but expanded on here. The problem is represented in Fig. 8.4. The obvious objective of pricing policy is to increase off-peak demand and, if necessary, ration peak demand.

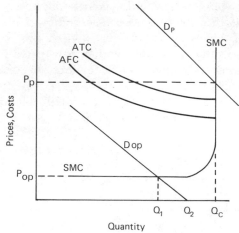

Fig. 8.4 Peak-load pricing.

We can distinguish two types of peak-load problem. A 'shifting peak' occurs when demand can be diverted from peak to off-peak times, whilst a 'firm peak' means that any demand lost from peak time does not switch to the off-peak time, but is lost to the supplier altogether. Given the well-established time-dating patterns of recreational activity noted in Chapter 2, the peak-load problem of sports facilities is most likely to be a firm peak.

One way in which many indoor, public sector, sports facilities have overcome off-peak under-utilization is dual use, i.e. weekday day-time use by schools, or, on a similar principle, joint provision. This still leaves holiday time under-utilization and problems of access for non-school users in the week, but many studies point to the greater cost effectiveness (implying capacity-utilization) of such dual use arrangements, as we shall see in greater depth in the next chapter. In effect these arrangements shift D_{op} in Fig. 8.4 outwards. There remains the problem, of course, of setting a price for educational users of a public facility. We suggest that on merit good grounds the recommendations made for off-peak users below might equally apply to schools use.

If dual use is not possible on a large scale, as is the case for many purpose built public sector facilities, then peak load pricing principles are of particular relevance. Taking peak demand first, in Fig. 8.4 the peak demand at capacity-utilization (Q_c) would accept a relatively high price, i.e. P_p. A price of this type, blatantly 'playing the market', would not only eliminate excess demand, but also provide an opportunity to earn revenue in excess of operating costs which may be used to cross-subsidize more socially 'deserving' parts of the facility's operations. This would mean penalizing peak demand users. Such 'surplus' revenue may alternatively be seen as contributing towards fixed costs or capital costs, in the manner of the partial overhead pricing.

Off-peak demand is likely to be characterized by some of the recreationally disadvantaged users identified in Chapter 4, i.e. elderly people, women with young children, unemployed, handicapped etc. In Fig. 8.4 it is apparent that where the off-peak demand cuts marginal cost, this cost is low – if a facility is open and half empty it costs very little extra to admit one extra user. Most costs are fixed. There does, indeed, seem to be a happy coincidence, for the public sector at least, in off-peak under-utilization. A low off-peak, marginal cost price at P_{op} would attract groups that are, in the main, recreationally disadvantaged.

Indeed at least one English authority, Nuneaton, has gone a relatively small step further and reduced prices to zero on social criteria, thus maximizing use at off-peak times (Q_2 in Fig. 8.4) and furthering two objectives with one move. In Nuneaton a 'passport' scheme, discriminating in favour of local residents, is accompanied by zero prices for selected groups. In its first year, free use for those under 18 years of age, senior citizens and the handicapped caused attendances to more than double for some activities in certain facilities.

Although this discussion has been set in the context of public sector facilities, private facilities would do their reputation and their revenues no harm by engaging in such off-peak pricing, and many do so in practice. Clearly such pricing needs to be accompanied by effective marketing to particular target groups, since home-based people often follow similar time-dating patterns in recreation to working members of the family. Such patterns need to be broken down by more than just price attractiveness. Indeed, the Audit Inspectorate (1983) concluded that:

'the actual level of off-peak prices, whilst important, is not as significant as . . . other factors in attracting off-peak utilisation.'

These other factors are the geographical ease of access to off-peak users, community awareness of the discrimination, coaching and leadership schemes and special interest packages, most of which are directly malleable by appropriate marketing tactics.

8.5 Two-part tariffs

The peak-load pricing suggestions above imply that peak-time users contribute to fixed (capital) costs whilst off-peak users at most contribute towards operating costs of provision. This may be seen as unfair discrimination against peak-time users, some of whom will be poor even though they are in full time jobs.

An alternative pricing policy, therefore, is to ask all users to pay a fixed charge plus a charge per activity time period. Such pricing is often found in UK indoor facilities with the fixed charge being either a membership fee or a standing charge for entry into the facility. Two-part tariffs of this type exist in many parts of the public sector (for example, electricity and gas supply in the UK) and can be seen as a compromise between the theoretical ideal of marginal cost pricing and the practical need to break-even or minimize losses in the long-run. So the activity price relates to the marginal cost of provision, and the fixed charge is designed to contribute to fixed costs.

In sports facilities, as we have emphasized in the previous chapter, fixed costs are likely to be the dominant part of total costs. In such circumstances, the fixed component of a two-part tariff will either have to be very high to cover such fixed costs, for example, membership fees in many private golf clubs, or it will make only a small contribution to fixed costs, as in most public sector facilities. By the same reasoning, however, any normal charge per activity time period is likely to more than cover the short-run marginal cost of providing that activity, this being very low. Hence a further contribution will be made to fixed costs. The net effect of such a two part tariff, therefore, is very similar to the partial overhead pricing mentioned earlier.

8.6 Willingness to pay

The analysis so far has been mainly concerned with how suppliers set rational prices. Little has been explicitly said about the recreational consumer's willingness to pay direct prices. Recent 'liberalist' economic writing has been severely critical of the hidden, indiscriminate, undisciplined prices paid by consumers and non-consumers alike in the form of taxes. Seldon (1979) typifies this attack when he suggests:

'The mechanism is quite clear and simple : if you pay directly for something in the market you buy ('demand') less than if you pay indirectly to government through taxes, because you then think its price is nil – that it is 'free' . . . you know how much you pay if you pay by price . . . paying by price requires a conscious decision to buy or not to buy . . . paying by price teaches care in comparing values . . . price enables you to pay for each commodity or service separately.'

Even the standard argument against direct charges – that they prevent access to a service by the poor – is comprehensively challenged by Howard and Crompton (1980). They base their challenge on three points. Firstly, property taxes are regressive, so that it can be argued that for the poor the option of paying directly is more equitable than the compulsion of paying proportionately more of their incomes for a facility than wealthier tax payers. Secondly, a discriminating consumer subsidy would more effectively improve access to any disadvantaged groups than indiscriminate producer subsidies. Finally, most evidence confirms that low income groups do not use recreational facilities much anyway, even when prices are heavily subsidized. So it is inequitable for them to pay taxes and subsidize wealthier users. Such equity arguments are considered in more detail in Chapter 10.

A household survey conducted for the Bureau of Outdoor Recreation (1976) lends some support to these arguments from the consumers' side, at least in the context of outdoor recreation. Some of the results are reproduced in Table 8.4.

Table 8.4. *Preference for more direct charging in USA outdoor recreation.*

	Percentage preferring more direct charging
Age	
16 – 24	52
25 – 34	56.3
35 – 54	61.9
55+	76.1
Income ($)	
Under 5000	67.2
5 – 9999	63.2
10 – 19 999	62.1
20 000+	53.9
Participation intensity	
Non-participants	76.9
1 – 2 activities	66.8
3 – 5 activities	58.6
6 – 8 activities	51.5

From: Bureau of Outdoor Recreation (1976).

Even in younger and wealthier groups a slight majority favoured more direct pricing, whilst for older and poorer groups and amongst non-participants generally, two thirds to three quarters of respondents wanted more direct pricing. By way of comparison, a parallel survey of local authority administrators confirmed that it is on the supply side that the allegiance to 'free' (i.e. tax-based prices) use is at its strongest – about 60% thinking that users should only pay for particular facilities, like overnight lodging, golf and tennis.

The Coopers and Lybrand report on local authority pricing in the UK (1981b) also suggested that administrators are far too timid of testing the market by direct pricing. Whilst such sentiments are symptomatic of an era of financial restraint, they do legitimately challenge the unthinking continuation of blanket subsidies and zero or very low prices in recreation. It is quite possible that consumers are willing to pay more directly for recreational services. It is also likely that this willingness can be manipulated by effective marketing of these services, and it is to this that we turn next. In the meantime it must not be forgotten that there are also well-argued aspects of market failure (see Chapters 1 and 10) which have led to the traditions of 'free' use and payment via taxes. Reaching a compromise between the two sets of arguments, liberalism and intervention, is made all the more difficult by the lack of relevant quantitative information on the values involved.

8.7 Marketing principles and practice

We now put the pricing decision into its wider perspective, 'marketing'. This term covers much of the interface between consumers and suppliers and because of this broad scope many of its component parts are covered elsewhere in this book. To avoid repetition, therefore, this section will be patchy and only attempt to fill the gaps left by more specific sections elsewhere. A representation of the whole marketing scenario is attempted in Fig. 8.5, which is adapted from Howard and Crompton (1980).

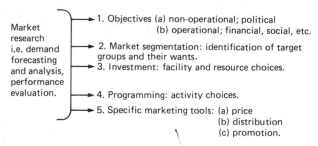

Fig. 8.5 The marketing system in recreational services.

8.7.1 Objectives

We have noted elsewhere in this book that it is unlikely that efficiency and equity in provision of recreation services will be achieved in the absence of systematic, specific policy objectives. At the political level these are likely to be non-operational. They must be converted into operational objectives by administrators and managers closer to the actual resource or facility. Without such operational objectives it would be impossible to judge whether or not the aims of the service are being achieved; there would thus be no yardsticks by which to make managerial decisions.

In the private commercial sector it is relatively easy to achieve operation, quantification and evaluation of financially orientated objectives. It is to this sector that most marketing principles are devoted. In the public sector, however, the more appropriate set of objectives is social, and as Henry (1983) states:

'The role of marketing in improving efficiency in the achievement of social (rather than financial) objectives is one which has been largely neglected in the marketing literature which relates to public services.'

We have noted that the introduction of social objectives has a complicating effect on the decision-making environment. This would appear to act as a deterrent for politicians, administrators and managers alike. In a study of 49 UK public sector leisure centres, Cowell (1979) found that for many centres the objectives had not developed past the political, non-operational stage, and in some even these had not been specified, leaving managers to use their own judgement about what to aim for. Only a quarter of the sample had written objectives, but these were not reviewed systematically in the light of any performance evaluation.

8.7.2 Market segmentation

Most modern marketing texts stress the consumer orientation of marketing. At an early stage it is necessary to identify which client groups are to be targeted to conform with the objectives set. These target groups then need to be analysed to identify the characteristics of their recreational demands. As we have indicated in Chapter 4, it is important to distinguish whether non-participation is because of binding con-straints or because of preferences by target groups. This is particularly critical for those target groups consistent with social objectives, for example, elderly people, mothers with young children, handicapped, ethnic minorities, unemployed. Once target group preferences and motivations have been identified, a rational, 'consumer sovereignty' foundation is laid for facility development and activity programming.

Evidence suggests that market segmentation is a common practice in recreation provision, even in the public sector. Fortunately, social objectives like 'sport-for-all' can be targeted at specific recreationally disadvantaged groups such as those just mentioned. The fairly responsive reaction of UK local authorities to the 'new' problem of high unemployment illustrates the point (Glyptis and Riddington, 1983). However, it does appear from the evidence of Chapters 3 and 4 that certain social target groups have not been marketed successfully by the UK public sector – notably the elderly, women and lower socioeconomic groups. Moreover, although identification of target groups is well-established, analysis of their wants is much less developed. In Cowell's study only 7 out of 49 centres had undertaken demand assessment studies. Even when they are done, such studies are 'one-offs' and are often not specifically designed to provide information on the prefer-ences of individual target groups.

8.7.3 Facility and resource choices

Once again basic market research is necessary before the 'right' recreation resource or facility can be opened in the 'right' location for use by the target groups identified. Most of such information requirements are reviewed elsewhere (Chapters 3, 4, 5 and 9). However, it is worth highlighting one important concern in the planning and marketing of facilities that we have not dealt with before, i.e. quality and atmosphere. Howard and Crompton (1980) indicate that this is one of the major differences between public and private sector facilities – the former being too cost-conscious and functionally minded to think much about atmosphere, the latter being more sensitive to the aesthetics of recreation supply.

Howard and Crompton distinguish between two types of factor which influence quality. 'Dissatisfier' factors at their best are neutral to participant satisfaction, and at worst ruin the recreational experience, for example, temperature, cleanliness and security. 'Satisfier' factors on the other hand, can make a positive contribution to participant satisfaction by stimulating such senses as excitement, relaxation and competition. This is an important distinction for marketing. The satisfier factors are directly related to the motives of recreationalists. They are the marketing equivalent of Scitovsky's theory of skilled learning which we reviewed in Chapters 2 and 3. In this theory optimum arousal is chiefly determined by novelty, and can be boosted by investment in leisure consumption skills. The satisfier factors add other aesthetic considerations to the determination of arousal levels.

The impression that public sector facilities are relatively backward at promoting satisfier factors, and indeed are often accused of not even getting dissatisfier factors right, is symptomatic of a more fundamental policy problem. This is that such facilities are still prone to out-moded product orientation in their marketing – i.e. providing what they think the consumer ought to have, or even worse, providing by custom and practice their resources and facilities whether the consumer likes them or not. In such an environment there is going to be little time spent on assessing consumer satisfaction, or thinking of higher order arousal or satisfier factors like quality and atmosphere. Another symptom of product orientation is the provision of facilities according to national standards of provision, such as those reviewed in Chapter 5. Such standards are indiscriminate and thus have only coincidental relevance to consumer recreational wants in different localities.

8.7.4 Programming

We have already indicated (Chapter 7) that the choice of activities is crucially dependent on the objectives of a facility or resource, but it is worth stressing the point again. The Sports Council (1982) provide a good example of inter-related objectives, target groups and activity choices at a national level, as shown in Table 8.5.

Table 8.5. *UK Sports Council's 'concentration of resources programme'.*

| | Market Potential | | | |
	Relevant sex	Total population	Target Group 1 (13-24 years)	Target Group 2 (45-59 years)
1981/2 to 1984/5				
Basketball	Both	Little	Good	Little
Judo	Both	Little	Good	Little
Gymnastics	Both	Little	Modest	Little
Cricket	Mainly male	Modest	Fair	Little
1982/3 to 1985/6				
Netball	Mainly female	Modest	Good	Little
Tennis	Both	Considerable	Good	Good
Bowls	Both	Considerable	Good	Good
Table tennis	Both	Considerable	Good	Good
1983/4 to 1986/7				
Keep fit	Both	Good	Good	Good
Movement and dance	Both	Considerable	Good	Good
Swimming (proposed)	Both	Good	Good	Good
Rambling (proposed)	Both	Good	Good	Good
1984/5 to 1987/8				
Volleyball	Both	Modest	Good	Modest
Badminton	Both	Good	Good	Fair
Cycling	Both	Good	Good	Modest
Squash	Both	Good	Good	Modest

From: Sports Council (1982).

The objective of increasing participation and loyalty to sport is translated into operational meaning by the choice of two target age groups. Each, according to the Sports Council, 1982:

'are at points of major change in life patterns, when new behaviour and attitudes are formed. Thus any sports participation developed at these times is more likely to carry over into later periods of life.'

It is unfortunate, however, that even the choice of sports in Table 8.5 reflects a bias towards the younger, more approachable target group. Half the sports are recognized as having only little or modest potential for the older age group.

Another dimension to the choice of activities is a standard concept known as the product life-cycle, and is illustrated in Fig. 8.6.

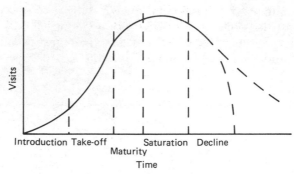

Fig. 8.6 The product life-cycle.

Although it is virtually impossible to predict accurately the time-span of an individual activity's life-cycle or any component therein, the concept is a useful one and approximate timings should be possible. It introduces predictability into the sequential planning of marketing strategies, since different mixes are needed at different stages of the life cycle. For example, as an activity moves from its introduction, through take-off to maturity, so the promotional effort declines. Management attention switches to re-packaging the activity to give it fresh appeal to existing clientele, for example, new competitions and membership deals. As saturation is reached the emphasis is likely to be on increasing or retaining the loyalty of existing participants and raising the frequency of their visits.

The product life-cycle also raises the notion of a balanced portfolio of activities, i.e. not all declining at the same time. This serves to reduce the risk of overall decline, just as a normal portfolio of assets does. It highlights another deficiency in marketing more apparent in public than private facilities, according to Howard and Crompton. This is the reluctance to eliminate programmes at the end of their life-cycle. The development of new programmes is thus unnecessarily constrained, being crowded out by old programmes that are past their peak.

Howard and Crompton suggest that:

'it is likely that a small proportion of an agency's services account for a large proportion of the overall satisfaction and attendance generated. This principle confirms that it may be possible to remove many programs without much adverse impact on a clientele.'

Whilst this is often the case, it runs counter to a prime social objective commonly found in public sector facilities which was identified earlier in this book and expressed by Cowell and Henry (1979):

'to maximise the recreation opportunities for people in the area by providing as wide a range of activities as possible.'

Nevertheless, the point remains that a large array of activities spreads managerial and marketing resources thinly. This is likely to handicap performance in any single activity; it also increases the danger of crowding out new developments and therefore harms the image of a facility as a dynamic institution.

Elimination of programmes and facilities, however, can only be achieved rationally and systematically if evaluation of performance provides suitable evidence. Such evidence would also help the 'demarketing' that must accompany elimination. This is the persuasion of both internal members of the organization and external parties such as clients and politicians that elimination is fully justified. When such demarketing is not taken seriously, problems may arise, such as the case of an old swimming pool in Fulham, London. In the late 1970s a decision to knock down the old pool and replace it with a new one of considerably higher quality was countered by an eight-month occupation of the old pool by faithful clients! Clearly market research is important to demarketing as well as marketing, but it is this market research element in the process that is weakest – particularly in local government. According to the Audit Inspectorate (1983):

'There is generally very little knowledge or research on where users live; how often they use facilities; who they are . . .; how satisfied they are; what additional facilities they require; and other significant questions.'

8.7.5 The marketing mix

Although this is conventionally seen as a mixture of product, price, distribution (or place) and promotion, we will only concentrate here on the last two. Product (i.e. facilities and activities) and price have been covered in preceding sections. There are inter-dependencies in this marketing mix. Price, for instance, serves as an instrument of distribution and promotion. Table 8.2 demonstrates various distributive roles for price, including one example of higher prices used as a deterrent to visitors living outside the providing authority. A low entry price is also one of the four main elements of a promotion package.

Efficient distribution means reaching the target groups with the product and improving access in its broadest context. This will involve locating activities in areas relevant to specific target groups, offering activities at appropriate times, and employing suitable differentiation between users in programmes. Physical location of facilities is crucial for efficient distribution of activities. Unfortunately this factor is usually pre-determined before a manager is even employed, and in the UK public sector, as Cowell (1979) points out:

'The siting of most centres had originally been based upon the availability of land . . . over two thirds of those interviewed expressed some weakness inherent in their present site.'

Despite this constraint, other policies can control physical access – either encouraging or inhibiting it. Typical among these are traffic restrictions and availability of overnight facilities in national parks, car parking at urban facilities and transport arrangements for the disabled.

Opening times is an access factor under more complete control by either facility management or central administrators, but there is little evidence of experimentation with early morning or late evening opening, and in the UK it is not unusual to find public sector facilities closed on bank holidays. The potential for marketing off-peak target groups identified earlier has also been generally under-exploited. In the present financial climate an easier option is to reduce opening times to save on operating costs, but of course the easiest option is not always the one most consistent with objectives.

Regarding differentiation of users, certain ethnic groups need to be isolated for religious reasons (see, for example, Henry, 1983) whilst other disadvantaged groups like the unemployed, elderly or disabled may need to be deliberately and subtly integrated into less differentiated programmes to help overcome stigma problems. Another common segregation, again critically dependent on consumer wants, is based on skill levels. Scitovsky's theory (see Chapter 2) indicates that without adequate differentiation by skill, problems of under-arousal (boredom) and over-arousal (fear) will deter future participation.

An effective promotion package will depend on which stage of the product life-cycle a programme has reached, but the major elements of such a package – price, advertising, publicity and personal contacts – all have roles to play. Howard and Crompton suggest that the public sector relies too heavily on the last two of these elements, primarily because of their low cost. They also demonstrate the irony and fallacy of this imbalance, since one major role of advertising and loss leaders is to reduce net costs in the long run by increasing revenue! Both the Audit Inspectorate and Cowell demonstrate that the problem of imbalanced and inadequate promotion is common to the public sector in the UK as well:

'Most leisure centres have very small budgets with which to market facilities. It seems that members and senior management may not appreciate the relationship between advertising and promotional effort and attendance levels and are unwilling to sanction adequate budgets' (Audit Inspectorate, 1983) and 'sometimes even small budgets were underspent. There seemed to be little understanding of the value of variable approaches which could be taken to reach and influence markets, or of the varying effectiveness of the various promotional means.' (Cowell, 1979).

To be fair though, there are also well-documented cases of very effective marketing in the public sector. An example in the UK is the expanding programme of 'sports leadership' schemes – a straightforward application of the promotion technique of using 'opinion leaders.' Such schemes have been particularly successful in drawing young and ethnic minority target groups into formal participation.

8.7.6. Market research

It is all too convenient, less costly and uncontentious to avoid market research in recreation service provision. Many authorities and institutions follow this approach. In Cowell's study of UK local authority leisure centres (1979) only a seventh of the sample had at any stage undertaken user surveys and none had investigated non-users, to better understand why people did not visit the centre. Furthermore the user studies lacked continuity, being ad hoc, piecemeal investigations.

At all the stages of marketing identified above, a recurrent weakness is that there is little demand forecasting and analysis, and little evaluation of the effects or success of existing programmes. Two of our Chapters deal directly with these issues, so we will not repeat the arguments here. For forecasting and planning information, readers should refer to Chapter 5. Specific consideration of performance evaluation is contained in Chapter 9.

8.8 Conclusions

We have been very hard on the public sector in this chapter. The intention behind our criticism is not, we hope, destructive. We would like to think that our analysis indicates the means by which substantial improvements can be made in the allocative efficiency of recreational service suppliers of all types. In part the unfavourable public sector impression derives from the lack of private, commercial sector or voluntary sector evidence. However, we think it likely that more efficient practices are the norm in the commercial sector. We conclude, therefore by reviewing the possible reasons for the inadequate, ad hoc nature of public sector pricing and marketing – some of which are inevitable and unavoidable.

A fundamental gap in pricing and marketing policy for the public sector seems to be the lack of a consistent set of explicit objectives. Local authority managers have little incentive to manage-by-objectives unless political preferences are revealed. The existence of social responsibilities only adds to this problem since many are easy to express politically, for example, 'serving the community's leisure needs', but not so easy to put into operation. Without the survival incentive, a manager will be all too tempted to operate in an incrementalist, custom-and-practice manner. The nature of bureaucratic decision making does not help efficient management either. When responsibilities are split between the line manager and a hierarchy of administrative and political levels above, decision-making is extended at best, and non-existent at worst, i.e. the X-inefficiency problem.

Marketing also suffers from the cost-consciousness of local authority councillors. All expenditure is conspicuous, and expenditure on promotion is often slurred with the tag of being a waste of money because 'nothing tangible' results from the expenditure. This weak bargaining position is exacerbated by the lack of professional, managerial skills in the public sector recreational services field, something which caused the UK government to set up the Yates Committee to look into professional training for recreational management. The weakness is particularly acute in specialist management areas such as marketing. Few leisure facilities are large enough to justify a marketing specialist, which led the Audit Inspectorate to recommend the part-time employment of such skilled personnel. However, most local authorities' recreation departments are large enough to sustain such specialist posts and this development is spreading steadily.

Another excuse, offered by Cowell (1979), is that marketing in services, and modern public sector recreation provision are both relatively new fields, and the assimilation time for such specific skills as these is likely to be fairly long. Finally, it must be said that local authority administrators are not fools. If, for example they perceive that raising more revenue by increasing pricing and marketing efforts will only lead to their central government, tax-based subsidies being reduced by the same proportion, then there is little incentive to change. If by increasing the cost recovery of a facility, there is increased danger of that facility being 'privatized' then, again there is a disincentive to improve financial performance. This highlights a fundamental criticism of the public sector – that without the incentive to survive, its objectives, behaviour and performance are always likely to be sub-standard. On this point other books have been written and we leave the question open to them.

Finally, we would like to emphasize that although this chapter has aired many commercially orientated views with respect to pricing and marketing, it is not our intention to attack the principles on which loss making recreation facilities are founded. There may be very good reasons for increasing or decreasing prices, and for raising or lowering subsidies. What this chapter demonstrates is the need to justify any such moves on clearly specified grounds. If, as we suggest, public sector supply is not allocatively efficient, then regardless of its objectives its performance may be improved by the adoption of some basic, rational pricing and marketing criteria, such as those reviewed above.

9 Investment appraisal, cost effectiveness and recreation budgeting

9.1 Introduction

A rational investor in the production of sports goods or services will seek the maximum return on such investment. Having made the investment, he will be interested, all other things being equal, in minimizing the costs of provision. However, such rationality is not necessarily easily achieved and it is sadly the case that many new recreation projects are not preceded by proper investment appraisal and recreation facilities are often not provided cost-effectively. Furthermore, the annually recorded budget information in the organizations that make these investments is not conducive to achieving efficient production.

The purpose of this chapter, therefore, is threefold. Firstly we demonstrate how the lifetime viability of a recreation project can be assessed. Secondly we review possible criteria by which to judge the cost-effectiveness of a recreation facility. Finally, since cost-effectiveness monitoring should be a repetitive exercise rather than a piecemeal check, we consider budget information systems – notably output and programme budgeting – which are appropriate as management aids rather than simply being records of the legitimacy of expenditure in an organization.

In dealing with investment appraisal we include normal entrepreneurial consideration of profitable opportunities – such a decision being similar to any other commercial investment decision. In the public sector, however, other considerations draw attention to the particular characteristics of sport and recreation services, as listed in Chapter 1. For instance, zero pricing of many facilities means the lack of an essential yardstick by which to decide how many facilities to supply. Merit good and public good aspects also confuse the straightforward financial approach. So decisions to invest in new recreational facilities or events are likely to be much more difficult to appraise in the public sector. Similarly, decisions relating to cost-effective provision of recreational services will be more complicated in the public sector for the same reasons – for example, such decisions as changes in manning, administrative procedures, programming policies or marketing targets.

9.2 Investment appraisal

9.2.1 Discounting*

We assume the profit-maximizing motive for the commercial recreation investor, in which case he would choose, subject to a likely capital rationing constraint, the project with the highest financial rate of return. The investment appraisal technique suitable for this purpose is called discounting. Discounting is remarkable for the universal acclaim given to it in economics and management texts, and its consistent lack of use in practice.

There is evidence that particularly in smaller, commercial organizations some form of pay-back criterion is preferred to assess the viability of an investment. Pay-back at its simplest considers the time period in which alternative investments are likely to pay back their original outlays – usually three to five years is the maximum considered. As an investment criterion it has one asset – it is easy to calculate and understand. In all other respects it is inferior to discounting. Only discounting accurately considers the different life-times of different projects, the different time-profiles of benefits and the fact that earlier returns have a higher value than later returns of the same cash amounts. The last of these considerations arises from two characteristics of the use of money. Firstly, it has an opportunity cost – even if it is only putting it on bank deposit to earn interest. Secondly, money generates a myopic time-preference for most individuals, firms and society in general, such that early returns are preferred. This time-preference usually derives from uncertainty and the diminishing marginal utility of money as incomes rise with economic growth.

The purpose of discounting is to reduce all estimated costs and benefits to values appropriate to one moment in time – usually the present day. This is done by using a rate of interest in the opposite direction to that by which present sums of money earn interest over time. So, for example, with a rate of interest of 10%, £110 in a year's time becomes £100 in present day values. The two most common discounting

---

* For a fuller discussion of formal investment appraisal techniques, readers are advised to consult Hawkins and Pearce (1971).

techniques are net present value and internal rate of return. A simplified form of net present value can be represented by:

$$\sum_{t=0}^{n} \frac{B_t}{(1+i)^t} - C_o$$

i.e. $\dfrac{B_1}{(1+i)} + \dfrac{B_2}{(1+i)^2} + \dfrac{B_3}{(1+i)^3} \cdots + \dfrac{B_n}{(1+i)^n} - C_o$

Where B = net benefits for each year
$\quad\quad\ C_o$ = capital cost of project at present day prices
$\quad\quad\ t$ = years
$\quad\quad\ t=0$ = present day
$\quad\quad\ n$ = lifetime of project
$\quad\quad\ i$ = rate of interest used to discount = discount rate

A critical choice is that of the rate of discount, since the appropriate opportunity cost of money lies somewhere in an array of interest rates to be found in any capital market. Time-preference rates are even more ill-defined, especially for society as a whole, when proper consideration for future generations is attempted. One pragmatic option is to use a realistic range of discount rates in separate estimates. This is one form of sensitivity analysis, testing the sensitivity of the overall result of the appraisal to changes in a key variable. If a project's net present value ranking is favourable and robust in the face of such a sensitivity analysis, then there is less cause for concern than for a project whose net present value ranking deteriorates substantially as the discount rate is increased.

The internal rate of return method is similar, but here the interest rate is calculated such that the net present value equals zero, i.e. solving for r in the formula

$$\sum_{t=0}^{n} \frac{B_t}{(1+r)^t} - C_o = 0$$

r being the internal rate of return that represents the marginal efficiency of the investment project. The larger the internal rate of return, the more worthwhile the project. The rate can be compared with other projects and with the interest rate that can be earned elsewhere, but again the question arises of which interest rate to use for comparison. For a public sector project the choice of a *social* discount rate is particularly difficult and has aroused much debate. Should it be based on the long-run, risk-free interest rate on government securities, or is this too conservative? Are any interest rates from imperfectly competitive and volatile capital markets appropriate for discounting over, say, a 25 year period?

Do different sources of finance for public sector investments imply different opportunity costs? We have assumed such cost differences do occur, in Chapter 7. In the UK, until recently, the central government actually recommended the use of a specific test discount rate, but although this may have simplified the choice there was no ready explanation of how this discount rate was chosen.

9.2.2 Cost benefit analysis*

Another set of problems involves the calculation of likely benefits and costs from each alternative project. The easier of the two might appear to be capital costs, since they occur sooner, are tangible and more predictable.

However, in the public sector at least, there is frequently a problem of cost escalation between the time of the original investment appraisal and the completion of construction (see, for example, Hartley, 1980). This, of course, depends on such circumstances as inflation, unforseen technical problems and the degree of deliberately low bidding by contractors to capture the tender for the job – all of which are unpredictable in the normal recreation investment gestation period of up to five years.

Another complication arises from the links between capital costs and eventual benefits, since if, for example, a sports centre is built according to a fixed contract, i.e. little cost escalation, any design faults are unlikely to be remedied and demand may suffer. A flexible contract may cause cost escalation, but benefits may be enhanced by such flexibility. Yet another problem is that of common costs – a project may have common and largely inseparable costs associated with a variety of outputs, for example, a reservoir contributing to water supply and electricity generation as well as a variety of recreational activities. Separate identification of the recreational aspects of such a project, for comparison with other recreation projects, would involve a largely arbitrary separation of common costs.

Benefit estimation depends critically on two considerations already examined in this book – demand forecasting and pricing decisions. As we have seen in Chapters 5 and 8, in practice there is little evidence of rational pricing criteria in operation in public sector recreation provision, at least in the UK, nor of consistent demand forecasting. If these two fundamentals for rational investment appraisal are missing, then such appraisals are likely to have wider error margins than are necessary. Given the uncertainty involved in medium and long-term .demand forecasting, these error margins are already going to be large.

---

* For a fuller discussion of cost-benefit analysis principles and applications, readers are advised to consult Sugden and Williams (1978).

For public sector investments, cost and benefit estimation is particularly difficult since social welfare is the objective to be maximized, not just financial profit. The technique frequently employed in such cases is cost-benefit analysis. This attempts to put values not only on likely financial returns, but also on other primary and secondary costs and benefits. Another primary benefit is the willingness to pay, of future customers, over and above the price charged, i.e. consumer surplus. This may change for existing sport and recreation participants, and be newly created for extra participants attracted by the additional facility.

In the case of those facilities for which no price is going to be charged – typically the case for national and urban parks – the entire primary benefit estimation is one of consumer surplus. Although other methods have been used to value this surplus, the technique which has been most commonly employed by academics is the Clawson demand curve. Unfortunately it has not been, and is unlikely to be, as commonly used by recreation investors in actual investment appraisals. This is undoubtedly due to the complications involved in a full scale Clawson exercise and the major criticisms levelled at the technique, as reviewed in Chapter 5, (see also Baxter, 1979; Curry, 1980; Gibson, 1978). Because of the continuing use of the method in economic analysis of recreation benefits, it is worth featuring one example. This is one of the most ambitious benefit estimation exercises to be attempted in the UK, by Mansfield (1971); see Case Study 1.

Case study 1. The Morecambe Bay Barrage, UK
This was a proposed project with three purposes – transport, water supply and recreation. Mansfield attempted to estimate only the recreation benefits, the major problem being that the exercise was akin to a true investment appraisal, unlike many other recreation benefit estimates, in that the facility did not exist at the time. Therefore, there was no facility specific demand data.

Instead, demand data was derived from surveys at a 'similar' recreation resource nearby – the Lake District. Mansfield estimated two effects on recreation trip making arising from the Barrage, both of which are represented in Fig. 9.1.
Because the Morecambe Bay area is closer than the Lake District for many recreationalists, the lower travel price would cause a diversion from the Lakes to Morecambe Bay – this is the diversion effect which reduces demand for the Lake District from OT_{L1} to OT_{L2}. The Barrage would also create a totally new recreational demand, as any new facility does – the generated or induced effect. This effect is taken from the Lake District demand curve (assuming the two areas have similar demand curves) and is represented by OT_{L1} to OT_B. The values of the consumer surplus changes associated with these changes in demand are represented by the areas indicated in Fig. 9.1

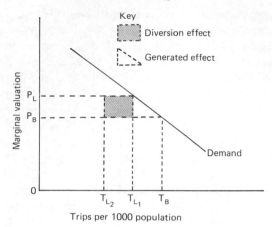

Fig. 9.1 Recreation benefits from the Morecambe Bay barrage.

This exercise required heroic assumptions and was only really part of a full cost-benefit analysis. The assumption was made that the two recreation resources are homogeneous – hence the generated effect for Morecambe Bay is taken from the Lake District demand curve. However, it can be argued that the two resources cater for different recreational activities, one being coastal and the other mountainous. This modification – treating the two resources as heterogeneous – was in fact adopted by Mansfield in a sensitivity analysis used for the diversion effect estimate. Whereas a high estimate assumed the maximum diversion (the area indicated in Fig. 9.1) a lower estimate assumed only a proportion of those with financial reason to divert would in fact do so, because of the heterogeneous nature of the two resources. Another assumption vital to the estimates was of car ownership during the life-time of the project. The use of forecasts made in 1966 involved error margins large enough to justify another sensitivity analysis, although this was not done.

Because of its concentration on benefit estimation, this study lacks the full dimensions of a cost-benefit analysis. It did not consider the allocation of common costs to recreation and the other functions of the project. It did not, as transport planners did, consider a selection of possible alternative barrage schemes. Nor did it consider other recreation schemes to see if they would yield recreation benefits more cost-effectively. Anderson (1975) did consider an alternative project with similar types of recreation benefits and found it to have greater potential benefits than the Morecambe Bay Barrage. Finally Mansfield's study did not even consider all relevant benefits; another one of some importance may have been the external one of relieved congestion in the Lake District.

Despite its problems, Mansfield's work does demonstrate that it is possible to estimate values for primary social benefits from a not yet existent recreational resource. It remains the case, however, that the Clawson method seems impractical to investors, if not to professional economists. Disenchantment with the method amongst some of the latter has led to attempts to measure consumer surplus directly, without having to identify the demand curve. This is done by asking people about their 'willingness-to-pay' for a facility, thus obtaining individual measures of consumer surplus. Such surpluses can then be aggregated to the whole population of participants, generating the primary benefit estimate for the facility.

However, surveys depend too much on the dubious accuracy of respondent's answers to such hypothetical questions as what they would be willing to pay for a recreational experience, or what they would need in compensation to stop participating at a particular site or facility. In particular, because free outdoor facilities have public good characteristics, respondents may play the free-rider role. This would cause them to undervalue their recreation experience in the hope that others (for example, the government) will pay more for the facility, whilst the free riders pay the minimum necessary. For a comprehensive review of this 'willingness-to-pay' approach to benefit estimation, see Meyer (1975), and for an example in recreation, see McConnell (1977).

The only other major type of alternative to the Clawson method for benefit estimation is to use utility analysis to estimate indifference curves, with the help of detailed information of a more objective kind than the direct 'willingness-to-pay' questions. This information concerns the relationship between individuals' utility and key variables such as distance travelled, income and intensity of preference. It is acquired by simulations of recreational choices, with questioning to expose individuals' utility/indifference curves concerning the choices on offer. The indifference curves are used to either calculate consumer surplus directly or to generate demand curves from which consumer surplus calculations are made. For examples of this approach, see Sinden (1974) and Sinden and Wyckoff (1976).

Because the choices are made in a simulation, the problems of the more direct 'willingness-to-pay' questioning are diminished. The other main advantage of this approach is that it requires less heroic assumptions than the Clawson method. However, computationally it is just as complicated and therefore inaccessible to practitioners, and it also shares another weakness of the Clawson method in being more suitable for benefit estimation for existing resources rather than proposed ones.

As well as primary benefits to actual producers and consumers involved in a recreation project, cost-benefit analysis also attempts to measure secondary costs and benefits for external, third parties. These include the externalities reviewed in Chapter 1. In the case of a proposed neighbourhood recreation centre in an inner city, for instance, one external benefit of some importance may be reduced crime and vandalism, particularly by youths in the local area. If these benefits are considered potentially important, some attempt should be made to value them when conducting a cost-benefit analysis of the project. Unfortunately this is rarely, if ever, attempted in such recreation investment appraisal, despite the recording of fairly reliable statistics on the incidence and costs of crime and vandalism. It is left to piecemeal, academic studies to furnish the few empirical details we have of the value of such externalities as reduced vandalism, regional multiplier effects, rising land values near recreation facilities, option demands and congestion costs. In many cases the physical measurement of these effects is possible but the valuation of them presents difficulties.

The problem is that externalities, by their very nature, have no market prices and are often intangible as well. They therefore have to be assigned shadow prices (also known as surrogate and imputed prices), a process which involves value judgements and invites criticism. The most common strategy in shadow pricing is the survey – asking people what they would pay if there were a market for a commodity, or to preserve a social, external asset, or what they would want in compensation for any social loss. Another tactic is to examine the changing values of economic agents; for example house prices in an area very well endowed with recreation facilities – although clearly such prices are dependent on many other variables. At the very least, projects could be ranked on the criteria of relevant externalities, by experts' opinions, as a supplement to the valuations achieved by cost-benefit analysis. Alternatively a range of possible values can be introduced for each externality, as a sensitivity analysis.

Another problem of relevance to any public sector investment appraisal is a distributional one, i.e. which individuals receive the benefits and suffer the costs? If, for instance, as our demand chapters indicate, the major recipients of benefits from a recreation project are going to be not the poor, but largely the middle classes, is this an equitable project? It may be that society, whether local or national, or its elected representatives, prefer projects where the benefits fall largely on more disadvantaged people. A good example of such a project is featured in our Case Study 2 below. The question is, should such a project be evaluated alongside more middle-class projects with no formal recognition of the distributional differences between the projects? If such distributional questions are important, then a decision has to be made whether or not to include them explicitly in the cost-benefit analysis calculations. The major arguments against this explicit adjustment are that it unnecessarily complicates an already problematic technique, and there are government mechanisms specifically designed to deal with distributional matters, i.e. tax and social security.

The convention in practical cost-benefit analysis is, in fact, to ignore distributional questions – assuming implicitly, therefore, that all recipients of benefits have the same marginal utility of income. However, this is conceptually unacceptable, and if the incomes of benefit recipients can be identified then some allowance for distributional bias in benefit allocation is fairly simple. Benefits can be divided into recipient income groups and multiplied by appropriate distributional weights. These weights could, for example, be the ratio of average income to the recipient group's income, or the inverse of appropriate marginal rates of taxation. Their effect would be to relatively enhance the sum of benefits for those below average income, and relatively reduce the calculated benefits for those above average income. Of course if such an adjustment were made in one cost-benefit analysis, it would also have to be made for all other project appraisals being considered by the organization in order that they be comparable.

A major problem with such an adjustment is that it makes explicit a consideration that is rarely brought to the surface in public policy – the notion of a fair distribution of income; moreover it does so in a way that is essentially normative. Another exercise which makes distribution considerations explicit is demonstrated by Weisbrod (1968). He calculates the distributional weights implicit in past USA government investment decisions concerning water resource projects. This involves calculation of those weights necessary to generate a ranking of projects that matches the order in which they were actually undertaken. Strictly speaking, of course, the exercise, being ex-post, may seem of little relevance to practical project appraisal. However, by disclosing the implicit distributional weights, it serves to bring to the attention of future social investment decision-makers the inescapable fact that a distributional bias is implicit in every investment. Weisbrod (1968) also illustrates this important point with reference to the distribution of recreation benefits in two beach erosion studies in Ohio and Connecticut.

Whilst all the above comments relate to income distribution, bias may also occur by age, race (which Weisbrod considered) and sex – all of which might be made explicit. We consider further the issue of equity in recreation provision in the next chapter.

9.2.3 Risk and uncertainty

We have already introduced the idea of sensitivity analysis, in the use of a variety of discount rates and shadow prices in calculating net present values. In any forecasting exercise, such as investment appraisal, error margins in estimates are likely to be high. Where probabilities of outcomes can be calculated, the situation is one of risk. Where such probabilities cannot be calculated, there is uncertainty. Sensitivity analysis is particularly appropriate to the latter case, since by feeding in reasonable extreme values for key uncertain variables, some estimate can be made of the implications for project choice, and even the financial or political survival of the sponsoring organization.

Regarding the Clawson method, Smith (1971) found the results to be sensitive to different assumptions about the value of operating costs for private cars, and the value of time, particularly when only a few distance zones were delineated. When the number of zones in Smith's study was increased from 8 to 27, the sensitivity was very much reduced. Where probabilities can be assigned to outcomes, i.e. risk, it is possible to calculate an expected value, as Table 9.1 demonstrates.

Table 9.1 *An example of expected value calculation*

(1) Outcome, for example, net present value (£)	(2) Assigned probabilities	(3) =(1) × (2) (£)	(4) Expected value = Σ (3) (£)
10 000	0.2	2000	–
6 000	0.5	3000	–
3 000	0.2	600	5800
2 000	0.1	200	–

Another less discriminating method of dealing with risk is to add a risk premium, of one or two per cent, to the discount rate. Whilst simple to operate, this does penalize those investments whose returns are spread over a longer period; it is not necessarily the case that such investments are riskier than those which pay back more quickly.

9.2.4 Other investment considerations

Recreation investment appraisals, be they straightforward commercial ones or public sector cost-benefit analyses, should properly be comparative, and consider all relevant costs and benefits. However in practice, projects are often considered in isolation rather than in comparison to alternatives, and also some recreation studies have concentrated almost entirely on benefit estimation. Mansfield's study falls into both of these categories, but never purported to be a full cost-benefit analysis.

Serious doubts exist about the practicality of cost-benefit analysis as an off-the-shelf investment appraisal technique, especially for recreation projects which will involve heavily subsidized or free services and a number of externalities. For one thing, the scope of such an analysis, if it were to properly consider a range of alternative projects and all relevant social costs and benefits, is likely to be much too large for an average local authority to handle – they are unlikely to possess the expertise or the planning time. Furthermore, the uncertainty in the estimates and criticisms of methods such as the Clawson technique may not justify the time and effort expended, nor even the contracting out of such an appraisal to consultants. A related doubt in assessing the value of cost-benefit analysis is that political opportunism may in many instances be a more important influence on the approval and financing of a recreation project than a rational appraisal. At the very least the technique is open to bias in its use by planning departments, to the extent that it is used to firm-up the political case for support.

Despite these problems, the technique of cost-benefit analysis is an attempt to fill a void and minimize the number of unquantified variables relevant to a social investment decision. Furthermore, there are examples of the technique that are on a more practical scale for local authorities. These cover all the major costs and benefits without making too many heroic assumptions and without taxing the resources of the appraising department too much. Good examples of such case studies are to be found in Kavanagh, Marcus and Gay (1973), and we feature one of these in Case Study 2.

Case study 2. Summer Youth Camps in Los Angeles, 1968-71
These youth camps were of short duration, so that most costs and benefits occurred in the same year, making discounting less critical. They also generated changes to important social or external costs and benefits. Since they were camps for poor, ghetto youths, the distributional bias was less likely to be a cause for concern than other recreational schemes. The main costs and benefits estimated were as follows:

1 Recreation costs
    (a) Direct programme costs – salaries, food, travel, expenses, etc.
    (b) Private costs – time and transport of campers and parents;
                    – policing costs for residences near camp.
    (c) Social costs – damage to property and people near camp.
    (d) Facility opportunity costs – imputed rents and tax losses.
2 Recreation benefits
    (a) Market value of recreational experience.
    (b) Reduced damage to property and people in home districts
                    – during camp period;
                    – in the following year.
    (c) Reduced public policing and court costs in home district
                    – during camp period;
                    – in the following year.
    (d) Reduced high-school drop-out rate.

Estimates were made for two scales of project, and for three years of the programme. For discounting, three discount rates were used – 4, 6 and 10% – although this did not influence the overall result, which was favourable. Assumptions had to be made for every category of costs and benefits listed, and one or two are worthy of comment. Many of the costs were common costs, since the camps were not only recreational but also for the purpose of work study and job training. The subsequent decision to allocate 40% of the programme costs to 'recreation' was arbitrary, but reasonable.

Similarly the benefits were common benefits and it is interesting that a different, arbitrary allocation of 50% of the benefits of reducing damage to property and people was assigned to the recreation programme. The reasoning for this was that recreation was likely to be a much stronger attraction for youngsters than the other work-related elements of the camps. However, if this was the case, common costs should have been allocated more to the recreation programme as well. Another interesting assumption concerns the market value of the recreation experience. As the summer camps were free and for very low income clients, there was an implicit weighting up of these benefit estimates because they were based on sample prices charged for private camps. However, distribution-al considerations were not made explicitly in any of the cost and benefit calculations.

The results of this cost-benefit analysis showed positive net present values for both options, no matter what discount rates were employed, with the larger scale camps having the highest values. The results could have been compared with other alternative projects although the original study did not do this.

Finally, the relationship between investment appraisal and capital rationing is a Catch-22 situation in the public sector. Ideally the capital constraint needs to be identified before projects are considered, so that only ones of a size within the constraint are appraised. In practice, however, it is only after feasibility is established that funding is approved or rejected by, for example, national government depart-ments. Also, the availability of public sector capital funds can fluctuate considerably from year to year because of government macroeconomic policies, thus making rational planning all the more difficult.

Table 9.2 demonstrates the volatility of capital spending on sport and recreation in the UK local authority sector, by comparison with current on 'revenue expenditure'. In the early 1970s the 'tap' was on, but after agreement with the IMF on the terms of a large loan, the British government tightened monetary control. The effect can be seen in 1976 to 1978, with actual reductions in cash spent, despite high inflation rates, thus causing real capital spending to fall substantially. These cuts were easily imposed in the UK by a central government that manipulated local authority capital spending with an extensive system of loan sanctions. It now cash limits the capital funds given to local authorities. From 1978 to 1981, this spending recovered in sport and recreation services, but in 1981/2 a fall in the absolute spending level occurred again – this time not because of loan sanctions, but more probably because local authorities could not afford to run facilities from their revenue accounts even though they might be able to get funds to build them.

Table 9.2 *Local government expenditure on sport and recreation, UK, 1975/76 to 1981/82*

	Real revenue expenditure* (£)	Percentage change	Real capital expenditure (£)	Percentage change
1975/6	275.5	–	95.2	–
1976/7	269.8	– 2.1	71.3	–25.1
1977/8	257.7	– 4.5	52.1	–26.9
1978/9	270.7	+ 5.0	56.7	+ 8.8
1979/80	298.2	+10.2	70.2	+23.8
1980/1	301.3	+ 1.0	78.7	+12.1
1981/2	286.8	– 4.8	59.2	–24.8

* Deflated by retail price index, (1975 = 100).
From: Local Government Financial Statistics.

Despite the many problems reviewed in this section, we must end it with a plea on behalf of rational appraisal methods. Only by habitual, systematic application of investment appraisal techniques will the basis of investment decisions be improved. Such application should also, in due course, iron out many of the problems associated with the methods. It is necessary to assess the life-time viability of recreation projects before they are developed, if only to prevent organizations being saddled with investments that do not fulfill their true potential. Proper investment appraisal also lays an efficient foundation for continuous monitoring of cost-effectiveness once the project is under way, and it is to this assessment of annual viability that we now turn.

9.3 Cost-effectiveness

At its simplest this is an exercise to determine whether or not a service is being provided, or an objective being met, at minimum cost. However, the term cost-effectiveness is also used in the context of a limited cost-benefit analysis – for example, an assessment of the different benefits to be derived from investing the same amount of resources in different projects, or the costs of achieving different levels of output. We shall concentrate in this section on the simple interpretation, because we are interested in regular decisions about effective use of resources within existing recreation programmes.

The most common measure of cost-effectiveness used to date in the UK is the ratio of the number of admissions to a facility in one year to its annual costs – either operating costs or total costs. This ratio has been used both this way and in its reciprocal form – one giving the visits per £ of costs, the other giving the costs per visit. Two studies in particular have analysed the cost-effectiveness of indoor sport and recreation facilities – by the Scottish Sports Council (1979) and Coopers and Lybrand Associates Ltd, (1981a) The former study examines cost-effectiveness, as measured by the ratio for different sizes of facility, different types i.e. pools, dry centres and wet and dry centres, and different locations, i.e. city, small town, urban, suburban. The latter study concentrates on the differences in cost-effectiveness between joint provision centres (i.e. jointly provided by both the recreation and education sectors of local authorities) and separate, sole provision centres, but also considers the size and type of facility.

Some of the cost-effectiveness evidence from the Scottish study is presented in Table 7.3. One important implication of the analysis accompanying this table is that the simple ratios hide many other considerations and it is possibly misleading to take such evidence at face value. In the case of different sizes of facility the quality of the product may differ; in the case of different locations there may be inescapable land and capital cost differences. All-in-all the Scottish evidence does not point to any consistent differences in cost-effectiveness with respect to size and location of facilities, but the type of facility does seem to be significant – wet and dry centres performing consistently well.

In their study of joint provision, Coopers and Lybrand (1981a) present evidence that joint provision is almost twice as cost-effective as separate provision. Their main results are reproduced in Table 9.3.

Some of these results are inconsistent with the Scottish Sports Council's findings, for example, with respect to type of facility. However, all the data in Tables 7.2 and 9.3 refer to averages and it is important also to look at the range, since the smaller Scottish sample may fall within an acceptable range. Unfortunately the Coopers and Lybrand study gives no indication of the range of results within any one type or size of facility. In the Scottish Study, however, there is considerable range of operating costs per visit for dry centres (25 – 93p) as we have already discussed in Chapter 7.

Another problem with the use of this cost-effectiveness ratio is that it ignores considerations such as pricing, programming and other management policies, like attitudes to minority groups. It is, in fact, a pseudo measure of capacity-utilization, and can be improved, assuming normal demand responses, simply by lowering prices. A free facility

Table 9.3 *Cost-effectiveness in joint and separately provided sports centres, UK, 1981.*

Type of centre	Type of control	Cost-effectiveness (i.e. visits/operating cost)
All	Joint	2.7
	Separate	1.5
Dry	Joint	4.9
	Separate	1.5
Wet and Dry	Joint	2.1
	Separate	1.5
Small	Joint	3.3
	Separate	1.4
Medium	Joint	1.7
	Separate	1.7
Large	Joint	3.2
	Separate	1.3

From: Coopers and Lybrand, 1981a.

would in this respect maximize cost-effectiveness since it would maximize capacity-utilization, all other things being constant. Clearly some additional consideration needs to be made of the revenue implications and both of the studies mentioned take up this point.

It would be expected, given the comment just made, that the most cost-effective centres would be those whose cost recovery from direct charges was lowest, indicating that their prices are very low. However in both studies this expectation is refuted. In the Scottish study a Rank Correlation coefficient of 0.99 can be calculated for 20 centres' ranking for cost-effectiveness and cost recovery, and in the English study centres with higher cost-effectiveness also tend to recover higher proportions of their operating costs. Coopers and Lybrand suggest two reasons for this apparently curious finding. Firstly, entry prices are generally highly subsidized, so minor variations in prices between centres make no difference to relative usage (a point we have noted in Chapter 4). Secondly, centres charging slightly higher prices may also be more commercial in their objectives, and hence achieve higher capacity-utilization. It must be said that whilst the evidence is fairly conclusive there are notable exceptions to the rule; for example, the most cost-effective centre in Coopers and Lybrand's sample recovered only just over 20% of operating costs in direct revenue – compared with an English average of 34% – due to much lower than average entry prices.

Whilst the cost-effectiveness ratio is useful for such analysis it must be stressed that it is inadequate on its own. There may be other more precise measures of capacity-utilization, as we have shown in Chapter 7. The Coopers and Lybrand study used no other actual empirical results, so that whilst mention was made of other private and social costs – such as administration problems, and lack of access during school time for certain disadvantaged groups in joint provision facilities – the lack of quantification left the ratio data in a stronger position than it otherwise might have held for interpretation purposes.

Other indicators of cost-effectiveness do not relate to capacity-utilization because they do not require information on admission numbers, which is quite often either difficult to obtain or inaccurate. Stabler (1982) has initiated work in England using information from the accounts of local authorities in the form of ratios, to help assess the efficiency of provision. Examples of these ratios, and some English public sector averages, are given in Table 9.4.

Table 9.4 *Cost and revenue ratios for performance monitoring: preliminary estimates, UK, 1979/80.*

Ratio	Separate provision (%)	Joint provision (%)
Total income/Total costs	37	55
Fees and charges/Total costs	29	28
Total income/Operating costs	55	61
Fees and charges/Operating costs	43	38
Staff costs/Operating costs	53	55
Debt charges/Total costs	30	22
Operating costs/Total costs	67	74

From: M. J. Stabler, 1982.

Other financial ratios of use may be administrative expenses/fees and charges, and fees and charges/fixed assets. Such ratios can be recorded quite easily by separate facilities or by organizations with control over different types of facility, such as the joint and separate provision in Table 9.4. The 'average' values in this table provide a standard by which to compare individual 'performances'. Such a comparison may promote discussion of, for instance, whether an abnormally high (or low) subsidy is a policy decision or an 'accident', or whether an exceptionally high ratio of staff costs to operating costs is explicable in terms of special circumstances, for example excellence or sports leadership schemes.

Obviously estimates of such ratios for an organization need to be put in context before they become meaningful. The two bits of qualifying information necessary for this purpose are the objectives of the organization, and the 'normal' range to be expected in the ratios' values across many facilities and authorities, some of which Stabler suggests. If such ratios were monitored consistently for individual facilities, they could be compared more meaningfully with the performance of other facilities in similar circumstances, and over time.

A wide range of financial ratios are also recommended by the Audit Inspectorate (1983) on the grounds that they would:

'provide a yardstick by which to monitor financial and operational performance, to assess the potential effect of decisions, to focus on problem areas and to assist in forming a judgement on 'value for money' performance.'

Unlike Stabler, the Audit Inspectorate does not estimate average or typical values for the ratios; but as it points out:

'primarily designed to present key information to the on-site management, performance statistics may also be useful to people not involved in the detailed day-to-day running of centres (Director of Recreation, Chief Executive, members, auditors, rate payers).'

In other words such indicators have a great deal of value in their own right, as well as in comparison over time or with other facilities' performances.

The notion of cost-effectiveness implicit in the use of such ratios goes further than providing the service at a minimum cost per visit, as implied by the first ratio used above, in Table 9.3. It leans more towards the conventional commercial objective of a rate of return. This would not seem unreasonable since most urban recreation facilities generate some direct revenue and in the current economic climate this financial objective is assuming greater importance. As Stabler in a later paper (1984) points out, many sports services, even within the public sector, are straightforward commercial services, and as such are suitable for the use of standard accounting ratios – for example, profit/sales, cost of sales/sales, sales/stock and sales/capital employed, etc. This is particularly the case for catering and bar services and may well be applicable to more commercially orientated activities, for example, popmobility, health suites and squash. For less revenue conscious parts of recreation provision, Stabler suggests a fund accounting approach to financial performance monitoring, i.e. deciding on the subsidy to be offered for a particular service and operating within that subsidy.

Another angle on cost-effectiveness can be borrowed from our earlier discussion on cost-benefit analysis. If recreation facilities have specific objectives concerning the type of people to benefit, it would seem logical to continuously monitor users to establish whether or not, for example, underprivileged groups are increasing or decreasing their representation, for example, in the manner of the grid approach (see Chapter 5, Section 4). Other performance ratios may reflect such social objectives, although they would almost certainly involve more sophisticated user records – for example, ratio of females/total users, expenditure on unemployed programmes/total costs, staff time spent on social programmes/total staff time. If such ratio information is to be of any use it must be comparable from year to year, between facilities and, hopefully, between authorities. Only then will norms be established as yardsticks by which to judge a facility's performance.

All of the ratios mentioned above are deficient in one respect. This is that they are all averages, probably over a year's operation. For many decisions in the operation of sport and recreation facilities a more appropriate performance ratio would relate to marginal costs and revenues, or at least incremental or avoidable values (see Chapter 7). These dimensions would be directly pertinent to such changes as the extension of a facility, the expansion of a programme in time and/or user numbers, the installation of new equipment and streamlined manning arrangements.

In each of the three aspects of cost-effectiveness identified, different objectives were made explicit – i.e. capacity-utilization, cost recovery and attracting disadvantaged users. Besides monitoring the performance of an organization in relation to such objectives, a role of cost-effectiveness studies is also to assess different ways in which minimum standards of performance can be achieved, and to identify the least-cost methods. Joint provision may, for many local authorities, be the most cost-effective method of achieving high capacity-utilization, but not for catering for disadvantaged groups. It is necessary to use cost-effectiveness analysis in relation to all major objectives of a recreation service, before rational decisions can be made about consistent and efficient policies.

The use of conventional budget information by Stabler is, in a sense, pessimistic about the quality of management information regularly produced by government recreation services. Furthermore, even this budget information is often inconsistent between authorities. There is a lack of agreement on the exact make-up of capital and operating costs, gross and net costs, and the means of accounting for debt charges and payments between authorities. The following section of this chapter, therefore, is extremely optimistic, since it recommends additional budgetary information for the purpose of improving managerial decision-making.

9.4 Output and programme budgeting

Conventional budgets (termed line-item budgets in the USA) are based on inputs. Primarily designed for the purpose of financial control, they list the major types of inputs and the annual expenditure on these inputs. A classic English example is given in Table 9.5.

In this budget there is not even delineation of separate recreation facilities. The problem with this type of budget is that although it is reasonable for financial control, it is almost useless for management decision-making. To detect inefficiency in expenditure, i.e. waste of resources, requires a mixture of accounting and detective skills; to detect ineffective expenditure, i.e. failure to attain goals, is impossible.

At the very least such input budgets should be accompanied by some indicators of performance and by some basic adjustments and additions

Table 9.5 *Conventional input budgeting : An example – General rate fund revenue account for the year ended 31st March 1982.*

Expenditure			Income		
1980/81 (£)		1981/82 (£)	1980/81 (£)		1981/82 (£)
Parks and recreation committee			Parks and recreation committee		
	Parks and Open Spaces			*Parks and Open Spaces*	
1 476 155	Employees	1 545 993	3 044	Government Grants	3 044
237 393	Premises	246 534	991	Sales	476
132 018	Supplies and Services	111 174	34 834	Fees and Charges	40 070
172 618	Transport & Movable Plant	159 416	12 830	Rents	17 162
98 832	Establishment	73 564	112	Miscellaneous	5 591
86 128	Debt.Charges	77 282			
2 203 144		**2 213 963**	**51 811**		**66 343**
	Outdoor Sports Facilities			*Outdoor Sport Facilities*	
46 608	Employees	64 072	–	Fees and Charges	214
25 999	Premises	10 035	11 587	Rents	10 080
2 740	Supplies and Services	4 104	6 634	Miscellaneous	3 615
7 436	Transport & Movable Plant	8 807			
8 191	Establishment	22 957			
14 931	Debt. Charges	24 681			
105 905		**134 656**	**18 221**		**13 909**
	Indoor Sports Facilities			*Indoor Sports Facilities*	
55 215	Employees	49 972	22 273	Fees and charges	24 433
31 006	Premises	27 880	53	Rents	52
4 367	Supplies and Services	4 131			
1 272	Transport	1 300			
2 127	Establishment	12 705			
6 121	Debt. Charges	5 933			
100 108		**101 921**	**22 326**		**24 485**
	Swimming Pools			*Swimming Pools*	
322 229	Employees	321 564	3 489	Sales	3 753
244 745	Premises	245 389	131 050	Fees and Charges	141 088
31 101	Supplies and Services	31 293	2 073	Rents	2 050
576	Transport	189			
22 416	Establishment	54 712			
174 560	Debt. Charges	168 948			
795 627		**822 095**	**136 612**		**146 891**

From: Stoke-on-Trent City Council Accounts, 1981/82.

to the data. Besides Stabler's ratios, we recommend the monitoring of trend data for costs and revenues over a few years at constant prices as well as in cash, so that a picture of changing real expenditure and income is presented. It would also be of use to know the average error margins between estimates and out-turns, and some comparative data – for example, average expenditure and income per head figures from similar areas and from the region and the country as a whole. Further time series data could be estimated for key workload indicators, for example, numbers of admissions; numbers of acres of open space, park land, playing fields; total areas of indoor facility space; population statistics for peak recreational activity ages.

Much more ambitious than such minor amendments is the principle of output budgeting which would re-allocate all the cost items in Table 9.5 to functional objectives and their associated outputs for the recreation service. An output budgeting procedure would look something like the following:

1. Define operational objectives and associated output targets.
2. Allocate all costs to these output targets – i.e. functional costing.
3. Judge effectiveness of present programmes in achieving objectives, i.e. with the use of cost-effectiveness criteria.
4. Evaluate alternative methods of achieving objectives – i.e. cost-efficiency or small cost-benefit analyses.
5. Systematically review and plan objectives, targets and resource use.

Whereas such a system is feasible for some programmes, for example health, defence and policing, there are considerable doubts about its applicability in recreation. One major problem is the definition of output targets. Many recreation outputs are either intangible, or inextricably linked to other policies, for example education, health or housing. Even the straightforward concept of capacity is difficult to define and measure, as we saw in Chapter 7. Nevertheless, output-related targets are not totally inconceivable, for example, the percentage of children of a certain age able to swim a certain distance, accident rate per activity hour, percentage utilization of each activity space, percentage participation by disadvantaged groups, maximum household distance from certain amenities.

A workshop on effectiveness in public sector outdoor recreation in the USA (Driver and Rosenthal, 1981) categorized three types of output with which inputs might be associated. Activity outputs are most easy to identify but actual output is poorly defined, for example, the wide range of skills and motives for walking and swimming. Such activity 'outputs' are in fact programmes and are more appropriate to the programme budgeting discussed below. The second output type is the setting or environment provided, for example, social, isolated, scenic and easily accessible. Such outputs are relatively easy to identify in relation to facilities. The third and most recommended output is also the most difficult to identify. This is the experience output, for example, relaxation, social interaction, physical exertion, risk and solitude. For budgeting purposes this output type is impractical, because experiential attributes like those mentioned are shared by many activities and facilities and are difficult to quantify for monitoring purposes. The first of these problems is common costs, which is a major problem with all output budgeting.

Such problems as these have led to a more feasible option being employed for recreation and other government budgeting, particularly in the USA. This is programme budgeting (often termed PPBS –

planning, programming, budgeting system) an example of which is to be found in Los Angeles, as reported by Kavanagh, Marcus and Gay (1973) and is reproduced in Table 9.6.

Table 9.6 *Programme budgeting : An example.*

	($ thousands)		
	Present oriented	Future oriented	Total
Services for Consumption	8 596.1	6 140.6	14 736.5
Extended-use programs	6 716.0	1 683.1	8 398.9
Athletic programs	4 597.7	1 091.1	5 688.6
Cultural programs	980.1	37.0	1 017.1
Environmental programs	1 138.2	555.0	1 693.2
Casual-use programs	1 880.1	4 457.5	6 337.6
Leisure enjoyment	1 508.4	4 359.0	5 867.4
Beautification	371.7	98.5	470.2
Services for human capital development	567.4	4.8	572.2
Skill development programs	150.2	4.8	155.0
Athletic	63.0	0.0	63.0
Cultural	44.9	1.5	46.4
Environmental	5.3	3.3	8.6
Other	37.0	0.0	37.0
Remedial programs	417.2	0.0	417.2
Educational, psychological	49.8	0.0	49.8
Physical, althletic	200.0	0.0	200.0
Social, job rehabilitation	167.4	0.0	167.4
Not elsewhere allocated	1 745.8	306.4	2 052.2
Administrative	1 258.2	28.4	1 286.6
Equipment	319.0	101.7	420.7
General construction, development	0.0	182.1	182.1
Miscellaneous	162.8	0.0	162.8
Total	$10 903.5	$6 457.6	$17 361.0

From: Kavanagh, Marcus and Gay, 1973; County of Los Angeles, Department of Parks and Recreation, 1966/7 Financial Statement.

Programmes are more easily identifiable than outputs. In this example the programmes are based on consumer behaviour and motives – for example, casual consumption, consumption involving greater, repetitive time commitments, and skill acquisition. As Kavanagh, Marcus and Gay point out, alternative programme formating could develop along the lines of types of users, for example, by age, affiliation, geographical distribution, socioeconomic group. With many such alternatives the problem of common costs becomes a major one again and without very sophisticated and probably intrusive monitoring of users the cost allocation would be essentially arbitrary.

The most likely form of programme budgeting, found in practice in the USA, records costs and revenues for types of activity and for functional areas; although this segmentation does not necessarily conform logically to the objectives of the facility. Again the problem of common costs is the most likely deterrent to the development of full programme budgeting, although there are sports centres with activity-based functional costing. The Spectrum Arena at Warrington, UK, is one example with each activity in two sets of programmes – commercial and community recreation – costed out as far as possible. The functional costing, or cost-centering, is achieved by a number of methods, as reviewed in Chapter 7. So long as revenue is similarly allocated then activities can be aligned to specific objectives and appropriate financial and participation targets formulated. Adjustment of policies and targets then becomes a much more straightforward, information-based routine, so long as the functional costing is a regular systematic procedure. Furthermore, the information basis of such decisions would be improved in quality if it were marginal or incremental, as well as in the form of annual averages. Decisions, after all, are not made once a year.

An even more radical approach to budgeting is the zero-base budget, which requires the whole budget to be justified each year. This contrasts completely with incrementalism, where only marginal changes are made to the overall budget and the single most important determinant of the budget is what expenditure occurred in the previous year. In practice it may be that zero-base budgeting is too demanding. Howard and Crompton (1980) claim 'there is little evidence of its widespread adoption in the public sector'.

One can question the validity of an annual respecification of all objectives, priorities and productivity targets. Output or programme budgeting is not only less ambitious, but is also a form of rolling programme whereby continual reappraisal takes place but not for the entire budget – only for those items to which either the data or decision-makers draw attention. In this sense it is related to what Howard and Crompton refer to as a 'modified zero-base budgeting system', where only selected, 'discretionary' parts of the budget are taken back to square one for complete reappraisal.

It may be, therefore, that programme budgeting and modified zero-base budgeting are more suitable to firms operating in a 'bounded rationality' circumstance. Time and resource constraints may forestall budgeting systems which involve more sophisticated techniques such as zero-base budgeting. This seems an appropriate judgement given the exceedingly slow take-up of even programme budgeting in both the UK and the USA, especially the UK.

Common to all suggested improvements in budgeting is another push in the direction of rational decision-making. The aim is to justify expenditures with reference to objectives and generate information which can help recreation managers to improve the quality of their decision making and achieve objectives more cost effectively. The most popular budgeting method is still one which suggests that inertia rules OK.

9.5 Conclusions

One of the most commonly used words in this chapter must be 'rational'. Moreover, in an attempt to demonstrate that rational decision-making can be improved, we have linked it inexorably with more quantitative information needs. It is only right therefore that we conclude with some words of warning. We do not recommend numbers for numbers sake and there is always the danger that the 'misplaced concreteness' of quantitative information may, in fact, distort decision-making away from a rational solution. Furthermore, the quality of the data is undoubtedly more important than the quantity; it is all too easy to present impressive data sets with inadequate explanations of major assumptions implicit in the estimates and likely error margins. It must also be said that quantitative information is only one input to the decision-making procedure. It happens to be one that we feel is woefully inadequate, but our desire to see this situation improve is not to be mistaken for a desire that it become the be-all and end-all of recreation decision-making. We hope that by improving this information the standard of political, managerial and media debate will also rise.

As it is, we are left with rather sad indictments such as that of Cowell (1979), with respect to public sector indoor facilities in the UK:

'The absence of clear, measurable objectives for centres or for individual staff meant that evaluation efforts are very subjective. 'Success' was usually identified with not overspending budgets, with reducing deficits and with absence of complaints.'

Section four

Contemporary issues in sport and recreation

10 The role of government

10.1 Introduction

Throughout Section 3 we have examined the behaviour of the public sector on the supply side of the recreation market. In this chapter we return to the global objectives of government in this area and consider the various means through which these objectives may be achieved. We attempt to use economic theory to indicate 'optimum' government intervention in the sense of successfully achieving policy targets. We then compare these optimum policy solutions with the actions of government in the recreation market in Britain. Through this comparison we reveal various problems with recreation policy and the instruments used in its implementation. We begin by considering the two objectives of government: the efficiency objective and the equity objective.

10.2 The efficiency objective

Government has the objectives of achieving efficiency in the allocation of resources both to and within the recreation market. Under certain conditions the efficiency objective can be achieved without specific government intervention. These conditions are those that define the perfectly competitive ideal with rational consumers, armed with perfect information, making decisions so as to maximize utility. In simple terms the role of government, as regards the efficiency objective, is to correct for market failures that prevent the achievement of this ideal competitive allocation of resources.

In Chapter 1 we identified several types of market failure in the sport and recreation market. We described a wide spectrum of recreation goods, ranging from quasi-public goods, such as National Parks, at one extreme, to private goods, such as sports equipment at the other. As we move from public to private across this spectrum we expect to see diminishing government involvement. At one extreme, the provision of pure public goods, the traditional view is that 'free-rider' behaviour will prevent the private sector from providing efficient output levels, and provision by government at zero price could be the optimum solution. In the case of pure private goods the government would not normally interfere with the market allocation as long as monopoly elements were not present.

The major reason for government involvement, though, in the finance and provision of recreation is the externalities associated with participation. These external benefits result in the free market producing a sub-optimal level of output of recreation opportunity. We then need to consider what is the best way for the government to correct for this market inadequacy.

10.3 Efficient government intervention

We have already considered the principles of public sector pricing for goods that generate externalities in Section 8.3 and Fig. 8.2. The conclusion seemed to be that because of the external benefits associated with consumption, government would subsidize the price to raise consumption above the market-determined level. Culyer (1980) presents a more detailed analysis of efficient subsidization of a merit good, such as recreation, which also tackles the problem of catering to need, rather than demand.

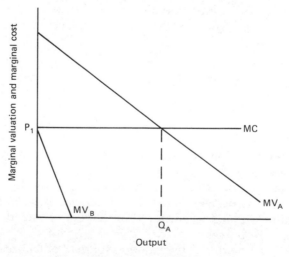

Fig. 10.1 Participation without subsidy.

Fig. 10.1 represents a market with two consumers A and B, with different valuation curves, MV_A and MV_B, for recreation. These curves show that A receives considerable utility from participation, and if price is set equal to marginal cost at P_1 he will consume Q_A. B on the other hand, has much lower marginal utility from recreation participation, and if the price is P_1, he will not participate at all. For him, there is no level of consumption where his marginal utility exceeds the price. Thus if recreation was allocated through the free market, A would participate, and B would not. However for a good that is regarded as a need this is not an acceptable situation.

For merit goods, effective demand is not an adequate reflection of an individual's need. In Chapter 3, we indicated the difference between need and demand, the main point being that assessment of need involves a judgement being made 'independently of the receiving individual's preferences' (Culyer, 1980). Even though consumer B chooses not to consume the good, society believes that welfare would be increased if everybody consumes some minimum quantity. Education is a merit good and this minimum level of consumption is enforced through legislation. It would be unrealistic to legislate to achieve the same result in the recreation market, and therefore normally the government encourages consumption through subsidies.

If Q_B in Fig. 10.2 is the minimum desired consumption level for the merit good, then B will only consume to this level if he is offered the good at price P_2. This XY represents the efficient level of subsidy to B. The important point is that it is only necessary to subsidise B; A already consumes greater than Q_B without subsidy. Government expenditure would be P_1P_2YX and both consumers would consume at least the desired minimum level.

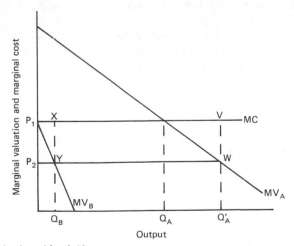

Fig. 10.2 Participation with subsidy.

Let us now look at what would happen if the government subsidized every unit of output, with a general reduction in price from P_1 to P_2. B would still consume Q_B, but A's consumption would increase to Q'_A. Total public expenditure on subsidies to this good would be (P_1P_2YX + P_1P_2WV). Out of this public expenditure P_1P_2WV would go to A, and P_1P_2YX would go to B. By subsidizing supply in this way, rather than demand, public expenditure is expanded considerably and the main beneficiary is consumer A. If the government objective is to achieve a minimum level of consumption for all, then the extra expenditure of P_1P_2WV adds nothing to the achievement of this objective. The clear implication is that as long as tastes vary for the merit good, then differential demand subsidies, and not supply subsidies, are the efficient solution.

Even if every consumer generates an external benefit by participation, the efficient result would not be equal subsidies to all. This is because consumers will have different preferences and some may well participate without subsidies since their private valuation is sufficiently high. Thus subsidies should be concentrated on those consumers least likely to consume the good without such financial encouragement. In fact, we can go further. In Chapter 3 we showed that demand for sport and recreation is positively related to income; the higher the income, the more likely a person will participate. Thus A's marginal valuation curve can be identified with the richer consumer and B's with the poorer consumer. The policy implication is therefore that the subsidy ought to vary inversely with income. Since demand is also strongly related to age, sex and other socioeconomic characteristics differential subsidies on the basis of these variables are also consistent with the analysis.

There are difficulties though in implementing such a policy. The above analysis suggests different subsidies to different consumers. The policy-maker is normally faced with a choice of subsidizing one activity rather than another, or one type of facility as against another. The economic analysis cannot distinguish which activities or facilities to subsidize unless detailed information is available on consumer preferences for these activities and facilities. This also raises the problem that any information we may have is expressed demand, which is related to a particular pattern of supply. Thus the observed preference structure may be substantially different from actual consumer preferences.

The information requirements for efficient subsidization, therefore, are exceedingly large, and in general such information will not be available to the policy-maker. However, the analysis above does provide a theoretical principle by which to judge the success of actual subsidy policies. However, efficiency is not the only government objective. Government also intervenes in the market system for equity reasons.

10.4 The equity objective

Specific distributional objectives for policy are rarely made explicit by governments. To do so would be vulnerable to attack because there are many attitudes to be taken on equity. Le Grand (1982) indicates five distinct types of equity objective as possible guidelines for the distribution of public expenditure.

1. *Equality of expenditure*: all consumers receive equal shares of public expenditure on a particular social service. Although this is likely to conflict with the efficiency objective discussed above, it has the advantage of relatively easy measurement. All that we need to know is how total public expenditure on sport and recreation is distributed over all members of society.

2. *Equality of final income*: public expenditure is allocated to favour the poor so that final income (original income plus subsidies) is distributed more equally than original income. This implies that subsidies should be inversely related to income which is consistent with our efficiency objective for recreation.

3. *Equality of use*: all 'relevant individuals' consume the same amount of the service after the subsidies. 'Relevant individuals' refers to the different needs of the individual for the service. So, for instance, for health, this objective implies equal use for those in similar states of ill-health. Another way of expressing this is 'equal use for equal need'. It seems reasonable to assume we all have the same 'need' for active recreation initially, therefore the policy implication is that subsidies should be specifically directed at the 'recreationally deprived' which as we have seen are the elderly, especially women, ethnic minorities, and young non-working mothers with small children.

4. *Equality of cost*: subsidies allocated so that all consumers face the same cost (time and money cost) per unit consumed. Another way of putting this is equality of access. For recreation, an important aspect of total cost is the travel cost and therefore it is not just the pricing of a facility, but its siting, that will be important for the fulfilment of this objective. It is a mistake to assume that equal prices charged to all implies equality of access.

5. *Equality of outcome*: subsidies should be allocated to promote equality of outcome associated with a particular service. This assumes a production function type of relationship between a social service and a state of well-being. In the case of health, for instance, this objective implies that consumers should end up with equal health status as a result of public subsidies. For recreation, outcome in this sense would be difficult to measure because of the difficulty of a precise definition of the relevant production function.

10.5 Equitable government intervention

Given the diverse nature of the specification of the equity objective then government intervention could be said to be equitable to some extent if greater equality in any of the senses referred to above had resulted from government policy. For recreation this requires accurate information on the distribution of incomes by participant and facility user. However it also requires a judgement on what the distribution would have been without government intervention. As Le Grand (1982) points out, it is not enough to compare the present distribution with the distribution before subsidy, because the initial distribution would have changed over time anyway, even if there had been no government intervention. The evaluation then of whether government intervention has been equitable or not requires the comparison of the existing distribution with a hypothetical distribution (i.e. the one that would have pertained if government had not interfered with the market allocation). Obtaining estimates of the latter can be little more than educated guesswork and therefore accurate quantification of the extent of redistribution is virtually impossible.

Despite these problems it is fairly uncontroversial to say that equitable government intervention should redistribute resources from the rich to the poor. That is, we should expect subsidies to be inversely related to income as in the efficiency case.

10.6 Evaluation of public expenditure on sport and recreation

The major aspects of public expenditure on sport and recreation were outlined in Chapter 6. Local authorities provide the major financial support through the revenue subsidy. Table 6.4 shows how the level of subsidies varies from one facility to another. The pattern of subsidies is substantially different from the USA since very little public expenditure is involved in providing wilderness and large countryside areas. In Britain such areas are normally privately owned and the government role is mainly one of conservation, control and where possible, ensuring public access. Thus it is subsidies to mainly urban, and increasingly indoor, facilities that account for the major share of public expenditure on recreation.

It is clear that the general method of subsidizing sport and recreation is through the supply-side of the market. Many facilities are provided by the public sector with prices set at below cost (see Table 8.3). Although this supply approach to subsidy policy seems to conflict with our earlier theoretical reasoning, it is possible that the overall policy objective may still be achieved. It is possible that this method actually results in the people most in need of subsidies actually receiving the greatest help.

There are several ways in which we can assess whether or not this is the case.

One direct way is to look at the relationship between sports participation and income, and the extent to which this relationship has changed over time. Data from the General Household Surveys for 1973 and 1977 allow us to do this to some extent. Table 10.1 looks at how sports participation, both indoor and outdoor, varies over the income distribution.

Table 10.1 *Sports participation rates by total household income*

	Income			
	Poorest 25%	Next 25%	Next 25%	Richest 25%
Outdoor				
1973	11	16	20	24
1977	16	25	31	37
Indoor				
1973	4	10	13	15
1977	7	23	26	31

From: Own estimates from General Household Surveys, 1973 and 1977.

The table indicates that participation rises sharply with income and also that between 1973 and 1977 there was no tendency for the relatively worse off to expand their participation at a faster rate than other groups. However if we look at participation by socioeconomic group then an apparently different picture emerges. Table 10.2 does this for 1973 and 1980. On the basis of this evidence subsidy policies in the 1970s certainly seem to have made participation more equal, particularly for indoor activities, the sector that has had the major increase in subsidies. However if we take a closer look at indoor sport, sport by sport, it is not quite so straightforward.

Table 10.2 *Adult sports participation rates by socioeconomic group*

	Professional and managerial	Other non-manual	Skilled manual	Semi and unskilled manual
Outdoor				
1973	27.8	19.0	18.3	9.9
1980	47.5	37.6	34.8	24.6
Indoor				
1973	13.4	10.8	11.8	5.7
1980	33.8	30.4	33.1	23.9

From: General Household Surveys, 1973 and 1980.

Table 10.3. *1980 adult sports participation rates for indoor sports by socioeconomic group*

	Professional	Employers and Managers	Intermediate non-manual	Junior non-manual	Skilled manual	Semi-skilled manual	Unskilled manual
Badminton	4.5	2.9	3.9	3.3	1.3	1.0	0.5
Squash	10.6	4.9	4.4	2.3	1.7	0.5	0.2
Swimming	11.5	6.5	9.5	7.1	5.5	4.0	2.5
Table tennis	3.2	2.0	2.7	1.8	2.0	1.1	0.7
Keep-fit, yoga	2.1	1.1	2.8	2.8	0.6	1.4	0.6
Billiards/ snooker	6.7	7.3	4.1	4.0	11.6	6.0	5.0
Darts	5.8	6.4	5.3	5.5	11.4	6.8	5.3

From: General Household Survey, 1980.

Table 10.3 shows a finer breakdown by socioeconomic group for the major indoor sports. The first group are the sports generally associated with sports centres and show a clear non-manual/manual split in participation rates, even surprisingly for a sport such as swimming. It seems very apparent that the reason we have the seemingly healthy picture of Table 10.2 is due essentially to just two sports billiards/ snooker and darts which have heavy manual involvement, particularly from the skilled manual class. These activities receive virtually no subsidies at all and are rarely provided for in public facilities. This illustrates a point we made earlier in Chapter 8. Manual workers are a target group for recreation policy and yet little attention has been paid to their recreation preferences. Table 10.3 shows that manual workers have very different preferences towards recreational activities than non-manual workers. When we look at the pattern of public provision we see that it is the preferences of the non-manual workers that are catered to. In general, the preferences of manual workers are satisfied by profit-making, commercial recreation suppliers.

All the evidence of Chapter 4 on facility use indicates that indoor sports centres are used disproportionately by professional and non-manual workers. Amongst manual workers, it is only the skilled ones, normally the higher paid, who use the centres to any great extent. This evidence seems to suggest that recreation policy in Britain has led to the same situation that Le Grand found with all the major social services public expenditure programmes. His conclusions are rather pessimistic:

'Public expenditure on health care, education, housing and transport systematically favour the better off, and thereby contributes to inequality in final income. It has not created equality of cost (or equality of 'access') and indeed in some cases has made cost differences worse; there persist substantial inequalities in outcomes. For several of the services there has not been even a reduction in the relevant inequalities over time. Nor does there seem to be more prospect of retrieving the situation through any piecemeal reform.'

We saw in earlier sections that although efficiency and equity considerations are normally treated as separate issues, for sport and recreation these objectives lead to the same policy conclusions, that subsidies should be allocated in inverse proportion to income. The evidence we have cited suggests that the objectives have not been achieved particularly for indoor sport. Indoor facilities, the large growth area over the last decade, are used predominantly by the better-off. We must analyse more closely why this is the case. In particular, we need an answer to the following question: do low income people fail to use subsidized recreation facilities because of a binding budget constraint (i.e. they cannot afford to use the facilities, even at the subsidized price), or is it simply because they do not wish to use them (i.e. their preferences are for other types of leisure activity)?

If the under-representation of low income groups is due to the income constraint then there is something wrong with the present method of subsidy since it is not alleviating the constraint. This represents a pricing policy failure. If it is due to different preferences by low income groups then the subsidies are being spent on the wrong facilities. If recreation is a need, then we have to find out what type of facility the recreationally disadvantaged require, and stop subsidizing facilities that cater to the preferences of the better-off. If preference is the reason for the failure of government recreation policy, then it is a marketing failure. The actual explanation is probably some mixture of both pricing and marketing failure. What can be done to rectify the situation?

First of all, how do we correct for pricing policy failure? Our earlier analysis of efficient government intervention points out the specific error nade in subsidy policy. Figure 10.2 shows that if consumption is encouraged by a supply-side subsidy that reduces prices for everybody, then most of these subsidies will be received by those with the highest expressed demand for recreation i.e. the better-off. What is really needed to encourage consumption by lower-income groups is differential demand subsidies to these consumers. Not only is such a policy consistent with the efficiency and equity objectives, but also these objectives are achieved at minimum cost to public expenditure as Fig. 10.2 clearly demonstrates.

There are problems though in implementing differential demand subsidies *Recreation and Deprivation in Inner Urban Areas* (Department of the Environment, 1977) clearly describes the problems where:

'various experiments have been tried to attract those from the lower socioeconomic groups into sports centres but they have generally not been successful.'

Research and experimentation is needed with direct demand-side subsidies.

Voucher policies have been suggested for many years for education and have normally been associated with right wing economists. They have been attacked by others because of the danger of a two-tier education system developing. However, such a voucher policy for recreation is not open to attack on the same grounds. Such a two-tier system already exists, and it favours the better off. A voucher system would operate by giving vouchers to recreation facilities, public and private. The owners of the facilities would then redeem the entrance price by exchanging the vouchers for cash from the government. Willcox and Mushkin (1972) discuss detailed administrative arrangements that can be devised for operating such a scheme, including a credit card approach, which might eliminate the problem of social stigma, that is often the downfall of such schemes.

Although the voucher idea is, in theory, closely in tune with the efficiency principles laid down earlier, some evidence suggests that, in many cases, resistance to facility use by certain target groups is too great to be overcome by a simple price reduction. In other words, direct demand subsidies will not always solve the problem. In this situation we are faced by marketing failure.

How can we counter marketing failure? We discussed this earlier in Chapter 8. The solution is to market to specific target groups and not to the whole market. This can be done by subsidizing supply, but making sure that the supply is restricted to the target groups. One way of doing this is to subsidize facility provision at the workplace. In Chapter 6 we presented some evidence to indicate that, in the United States, industrial recreation facilities were highly successful. The incentive there seems, however, to have been that firms find such facilities pay for themselves in terms of increased productivity: that is, they are internalizing the externality. There seems at least to be a strong argument that facilities provided at the workplace are much more likely to overcome the social, time-cost, and travel-cost barriers to greater participation by lower-income, manual workers. We really need further evidence in order to judge if this is the case.

Some examples of a similar policy of subsidizing supply, where the supply is likely to be restricted to a target demand group, already exist. The Sports Council's 'Urban Deprivation' programme concentrates on providing equipment and motivators in deprived urban areas. Another Sports Council initiative, the 'Football and the Community' scheme, was designed with the idea of using the attraction of professional football clubs, and the charisma of the players, to attract relatively deprived teenagers into active recreation. We discuss this scheme further in Chapter 12, and Table 12.2 provides some evidence that as long as objectives are clearly specified, it is possible to succeed. Provision of facilities alone is not enough to achieve success. Much depends on the enthusiasm and ability of the leaders of the programmes.

10.7 Conclusions

Throughout this book, we have analysed many aspects of the public sector in sport and recreation. In this chapter, we have concentrated on the objectives of recreation policy and assessed the extent to which these objectives have been achieved.

A major role of government is to correct for private market failure. In Chapter 1 we discussed the causes of market failure in the recreation market. Certain facilities are, at least to some extent, non-rival and non-excludable (for example, National and Countryside parks) and therefore we expect to see the government involved in the provision of these collective goods. The other major area of market failure relates to the existence of externalities associated with recreation participation. Most indoor sports facilities are private goods in the sense of being both rival and excludable. However we may expect government involvement in the provision or subsidy of such private goods as long as this government intervention increases social welfare by maximizing the external benefits of participation. Recent developments in recreation policy have emphasized the 'recreational need' concept, as Dower *et al*. (1981) indicate:

'Leisure is a major area for satisfaction in peoples' lives. Provision for leisure may be seen as an element in a caring society: it may be used to counteract personal and social alienation. The idea of leisure and enjoyment for all, and of leisure and recreation as a social service has become widely accepted.'

A clear statement of the role of local authorities in recreation provision is made in the Chairmen's Policy Group paper *Leisure Policy for the Future* (1983):

'Local authorities have, among leisure providers, a unique responsibility to the quality of life of all citizens. Recognition of this role is increasingly reflected in efforts by local authorities to understand the needs of their communities; to encourage and assist the work of all leisure providers; and to serve those needs which others do not meet.'

These two quotes show that recreation, the major area of public expenditure in leisure provision, is now regarded as a need in the same sense as housing or education. Chapter 6 charts the rise in public expenditure (mainly local authority expenditure) that was directed at the recreational needs of communities. The statistics clearly reveal that a major share of this rising expenditure went to indoor facilities.

In this Chapter we have pointed out a crucial flaw in the thinking behind such recreational policy. Even if we regard recreation as a 'need', it is naive to expect that building facilities, and offering recreation services at subsidized prices is an ideal way to cater to that need. If need is defined as some minimim level of consumption for all, as the 'Sport for All' slogan seems to suggest, then Fig 10.2 shows how the government should cater for that need. It also shows that the inefficient way to spend public money is to subsidize every consumer, since some consumers will consume above the desired minimum, without subsidy. Unfortunately, this had tended to be the way that most recreation subsidies have been spent.

It is not only inefficient but also inequitable when the main beneficiaries of the subsidies are the better-off. Figure 10.2 predicts that with supply-side subsidies, this is exactly what would happen. The evidence presented in this Chapter, and elsewhere in the book, indicates that this is what has happened with most of the new facilities that were built in the 1970s. It is particularly inequitable when the revenue to pay for the subsidies is raised from a rating system that is regressive. In general, we should redistribute from rich to poor, and not the other way round.

Given the political swing to public expenditure control in the 1980s, such policy failure provides valuable ammunition for those who wish to reduce subsidies to a minimum. It is an easy solution when objectives have not been achieved, to throw out the objectives. A more correct policy would be to examine what has gone wrong with the means of achieving the objectives and to change the means, but retain the objectives. We have identified the problem as pricing or marketing failure, or some combination of the two. An understanding of the principles of Chapter 8 should help future public investment to yield greater social returns.

11 Sport Sponsorship

11.1 Introduction

In Chapter 10 we examined the economic aspects of public subsidies to sport and recreation. Yet for many sports, the public sector is not the major source of non-revenue income. The sponsorship of sport provides private market 'subsidization' to sport and recreation, and in many ways this sponsorship is a very close substitute for government subsidies. In times of government expenditure restraint sport agencies try hard to switch from declining public support to private sources. But how similar are these two methods of assisting the finances of sport? Although the receiving agency may regard the two sources of income as very much inter-changeable, the motivation of the organizations supplying the funds is very different. In this chapter we analyse the sponsorship decision and the various economic issues that relate to this decision.

In order to illustrate this analysis we use data from the very few, mainly British, investigations into sponsorship. Our main source of information is the comprehensive study carried out by the Central Council of Physical Recreation's Committee of Enquiry into Sports Sponsorship, *The Howell Report* (CCPR, 1983). Another major source material is the Economist Intelligence Unit's report, *Sponsorship 1980* (Simkins, 1980). Our aim is to use the information contained in these and other sources to move towards an economic analysis of sports sponsorship. However before we do this it is necessary firstly to define what we mean by sponsorship, and secondly to give a brief description of its development and major characteristics.

11.2 What is sponsorship?

The Howell Report defines sponsorship as:

'the support of a sport, sports event, sports organisation or competition by an outside body or person for the mutual benefit of both parties.'

The overall conclusion of the report was that:

'the sponsorship of sport provides a service to the whole of sport and to the community which sport serves; in this respect therefore it also serves the public interest.'

These quotes suggest that sponsorship is very similar to subsidization and hints at the view that it is also a form of private market charitable support. However there is much more to it than that. From the point of view of the sponsored sport, this may be true. But the sponsors' aims are often purely commercial.

Simkins picks out three characteristics of sponsorship: the sponsor makes a contribution, in cash or in kind, to the sport; the sponsored activity is not part of the main commercial operations of the company; and thirdly, the sponsor expects a return in terms of publicity which does not reflect adversely on the sponsor. This last characteristic puts sponsorship firmly in a similar position to advertising expenditure. However Simkins suggests that it is not the same as advertising since she defines advertising in a way that requires the company's name or product to be specifically placed and paid for. For sponsorship, such publicity for the company's name arises without a specific fee and from an activity outside its main operation.

Although we take Simkins' point that sponsorship expenditure is different in kind from advertising expenditure, we believe that the economic behaviour of the sponsors will be similar for sponsorship expenditure as for advertising. That is, we argue that some understanding of the behaviour of sponsors can be gained from the economics of advertising literature, although as we will see, the analysis has to be slightly changed to take into account the special features of sports sponsorship.

Sponsorship is a very varied activity. We tend to regard it as a relatively new phenomenon and yet there are examples in cricket going back over 120 years. *The Howell Report* catalogues the case of Spiers and Pond, an Australian catering firm, who sponsored the first England tour of Australia in 1861/62 and made a profit of £11 000 from the deal. Sponsorship may involve ground advertising, player sponsorship, shirt advertising, competition sponsorship, event sponsorship and can range from top international events such as the Olympic Games down to the most humble local team. The main characteristic though is that the name of the sponsor will appear boldly and often this is emphasized by media coverage of the occasion. This form of commercial involvement in sport has seen a rapid rise over the last ten to twenty years culminating in massive sponsorship activity of the Los Angeles Olympics in 1984. Before we analyse the economic aspects of this activity it is worth charting its growth over recent history.

11.3 The growth of sports sponsorship

The estimated growth of sports sponsorship in the UK from 1971 to 1983 is shown in Fig. 11.1. By the very nature of sponsorship, these estimates are subject to a very wide degree of error. However it is fairly clear that there has been steady growth in the amount of money spent in sponsorship in the UK throughout the 1970s. Even after allowing for inflation this represents a real increase in resources for supporting sport from the commercial sector. These figures actually represent 'visible' sponsorship or cash support openly revealed by the sponsors. These are good reasons to expect that this is a serious under-statement of the true amount of resources involved.

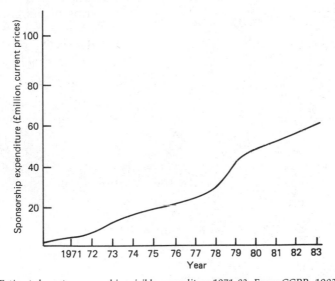

Fig. 11.1 Estimated sports sponsorship: visible expenditure 1971-83. From: CCPR, 1983.

Many sponsorship deals will never be revealed in statistics because they are at a local or regional level and involve sponsorship arrangements between relatively small firms and small local sports organizations. The CCPR tried to find out through a questionnaire study, how important these local expenditures were and estimated that they could account for up to 25-27% of the national total. Thus the figures above could all be adjusted to this extent by this invisible aspect of sponsorship expenditure

Probably the main reason why the 'visible' figure is such an under-estimate is that firms have to devote many more resources to the sport than is actually revealed in money expenditure figures. Often a large amount of time and resources of the promotion and marketing departments of companies are taken up with sponsorship arrangements. Also there are expenses associated with printing, publicity and entertainment which are in addition to the agreed sponsorship support.

If we take all of these 'invisibles' into account then sponsorship expenditure on sport is probably close to £100 million. Having said this, it should also be pointed out that such expenditure for any one company will only be a small percentage of the total advertising, promotion and public relations budget. Schweppes, who regard sponsorship as an important part of their operations estimate that such expenditure accounts for about 3½% of the marketing budget (*Financial Times*, 1979). Very few firms devote as much as 10% of their marketing budget to sponsorship and then only for short periods.

There is great variety in the types of sponsoring company and the level of expenditure involved. Also there is a tendency for firms to move from zero sponsorship to significant levels overnight such as the Milk Cup sponsorship arrangement in soccer, the Canon Football league sponsorship deal, and the Cornhill Test sponsorship. Equally other firms with significant sponsorship, established over many years, suddenly drop out. Examples are Rothmans, Colgate-Palmolive and recently Schweppes, Prudential and Gillette withdrawing from cricket sponsorship. However we can identify certain important industries in sponsorship. The Tobacco industry not only provides the largest total sponsorship figure (estimated at over £10 million in 1983; Moller 1983), but also this industry spends the highest proportion of its total industry advertising budget on sponsorship. The alcoholic drinks industry is the next largest sponsor. Other industries having significant sponsorship expenditure are soft drinks companies, oil companies, banks and insurance companies and a variety of broad leisure industries (for example, bookmakers and motor sport related industries).

We have similar problems in identifying the most sponsored sports since one large deal can move a sport from low down in the sponsorship table to near the top (for example, the Canon League sponsorship in soccer). However it is not difficult to identify the leader, which is motor sport, having sponsorship to the order of £20 million in 1982. This one sport accounts for about 40% of total expenditure on sponsorship. Simkins (1980) estimated that horse racing attracted the second highest sponsorship income. However by 1982 soccer was clearly second with an estimated sponsorship income of nearly £12 million. This represents a staggering rise in sponsorship of this sport, mainly caused by a definite policy decision to try and attract large sponsors because of the financial crisis in the sport. Table 11.1 looks at the sponsorship income of other sports in 1982.

Table 11.1. *Sponsorship revenue by sport, 1982.*

Sport	Sponsorship income (£000s)
Motor sport	19 450
Association football	11 915
Horse racing	2 320
Cricket	2 077
Golf	1 816
Tennis	1 228
Athletics (including marathons)	1 194
Equestrian	1 033
Power boat racing	950
Snooker	847
Greyhound racing	656
Cycling	575
Rugby	423
Gymnastics	400
Rugby Union	382
Darts	375
Basketball	335
Yachting	225
Badminton	221
Angling	179
Bowls	179
Swimming	175
Squash	138
Ice skating	135
Rowing	132
Skiing	120
Other sports	1 443
Total	**48 923**

from: CCPR (1983)

11.4 The sponsorship decision of the firm

We now attempt to analyse why firms sponsor sport. The analysis is based on the economics of firm behaviour in respect of the advertising decision. To begin with we will assume that the sponsorship is identical to advertising expenditure by the firm and gradually move away from this position as we progress. Equating sponsorship with advertising allows us to draw on the literature of the economics of advertising. The initial analysis of the advertising decision assumes the firm to have the overall objective of profit-maximization. Advertising aims to move the demand curve of the product to the right, although at the same time the costs of advertising will raise overall costs. Advertising increases profits as long as the increased sales revenue more than matches the increased cost. In fact Koutsoyiannis (1982) indicates that such profit-maximizing behaviour by a firm is not inconsistent with a simple rule of thumb that sets advertising expenditure as a constant proportion of revenue.

This rather simplistic view of advertising yields the direct conclusion that 'successful' advertising leads to increased sales. It is also relatively easy to test since 'unsuccessful' firms will cease to advertise and hence we should find a strong positive relationship between advertising expenditure and the rate of growth of sales. Many studies have attempted to estimate the effect of advertising on sales but few have established any relationship at all. Koutsoyiannis (1982) reviewing all the empirical studies on the advertising-sales relationship concludes: 'that the effects of advertising on buyers have not been theoretically or empirically established in a satisfactory way.'

This economic research has indicated that one of the greatest problems with the advertising decision of the firm is the uncertainty associated with the returns of this expenditure. This may explain why rules-of-thumb such as setting a constant advertising-sales ratio are the order of the day with firms adjusting advertising expenditure to changes in revenue rather than revenue reacting to changes in advertising expenditure.

This risk or uncertainty associated with the advertising decision is compounded by the view of some writers (Palda, 1964; Heflebower, 1967) that advertising should be treated as an investment, because it yields returns over several periods of time. They argue that advertising is the main means by which a firm builds its name and goodwill over time. The longer the period of time over which the revenue stream is affected the greater the risk and uncertainty associated with the advertising decision. Also this view indicates that return to advertising involves immeasurable variables such as 'name and goodwill', and we will have more to say on this later.

With this background of economic theory relating to the advertising decision of the firm we now return to sponsorship. Sponsorship can be viewed as part of profit-maximizing behaviour of a firm. In this context the primary motive is increased sales. The risk and uncertainty of revenue response to advertising expenditure would lead firms to diversify into alternative marketing strategies, of which sponsorship is one.

All the evidence on sports sponsorship by firms indicates that this type of marketing/advertising behaviour is highly risky in terms of expected returns. John Carson (*Financial Times*, 1979), then Schweppes marketing manager, was reported as saying at a conference on sponsorship organized by Marketing Week:

'Despite my known desire for better information, no market research company has come forward with a satisfactory method of evaluating spending on sponsorship.'

He hinted that he would pay somebody good money to do it.

Because of the riskiness of this type of marketing strategy we would expect some involvement (since returns could conceivably be large) but not too much. This is consistent with the observed behaviour of firms to keep sponsorship activity below 5% of total marketing expenditure.

However for some industries we could expect a much higher involvement in sponsorship. This is not necessarily because it is any less risky for these industries, but rather that other forms of advertising strategies are prevented. In this case, in order to maintain a given advertising expenditure/revenue ratio then expenditure on sponsorship will have to increase. The tobacco industry, the main sponsors in the UK, are the prime example of this form of firm behaviour. Moller (1983) quotes the figures:

'Certainly the tobacco industry has the funds to play for high stakes. On direct advertising each year, it now spends £85 million, in sponsorship of sports and the arts, in excess of £10 million.'

Because cigarette advertising is banned on television, this form of marketing strategy is often the only alternative.

Another quote from Moller illustrates how important this would be for cigarette manufacturers:

'One of the greatest coups has been the annual Embassy World Professional Snooker Championship. During a 17 day period in April and May last year, no fewer than 81 hours' coverage was given on television to an audience of up to 10.8 million. For a sponsorship outlay of less than £2,000,000 Embassy gained a form of advertising that, at average television commercial rates, would have cost some £68 million.'

We have characterized sponsorship behaviour by firms as a response to risk and uncertainty in the advertising-sales relationship. This implicitly assumes that the major objective of the firm is profit-maximization. However there are other objectives of the firm that can also be related to sponsorship behaviour. Many of these alternative objectives could be related to long-term as opposed to short-term profit-maximizing behaviour, but others are really, in a modern business environment, ends in themselves.

Simkins suggests five reasons why firms sponsor: publicity; building the corporate image; public relations and contact with the local community; entertainment and trade relations; and marketing and promotion. Publicity, marketing and promotion come under the broad heading of advertising as discussed above. Marketing expenditure aimed at building the corporate image is increasingly noticeable in Britain. It is closely associated with the investment motive for advertising that we referred to earlier in the work of Palda (1964) and Heflebower (1967). It is also often associated with some of the industries that are closely connected to sponsorship, banks, insurance companies and oil companies. Part of the reason may be a fear of nationalization but we would also expect some knock-on effect to sales. Since sport has a healthy image, the idea is to carry over the image to the company and the product. Strength, competitiveness, the will to win are part of both sport and the competitive business environment. By associating elite performers with the product, the aim is to create an elite image for the company. There are several notable examples where this aim has gone badly wrong. Chrysler's attempt to link their name with the Scottish World Cup team in the 1978 World Cup in Argentina went badly wrong. Not only did the team produce poor results on the field but the disappointment was further compounded by newspaper stories of drunkenness and drug-taking.

Public relations and contact with the local community is an objective that is most likely to be associated with small sponsorship deals at the local level rather than large, well publicized deals. The rapid increase in marathon running over the early 1980s has probably given a big boost to this type of sponsorship, but local soccer teams and cricket teams now actively search for sponsors and many firms are willing to give small amounts to sporting teams in the local area. They can expect little advertising-type return from this, but such sponsorship could be useful politically if for instance the firm wishes to expand and needs planning permission for a new development. Contributing to the community in terms of sports sponsorship could then be a useful asset at a public inquiry.

In many ways though, it is entertainment and trade relations that many marketing managers regard as the most important motive for sponsorship. Even here there is a link with sales or profit-maximization, since the people the firm wishes to entertain are its customers, and the object of the entertainment is the signing of a contract. The attraction of sport is the facility to entertain customers at national, prestigious, sporting occasions while at the same time having access to the best boxes, boardrooms, and the like due to the firm's sponsorship. This is particularly the case with big motor racing or horse racing occasions, but also applies to football matches, tennis tournaments and cricket.

Because of the multiplicity of objectives associated with sponsorship it becomes very difficult to monitor whether or not the sponsorship has been successful. If it were simply a matter of profit maximization, or even sales maximization, some testing would be possible. Even then, as our quick look at the advertising literature shows, establishing any clear statistical links with this expenditure and sales is very difficult. Gillette has pioneered work in the evaluation of the effects of sponsorship expenditure and some market research companies also now experiment with various ways of measuring returns.

Gillette tends to rely on social survey methods and attempts to measure increasing awareness of the company's name through its sponsorship activity. Unfortunately their research has indicated that consumers are often more likely to associate Gillette with sport (particularly cricket) than they are with safety razors. The other problem Gillette found was that public consciousness of the company's sponsorship was not cumulative year after year. Repeated sponsorship of the same competition (for example, the Gillette Cup) seems eventually to prove unproductive in reaching new consumers, as awareness levels reach a plateau and then stay there, or even fall away.

On the other hand Cornhill, with their sponsorship of Test cricket, showed how new sponsorship deals can have a dramatic effect on public awareness of the company's name, as this quote from *The Howell Report* indicates:

'When it began sponsorship of the Cornhill Test series in 1977 the company rated twelfth among UK insurance companies and a survey showed that the public's 'spontaneous awareness' was 2%. After five years of the sponsorships that awareness had increased to 17%.

Cornhill analysed the benefits from this sponsorship in 1981. During 140 hours of television coverage the company received 7,459 banner sitings on screen and 234 verbal mentions. In addition, there were 1,784 references on radio, 659 in the national press and 2,448 in the provincial press. There were also unexpected bonuses of publicity which included the 21 million telephone calls to British Telecom's cricket score service in 1980.

The 250 tickets which Cornhill receives for each Test Match are also a valuable aid in customer contact. Cornhill's brokers tell them that policies are now much easier to sell as a result of the greater awareness of Cornhill's name and enhanced reputation and Cornhill itself estimates that an increased annual premium income of £10 million could be attributed to the sponsorship.'

This quote also indicated alternative methods of measuring the achievements of sponsorship expenditure, which is to monitor newspapers and television and count the number of column inches or television time that the company gets as a result of the sponsorship. This media coverage can then be costed at the price that similar space and air time would have cost if purchased at market rates. We have already mentioned Moller's estimate of £68 million for Embassy's media coverage in the 1982 World Professional Snooker Championship. *The Howell Report* details more closely where the media coverage came from:

(a) Banners, sited over the competitors' rest alcoves took up as much as one-eighth of the screen when the camera zoomed-in during actual play. During 17 days of competition there were more than 90 hours of scheduled viewing which grew to almost 100 hours when late-night programmes were allowed to over-run.

(b) Verbal mentions were certainly more than two per programme during many longer transmissions, especially those covering six hours. There were 78 scheduled programmes with at least an entitlement of two mentions each for a minimum of 156 mentions.

(c) Radio Times gave 28 mentions to Embassy in the published programme billings for the last 10 days, with as many as three on a single page.

(d) Written captions of latest positions appeared regularly and Embassy was always in the heading.'

These two examples, Cornhill and Embassy, indicate clearly that benefits to the sponsoring firm can be substantial and that it is possible to put some monetary valuation on these benefits. However many sponsorship deals do not involve such tangible benefits, and such deals cannot be so clearly explained on commercial grounds. Richard Butler, director of Extel Public Relations Sponsorship Division, whose clients include Calor Gas, Courage, Asda and Texaco, probably summed up the general feeling of marketing managers towards sponsorship:

'We feel that sponsorship PR must be seen to be a valuable part of the total marketing mix of any go-ahead company and should be pursued in conjunction with all the other elements such as boarding, advertising, identification, sales presentations, promotions and exhibitions. Sponsorship must be a business deal which is to the advantage of both the sponsor and the sponsored and must be geared to achieve the sponsor's defined objectives.' (CCPR, 1983).

This quote is well in line with our analysis above that emphasises the diversification of marketing techniques, not only in relation to diverse objectives, but also because of the uncertainty associated with the results of any one technique. For a more cynical view on why firms sponsor, we can quote John Carson from Schweppes:

'Marketing people are all failed sportsmen or actors. I'm sure that's where it all started.' (*Financial Times*, 1979).

11.5 The benefits and costs to the sponsored activity

The benefits to the sponsored activity seem fairly obvious, they receive payment from the sponsoring firm and this revenue is an important source of income. In Chapter 6, we analysed the importance of voluntary non-profit organizations in sport and Weisbrod's analysis (1978) of such organizations indicates the importance of alternative income sources. A sport's governing body, or even an individual sports club, must raise its income from government subsidy, sponsorship, membership fees, or ultimately from selling its product (i.e. sales of admission tickets to sporting events). To some extent one form of income is a substitute for another. If sponsorship income is increased then sport can become cheaper to the participant (lower membership fees) or the spectator (lower admission charges). In a way then sponsorship is a form of private market subsidy to sport.

Income though is not the only benefit to the sponsored sport. We have seen that sponsorship is a form of publicity and advertising for the sponsor. In this process though the sport is also receiving publicity. A sponsor will normally be willing to take steps to improve publicity for the sponsored event and this automatically widens the market for the sport as well as for the product of the sponsoring company.

In the UK, the startling rise in the popularity of snooker indicated how this 'joint publicity' effect can create a virtuous circle of expanding demand for both product and sport. In the early 1970s, snooker was a low interest sport with little media coverage. Sponsorship allowed the sport to move from smoky rooms to lavish surroundings for big competitions (most notably the Crucible Theatre, Sheffield). These surroundings attracted more media, in particular television, coverage, which itself attracted more sponsors, giving higher prize money. The higher prize money and media coverage generated much wider interest which further encouraged the television companies and the sponsors, thus giving another boost to the upward spiral. Sponsorship then was a necessary condition for the promotion of the sport itself. By 1983, snooker was the fourth most televized sport in Britain, and had the second highest participation rate for an indoor sport. Thus income, publicity and promotion for the sport are the main benefits to the sponsored sport.

There may well be costs, however, to the sponsored sport. Sponsorship is essentially a commercial activity and the sponsor expects a commercial rate of return on his investment. Because of this, sponsors may require some sort of control over the sponsored activity. Head (1982) comments:

'it is not difficult to predict that sponsors who feel they are getting a raw deal will either lose interest altogether or demand much greater control. By then we shall have moved into full scale promotion in which sport is run for the benefit of the promotion company and not primarily in the interests of sport itself.'

This quote illustrates the underlying danger of the conflict in objectives between sponsor and sponsored. There is a worry over whether sponsorship somehow reduces the integrity of sport. Various questions are raised in this debate. Should the sport become more professional and commercial to satisfy the wishes of the sponsors? Should the rules of a sport be changed to make the game more interesting to television?

Some changes brought about by sponsorship are clearly beneficial and have attracted new audiences. The case of snooker above is a good example. Others have been less welcome. Events created to provide sponsorship vehicles are not always in harmony with sporting programmes. Over-exposure on television can have damaging effects. All this can lead to the detriment of the long-term interests of sport. At the time of writing there are serious reservations expressed over the massive sponsorship of the Los Angeles Olympics.

Some commentators referred to the 1984 Olympics as the '$Olympics'. (*The Observer*, 1984). The scale of the sponsorship involved is illustrated by this quote:

'US corporations are sinking $500 million into this summer's 23rd Olympic extravaganza in return for the right to use the games as a market-stall for their products. They mean to get their money's worth. This list runs through 30 major companies that have put down a minimum of $4 million apiece for 'exclusive rights' to use Olympian phrases and logos to market their wares. For most sponsoring firms, that $4 million is just a down payment. McDonald's the Big Mac people, forked out a further $6 million to build Los Angeles a new swimming stadium. ABC-TV paid a staggering $225 million for T.V. rights.' (Observer, 1984).

Although sponsorship on this scale meant that for the first time for many years the national and local government of the country staging the Olympics were not faced with a massive bill, many felt that the Olympic ideal had been lost in the race to attract sponsorship. The Mayor of Olympia in Greece, home of the Olympic flame, felt so strongly that he threatened to prevent the flame leaving Olympia since the LA Olympic Organizing Committee had sold off sections of its journey across the United States at $3000 a kilometre.

Probably one of the most serious problems though with sponsorship is that the sponsor, in order to gain maximum publicity, is normally only interested in the top, most prestigious, events and the elite performers, the superstars. This creates several problems. First a conflict arises between the willingness of companies to sponsor elite sportsmen, and the rules of international sports federations on the amateur status of competitors. The current situation here is very confused with some sports allowing sponsorship money to be used for certain expenses and other sports allowing trust funds to be set up.

Secondly, the top competitors are often subject to a too crowded schedule in order to satisfy the demands of the sponsors. Such problems have been felt particularly in the early 1980s by Steve Ovett and Sebastian Coe who both attracted sponsors with little difficulty. Problems arose in fulfilling the sponsor's expectations and managing to keep to rigid training schedules for international competition. Both runners seemed to lose competitive edge at various times through over-indulgence in heavily sponsored world record attempts.

Thirdly, conflicts arise between the governing body of a sport and the competitors because of sponsorship deals. Sponsorship of individual competitors often leads to a situation where the governing body receives no income from the sponsorship deal. The governing body has responsibility for the sport right down to grass roots level and may feel that it has the right to a share in the sponsorship money received from use of its competition. Such conflicts are often exacerbated by specialist agencies that arrange sponsorship deals between competitors and companies. These agencies sometimes cut across the responsibilities of the governing bodies by staging their own events, but essentially by putting themselves between the sport and the individual competitor, they create a possible area of conflict.

Another problem for the sport is the lack of continuity that characterizes much sponsorship activity. Sponsors often withdraw from a sport with very little notice. The *News of the World* withdrew its sponsorship from Athletics in 1968 and a major part of the sports' income disappeared overnight. This volatility in income can cause serious problems for a governing body of sport. The Gillette Cup, a pioneering knock-out competition of one day games, became so successful that Gillette could not afford to continue with the sponsorship and withdrew after nearly twenty years in 1981. As *The Howell Report* comments:

'There is an important lesson here for sport, companies have to take hard commercial decisions about their investments. Gillette fully appreciated that the very success of the competition which it had initiated meant that its value to sport was not probably more that its own sponsorship would sustain.'

This raises another important point. In order to achieve the sponsor's commercial objectives it may be necessary to continually change events. Gillette changed to sponsor the London Marathon, which it then dropped after two years. Similarly, Prudential and Schweppes both withdrew from cricket sponsorship in 1983.

This volatility in sponsorship incomes means that sports have to be wary of dependence on sponsorship as a whole, and in one sponsor in particular. *The Howell Report* suggested that:

'governing bodies should guard against an over-reliance upon sponsorship income and should maintain as wide a portfolio of sponsorship as is practical in order to minimise the dangers when sponsors end their involvement.'

A final problem with sponsorship is the association of sport with tobacco, gambling and alcohol, three industries which provide the bulk of sponsorship money. Our model of the sponsorship decision by the firm indicates that it is the banning of other forms of advertising for tobacco products that directly leads to more sponsorship money being available from this industry. Here we have a conflict: an activity, sport, that is actively encouraged because of the positive externalities generated by participation, becomes linked with other activities, smoking, drinking and gambling, that are known to have a negative externalities associated with their consumption.

A 'voluntary agreement' between the government and the tobacco industry limits levels of sports sponsorship and types of sponsorship (for example, sports competitors are not allowed to display company or board names on clothing for televised sports events). Despite this there is a controversy over whether tobacco advertising should be allowed in sport and this creates yet another conflict between the aims of the sport governing body (to promote healthy activities) and the need for finance.

The discussion above shows that sponsorship can be a mixed blessing to the sport and there is not always a net surplus of benefits over costs.

11.6 Sponsorship and public subsidies

We began this Chapter by suggesting that sport sponsorship could be a substitute for public subsidies. In some circumstances they can be one and the same thing. Nottingham City Council sponsored Jayne Torvill and Christopher Dean with an annual income of £14000 from 1980 to their successful World and Olympic ice-dance championships in 1984. This sponsorship allowed them to give up their full-time jobs and concentrate totally on training and competitions. *The Howell Report* estimated sponsorship from local authorities to be in the region of £2 million per year. Sponsorship by local authorities is part of the total subsidy to sport provided by the public sector and it is only referred to as sponsorship because the subsidy is directed at elite performers or specific events, rather than the more familiar facility-related subsidy. Since we have this overlap between the two alternative forms of finance to sport it is useful to consider the major differences between public subsidies and private sponsorships.

The first major difference is ·in the objectives of the suppliers of finance for sport. Government subsidizes sport in the interests of broad social objectives, to improve resource allocation to an activity that generates positive externalities. By the nature of the externalities this involves subsidies at both the elite level of sport and at the basic participation level. However, in absolute terms it is the latter that accounts for the major share of total subsidies to sport and recreation.

On the other hand, income from sponsorship comes from commercial operations that aim essentially to increase the sales of their own product. Although there may be subsidiary objectives, if sponsorship does not result in increased sales in the long-run then it is likely to end. For this reason, it is concentrated at the upper end of the sports market.

Top international sportsmen in popular sports, and important international events that attract television coverage, are unlikely to find
difficulty in attracting willing sponsors. Sponsors are unwilling, in
general, to subsidize the construction and operating costs of the facilities
that increase the opportunities for sports participation for the general
population.

In some ways, the objectives of the government and the sponsor are
complementary. Both want sport to be successful and have a good
image, since the image of the sport, for the sponsor, is intrinsically tied
up with the image of the product they are trying to sell. But there is an
essential difference in the role that the two forms of finance provide for
sport. The private sector is willing to provide the finance for those
activities and those competitors that have already proved to be
'winners'. In many ways much sponsorship money finds its way into
the pockets of the elite performers and does nothing to alter resource
allocation: it is that part of income that economists term 'economic rent'.
That is, if these competitors did not receive this income they would still
remain within the sport. It just serves to make them better-off. This is
illustrated in Fig. 11.2.

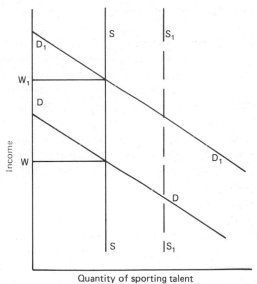

Fig. 11.2 *Economic rent and sponsorship income.*

Elite performers, at any point in time, are restricted in supply, as
indicated by the inelastic supply curve SS. Sporting success at national,
or international level for these performers attract sponsorships, which
increases the demand for their services, moving the demand curve from
DD to $D_1 D_1$. The main result is that the income of the elite performers

increases from W to W_1. This extra income is 'economic rent'. There are many examples of sponsorship deals designed specifically to increase the incomes of elite performers in this way. The Cornhill Tests sponsorship was designed to raise the income of Test players to combat the attraction of Kerry Packer's World Series Cricket.

However, sports sponsorship does differ from this conventional analysis of economic rent. Figure 11.2 suggests that sports sponsorship payments only serve to increase the income of the sponsored sportsmen and sportswomen. It is well-known that international sporting success in any sport leads to an upsurge of interest in that sport which often generates further champions in later years. That is, in time the sponsorship may eventually lead in a shift in the supply curve from SS to $S_1 S_1$.

This analysis suggests that we can characterize sponsorship as a private market subsidy that, maybe unintentionally, corrects for one aspect of market failure analysed earlier. The social demand for international sporting success may well be catered for by sponsorship money since the sort of publicity that arises from such success is just the sort of attraction needed by the sponsor to sell his product. There is still a role for government subsidy, though, even at this elite end of the market.

As we have seen sponsorship is a rather patchy and random process that leaves some sports and some performers well-supported but others struggling for finance. Often the decision over which sports to sponsor is media-determined, with firms only willing to provide sponsorship if there is guaranteed television coverage. Squash is a sport that has found it difficult to attract sponsorship because it has not proved a popular television attraction. There have been attempts to change the court and the colour of the ball in order to make it more attractive to television, and hence to sponsors. The main point though is that even at the elite level, sponsorship will leave substantial gaps in terms of financial support for sport, and government must fill these gaps.

One attempt to do this was through the establishment of the Sports Aid Foundation. This is an independent organization, set up with the support of the Sports Council, whose aim is to channel sponsorship money to aid the training and preparation of elite performers. It essentially tries to give financial help to those sportsmen and women who cannot find personal sponsorships: that is, it is trying to fill the gaps referred to above. Unfortunately from 1976-83 the Sports Aid Foundation only managed to raise £2½ million, which included an initial grant of nearly £½ million from the Sports Council. *The Howell Report* concluded that:

'the response from industry, commerce, and the public has been disappointing and that the Foundation has not reached the level of success which had been anticipated.'

Our analysis indicates that this is exactly the outcome we would expect. Given the objectives of the sponsors, the private sector will always leave certain parts of the market under-supplied with finance. The solution to this problem will have to be some sort of public subsidy. To the extent that at least part of the finance of elite performers is taken over by the private sector, the role of government is eased.

On the other hand, other aspects of market failure, mainly related to participation at the grass roots level, has proved unattractive to sponsors. This reinforces the conclusion of Chapter 10, that Government intervention needs to be at the lowest level of sport, that is at grass roots level, and for facility provision. Government needs to direct resources at the lowest level of the hierarchy in order to generate the elite performers that the private sector will then finance. Government still has a role in administration and policing of private sector support at the elite level, in controlling the type of products that sponsors try to sell using sport, and in filling in the gaps in support for less popular recreation pursuits which cannot attract sponsorship.

Our analysis of public support for sport and recreation suggests that demands for government finance for sport are always likely to be greater than the available supply. The analysis presented here suggests that some of the demands can be met by the private sector, allowing the government to concentrate its help where it is most needed. The Los Angeles Olympics provides the prime example of this point, where for the first time, the private sector sponsorship covered virtually all the costs. Many people did not like the resulting heavy commercial involvement. As we have pointed out earlier, there are costs to the sponsored activity in sponsorship. However the clear implication is that you have to cater to the needs of the private sector if you wish to attract their finance. In time of strict government financial restraint, this may be the only option.

11.7 Conclusion

Our aim in this chapter was to investigate the extent to which economic analysis can help us to understand the issues involved in sports sponsorship. The analysis is still incomplete but there are certain statements that can be made. We view sponsorship as one marketing strategy in a mixed portfolio of strategies. We have quoted several cases where this strategy has proved to be highly successful. However, in general, all marketing strategies are characterized by risk and uncertainty and therefore we expect firms to have a diversified portfolio. Other things being equal, those industries generally noted for high advertising/marketing budgets will also be the ones having the highest sponsorship expenditure. Since sponsorship is a high-risk marketing strategy, we expect it to take a small share of the marketing budget. However, where other advertising routes are restricted (for example, tobacco) then this share will normally rise.

As with any marketing strategy, the ultimate aim is increased sales. The sponsor will therefore look for the competition, event, or competitor likely to give his product greatest exposure. This will in turn depend on the media, in particular television coverage.

Sponsorship, therefore, tends to be limited to the top end of the sports market. This is not necessarily in conflict with overall government objectives with respect to sport since it allows public subsidies to be channelled specifically to those areas where the private market has 'failed'.

12 The economics of professional team sports

12.1 Introduction

The literature on the economics of professional team sports has grown steadily after articles first started to appear in the 1960s. Most of the literature has been generated in North America and deals with the specific problems associated with the major American professional team sports, American football, baseball, ice-hockey and basketball. Much of the analysis developed in North America has also been applied to UK professional team sports, in particular to football and cricket.

In this chapter we do not attempt to give a comprehensive review of the literature since this is available elsewhere (for example, Sloane, 1980 or Cairns, 1983a). Rather we aim to show that much of the analysis developed earlier in this book is directly relevant to professional sport. Consequently we adopt the same framework as our earlier analysis, by first looking at the demand for professional team sports, and then at the supply-side of the market. Many of the theoretical principles we discuss are relevant to all professional team sports but we focus specifically on football not only because it is the major professional team sport in Britain but also because since at the time of writing this sport is passing through a serious financial crisis. It therefore provides a useful testing ground for the economic theory, in that it enables us to assess whether the theory offers appropriate policy solutions.

12.2 The demand for professional team sports

As a starting point to the analysis of demand we can return to the demand function of Chapter 3 where the quantity demanded of Activity A (Q_{DA}) depends on price of the activity (P_A), the prices of other activities (P_1, P_2, . . ., P_n) and the level of the consumer's income (Y). The activity we are concerned with here, is not participation in sport, but spectating at professional football. We can measure this demand in much the same way as before, that is the percentage of the population that watches football. Again the General Household Survey provides a database for the analysis. As we will see, however, less interest has been placed on this cross-section analysis than on the time-series behaviour of demand.

At the cross-section level, spectating at sport reveals a very similar pattern to participation. More men than women attend football matches; spectating, like participation, declines with age; and spectating is positively related to income. Table 12.1 indicates this pattern.

Table 12.1 *The relationship between spectating at soccer and sex, income and age.*

	Percentage engaging in the activity in the four weeks prior to interview
Sex	
Male	7
Female	1
Total	**4**
Income (£ per week)	
Up to 20	1
20.01-40	1
40.01-60	3
60.01-80	4
80.01-100	4
100.01-150	6
over 150	6
Total	**4**
Age (years)	
16-19	8
20-24	6
25-29	6
30-34	5
45-59	3
60-69	3
over 70	1
Total	**4**

From: General Household Survey, 1977.

Given the similarity between the football spectating demand function and the participation demand function at the cross-sectional level we might expect to see a picture of rapidly expanding demand over time that we saw for participation. In fact, the reality is just the opposite. Figure 12.1 plots the steady decline in attendances from the peak of 41.3 million in the 1948-49 season. Except for a brief reversal following England's World Cup success in 1966, attendances have fallen steadily since then, so that they stood at only 20 million in 1981/82. The crisis in the 1980s was caused by a particularly sharp increase in the rate of decline of attendances after 1979.

How is it that an activity, that from the cross-sectional evidence, seems to be income-elastic shows such a steady decline over a period when incomes have been steadily increasing? We have seen this conflict between cross-sectional and time-series evidence earlier in Chapter 3 and again in Chapter 5. At any point in time availability of leisure time and choice of leisure activities is fixed to the consumer. In these circumstances it is not surprising that any leisure activity (including spectating at football) shows the characteristics of a normal good. We gave several explanations for this pattern of behaviour in Chapter 3. However, over time the two crucial factors, availability of leisure time and the choice set of leisure activities, change dramatically. Another important factor that changes over time is fashion in leisure activities.

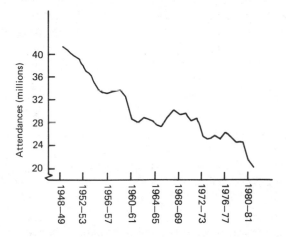

Fig. 12.1 Football League attendances 1948/49-1983/84. From: Rothman's Football Yearbook.

Squash became the fashionable sport of the 1970s. Marathon running has taken over in the 1980s. It is quite possible therefore for an activity to have a positive income elasticity over the cross-section, but a negative income elasticity over time. This argument would suggest then that part of the explanation for the fall in attendances is due to consumers switching to other leisure activities when faced with more leisure time and more income.

However, there are other influences on demand, besides income. We saw in Chapter 3 that own-price and cross-price elasticities for any activity are difficult to estimate. In a spectator sport such as football, these problems are compounded by other factors. Simple demand-price relationships (i.e. demand curves) are inappropriate since consumption is spread over a whole season, so there is a time dimension to the demand curve. Also consumption is geographically spread which means that each game has a localized market, and in addition, whatever the price of admission, the price faced by the consumer will be different depending on the distance he lives from the ground (because of the time and travel component in total price). Each club therefore has an aspect of local monopoly power. Finally it is possible in some circumstances for spectators to watch the game at home on television at virtually zero marginal cost. Although the nature of the product may be changed by television it must remain a very close substitute.

Wiseman (1977) has added another aspect to the demand-price relationship, the quality factor. One of the major problems in estimating the influence of price is that there is no price variation from club to club. However, Wiseman suggests that the consumer (i.e. the spectator) takes into account not only the entrance charge (P) but also the expected quality of the game (R). The decision on whether or not to attend is based on the 'expected real price', P/R. With an entrance charge fixed by the League, the influence of quality is crucial in determining variation in attendance from one club to another.

However all the above factors have been given secondary importance in the literature to another feature of the demand for professional team sports. Uncertainty of outcome is the key to demand identified by economists. El-Hodiri and Quirk (1971) state that:

'the essential economic fact concerning professional team sports is that gate receipts depend crucially on the uncertainty of the outcome of the games played within the league. As the probability of either team winning approaches one, gate receipts fall substantially, consequently, every team has an economic motive for not becoming too superior in playing talent compared to other teams in the league.'

Economists have highlighted this as the crucial feature of the professional team sport industry that distinguishes it from all other industries. The conventional textbook firm in economic theory has an interest in increasing its market power and ultimately it maximizes its own interest (and profit) when it achieves maximum market power as a monopolist. In professional team sport once a team becomes a monopolist, revenue would disappear altogether; output would be zero since it would be impossible to stage a match.

One major function of the league is to ensure that no team achieves too much market power, or excessive dominance. The league therefore aims to restrict competition. This explains why price competition between clubs is effectively prevented. Other non-competitive characteristics of professional team sports' leagues include labour market restrictions giving clubs property rights in players and the pooling of revenues so that poorer clubs are cross-subsidized by the richer ones. As Noll (1974) points out:

'Nearly every phase of a team or league is influenced by practices and rules that limit economic competition within the industry. In most cases government has either sanctioned or failed to attack effectively these anti-competitive practices. Consequently professional team sports provide economists with a unique opportunity to study the operation and performance of an effective and well-organised control.'

Despite almost universal acceptance by economists writing in this area, that uncertainty of outcome is the key to demand analysis in professional team sports, there has been little conclusive empirical evidence in support of this contention. Cairns (1983a) reviews the empirical studies that have been carried out and indicates that uncertainty of outcome has been measured by two types of variable: measures of relative team quality and closeness of competition. A relative quality measure would be the percentage of games won over a season as used by Noll (1974). Closeness of competition can be represented by the difference between the competing teams' league positions, as used by Cairns himself in his own demand studies (Cairns, 1983b). Measures of relative quality normally have shown significant positive effects on demand, but closeness of competition variables are normally not significant. It could be argued that a measure of relative quality is not representing uncertainty of outcome at all but instead is a proxy for Wiseman's quality adjusted price discussed above. Thus a significant coefficient for a variable of this type is not evidence in support of the uncertainty of outcome hypothesis. Having said this, it should be pointed out that Cairns' (1983b) study of the demand for Scottish football found 'clear but limited evidence in favour of an uncertainty of match outcome hypothesis'.

We are not here arguing against any influence for uncertainty of outcome. Our argument is that economists have been rather too enthusiastic, having created the idea, to accept that it is the single most important determinant of demand. The weight of the evidence does not support this.

Our discussion has tended to suggest that it is the global demand for sport that we are interested in. This is true in the context of the financial crisis currently facing football. However there is an important microeconomic aspect to demand analysis. Each individual club is mainly concerned about its own home gates. The relevant variables affecting this demand are similar to those we discussed in Chapter 4, when analysing the demand for individual sports facilities, that is locational factors. The size of the local market, in terms of population, is obviously of crucial importance in determining potential demand. Table 12.1 shows that spectating at football matches is closely related to age, sex and income and therefore the socioeconomic mixture of the population is just as important as its overall size. Also the number of clubs competing in the local catchment area will influence the size of each club's attendances. It is factors of this type that explain to some extent how clubs such as Manchester United, Aston Villa and Coventry City have maintained good attendances even when spending seasons in the lower divisions of the Football League.

Finally, an obvious determinant of a football club's demand is playing success. In general, other things being equal, the more successful the club, the higher the attendance. This is in obvious conflict with the uncertainty of outcome hypothesis discussed above. Whereas each club can maximize its attendances by maximizing the number of wins, the league as a whole may suffer by a reduced uncertainty of outcome. This conflict is really a feature of the supply-side of professional team sports to which we now turn.

12.3 The supply side: the professional team as a firm

In many ways the British professional sports team resembles any other firm. All professional football teams, except for Nottingham Forest and Tottenham Hotspur, are private limited liability companies, with shareholders, a Board of Directors and a manager. The manager will not normally be involved in the day-to-day financial business of the club, though, and his main concern is the performance of the team. He is also prevented from sitting on the Board since FA rules prohibit payment of fees to Directors. Shareholders in a firm are normally interested in maximizing the return on their investment either through capital gains or through dividend payments. As Sloane (1971) points out:

'it is unlikely that football club shareholders are primarily interested in financial gain since income from this source is severely limited by an FA rule which specifies that the maximum dividend payable in respect of any year shall be 7½% (or 5% free of income tax) and many clubs in fact pay no dividends.'

Thus there are structural features suggesting that clubs are different from a normal firm. But it is in the objectives of football clubs that we find the major difference from a conventional business firm.

In North America profit maximization is the clearly established objective. Noll (1974) concludes that:

'there is no evidence that the prime motivation of the vast majority of the owners is any consideration other than profits.'

A similar statement would not be true for British professional team sports. The PEP Report on Professional Football (1966) stated that the objective of the football club is:

'to provide entertainment in the form of a football match. The objective is not to maximise profit but to achieve playing success while remaining solvent.'

Many league clubs operate at a loss and only stay in existence through directors' donations, supporters club activities, transfer fee revenues and increasingly through the use of lotteries.

Sloane (1971) regards utility maximization as the objective of most clubs. He suggests that supporters and directors are willing to outlay money without regard to pecuniary rewards, playing success being the ultimate objective of the clubs. His theory is that clubs strive to maximize utility subject to financial viability, or a maximum security constraint.

Wiseman (1977) indicates that the motives of Directors may not be too dissimilar to those we identified for sponsorship in Chapter 11:

'Club directors are often fanatical supporters and find their involvement a rewarding hobby in itself. But of course philanthropy is not all. Directors are given the best seats, free boardroom hospitality and the chance to mix with men in similar positions as themselves. In addition to these social and business contacts, a directorship (and especially a chairmanship) of a league club is excellent for a man's prestige, local standing and business.'

Wiseman goes on to suggest that, whereas profits are not the objective, the pursuit of playing success can lead to larger attendances, and hence greater revenue. This might indicate that utility maximization and profit maximization objectives may yield the same predictions. However Sloane (1971) argues that the utility maximization objective will give quite different predictions to that of profit maximization. He quotes Rottenberg (1956) who suggests that a profit maximizing club may not want to maximize playing success:

'It should not be thought that wealthy teams will invariably want to assemble winning combinations of players...A team will seek to maximise the difference between its revenues and its costs. If this quantity is maximised, for any given club, by assembling a team of players who are of lower quality than those of another club in its league, it will pay the former to run behind.'

Such 'running behind' would not occur under utility maximization. However, it is difficult to envisage how a club could maximize profits in the Football League by this type of behaviour. There are many examples of clubs that have assembled 'a team of players...of lower quality', often by deliberately selling star players in order to raise revenue. The end result has tended to be relegation to a lower division, reduced attendances and lower profits (or more likely, bigger losses). Cairns (1983a) concludes that:

'it is not clear that we are capable in principle of empirically distinguishing utility and profit maximising behaviour.'

In fact the argument over objectives is more concerned with the behaviour of the league than with the individual club, but this involves a discussion of market failure which we leave to the next section.

Although the literature has concentrated on objectives in professional team sports there are other supply-side issues that are closely related to our analysis in Section 3. One issue is raised by Wiseman (1977) in discussing club behaviour aimed at maximizing profits when demand is dependent on the quality adjusted price (P/R). His analysis is reproduced in Fig. 12.2. Demand increases as R, the quality of the performance, increases since the real price (P/R) falls. If the league controls P, then the club will aim to increase R. The obvious way to do this is to buy new players. Alternatively the club may decide to improve quality by offering better seating, better catering facilities, or generally more luxurious surroundings. However either of these options increases costs and the average total cost curve shifts to the right. For the policy to be successful crowds must increase more than proportionately to the increase in costs.

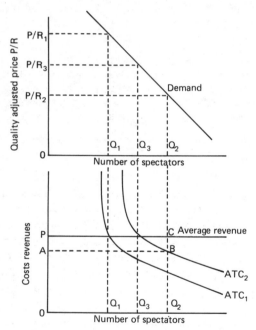

Fig. 12.2 Profit maximization when demand is dependent on quality adjusted price. From: Wiseman, 1975.

If Q increases to Q_2, then the club will receive a profit (compared with its initial break-even position at Q_1 and P/R_1). However if Q increases by less than Q_3, then the club will make a loss.

Wiseman's analysis reveals several features of the supply decision of the firm. First of all it reinforces our earlier point that profit maximizing behaviour by the club can lead to the club aiming to maximize playing success. Secondly it illustrates the uncertainty aspect of decision making. There is uncertainty over how increased expenditure will generate increased quality. There is also uncertainty as to how demand will respond to increased quality. Thirdly it illustrates the similarity between the cost structure of a professional football club and that of a sports facility as analysed in Chapter 7. The average total costs decline continually up to capacity output (i.e. the ground filled to capacity), showing that fixed costs are the most important element of costs.

In fact our analysis of Chapter 7 becomes directly relevant to the current problems of professional football clubs. We defined output as capacity, and this clearly indicates that the problem with professional football is low capacity utilization (or putting it another way, too many empty grounds). Although this seems a rather obvious statement, it is something that has been missed in the literature. One of the reasons for this is Rottenberg's (1956) original definition of output in professional team sports:

'Two teams opposed to each other in play are like two firms producing a single product. The product is the game, weighted by the revenues derived from its play. With game admission prices given, the product is the game, weighted by the number of paying customers who attend. When 30,000 attend the output is twice as large as when 15,000 attend. In one sense, the teams compete; in another they combine in a single firm in which the success of each branch requires that it be not 'too much' more efficient than the other. If it is output falls.'

This definition confuses supply with demand, and any analysis that uses such a definition is likely to be equally confusing, but more importantly, wrong. If a football ground holds 50000 spectators then this is the output supplied by the club when a game is held. The supply curve is totally inelastic at an output of 50 000. If a club has a low degree of capacity utilization, then it has two choices. Either it adopts a policy aimed at increasing demand as outlined in Fig. 12.2 or it reduces capacity to meet existing demand by moving to a smaller stadium.

Other characteristics of the supply of sporting opportunities, as discussed in Section 3, are equally relevant here. The peak problem is particularly acute in professional team sport, with the capital invested only utilized on average for 90 minutes per week. Thus for efficiency reasons, clubs should look for alternative uses for their stadia in the long off-peak periods (i.e. any time other than Saturday afternoons). These rather simple economic arguments have tended to be passed over in the literature mainly because interest has been focused on a particular type of externality that has been associated with professional team sports.

12.4 Market failure in professional team sports

The externality relates to the conflict between the interests of the league and the interests of each individual club. To understand the externality argument we must go back to our earlier discussion on the uncertainty of outcome. To preserve uncertainty of outcome the league will aim to achieve rough equality of playing strengths of competing teams. However a problem arises since market forces set up a virtuous circle for winning teams with playing success generating higher attendances, hence ensuring more revenue with which to buy better players, guaranteeing yet further success and so on. Other teams get involved in a vicious circle of playing failure, falling attendances, and having to sell star players to generate revenue, making it even more difficult to achieve success. Thus profit maximization for a particular club conflicts with the joint profit maximization objectives of the league. When a team becomes much better than average, there are diseconomies external to that team, but internal to the league, because attendances for the league drop off as uncertainty of outcome is reduced.

Jennett (1982) indicates that the league can correct for this externality by acting as a cartel to counteract the natural direction of market forces. In particular they operate a policy of 'cross-subsidization', taking wealth off richer clubs and giving it to poorer clubs. Success in this policy can break the virtuous/vicious circles and maintain stability. If the league is successful in carrying out this policy there is no need for government intervention to correct for market failure since the externality is effectively internalized. The externality argument is important since it is the justification for various restrictive practices (for example, players contracts) adopted by the league and also is the basis of the income redistribution mechanisms such as the equal sharing of revenue from television rights.

There are several major problems caused by this over-concentration on the uncertainty of outcome externality. Some of these problems arise from the fact that the original analysis related to the North American market. What is true for American team sports is not necessarily true for their British equivalents. In Britain the sporting environment is totally different and there are other aspects of market failure in addition to the uncertainty of outcome externality. One major criticism of the analysis above is that it makes the implicit assumption that uncertainty of outcome has an important effect on attendances. As we indicated earlier, the evidence is not conclusive on this.

Secondly, the analysis above ignores international competitions by the clubs which requires the teams competing to become very strong. The three European Cup competitions have become the most important prizes for British clubs after successes in the 1960s and the 1970s. To beat teams like Juventus, Hamburg and Barcelona, teams that can afford to attract the best footballers in the world, British teams must match them by a concentration of talent in a few top teams. Profits from European competitions can be very large, and success in Europe for British teams can have beneficial spin-off effects in attendances at domestic league fixtures. Thus joint profit maximizing behaviour from the point of view of domestic leagues will not necessarily maximize profits when all competitions are taken into account.

This argument can be taken further. It is interesting that the only occasion that the long-term decline in attendances in the Football League was reversed was in the years immediately following England's World Cup success in 1966. It may well be that success of the league depends on international success, in particular in the success of the national team. There is an analogy with international trade theory here where success of home industries depends crucially on the success of home companies in international markets. The analogy is relevant in Europe but not in the United States since the major professional team sports in the USA are only played professionally in North America and therefore international competitions of the status of the World Cup and European Championship simply do not exist.

International sporting success as we saw in Chapter 1 is a public good. By concentrating attention on the uncertainty of outcome externality, the literature has failed to recognise the importance of this public good aspect of market failure. This is a form of market failure that is unlikely to be internalized by league action. We might expect to see some government intervention here to stimulate international success but as we concluded earlier, this is an area where we would expect sponsorship to provide financial resources. This is exactly what happened in cricket. When the Kerry Packer rival league organization threatened to drain away talent from the national side, Cornhill Insurance provided the financial incentives to retain the major players in a sponsorship deal that was highly successful for both sponsor and the sport.

Another aspect of market failure is suggested by Gratton and Lisewski (1981). They suggest that the public good aspect of international sporting success has a parallel in the success of the local team. In the same way that success for the English football team or English cricket team generates benefits throughout England, success for a local football league team or county cricket team generates benefits throughout the area. That is, success of a local club is a local public good.

They quote evidence from Derrick and McRory (1973), who studied the effects on the people of Sunderland of the FA Cup Final victory of Sunderland Football Club in 1973. This study indicated the wide-ranging benefits to the local community that resulted from the team's success. There was an upsurge of pride in Sunderland. This was particularly important for a small depressed area with high unemployment, an area that for so long had felt in the shadow of nearby Newcastle. Other effects pursued by the study were on shops, offices and factories. Companies reported greater productivity due to a more enthusiastic atmosphere in the labour force. A local colliery reported a decrease in absenteeism, improved punctuality and work rate, and better labour relations.

Such local community attachment and involvement in the local professional team has a strong history and tradition in the UK, much more so than in North America where movement of franchises, the right of a club to locate in a particular city, is relatively common. The association of the community with the team suggests that it may be the existence of the club, rather than just its success, that is a collective good. There is some evidence that this is the case. In 1983 Robert Maxwell, Chairman of Oxford United, tried to merge Reading and Oxford football clubs. A new stadium was to be built at Didcot, about half-way between Reading and Oxford. There was tremendous opposition to the plan from both communities culminating in demonstrations and a pitch 'sit-in' which delayed the start of an Oxford league fixture. The outcome was that a consortium was organized to take over Reading FC, and the new owners withdrew from the Maxwell plan. We could identify aspects of option demand in this example. Many people were willing to fight to maintain the existence of their local club even though they did not attend matches regularly.

Gratton and Lisewski (1981) make the general point that the existing literature on the economics of professional team sports has ignored the spatial aspect of the market. Each club has some element of local monopoly power and there is some degree of 'brand loyalty', that is community attachment to the local team. The model of the league operating as a cartel with the objective of maximizing joint profit seems to ignore these aspects.

If the existence of a local team has collective good aspects, we might expect to see some government involvement in the provision of the good. However we saw in Chapter 6 that the voluntary sector is also involved in the provision of collective goods. If Gratton and Lisewski's arguments are valid we would expect football clubs to have a 'collectiveness index' (see Chapter 6) significantly different from zero indicating that the clubs were in the voluntary sector rather than the commercial sector, and therefore involved in the provision of collective consumption goods. Gratton and Lisewski (1982) cite the example of Port Vale FC. They received £174 890 from 'Donations and the Development Fund' in the 1980/81 section. This compares with gross gate receipts for the season of £101 978 (Port Vale Annual Report, 1981). In fact, the collectiveness index for this club in 1980/81 was 25%, which puts it firmly in the voluntary sector on Weisbrod's criterion.

In summary then, we can see that the economics of professional team sports has revolved around a particular type of market failure, the uncertainty of outcome externality. This externality may well be important for professional team sports in North America but there are strong arguments, and some evidence, that other forms of market failure are more relevant to the UK situation. The debate over the causes of market failure in professional team sports is important because it conditions the appropriate policy response, to which we now turn.

12.5 Policy

Sloane (1980) stresses the importance of the 'uncertainty of outcome' externality and the need for the league to operate stronger anti-competitive controls to prevent domination by one or a few teams. This would involve greater cross-subsidization than currently exists. The following quote from Sloane (1980) indicates the policy prescription:

'The more the uncertainty of the results of the games, the higher the public demand for the sport. The more equal the quality of competing teams, the more the uncertainty of the result. Uncertainty of result is threatened by the tendency of wealthy clubs to enjoy a virtuous circle of playing success and rising revenue, and others to be caught in a vicious circle of relative poverty and playing failure. To diminish this possibility sports league organisations claim justification for operating as cartels, redistributing revenue among member clubs, restricting price competition between them, and limiting their property rights in players. With the recent weakening of labour market controls in professional team sports, revenue sharing may have become even more necessary to promote equality of performance among clubs.'

In applying these principles to British Football, Sloane criticises British League organizations for failing in this essential task of maintaining uncertainty of outcome and accuses them of being 'unenterprising and unimaginative' and doing little more than preventing competition in the drive to increase attendances. In order to achieve rough equality in revenue potential Sloane suggests some of the smaller clubs will have to close down as population changes have made them no longer viable. Other clubs may have to move to areas of new population development (for example, new towns such as Milton Keynes). The end result would be a smaller league, with each division made up of clubs with equal opportunity for attracting high attendances.

Although this scenario fits closely with the analysis of professional team sports as developed in the mainly American literature there seems to be serious problems in applying it in the UK. One problem has already been mentioned. Robert Maxwell tried to do just as Sloane suggests by moving Oxford United and Reading and merging the two clubs together under the new name of Thames Valley Royals, and siting the club at a new location in Didcot. The local attachment to both clubs was so strong that within weeks the considerable resources of Robert Maxwell were defeated and the two clubs remained separate entities (both highly successful, by the way, in the following season, as though the uniting of local resources to counter the threat lead to more playing success).

The other problem with Sloane's solution is that the decline in attendances, as Fig 12.1 shows, is a steady long-term decline since 1945, except for the hiccup immediately after 1966. This steady fall cannot be explained by the 'uncertainty of outcome' hypothesis. Uncertainty of outcome will have fluctuated up and down over such a long period and it is unreasonable to suggest that it has been in trend decline, and hence caused the drop in attendances.

The question then arises of why this decline in attendance has occurred and what solutions are available. Our view is that it is no coincidence that all the trends we have identified earlier – greater participation in active sports and recreation, more leisure time – occurred at the same time as the decline in attendances at professional team sports. It is primarily the competition from other leisure pursuits that has attracted spectators away.

On the other hand our analysis of the option demand associated with local soccer teams indicates that people would not be happy to see their local team disappear. The logical suggestion is that clubs should therefore diversify their portfolio of leisure producing activities rather than specializing in producing a game of football once a week. If demand for active sports is increasing, as demand for spectator sports declines, then clubs themselves could provide facilities for participation. In many ways they are in an ideal position to do this. Not only do they possess suitable facilities that are in general severely under-utilized, but they also possess the professional staff needed for coaching and leadership in sport.

The players and coaching staff have the charisma and ability to attract certain sections of the population that other policies may fail to touch. Vandalism and delinquency are particularly associated with British football supporters, and yet the few people that have influence and leadership qualities in this sub-culture are the players themselves. In solving the option demand externality such a policy may also yield the return to participation that we mentioned earlier, reductions in vandalism and delinquency.

If the clubs were to diversify into general suppliers of sport and recreation opportunities, they should then qualify for financial support from the government. We saw in Chapter 10 that there are serious problems with current subsidy policies since the main beneficiaries seem to be those in least need of financial help. Several problems would be solved by such joint action of government and professional clubs. The clubs can extend their facilities to broaden their revenue producing activities; the peak demand problem is less acute since revenue is raised throughout the week, rather than just on a Saturday afternoon; the capital facilities and human resources of the club are used more productively; and attendances for the club's matches may well increase by broadening the base of the club's support. From the government's point of view it fits in with our suggestion in Chapter 10 that government should subsidize supply, but a type of supply that by its nature would be restricted to the target groups. The football clubs have a specific locational advantage in that many are sited in inner city, recreationally deprived areas. Also, many of the groups that policy aims to reach already identify with the football club.

There is some evidence that such a policy would prove successful. In 1978 the government made a special grant available to the Sports Council for the development of facilities at professional football and rugby league clubs that would be open to the public (the 'Football and the Community' scheme). Over £3 million of public money was spent and 39 sports schemes linked with clubs were established. Although the initial grants and initiative came from the government and the Sports Council, there was no continuing finance from this source. In some cases the local authorities continued to subsidize the facilities for community use when Sports Council funding was terminated. The 'Football and the Community' scheme provides an ideal testing ground for the ideas discussed above. The initial monitoring of the schemes by Ingham (1984) revealed tremendous variety. However at one club, Portsmouth FC, the results provide a startling contrast to our discussion of other subsidy policies in Chapter 10. Table 12.2 provides a socioeconomic outline of the major users. These are the complete opposite to those we looked at in Chapter 4 for local authority sports centre users. The scheme at Portsmouth was encouraged by the local authority, and was enthusiastically pursued by Portsmouth FC.

No other scheme was quite as successful as the Portsmouth one, and some were totally unsuccessful. However this one example illustrates that local authorities and professional sports clubs can work together to achieve their dual ambitions. The club can receive public subsidies to enhance their facilities, local authorities can use the charisma of the club to reach sections of the population that they would otherwise fail to reach.

This example is only one aspect of the policy of diversification into a broader leisure provider by the football club. However it does illustrate

Table 12.2 *The Football and Community Scheme: Case study of Portsmouth Football Club.*

	Percentage of people using scheme
Social class of user	
AB	0
C1	8
C2	33
DE	50
Other	9
Total non-manual	**8**
Total manual	**83**
Mode of travel of user	
Walking	95
Car	3
Bicycle	3
Bus	0
Other	0

From: Ingham, 1984.

that government and professional clubs can both achieve their objectives, but they are more likely to do it working together than working separately.

12.6 Conclusion

The economics of professional team sports has developed completely separately from the broad area of recreation economics, which has been the subject matter of this book. An assumption has been made that a professional team sport is a commercial activity and therefore the economists' analysis has been concerned with how the clubs can maximize profits and achieve commercial objectives. Such analysis is useful in understanding the American professional team sports industry. Our argument is that American models of professional team sports are inappropriate in the British context. Whereas American professional team sports are experiencing demand conditions and have experienced steady growth throughout the post-war period, Britain's main professional team sports, football and cricket, have been in steady trend decline. The objectives of British professional clubs are different than their American counterparts. Most importantly the major aspect of market failure that the analysis rests on, the uncertainty of outcome externality, is not of over-riding importance in Britain.

Other aspects of market failure are more relevant to the British scene. In fact the public good and externality arguments that are outlined in Chapter 1 are also relevant to professional clubs. There is little difference in Sebastian Coe winning an Olympic gold medal, and England winning football's World Cup. Both generate collective consumption benefits. In fact the word 'professional' is irrelevant to the analysis. The England football team is the elite echelon of the hierarchy of football participation, as Sebastian Coe is at the top of the athletics participation hierarchy.

Professional clubs are therefore firmly on the supply-side of the sport and recreation market. We have tried to show in this chapter that the economic analysis of the supply-side that we presented in Section 2 is equally applicable to professional sports clubs. The policy prescriptions that follow from this analysis are more likely to reduce the financial problems of professional clubs than any quest for increased uncertainty of outcome.

References

Alden, J.W. (1978), The nature and extent of moonlighting in GB. Paper given to *SSRC Labour studies group*, London.

American Recreation Coalition (1983), *Outdoor Recreation in America, a Profile*, American Recreation Coalition, Washington DC.

Anderson, R.W. (1975), Estimating the recreation benefit from large inland reservoirs, in *Recreation Economics and Analysis*, (ed. G.A.C. Searle), Longman, London, 75-88.

Audit Inspectorate (1983), *Development and Operation of Leisure Centres: Selected case studies*, HMSO, London.

BBC (1965), *The People's Activities*, BBC, London.

BBC (1978), *The People's Activities and Use of Time*, BBC, London.

Baxter, M.J. (1979), *Measuring the benefits of Recreational Site Provision; a review of techniques related to the Clawson Method*, Sports Council/SSRC, London.

Becker, G.S. (1964), *Human Capital*, Columbia University Press, New York.

Becker, G.S. (1965), A theory of the allocation of time. *Economic Journal*, **75**, 3.

Birch, J.G. (1972), *Indoor Sports Centres*, Sports Council Study No. 1, London.

Bradshaw, J. (1972), A taxonomy of social need, in *Problems and Progress in Medical Care*, (ed. G. McLachlan) Oxford University Press, Oxford.

British Travel Association/University of Keele (1967), *The Pilot National Recreation Survey*, London and Keele.

Buchanan, J.M. (1965), An economic theory of clubs. *Economica*, **32**, 1-14.

Bureau of Outdoor Recreation (1976), *Evaluation of Public Willingness to pay User Charges for Use of Outdoor Recreation Areas and Facilities*. US Department of Interior, Washington DC.

Burton, T.L. (1971), *Experiments in Recreation Research*, George Allen and Unwin, London.

Business Monitor Series, *Sports Equipment PQ494.3 and PQ494.2 Quarterly Series*, Government Statistical Service, HMSO, London.

Butson, P (1983), *The Financing of Sport in the UK*, Sports Council Information Series, No. 8., London.

CCPR (1983), *The Howell Report*, Central Council for Physical Recreation, London.

Chairmens Policy Group (1983), *Leisure Policy for the Future*, Sports Council, London.

CIPFA (1981), *Leisure and Recreation Statistics, 1981-82 Estimates*, Chartered Institute of Public Finance and Accountancy, London.

Cairns, J. (1983a), Economic analysis of league sports – a critical review of the literature. *University of Aberdeen, Department of Political Economy Discussion Paper No. 83-01*, Aberdeen.

Cairns, J. (1983b), Demand for Scottish football, 1971-1980. *University of Aberdeen, Department of Political Economy Discussion Paper No. 83-03*, Aberdeen.

Canada Fitness Survey (1983), *Fitness and lifestyle in Canada*, Ottawa.

Cicchetti, C.J. (1973), *Forecasting Recreation in the US*, Lexington Books, Lexington, Massachusetts.

Cicchetti, C.J., Seneca, J.J. and Davidson, P. (1969), *The Demand and Supply of Outdoor Recreation: An Econometric Analysis*, Bureau of Outdoor Recreation, Washington DC.

Cicchetti, C.J., Smith V.K., Knetsch, J.L. and Patton, R.A. (1972), Implications of the indentification problem, *Water Resources Research*, **8**, 840-850.

Clawson, M. (1959), *Methods of Measuring the Demand for and Value of Outdoor Recreation.* Resources for the future, Reprint No. 10, Washington DC.

Coopers and Lybrand Associates (1981a), *Sharing Does Work, The Economic and Social Costs and Benefits of Joint and Direct Sports Provision*, Sports Council Study No. 21, London.

Coopers and Lybrand Associates (1981b), *Service Provision and Pricing in Local Government*, Studies in local environmental services; commissioned by the Department of the Environment, HMSO, London.

Council of Europe (1980), *European Sport for All Charter*, Strasbourg.

Countryside Commission (1982), *Participation in Informal Countryside Recreation: a comparison of two national household surveys of informal countryside recreation (1977 and 1980)*, Countryside Commission.

Cowell, D. (1979), Marketing in local authority sport, leisure and recreation centres, *Local Government Studies*, **5**, 31-43.

Cowell, D. and Henry, I. (1977), Marketing of local authority sports centre services, *European Journal of Marketing*, **11**, no.6, 445-459.

Cullis, J.G. and West, P.A. (1979), *The Economics of Health: an introduction.* Martin Robertson, London.

Culyer, A.J. (1980), *The Political Economy of Social Policy*, Martin Robertson, London.

Curry, N. (1980), A review of cost-benefit techniques in rural recreation planning, *Gloucestershire Papers in Local and Rural Planning*, Issue No. 7. Gloucestershire College of Arts and Technology.

Department of the Environment (1975), *Sport and Recreation*, Cmnd 6200, HMSO, London.

Department of the Environment (1977), *Policy for Inner Cities*, Cmnd 6845, HMSO, London.

Derrick, E. and McRory, J. (1973), Cup in hand : Sunderland's self-image after the Cup, *University of Birmingham, Centre for Urban and Regional Studies, Working Paper no. 8*, Birmingham.

Dower, M., Rapoport, R., Strelitz, Z. and Kew, S. (1981), *Leisure Provision and People's Needs*, HMSO, London.

Driver, B.L. and Rosenthal, D.H. (1981), *Measuring and Improving Effectiveness of Public Outdoor Recreation Programs*, George Washington University, Washington DC.

Duffell, J.R. (1975), Car travel 1965-75 with particular reference to pleasure travel and highway planning. *Traffic Engineering and Control*, **16**, 12.

Duffield, B.S. (1975), The nature of recreational travel space, in *Recreation Economics and Analysis*, (ed. G.A.C. Searle), Longman, London, 15-35.

Duffield, B.S., Best, J.P. and Collins, M.F. (1983), *A Digest of Sports Statistics*, Sports Council Information Series, No. 7, London.

Edwards, A. (1981), *Leisure Spending in the European Community : Forecasts to 1990.* Economist Intelligence Unit, Special Report, No.93, London.

El-Hodiri, M. and Quirk, J. (1971), An economic model of a professional sports league. *Journal of Political Economy*, **79**, 1302-1319.

Elson, M.J. (1977), The poverty of leisure forecasting, in *Forecasting Leisure Futures*, (eds. J. Howarth and S. Parker), Leisure Studies Association, London.

Elson, M.J. (1979), *Countryside Trip Making*, Sports Council/SSRC, London.

Fentem, P.H. and Bassey, E.J. (1978), *The Case for Exercise*, Sports Council, London.kl

Fentem, P.H. and Bassey E.J. (1981), *Exercise: The Facts*, Oxford University Press, London.

Financial Times (1979), *A Swag of Sponsors*, October.

Fishwick, F. (1979), Overtime working – a matter of public concern. *Management Decisions*, **17**, no.3, 265-272.

Fitton, M. (1979), Countryside Recreation – the Problems of Opportunity, *Local Government Studies*, **5**, 57-90

Flegg, A.T. (1976), Methodological problems in estimating recreational demand functions and evaluating recreational benefits, *Regional Studies*, **10**, 353-362.

Gershuny, J.I. (1978), *After Industrial Society? The Emerging Self-Service Economy*, Macmillan, London.

Gershuny, J.I. (1979), The Informal Economy; its role in post-industrial society, *Futures*, **12**, no.1, 3-15.

Gershuny, J.I. and Thomas G.S. (1980), *Changing Patterns of Time Use*, University of Sussex, Science Policy Research Unit, Brighton.

Gibson, J. (1978), Recreational land use, in *The Valuation of Social Cost*, (ed. D.W. Pearce), Macmillan, London.

Glyptis, S. and Riddington, A.C. (1983), *Sport for the Unemployed: a review of local authority projects*, Sports Council Research Working Paper 21, London.

Godbey, G. (1975), Anti-leisure and public recreation policy, in *Sport and Leisure in Contemporary Society*, (eds. S. Parker, N. Ventris, I. Howarth and M. Smith), Polytechnic of Central London, London.

Gratton, C. (1979), The demand for sport, unpublished paper given to the *Conference of the Association of Polytechnic Teachers in Economics (APTE)*, Plymouth.

Gratton, C. (1984), Efficiency and equity aspects of public subsidies to sport and recreation, *Local Government Studies*, **10**, 53-74.

Gratton, C. and Lisewski, B. (1981), The economics of sport in Britain: a case of market failure? *British Review of Economic Issues*, **2**, 63-75.

Gratton, C. and Lisewski, B. (1982), The economics of sport in Britain: a reply. *British Review of Economic Issues*, **4**, no.1, 103-108.

Greenley, D. A., Walsh, R.G. and Young, R.A. (1981), Option value: empirical evidence from a case study of recreation and water quality. *Quarterly Journal of Economics*, **XCVI**, no.4, 657-673.

Grossman, M. (1972), On the concept of health capital and the demand for health. *Journal of Political Economy*, **80**, no.2, 223-255.

Hartley, K. (1980), Towards better cost estimation. *Public Finance and Accountancy*, 16-19.

Hawkins, C.J. and Pearce, D.W. (1971), *Capital Investment Appraisal*, Macmillan, London.

Head, V. (1982), *Sponsorship: The Newest Marketing Skill*, Woodhead-Faulkner, Cambridge.

Heflebower, R. (1967), The theory and effects of non-price competition, in *Monopolistic Competition Studies in Impact*, (ed. R.E. Kuenne), Wiley, London.

Henry, I. (1983), Societal marketing and public sector leisure services, *Leisure Management*, **3**, 2-3.

Hillman, M. and Whalley, A. (1977), Fair play for all: a study of access to sport and informal recreation. *Political and Economic Planning*, **43**, no.571.

Holbrook, M.B. (1980), Representing patterns of association among leisure activities: a comparison of two techniques. *Journal of Leisure Research*, **12**, no.3, 242-256.

House of Lords (1973), *Second Report from the Select Committee on Sport and Leisure*, HMSO, London.

Howard, D.R. and Crompton, J.L. (1980), *Financing, Managing and Marketing Recreation and Park Resources*, Wm.C.Brown, Dubuque.

Ingham, R. (1984), *Football in the Community*, Sports Council, London.

Jennett, N. (1982), Economics of sport in Britain: a comment. *British Review of Economic Issues*, **4**, no.1, 93-102.

Kalter, R.J. and Gosse, L. (1970), Recreation demand functions and the identification problem. *Journal of Leisure Research*, **12**, 43-53.

Kavanagh, J.M., Marcus, M.J. and Gay, R.M. (1973), *Program Budgeting for Urban Recreation; Current Status and Prospects in Los Angeles*, Praeger, Los Angeles.

Koutsoyiannis, A. (1982), *Non-Price Decisions*, Macmillan, London.

Lancaster, K. (1966), A new approach to consumer theory. *Journal of Political Economy*, **74**, 132-157.

Le Grand, J. (1982), *The Strategy of Equality : Redistribution and the Social Services*, George Allen and Unwin, London.

Leibenstein, H. (1966), Allocative efficiency versus X-efficiency. *American Economic Review*, **56**, 392-416.

Leisure Consultants (1980, 1983), *UK Leisure Markets*, Henley Centre for Forecasting, London.

Linder, S. (1970), *The Harried Leisure Class*, Columbia University Press, New York.

McConnell, K.E. (1977), Congestion and willingness-to-pay : a study of beach use. *Land Economics*, **53**, 195-219.

Mansfield, N.W. (1969), The estimation of benefits accruing from the construction of a major recreation facility, in *IMTA, Cost-Benefit Analysis in the Public Sector*, Institute of Municipal Treasurers and Accountants, London.

Mansfield, N.W. (1971), The estimation of benefits from recreation sites and the provision of a new recreation facility. *Regional Studies*, **5**, 55-69.

Marshall, A. (1885), *Principles of Economics*, Macmillan, London.

Martin, W.H. and Mason, S. (1979), *Broad Patterns of Leisure Expenditure*, Sports Council/SSRC, London.

Martin, W.H. and Mason, S. (1980), *The UK Sports Market*, Leisure Consultants, Sudbury.

Meyer, J.R. and Kuh, E. (1957), How extraneous are extraneous estimators? *Review of Economics and Statistics*, **39**, 380-393.

Meyer, P.A. (1975), A comparison of direct questioning methods for obtaining dollar values for public recreation and preservation. *Technical Report Series*, No. PAC/T-75-6, Canadian Marine Service, Ottawa.

Mishan, E.J. (1982), *Introduction to Political Economy*, Hutchinson, London.

Moeller, G.H. (1975), The Delphi Technique : An approach to identifying events that will shape the future of outdoor recreation, in *Indicators of change in the Recreation Environment*, (ed. B. Van-der Smissen), Pennsylvania State University, Pennsylvania.

Moller, D. (1983), Sponsorship: Tobacco's Deadly New Ingredient. *Readers' Digest*, **121**.

National Trust (1983), *Annual Accounts*, 1982.

Noll, R.G. (1974) (ed.), *Government and the Sports Business*, Brookings Institution, Washington DC.

North West Sports Council (1972), *Leisure in the North West*, Salford, North West Sports Council.

North West Sports Council (1978), *Moss-Side Leisure Centre: a study of a sports centre in an Inner City Area*, Manchester.

Observer (1984), *The $ Olympics*, 5 February.

Office of Population Censuses and Surveys (1976), *The General Household Survey*, 1973, HMSO, London.

Office of Population Censuses and Surveys (1979), *The General Household Survey*, 1977, HMSO, London.

Office of Population Censuses and Surveys (1982), *The General Household Survey*, 1980, HMSO, London.

Olson, M. (1965), *The Logic of Collective Action : Public Goods and the Theory of Groups*, Harvard University Press, Cambridge, Massachusetts.

Owen, J.D. (1979), *Working Hours: An Economic Analysis*, Lexington Books, Lexington, Massachusetts.

PEP (Political and Economic Planning) (1966), English professional football, *Planning*, **32**, no.496.

Palda, K. (1964), *The Measurement of Cumulative Advertising Effects*, Prentice-Hall, London.

Peacock, S. (1979), *Capacity, Intensity of Use and Programming of Multipurpose Areas in Indoor Sports Centres*. Sports Council Research Working Paper 13, London.

Peacock, A.T. and Godfrey, C. (1973), Cultural accounting. *Social Trends*, **4**, 61-65.

President's Commission on Olympic Sports (1977), *Executive Report*, Government Printing Office, Washington DC.

Proctor, C. (1962), Dependence of recreation participation on background characteristics of sample persons in the September 1960 National Recreation Survey, in *Appendix 'A',ORRRC Study Report, No.19*, Washington DC.

Roberts, K. (1978), *Contemporary Society and the Growth of Leisure*, Longman, London.

Roberts, J. (1983), Playing at work, *Leisure Studies*, **2**, 2.

Rodgers, B. (1977a), *Rationalizing Sports Policies; Sport in its Social Context : international comparisons*. Council of Europe, Strasbourg.

Rodgers, B. (1977b), Forecasting : the last of the black arts? in *Forecasting Leisure Futures*, (eds. J. Howarth and S. Parker), Leisure Studies Association, London.

Rodgers, B. (1978), *Rationalising sports policies: Sport in its Social Context: Technical Supplement*, Council of Europe, Strasbourg.

Romsa, G. and Hoffman, W. (1980), An application of non-participation data in recreation research : testing the opportunity theory. *Journal of Leisure Research*, **12**, no.4, 321-328.

Rosenthal, S.R. (1980), Risk exercise, *Stress*, **1**, 37-40.
Rosenthal, S.R. (1981), Risk exercise and youth of today. *Stress*, **2**, 9-14.
Rosenthal, S.R. (1982), The fear factor. *Sport and Leisure*, **23**, 61.
Rottenberg, S. (1956), The baseball players' labour market. *Journal of Political Economy*, **64** 243-258.
Sandler, T. and Tschirhart, J.T (1980), The economic theory of clubs : an evaluative survey. *Journal of Economic Literature*, **XVIII**, 1481-1521.
Scarman, Lord (1981), *The British Disorders 10-12 April 1981*, Cmnd 83427, HMSO, November.
Scitovsky, T. (1976), *The Joyless Economy*, Oxford University Press, New York.
Scitovsky, T. (1981), The desire for excitement in modern society. *Kyklos*, **34**, 3-13.
Scottish Sports Council (1979), *A Question of Balance*, Scottish Sports Council, Edinburgh.
Seldon, A. (1979), Micro-economic controls – disciplining the state by pricing, in *The Taming of Government*, (eds. S.C. Littlechild, G. Tullock, A.P.L. Minford, A. Seldon, A. Budd and C.K. Rowley). Institute of Economic Affairs, London.
Settle, J.G. (1977), *Leisure in the North West : a tool for forecasting*, Sports Council Study No.11, London.
Shucksmith, D.M. (1980), Petrol prices and rural recreation in the 1980s. *National Westminster Bank Review*, 52-59.
Sillitoe, K.K. (1969), *Planning for Leisure*, Government Social Survey, HMSO, London.
Simkins, J. (1980), *Sponsorship 1980/81*, Economist Intelligence Unit, Special Report No.86, London.
Sinden, J.A. (1974), A utility approach to the valuation of recreational and aesthetic experiences. *American Journal of Agricultural Economics*. **56**, 61-72.
Sinden, J.A. and Wyckoff, J.B. (1976), Indifference mapping : an empirical methodology for economic evaluation of the environment. *Regional Science and Urban Economics*, **6**, 81-103.
Skjei, S.S. (1977), Identification in the estimation of recreation demand curves from cross-section data : how important is it? *Journal of Leisure Research*, **9**, no.4, 301-309.
Sloane, P.J. (1971), The economics of professional football : the football club as a utility maximiser. *Scottish Journal of Political Economy*, **18**, 121-146.
Sloane, P.J. (1980), *Sport in the Market*, Institute of Economic Affairs, London.
Smith, R.J. (1971), The evaluation of recreation benefits : the Clawson method in practice, *Urban Studies*, **8**, no.2, 89-102.
Smith, M.A. and Simpkins, A.F. (1980), *Unemployment and Leisure : a Review and Some Proposals for Research*, University of Salford, Centre for Leisure Studies, Salford.
Sports Council (1982), *Sport in the Community . . . The Next Ten Years*, Sports Council, London.
Stabler, M.J. (1982), The provision of sport and recreation in an English rural district, a preliminary report, paper given to Sports Council/SSRC Conference, *Economic Issues in Recreation and Leisure*, University of Kent.
Stabler, M.J. (1984), The use of performance indicators in the management of leisure centres, paper given to Leisure Studies Association Conference, *Leisure Politics, Planning and People*, University of Sussex.
Stewart, I.M.T. (1979), *Reasoning and Method in Economics*, McGraw-Hill, London.
Stottlemeyer, R. (1975), Estimating carrying capacity for the National Parks, in *Indicators of Change in the Recreation Environment,* (ed B. van-der Smissen), Pennsylvania State University, Pennsylvania.
Sugden, R. and Williams, A. (1978), *The Principles of Practical Cost-Benefit Analysis*, Oxford University Press, Oxford.
Szalai, A. (1972), *The Use of Time*, Mouton, The Hague.
Toyne, P. (1974), *Recreation and Environment*, Macmillan, London.
Treasury, UK (1983), Relative prices over twenty years. *Economic Progress Report*, No.161, Treasury, London.
US Department of Commerce (1980), *Statistical Abstract of the US*, Bureau of the Census, Washington DC.
US Department of the Interior (1979), *The Third Nationwide Outdoor Recreation Plan*, Washington DC.

US News and World Report (1981), *Our Endless Pursuit of Happiness*.

US Travel Data Center (1983), *Economic Review of Travel in America*, US Travel Data Center, Washington DC.

Veal, A.J. (1975), *Six Examples of Low Cost Sports Facilities*, Sports Council Study No.20, London.

Veal, A.J. (1980), *Trends in Leisure Participation and Problems ofac Forecasting : The State of the Art*, Sports Council/SSRC, London.

Veal, A.J. (1982), Planning for Leisure: Alternative Approaches, Papers in *Leisure Studies*, No.5, Polytechnic of North London, London.

Veal, A.J. (1985), *Using Sports Centres*, Sports Council, London (in Press).

Vickerman, R.W. (1975a), Demand and Derived Demand for Recreation, *Hull University Economics Research Papers*, No.5, Hull.

Vickerman, R.W. (1975b), *The Economics of Leisure and Recreation*, Macmillan, London.

Vickerman, R.W. (1980), The New Leisure Society: an economic analysis. *Futures*, **12**, 191-199.

Weisbrod, B.A. (1968), Income redistribution effects and benefit-cost analysis, in *Problems in Public Expenditure Analysis*, (ed. S.B. Chase Jr). Brookings Institution, Washington DC.

Weisbrod, B.A. (1978), *The Voluntary Non-Profit Sector*, Lexington Books, Lexington, Massachusetts.

Whaley, B. (1980), *Sports Centre Planning in England and Wales: Special Study of Torfaen*, M.Phil Thesis, Centre for Urban and Regional Studies, Birmingham University, Birmingham.

Willcox, M. and Mushkin, S. (1972), Public pricing and family income: problems of eligibility standards, in *Public Prices for Public Products* (ed. S. Mushkin), Urban Institute, Washington DC.

Wiseman, N.C. (1977), The economics of football, *Lloyds Bank Review* 29-43.

Yates, A. (1984), *Recreation Management Training Committee : Final Report*, HMSO, London.

Young, M. and Willmott, M. (1973), *The Symmetrical Family*, Routledge, London.

Author index

Subject index

Le miroir des femmes

II

Roman, Conte, Théâtre, Poésie
au XVIe siècle

LUCE GUILLERM, JEAN-PIERRE GUILLERM
LAURENCE HORDOIR, MARIE-FRANÇOISE PIÉJUS

Le miroir des femmes

II

Roman, Conte, Théâtre, Poésie
au XVIᵉ siècle

PRESSES UNIVERSITAIRES DE LILLE

Le miroir des femmes / Luce Guillerm, Jean-Pierre Guillerm, Laurence Hordoir, Marie-Françoise Piéjus.— Lille : Presses Universitaires de Lille, 1984, 256 p.— 24 cm.

2 : Roman, conte, théâtre, poésie au XVIᵉ siècle

ISBN 2-85939-235-1
— FEMME. 16ᵉ s.
— 396

© Presses Universitaires de Lille
ISBN 2-85939-235-1

Livre imprimé en France

Introduction

Les textes narratifs que nous avons réunis s'organisent, comme nous l'avons précisé, autour du centre vide de la production proprement française à la fois restreinte et notoire : Jeanne Flore, Hélisenne de Crenne, Marguerite de Navarre, Rabelais aussi. Des contes, un roman, un texte « inclassable »..., on les trouvera aisément dans des éditions modernes. L'apport étranger est en revanche considérable et méconnu qu'il s'agisse de ce que Reynier a nommé « roman sentimental » ou de ce qui peut se constituer comme « roman pastoral » ou encore de la surprenante relance du roman de chevalerie par l'Amadis de Gaule. Une part importante de la prose en français s'élabore dans la pratique des traducteurs et le privilège traditionnellement accordé aux productions poétiques de la Pléiade occulte le phénomène capital de la formation de la prose narrative.

Pour nous en tenir aux représentations de la femme et à la première section de ce volume, une remarque s'impose : les textes réunis figurent pour la grande partie dans le répertoire du « roman sentimental » de Reynier. L'adjectif en fait rend mal compte de ces textes. D'abord parce qu'en nombre de ces romans empruntés à l'Espagne ou à l'Italie, le plaisir dominant semble bien être celui de la ratiocination. La prison d'amour, Arnalte et Lucenda, les deux Flamette, le Philocope s'adonnent au débat, voire au débat allégorique. Le texte que traduisit Maurice Scève s'encombre à tel point de raisonnements justificatifs ou accusateurs qu'il en acquiert une sorte d'étrangeté fascinante. Des casuistiques immobiles et jouissives prennent le pas fréquemment sur ce qu'on appelle « roman ». L'histoire s'encombre non pas tant des détours et rebonds du romanesque mais surtout de l'inflation demesurée d'une scolastique ludique. Rien de très « roman sentimental » là-dedans.

Et cependant le « sentiment » est bien présent mais sous un mode particulier : la souffrance. En marge des poésies platonisantes et/ou pétrarquisantes, les romans semblent assumer la part plus ouverte et plus vulgaire des mises en scène clairement sado-masochistes. Le roman sentimental se termine mal, rien de plus pertinent que l'achèvement de la Flamette à cet égard. On y meurt dans la solitude, le désespoir, la renonciation suicidaire à la vie sociale. Arnalte meurt comme meurt Leriano, comme meurent Pamphile et Grimalte fascinés par le désert et la régression bestiale. La narration n'émerge des plaisirs du débat que pour conduire à ces issues déchirantes et à ces spectacles de folie et de cruauté. La chasse infernale de Nastagio degli Onesti s'inverse chez Juan de Florès qui fait déchirer son Appiano par les Furies pour l'honneur des Dames... mais la violence n'est pas toute en ces spectacles. La pause narrative en est toute chargée et il n'y a guère de solution de continuité entre le débat et la « complainte ». Sentimentaux ces romans le sont par l'exhibition de la plainte, du ravage pas-

sionné, la mode baroque du « lamento » s'élabore en ces textes mettant en scène inlassablement la femme productrice de longues séquences de misère, de folie et de culture. Le modèle vient de loin, c'est Didon hurlant jusqu'à la mort sa douleur. Beauté lyrique et plastique des larmes de la femme, il faudra à Hélisenne de Crenne frayer dans cette littérature un roman « sentimental » écrit par une femme.

Les textes que l'on peut considérer comme fortement centrés sur la représentation de la faute et de la souffrance constituent un ensemble qui possède également une cohérence chronologique. Il s'agit en effet de textes traduits ou produits dans les années 30 du XVIᵉ siècle, ce qui ne fait pas oublier qu'ils purent bénéficier d'une réception prolongée tout au long du siècle mais sans apport nouveau appréciable. C'est donc ainsi que s'amorce le vaste mouvement d'assimilation de textes « littéraires » issus des langues modernes espagnole et italienne.

Par rapport à ce premier ensemble nous en situons deux autres : celui des textes « chevaleresques », celui des textes « pastoraux ». Il s'agit là bien entendu de regroupements assez largement arbitraires, fondés sur l'approximation concernant des « contenus » narratifs et ignorants parfois des hétérogénéités flagrantes : prose, poésie, récit, théâtre. Il est aussi trop évident que les textes centrés sur la souffrance peuvent comporter de très importantes séquences d'errances romanesques, comme aussi bien il peut arriver qu'un chevalier se retrouve chez les bergers ! Néanmoins, l'aventure chevaleresque comme la pastorale peuvent présenter des éléments significatifs justifiant la distribution observée.

Tout d'abord dans la résistance qu'ils offrent en commun à l'arbitraire thématique qui est le nôtre. La représentation de la femme devient comme insaisissable, elle est partout et nulle part, se dérobant dans une représentation elle-même relativement floue qui est celle de situations d'amour. C'est l'effet de l'amincissement des personnages par rapport à ceux des premiers textes, ce n'est plus la représentation psychologique qui domine et organise fortement le texte, l'intériorité feinte du personnage tend à s'effacer, tout spécialement dans le récit de l'aventure chevaleresque.

Autre mise en échec de l'anthologie : le caractère proliférant des textes et le fait, non moins évident, qu'il faudrait largement déborder les limites chronologiques du XVIᵉ siècle. L'Amadis ouvre en 1540 une suite ininterrompue de traductions, d'imitations, une arborescence magnifique et fastidieuse d'innombrables Primaléons, de multiples Palmerins, histoires indéfiniment prolongées à la manière de l'épopée médiévale mais avec les moyens techniques de l'imprimerie racontant les aventures des aïeux, des enfants, petits-enfants, neveux, etc... Le tout nous menant par de lentes et obscures transmutations vers Le grand Cyrus quelque cent ans après le premier Amadis. De même, la traduction en 1544 de L'Arcadie de Sannazaro n'est qu'une préfiguration de l'essor de la pastorale qui conduit à l'Astrée. Autant de problèmes que nous ne pouvons envisager. Néanmoins, une répartition chronologique là encore peut s'esquisser, c'est autour de 1540 que se produit la « relance » de la littérature chevaleresque, alors que l'essor de la pastorale se date bien plutôt de l'extrême fin du siècle.

Chevaliers et bergers organisent deux systèmes de représentation codée dont l'effet premier est de dérober l'espace « réaliste ». La cité « réelle » s'aperçoit sans doute mais c'est bien contre l'idéalisme attendu d'abord. Répartissant emblématiquement les deux pôles de la structure féodale, ces littératures ne connaissent que des espaces et des temps inexistants et ne retiennent du présent que les ornements qu'élaborent les premières sociétés de spectacle que sont les Cours du temps.

Est-il pertinent de constater que ce n'est pas Marignan qui suscita le renouveau du goût pour la littérature chevaleresque mais la fin d'un règne qui ne fut, au bout du compte, pas si glorieux que cela ? Comme si, alors que Charles Quint venait d'accomplir d'Espagne en Flandres une chevauchée qu'on n'avait pas pu empêcher, il restait du moins place pour l'aventure brillante, la parade décorative, le faste imaginaire, la gaîté un peu folle de ces chevaliers décidément inexistants. Ce qui est frappant est d'ailleurs que le « genre » n'était nullement inexistant en France, loin de là. Il végétait semble-t-il mais L'histoire de Maugis d'Aigremont et de son frere Vivien comme Les proesses et faicts merveilleux de Huon de Bordeaux furent réédités tout au long du siècle. Peut-être manquait-il à ce vieux fonds l'illusion d'une rupture, le prestige d'une altérité exotique, le goût propre à ce qui est connu quand il paraît venir de loin. Les textes chevaleresques visèrent une clientèle de prestige, ceux du vieux fonds en revanche glissaient vers la consommation populaire, vers la future Bibliothèque bleue. Toujours est-il que les romans de chevalerie revinrent à la mode en offrant avec leur nouveauté le plaisir d'une reconquête culturelle, on s'appliqua en effet à soutenir que l'Amadis n'était qu'un vieux texte picard ravi par les Espagnols et enfin rendu aux Français ; sous le Philocope au nom énigmatique on retrouva Fleur et Blanchefleur ; quant au Roland de l'Arioste, l'imprimeur de la traduction se dit aussi bien serviteur de la maison d'Este que travaillant à rendre « aux Gaulois leur inestimable gloire ».

Dans cette revanche culturelle que s'assure la société de cour, la cruauté est moins importante que le plaisir le plus simple. Le « pays des femmes homicides » de l'Arioste témoigne de la complexité du poème italien qui absorbe dans son espace des pratiques hétérogènes. Ce qui apparie davantage les textes est le goût pour la description somptueuse et coquine. La femme, sous un mode toujours discret, souvent « courtois », est un objet complaisamment donné à voir. Elle est belle, désirable, désirée et autrement qu'en pensée. Du regard on passe volontiers aux actes, les textes jouent constamment sur l'imagination érotique. La scène suggestive vient rythmer le cours de l'errance héroïque. Cela n'exclut pas pour autant la casuistique subtile, treize demandes d'amour ornent le Philocope, quant *à Oriane, elle est aussi agréable à entendre qu'à voir, et plus encore à lire, si du moins on est sensible aux charmes du néo-platonisme. Le texte fait donc de la femme un objet de désir associant élégamment le corps, le vêtement, la culture. Tout cela n'est pas neuf mais rénové, apte à séduire un public en quête de lectures d'évasion élégantes.*

Les moralistes tonnèrent universellement contre une telle littérature de plaisir. La pastorale est plus ambiguë dans la mesure où peuvent s'y croiser l'idéal ascétique et l'aspiration libertine.

Le chevalier constitue l'instrument de rêve d'une culture, le berger est plus largement le contre-point régressif opposé à la conscience d'une civilisation qui se pense comme perfectionnée. Rien n'est plus récurrent que la nostalgie pastorale et son mélange d'austérité quant à la consommation et de bienheureuse dépense sexuelle. Rien n'est plus culte que cette dénégation de la civilisation, rien de plus profondément mondain... C'est du sein des Cours que Guevara prêche le Mépris de Court et la louange de vie rustique, l'un des grands succès de la littérature morale du temps. Rien n'est donc plus disposé aux merveilles des codes rhétoriques que la Nature.

Autour du centre vide laissé par l'absence de Daphnis et Chloé, *texte trop répandu pour que nous ayons besoin de le reprendre ici, nous avons convoqué des séquences diverses qui marquent les possibles investissements de la pastorale. Il s'y perçoit essentiellement le débat entre la fascination de la liberté sexuelle et la nécessité morale, sociale, théologique du mariage. C'est un couple dont la légitimité est dûment vérifiéeque Lemaire de Belges, témoin vénérable en ces choses, voue aux plaisirs du camping sauvage. C'est de même pour la plus grande gloire du couple post-tridentin que Guarini joue avec le libertinage des rustiques. Il s'y perçoit aussi l'importance des modèles culturels, qu'il s'agisse de l'églogue latine dans le cas des Bergers de Sannazaro ou des théoriciens de l'amour dans les discours de la docte bergère de Montemayor.*

Par rapport à ces domaines des lectures françaises dans lesquels l'apport étranger est considérable pour ne pas dire prédominant, le domaine des Contes apparaît en revanche comme puissamment intégré à la tradition littéraire française. Un volume de la Bibliothèque de la Pléiade consacré aux Conteurs français *du* XVIᵉ *siècle en témoigne.*

Des Cent nouvelles nouvelles *à l'*Heptaméron, *le conte français s'impose et relègue l'apport étranger à bon droit semble-t-il.*

Il n'en reste pas moins que la production nationale affiche parfois dans ses titres mêmes l'importance de textes étrangers dont elle est, proche ou fortement médiatisée, la réécriture. Le Décaméron *n'est cependant pas le seul apport puisque l'Italie continue à produire des recueils de narrations brèves qui sont rapidement intégrés par la traduction à la bibliothèque française avec un succès de lecture et non moins de réécriture très notable, qu'il s'agisse de Bandello ou de Straparole. Ceci sans parler des retombées plus lointaines, celles du* XVIIᵉ *siècle, celles aussi dans d'autres cultures européennes.*

Alors que les romans chevaleresques ou pastoraux pouvaient tendre à intégrer dans le continu narratif les représentations de la femme que les romans sentimentaux tendaient encore à exhiber sous le jour du débat, les contes et nouvelles s'organisent à partir de situations fortement caractérisées qui très volontiers manifestent une donnée particulière des systèmes de représentations. Certes, il s'agit souvent d'un défaut des femmes dont la lascivité qui est privilégiée comme origine de multiples et inlassablement répétées bonnes histoires de coucheries. Cependant, ce qui caractérise aussi l'espace particulier que constitue le recueil des contes est d'une part la polyphonie et d'autre part une problématique « liberté ». Polyphonie dans la mesure où des voix diverses se font entendre et où des contrastes, voire des contradictions, sont de règle afin que la rencontre des devisants soit variée en agréments. Aussi n'est-ce pas sans arbitraire qu'un conte est soustrait à un ensemble, surtout lorsque c'est à fin d'édification conformiste comme ce fut le cas avec l'histoire de Grisélidis. Liberté dans la mesure où les « gaillardes » qui caractérisent le conte sont souvent les protagonistes de l'histoire et où elles ne sont nullement accablées, au contraire. L'espace du conte, comme celui de la comédie, est permissif, il exhibe la transgression même s'il la neutralise partiellement par le rire. La « prude femme » parle, agit, mène son plaisir, affirme haut son droit au contentement sexuel... Tout cela est certes ambigu, fait pour susciter le rire. Tout cela côtoie somme toute paisiblement les réalités à la fois répressives et sans doute aussi parfois fort libres. Il reste que ces histoires drôles et fortes, honnies par les cagots, sont comme l'unique place en littérature où s'accomplit une prise en compte d'une sorte de contre-culture qui résiste sourdement au développement des représentations exemplaires. Place unique en prose narrative, conviendra-t-il de dire, puisque le développement de la comédie « moderne », sous l'égide des modèles antiques ou étrangers nous fait retrouver un problème semblable.

Avec la présence de quelques textes dramatiques nous avons voulu cependant moins donner une place à un « genre » qu'indiquer une insistance — relative bien entendu — de représentations violentes, expressionnistes serait-on tenté de dire, des problèmes féminins dans une période particulière qu'on peut définir comme le dernier quart du siècle, à quelques années près. Nous privilégions ainsi la traduction de La Célestine par Jacques de Lavardin sans ignorer qu'une autre bien antérieure fut produite et nous provoquons le côtoiement de textes hétérogènes, peut-être d'ailleurs inclassables... Que faire du Corbaccio ?

La traduction en 1571 du texte de Boccace est de prime abord un étonnant anachronisme. Cette « invective contre une mauvaise femme » aurait dû être traduite beaucoup plus tôt, tant elle semble l'effet d'une culture médiévale que le célibat consacré névrose. Or cette hantise effrayante de la chair et plus encore du corps survient alors qu'on aurait cru les acquis de la Renaissance irréversibles. Mais la Célestine elle aussi revient et avec elle se développent les comédies nouvelles. Autant de modes qui interrogent le discours moral, qui l'agressent d'autant plus sans doute qu'on est désormais en période « post-tridentine » et que la réaffirmation solennelle de la croyance et de l'idéologie morale est plus urgente. Il ne faut pas perdre de vue que ce dernier quart de siècle voit aussi « revenir » Plutarque que La Boétie traduit l'année même où l'on publie la traduction du Corbaccio, traduction qui précède de peu celle des Œuvres morales de Plutarque par Aymot et une nouvelle traduction de Luis Vivès. On continue d'ailleurs aussi à platoniser fort doctement. Quant à l'idéalisme romanesque, il galope d'Amadis en Primaléon en attendant d'aller de Diane en Aminte. Est-ce hasard cependant si c'est aussi l'époque où Benoist traduit saint Jérôme, où il renouvelle la condamnation usée des ornements des femmes comme celle, bien inutile, de « la familière fréquentation et alliance des hommes du monde » (1573, 1580). Puritanisme protestant certes, mais Jacques de Lavardin traduit lui aussi saint Jérôme en 1585.

Cependant le « Songe » est cauchemar et ce qui nous semble intéressant dans l'invective c'est qu'elle ne soit pas abstraite, purement morale ou théologique, qu'il n'y ait pas simple reprise d'un catalogue et d'une ratiocination. Le Songe sue l'angoisse, il pue la mort. La béance putride du Labyrinthe dénude le corps de la femme mais c'est tout corps qui s'y reconnaît en tant que la mort s'y voit et s'y vit. La femme est plus que jamais corps mais corps qui n'est pas celui d'Eve, la chair cède à la matière, parfois à la viande.

La maquerelle, la « Célestine » emblème de toutes celles qui se mettent à pulluler en cette fin de siècle où le théâtre comique se développe en attendant la littérature qu'on dira picaresque, se dépense non seulement en messages et en courtages mais en fards et en onguents, elle s'applique à couvrir d'odeurs la puanteur menaçante des corps. Alchimiste profane, son art au service des femmes dénie la mort pour piéger le désir. Cependant, l'apprentie courtisane des Tromperies de Larivey, Dorothée, renvoie le compliment, c'est l'homme, qui plus est le Médecin, qui pue, qui est « le vieil pourry » que l'argent ne parfume pas, car l'argent est le fard de l'homme. Charognes donc et libidineuses, puantes comme l'Ambroise de La veuve qui double l'inefficacité de la richesse de celle des parfums, ne laissant pas de jour qu'il n'aille « chez maistre René, le parfumeur ». Au terme des voleries des courtisanes, l'Arétin l'atteste, c'est encore sur les parfums qu'on tombe. Tout semble intensément se boucler sur l'odeur. C'est aussi à l'ambiguë alchimie des fards qu'en 1573, on l'a vu dans le premier volume, l'Instruction pour les jeunes dames sacrifie l'édification morale.

Vendeuse de fard, bricoleuse de pucelage, semeuse de vérole, contrefaçon de médecin comme la Méduse du Fidelle de Larivey dit être, la maquerelle brûle son corps et celui des autres, hommes et femmes, aux feux d'un désir que les raisons et les fictions n'assument pas. Peut-être faut-il penser qu'en ces années, le débat d'idées vient ravager les corps. Les pratiques littéraires hétérogènes que nous rassemblons ici d'autres réalités peuvent les motiver. Lorsque dix ans après la traduction de La Célestine, Jean Bodin publie sa Démonomanie des sorciers, on sait que le texte ne resta pas lettre morte. Comment oublier que 1572 est aussi la date de la Saint Barthélémy, une nuit où l'odeur des corps dût être plus forte que celle de tous les parfums.

Le dernier quart du siècle se caractérise enfin par une « relance » de la production littéraire féminine qui peut d'abord apparaître comme une réaction au déploiement satirique que nous venons de mentionner. Certes, les femmes qui publient alors n'ont pas la renommée de celles, bien connues et il faut le reconnaître à juste titre, qui publièrent leurs écrits entre 1540 et 1550. C'est d'ailleurs cette notoriété même des unes, Marguerite de Navarre ou Louise Labé, qui les a fait exclure de cette anthologie, quand l'obscurité des autres, Mes dames Des Roches, Liébaut, leur vaut au contraire d'y figurer.

On pourra disputer longuement sur la portée exacte de tels écrits. On ne peut s'empêcher de constater que cette production à bien des égards s'inscrit dans le ressassement idéologique qu'on a constaté, Les misères de la femme mariée répondent, et c'est symptomatique, aux Stances du mariage de Desportes, celles-ci inspirées par les Quinze joies de mariage. Cette programmation des textes accable. Cependant, c'est malgré tout la première fois qu'une réponse féminine est donnée et que ce n'est pas une voix d'homme qui répond. Quant aux Œuvres des dames Des Roches si elles n'ont ni pensées profondes ni forme originale, elles témoignent néanmoins d'une ambition nouvelle de l'écriture féminine dans les « genres » littéraires qui sont visés. Au terme du siècle, la conclusion demeure contradictoire.

J.P.G.

Note

Comme nous l'avons explicité dans le premier volume du Miroir des Femmes, nous avons cherché avant tout à donner à lire des textes rares, peu accessibles. On repérera donc dans ce choix de textes « littéraires » d'évidentes lacunes. La plus considérable concerne la poésie amoureuse qui pour l'essentiel étant d'origine française se trouve très largement éditée. Quant à Pétrarque, une publication prochaine de la traduction du Canzoniere par Vasquin Philieul le rendra accessible dans la version qui l'intégra aux lectures françaises du XVIe siècle.

Romans sentimentaux

Æneas Sylvius Piccolomini, L'histoire d'Eurial et Lucresse, 1444-1497.

Ce premier texte est un repère historique, celui d'un moment très précoce où quelque chose se constitue qui peut être perçu soit comme encore très « primitif », soit comme annonçant déjà l'avenir. Il s'agit d'un emprunt moderne, mais c'est à un texte néo-latin, c'est déjà un roman mais on le traduit partiellement ou totalement en vers... A. S. Piccolomini écrivit son De duobus amantibus *en 1444, une trentaine d'années plus tard Octovien de Saint-Gelais en donnait une traduction en vers que devait suivre en 1497, trois ans plus tard, celle d'un certain maître Antithus. En 1551, Jean Millet produisait une nouvelle version du texte qui, par ailleurs, était traduit en italien, espagnol, allemand, anglais, hongrois... Bref, un grand succès « moderne », l'un des premiers à manifester la puissance de l'imprimerie non dans le domaine des textes fondamentaux de l'humanisme mais dans celui de ses divertissements. Faut-il penser néanmoins que ce type d'ouvrages reste de peu de prix ? En dépit d'une indubitable diffusion les exemplaires sont rares et la Bibliothèque nationale par exemple ne dispose pas de la traduction que nous avons utilisée.*

Si Piccolomini n'était pas Boccace et qu'en conséquence le statut de son texte n'était sans doute pas celui des textes de l'illustre Toscan, il n'en est pas moins un personnage considérable, rien moins que le futur pape Pie II, le grand humaniste siennois, le fondateur de Pienza, une utopie urbanistique réalisée à demi, un pape « pieux » comme Enée faute, dit-on, d'avoir osé prendre pour nom Formose...

L'histoire d'Eurial et Lucresse est fort simple. Un beau cavalier séduit une bourgeoise de Sienne. Il l'abandonne pour remplir son devoir auprès de l'empereur. Lucresse en meurt de douleur, quant à Eurial l'empereur tente de le consoler en le mariant. La moralité est évidente : Mesdames méfiez-vous des amours d'occasion. Piccolomini, bon connaisseur des Latins, brode sur un schéma qui pourrait conduire à une épure tragique. En fait, il mêle au lyrisme passionné le burlesque du conte, le souvenir des Nobles dames malheureuses et les plaisanteries comiques et ses chants d'amour ont de vagues relents liturgiques !

Le dispositif narratif demeure relativement archaïque, un « acteur » sert de récitant, assurant la liaison entre les dialogues et les échanges de lettres. Le mélange de prose « épylogalle », de rimes « desdascaliques » et de rimes « dédaliques » fait de la traduction un exercice rhétorique dont le plaisir s'entremêle à celui du romanesque.

Les extraits qui suivent sont repris de l'exemplaire de la Bibliothèque Méjanes d'Aix-en-Provence qui a bien voulu en autoriser la reproduction.

J.P.G.

S'ENSUIT L'ISTOIRE DES DEUX
VRAYS AMANS
EURIAL ET LA BELLE LUCRESSE

S'ensuyt l'ystoire de Eurial et Lucresse
compilée par Enée Silvius et translatée
en françoys par Maistre Antithus
chapellain de la sainte chapelle
aux ducz de Bourgoigne à Digon
à la priere et requeste des
Dames
Paris, Michel Lenoir
1497

*La rencontre d'Eurial et de Lucresse est suivie par un échange de lettres
entre les deux jeunes gens. Choquée d'abord par le fait que la première lettre d'Eurial lui ait été transmise par une maquerelle notoire, Lucresse
brûle la lettre, elle accepte néanmoins peu après une bague et surtout à
chaque fois elle répond...*

Response par Lucresse à la replique d'Eurial

Très voulentiers de mon cueur t'aymeroie
Et te vouldroye de mon pouvoir complaire
Mais je congnois que je m'abuseroye
Devant mes yeulx le voy par exemplaire
Car maintes dames pour plaisir vouluntaire
Bien ont eu piteuse destinée
Comme Dido, Ariadne et Medée.
    Les dessus dites pour estrangiers amer
Se sont trouvées en grant peine et douleur
En avalant le faulx breuvage amer
De Cupido et de sa grant chaleur
Par quoy concluz d'eviter ce maleur
Car se j'aymoye de voulenté entiere
Je ne tiendroye ne mode ne maniere.
    Finablement congnois clerement
Que longuement ne peulx demourer cy
Je feroye donc trop oultrageusement
Se promptement m'abandonnoye ainsi
Parquoy concluz pour eviter soucy
Laisser amours : toutesfoys je t'envoye
Ce don : priant à Dieu qu'il te convoye.

Les lettres receues par Eurial à tant ne se voulut taire ains repliqua en la maniere qui s'ensuyt.

Dieu te salve la maistresse de mon cueur ainsi que par tes lettres m'a saulvé la vie, combien que en doulceur d'icelles ayez voulu mesler quelque peu de amertume toutesfois je espere que après que m'auras ouy que tu te adoulciras, j'ai receu tes lettres par lesquelles me prie que cesse de toy aimer, pour que à toy n'affiert d'aymer ung estranger, et à ce propos recitent les exemples de plusieurs femmes qui pour estrangiers aymer se sont trouvées piteuses et désolées. Se tu vouloye me faire d'amour desister, tu ne debvoye point si orneement ou elegamment escripre, car d'une petite estincelle tu as fait ung grant feu inextinguible. Et en lysant ta lettre j'ay congneu loyaulté et intelligence avec sapience conjoinctes en toy, et me seroit à present aussi possible de non toy aymer, comme au soleil de laisser son cours, aux montaignes estre sans neiges, et la mer sans poissons. Au regard des exemples des femmes qui par les hommes ont esté deceues pour une qui a esté ainsi trompée : j'en trouveroye à l'opposite dix hommes depceuz par femmes : comme Troylus le filz du roy Prian par Briseyda et plusieurs aultres telz. Que dirons nous de Circé qui par enchantemens muoit ses amys en diverses especes de bestes : combien que ce seroit erreur se pour aucunes en petit nombre on jugeoit les autres toutes semblables. On pourroit aussi donner plusieurs autres exemples comme Anthenor et Cleopastre et mains aultres dont à cause de brieveté pour le present me tays. Ovide recite paraillement que après la destruction de Troye la grant plusieurs des Grecz furent prins d'amours : lesquels jamais ne retournerent en leurs pays mais habandonnerent royaulmes et seignouries pour obeyr à leurs dames. Pour ce Lucresse m'amye considere ces exemples en delaissant ceulx qui contrarient à noz amours. Ma pensée est tellement en toy fichée que je t'aymeray et à perpetuité seray tien. Ne me appelle plus estrangier, car jamais n'auray aultre pais fors là où tu seras, et trouveray le moyen d'estre commis et lieutenant de par Cesar en ceste province, donc ne te doubtes de mon departement, car ainsi qu'il est impossible de vivre sans cueur aussi m'est il de vivre sans toy. Pourtant prens pitié de ton serviteur, qui font devant toy par peines intolerables comme la neige devant le soleil. Tu m'as osté l'usaige de boire et menger et de dormir : Car incessamment à toy je pense. Donc ma très honorée dame se tu me use de si grant cruaulté pour trop aimer que feras tu à ceulx qui mal te vouldront. Pourtant mon salut et refuge recoys moy en ta grace, autre chose ne desire fors que tu me puisse nommer ton serviteur. Et à Dieu ma seulle esperance.

L'acteur

Lors com la tour dedans rompue
Qui par dehors est toute entiere
Se trouva Lucresse abbatue
Et ravie en ceste matiere
Et rescripvit en telle manière

℄Pourtant me fault trouuer moyen
Dacquerre deurial sa grace
Amour ma mis en son lien
Lie deung desir qui tout passe
Dont ilest force que le face
Nulautre ne me peult guerir
Te ce faire prendray laudace
Car languir Vault pis que mourir.

ors disposa dame lucresse
Te declarer son poure cas
a print en soy mesme hadiesse
Pour en parler a zosias
En disant quelle ne cuide pas
Que de cecy fist iamais bruyt
Dont pour recouurer son soulas
Luy dist tout franc ce qui sensuyt. Lucresse
Dsiasmon bon seruiteur
En qui iay toute ma fiance
Je te requier de tout mon cueur
Que tu sois demon aliance
Il ya Vng mignon de france
Que tu Vois passer plusieurs fois
Auec cesar comme ie pense
Que me dye se le congnois

A Eurial par motz exprès
Comme vous verrez cy après.

Lucresse

Or n'est loisible que puisse plus fouyr
Na ton vouloir en riens contrarier
Mon doulx amy à toy vueil obeyr
Mon cueur se veult avec le tien lyer
Ne vueilles donc à jamais oublier
Se que promis as par ton escripture
Puis que me metz en si grand adventure.
  A toy me donne, à toy prens mon refuge
Tu tiens mon cueur en vraye possession
Dès maintenant ne quiers aultre confuge
Fors demourer en ta dilection
Tu es ma joye et ma protection
Preserve moy d'annuy et de dangier
Car à jamais ne te vouldroye changer.
  Garde la foy qu'ung amant doit avoir
Quant aymer veult de franc cueur loyalment
Et de ma partie je feray mon devoir
Accomplissant ton vueil entierement
Et à Dieu soyez mon très doux pensement
Qui en soulas longuement te maintienne
Avec celle qui se dit du tout tienne.

Le consentement obtenu il reste à organiser un rendez-vous, à quoi s'emploie un frère bâtard de Lucresse.

  A l'eure que Apolo rend à chascune chose sa couleur le jour prefix et desiré par Eurial et Lucresse venu se trouva ledit Eurial en la compaignie des portefais, et marcha avec eulx en la maison de Lucresse chargé de son sac plein de blé et après ce que ou garnyer l'eut deschar voulut descendre le dernier ainsi que par ledit Zosias luy avoit esté dit. Et quand il se trouve à l'endroit de l'uys de la chambre le boute combien qu'il semblast estre fermé, et entra dedens ladicte chambre où il trouva Lucresse toute seulle qui besoignoit en soye : et en approchant d'elle commença à la saluer. En disant

O mon espoir et mon seul souvenir
Il me souffist que te puisse tenir
Entre mes bras pour eternelle joye
Eureux je suis quant j'ay peu parvenir
A ce hault bien de m'amye detenir
Maintenant peult mon cueur cryer montjoye
Car en ce monde rien je ne desiroye

Fors vous mamours que voy devant mes yeulx
Dont suis frapé et ravy jusques ès cieulx.

L'acteur

De prime face se trouva Lucresse toute esbahye : cuydant mieulx veoir ung esperit que son amy Eurial. Car elle n'avoit peu croire que ung tel et si grant homme se fust exposé à si grant dangier, mais après que Eurial l'eust par plusieurs fois baisée et accolée elle le congneut et luy dist en telle maniere

Lucresse

Las mon amy soulas et desir
Sur tous vivans je t'ay voulu choisir
Pour vray amy et loyal serviteur
Donc à ceste heure fays de moy ton plaisir
Embrasse moy à coup viens moy saisir
Car deux corps sommes et si n'avons qu'un cueur
L'eure est venue que fortune et bonheur
Nous ont donné povoir et faculté
Pour accomplir d'amours la volupté.

Cependant que Eurial et Lucresse cuidoient recevoir le hault bien et souverain gardon d'amours Zozias qui faisoit le guet vint hurter à la porte de la chambre et leur dist Gardez vous povres amans de Menelaus qui vient en ceste chambre. Pour laquelle chose celez vostre cas au mieulx que vous pourrez si que par cautelle cest homme soit abusé car de saillir hors pour ceste heure n'est possible. Lors dist Lucresse à Eurial Mon amy il y a dessoubz nostre lit une musse très secrette en laquelle nous mettons toutes nos precieuses choses. Entrez dedens secretement et gardez de vous remuer, de toussir ne de cracher en facon que ce soit. Lors Eurial très douteux de ce qu'il avoit à faire voyant que autre remede n'y avoit obeist au commandement de Lucresse Et ce fait Lucresse va ouvrir tous les huys de la chambre et retourna à son ouvrage de soye. Adonc Menelaus et ung aultre home de la cité entrerent en la chambre pour querir aucune lettre qui à la chose publicque appartenoit. Et quand ilz ne la trouverent point Menelaus dit quelle devoit estre en la musse où estoit Eurial et demanda à Lucresse de la chandelle pour y regarder, desquelles parolles fut moult espouvanté Eurial et presque perdit le sens doubtant que Lucresse n'eust faicte ceste emprinse pour le decevoir et dist en soymesmes ce qui s'ensuit.

Eurial

O fol abusé et infame
Que pourra dire l'empereur

Mourir te fault pour une femme
A grant blasme et à grand deshonneur
O faible et desordonné cueur
Qui t'a fait cy venir loger
Dieu mon souverain createur
Preserve moy de ce dangier
    O fol remply de vanité
Chascun congnoistra ta folye
Par tout à perpetuité
Sera ta renommée faillye
Vilipendée orde et soillée
Et d'honneur tousjours estrangier
Glorieuse Vierge Marie
Preserve moy de ce dangier
    O faintise deception
Qui m'a mis en ce desarroy
O grief desolation
Obscur et tenebreux charroy
Je suis icy prins à l'arroy
Près de la mort pour abreger
Pourtant Jhesus souverain roy
Preserve moy de ce dangier
    Prince jamais en tel conroy
Ne feuz vueille ce dueil changier
Humblement je me rens à toy
Preserve moy de ce dangier

L'acteur

Or est il assavoir que nonobstant que Eurial en l'ymagination que avez ouye et Lucresse de son costé n'en estoit pas moins travaillée laquelle n'estoit point seulement tant crainte de soy comme de son amy Eurial Or est vray que de tous perilz et cas soudains l'engin de femme est plus prompt à trouver remede que celluy de l'homme comme à ce besoing bien le monstra Lucresse car par soudain advis destourna son mary de regarder en sa musse en disant et affermant qu'elle avoit veu mettre certaines lettres en ung petit coffre qui estoit sur une fenestre, et pource regardons se celles que vous querez y seroient point. Adonc courut legierement au dict coffre et faignant de l'ouvrir le getta du hault de la fenestre en la rue puis comme femme esbahye commenca à crier et dist à son mary. Ha mon amy Menelaus le coffre où sont noz meilleurs bagues est cheut en la rue ainsi que je l'ouvroye pour cercher les lettres que vous demandez pourtant avancez vous de courir que le coffre et les bagues ne soient perdues et je regarderay par la fenestre que nul n'y mette la main. Sur ce point cy est à noter l'audace femenine et se bon vous semble adjoutez foy à tout ce qu'elles vous diront, et tout bien considéré trouverez que en ce cas les hommes especialement les mariés sont plus souvent eureux que sages car nul est tant soit saige clervoyant qui de femme n'ait esté trompé et deceu. Et pour retourner à nostre propos, Menelaus et son compaignon descendirent hastivement pour aler querre le dit coffre à causes des bagues et lettres qui estoient dedans. Or estoit la maison haulte parquoy Eurial eut assez espace de changer lieu et place : lequel par le conseil de Lucresse se mist en ung autre lieu. Menelaus et Bretus vont revenir et apporter le dit coffre puis sercherent en la musse où il estoit par avant mussé et trouverent les lettres qu'ilz queroient puis s'en vont et commenderent Lucresse à Dieu. Lors ne fut Lucresse negligente d'aller fermer les huys et puis se transporta vers Eurial disant ainsi

Lucresse

Viens dehors mon amy parfait
Ma fontaine et source de joye
Par qui mon cueur est tout refait
Tu es mon soulas et ma joye
Viens que je tiengne et te voye
Mon seul bien et mon seul plaisir
Sans danger peulx aller par voye
Et acomplir tout son desir
    Se fortune par sa faintise
Nous a cuidé estre contraire
Cupido qui nous favorise
L'a incontinent fait retraire
Viens dehors nous avons beau faire
Embrasse moy mon souvenir
En oubly metz tout nostre affaire
Car à ton gré me peulx tenir

L'acteur

Alors ne se peut contenir
Eurial mais va l'embrasse
Et ne se scavoit maintenir
Voiant de beaulté l'outrepasse

. . . .

Juan de Flores, L'Histoire d'Aurelio et Isabelle, 1495-1530.

Le second roman de Juan de Flores, Historia de Grisel y Miravella, *fut d'abord traduit en Italien sous le titre de* Historia de Isabella e Aurelio. *Le texte en français, qui paraît en 1530, est traduit de la version italienne. Tout au long du siècle, de nombreuses éditions souvent bilingues, voire quadrilingues, témoignent de l'exceptionnel succès de ce roman. L'*Histoire d'Aurelio et Isabelle, *autrement intitulée le Jugement d'Amour, est, comme le souligne Reynier, « de beaucoup le plus lu de tous les romans étrangers ».*

Le sous-titre de l'édition que nous utilisons explicite une des raisons de cet engouement : Histoire d'Aurelio et Isabelle, *« en laquelle est disputé qui baille plus d'occasion d'aymer, l'homme à la femme, ou la femme à l'homme ». Débat casuistique, dispute rhétorique sur un des thèmes obligés de la « querelle »... Mais la rhétorique trouve ici son lieu de déploiement dans un dispositif narratif qui en exhibe la violence latente : c'est d'un procès qu'il s'agit, et dont la sentence doit être sentence de mort, conformément sans doute à des modèles archaïques, mais que l'époque, nous l'avons souligné, s'est complue à réactiver.*

Le roi d'Ecosse, ayant surpris les amours clandestines d'Isabelle, sa fille, qu'il refuse de marier et séquestre, et d'Aurelio, décide qu'ils seront jugés selon la loi commune en Ecosse, qui veut que soit puni de mort « celuy des deux qui a donné à l'aultre plus grande cause de commettre telle meschanceté ». Mais chacun des deux amants se déclare seul coupable. On généralise donc le débat, et on choisit deux avocats célèbres : Hortensia pour les femmes, et Affranio pour les hommes. A l'issue du fort long procès, Affranio est déclaré vainqueur et Isabelle condamnée à être brûlée. Mais Aurelio se jette le premier dans les flammes. C'est donc la volonté du ciel : Isabelle sera épargnée. Mais, refusant de survivre à son ami, celle-ci se jette dans la cour aux lions. Le texte pourrait s'arrêter sur cette « déplourable fin ». Mais l'auteur de la continuation tragique de la Flammette aime les redoublements sinistres à signification ambiguë. Si le récit lui-même, contre les résultats du procès, hésite et ne choisit pas de coupable, les deux amants rivalisant dans l'amour et la mort, le rebondissement final donne aux femmes la victoire ultime : conduites par la reine en personne, elles font payer à Affranio, par un horrible supplice, son triomphe d'orateur.

Nul doute que cette apparente contre-épreuve de Nastagio degli Onesti se retourne aisément en démonstration atroce du sadisme féminin (dans Grimalte y Gradisa, *Flammette brûlait en enfer), mais il reste qu'entre ces deux « victoires », celle de la parole de l'homme et celle du corps déchaîné des femmes, le texte hésite, ouvrant l'espace où viennent jouer les deux faces complémentaires de l'impensable dialogue ; l'amour impossible, et la fantasmatique sado-masochiste.*

Nous reproduisons ici, en plus de la fin du texte, un échange de répli-

ques entre *Affranio* et *Hortensia* au cours du procès. Le débat porte sur la question centrale des rapports de l'homme et de la femme dans la conquête amoureuse. Toujours présente, et éclairant les utilisations respectives de l'argumentation par les deux avocats, la question de l'honneur, ou plutôt des deux sortes d'honneur, fort différentes selon qu'il s'agit de l'homme ou de la femme.

L.G.

HISTOIRE D'AURELIO, ET ISABELLE

en italien et françoys :
En laquelle est disputé qui baille plus d'occasion
d'aymer, l'homme à la femme, ou la femme à l'homme.

Plus la Deiphire de M. Leon Baptiste Albert, qui enseigne
d'éviter l'amour mal commencée.
A Lyon, par Benoist Rigaud.

1574

Hortensia en ceste maniere commença.

Bien que vostre renommée, Affranio, à nous ne fust cogneüe, comme à present elle appert par voz œuvres, non pourtant veux je plustost vaincre le fort & malicieux que le simple & debile : & comme plus courageusement vous vous saurez defendre, à moy plus grande louange sera, savoir vous condamner. Or quant à ce que vous dites, que nous autres pour accomplir nos appetis, mettons toute crainte & honneur en arriere, je respond que contre voz subtiles tromperies & fallaces, nulle est de nous qui puisse faire rempart, ou qui d'elles defendre se sache : & si aucune presume se preparer à la defendre, vostre obstinée iniquité de telles & si merveilleuses fallaces va usant : que là où est la plus grande & excellente chasteté, là moins y peut avoir de resistence. Et pource, comme c'est chose certaine, que les Dames sont de moindre discrétion & jugement que les hommes, cela a faict nostre sexe, au vostre subject. Mais di moy, qui merite plus grand peine de la commise erreur, ou celuy qui a plus grande cognoissance de la coulpe, ou celuy qui en a le moins ? Parquoy je concludz que vous autres estes mieux cognoissans le mal, & vous mesme soycz juge, qui merite plus de mal de nous deux. Mais laissons cecy. Ne voyons nous communement entre les bestes irraisonnables les masles plus que les femelles estre beaux ? Et pour ceste heure je prendray en exemple le paon, luy non content de la beauté des plumes, dont il est couvert, pour complaire de plus en plus à la paonne (qui au prix de luy sans comparaison est plus laide) met en roüe ses plumes dorées : neantmoins la paonne encore veut estre priée. Et en recompense de ce que le paon plus se travaille de luy plaire, plus elle ne le daigne regarder : aussi la plus grande part des femelles, autant d'oiseaux comme de bestes, veut estre priée. Lesquelles après ny pour crainte, ny pour dommage jamais n'abandonnent leur masle. Et ce pource que l'inclination naturelle leur enseigne de tenir cheres leurs propres choses, & que le requerir appartient aux masles. Et ainsi vous hommes, estes de la semblable qualité : car non moins que bestes brutes sans raison, estes reveilleurs de tous telz desirs. Donc par ce que j'ay dict assez appertement, est certain que la deffence est à nous, & le requérir est vostre. Et le tant de peines, melancolies, travaux et entreprises que pour nous dites que faintement monstrez, font assez clere foy, que plus grande folie est la vostre. Et en n'aymant aucunement, faire que nous tombions aux bouches du populaire, pourtant si quelcune se laisse vaincre, c'est par amour. Donc il est cler selon les grands defaux & perilz que nous autres tenons, que si amour ne nous forçoit, que sans estre requises, jamais ne seroit possible, d'avoir de nous victoire. Mais vous hommes, qui sans aimer monstrez amour, voyez combien vous estes dignes de punition ? qui donnez consentement au mal sans vous delecter d'iceluy. Mais que les Dames forcées par amour se laissent vaincre, je ne voy comment on les puisse dire errer, pource qu'à chose si debile, comme sont les Dames, donner & charger si grand faiz, il leur est force d'y ployer ny ne peut Dame aucune voz damnables conseils ouir, qu'en prenant quelcun pour bon ne luy soit nuisible. Mais maudictes soit celle generation, qui toutes ses pensées contre nous adresse à la plus maulvaise part : & est cause, que ceux mesmes, qui pour garde nous sont donnez, nous sont les plus dommageables, & à nos honneurs plus contraires. Et à ceste heure regardez, combien peut vostre iniquité. Que si aucune de grande vertu douée, de vous se saura defendre, elle pourtant ne saura de voz mordantes langues se garder. Car pour vous vanter, quand avec quelques vos amis estes assemblez, vous dites que des Dames, avez eu assez plus que ne seustes demander. Contre telle meschanceté, que pourrons nous faire ? vrayement contre cecy je ne trouve aucune expedience, car sans que nous commettions peché vous nous blasmez : & encores qu'il ne se face, toutesfois il se diz, & par ainsi toutes, ou en la reputation ou en œuvres sommes de vous diffamées. Qui me fait croire que les tourmenteurs d'enfer ne pouroyent plus faire en leur office, que nous hommes faites au vostre. Car encores que les chastes nonnains allent evitant toutes tentations, si ne peuvent elles à peine, des vostres se ramparer, & estiment vos meschancetez estre meilleures que les saints exemples ; en sorte que les jeusnes, abstinences, & dire pseaumes & oraison pour se defendre de vous, peu leur sont profitables, pource que plus vaut une vostre fauce parole que plusieurs veritables predications. Comme donc se defendront celles qui au milieu de leurs ennemis conversent & praticquent ? Et cecy ne sera à autre raison, si ce n'est que les deputez juges (par estre hommes) ne se laissent aveugler d'affection, qui tous vous oste les yeux. Mais si la vérité est honnorée, d'icy vous partirez avec peu d'honneur, & serez condamné : au moyen dequoy vostre obstination cessera desormais de plus dire : & comme Dieu pour les bons souffrit mort, vous au contraire estes venu endurer & satisfaire pour les ribauts. Là ne s'arresta Affranio, mais voyant que Hortensia se taisoit, ainsi dit.

Si vous dictes que plus grand louange vous sera attribuée, de m'avoir condamné, pource que je suis fin & reputé plus savant que les autres. Je veux aussi que vous sachez que je ne feray pas grand estime, & ne prendray guere grand peine de vous surmonter. Et comme aux meslées amoureuses vous estes faciles à conquester, ainsi croy je qu'en tous autres vous le devez estre, & beaucoup plus en cestuy cy, où si grand occasion de verité s'offre. Il me semble toutesfois (si j'ay bonne souvenance) que vous avez dit un exemple du paon, le tirant à vostre propos, lequel entre vous Dames ne peut avoir place, pource que nature vous a enrechies plus entierement de gratieuses beautez, qu'elle n'a les hommes. Et ceste louange je vous donne volontiers, attendu qu'elle duit tant à mon propos, mais vous non contentes de la liberalité de nature, pour mieux dorer la chose dorée, vous cherchez bagues de grand prix, riches vestemens, et fard de diverses sortes. Ces choses donc à quelle fin les faites vous ? Pour certain il est assez notoire, que vostre parement pompeux à vous autres est plus delectable roue qu'à la paonnesse ne semble la queuë, chargée d'ieux, du paon : & à cette occasion on dit communement, qu'on ne sauroit rien veoir au monde si beau que desirer les Dames & damoiselles richement acoutrées, & cela peut servir à mon propos. Et puis que nous tendons à savoir lequel plus l'autre incite à l'amour, cecy manifestement je prouve, pource que la meilleure de vous & plus sumptueusement habillée plus d'occasion donne à aimer, & à cela ne se peut raison contraire. Toutes les autres choses par lesquelles des hommes vous lamentez, ne concluent autre chose en nostre pensée, sinon à chercher nouvelles façons, par le moyen desquelles tromper nous vous puissions : mais cecy je ne veux defendre & ne desire, et aussi je ne le condamne, pource que (comme j'ay dit) entre nous qui plus de vous acquiert est des autres le plus loué. Mais s'il plaisoit à Dieu mettre nouvelle loy au monde, et faire que tous les hommes fussent d'un vouloir, de demeurer quelque temps sans vous desirer à fin d'esprouver vostre vertu, tant peu d'elle je me confie, & encores moins que je ne dy, que certain je suis que vous voyant n'estre plus priées, la necessité vous feroit heritieres de nostre office. Mais vous estant adverties, qu'il nous appartient vous requerir & poursuivre, vostre prudence vous monstre que vous vendez bien cher ceste poursuite. Et tant plus que vous congnoissez nostre condition, car nous prisons tousjours celles sus les autres, qui se font plus chapperonner & prier. Car si nous monstrions avoir plus aggreable celle qui plus tost se rend à nous, certainement nous serions excusez de prendre tant de peine. Mais vous savez bien qu'il vous plaist plus d'estre envers nous desdaigneuses, & cela vous est grande occasion d'estre honnestes, mais ne croyez pourtant que moy, qui vous cognoy bien, en ce cas puisse estre trompé, d'autant que comme plus vous monstrez desdaigneuses, plus me donnez lieu de souspeçon, puis que je say que plus le desirez, quand plus vous vous monstrez ritreuses. Et pourtant si par fortune advenoit que nostre liberté de vous nous fust ostée, je suis certain que sans honte vous nous prieriez comme nous faisons avec vous. Mais qui se trouveroit si fourni de force que de voz mains peust fuyr ? veritablement si ce advenoit (tant je me fie en vostre souverain savoir), que vous nous feriez chercher par les forests & montaignes : encores que preferement avec si grand danger & avec si grand deshonneur vous le fassiez, toutesfois le faictes. Donc par ce que j'en ay experimenté, je vous dy que plusieurs choses perilleuses sont passées touchant ceste matiere, & qui sont advenues à moymesme, lesquelles je tairay, si de vous ne suys contraint à les dire. Ainsi vous povez veoir que vous ne povez refrener à present de babiller. Que feriez vous si les resnes vous estoyent allongées ? Je sçay certainement que tout vostre travail n'est autre chose, sinon que nous n'estimons pas tant ce mal, qui tant vous plait comme vous faictes. Et pource, la honte vous tourmente sans cesse, pource qu'elle ne vous permet ce que tant vous est aggreable. Par quoy on voit journelle-

ment dames de grand estat se soubmettre au gré de leurs moindres serviteurs, & si j'eusse voulu avoir esgard à toutes celles qui à moy se sont
offertes, non une-fois, mais mille & mille, me fusse perdu, & ruyné, mais
raisonnablement j'advisay ce que me devoit suffire, laissant toute charge
dommageable. Or je ne veux plus donner lieu à mes raisons, attendant
que selon que vous vous plaignez de nous autres pareillement vous plain-
drez de voz honneurs, sans donner occasion que les faultes qui sont encores incongneues soyent manifestes à tout le monde.

Fin du roman
(Hortensia à Affranio)

Et pour tant d'icy en avant, ostez de vostre entendement toutes ces pensées amoureuses, & vous pourvoyez de vraye contrition & patience contre la mort : car aujourdhuy par celles que vous avez offensées, vous rece-
vrez cruellement la mort. Et bien que leurs forces soyent feminines & foi-
bles, si n'ont elles pourtant jamais de nul esté offensées, qui à la fin soit
demouré sans offense. Et à fin que vostre mort soit exemple aux autres
d'aspre chastiement, nous avons cherché façon de la faire tant cruelle,
qu'en pensant les tourmens que vous avez à souffrir, je m'espouvente.

L'AUTHEUR

Pendant qu'Hortensia disoit ces raisons, la royne qui, accompaignée de
ses damoiselles, estoit cachée pour tourmenter Affranio, entra en la chambre où il parloit. Et soudainement toutes d'une flotte jetterent le pouvre
Affranio en terre : & tant estroictement luy lierent les mains & les pieds,
qu'il ne pouvoit faire aucune defence. Et après qu'elles l'eurent lié, elles le
despouillerent de ses vestemens. Et à fin qu'il ne peust crier, soudainement avec je ne say quoy lui estouferent la bouche. Ainsi tout nud fut
Affranio à un pilier bien lié, là où chacune d'elles cherchoit nouvelles
inventions pour plus fort le tourmenter. Il y en eut qui avec tenailles toute
ardantes, autres avec les ongles & dents comme enragées le depeçoyent.
Ce pendant il estoit plus que demy mort : & pour plus accroistre sa peine,
ne le voulurent si soudain occire, à fin que les cruelles & dangereuses
playes se refroidissent, & que plus de martire luy donnassent, quand elles
recommenceroyent à luy en faire de nouvelles. En ceste sorte elles estant
lassées de l'affliger, la Royne & toutes ses damoiselles se mirent à leur
aise, & soupperent auprès de luy, à fin que mieux il les veist. Là où
racompterent toutes ses meschancetez, toutes les œuvres malicieusement
par luy faites : chacune concluoit devant la Royne qu'elles ne savoyent de
combien de mortz homme si mauvais devoit estre puny, parlant chacune
de celle que plus elle estimoit. Et pourtant entre les dames se traictoyent
telles choses, lesquelles (comme je pense) donnoyent plus grand martire
au mal d'Affranio que n'eust fait la mesme mort. Et ainsi d'autant que son
œuvre le requeroit, d'autant souffroit il peine de leurs paroles. Mais après
que les tables furent levées, la Royne et les dames derechef se mirent
ensemble pour donner à Affranio très amer soupper. Et fut si bien servy

de divers tourmens en lieu de fricassée, de gibier & autres viandes, de dames & du maistre d'hostel, que je ne say comment se pourroyent escrire tant & si differentes affliction qu'elles luy feirent. Et dura cela jusques à ce que le soleil apparut le lendemain en orient. Et après qu'elles luy eurent desrompu la chair jusques aux os, elles jetterent le reste dedans le feu. Ce qu'après qu'il fut du tout consommé, chacune d'elles print un peu de la cendre pour garder comme relicque, & l'enchasserent en petis vaisseaux d'or, à ce convenables. Et y en eust aucunes d'elles qui la portoyent au col en lieu de joyaux, à fin qu'ayans plus souvent memoire de la vengeance faite, elles eussent plus de plaisir. Ainsi donc la grand malice d'Affranio donna aux dames victoire, & à luy payement de ses merites.

Fin de l'histoire d'Aurelio & Isabelle

Jean Boccace, La Flamette amoureuse, 1343-1532

*Une « complaincte », traduction de l'*Elegia *boccacienne, « très piteuse » dans l'édition parisienne, des « tristes amours » dans l'édition lyonnaise. Redondance de la douleur et du lyrisme. Flamette abandonnée pleure l'infidèle et l'infidélité qui d'abord fut sienne. Peu de péripéties chez Boccace, moins encore dans la traduction française qui omet les rebonds ultimes de la narration. Une rencontre, un « coup de foudre », la passion, le départ, l'exaspération du désir et du remords, la plainte, l'écriture enfin, dédiée aux Dames.*

Le texte fut composé vers 1343, la traduction publiée en 1532. Introduction retardée d'une narration en prose inaugurée par Boccace deux siècles auparavant, proposant dans la simplicité du contenu narratif romanesque une écriture complexe, ambiguë, perverse peut-être puisque cette confession autobiographique d'une femme saisie par le désir, c'est un homme qui l'écrit. Un homme qui prend en charge la culpabilité rétrospective et en même temps l'avidité maintenue d'un désir de vivre et d'aimer. Un nœud plus important peut-être que l'implication moralisante : danger des passions, surtout chez les Dames, qu'elles s'en gardent, si possible...

Malheur à la femme qui cède dit la morale, plaisir pour l'homme qu'elle cède, plaisir aussi qu'elle souffre. Coïncidence, la même année, l'énigmatique Jeanne Flore adapte en ses Comptes amoureux *(cf. l'édition dirigée par G.A. Pérouse aux Presses Universitaires de Lyon, 1980) des nouvelles du* Décaméron *qu'une thématique réunit : la punition de la Dame qui s'est refusée. Deux versants contradictoires et complémentaires qui aboutissent à la même exhibition de la souffrance féminine. Boccace préside, autorise des spectacles également cruels. Les déchirements de la femme par les chiens répondent aux larmes dévorantes dans ces mises en scène de la contradiction entre l'errance du désir et les nécessités de l'appropriation jalouse et/ou de l'institution matrimoniale.*

La traduction de 1532 eut trois éditions mais son succès se mesure surtout à ses retombées : la traduction par Maurice Scève de la suite espagnole du roman italien en 1536, l'émergence enfin du premier roman « sentimental » français en 1538, avec Les angoysses douloureuses qui procèdent d'amour *d'Hélisenne de Crenne.*

Le texte italien n'est pas facile, la traduction s'en ressent. L'écriture est comme rétive devant un objet, un « genre » qui ne lui est pas familier. L'infatigable Gabriel Chappuys se chargea en 1585 de produire une édition bilingue « pour l'utilité de ceux qui désirent apprendre les deux langues ». Nous avons préféré nous en tenir à la version de 1532 puisque c'est elle qui fut d'abord productive et qui permet de se reporter au texte d'Hélisenne (édité par Paule Demats en 1968, les Œuvres *étant par ail-*

leurs reprises en « reprint » chez Slatkine). Nous avons dû confronter l'exemplaire gothique de Lyon à celui « moderne » de Paris.

J.P.G.

FLAMMETTE

Complaincte des tristes amours
de Flammette à
son amy Pamphile
translatée d'italien en françoys.
Lyon, Cl. Nourry

1532

CHAPITRE PREMIER

auquel dame Flammette recite l'occasion de son amour envers son amy Pamphile avec familiere collocution d'elle & sa nourrice.

[...] Ce jour là estoit une feste solennelle à tout le monde, parquoy je me aornay de plusieurs sortes de drapz d'or, et de drapz de soye, cuydant bien estre semblable à l'une des troys deesses, que vit Paris au val de Tenedon, me appareillay pour aller à la feste et cependant que je me miroys comme le paon en ses belles pleumes ymaginant plaire aux aultres comme à moy mesmes, je ne sçay comment tumba du chappelet ou couronne que portoys sur ma teste une fleur qui en fut tirée, comme je croy par main celeste, et volunté des dieux, et cheut à terre près de mon lict, mais je la reprins et la mys dessus ma teste sans penser aux presages et demonstrances occultes des dieux, et m'en allay. O dolente quel plus grand signe d'infortune me pouvoyent ces dieux envoyer : Certes cecy suffisoit avec le precedent songe pour me demonstrer que celluy jour je debvois perdre ma liberté et franchise, et que de dame seigneurialle debvoys devenir serve et subjecte. O si j'eusse eu l'entendement, se j'eusse congneu celluy jour me estre malheureux comme il advint je l'eusse passé sans saillir hors de ma chambre. Mais quant les dieux sont courroucez ou veullent pugnir aulcun, combien qu'ilz leur envoyent quelques signes ou demonstrances pour les inconveniens et dangiers à venir, toutesfoys ilz les privent de la congnoissance et leur ostent l'entendement, et par ainsi en ung moment ilz monstrent de faire faictz et font vengeance de leur ire, et par ce suyvant ma bonne fortune sans nul soucy ou consideration de telz presages saillis hors, et en grande compaignie cheminay gentement jusques à l'eglise où jà estoit commencé le divin service.

Par longue usance en consideration de ma noblesse m'estoit gardé lieu en l'esglise assez excellent, auquel après que fuz assise, gettay le regard de mes yeulx entour de moy et vis multitudes d'hommes et femmes en diverses tourbes faire divers actes, les ungs par saincte devotion prioyent Dieu, les aultres regardant par desir amoureux les plus belles dames en faisant regars par grand affection, je ayant apperceuz plusieurs tant hommes que femmes retournant leur veue sur moy comme si lors Venus ou Minerve feussent entrées nouvellement au temple, et mesmement plusieurs hommes venoyent en circuit autour de moy collaudant ma beaulté dont j'estoys fort contente me glorifiant en moy-mesmes et faignant regarder aultre part, prestoys l'oreille escoutant leurs ditz et aucunesfoys monstrant y prendre plaisir leur gettoys doulx, et amoureulx regardz desquelz prenoyent esperance et s'en glorifioyent.

Cependant que en telle guise et en varietez de mes pensées prenoys plaisir vehement à telles legieres vanitez cuydant que ma jolye beaulté prist et captivast les hommes, mais moy mesmes fuz miserablement et follement prinse, et jà estant prochaine au douloureux point où ma joyeuse et plaisante jeunesse debvoit estre convertie en vie trop angoisseuse et pire que la mort, ne sçay de quel esperit ou fantaisie enchantée par honneste gravité levay mes yeulx et regardant oultre la multitude des jeunes gens estant entour de moy oultre et par dessus ung traversant et agu regard choisy et advisay ung jeune gentil homme à moy estrangier que jamais n'avoys veu, apuyé à une coulonne de marbre droictement devant moy, ne sçay si c'estoit par predestination fatale ou aultrement lequel par sa maniere et contenance estimay beaucoup, ce que jamais ne m'estoyt advenu de nul aultre, car selon mon opinion et jugement, qui encores n'estoye d'amour surprinse, il estoit de très belle forme en ses gestes et contenances, plaisant, honneste en son habit et estat, ayant la premiere barbe crespe et blonde, donnant manifeste demonstrance de sa gentille jeunesse et luy estre gracieux, aimyable et constant. Après que ainsi soubdainement le veis, je regarday et choisis les aultres jeunes hommes assistans l'ung après l'aultre. Mais mon œil par force retournoyt à luy et n'avoys puissance qu'à grand peine d'en retirer mon regard : car desjà avoys en mon cueur sa beaulté, gentillesse, grace et honnesteté, et estoit sa semblance, effigie, ou similitude paincte et descripte en ma pensée qui celleement et taisiblement retiroit mes yeulx à la regarder, et lors que m'en vouloys plus garder, plus d'occasions venoient en ma pensée de prendre plaisir à la veoir. Et souvent en regard simple et bening regardoys plus fermement et par grande affection s'il me regardoit, ne me doubtant des dangereux latz et dars d'amour, rencontray de mes yeulx les siens qui les myens transpercerent jusques au cueur. Et me semble que par icelluy reciproque regard, il me disoit telle parolle — Ma dame vous estes mon seul bien et ma seule beatitude —, je ne mentiray point celle seule doulce ymaginée parolle me fut si delectable qu'elle tira de mon cueur ung gracieux et tendre souspir, qui rapporta de ma pensée telle parolle — et vous la myenne —. Et soubdainement retournée en moy mesmes la reprins, mais le cueur retint en soy ce que ne se pouvoit exprimer par dehors, et s'il eust esté gecté j'en feusse par adventure encore en liberté et dès l'heure je donnay à mes yeulx plus liberal arbitre de regarder seullement celluy dont j'estoys blessée, qui paravant estoit vacabond par tout. Et certes si les dieux qui ont congnoissance de toutes choses jusques à la fin ne me eussent osté l'entendement je ne pouvoys encore estre à moy et en ma liberté, mais toute congnoissance de raison rejectée et laissée, je suyvy l'appetit de ma sensualité, et devins subitement apte et facile d'estre prinse, et subjecte à volunté, parquoy ainsi que la flamme du feu, qui d'elle mesmes saulte d'une part à aultre, tout ainsi les rays de la lumiere subtile de ses yeulx transcourut à moy et frappa les miens, et ne sçay par quelle voye subtillement entra jusques à mon cueur dont je demouray très contente à son soubdain advenement duquel je voulus revocquer et attraire les puissances exteriores. Mais je devins toute froide palle et lassée. La demeure ne fut pas longue que la contrariété survint et ne senty las seullement l'ardeur fervante au cueur, mais les yeulx retirerent la chaleur vehemente, qui chassa de moy la palle couleur, et devins vermeille et chaulde comme feu et en cuydant considerer dont ce me procedoit, fuz contraincte de souspirer, et de celle heure ne peuz jamais avoir aultre pensée sinon de pouvoir faire plaisir et complaire à celluy que j'avois veu, et lequel j'aymois de si grand amour que rien plus.

Et luy aussi sans faire semblant et sans muer lieu cautement regardoit ma contenance et comme expert en amoureuse bataille, congnoissant par quelles armes il pourroit la proie desirée prendre à toute heure par humble semblant se demonstroit pitoyable et plain de amoureulx desirs. O combien de decevance estoit cachée en telle piteuse et faincte maniere comme je congnoys à présent par les effectz qui demonstrent estre partiz de son cueur.

Et afin que je n'aille racomptant tous ses gestes et actes plains de tromperie et faulceté, ou par sa finesse, ou que les dieux par leur vouloir fatal l'ont ainsi ordonné, suis allée en telle adventure que subitement et de telle sorte non opinée que je ne pourroys dire, me trouvay et suis encore prinse et liée de ardente amour.

O mes piteuses et bonnes dames. Ce fut d'oncques celluy qui mon cueur a estimé plus que nul autre entre tant nobles, beaux, preux et jeunes gentilz hommes et non pas seullement ceulx qui là estoient presens, mais de toute ma ville et cité de Naples lequel je choisy seul et dernier pour seigneur de ma vie, c'est icelluy que j'ay aimé et ayme plus que nulle aultre chose qui soit au monde.

Ce fut luy qui debvoit estre premier commencement et l'occasion de tous mes maulx, et comme je pense de ma damnable mort. Celluy fut le jour auquel premierement de dame honnorée, je devins miserable, serve, esclave et subjecte. Ce fut le jour où premierement je congneu amour dont jamais n'avoys eu congnoissance. Celluy fut le jour auquel premierement le venin de Venus contamina et empoisonna mon cueur pur et chaste. O moy miserable combien fut celluy jour là faict ennemy à mon honneur. Mais les choses passées mal faictes se peuvent trop mieulx et plus voluntiers plaindre et blasmer que non pas amender. Toutesfoys je fuz prinse et quoy que ce fust ou furie infernale qui saillit d'enfer pour me tourmenter griefvement, ou fortune à moy ennemie et de la mienne chaste felicité envieuse insidiante, celluy jour avec infaillible esperance de victoire s'en peult vanter et resjouyr.

Ainsi prinse doncques par telle maniere de nouvelle passion et peine estonnée et contraincte de ce furieux et ardent feu, estoys assize entre toutes les aultres jeunes dames au sainct et divin office, lequel à peine pouvoys ouyr et point ne l'entendoys ne semblablement les propos, raisons, et divises de mes compaignes, mais estoit toute ma pensée occupée de l'amour soubdaine et nouvelle qui continuellement estoit en l'œil ou en ma pensée le jeune et nouvel amy, et ne sçavoys dont me venoit si fervent desir [de le voir plus près de moi] et blamoys en moy mesmes la longue demeure qu'il faisoit sans soy remuer comme faisoyent les aultres puis

estimoys que c'estoit par craincte, ce dont il usoit à cautelle. Et si
m'ennuyoient les aultres jeunes gens estant devant moy, par entre lesquelz
j'en regardoys celuy que mon cueur aymoit dont les ungs cuydoient que
mon regard se adressast et tirast à eulx, et que par adventure j'en feusse
amoureuse.

Cependant fut finy l'office solennelle et jà mes compaignes estoient
levées et congneu qu'il falloit partir, à grand peine retiray mon esperit qui
vacquoit autour du plaisant et aymé jeune ymage.

Et quand je fuz levée avecques les aultres retournay mon œil qui ren-
contra le sien demonstrant que ce departement estoit ennuyeux, de là
nous despartismes avecques douloureux soupirs. O dames piteables qui
pourroit croire estre possible que en ung moment ung cueur peust estre si
fort altéré.

Qui pourroit dire que personne ayt jamais veu si soubdainement et de la
premiere veue aucun estre amoureulx en sorte que le departement en desplaise ? Qui imaginera que par ung seul regard on puisse laisser et hayr
toutes aultres choses qui paravant ont esté plaisantes. Certes nulluy, sinon
qu'il ayt esprouvé comme j'ay faict. Hée lasse amour usoit desjà en moy
comme encores faict de crudelité qui oncques ne fut ouye, et me contrai-
gnoit à nouvelle loy differente de toute aultre, j'ay ouy dire plusieurs foys
que aux aultres le commencement d'amour vient de legiers plaisirs et qui
après qu'ilz sont nourryz par longues et continuelles pensées accroissent et
augmentent leur force, à moy n'est ainsi advenu mais tous telz et en telle
sorte qu'ilz entrerent en mon cueur tout ainsi qu'ilz y sont demourez et
demeurent, amour a eu de moy dès le commencement toute entiere possession. Et tout ainsi que le boys verd à peine reçoit la flamme, et ardeur
du feu, mais après qu'il l'a receue la tient, et garde plus longuement, et
rend plus grande chaleur. Tout ainsi m'est advenu qui au paravant tempt-
tée, priée, et poursuyvie fuz de plusieurs, non vaincue d'aulcun fol plaisir.
Finablement fuis prinse d'ung seul regard par ardent desir. Puis que ainsi
est je garderay fidelité plus que nul autre en cest embrasement où à present suis de ce jeune. Et laissant maintes et diverses pensées qui descou-
roient toute celle matinée par ma fantaisie, je vous dis que mon esperit
eschauffé de fureur et ma volunté qui tousjours avoit esté franche et
libere, fut faicte serve et subjecte m'en retournay sans parler, et quand me
trouvay en ma chambre seulle et oysive chargée de divers pensemens et de
grandes sollicitudes fuz incessamment aiguillonnée de la beaulté imaginée, et paincte en ma fantaisie du plaisant jouvenceau considerant la miserable peine où j'estoys si soubdainement entrée.

Finablement feiz en moy mesmes resolution que si je ne pouvoys chasser amour, au moins le gouverneroys secrettement et saigement en mon
triste cueur qui est si difficile chose à faire qu'on ne le pourroit croire qui
ne l'auroit bien experimenté, et ne croy pas que aultre l'en peust faire que
Amour luy mesmes, et demouray ferme en tel propos et si ne sçavoit-on
comment ne de qui j'estoys amoureuse.

Long seroit à racompter, et difficile combien et quelz pensemens j'avoys
de telle amour. Mais je m'esforceray d'en eclairer aucuns qui me advinrent
oultre ceux qui ont accoustumé venir aux amoureulx. Après doncques
que j'euz laissé et oublyé toutes les aultres choses je n'avoys rien plus cher

que de penser à la beaulté du jeune gentil homme que j'aymois, et me sembloit que en perseverant en telles pensées on pourroit presumer ce que vouloys celer et puis me reprenoys moymesmes, mais telle reprehension ne me servoit de rien. Ains donnoit à mes desirs place et lieu, par lesquelz j'appetoys et desiroys sçavoir qui estoit celluy que j'aymois, ce que sceuz subtillement, qui me fut chose très agreable. Et lors je commencay à aymer riches et triumphants habillemens, et diversitez d'habitz, desquelz auparavant ne me challoit, pensant que je luy plairoys plus quand je seroys bien joliement aornée. Et quand je vestoys mes beaulx habitz enrichis d'or, de pierrerie, et aultres aornemens je m'estimoys trop plus valloir. Et commencay à frequenter plus que n'avoys de coustume, les temples, festes, jardins, compaignies, et lieux où se trouvoyent les jeunes gens pour les veoir ou estre veuë et désirée. Non pas sans que premier eusse prins conceil de ma beaulté, grace et contenance à mon mirouer avant que partir de ma chambre. Car certes je perdis l'esperance que j'avois eu en ma premiere nature, et trouvoys de jour en jour nouvelle artifice pour ayder et croistre ma naturelle beaulté pour estre plus elegante ou resplendissante. Et appetant plus d'honneur que devant, m'efforçay d'estre plus courtoise aux aultres dames, affin qu'elles feussent plus faciles à me faire honneur tel ou plus grand qu'il me sembloit appartenir à mon estat et noblesse. Et que par ce, celluy que j'aymois tant eust plus grande estime de moy et avec ce commencay à fuyr avarice où par nature, comme toutes les aultres femmes paravant j'estoys subjecte tellement que j'aymoys mes choses, comme si elles ne feussent miennes et devins liberalle, hardie, et audicieuse, delaissant toute craincte pudique, vergogne, modesteté, et feminine honnesteté. Et aussi mes yeulx qui jusques à icelluy temps usoient de simple et honneste regard furent changez et convertiz à regardz impudiques et artificielz, et pour abreger, je changeay mes complexions, façons, gestes, vouloir, et manieres en opposite sorte, commes celles dames qui se sont trouvées en telz accidens.

Je croy veritablement que jamais l'amour de Tisbée envers Pyradmus ne fut plus fervente combien que par la grand ardeur d'amour s'exposast au peril et dangier de la mort. Car pour l'amour de celluy en qui avoys mis mon cueur n'estoit chose au monde que je ne feisse liberalement jusques à vouloir mourir pour luy si l'occasion de la mort se feust offerte à moy tant estoys de son amour esprinse comme je monstroys par indices evidentz, gestes, exterieurs et manieres de dire, et de faire declaratives de ma très vehemente amour.

Quant celluy que j'aymois se trouvoit en compaignies d'aultres jeunes gens hardiz et audacieux, il se monstroit plus modeste et craintif, et comme s'il eust sceu le propos de mes pensées sembloit qu'il voulsist celer l'amoureuse flamme de notre cueur et me regardoit de discret, secret, et saige regard, et sans mentir quant je voyois sa prudente et saige contenance l'amour croissoit en mon cueur si puissante que mon esperit ne la pouvoit soubstenir comme si le feu d'amour feust allumé par toutes mes puissances. Mais si le commencement de sa veue m'estoit delectable et plaisant la fin en estoit trop plus triste, car quand mes yeulx estoient privez de leur allegresse et plaisir, ilz donnoyent à mon triste cueur trop ennuyeulx desplaisirs, et douloureuse occasion et desplaisans souspirs qui

me mectoyent hors de moy mesmes comme esvanouye me ostoyent tous
sentement et congnoissance, tellement que ceulx qui me voyoient s'esmer-
veilloyent de si soubdaine mutation par ce qu'ilz ne savoient tel accident
d'amours estre venu, et quant venoit la nuict heure de repos, j'estoys tourmentée continuellement comme femme furieuse et ne pouvoys dormir.

Juan de Florès, La déplourable fin de Flamette, 1495-1536.

La Flamette de Boccace n'avait pour fin qu'un épuisement de la plainte dans la convocation traditionnelle du souvenir des Dames illustres et malheureuses et dans l'envoi, à fin d'exhortation morale, du livre aux Dames d'aujourd'hui. Le traducteur français avait d'ailleurs omis ces chapitres. L'Espagnol Juan de Florès s'employa vers 1495 à donner au texte, après maints épisodes romanesques, une fin tragique. Le Breve Tratado de Grimalte y Gradisa fut traduit en 1536, peu après le texte de Boccace et le titre de la traduction explicite la volonté de clore un texte initialement dépourvu d'une catastrophe finale, conformément d'ailleurs à la nécessité structurelle de l'autobiographie fictive.

Florès distancie donc l'histoire intime, invente un dispositif narratif à la fois complexe et naïf. Une jeune dame, Gradisse, émue par le récit des peines de Flamette, a conçu une violente rancune contre les hommes. Elle enjoint à son ami Grimalte de partir à la recherche de Flamette et de se mettre à son service afin de l'aider à reconquérir Pamphile. Grimalte retrouve les protagonistes du roman de Boccace mais ne parvient pas à convaincre Pamphile. Flamette en meurt de désespoir. Grimalte défie alors Pamphile mais celui-ci, converti au repentir par la mort de Flamette, refuse le combat et s'enfuit au désert. Gradisse ne se satisfait pas de cette situation, renvoie son serviteur à la recherche de Pamphile. Après vingt-sept années d'errances, Grimalte retrouve Pamphile en Asie, menant une vie de bête sauvage. Grimalte décide alors de l'imiter. Le récit s'achève sur un tableau de folie désespérée et sur l'apparition de Flamette brûlant en enfer.

Maurice Scève donna du texte une traduction de lecture difficile ; elle figure dans l'édition des Œuvres complètes publiée en 1974 au Mercure de France ; on trouvera par ailleurs dans les Etudes sur le XVIᵉ siècle d'A.M. Schmidt une analyse du texte. Tout cela aurait pu nous conduire à éliminer ce texte s'il ne nous avait pas paru compléter très exemplairement ces premiers essais d'une prose narrative française aussi bien par l'embarras de l'écriture humaniste que par l'inflation extravagante de la ratiocination et que par l'étrangeté sauvage du dénouement.

L.G., J.P.G.

LA DEPLOURABLE FIN
DE FLAMETTE

Elégante invention de Jehan de Flore,
espaignol,
traduicte en langue françoyse

Paris, D. Janot

1536

Pamphile de rechef remonstre à Flamette par vives raisons qu'elle se doibt déporter de ses ardantz desirs, car il n'est deliberé la secourir.

CHAPITRE XIX

Il m'est bien tout notoire (O le seul bien de ma vie) l'affection que tu me portes. Toutesfois si ta superabondante amour n'est egalle à la mienne trompeuse, je ne te suis pour cela occasion de ta mort, mais plustost je te seroys obligé, si de nouvelle façon de vie je te enhortois, & ne penses point que je craigne ta mort, mais ta grand vergongne me faict plus couhart que ta heureuse fin. Pource que nul dolent se doibt douloir sinon celluy qui mauvaise renommée emporte. Voy par exemple les anciens Romains, qui desprisoient la vie pour mourir honnorablement. Mais si la cruelle mort (que tu dis estre appareillée de recevoir) te vainct ne te seroit donné telle louenge comme à celle de Lucresse, de laquelle en sera perpetuelle memoire, dont la fin d'elle est une louenge et exemple de ceulx qui vivent bien, puis, ce que nous debvons garder, & qui nous faict plus d'honneur, le debvons bien tenir, plus cherement je ne sçay quel remede tu te peulx donner, car la personne qui en tout est cause de ses erreurs (et non autre) comme toy, je suis asseuré qu'elle en sera grandement blasmée, car ceulx qui sont de grand extime, sont plus notez en leurs ouvraiges, que ceulx des basses conditions, pource que ceulx qui sont de bas lieu ne peuvent de hault tomber. En maniere que pour estre plus extimée que nulle autre comme tu es, comment sera possible que en estrangieres terres, & en erreurs tant apparentes tu puisses estre mise en oubly ? Regarde que les nobles & grandes dames doibvent estre plus obligées à garder l'honneur d'autruy, que le leur propre, & n'est mal si grief que celluy là, & tu sçays bien que nostre vice a esté commis en ung pays, & tu le veulx faire publier & apparoistre par tous les autres, & toy mesme n'es tu pas plus tenue à vertu que à la vie, voyant que toy ainsi deshonnorée veulx provocquer les autres à tel deshonneur ? Et si de toy tu n'as remors, ayes doleance de l'honneur de ton mary, auquel ce sera ung pardurable deshonneur, qui est plus grief que la mort. Renouvelle donc ta pensée en ton nouveau juge-

ment, & retourne à recouvrer ta vie. Ne veuilles permettre de aneantir tes
honneurs & celluy là des autres, car il est tout clair, que tes desordonnez
appetitz, & frivolles voluntez ne meritent aucun remede, ny du ciel te
peult venir, si tes œuvres ne ameilleurissent. Par ainsi ce que tu endures
est juste, & voy combien que l'affection induyse les hommes, toutesfois
ilz suyvent plustost la raison que les femmes, en evitant les delictz de leurs
voluntez, & ce qui est oultre raison affectionnée, tant plus ilz ont l'œil à
s'en garder, & ce plus souvent, quand ilz accommencent à aymer, comme
à present sont tes desirs. Pourtant de ce que je te prie, c'est pour ton bien
salutaire, & tu penses que je le face pour non avoir amytié en toy. Toutesfoys (comme desirant ton bien) il ne convient te condempner, car certainement il est vray que je ne suis prins aux lacz d'amour pour ceste heure, &
ma descretion est plus prompte pour donner conseil, que de tumber aux
erreurs où tu es, & si tu veulx dire, que quant j'estois amoureux de toy,
autre chose te conseilloient mes parolles, je confesse estre verité. Car alors
comme hors du sens je disoys ce qu'il me sembloit, & à ceste heure que
je congnoys entierement la raison, verité & conscience m'obligent de te
oster hors du chemin, que tu ne puisses estre trompée de ce tyrant & cruel
amour, non seullement toy mais tous ceulx qui le veullent ensuyvre, & ne
croy qu'en ce temps là je te disoye autre chose, sinon ce qui estoit en ma
volunté. Car non moins que toy mesmes je le croioye, pour estre aussi
bien trompé d'icelluy amour que toy mesmes. Et toutesfoys (là comme tu
me disoys qu'il n'y a amour là où il n'y a point d'affection) juste sentence
s'en doibt prendre. De laquelle chose je te prie que tu te tiennes pour vaincue avant que ma forte sentence te condamne, dont ne sera vallable nulle
appellation, & retiens bien mes parolles, comme de celles là par lesquelles
je t'ay vaincue, & regardes comment toutes les choses (voire efforcées)
perissent. Par ainsi nostre amour ne debvoit estre perpetuelle, ains debvoit avoir fin, en maniere que je ne scay où tu as eu meilleur temps, que à
ceste heure de laisser tes superflues faintises, & ne veuilles plus publier
nos faultes & erreurs desjà publiées, & combien que mes conseilz soient
ennemys de tes desirs, après quant tu seras à ta bonne congnoissance
retournée, tu loueras ce que à ceste heure tu abhorris & desprises, & me
seras à tenue pour avoir tant bien pourveu à tes honneurs, & pense sans
doubte, que selon ton grand estat, je ne vouldrois moins que toy avoir
nouveaulx plaisirs, & me associer au joyeulx passetemps passez. Toutesfoys j'ayme mieulx souffrir & endurer en m'efforceant contre les flammes
d'amours, qui sont abregement de vie & d'honneur, que d'acomplir ta
volunté. Non point que (tant pour mes perilz, comme pour les tiens) je
craigne de ce faire, car en mourant je remains en honneur, pour estre
secourable au besoing de tes honnorables louenges, lesquelz (comme deffenseur d'iceulx) je veulx deffendre. Et comme je congnois mieulx ton
peril que toy (si je donnoys lieu à icelluy) je serois jugé pour vray meur-
trier de toy, si a ce que tu requiers je consentoye, & ne fais nul doubte à la
perdition de ton honneur, si à ce remede tu ne obeys. Car comme si tu
estoys morte dès à ceste heure je te pleure.

Comment Flamette indiciblement et grandement remonstre à Pamphile
le tort qu'il a eu de la laisser, veu ses promesses & jurementz, pourquoy
elle n'a plus de espoir en luy.

CHAPITRE XX

O malheureuse celle qui te tient pour amy. Mais dis moy, estoient ilz
telz tes conseilz, quant par amours me requerois ? Les perilz (avecques
lesquelz maintenant tu te excuses) n'estoient ilz au monde lors, comme ilz
sont à ceste heure ? & en ce temps là n'y avoit il aucun cas que tu craignis-
ses, sauf la craincte de ne me pouvoir avoir ? Lors (pour certain) tout ton
penser estoit à me servir, ce que tu as maintenant bien oublié. Qui monstre bien clerement que là où regne couardise, amour n'y est. Par ainsi plusieurs inconveniens tombent sur les froides voluntez, mais qu'est ce à dire
(Pamphile) que en estrange pays, & entre tes ennemys, en desprisant tous
les dangiers du monde, plusieurs foys tu monstrois tes effors, et si osois
bien me poursuyvre ? Dont vient cela que maintenant tu me tiens en ta
terre avecques la faveur de tous les tiens, tu soys si paoureux & couart ?
En quel lieu seras tu desormais plus hardy ? & si alors que tu me poursuy-
vois, l'on te povoit presumer fort audacieux & magnanime, mais ce
n'estoit que amours qui te donnoient couraige de ce faire. Que diray je à
ceste heure, fors que je voy bien que tu n'as plus d'amytié ny valeur, et que
ta qualité & hardiesse est en grand couardise changée ? Bien je t'advise
que la chosc la plus estimée entre les hommes, c'est d'estre courageux, &
ce que plus agrée aux princes, & dames te deffault maintenant, dont suis
contraincte prendre soucy en autres choses trop plus ameres, pource que
je viens à congnoissance de mon grief mal, lequel tu meritois mieulx, pour
estre estimé de peu de valeur, que moy, pour estre desaymée. O si ce
cruel, & non piteux envers moy amour, qui tant griefvement me faict languir, vouloit estaindre ses flammes, lesquelles (combien que jc lc vueille)
ne les puis temperer, pour raison que me y puisse induyre. Mais toy Pamphile, as tu eu la hardiesse de encores fraulder ta nouvelle amye ? Pour
laquelle je suis délaissée, en laquelle esmeue de pitié je la vouldroys adviser de tes fallaces, & lui manifester mes calamiteuses peines à celle fin que
tes mauvaisetiez ne luy fussent cachées, & lui dire comment tu scais bien
contrefaire (quand tu veulx) le visaige triste & appassionné, persuadant à
tes parolles, contrefaisant le mort, transy, dont tu me faisois croire que je
faisois myracle à te ressusciter. O mauvais, malicieux, comment faisois tu
le dolent, là où il ne te douloit ? Je te regarde & ne scay où tu povois
cacher tant de manieres fallacieuses pour me tromper avecques tes exces-
sives importunitez, & ce que je croy que oncques ne fut dit, tu l'as bien
sceu dire à ton advantage, & si telle grace tu avois à ceste heure en te
excusant, comme tu avois lors en me priant, je te croyrois comme je feis.
Car pour certain tu estoys plus doulx à lamenter tes maulx, que tu n'es en
te excusant d'iceulx. Mais je te voys à présent tant mué, que je fais doubte
que tu ne soyes point le mien Pamphile, qui souloit estre en mes consola-
tions tant cher amy : & vrayement je ne croy point que tu le soyes, ne
Dieu ne le consent, ny permet, & ne pense que fortune me l'eust si tost
desrobé. Combien que clerement le veisse à grand peine le scauroys je

croire. Car elle auroit plus de douleurs de ta mutabilité, que ne auroit de ta peine, & n'est possible que tu soyes mon Pamphile, ne qu'il me peust à present dire telles choses. Mais plutost je croy que tu soyes ung autre qui se nomme ainsi, lequel (par juste raison) avecques aucune sienne amye est en debat. Laquelle ayant par adventure meffaict, vous luy donnez telz guerdons comme je voy. Mais moy je ne congnoys chose que j'aye meffaict à mon amy, saulve que je l'ay (peult estre) trop aymé : & puis que ce n'est peché, je ne merite telle peine, ny moins je le congnoys tant injuste que (en non meritant chose aucune) il voulust que je souffrisse peine. Par ainsi il est verité que tu es celluy là, & à moy paovrette tu ne le veulx dire. Car il vault beaucoup mieulx que en doubtant je travaille, que estre certaine & je meure. Voyant que il ne seroit mestier autre cousteau pour ma mort, fors ta grand descongnoyssance, & du peril de mon mary, qui te mect en si grand soucy, je n'en fais tant de doubte que toy, pource que toutes celles qui pechent ne sont si soubdain pugnies. Principallement que moy pour mon adultere seroys beaucoup plustost sauvée par penitence que par mort, & Dieu & fortune useroient plus de cruaulté que de justice, si autre pugnition vouloient faire, sinon à toy, pour satisfaire aux viles erreurs que tu as commis si detestablement envers les femmes, & pour ceci le Ciel, & la Terre se debvroient contenter de tant de maulx que j'ay souffert, sans desirer encores ma mort, en tant que tes parolles ne me peuvent mieulx tromper, que elles ont faict par cy devant, & que tu me tiennes pour si simple & ygnorante, que tu me vueilles faire entendre, que je te soye obligée. Tu laisses ce que tu as crainct, qui est le contraire, en me voulant gecter hors du feu. Tu me fais beaucoup plus brusler en icelluy, par tes desloyaulx propos. Car si vrayement tu estoys bien parfaict en bonté, & aussi en equité, par toutes raisons Loyaulté seroit par toy conservée envers moy, & plus grande que je ne merite, ou sinon que les guerdons & bien meriter me fuyent comme mes ennemys. Après tu scais combien à plusieurs grandz personnaiges ma veue a esté aggreable, & à ceste heure je suis tant envers toy courroucée & ennuyeuse. O dolente que je suis, que chascun par toy tenoys en desdaing. Mais dis moy Pamphile, les festoyementz que tu as receu en nostre pays, estoient ilz de telle sorte comme ceulx là que je recoy presentement, là où je suis venue seullement pour te veoir ? & tu sans vergongne me veulx ainsi envoyer. O infortunée dis moy, de telles recompenses fuz je oncques meritante ? Prens y regard au secret de ton cueur, & comme toutes tes faultes sont hideuses & deshonnestes, tu les vueilles juger. Dont je croy qu'il te viendra une si grande repentence & abhorrissement, que je crains fort que de tes propres mains tu ne te tues, & prendz y donc advis que meilleur remede que desespoir tu peulx prendre. C'est que en estant mien tout le malheur & erreur susdit tu les abolis, souldes, & gueris. Mais quelle folie est à moy, te vouloir degecter de ce que tu te prises & confermes ? Puis que je suis certaine que en te mocquant de moy tu t'en glorifieras ? Plaise à Dieu que le plus grand bien que tu puisses avoir en ceste vie soit, que tu me voyes mourir. Dont demourera à moy pour descharge & memoire de mon meffaict, ce que je t'ay creu & obey. O povrette, appassionnée femme mal fortunée, qui penseroit en tes parolles, qui sont à present sagettes qui percent mon cueur ? Mais qui eust esté tant saige, que tes grandes adulations n'eussent vaincu ? Par ainsi j'entendz bien que si tousjours mais tu me vouldrois vaincre par tes deceptions, me donnant à entendre le contraire de la verité, dont bien tard m'est venue la congnoissance, que tu es, & pour qui tant grands choses j'ay perdu. & ne scay avecques lesquelz aveuglez yeulx je n'y ay pris regard jusques à ceste heure. Car pour certain si j'eusse veu si clairement au commencement, jà ne me feusse laisser vaincre. O Pamphile je ne scay quel bon remede je puisse faire pour te desaymer, jacoit ce que tes œuvres m'y aydent, mais je ne le puis faire. Doncques si ma fortune veult que cecy soit cause de ma perdition comme tu diz, pire sera la journée de ma perte, & nulle chose qui me puisse faire honneur, je ne veulx avoir. Car celle qui a beaucoup perdu pour toy, peult bien mettre en oubly les moindres : & si ce deshonneur me donne la mort que tu m'as annoncée, vienne hardiment pour la fin de mes douleurs, car il ne me sera grief à la souffrir, pour laquelle tu vivras joyeusement sans que nulle te tourmente, en accomplissant tes desirs avecques ta neufve amye jusques à tant ennuyé (comme tu es de moy) je te voye, en luy donnant le guerdon que de toy j'emporte. Mais puis que ainsi est, finablement je ne veulx estre tant secrete en tes erreurs, c'est que je te prie de ne vouloir plus user de tant grands superfluz juremens à celle que tu vouldras tromper, comme tu as faict à moy, tant pour non rengreger tes pechez et coulpe, que pour aussi à celle fin que je ne soye le porte enseigne d'icelles malheureuses.

Grimalte recite les terribles visions de Flamette qu'il veit la premiere nuict, luy estant aux desertz avec Pamphile.

CHAPITRE XLII

Après que Pamphile m'eut ainsi demonstré sa passion, je (pour certain) voyant ses angoysses plus grandes que ne se peuvent penser, avecques mon taire luy accorday la raison qu'il avoit de se tourmenter & affliger : & ainsi se lamentant, & moy perseverant passasmes tout ce jour, & venue que fut la nuict ennemye de tous tristes cueurs, fut festoyé de telles festes solemnelles pour ma bien venue, qu'il affiert à une ame damnée. Qui fut d'une très obscure nuict bien tenebreuse, en la plus froyde montaigne (se me semble) que je fus oncques, pour non avoir accoustumé d'aller ainsi tout nud, pource que ma chair sentoit la force du grief vent froid, & ce m'estoit ung delict, en comparaisons des espoventables visions que celle nuict nous suyvoient en ceste espoisse montaigne. Qui estoient espoventables crys de Flamette très apparentz, avecques douleurs & gemissementz, que nous oyons d'elle, & dès qu'elle fut près de nous approchée, acompaignée la veisme de gens abhominables, dont j'avoye si grand horreur que je ne la sceu veoir. Car la difformité de leurs visaiges, avecques la muance de leurs regardz me deffigurerent plus que la vie travailleuse que j'avoye passée, pource que de leurs bouches sortoient ardantes flammes, si grandes, & avecques ung horrible sifflement, que qui ne l'eust veu, ne le scauroit croire. Concluant que les infernaulx feux que de leurs yeulx, & oreilles sortoient l'obscurité de la nuyt en grande clarté rendoient. D'où la force

de leur grand resplandeur ne me laissoit congnoistre entierement la
maniere qu'estoit Flamette, je dis, car elle estoit de diverses couleurs couverte & enlevée, tellement que je le allay veoir, & elle commença à crier
mon nom, avecques propos de me dire quelque chose, n'eust esté la
grande empesche que luy faisoient ceulx qui la poursuyvoient, & congneu
bien que par force ilz revoquerent ses parolles, pource qu'ilz veoient
auprès d'elle son désiré Pamphile, & là en la tourmentant applicquoient
leurs cruaultez, & pour non tant donner de peine aux liseurs, je ne veulx
compter au long ses griefves mesadventures. Car ilz faisoient tel tourment
en elle que de pure compassion je me cuiday tirer les yeulx hors de la teste,
& ne les povoye tant cacher & clore, que ses gemissementz ne me feissent
bien souvent la regarder, & plusieurs foys luy voulu ayder, mais mes forces tant flacques contre iceulx demonstroient paouvre victoire, de sorte
que aucunes foys ilz la lassoient, & moy (comme son deffenseur) offen-
doient & tourmentoient : & après que la plus grand part de la nuict Flamette eut passé avecques une grand raige, ilz la meisrent au plus hault
d'une cherrue, que deux chevaulx noirs menoient, & des appareilz que je
vey là pour tourmenter la plus que tourmentée Flamette, je m'en tairay,
pour estre chose incredible, & après ainsi estre mise toute nue, monstre-
rent à Pamphile, comment sa descongnoyssance l'avoit mise & muée, de
ce qu'elle souloit estre. & je dis en verité que (selon que par veue j'ay peu
congnoistre) ce estoit la mort, ou ses effectz sembloit, & plus horrible que
les raiges infernalles se monstroit de telle sorte. De autant qu'elle me sembloit en sa vie gracieuse & allegre, d'autant plus elle me donnoit de peine
à ceste heure là à la veoir, dont je ne scay que dire, car en toute ma vie je
ne scauroye suffire à racompter ce que de sa figure m'apparoissoit : &
après qu'elle eut donné à congnoistre à Pamphile combien l'amour d'elle
estoit envers luy, & ayant passé par tant de mondes pour son amour, &
combien elle souffroit pour luy, à celle fin qu'il recordast s'il souffroit la
moytié de ce que sa cruaulté meritoit, en especial pource que la desesperée
mort de Flamette estoit condampnée aux peines infernalles à toujours-
mais, & Pamphile payoit sa penitence en ceste briefve vie mondaine, pour
laquelle amour il y a eu ce que d'amours se merite, & au besoing n'a voulu
avoir pitié d'elle, que au moins il voulust prendre pitié, laquelle certes il
avoit grande comme pour certain j'apperceuz en luy l'avoir telle que ung
bon cueur pitoyable doibt avoir.

Diego de San Pedro, Arnalte et Lucenda, 1491-1539

Les deux romans par lesquels est essentiellement connu Diego de San Pedro, el Tratado de los amores de Arnalte y Lucenda, *et la* Carcel de Amor *(1491 et 1492) sont contemporains de ceux de Juan de Flores et obéissent, dans l'Espagne de cette fin du XVᵉ siècle au même courant romanesque, marqué par la* Flamette *de Boccace et le texte d'Aeneas Sylvius.*

Arnalte y Lucenda *constitue la première ébauche de la* Carcel de Amor *: moins élaboré, moins connu, semble-t-il, en Espagne tout au moins, il utilise une fiction narrative plus simple, celle du récit retrospectif, assumé par le héros lui-même, qui conte à l'auteur son histoire, tout entière colorée par son issue malheureuse. Complainte, donc, surtout, comme la* Flamette, *mais la victime est l'homme, et la femme est la dame sans mercy. Point d'amour adultère, d'ailleurs l'obstacle vient de la dame elle-même. Elle se refuse longtemps, et l'amant mène sa longue quête, aidé par son ami Yerso à qui il a confié son desespoir. Et lorsqu'enfin il croit venue la fin de ses tourments, et qu'elle consent à le voir, il apprend soudain qu'elle s'est mariée, contre son gré, avec Yerso. Il défie le traitre, et le tue en combat singulier. Lucenda le repousse alors, pleure son époux défunt, et s'ensevelit dans un monastère.*

Au service de cette sombre histoire, une mise en scène macabre : comme les héros de Juan de Flores s'en iront mourir au désert, Arnalte, chevalier triste, s'est fait construire une demeure toute noire dans un paysage sinistre, et son tombeau l'attend tout près. C'est dans cet endroit qu'il parle : et son récit nous vient de la mort même, dont est cause la femme, capricieuse et cruelle.

Le traducteur français, Herberay des Essars *(qui traduisit aussi l'*Amadis de Gaule, *et l'*Horloge des Princes*) donne à sa version, en 1539, un sous titre qui insiste sur cette interprétation de l'œuvre : « l'Amant mal traité de s'amye ». Mais, au moins autant que cet imaginaire de la mort, ce qu'autorise ici la structure de quête impossible, de retards et de refus injustifiés, c'est le déploiement d'une rhétorique amoureuse complexe et artificieuse, qui fut sans doute largement déterminante dans l'accueil que le public français fit à ce texte : presque vingt éditions entre 1539 et 1583.*

Nous donnons ici un bref exemple de cette rhétorique, sous la forme de la première conversation qui oppose Arnalte et Lucenda, dans une église où Arnalte, déguisé en damoiselle a réussi à s'approcher de sa Dame.

L.G.

PETIT TRAITE
DE
ARNALTE ET LUCENDA

autrefois traduit de langue
Espaignole en la
Françoyse,
et intitulé
L'Amant maltraité de s'amye
par le Seigneur des Essars, Nicolas de
HERBERAY

Paris, J. de Marnef
et J. Longis

1546

Ah ! Lucenda, Si j'avois autant de sçavoir, pour de toy me plaindre, que tu as de pouvoir à me faire douloir, je ne serois moins sçavant que tu es belle. A ceste cause, je te suplie ne prendre garde à ce que je te diray : mais à la passion de mon cueur, & à l'abondance de mes soupirs, lesquelz maintenant je te presente, pour estre tesmoings de mon martyre. Je ne sçay quel gaing tu esperes de ma perte, ne quel bien de mon mal. Je t'ay escrit que je suis tout tien, & par grand despit as mis ma lettre en pieces. Bien te devoit suffire d'avoir fait le pareil à ma vie par ta grande beauté. Tu devois donc luy laisser faire son message. Lors par icelle eusses sceu en quantes passions j'ay vescu, de puys que je te vy. Ne persevere (je te prie) en si outrageux propos : car trop s'endommageroit ta renommée, & destruirois ma senté. Ou veux-tu chercher excuse valable, pour te servir en ceste estrange façon de faire ? Tu entends les angoisses, avecq'lesquelles ma langue te demande remede, & sçais combien la vertu & la rigueur sont differentes en condicion, & que tu ne peux estre vertueuse, sans estre benigne & gracieuse : Puys doncq' qu'avecq' si peu, que ta seule parole, tu peux satisfaire & recompenser mes services, ne me la denie. Car je ne desire plus grand bien, que ton consentement me pouvoir dire ton serviteur : veu qu'avecq' ceste gloire d'estre tien, le mal que j'ay par toy receu sera satisfait. Mais tu me tiens en grand esbahissement, comme pour si peu de chose, tu consens, si longuement estre importune. Regarde que desjà mes soupirs te font congnoistre, que le peu de ma resistance (veu le rude combat que tu me livres) est si mal ediffié qu'il est plus prest de tost tomber, que pour servir de forteresse à ma vie. Et si tu penses que pour parler à moy (craignant fouler ton honneur) soit à toy trop entreprins, garde en cela te decevoir : car tu recevrois plus de blasme à me faire mourir qu'à fidelement me remedier. Ne veuilles doncq', Lucenda aquerir le nom d'homicide. Ne veuilles, je te suplie, pour si peu de pris, perdre serviteur, & service affectionnez. Je ne sçay plus que te dire pour te faire cer-

taine de mon mal : car je suis nay, non pour acertener : Mais pour estre
fait certain : ayant plus aprins à me douloir qu'à trouver remède. Et
pource que mon vouloir & ton excellence n'ont point de mesure, je ne
veux par long propos te donner ennuy. Suffise toy de voir à veuë d'œil,
que si m'esloignes l'esperance, brieve sera ma vie. Et n'ayant quasi finy
mon propos, d'une voix tremblante me va respondre :

Tu penses bien, Arnalte, par tes propoz affectez, vaincre la force de ma
vertu : mais si ainsi est, tu t'abuses. Car tu dois sçavoir, que je n'ay moins
de confiance à mon peu de defense, que tu as en tes grandes persuasions.
A ceste cause, je te conseille te deporter de telle demande, puys que tu
peux congnoistre, que tu feras saigement. Et à fin que tu en sois plus
asseuré, tu dois croyre, qu'il n'y a force au monde, qui puisse froisser la
porte de mon deliberé propos : par ainsi tu peux voir que tu te mettras
hors de grand labeur, te deportant de telle requeste. Et si à présent j'ay
voulu te respondre, ç'a seulement esté, à fin que n'ayant de moy nulle
asseurance, tu n'esperes nulle recompense : Car en tel cas, l'esperance par
sa condition prolonge plus, qu'elle ne satisfait. Par ainsi tu voys qu'en celà
le desespoir conforte, & le contraire (par un entretien) lasse & estraint.
Et si en mes paroles je ne te montre la rigueur que je devrois, c'est pour
aucunement satisfaire à ta foy, laquelle je congnois. Toutesfois je ne te
veux nier que tu m'aymes, puys que tu me cherches plus que je ne veux.
Ainsi de ces travaux tu seras mal guerdoné. Car je te declare, qu'autant
sera spacieuse l'esperance, comme ta demande m'est importune. Et
pource que (peult estre) tu penseras, que puys que mes paroles sont douces, que mes œuvres ne seront rigoreuses : pour ne te tromper, je te dy
que si du tout ne renverses ton outrageuse affection, & que l'ordre d'icelle
ne pervertisse, je la mettray en main de tel, qui sçaura bien de toy se plaindre & se venger. A ceste cause, c'est mon desir, que sans differer tu sortes
de ce debat : Car tu vois, qu'il est meilleur promptement guerir, qu'à la
longue moyenner sa mort. De celà t'ay voulu aviser : pource que pour toy
y a plus de danger, que de remede. Pourtant loüe mon conseil. Et à fin que
tu ne dies que par paroles je t'aye abusé, je te declare, que grand mal t'en
adviendra, qui peu me sera. Doncques dès à present tu dois mettre en
repos tes desirs, & vivre en paix. Ce que je croy, que tu veux faire : veu
que selon que tes larmes, & tes affections me demonstrent, il te sera plus
agreable me donner plaisir qu'ennuy. Car si tu fais autrement, j'auray la
foy douteuse, que tu publies certaine : & causeras à toy dommage, & à
moy fascherie. Or à fin que desormais tes propoz soient autant discretz,
comme tes souspirs te tesmoignent amoureux, je ne veux plus t'enseigner
le chemin, que tu dois tenir, pour te faire plaisir.

Diego de San Pedro, La Prison d'amour, 1492-1552.

La Cárcel de Amor *fut connue plus tôt en France que le* Tratado de Arnalte y Lucenda, *grâce à la version italienne de 1513 qu'en donna Lelio Manfredi. La première traduction française, établie à partir du texte italien, parut en 1526. L'original espagnol fut publié à Paris en 1548, suscitant un remaniement de la version française. On a dénombré 4 éditions de la première version, et 9 de la seconde à partir de 1552, dont celle de 1583 ici reproduite.*

Du Tratado *qui fut son ébauche, Diego de San Pedro a repris le thème de la longue quête d'amour, et le retournement final tragique, la dame s'esquivant alors que tout semble devoir s'arranger. Mais le texte est beaucoup plus complexe et présente une intéressante utilisation de modèles narratifs hétérogènes. Il débute sur le mode allégorique, qu'apprécièrent sans doute les lecteurs du* Roman de la Rose *rajeuni par Marot, dont Galliot du Pré donna 5 éditions dans ces mêmes années, de 1526 à 1538 : S'étant égaré, le narrateur rencontre un chevalier (Desir) qui conduit vers la Prison d'Amour un triste prisonnier qui lui demande de le secourir. Il le suit jusqu'à la Prison, bâtie sur une pierre qui a nom Fidélité, soutenue par quatre piliers (Entendement, Mémoire, Raison et Volonté), et là, assis sur le siège Affection, sous la couronne de martyr tenue par deux Dames, Passion et Peine, le prisonnier, Leriano, conte son aventure. Le modèle chevaleresque prend alors le relai, associé à l'« analyse » sentimentale qu'autorise le recours au mode épistolaire, pour rendre compte de l'histoire fort compliquée des amours contrariées de Leriano et de Laureole, fille du Roi de Macédoine. Le narrateur se trouve lui-même pris dans l'intrigue, acceptant de servir d'intermédiaire entre les deux amants. Au moment où Laureole enfin vaincue est sur le point de déclarer son amour, un rival dénonce au Roi le commerce des deux amants : sur ses fausses accusations, qui mettent en cause l'honneur de Laureole, le Roi la condamne à mort. Leriano, qui a défié et tué le calomniateur en combat singulier, parvient à enlever Laureole, et à rétablir la vérité. Le roi va pardonner. C'est le moment que choisit Laureole pour décider qu' il est de son devoir de refuser d'épouser celui qui fut l'occasion, même innocente, de soupçons jetés sur son honneur. Le malheureux Leriano, d'autant plus malheureux qu'il comprend les raisons de sa dame, se laisse alors mourir de faim, et expire, non sans avoir d'abord bu dans une coupe les morceaux de la dernière lettre de son amie, et prononcé un long discours à la louange des dames (dernier genre rhétorique travaillé par ce curieux roman).*

C'est donc dans le sens d'un traitement ouvert de la thématique de l'honneur féminin que Diego de San Pedro a travaillé le motif de la cruauté capricieuse de la Lucenda du Tratado *: une autre raison sans doute, outre ce jeu sur des formes littéraires appréciées, du succès du roman.*

Nous avons choisi de donner ici les deux chapitres dans lesquels Leriano, sur son lit de mort, fait l'apologie des dames. On verra que chacun des arguments, pris isolément, n'a rien d'original. Mais leur accumulation qui nous paraît si disparate aujourd'hui (utilisation du christianisme à la limite du blasphème, arguments provenant de la thématique courtoise, sans oublier les bonnes raisons de type économique) illustre de façon particulièrement pertinente les rapports entre les textes de fiction et ceux des moralistes et des polémistes.

L.G.

LA PRISON D'AMOUR

en deux langages
espaignol et françois,
pour ceux qui voudront apprendre l'un par l'autre

Lyon. Rigaud.

1583

Et donnant commencement à l'intention que j'ay prinse, je veux monstrer quinze causes, par lesquelles errent ceux qui jettent leur langue contre
ce sexe, & vingt raisons pourquoy nous leur sommes obligez, & divers
exemples de leur bonté. Quant au premier, qui est de proceder par les
causes qui font errer ceux qui mal en disent, je fonde la première par telle
raison. Toutes les choses faictes par les mains de Dieu sont bonne neces-
sairement : car selon l'ouvrier doivent estre les œuvres. Parquoy estant les
Dames ses creatures, non seulement les offence celui qui les blasme, mais
blaspheme les œuvres de Dieu. La seconde cause est pource que devant
Dieu & les hommes n'i a peché plus abominable ni plus grief à pardonner,
que l'ingratitude. Quelle ingratitude doncques peult estre plus grande que
descongnoistre le bien qui par Nostre Dame nous est venu & nous vient ?
Elle nous delivre de peine, & nous fait meriter la gloire, elle nous sauve,
elle nous soustient, elle nous defend, elle nous guide, elle nous enlumine.
Par elle qui fut femme, toutes les autres meritent couronne de louange. La
tierce est pource que (selon vertu) est defendu à tout homme se monstrer
fort contre le foible : car si paraventure ceux qui langaigent contre elles
pensoient recevoir la defense & contradiction par leurs mains, pourroit
estre qu'ilz auroient moins de liberté en leur langue. La quatriesme est
qu'aucun ne peult dire mal d'elles, sinon qu'il feist deshonneur à soy
mesme, parce qu'il fut creé & fait aux entrailles de la femme, & est de sa
mesme substance : & aussi pour l'honneur & reverence que les enfans
doivent aux meres. La cinquiesme est pour la desobeissance envers Dieu,
qui a dit par sa bouche que le pere & la mere soyent honorez & reverez,
pour laquelle cause ceux qui touchent l'honneur des autres femmes meritent peine. La sixiesme est, pource que tout noble est obligé à soy occuper
en actes vertueux, autant en faicts comme en parolles : dont si les parolles
vilaines maculent la netteté, à grand peril d'infamie mettent leur honneur
ceux qui en telles pratiques gastent leur vie. La septiesme est, que quand
fut establie la chevalerie, entre les autres choses qu'estoit tenu à garder le
chevalier qui portoit armes, l'une estoit qu'il gardast toute reverence &
honnesteté aux dames : & par ceci se cognoit que chacun qui use du contraire, rompt la loy de noblesse. La huictiesme est pour oster l'honneur
d'un peril. Les nobles anciens avec tant grande subtilité gardoient les choses de bonté, & les tenoient en tel honneur, que de chose aucune n'avoient
plus grande peur, que de laisser d'eux memoire d'infamie : ce que gardent

comme il me semble ceux qui preposent la turpitude à la vertu, mettant
une mauvaise note à leur renommée par leur langue : car chascun est juge
en ce qu'il est, & en ce qu'il parle. La neufviesme & plus principale est
pour la damnation de l'ame. Toutes les choses prinses se peuvent satisfaire, mais à la renommée ostée la satisfaction est douteuse, ce que plus
amplement determine nostre foy. La dixiesme est pour eviter inimitié.
Ceux qui emploient leur temps à offenser les dames se font ennemis d'icelles : & non moins des vertueux, car comme la vertu & immodestie sont
differentes en propriété, elles ne peuvent demeurer sans inimitié.
L'unziesme est, pour les dommages qui procedent de tel acte malicieux :
car comme les parolles ont puissance d'entrer autant ès aureilles des simples comme des sages, eux oyans tant soient petites les opprobrieuses
parolles distes des dames, & se repentans d'avoir prins femme, leur font
mauvaise vie se departent d'elles, ou par aventure les tuent. La douziesme,
pour les murmures qui moult se doivent craindre estant un homme dif-
famé pource qu'il est mal disant : en places, maisons, & aux champs : &
quiconque soit il retire à luy son vice. La xiij est la raison du peril : car
quand les mal disans sont cogneuz pour telz, ilz sont tant hays de tous,
que chascun leur est contraire : & aucuns pour satisfaire à leurs amis,
pose qu'ilz ne le demandent, ni ne les en requerent, mettent les mains sur
ceux qui mettent leur langue sur tous. La quatorziesme est, pour la beauté
qu'elles ont, laquelle est de telle excellence, qu'encores que soyent com-
prinses toutes les choses que les mal-disans leur attribuent, il y a plus à
louer en une avec verité, qu'il n'y a à vituperer en toutes avec malice. La
quinziesme, pour les grandes choses dont elles ont esté causes. D'icelles
nasquirent hommes vertueux, qui ont faict œuvres dignes de louenge.
D'elles procedent les sages qui ont enseigné à congnoistre quelle chose
estoit en Dieu, en la foy duquel nous sommes sauvez. D'elles sont venus
les inventeurs qui ont basti citez, forteresses, & edifices de perpetuelle
excellence. Par elles sont venus les hommes tant subtilz qui cerchent toutes les choses necessaires pour la substance de l'humain linage.

LERIANO DONNE

aucunes raisons pourquoy
les hommes sont obligez
aux dames.

Tefeo, puis que tu as oui les causes pourquoy tu es coulpable, toy &
tous ceux qui suivent opinions tant erronées : toute prolixité laissée,
j'ajoute plusieurs raisons par lesquelles je m'offre prouver que les hommes
sont obligez aux femmes. La premiere desquelles est, pource qu'elles dis-
posent les simples & rudes à l'acquisition de la vertu de prudence. Et non
seulement sont sçavans les ignorans, mais les mesmes sçavans plus subtilz,
de sorte que s'ilz se font prisonniers de l'amoureuse passion, ilz estudient
tant pour leur liberté, que edifiant le sçavoir avec la douleur, ilz dient
parolles tant douces & bien composées, qu'aucunes fois de compassion
qu'elles ont, ils sont deliez d'icelle : & les simples de leur nature ignorans,

quand ilz se mettent à aimer, ilz entrent avecques une lourderie, & treuvent l'estude du sentiment tant subtil, que plusieurs fois en sortent sçavans : en maniere que les dames fournissent en eux, ce que default la nature. La seconde raison est, pource que par la vertu de justice, telles nous font tant bien souffrir, que les tourmentez d'amour (encores qu'ilz reçoivent peine oultre mesure) ont ceste vertu pour reconfort : eux justifians par ce que justement ilz souffrent : & non pour ceste seule cause nous font jouir de ceste vertu, mais pour une autre qui leur est naturelle. Ceux qui aiment fermement pour s'accomoder avec celles qu'ilz servent, cerchent toutes façons qu'ilz peuvent à cela propres, par lesquelz desirs ilz vivent justement, sans exceder les choses d'équalité pour ne se conformer aux mauvaises coustumes. La tierce est, qu'elles nous font dignes de la temperance : car à fin que ne leur soyons en horreur & fascherie, & par ce moyen venir à estre hahys d'elles, nous sommes temperez au manger & au boire, & en toutes autres choses qui suivent ceste vertu. Nous sommes temperez à la mesure, nous sommes temperez aux œuvres, sans que sortions un point hors de l'honnesteté. La quatriesme est pource qu'elles donnent la force à qui elle default, & l'accroissent à celuy qui l'a. Elles nous font forts pour souffrir, nous causent hardiesse pour accomplir, & nous donnent courage pour esperer. Quand le peril s'offre aux amans, aussi leur apparoit la gloire. Ils tiennent les effrayemens pour vice : & estiment plus la louenge de l'amie, que le loyer de vivre longuement. Par elles se commencent & achevent les hautlz & excellens faictz. Elles mettent la force à qui la merite, & à cela se peult juger si nous leur sommes obligez. La cinquiesme est, pour le bon conseil que tousjours elles nous donnent : car il eschet aucuncs fois qu'on treuve en elles un soudain admonestement, ce que nous autres avec longue estude & diligence cerchons. Leurs conseils sont pacifiques sans aucun scandale. Elles evitent beaucoup de meurtres, elles gardent la paix, refrenent l'ire, appaisent la colere, & leur advis est tousjours sain. La sixiesme, pource qu'elles nous font honneur : avec elles se traitent grans mariages, avec rentes & revenu. Et pource qu'aucun me pourroit respondre que l'honneur consiste en vertu, & non en richesse : je dis qu'elles sont autant cause de l'un que de l'autre : & nous donnent des presumptions & hardiesses tant vertueuses, que par elles nous acquerons les grans honneurs & louenges que nous desirons. Par elles estimons plus la vergongne, que la vie. Par elles estudions toutes les œuvres de noblesse : & par elles nous les mettons en la hautesse qu'elles meritent. La septiesme raison est, que nous separant de l'avarice elles nous accompaignent de liberalité, duquel œuvre nous gaignons la benevolence de tous, car comme elles nous font largement despendre ce que nous avons, nous sommes louez & tenuz en moult grand amour : & en quelconque necessité qui nous surviene, nous recevons aide & service. Et non seulement nous font prouffit à nous faire user de liberalité comme nous devons, mais nous mettent en meilleure garde : pource qu'il n'y a lieu où soyent les richesses plus seures, qu'en la benevolence des gens. La huitiesme est, pource qu'elles accroissent & gardent noz possessions rentes, lesquelles les hommes acquerent par fortune, & elles les gardent par diligence. La neufiesme est, pour la netteté qu'elles procurent en noz personnes, comme au vestir, au manger, & en tout ce que nous faisons. La dixiesme, pour les bonnes accoustumances qu'elles mettent en nous (une des principales choses de quoy les hommes ont besoing) & estant ainsi bien accoustumez, nous usons de courtoisie & fuyons la gravité : sçavons honorer les moindres & servir les plus grands. Et non seulement nous font bien accoustumez, mais bien aimez : car quand nous traictons chascun selon son merite, chascun nous donne ce que nous meritons. La unziesme est, pource qu'elles nous font estre gaillarts hommes. Par elles nous nous eveillons en vestemens : par elles nous estudions maintien & gestes : par elles nous nous aornons, de maniere que par industrie nous mettons en noz personnes la bonne disposition que nature nie à aucuns. Par artifice se dresse le corps, en portant l'habit avec maistrise. Et par le semblable se mettent les cheveux qui defaillent & amenuisent & engrossissent les cuisses, & jambes s'il convient le faire. Par les dames se trouvent les gentilz entailleurs, les ingenieuses borderies, & nouvelles inventions : de grans biens pour certain sont cause. La douziesme raison est pource qu'elles nous accordent la musicque, & nous font jouir de la douceur d'icelle : par elles se sonnent les douces chansons, par elles se chantent les vers elegans, par elles s'accordent les voix : Par elles s'aguisent & assubtilent toutes les choses qui consistent à chanter. La xiij. est par ce qu'elles accroissent les forces à ceux qui jettent les dardz & saiettes, la subtilité aux luiteurs, la legereté à ceux qui font tours d'agilité de corps, courent, sautent & font autres choses semblables. La xiiij. raison est, pource qu'elles conjoingnent les graces avec ceux, lesquelz (comme est dit) sonnent des instrumens & chantent pour elles, & tant se reveillent qu'ilz montent au plus parfaict qu'en icelle grace se peult acquerir. Les inventeurs mettent pour elles tant d'estudes en ce qu'ilz treuvent, que ce qui est bien dit font sembler meilleur : & tant subtilement s'aguisent l'esprit, que avec nouveau & gentil stil mettent en invention ou chanson ce qu'ilz veulent dire. La xv. & derniere raison est, pource que nous sommes enfans de femmes : par lequel respect nous sommes plus obligez que par aulcunes desdictes raisons, ni par beaucoup d'autres qui se pourroient dire. J'auroye beaucoup d'argumens pour monstrer combien nous hommes sommes redevables à ce sexe feminin : mais la disposition mienne ne me concede les dire toutes. Par elles s'ordonnent les joustes Royalles, les pompeux tournois & les joyeuses festes. Par elles sont les graces proufitables, & se commencent & finissent toutes les choses de gentillesse. Nous n'avons cause aucune par laquelle doivent estre de nous vituperées. O coulpe meritoire de grieve punition, que pource qu'aucunes ont pitié de ceux qui souffrent pour elles, ilz leur donnent telle desserte. Quelle dame de ce monde n'auroit compassion aux larmes que nous espandons & aux appassionnées parolles que nous disons, & aux soupirs que nous jettons, qu'elles ne donneroit foy aux jurées parolles ? Qu'elle ne croiroit à la certifiée foy ? Qu'elle n'esmouveroit les grandes liberalitez ? En quel cœur ne feroient fruict les deues louenges ? En quelle volonté ne fera muer la fermeté certaine qu'elle se pourra defendre de continuellement estre suivie ? Pour certain selon les armes avec lesquelles sont combatues, quand encores la moindre partie d'elles se defendist, ne seroit chose de soy esmerveiller : mais devroient celles qui ne se peuvent defendre estre plus tost louées pour piteuses que blasmées pour coulpables.

La reviviscence chevaleresque

Garcí Ordonez de Montalvo, Amadis de Gaule, 1508-1540.

Sans vouloir rentrer ici dans les controverses sur les origines de l'Amadis de Gaule, rappelons seulement que la première édition connue en espagnol, œuvre (ou remaniement d'un texte antérieur) de Garcí Ordonez de Montalvo), date de 1508.

Si l'on peut parler à cette époque de « best-seller », ce roman, à coup sûr en fut un, pour toute l'Europe du XVIᵉ siècle, et particulièrement pour la France. Servis par un excellent traducteur, Herberay des Essars, les éditeurs Longis, Janot et Sertenas, comprirent très vite quel parti pouvait être tiré de l'engouement du public pour ce roman de chevalerie attardé, un des rares livres de son espèce que les censeurs du temps, comme le curé de Don Quichotte, consentirent à sauver. Qu'il s'agit d'une opération commercialement rentable, on s'en aperçoit à mesurer les exigences croissantes du traducteur dans les contrats successifs qui le lient à ses éditeurs. Après Montalvo, ce sont ses continuateurs espagnols qu'Herberay traduit, pour les huit premiers livres, relayé pour les suivants par C. Colet, J. Gohory, G. Aubert... Les éditions se succèdent, de somptueux exemplaires in-folio illustrés des années 1540 à 1550, aux tout petits formats pour les dames de la fin du siècle, tant à Paris, qu'à Lyon ou Anvers. Et la traduction française sert de base à la plupart des versions européennes du temps.

Une précieuse indication sur l'utilisation qui put être faite de ce texte nous est fournie par les « Thresors d'Amadis », c'est « assavoir les Harengues, Concions, Epistres, Complaintes, et aultres choses les plus excellentes et dignes du lecteur françois » : recueils de morceaux choisis, très vite organisés par rubriques, et assortis d'une table des matières, destinés comme l'explique le compilateur anonyme de la première édition, à fournir aux bons esprits « le moyen et grace de harenguer, concioner, parler et escrire de toutes affaires qui s'offriront devant ses yeux ». La jeune noblesse française, précisent les éditions postérieures, trouvera là discours modèles, et lettres admirables, susceptibles de lui venir en aide dans les situations multiples et variées.

Ce roman semble donc avoir rempli une double fonction : manuel de civilité, code régulateur des rapports humains en société et spécialement dans la société de cour, et entretien rassurant, sur le mode de la fiction et sous des formes renouvelées, de la morale chevaleresque, rêve d'un monde régi par de toutes autres lois, et où une telle morale n'a plus guère de place réelle. La délicieuse infidélité de la traduction d'Herberay trouve d'ailleurs très exactement son sens dans ce double objectif. Il convient d'ajouter qu'aux yeux de bien des écrivains du temps, traducteurs, mais aussi poètes à la recherche des nouvelles beautés de la langue vulgaire, la prose d'Herberay des Essars figure comme l'exemple d'une inaccessible réussite, ayant atteint, écrit en 1546 Jean Maugin, à une « douceur de phrase, propriété de termes, liaison de propos, et richesse de sentences telle, que plu-

sieurs lisans cette *nouveauté de bien parler*, desperent en aprocher tant
s'en faut qu'ilz y puissent ataindre ».

Nous avons choisi à dessein deux passages où la veine descriptive et rhétorique du traducteur se donne libre cours, developpant et modifiant con-
sidérablement l'original espagnol : deux moments des amours d'Amadis
et de la princesse Oriane qui constituent le fil conducteur des premiers
livres.

Le dialogue amoureux du premier extrait (I, ch 15) joue subtilement sur
le heurt des deux rhétoriques ; le discours d'inspiration courtoise d'Amadis s'opposant au néoplatonisme de la réponse d'Oriane (élément parfaitement étranger au texte espagnol) : brillant maniement des mots et des for-
mules, pur jeu rhétorique qu'on rapprochera avec intérêt de la nouvelle
10 de l'Heptameron, dont les héros, Amadour (justement) et Floride sont
aux prises avec les mêmes contradictions discursives. On n'en saisira que
mieux l'humour du traducteur, qui feint de masquer et dévoile sans cesse
le véritable objet commun aux deux discours, souriant, de connivence
avec le lecteur, comme Oriane, lorsqu'elle découvre, au bout de tous ces
mots, « qu'elle n'a pas esté du tout entendue ».

La scène d'amour du chapitre 36 isole les deux amants dans un lieu
idéalement naturel qui rejoint la tradition médiévale. Mais si le frais val-
lon symbolise la nature tout entière où donner son sens à l'amour, il est
aussi, bien plus explicitement que dans les anciens romans, le retrait idéal
loin de la société qui juge, et la condition même de l'innocence de l'acte.
Et un autre regard se glisse, qui viole cette solitude, non pas pour la condamner, mais pour en jouir : ici encore, l'érotisme du texte est le fait du
seul traducteur.

                                                          L.G

LE PREMIER LIVRE
D'AMADIS DE GAULE,

Mis en françoys par le Seigneur
des Essars Nicolas de Herberay,
Commissaire ordinaire de l'artillerie du Roy &
Lieutenant en icelle, ès païs & gouvernement
de Picardie, de monsieur de Brissac,
Chevalier de l'ordre, grand Maistre &
Capitaine général d'icelle artillerie.

Paris, Estienne Groulleau

1548

CHAPITRE XV

[...] Venue l'heure de dormir, chascun se retira comme ilz avoient de coustume : et peu après voyant Amadis temps commode à son entreprise, se leva, et trouva Gandalin qui avoit ja mis son cas en ordre, parquoy il s'arma, et monterent à cheval, prenans leur chemin vers la ville. Et arrivez près le jardin, que Oriane le soir de devant avoit monstré à Gandalin, descendirent, et attacherent leurs chevaulx joignant une touffe d'arbres. Puis entrerent dedans le jardin, par ung trou que les torrens avoient nagueres fait à la muraille, et s'approcherent de la fenestre, que Oriane avoit monstré (le jour precedent) à Gandalin : lors frappa Amadis tout bellement contre. Pas ne dormoit à l'heure celle qui attendoit leur venue, ains ayant ouy le bruict, esveilla Mabile, et luy dit : Ma cousine, je croy que vostre cousin frappe à ceste fenestre. Mon cousin, respondit Mabile, il peult bien estre : mais vous avez plus de part en luy, que tout son lignaige ensemble. Lors se leva Mabile, et print ung flambeau qui estoit caché derriere une tapisserie, et esclaira à Oriane qui se leva, et ensemble vindrent ouvrir la fenestre où elles trouverent Amadis, non moins attendu que attendant. Si ilz furent bien aises, il ne s'en fault enquerir : car tous les contentemens du monde ne sont qu'ennuy en comparaison de celuy qu'ilz receurent de s'entrevoir. Et sans point de doubte, ilz en avoient tous deux raison : car oultre la nourriture qu'ilz avoient prise ensemble dès leur jeune aage, et leur premiere amytié, continuée par la souvenance et bonne opinion qu'ilz avoient tousjours eue l'ung et l'aultre, leur beauté estoit si grande, que quand ilz ne se fussent jamais entreveuz que lors, si avoient ilz, cause de s'entreaymer. Oriane qui l'attendoit s'estoit coiffée à son advantaige si proprement que jamais n'avoit esté mieulx pour la nuict, car par dessoubz ung blanc et delié couvrechef mis bien en arriere paroissoient les plus blonds et les plus crespes cheveulx que jamais feit nature. Sur ses espaules

avoit jecté ung manteau de toile d'or figurée, et rehaulcée de menues fleu-
rettes, decouppé et enrichy de la meilleure grace du monde. Et bien que de
soy, elle eust le plus beau, et le plus cler taint qu'il estoit possible, l'aise et
l'émotion en quoy elle estoit, luy avoient d'advantaige apporté une couleur si vive, et si belle, qu'il sembloit que nature se fust delectée à la faire
première en toute perfection. Je vous laisse donc penser quel jugement en
feit Amadis, lequel (quand bien elle eust eu moins de beaulté) l'aymoit
tant, qu'il eust trouvé en elle tout ce qui y estoit, l'y trouvant doncques et
l'aymant, ne sçavoit s'il se trouvoit luy mesme. Et devint si esperdu, que
son grand aise cuida (pour occuper trop de place en son cueur) en chasser
l'ame dehors. Dequoy elle s'apercevant, s'approcha, et parla la première,
disant : Monseigneur, si je vous ay donné la privaulté (contre mon devoir
et ma coustume) de me laisser voir en tel lieu, et à telle heure qu'il est,
vous en donnerez, s'il vous plaist, la coulpe à la seureté que m'a promise
de vous nostre premiere nourriture, et à la bonne opinion que depuis en
ont augmentée vos grandes vertus, qui ne vous ont acquis en moy moindre faveur, qu'en tous aultres lieux grande renommée.

Amadis pour ne demeurer muet, ayma mieulx ouvrir la bouche, et laisser sortir paroles à l'aventure, que se taisant, sembler ou peu estimer ce
grand heur, ou moins aymer qu'elle, qui avoit eu la force de commencer,
et deit ainsi : Madame, je ne me sens si favorisé de la fortune que je
n'estime l'honneur d'avoir esté des premiers en vostre service, le plus
grand bien qu'elle m'ayt jamais fait, ny ne me sens tant tenu à ma vertu,
que je ne reste trop obligé à ceulx qui font bon rapport de moy. Mais
quand bien l'ung ne l'aultre ne seroit point si ay je une amytié envers vous
si grande, et une servitude si affectionnée, que elle seule ne povoit riens
moins meriter que vostre fiance et privaulté : laquelle quand bien il vous
auroit pleu me donner encores plus grande, elle auroit bien peu accroistre
mon obligation, mais non point l'affection, qui est telle, que pour bien
que sçachiez faire, elle ne sçauroit augmenter, ny pour peine diminuer. Et
ne sçay s'il seroit bien seant à ung homme de confesser les estremitez en
quoy je me suis infinies fois veu par ceste passion. Le moindre ennuy que
j'en ay receu a esté la perte du repos, et avoir banny le sommeil de mes
yeulx, si ce n'a esté pour encores plus me travailler, me representant en
songe, ce que mon esprit voit et desire incessamment. Quantesfois m'est il
advenu pensant en vous, me ravir telement, que à ceulx qui me voyoient,
je semblois non seulement privé du sens commun, mais de la vie mesmes ?
Quelle femme, quel enfant bien batu, versa jamais tant de larmes, que
moy chevalier au milieu des plus fortes entreprises en ay respandues pour
vous, non pour ne me sentir avoir trop heureux subject en amour, mais
pour m'en sentir avoir trop peu de merite, et encores moins d'esperance ?
Et bien que ceste faveur que vous me faites de me daigner ouyr, soit plus
grande que je n'eusse osé l'esperer, si elle est si surmontée de ma passion,
que je ne puis exprimer la moindre partie de ce que je sens, et demeure ma
langue presque inutile, et non sachante son office, qui si bien et si longuement loing de vous avoit accoustumé de me servir. Mais à tout le moins
ceste impuissance de parler m'aydera à vous tesmoigner ce que toutes les
paroles du monde ne sçauroient assez au vray vous exprimer. Car tout
ainsi que toutes les aultres beaultez et perfections devant la vostre devien-

nent riens, ainsi devant mon affection, toutes les aultres puissances de mon ame disparoissent, et deviennent nulles. Vueillez donc, madame, par vostre courtoysie, supplier mon insuffisance, et deliberez de (avec pitié) me rendre la vie et moymesme, et conserver ce qui ne peult estre, s'il n'est vostre.

Ces paroles proferoit Amadis si interrompues de sanglotz et de frequentes larmes, qu'il declaroit assez qu'il n'y avoit point de fainte, et qu'il sçavoit plus souffrir que dire. Dont Oriane ayant compassion luy dit : Je ne fais doubte, mon amy, que vous ne m'aymez tant pour les peines qu'avez prises pour moy, que pour ce que vous dites. Et quand je n'en aurois nul enseignement de parole ne d'effect, si suis je contente de le croire, pource que mon cueur n'a d'aultre desir, et en cela me sens grandement satisfaite. Mais le tourment en quoy je vous voy, et l'impatience que vous vous donnez, trouble mon aise . car vous ayant asseuré par assez d'espreuves, et mesmes par ceste cy, que je vous ayme, il me semble que nous n'avez plus d'occasion de si fort vous affliger, et que vous deviez temperer vos peines, lesquelles (pour l'union de noz espritz) je sens non moins que vous mesmes. Si doncques vous ne les appaisez pour l'amour de vous, je vous prie le faire pour l'amour de moy, mesmement que ayant (s'il vous plaist) à nous entrevoir souvent, et en publicque, cela ne pourroit servir sinon à descouvrir ce que nous vouldrions estre incongneu, dont trop de mal nous pourroit advenir, et pour le moins empescher ce que nous desirons le plus. Madame, dit Amadis, j'ay tant de bien et de felicité de vous voir et ouyr, que ne me trouvant forces pour soustenir le fais de si grand contentement, je suis contraint de tomber dessoubz, experimentant non moindre la peine du non accoustumé plaisir, que celle de la continuelle tristesse, et m'esbahis comme j'ay peu ne mourir point icy. Si doncques je vous ai offensée de ceste transportation, pardonnez la à vous mesmes, qui m'avez apporté cest heureux malheur, et donné ceste nuysante medicine, et souffrez que usant d'elle plus avant, et de l'asseurance de vostre bonne grace, je m'accoustume peu à peu à la supporter, et à sçavoir vivre content, et excusez en ce grand heur mon apprentissaige, qui n'en sçait encores prudemment user. Amour est maladie, et soit il favorable, ou contraire, il ne peult estre sans passion, qui rend à chascun l'effect que vous reprenez en moy. Bien dites vous, amy, respondit Oriane, que vous estes encores apprentif, et bien le monstre vostre propos, qui ne voulez amour povoir estre sans passion. J'espere voir le temps, que vous ayant de luy encores plus grande et plus perfecte partie que vous n'avez, serez en plus grande tranquillité d'esprit, que peult estre vous n'estimez qu'on puisse avoir en ce monde : et ce ne vous adviendra par l'admiration de ce que pour ceste heure vous aymez le plus, et qui est le moins, mais par la fruition de ce où gist la felicité, la cognoissance dequoy unit et eslieve les espritz jusques au ciel. Et bien que j'aye encores si peu d'aage et d'experience que je ne me puisse exempter du mal dont vous plaignez, si ne suis je despourveue du desir de nous en voir ensemble dehors, et vivre quelque fois heureux et contens.

Ha madame, dit Amadis, l'esperance de celle heureuse journée me fera passer ceste penible vie en patience, supportant pour l'honneur de vous les peines intérieures le plus couvertement que je pourray, et entreprenant

celles de dehors le plus courageusement qu'il me sera possible : mais je
vous supplye me faire ceste grace de me dire quand elle sera. Bien cogneut
Oriane qu'elle n'avoit pas esté du tout entendue, et en soubzriant luy dit :
Elle est desjà commencée, mais vostre œil esblouy ne la voit point. Lors
commença Amadis à devenir pensif, tenant l'œil arresté sur elle : et elle
pour l'en divertir, meit la main hors du treillis, et empoigna la sienne, et
Amadis se meit à la baiser mille fois, sans sonner l'ung ne l'aultre ung seul
mot. Ce que voyant, Mabile, s'approcha et leur dit : Seigneurs, vous vous
oubliez. Amadis leva lors le visaige, la salua de bon cueur, et elle luy. Et
après quelques propos communs de sa bien venue, et du long desir qu'elles
en avoient eu, Mabile luy demanda combien il deliberoit demeurer en
celle court. Autant qu'il plaira à Madame Oriane, respondit Amadis. Ce
sera doncques tousjours, dit Oriane, et de ma partie vous en supplie, si le
Roy vous en requiert. Madame, dit il, s'il me fait cest honneur, je luy
obeiray et à vous, mais ce sera après longue dissimulation. Ce sera bien
fait dit Mabile, et ce pendant je vous prie nous voir souvent. Et voulans
continuer plus longuement leurs devis, Gandalin, qui faisoit le guet, veid
que l'aube du jour apparoissoit, parquoy dit à Amadis : Monseigneur, je
scay que je vous seray importun, mais il fault que vous en accusiez le jour.
Amadis n'en tenoit compte et prolongeoit son propos, mais Oriane
voyant que Gandalin disoit vray, et craignant qu'ilz ne fussent apperceuz,
dit à Amadis : Monseigneur, allez vous en s'il vous plaist, car il en est
temps, et ne m'oubliez vostre promesse. Lors print de rechef sa main, et la
baisa. Puis monta à cheval, et revint au boys trouver les deux seurs
damoyselles, lesquelles à grande requeste luy persuaderent d'aller delivrer
leur cousine que le Roy retenoit captive, jusques à ce qu'elle eust repre-
senté son champion, ce avoient elles entendu. Parquoy après avoir pris ce
jour repos, le lendemain retourna à la ville, en grande faveur et expectation de tout le monde.

CHAPITRE XXXVI

Et ainsi s'equipperent, et s'en partirent avec autant de plaisir que l'on
sçauroit estimer. Amadis conduisoit son Oriane tenant les resnes de son
pallefroy, et elle luy recitoit en cheminant la peur qu'elle avoit eue des chevaliers qui gisoient mors. Et telle, disoit elle, que je ne me puis encores
asseurer. Madame, respondit Amadis, trop plus grande a esté la peine que
j'ay receue d'une personne vive, et moins espoventable que les mortz, lesquelz ne peuvent faire mal, mais ceste là, pour sa beaulté, me fait mourir.
Encores que Oriane l'entendist bien, elle luy demanda : et qui est ceste
personne ? Vous, Madame, dit-il, qui me tenez en telle vie, qui est plus
penible que la mort. Mon amy, dit elle, jamais de mon consentement vous
n'eustes mal, et serois bien marrie de le vous avoir prochassé : car plustost
y remedirois, si j'avois le povoir. Madame, vous seule sans le prochasser
le m'avez fait, et vous seule en avez le remede, que je prochasse, et n'est
inconvenient que de si grande perfection, soit causée si extreme passion.
Mais si en vous y a la pitié que promet le reste de voz excellences, vous ne
vouldrez veoir en moy ce qui vous a despleu en voz ennemys : c'est la
mort, laquelle je n'eusse peu tant differer en si grand tourment, n'eust esté

la cognoissance que j'avais que vous n'aviez encores nulle opportunité d'y
pourvoir, et delivrer ensemble vous de vostre promesse, et moy de ce travail. Mais puis que l'occasion s'y offre, et que la fortune nous a eslongné
tout ce qui povoit empescher nostre contentement, je vous supplie,
Madame, ne nous estre plus contraire qu'elle, et vouloir user de sa liberalité, sçachant que l'occasion est chaulve, et qu'estant passée, on ne treuve
pas toujours par où la reprendre. Oriane (non tant pour ses raisons, que
pource qu'elle estoit en aussi grande peine que luy, et que s'il n'eust commencé, elle eust voluntiers fait l'office de requerir) luy dit ainsi : Grande
est la force de voz persuasions : mais plus grande est celle de l'amour que
je vous porte, qui me tient si esprise, que quand bien vous auriez moindre
occasion de demander, si suis je contente et contraincte de vous obeir, et
de me fier en vous de la chose que à grand peine je tenois seure en ma pensée. Bien vous prie je, que puis que vous me voyez si despourveue d'entendement, vous preniez la cure de conduire nostre fait si prudemment qu'il
soit incogneu, et que au moins ce qui aux hommes sembleroit mal fait, ne
le soit devant Dieu. Assez de protestations et remonstrances feit là dessus
Amadis : mais il ne falloit grande batterie à ville rendue. Ainsi sur ce propos arriverent en ung lieu assez près de la ville, où il y avoit ung bois fort
espes d'arbre. A l'endroit duquel grand sommeil print à Oriane, comme à
celle qui n'avoit oncques dormy la nuict precedente, et dit à Amadis : Je
vous asseure, mon amy, que l'envie de dormir me prend si fort que je ne
puis plus tenir. Madame, respondit il, descendons en ceste vallée où vous
reposerez. Et laissans le grand chemin, trouverent un petit ruisseau
bruyant doulcement, joignant l'herbe et les arbrisseaulx tout à l'entour,
qui donnoient grand umbraige au lieu. Là descendirent, et dit Amadis à la
princesse : Madame, s'il vous plaist, nous passerons icy la chaleur, et dor-
mirez tandis que la fraischeur viendra : et ce pendant j'envoyrai Gandalin
en la ville pour nous apporter vivres. Vous dites bien, respondit Oriane,
mais qui luy en baillera ? Il en empruntera, dit Amadis, sur ce cheval qu'il
menera, et retournera à pied. En bonne foy, respondit elle, nous luy
ferons mieulx. Il vendra cest anneau, lequel jamais ne nous servira si bien
qu'il fera maintenant. Et le tirant de son doit le bailla à Gandalin, qui s'en
partit et passant près d'Amadis, luy dit : Qui a temps à propos et le perd,
tard le recouvre. Amadis entendit assez pourquoy il le disoit, combien
qu'il n'en feit semblant, mais se print à desarmer. Et tandis, Oriane faisoit
estendre le manteau de la damoyselle de Dannemarc sur l'herbe, et se coucha dessus : puis se retira la damoyselle ung peu après dans le taillis, et
s'endormit comme celle qui en avoit grande envie. Ainsi demeura Amadis
seul avec sa dame, tant plein de grand aise (pour le bien qu'elle luy avoit
octroyé, qui estoit la perfection de ce qu'il eust sceu desirer) qu'il ne
povoit oster l'œil de dessus elle en se desarmant, qui le faisoit faillir, et
tant plus il avoit de haste, et moins il s'avançoit. Mais en fin estant en
pourpoinct, et à son aise, si ses mains avoient esté lentes en leur office de
le desarmer, tout le reste de ses membres ne l'estoit poinct : car il n'y avoit
celuy qui ne fust en son devoir. Le cueur estoit ravy en pensées, l'œil en
contemplation de l'infinie beaulté, la bouche au baiser, et le bras à
l'embrasser : et de tous n'en y avoit ung seul mal content, sinon les yeulx
qui eussent voulu estre en aussi grand nombre qu'il y a d'estoilles au ciel,

pour mieulx la regarder : car ilz ne pensoient suffire à assez clerement veoir chose si divine. Ilz estoient en peine aussi de ce qu'ilz ne voyoient poinct leur lumiere : car la princesse les tenoit clos, tant pour ne sembler avoir, sans raison, parlé de dormir, que pour la discrete honte que son grand plaisir luy apportoit, ne luy permettant oser veoir hardiement ce qu'elle aymoit le plus en ce monde. Et pour ceste mesme occasion, tenoit les bras negligemment estendus comme endormie, et avoit pour le chault laissé sa gorge descouverte, et monstroit deux petites boules d'albastre vif, le plus blanc et le plus doulcement respirant que nature feit jamais. Lors oublia Amadis son accoustumée discretion, et à la charge d'estre importun, il lascha la bride à ses desirs, si avantageusement, que quelque priere et foible resistance que feist Oriane, elle ne se sceut exempter de sçavoir par espreuve, le bien et le mal joinct ensemble qui rend les filles femmes. Grande fut l'astuce et bonne grace que eut la princesse de sçavoir si bien temperer son grand plaisir receu avecques une delicate et feminine plaincte de l'audace d'Amadis, et au visaige monstroit ensemble ung si gratieulx courroux, et ung si content desplaisir, qu'en lieu de consumer le temps en excuses, Amadis print encores la hardiesse de la rebaiser, et de luy donner nouvelle cause de le tenser. Ce que pourtant (voyant que c'estoit peine perdue, et qu'il estoit obstiné) elle ne feit poinct, mais convertit tout son propos à se rappaiser, et par leur advis donner ordre à povoir, le temps à venir, continuer leur jouyssance, si saigement que nulle partie du plaisir fust troublée par ennuy et empeschement. Dequoy ilz deviserent grande piece, entremeslant leurs paroles d'infinis baisers, et de plus delicates caresses dequoy amour se peult adviser. Ha combien de comptes luy feit lors Oriane des peines qu'elle avoit souffertes attentant ce jour, luy confessant des particularitez que aultre qu'elle et son desir n'avoit encores entendues. Combien aussi de choses luy dit Amadis pour luy tesmoigner son contentement, et l'asseurer de sa perpetuelle foy, tenant tous les travaulx qu'il avoit souffers pour bien heureulx, et trop bien recompensez. Et bien qu'en ce discours et plaisirs ilz eussent consommé la plus grande partie du jour, et qu'il devint tard, si estoient ilz si distraictz de tout aultre souvenir, qu'ilz n'en sentoient poinct le temps, ny leur souvenoit de jour ne de nuict, ne à peine d'eulx mesmes. Et quand Gandalin ne fust jamais survenu, ne la demoyselle esveillée, ilz ne s'en fussent souciez ne advisez : assez de vivres leur sembloit avoir de la jouyssance l'ung de l'autre, qui les passoit plus delicieusement que n'eust sceu faire tout le Nectar et l'Ambrosie de Juppiter, et assez bien servie estoit la princesse d'Amadis, sans sa damoyselle. Neantmoins l'ung et l'aultre survindrent, presque à mesme heure, qui fut cause que les deux amans se leverent, et se prenant par les bras, se meirent à promener le long d'une couverte allée qui estoit en ce bois. Et ce pendant Gandalin et la damoyselle de Dannemarc meirent ordre à leur menger sur une petite levée, tapissée de menue herbe, assez commode pour le lieu. Et combien que là n'y eust buffet d'or ne d'argent, comme chez les Roys Lisuart, et Perion, ny solennité de grans services, si s'estimerent ilz mieulx traictez que oncques paravant n'avoient esté. Et durant leur repas, voyant l'amenité de ce bois, et des fontaines, comencerent à ne trouver estrange que les Dieux eussent aultrefois habandonné le ciel pour venir habiter les forestz, et tindrent Juppiter saige pour avoir suivy Europa, Io, et ses aultres amyes, et Appolo avoir eu raison de devenir pasteur pour l'amour de Daphne, et de la fille d'Ametus. Et eussent voulu à l'exemple d'eulx demourer là, sans jamais retourner à leurs pallais, et royalles pompes, estimant les nymphes des bois plus heureuses déesses, que celles qui sur les autelz de marbre demeurent aux superbes temples des grandes villes. En telz propos passerent le temps qu'ilz furent à table : puis estans Gandalin et la damoyselle retirez, les deux amans recommencerent leurs plus agreables devis, provoyant bien par doulx effetz et paroles que nulle minute de temps fust perdue. Puis doncques qu'ilz sont si à leurs aises, nous les destourberons poinct, mais les y laisserons, et viendrons à parler de ce qui advient à Galaor, estant en la queste du Roy.

Jean Boccace, Le Philocope, 1336-1542.

Le Philicope *est le titre français donné par le traducteur Adrien Sevin au* Filocolo *de Boccace. Le roman parut une première fois en 1542. En 1555, deux éditeurs parisiens en donnaient concurremment une deuxième publication, dans la même version. Enfin, en 1575, la mode littéraire semble la remettre au goût du jour, puisque l'éditeur Gadoulleau la fait reparaître, toujours sous la signature de Sevin.*

Le succès de cette œuvre de jeunesse de Boccace s'explique peut-être avant tout par son thème. La célèbre légende de Floir et Blancheflor, dont la première version littéraire est due à un poète français anonyme du XIIe siècle, présentait une structure romanesque bien propre à susciter l'engouement populaire : deux enfants s'aiment depuis leur plus tendre enfance, tout les sépare. Elle est chrétienne et de naissance servile, il est fils de roi et sarrazin. Le caractère fatal et invincible de l'amour pourra donc s'affirmer à travers les innombrables obstacles que cette situation va engendrer.

Boccace donne à cette épopée amoureuse une dimension littéraire et idéologique nouvelle. Transposé dans l'antiquité, le conte originel devient une savante psychomachie, où les dieux de l'Olympe guident les cœurs des héros. Le milieu aristrocratique évoqué ici devient, par ailleurs le lieu privilégié où s'exerce, parallèlement à la fiction elle même, toute une réflexion théorique sur l'amour. Ainsi le livre IV nous transporte au sein d'un tribunal courtois où sont débattues treize « questions » sur l'amour sincère. (C'est cet aspect de l'œuvre qui avait été retenu dans une édition séparée des Treze elegantes demandes *d'amour, publiées au début du siècle.*

Les extraits que nous reproduisons ici appartiennent, en revanche, à des moments purement narratifs. Dans ces pages, les éléments informationnels, et même didactiques sur l'essence de l'amour et la beauté des femmes se présentent comme le moteur même de l'élaboration romanesque. Les deux passages choisis appartiennent respectivement aux livres I et II.

L.L.H.

LE PHILOCOPE

de messire Jehan Boccace
Florentin, contenant l'histoire
de Fleury et Blanchefleur.
Divisé en sept livres traduictz
d'Italien en Françoys
par Adrien Sevin,
gentilhomme de la maison de Gien.

Paris, Denys Janot

1542

La petite Blanchefleur, fille de citoyens romains morts en Espagne, a été recueillie et adoptée par le roi et la reine de ce pays. Elle est élevée avec leur propre fils, Fleury, né le même jour qu'elle.

La Royne recommenda cherement aux nourrices les petites créatures dont elle avoit incessamment grand soing. Or depuis que les nourrices leur furent ostées & qu'elles parvindrent à ferme aage, le Roy en faisoit très grande feste, & toujours les faisoit vestir egalement, de sorte qu'il n'aymoit la pucelle, de laquelle la beaulté croissoit de jour en jour que son fils Fleury : & sçaichant que la dame Citharée les avoit jà six fois environnez, il pourveut que là où nature auroit aulcunement defailly en culx, ilz peussent en estudiant recouvrer tel deffault par science. Et feit incontinent appeler un sage jeune homme nommé Richard, très expert en l'art de Minerve, qu'il commist pour enseigner les deux enfans affectueusement à bien lire, & semblablement Ascalion auquel il les recommanda & dist : Ayme ses deux enfans comme s'ilz estoient tiens & leur enseigne tout ce qui convient à gentilz hommes & nobles femmes, car ilz sont ma seule esperance & dernier terme de mon desir. Lesdictz Ascalion & Richard prindrent la susdicte charge & incontinent ledict Richard commença à son pouvoir d'executer la sienne, tellement qu'après leur avoit faict cognoistre les lettres, il leur feit lire le sainct œuvre du souverain poete Ovide, où il enseigne d'allumer diligemment les saintz feuz de Venus ès cueurs froids.

Adoncques les deux jeunes enfans comprindrent en leurs jeunes ans puerilles les delectables estudes & amoureux vers, esquelz la saincte deesse mere de Cupido se sentit affectueusement nommer & s'en glorifia en la presence des aultres dieux & ne voulant que si haulte & louable chose fust en vain sceue des deux enfans, elle enveloppa ses blans membres d'ung divin & celeste linge violet, environné de claire nue, & descendit hastivement sur le hault mont Citharée où elle trouva son cher filz qui trempoit ès sainctes eaux nouvelles sagettes auquel elle dist en digne regard. O mon doux filz il y a non loin des agües espaules du mont Appenin, en une ancienne cité nommée Marmorine comme j'ay sceu en noz haulx Royaulmes, deux jeunes enfans qui y estudient affectueusement les vers que tes forces font acquerir, & leurs chastes cueurs invocquent nostre nom & desirent estre noz subjectz, je t'advise que leurs visaiges rempliz de nostre doulceur s'appareillent trop plus à noz services qu'à cultiver les froides fleurs de Diane. Laisse donc ton œuvre pour entendre à plus grant chose, & te despoilles les legeres aeles : Puis comme jadis tu a pris la forme du jeune Ascanius dans la non complaincte Cartaige, revest toy ores de l'ancienne presence du vieil Roy pere de Fleury, & quand tu seras arrivé où ilz sont, embrasse les & baise estroictement par pure amytié, ainsi qu'il a accoustumé de faire, & metz en eulx ton secret feu, les enflambans l'ung l'aultre de sorte que ton nom ne se puisse pour nul accident oster de leurs cueurs. Et ce pendant j'occuperay le Roy que sa venue ne pourra manifester ta faincte forme. Lors Amour se despouilla des legeres plumes, & aux prieres de sa saincte mere, s'en alla au lieu qu'elle luy avoit dict, ou il vestit la faulse forme, & entra sous les royalles couvertures doulcement en la secrette chambre : il trouva lesdictz Fleury & Blanchefleur qui jouoyent puerilement ensemble. Ilz vindrent à l'encontre ainsi qu'ilz souloient faire, & à l'heure il print premierement Fleury, qu'il tyra à luy & le baisant amoureusement, il luy alluma au cueur ung nouveau desir qui le contraignit regarder & s'arrester plaisamment ès yeux verds & irradiens de Blanchefleur, laquelle Amour print pareillement & la regardant au visage il l'alluma avec ung petit soufflement non moins que Fleury, & après avoir esté là en leur compaignie ung peu il les laissa & s'en retourna prendre ses laissées aesles pour recommancer son labeur.

Les jeunes enfans ainsi rempliz de nouveaux desirs, s'entre-regardoient & esmerveilloient sans dire mot, tellement que de là en avant ilz n'estudoient à aultre chose, ne jamais s'en voulurent divertir pour quelque accident qui leur advint, tant le secret venin les avoit secretement penetrez.

Las, Blanchefleur quelle nouvelle beaulté t'est puisnaguere augmentée qu'il fault que tu me plaises tant, ce qui ne souloit estre ? & encore, mes yeux ne se peuvent maintenant rassasier de te contempler. Lors Blanchefleur respondit : Je ne sçay sinon que je puis bien dire qu'il m'est advenu en cas pareil : Et voy que la vertu des saintz vers que nous lisons devotement, allume de nouveau feu en noz pensées, œuvrant en nous ce que nous voyons ès aultres. Asseurement dist Fleury, je le croy aussy d'autant que tu me plais sur toutes choses. Certes tu ne me plais moins respondit Blanchefleur. Et estant en ce propos & leurs livres cloz, leur precepteur Richard entra en la chambre pour les endoctriner, lequel s'en apperceut aulcunement, & les en reprint griefvement, leur disant : Pourquoy voy je maintenant vos livres cloz ? Quelle nouveaulté esse, ne où est fuye la sollicitude de vostre estude ? lesdicts Fleury & Blanchefleur muerent leurs blans visaiges en couleurs de roses vermeilles, pour honte de la non accoustumée reprehension & ouvrirent leurs livres. Ce neantmoins leurs yeux qui desiroient plus l'effect que la raison, regardoient de travers leurs soubzhaitées beaultez, & leurs langues qui souloient appertement reciter les enseignez vers, erroient & vacilloient incessamment. Mais ledict

Richard bien advisé congneut incontinent à leurs faictz le nouveau feu allumé en leurs cueurs, ce qui luy despleut assez. Toutesfois premier que le dire, il voulut par experience estre plus certain de la verité, & à ceste fin il se celoit souvent où il pensoit qu'ilz ne le veissent, tellement que ce luy fut chose manifeste pour autant qu'en son absence il les veoit soubdainement clore leurs livres, embrasser l'ung l'aultre, & baiser simplement, bien qu'ilz ne passassent oultre car leur jeune aage ne congnoissoit encorez les secretz plaisirs.

Le roi d'Espagne a ordonné que Fleury fut séparé de Blanchefleur. Pour mieux lui faire oublier son amour, il charge deux demoiselles de sa cour de le séduire.

Ce jardin estoit très beau & plein d'arbres, fruictz, et fresches herbes qui estoient souvent enrosées de plusieurs fontaines. Or comme le soleil eut passé les regions meridionalles, les deux jeunes damoyselles legerement vestues (à cause du chauld) sur les delicates et blanches chairs & leur blonds cheveulx richement aornez, soubz esperance de mieulx plaire & acquerir si hault mary, y entrerent seulles, & chercherent les fresches umbres auprès d'une claire fontaine, où elles s'assirent attendans Fleury, lequel ainsi que la challeur du soleil defailloit sortit secretement de sa chambre vestu d'un riche manteau de tafetas & entra comme il souloit au jardin, & alla au lieu où il avoit autresfois veue la fleur blanche entre les espines, où il s'arresta longuement pensif. Chascune des deux damoyselles avoit un plaisant chappeau de fueilles de Bacchus, & parloient de Fleury qu'elles n'avoient encore apperceu, tellement que pour n'estre oysives, elles commencerent à dire à doulce & claire voix angelicque, une amoureuse chanson, tant qu'il sembloit que tout le jardin se meust de joye : Dont Fleury s'emerveilla fort & dist : Quelle est cette nouveaulté qui chante ores si doulcement ceans ? Lors il alla vers l'endroict où il les oyoit, & y estre arrivé il advisa entour la fontaine les deux jouvencelles. Elles estoient très blanches & avoient au visaige une petite et bien proportionnée couleur rouge. Leurs yeulx sembloient estoilles matutinalles : & avoient petites bouches vermeilles comme la rose, qui plaisoient moult en leur chant. Leurs dorez et blonds cheveulx crespes environnoient les verdes fueilles de leurs chappeaulx. Leurs testins estoient ronds et elongnés, & encores la pluspart de leurs corps se manifestoit au travers de leurs riches et legers vestemens. Elles estoient convenablement grandes et bien proportionnées en tous membres : brief, c'estoient les plus beaulx corsages du monde. Quoy voyant Fleury, il s'arresta fort estonné, mais aussi tost elles cesserent leurs doulx chantz, puis toutes joyeuses se leverent vers luy, & quasi honteuses le saluerent humblement. Lors Fleury leur dist : Les dieux vous concedent vostre desir. Auquel elles respondirent : Ilz le nous ont permis si tu t'y accordes. Pourquoy (dist il) avez vous au moyen de ma venue laissé vostre plaisir ? Elles respondirent de rechief. Pour ce que nulle chose nous est tant aggreable que ta presence & parolle. Certes ce me plaist fort dist Fleury. Lors s'assit avec elles sur les claires undes de la fontaine, les regarda diligeamment l'une après l'autre, s'efforçant en tout de leur complaire, & leur demanda : Jeunes damoyselles, dictes moy s'il vous plaist que vous attendiez ainsi seulles ? Veritablement respondit l'une nommée Edée, nous estions plus grande compaignie, mais les aultres convoiteuses de veoir d'advantaige nous habandonnerent en ce lieu quasi toutes lassées, & ne doibvent retourner que le soleil ne se couche : nous demourasmes voluntiers esperant vous veoir ce que la fortune nous a permis : Leur gratieuse compaignie pleust moult à Fleury, & se delectoit incessamment à les regarder & noter en con cueur les beaultez de chascune disant : Bien heureux sont ceulx que les dieux feront possesseurs de si grandes beaultez. Il les mettoit en divers propos amoureux, & elles luy. Elles estoient sur ses genoilz, dont l'une le baisoit, & l'aultre avoit le delicat bras sur son blanc col. Ses yeulx regardoient souvent au travers le blanc vestement, leurs coulourez membres : sa debile main en touchoit quelquefois le tetin, puis tastoit à grande joye chascune aultre partie de leurs corps, & elles ne luy deffendoient riens, parquoy il fut moult esbahy. Neantmoins il estoit tant aise que tout luy sembloit bien si qu'il ne luy subvenoit aulcunement de la miserable Blanchefleur. Or ayant esté longuement ainsi, une seule petite honte leur empeschoit l'effect qu'on ne pourroit desirer davantaige en la femme : mais le loyal amour qui sçait tout, se sentant offensé, ne souffrit cette injure estre faicte à Blanchefleur, laquelle ne fist oncques la semblable à Fleury : ains faillit incontinent avec ses agües sagettes dedans le cueur d'icelluy Fleury qui follement ployoit ailleurs, & luy feit tellement recongnoistre son erreur qu'il perdit soubdainement la parolle. A l'heure l'aultre damoyselle nommée Calmene leva sa blonde teste pour le regarder & luy dist : Helas Fleury dy moy l'occasion de ta couleur maintenant perdue ? Je te voy tout changé, as tu senty quelque mal ? Lors Fleury voulant respondre, se souvint de Blanchefleur qui en estoit cause, & jecta un très hault soupir disant : Las qu'ay je faict ? Puis se repentant, il se tourna les yeulx en terre, & commença à penser en son erreur, & disoit tout bas : Ha villain, non extraict de royalle lignée, quelle trahison as tu conspirée jusques à present ? Comment povoys tu pour ces dames ou aultres oublier Blanchefleur, jusques à en desirer choses deshonnestes, les touchant & leur desmontrant signe d'amours ? Hée meschant que toute douleur t'est bien deue, veritablement ton iniquité l'achetera bien cher. Pourquoy as tu osé te condescendre d'aymer celles dont la moindre partie de Blanchefleur est trop plus belle ? Et où il ne seroit ainsi, qui te pourroit aymer autant et perfaictement qu'elle ? Helas si elle le sçavoit elle ne te vouldroit plus veoir. Il se lamenta longuement en cette sorte, tellement que Calmene ignorant la cause s'en approcha, & voyant qu'il ne disoit plus aulcune parolle luy dist. Las mon amy responds moy, dy moy qui te faict souspirer amerement, & l'occasion de ton nouvel ennuy ? n'esloigne celle qui t'ayme plus que soy. A l'heure Fleury dist avec dolente voix, damoyselles vous plaise en l'honneur de dieu me laisser, car ma douloureuse pensée est ailleurs occupée. Il se fust levé n'eust esté qu'il craignoit leur faire honte : mais Edée lui dist : Quelle chose t'est si soubdain intervenue ? Tu parlois cy devant, tu demandois & respondois si privement, & maintenant il ne te plaist seulement nous regarder : Vrayement tu me fais bien esmerveiller. Toutesfoys Fleury ne disoit mot,

ains regardoit de l'aultre costé & les eslongnoit, mais elles s'en appro-
choient amoureusement : tant que Calmene laquelle brusloit jà oultre le
debvoir en l'amour de Fleury, & plus prompte qu'Edée le joignit et
l'embrassant luy dist. O gratieux jouvencel que ne recites tu la raison de ta
soubdaine melencolie ? Pourquoy nous refuses tu à present & nous esloignes, veu que ta compaignie nous est tant benigne ? n'est nostre beaulté
gratieuse à tes yeulx ? Veritablement les dieux s'en contenteroient, & ne
puis croire que Yo tant persecutée de Juno, fust plus belle lors quelle
pleust à Juppiter, ne pareillement Europe, laquelle si longuement luy
chargea les espaulles, non pas jamais aultres jouvencelles, bien que nous
en voyons le ciel aorné. Doncques pourquoy nous reffuses tu ? Et ainsi
avec plusieurs aultres divers & honnestes actes en souspirant, elles rete-
noient Fleury, auxquelles il dist. Damoyselles si oncques les dieux obtem-
perent à vostre plaisir, aymastes vous jamais ? A quoy elles respondirent.
Ouy, vous seulement, dont nous souspirons & sentons cette ardeur.
Vrayement dist Fleury, il appert evidemment que vous ne fustes jamais,
n'estes aulcunement amoureuses, non seulement de moy, mais de personne
au monde, d'autant qu'Amour ne permet au commencement, ne semblablement seuffre après aux amans pareille deshonnesteté qu'en vous, m'ayant
faict craintifz & les revet de chaste honte, tant que la longue frequentation
faict congnoistre leurs cueurs esgaulx & les voluntez pareilles.

Comme Palmerin fut voir vne

nuict ſa dame Polinarde, & du gracieux acueil qu'elle luy fiſt.
Chapitre XLIII.

Rbande tout reſiouy, ſ'en retourna pardeuers ſon
maiſtre, lequel quand il le vid, luy demáda: quelles
nouuelles il aportoit. Monſieur, reſpondit il, Dieu
vous face autant ioyeux, comme vous auez ocaſion
de l'eſtre. Qu'y a il ? diſt Palmerin, ie te prie dy moy
que c'eſt, ſans me faire plus ſonger. Adócq' luy reci-
ta de mot à mot les propoz qu'il auoit euz auec Polinarde, la cótenáce d'elle, la reſpóſe qu'elle luy auoit
faite, l'amour qu'elle luy portoit, & iuſques à la concluſion, qui eſtoit de ſe
trouuer la nuiⸯt enſuyuant au lieu acouſtumé. Grande ioye eut Palmerin
de tel meſſage, & luy diſt: Mon amy, ie cófeſſe maintenát te deuoir beau-

Ludovico Ariosto, Roland Furieux, 1516-1543.

Le Roland Furieux *est trop connu pour qu'il soit necessaire de le pré-*
senter aux lecteurs, et trop complexe pour qu'il soit possible de situer en
quelques mots, les passages choisis dans des développements romanesques
inextricablement enchevêtrés. Il ne saurait non plus être question de tra-
cer un tableau, fût-il sommaire, des personnages féminins du poème, figu-
res si nombreuses et si variées qu'elles meriteraient à elles seules une étude.
Nous nous sommes limités à reproduire les deux portraits complémentai-
res de la magicienne séductrice Alcine et d'Olympe, l'amoureuse volup-
tueuse, vues toutes les deux par les yeux de jeunes guerriers prêts à succom-
ber à leurs charmes. Ces deux descriptions ont représenté pour les poètes
français du XVIᵉ *siècle un modèle constamment présent et c'est pourquoi*
nous avons tenu à les donner ici, en dépit de la gaucherie de la traduc-
tion. L'épisode des femmes homicides nous emmène dans un pays mer-
veilleux où la hiérarchie des sexes se trouve inversée et aboutit à une
domination tyrannique dont l'évocation est pour l'Arioste l'occasion
d'une plaisante mise en garde à l'adresse de ses contemporains ainsi que
d'un hommage ironique à l'énergie féminine. Cet épisode caractérise
assez bien une mentalité, qui n'est pas nécessairement celle de l'auteur,
pour laquelle toute valorisation de la femme suppose de la part de celle-ci
un effort de mimétisme à l'égard des qualités masculines. L'histoire de
Joconde enfin, fort connue au XVIᵉ *siècle et traduite séparément en vers par*
Nicolas Rapin en 1572, est un récit dans la tradition réaliste qui stigma-
tise avec une indulgence désabusée l'infidélité insatiable des femmes : cette
satire représente un contrepoint ironique aux touchantes histoires
d'Angélique et Médor, de Richardet et Fleurd'épine, d'Isabelle et Zerbin.
Mais l'épisode ne se situe pas au même niveau de fiction que les aventures
précédentes : c'est un récit dans le récit, une parenthèse que les dames-
lectrices sont invitées à sauter, et qui ne saurait en rien altérer le respect
que leur voue l'auteur. Ainsi est conservée l'ambiguïté attachante de
l'œuvre, dont cette position à l'égard des femmes n'est qu'un exemple.
   Publié en 1516, le Roland Furieux *fut traduit en prose française en*
1543. Cette même traduction anonyme fut réimprimée en 1544, 45, 53,
55, 71 (revue et corrigée) et en 1576 (revue et corrigée par G. Chappuis).
Cette dernière version fut rééditée en 1577 et 1582. Les corrections de
Chappuis sont d'ailleurs fort peu de choses : pour les deux portraits que
nous donnons ci-dessous dans l'édition de 1544, elles sont inexistantes, et
se limitent à quelques termes modifiés pour les deux autres épisodes que
nous avons transcrits avec le texte et l'orthographe de 1576. Pour rendre
la lecture de ces extraits plus aisée, nous nous sommes contentés de rétablir
le découpage des strophes italiennes que les traducteurs avaient rassem-
blées en un texte très compact.
   A côté de cette traduction complète parurent de nombreuses traduc-
tions partielles, par exemple en 1555, les quinze premiers chants en vers

par Jean Fournier, ou des traduction qui isolaient délibérément un épisode traité comme un développement narratif autonome. De nombreuses imitations voyaient également le jour, dont les plus célèbres sont celles de Philippe Desportes (1572 rééditées chez Droz en 1936). Le succès du Roland Furieux *fut au total considérable et la traduction anonyme de 1543 se vantait de pouvoir surpasser celle qui apparaissait alors comme un modèle du genre, l'*Amadis *d'Herberay des Essarts. Ambition sans doute quelque peu surfaite car les octaves sonores de l'Arioste perdent beaucoup au passage à la prose et les nombreuses erreurs de la traduction suscitèrent des critiques qui prouvent que le texte italien était fort bien connu en France. C'est évidemment à lui que se sont référés les écrivains.*

M.F.P.

D'AMOUR FUREUR
ROLAND FURIEUX

Composé premierement en ryme thuscane par
messire Loys ARIOSTE
noble Ferraroys,
& maintenant traduict en prose
françoyse : partie suivant la phrase de
l'Autheur, partie aussi suivant le stile
de ceste nostre langue.

Lyon, Sulpice Sabon

1544

CHANT VII

Il s'agit du portrait d'Alcine, la fée qui séduit les hommes pour les transformer en arbres. L'hippogriffe a emmené Roger dans son île.

Seulement Alcine estoit plus belle, que les autres, ainsi comme le Soleil est plus beau, que les estoilles.

Elle estoit de personne aultant bien formée, que paintres industrieux sçauroient faindre, avec cheveulx blondz, & longz, & nouez. Il n'est Or, qui soit plus resplendissant ny de plus grand lustre. Une couleur meslée de roses, & de lys se respandoit par sa délicate face : & le joyeulx front estoit d'un yvoire poly, qui finissoit son espace avec juste fin.

Sous deux noirs, & tresdeliez sourcilz sont deux yeulx noirs, mais bien deux clairs Soleils piteux à regarder, & eschars au mouvoir : autour desquels semble que Amour se joue, & vole : & que de là il descharge toute sa trousse, & que visiblement il desrobe les cueurs. Delà aussi descend le né parmy le visaige en sorte que l'envie ne sçauroit trouver, où le reprendre.

Dessoubz celluy, quasi entre deux petites vallées, est la bouche esparse de nayf Cynabre : & là sont deux filletz de perles esleues, lesquelles une belle & doulce levre ouvre & clot : d'où sortent les courtoyses parolles, pour amollir tout cueur gros, et scabreux. Et là se forme ce suave rys, qui à sa poste ouvre le paradis en terre.

Le beau col est neige blanche, & la gorge laict : le col est rond, la poytrine pleine, & large, où deux pommes fermes d'yvoire, vont & viennent, comme l'unde à la premiere ryve, quand la plaisante aure combat la mer. Argus ne sçauroit veoir les aultres parties : au fort bien se peut juger ce qui se cache, estre correspondant à ce qui appert dehors.

Les bras monstrent leur juste mesure, & souvent se veoit la blanche main aulcunement longuette, & de largeur estroicte, où ne appert aulcun noud, & où aulcune veine n'excede. Et à la fin de sa personne se voit aussi le brief, sec, & rondelet pied : & son angélique contenance née au Ciel ne se peult celer soubz aucun voyle.

En toutes les parties de soy, elle avoit tendu un las, soit qu'elle chante ou parle, ou rye, ou chemine : & n'est merveille si Rogier en est pris, puis qu'il la se treuve tant benigne, & peu luy proffite ce que jà il avoit entendu par le Myrte, qu'elle estoit desloyalle, & maligne. Car il luy est advis que tromperie, & trahison ne peuvent estre avec si suave rys : mais bien croit qu'Astolphe fut transmué par ceste, pour ces faictz ingratz, & vicieux, & qu'il estoit digne de ceste peine, & de plus grande.

CHANT XI

Olympe, enchaînée nue à un rocher pour y être dévorée par un monstre marin, a été délivrée par Roland. Celui-ci raconte l'aventure d'Olympe au roi d'Irlande, Obert, qui se laisse aussitôt toucher par sa beauté.

& pendant qu'il parloit les beaulx yeulx serains de la Dame estoient pleins de larmes.

Son beau visage estoit tel que le ciel est aucunesfoys en la Primevere quand la pluye tombe, & en un temps le Soleil s'obscurcit autour du voyle nubileux, & comme le Rossignol alors chante doucement sur les verdz rameaulx, ainsi Amour aux belles larmes baigne ses plumes,

& en la torche de ses beaulx yeulx enflamme son traict doré, & au ruisseau l'estainct, qui descent entre fleurs vermeilles, & blanches. Et après qui l'a trempé tire de force contre le jeune garçon, lequel ny escu, ny double maille, ny escorce ferine peult deffendre. Car ce pendant qu'il demeure à regarder les yeulx, & les cheveux, se sent le cœur blessé, & ne sçait comment.

Les beautez d'Olympe estoient de celles qui sont plus rares, & non seulement avoit beaulx les cheveulx, le front, les yeulx, le né, la bouche, les joues, la gorge, & les espaulles : mais descendant en bas des tetins, les parties que la robbe souloit couvrir furent de telle excellence, qu'elles pouvoient possible estre preferées à tant qu'il en avoit au monde.

Elles vainquoient de blancheur la premiere neige, & estoient plus que yvoire au toucher doulces. Les tetins rondeletz sembloient laict, que à l'heure on oste des jonchées, & tel espace descendoit entre eulx, comme les umbreuses valées entre petis costaulz, lesquelles l'hyver en sa plus douce saison a remplyes de neige.

Les flancs relevez, & les belles hanches, & le ventre plein plus net que myroir & celles cuysses blanches sembloient estre faictes au Tour, par Phidias, ou par plus docte main. Vous doiz-je dire encor de ces parties, que toutesfoys elle desiroit cacher en vain ? Je diray en somme, que la teste jusques aux piedz toute beauté se voit en elle aultant que peut estre.

CHANTS XIX & XX

La vierge guerrière Marphise arrive avec ses compagnons dans une île étrange, le pays des femmes homicides.

Le vaisseau ne fut si tost surgi là (jà l'advis en estoit par toute la cité) que six mille femmes furent sus le port avec les arcs en main, & toutes preparées en habit de guerre. Et d'avantage pour oster tout confort de la fuite à tous ceux qui arrivent là, la mer se clot, entre l'un & l'autre chasteau : & pource il fut enclos de navires, & de chaines, qu'elles tenoyent tousjours prestes à tel usage.

L'une de ces femmes, qui d'ans se peut egaller à la Cumée d'Appolo, & à la mere d'Hector, fist appeler le patron, & luy demanda s'ils se vouloyent laisser oster la vie, ou s'ils vouloyent soumettre le col au joug, selon la coustume : car de ces deux partis il leur en falloit prendre l'un, assavoir de tous mourir là, ou de demourer captifz.

Il est vray (disoit-elle) que si entre-vous se trouvoit un homme si courageux, & si fort, qui osast prendre bataile contre dix de nos hommes, & les mist à mort, puis fust suffisant à faire l'office du mary avec dix femmes durant une nuict, il demourera nostre Prince : & vous en retournerez à vostre chemin :

& sera encore en vostre arbitre de demourer tous, ou une partie : mais avec pache, que qui voudra demourer, & estre franc, il faut qu'il soit mary de dix femmes. Mais aussi quand vostre guerrier ne pourra à un coup contre les dix ennemis, ou qu'il ne fournira la seconde espreuve, nous voulons que demouriez tous esclaves & lui perisse.

Où la vieille pensoit trouver crainte aux Chevaliers, elle y trouva audace : car chacun se tenoit pour tel, qu'il avoit esperance d'achever l'un & l'autre. Et à Marphise ne defailloit le cœur, bien qu'elle fust mal propre pour la seconde dance : mais elles estoit seure de suppleer avec l'espée, où la nature ne luy voudroit ayder.

La response premierement concluë par commun conseil, fut enchargé au patron de dire, qu'ils avoyent qui se pourroit mettre en place à leur volonté, & au lict. Ils levent les empeschemens, & le nocher s'approche, jette la corde, & la leur fait prendre, puis fait accouster le pont, dont les Chevaliers sortent armez, & tirent leur chevaux.

Et de là vont parmy la cité, & y trouvent les pucelles hautaines troussées à chevaucher par pays, & les voyent tenir les armes en place [1], comme font hardis champions. Là les hommes ne peuvent chausser eperons, ne ceindre espée, ny avoir chose d'armes, sinon les dix qu'elles faisoyent combattre contre l'un des survenans : & ce par respect de l'antique coustume que je vous ay dite.

Tous les autres hommes de l'Isle sont employez à l'eguille, au fuseau, au pigne, & autres tels mestiers, avec habit femenin, qui vont en bas jusques aux piedz, & qui les rendent mols & paresseux. L'on en tient à la chaine

---

1. Sur le champ de combat.

pour labourer la terre, & pour garder le bestail. Et à ce moyen il y a bien peu de masles, & seroit l'on fort empesché d'en nombrer un cent pour chasque millier qu'il y a de femmes en toute celle contrée.

Les Chevaliers voulans jetter le sort, qui d'eux devra combattre contre la dizaine ennemie, & la rendre vaincuë, & morte pour l'echapatoire commun : & après la nuict suyvant satisfaire à l'autre dizaine, ne proposent point de la sorte Marphise, estimant qu'elle trouveroit empeschement à la seconde joute du soir : car elle estoit inhabile à en avoir victoire.

Si voulut-elle toutesfois sortir [2] avec les autres : & sur elle, pour le faire court, cheut le sort. Elle disoit, j'y veux mettre premier la vie, que vous la liberté : mais ceste espée (& leur monstra celle qu'elle avoit ceinte) je vous donne pour assurance, que je vous deslieray tous les entrelas, à la sorte qu'Alexandre fit le noud Gordian.

Je ne veux qu'aucun estranger se plaigne jamais plus de ceste cité. Ainsi elle leur dit : & les compagnons ne luy sceurent oster ce que son aventure luy donnoit. [...].

Marphise triomphe de neuf chevaliers ; le dixième se défend vaillamment et une trève est décidée. Les voyageurs sont les hôtes de leur adversaire qui déclare s'appeler Guy le Sauvage.

Adonc, les Chevaliers demandent à Guy à quoy il tient qu'il y a si peu de masles en ce territoire, & s'ilz sont subjectz aux femmes, comme elles sont aux autres lieux aux hommes. Guy leur respond : Plusieurs fois j'ay ouy dire la raison, depuis que je demeure ici, & vous sera (selon que je l'ay ouye) recitée par moy, puis qu'il vous aggrée.

Au temps que les Grecz retournerent de Troye après les vingt ans que dura le siege, dix & dix autres furent par vents contraires agitez en mer avec trop d'ennuy : puis trouverent que leurs femmes avoient prins remedes aux tourments de si grande absence, car toutes avoient choisi de jeunes amys pour ne se refroidir seules au lict.

Ainsi les Grecz touverent leurs maisons pleines de filz d'autruy, & par commun advis pardonnerent à leurs femmes : car ilz sçavoient bien qu'elles ne pouvoient tant jeusner. Mais il convint aux enfans des adulteres pourchasser autre fortune ailleurs, car les marys ne veulent souffrir qu'ilz soient plus nourriz à leurs despens.

Au moyen dequoy les uns furent exposez, les autres tenus cachez de leurs meres, & soustenuz en vie : & ceux qui estoient jà en age, en diverses troupes departirent tous qui ça, qui là. Aucuns suivirent les armes, aucuns les estudes, les aultres les artz, d'autres labourerent la terre, maintz servirent en Court, & plusieurs garderent les brebis, comme pleut à celle qui gouverne ceste cité [3].

Entre les autres partit un jeune filz de Clitemnestra la cruelle Royne, estant de dix huict ans, frais comme un lys, ou rose nouvellement cueillie sus l'espine. Celuy arma un sien vaisseau, & se mit à piller la marine en compagnie de cent jouvenceaux de son âge, choisis par toute la Grece.

---

2. Participer au tirage au sort.
3. La fortune.

Or les Cretensois en ce temps, qui avoient chassé le crud Idomenée hors du Royaume, & pour s'asseurer le nouveau estat, faict congregation d'hommes, & d'armes : prindrent à bon gages Phalante (ainsi avoit nom le jeune homme) pour soldart, & tous ceux qu'il avoit avec soy. Ils le mirent pour garde en la cité Dittée,

Laquelle entre cent bonnes citez, estans ès Crete, estoit la plus riche, & la plus plaisante. Elle estoit tousjours de belles Dames amoureuses plaisante & recreative, de jeux qu'on y faisoit presque tousjours du matin jusques au soir : & comme celle noble cité fut de tout temps accoustumée de caresser les estrangers, elle fit à ceux cy tellement, que gueres ne resta à les faire encor Seigneurs de leurs propres maisons.

Ilz estoient de faict tous jeunes & beaux : car Phalante avoit esleu la fleur de Grece, en sorte que de premiere face ilz gangnerent le cœur des belles Dames : mesmement qu'ilz se montrerent non moins bons, & gaillards au lict, que beaux & polis de leurs personnes. Parquoy en peu de jours ilz se firent si aggreables à elles, que sus tout autre bien, ilz estoient aymez & cheris.

Après que la guerre pour laquelle Phalante estoit là conduit, fut finie, & la soulde militaire fut achevée, tellement que les jeunes gens n'eurent plus de quoy vivre, & de quoy s'entretenir, & pource ilz vouloient laisser la ville. Au moyen de quoy les Dames de Crete font le plus grand dueil du monde : & pour cecy rendent plus de pleurs, que si elles avoient leurs peres mortz au devant.

Les jeunes gens furent assez, chacun par soy, priez par leur Dames de demeurer : & ne voulans demeurer, elles s'en allerent avec eux, laissant & peres, & filz, & freres, ayans despouillé leurs domestiques de leurs plus riches bagues, comme sont pierres precieuses, & grandes sommes d'or : car la praticque fut tant secrette qu'homme de Crete ne sentit oncques la fuitte.

Et d'ailleurs si propice leur fut le vent, si commode fut l'heure, que Phalante print pour fuir, que plusieurs milles estoient sortiz hors, quand Crete se doulut de son dommage. Après par fortune ilz furent jetez en ceste contrée inhabitée & icy s'arresterent, & icy trouverent les fruitz meilleurs que leur larcin.

Ceste demeure leur fut par dix jours toute pleine d'amoureux plaisirs : mais comme souvent advient que l'abondance en un cœur jeune ameine facherie avec soy, ilz furent tous d'accord de demeurer sans femmes, & de se delivrer de telle peine : car il n'est peine si griefve à porter, comme d'avoir femme, quand on l'a à ennoy.

Eux qui estoient desireux de gain & de rapines, & de peu de despence, veirent qu'à paistre tant de concubines, il leur falloit autres choses, que haches & arcz. Et telle force eust celle opinion, qu'ilz laisserent icy seules les malheureuses, & s'en allerent chargez de leurs richesses, là où en la Pouille j'enten que sus la rive de la mer ilz edifierent la cité de Tarente.

Les femmes qui lors se veirent trahies de leurs amis, en qui elles avoyent plus de foy, demourerent par aucuns jours si estonnées, qu'elles sembloient statuës immobiles sus le rivage. Voyant après qu'elles ne tiroient aucun proffit de leurs cris, & infinies larmes, elles commancerent à pen-

ser, & avoir soucy, comment elles se pourroyent ayder en leur si grande
deffortune ;

& proposant parmy leurs advis, les unes disoyent qu'elles devoient
retourner en Crete, & plustost se donner à l'arbitre de leurs peres severes,
& de leurs marys offensez, que de se consumer de faim, & de mesaise aux
rivages desertz, & aux bois espouvantables : les autres disoient qu'il leur
seroit plus honneste de se noyer en mer, que de faire cecy,

& qu'il estoit moins de mal d'aller abandonnées par le monde, &
d'estre mendiantes, ou esclaves, que de s'offrir elles mesmes aux suppli-
ces, dont leurs mauvaises œuvres estoient dignes. Telz & semblables partis se proposoient les malheureuses, & chacun tousjours plus dur & grif.
A la fin une d'elles surnommée Orontée, laquelle tenoit son origine du
Roy Minos,

& estoit la plus jeune, la plus belle, & la plus discrette de toutes les
autres, qui avoit le moins failly (elle avoit aymé Phalante, & s'estoit donnée à luy pucelle, & pour luy avoit laissé son pere) se leva pour dire son
advis, monstrant au visage, & à la parole le cœur magnanime enflammé
d'ire : & reprenant le dire des autres, declara son advis, & en fit sortir
l'effect.

Elle fut d'advis de ne sortir point de ce pays là qu'elle congneut fecond,
& sain d'air, & avoir plusieurs clairs fleuves, obscur de foretz, & la plupart contenant belles & larges plaines, avec portz, & fosses, où les gens
estrangers estoient recouruz de peril, & de mal en la mauvaise fortune :
lesquels estrangers ores d'Afrique, ores d'Egypte leurs portoient choses
diverses, & necessaires au vivre.

Et pource elle fut d'opinion de s'arrester là, & faire vengeance du sexe
viril, qui les avoit si fort offensées. Elle veut que toute nef, laquelle con-
trainte des ventz viendra prendre port en leur pays, se mette en fin à sac, à
sang, & à feu, & qu'à un seul on ne soit courtoyse de la vie. Ainsi fut dict,
& ainsi conclud : & faicte ceste loy, fut dès lors mise en usage.

Soudain qu'elles sentoyent troubler l'air, elles couroyent armées sous la
marine, guidées par l'implacable Orontée, qui leur donna la loy, & se fit
leur Royne : & des nefz estrangeres chassées à leurs rivages, faisoient hor-
ribles feux, & rapines, ne laissant homme vif, qui en peust porter nouvelles en ceste part, ou en celle.

Ainsi elles vesquirent quelques ans solitaires, aspres ennemies du sexe
masculin : mais elles cogneurent après, qu'elles pourchasseroyent leur
propre dommage, si elles ne changeoyent telle façon de vivre : car si elles
ne font lignées d'elles, leur loy sera en brief nulle, & bien sotte : & def-
faudra avec le steril Royaume, où leur intention estoit de la faire eternelle.

Tellement que moderant un peu la rigueur, elles choisirent en l'espace
de quatre ans entiers dix beaux & gaillards Chevaliers de tous ceux qui
arriverent en ce lieu & lesquelz fussent bons guerriers pour durer en
l'amoureux jeu contre elles cent. Elles estoient cent en tout, & à chascune
de leurs dizaines fut ordonné un mary.

Premierement on en decapita plusieurs, qui furent peu fortz au parangon d'elles. Or donc (ainsi que vous oyez) elles retindrent ces dix pour
confors du lict, & du gouvernement de l'Isle, les ayant neantmoins auparavant bien esprouvez, & leur ayant fait jurer que si autres hommes

venoyent en ces portz, toute pitié estainte, les mettroyent égallement au fil de l'espée.

Depuis les femmes commencerent à craindre de trop multiplier d'engroisser, & après de faire trop d'enfants masles : car il pourroit tant naistre du sexe masculin, que après elles ne pourroyent resister contre eux, & à la fin le gouvernement du Royaume qu'elles ont si cher, seroit remis en main des hommes. Parquoy elles ordonnerent de faire en sorte, ce pendant qu'ilz seroyent jeunes, que jamais ilz ne leurs fussent rebelles.

A fin doncques que le sexe viril ne les subjugast, la loy abominable veut que chascune mere en retienne un seul avec soy : les autres ou que elles les noye, ou permute, ou vende du Royaume. Pour cecy elles en envoyent en divers lieux, & commandent à ceux qui les portent, qu'ilz en rapportent des femmes, s'ilz en peuvent troquer, sinon qu'ilz ne tournent point les mains vuides.

Encor ne nourriroyent elles pas un, si sans hommes elles se pouvoyent maintenir. Et ceste est toute la pitié, & toute la clemence, que la loy inique use plus aux siens, qu'aux autres : lesquelz elle condamne par egalle sentance, & seulement en cecy elle se mitigue, qu'elle ne veut, que selon la premiere coustume les femmes les tuent confusément :

Car si dix personnes, ou vingt, ou plusieurs arrivoyent là à un coup, ilz estoyent mis en prison. Et d'un par jour sans plus, l'on tiroit la teste par sort pour l'occire, & le sacrifier au temple horrible, que Orontée avoit faict faire, où elle erigea un autel à la Vengeance : & par sort aussi le cruel office estoit permis à un des dix pour en faire le sacrifice.

CHANT XXVIII.
Histoire de Joconde

Un chevalier romain, Joconde, et Astolphe, le puissant roi des Lombards quoique tous deux très beaux se sont vus trompés par leurs femmes.

Laissons (dist Joconde) ces ingrates, & esprouvons si les autres sont ainsi molles, & aux autres faisons leur ce de leurs femmes, qu'autres ont faict des nostres.

Nous sommes tous deux jeunes, & de telle beauté, que facilement nous ne trouvons noz semblables. Quelle femme doncques sera qui nous use de rigueur, si elles ne se peuvent deffendre contre les laids ? Et si beauté n'y vaut, & jeunesse, au moins il nous vaudra de les avoir par argent. Parquoy je ne veux sans doute que tu retournes, que premierement tu n'ayes eu la despouille ample de mille femmes d'autruy.

Aussi la longue absence, & voir divers lieux, & practiquer d'autres femmes dehors, semble que souvent cela descharge le cœur des amoureuses passions. Le Roy loue l'advis, & ne veut que l'allée se prolonge plus, mais en peu d'heures avec deux escuyers seulement outre la compagnie du Chevalier romain, se met en voye.

Ainsi desguisez chercherent Italie, France, le païs des Flamans & Anglois, & autant qu'ilz en trouvoient de belles, ilz les trouvoient toutes courtoises à leurs prieres. Ilz donnoient, & l'or donné servoit d'estraine, & d'arres, & souvent remboursoient leur argent : car ilz en prierent maintes, & d'autres-tant furent souvent priez.

Doncques sejournant un moys en ce pays, & deux en l'autre, ilz s'acertenerent par vraye experience, que non moins se trouvoit foy & chasteté aux femmes d'autruy qu'aux leurs. Après aucun temps il ennuia à tous deux de pourchasser tousjours chose nouvelle mesmement qu'ilz ne pouvoient aisément entrer en maison d'autruy sans hazard de mort.

Il est meilleur (disoit le Roy) en trouver une, qui de face, & de mœurs soit aggreable à tous deux, & qui nous satisface communement, sans que nous en ayons jamais jalousie ensemble. Pourquoy crains tu qu'il me desplaise de t'avoir plustost en compagnie qu'un autre, veu que tu sçais bien, que je sçay qu'en toute la grande multitude des femmes, n'en est une, qui soit contente d'un seul ?

Une seule, sans nous efforcer (mais seulement quand nature nous incitera) nous suffira pour en jouir en joye, & à plaisir : nous n'en aurons jamais question ne debat. Et ne croy point qu'elle se puisse douloir, car si toute autre avoit aussi deux maris elle seroit plus fidele à deux, qu'à un, & possible ne se orroient tant de querelles :

De ce que le Roy avoit dict, sembla que le jeune Romain en fut très content. Doncques arrestez en tel propos errerent plusieurs montagnes, & maintes plaines. A la fin trouverent selon leur intention une fille d'un hoste Espagnol, qui tenoit logis au port de Valence, belle de presence & de contenance.

Son âge tendre estoit encor sus la fleur de sa primevere, & le pere estoit chargé de plusieurs filz, & ennemy mortel de la pauvreté ; parquoy fut legere chose à l'induire de leur octroyer sa fille en pouvoir de la mener où bon leur sembleroit, puis qu'ilz luy avoient promis de la bien traicter :

Ils prennent la fille, & en ont à plaisir, ores l'un, ores l'autre en charité, & en paix : non autrement que les souffletz d'une fournaise donnent le vent l'un après l'autre. Et pour voir toute Espagne s'en vont delà, & après passerent au Royaume de Siphax, & le jour qu'ils partirent de Valence, vindrent loger à Zattine.

Or là eux, comme maistres vont voir les rues, les palais, les lieux publiques, ainsi qu'estrangers qui ont de coustume de prendre semblable soulas en toutes villes où ilz entrent : la fillette demeure avec les valets. Les uns accoustrent les lictz, les autres les chevaux les autres ont soucy que le souper soit prest au retour de leurs Seigneurs.

Or en ce logis demeuroit un garçon pour valet, qui autresfois avoit demeuré en la maison de la jeunette au service du pere, & aux premiers ans fut amoureux d'elle, & jouit de son amour. Ilz se cogneurent bien, mais ilz n'en firent semblant : car chascun d'eux craignit d'estre apperceu : mais aussi tost que les maistres, & la famille leur donnerent lieu, ilz commancerent de parler ensemble.

Le valet luy demanda où elle alloit, & lequel des deux Seigneurs elle avoit pour amy. Flamette (ainsi avoit elle nom, & le garçon, Legrec), luy dict tout le faict. Doncques quand j'esperoy (luy dist aussi Legrec) que le temps deust venir de vivre avec toy, ô Flamette, âme mienne, tu t'en vas ores, & ne sçay si jamais je te reverray.

Mes intentions douces se font ameres, puis que tu es à autruy, & puis que tu t'eslongnes de moy quand j'avoy deliberé (ayans aucuns deniers en grand labeur, & grand sueur gangnez, & lesquels j'avoy espargnez de mes salaires, & des bien-allées de maints hostes) de retourner à Valence, & te demander à ton pere pour femme, & t'espouser.

La fillette se serre les espaules [1], & respond qu'il fut trop tardif à venir. Legrec ce oyant pleure, & en partie aussi use de faintise, disant : Me veux tu (disoit-il) laisser ainsi mourir ? Au moins avec tes bras ceins moy les flancs, & laisse moy descharger si grand desir. car tout moment que je demeure avec toy devant que tu partes, me faict mourir content.

La fille piteuse respondant : Croy (disoit-elle) que je ne le desire moins que toy : mais je n'y compren ne temps, ne lieu icy, où nous sommes au milieu de tant d'yeux. Legrec repliquoit : Je suis tout certain que si tu m'aymes un tiers de ce que je t'ayme, tu trouveras au moins ceste nuict lieu, par lequel nous pourrons jouir un peu ensemble des bien d'Amour.

Comment le pourray-je (luy disoit la fille) car je couche la nuict au milieu de deux, & ores l'un se jouë avec moy, & ores l'autre, tousjours je me trouve aux bras de l'un ? Cecy (respond Legrec) ne te sera impossible : car je te sçauray bien oster cest empeschement & te faire sortir du milieu d'eux pourveu que tu le veuilles, & si tu le dois vouloir [2], si tu me plains.

Elle pense un peu, & puis luy dict qu'il s'en vienne donc, quand il cuidera que chacun dorme : pleinement l'informe, comme il le convenoit faire à l'aller, & au retourner. Legrec (comme elle luy a enseigné) quand il sent que toute la tourbe dort, vient à l'huis, & le pousse, & il s'ouvre : il entre tout bellement, & va à taston avec le pied.

Il faict grand pas, & tousjours sus le pied derriere se soustient tout, en sorte qu'il semble qu'il craind de marcher sus verre, & qu'il doit marcher sus un œuf, & non sus terre, & tient aussi la main devant, & va ainsi branlant jusques à ce qu'il trouve le lict, & du costé des pieds tout doucement se pousse souz la couverture la teste premiere,
& vint entre les deux jambes de Flamette, qui gisoit à l'envers. Et quand il fut pair à pair il l'embrassa estroictement, & dessus elle se tint jusques auprès du jour, chevauchant fort, sans estrieu : si ne lui convint jamais changer de beste : car ceste luy semble qu'elle trotti si bien qu'en n'en veut descendre de toute la nuict.

Joconde, & le Roy avoient entendu le chaplis qui tousjours fit branler le lict, & l'un & l'autre d'une erreur deceu croyoit que celuy fust son compagnon. Après que Legrec eut achevé son chemin, il s'en retourna, comme il estoit venu : adonc le Soleil jetta ses raiz de l'Orison, & fit lever Flamette.

Le Roy dist à son compagnon en le gaudissant : Frere, tu dois avoir faict grand chemin : & est bien temps que tu te reposes, quand tu as esté toute la nuict à cheval. Joconde luy respond le semblable, & dist : Tu me dis ce que je te devroy dire, & à toy touche [3] de te reposer & prou te face, car toute la nuict tu as chevauché à haste.

---

1. Italianisme, hausser les épaules.
2. Tu dois bien le vouloir.
3. Il te convient.

Et moy encor (suivit le Roy) sans faute j'eusse laissé courir mon chien pour un coup si tu m'eusses presté un peu le cheval tant que j'eusse faict mon affaire. Joconde repliqua : Je suis ton vassal, & peux faire, & rompre pache avec moy : parquoy il ne convenoit jà user de telz signes, & me pouvois dire, laisse la.

Tant repliqua l'un, & tant respondit l'autre, qu'ilz sont en grand debat ensemble, & des motz viennent à un parler qui pique : chascun d'eux se fachoit d'estre moqué : ilz appellent Flamette (qui n'estoit loin, qui craignoit d'estre descouverte de la fraude) pour eux faire dire à l'un & l'autre en face ce que tous niant sembloient mentir.

Dy moy (luy dist le Roy avec un fier regard) & n'ayes crainte de moy, ne de cestuy : qui est celuy si gaillard, qui toute la nuict a jouy de toy sans en faire part à autruy ? Tous deux attendoyent la responce, cuydant l'un de prouver l'autre menteur, quand Flamette se jetta à leurs piedz, incertaine de plus vivre, se voyans decouverte,

& leur en demanda pardon, de ce que esmeuë de l'amour qu'elle avoit porté à un Jouvenceau & que vaincuë d'un cœur tourmenté, qui pour elle avoit beaucoup souffert, ceste nuict elle estoit tombée en celle erreur. Puis suyvit sans dire mensonge, comment elle s'estoit conduite entr'eux avec espoir que tous deux creussent que ce fust son compagnon.

Le Roy & Joconde se regarderent en face, de merveille & d'esbaïssement confus : si leur sembla n'avoir jamais ouy qu'autres deux fussent oncques ainsi deceuz. Puis ilz jetterent egallement une si grande risée qu'à bouche ouverte, & yeux clos, pouvant à peine r'avoir leur alaine, se laisserent choir en arrière sus le lict.

Après qu'ilz eurent tant riz qu'ilz s'en sentoient douloir l'estomac, & pleurer les yeux, ils dirent entr'eux : Comment pourrions nous garder que nos femmes ne nous le facent, si nous ne pouvons garder ceste cy estant entre nous deux, voire si estroitement qu'elle touche l'un & l'autre ? Si le mary avoit plus d'yeux que de cheveux, il ne pourroit faire qu'il ne fut trahy.

Nous en avons esprouvé mille, & toutes belles, & si n'en fut jamais une entre tant qui nous contredit, & si nous esprouvons encor les autres, elles seront sans doute semblables : mais ceste cy suffise pour la derniere preuve. Nous pouvons donc croire que les nostres ne sont point plus mauvaises, ne moins chastes que les autres, & si elles sont comme toutes les autres, sera bon que nous retournions devers elles, & qu'elle soient nostres comme devant.

Après qu'ilz eurent conclud cecy, firent appeller par Flamette mesme son Amant, & en presence de plusieurs la luy donnerent pour femme, & luy donnerent douaire suffisant : puis monterent à cheval, & tournerent leur chemin, qui estoit en Occident vers Orient, & s'en retournerent vers leurs femmes desquelles ilz ne prindrent oncques puis fascherie.

ΠΑΝΤΩΝ ΤΟΚΑΔΙ

Les Bergers

Jean Lemaire de Belges, Les illustrations de Gaule et singularitez de Troye, 1509.

On connaît mieux Jean Lemaire de Belges comme poète rhétoriqueur que comme «historien». Si du moins il faut tenir pour historien l'auteur des Illustrations de Gaule. *Le propos justificatif du livre fait, il est vrai, état du désir de rétablir la vérité, de produire contre la légende adultérée une « histoire restituée véridique ».*

Quelle vérité ? quelle « histoire » ? La question se pose même si l'on tient compte de ce que l'histoire n'est pas pour un homme du XVI⁰ siècle ce qu'elle est pour nous. D'emblée le texte de Lemaire de Belges s'avoue pour décoratif et agréable tout autant qu'idéologique et moral, plus encore une curieuse insistance présente le texte comme convenable aux Dames non seulement à la dédicataire, Marguerite de Bourgogne, mais aux « princesses, dames et demoiselles et autre noblesse feminine de la dite langue Françoise ». Ce sera pour elles, « occupation volupteuse et non pas inutile ». Autant dire que cette « histoire » pour les Dames ne saurait répondre à ce que l'on attend de l'Histoire... quand on est un homme, fût-ce un homme du XVI⁰ siècle.

Il n'est pas jusqu'au propos idéologique qui ne renchérisse sur cette particularisation féminine de l'histoire quand le scripteur place son texte non sous le jour des armes et des lois mais sous celui de la paix, sous le jour de l'éducation d'un jeune prince mais surtout celui de l'éducation de ses amours. C'est dans cette lumière ambiguë qu'il faut sans doute lire cette recherche proprement fabuleuse des origines les plus lointaines et les plus vraies de la concorde qui doit régner entre l'Empire et le royaume de France. Une origine familiale garantit cette harmonie récente, greffant de prodigieuse manière la Fable et la Vérité chrétienne. Lemaire de Belges découvre en Noé le patriarche le Janus latin, en Cam Zoroaste, Pan et Saturne tout ensemble et par cette opération allégorique, la vérité fondamentale : à savoir que Français et Germains ont même origine et sont également parents des héros troiens...

Quel que soit l'intérêt d'une telle opération quant aux idéologies politiques du moment comme par rapport à la formation des pratiques humanistes, il faut souligner que Lemaire de Belges demeure résolument dans une optique qui n'est pas celle de l'homme. Ne serait-ce qu'en arguant d'un singulier prétexte justifiant l'origine de son texte. Ce n'est pas la lecture qui l'aurait conduit à écrire mais la vue d'un décor, celui des tapisseries ornant les « salles et chambres royalles ». Diffusion donc par imagerie de l'histoire, rappel de ces prestigieuses bandes dessinées qui, tissées à Tournai à la fin du XV⁰ siècle, illustraient le Recueil des histoires de Troie *de Raoul Lefevre et ornaient en effet les palais de Charles le Téméraire, Henri VII, Mathias Corvin ou Charles VIII (cf. G. Souchal,* Chefs d'œuvre de la tapisserie du XIV⁰ au XVI⁰ siècle, *Paris, 1973). Or « toutes peintures et tapisseries modernes de quelque riche et coustengeuse estoffe*

qu'elles puissent estre, si elles sont faictes après le patron des dites corrom-
pues histoires, perdent beaucoup de leur estime et reputation. ». Le lieu de
restitution de l'Histoire n'est pas la Librairie mais la Chambre.

De même encore, la subversion rapide des fabuleuses généalogies et du
propos d'ensemble, qui devait conduire jusqu'à l'époque moderne, par les
délices romanesques de l'histoire de Paris qui occupent l'essentiel du Livre
I. Certes il s'agit d'une « enfance palladienne » bien propre à former, sous
l'égide de Marguerite, un neveu qui s'appella plus tard Charles Quint
mais si l'on n'oublie pas absolument les chasses et les armes, ce sont les
amours que relèvent les préambules : « c'est à savoir en donnant franchement son cœur à une seule chaste Nymphe, ou demy déesse, par loy de
mariage (et non autrement) avec laquelle il hantera (par gayeté amoureuse) les bois et les foretz, en habit de veneur ». Alors que l'espace des
tapisseries nous apparaît encombré et dominé par la violence des enchevê-
trements et des lignes acides qui illustrent les épisodes de la guerre, ce qui
domine ici est bien le « pastoureau » en sa « douce simplesse sans rusticité
ne malice », un imaginaire tout autre qui ouvre sur la pastorale volup-
tueuse même si elle est moralisée, une espace de rêve érotique vient dérober la vérité et l'histoire. Triomphe des Dames... telles que les veulent les
hommes.

J.P.G.

LES ILLUSTRATIONS DE GAULE
ET
SINGULARITEZ DE TROYE

Avec les deux epistres de l'amant
verd

Paris, Fr. Regnault

1523

CHAPITRE XXVII

Du louable contenement de Paris Alexandre en son mariage. De la grant amour mutuelle, qui estoit entre luy et sa femme. Et des deux enfans qu'il eut d'elle, avec allegations suffisantes pour prouver qu'elle estoit sa femme legittime. Et une explanation notable, que c'est à dire Nymphe à parler proprement. Avec probation de la noblesse d'icelle nymphe Pegasis Oenone.

Le noble Paris Alexandre et sa compaigne Pegasis Oenone demenoient vie si amoureuse et si plaisante que c'estoit un grand soulas de les veoir, souventes fois se reposoient ou meillieu de leurs troupeaulx soubz le doux umbraige des hayetes fueillues, et soubz l'espesseur des branchettes des arbres : Ne jamais l'ung ne fut veu sans l'autre. Et quant ce vint que le riche temps d'automne eut mis en grenier tout son tresor et amas frutueux de l'année pour le vivre et provision des animaulx marchans sur terre, et que tous arbres furent despouillez de leur beaulté verdissante, Vulturnus le froid vent venant de septentrion comme precurseur vint annoncer triste nouvelle (de) froidure hyvernalle. Et cifflant de sa griefve alaine escroloit les gros troncz des haultes foretz. Et son compaignon Boreas congeloit la liquitité des fleuves decourans et les transformoit en chrystal immobile. Alors les deux amans se tapissoient en leurs petites maisonnettes pastoralles, ayans pour tout habillement à resister contre l'impetuosité du froit hiemal des peaulx de mouton houssues de leur toison, et bien garnies de laine. Et se contenoient dedans les bordes champestres couvertes de chaulme ou d'esteulle, dont les chevrons fleschissoient aucunes fois de foiblesse pour la pesanteur de la neige qui de nuyt cheoit dessus, et ilz se gisoient non pas en coustres de plume de duvet, mais en povres materatz farsis de paille, ou de fueilles de chastaignier esquelz ilz se reschauffoient du feu d'amoureuse exercitation. Adonc les troupeaulx beslans et mugissans par faulte de pasture tous herissez et racroupis de froit se contenoient dedans les estables, et on leur administroit foing et fourraige pour leur sustentacle. Mais nonobstant la rigueur de froidure, Paris impacient de ce jour, mesprisant glaces et bruynes par souventes fois faisoit bondir son cor, et assembloit ses compaignons pour aller à la chasse, et la belle nymphe par semblable couraige le suivoit parmy la montaigne : et souventes fois luy aidoit à mener les chiens ou tendre les retz et les filez. Et luy enseignoit les cavernes des rochiers là où les bestes paisibles et non dangereuses avoient accoustumé de repairer. Mais des autres bestes cruelles et furieuses elles admonnestoit tousjours Paris de fouyr les duyeres en luy racontant l'hystoire du malheureux jouvenceau Adonis.

Adonis (disoit-elle) mon amy fut filz de Cynara roy de l'isle de Cypre (laquelle n'est pas trop loing de ce pays) engendré incestueusement en sa propre fille Myrrha, mais il estoit si beau et si plaisant que Venus la deesse en fut de tel desir attaincte qu'elle (le) suyvoit communement allant à la chasse parmy les bois et les foretz comme je fais toy. Et pour la souveraine amour et plaisir total qu'elle avoit mys en luy, l'advisoit maintesfois de se garder des bestes qui sont fieres et rebelles armées d'ongles et dentz, et de cruaulté mortelle et perilleuse. Mais ce nonobstant ung jour entre les autres l'enfant trop hardy et peu robuste non tenant compte d'exhorations salubres de sa dame (pour lors absente) s'aventura d'envahir ung terrible senglier, grant et orgueilleux à merveilles. Lequel irrité des chiens et escumant horriblement pourfendit l'enfant par grant oultrage et le mit à mort piteuse. Dont la deesse quant elle en fut advertie fut si dolente qu'elle le plora long temps amerement et desrompit ses beaulx cheveux aureins. Et se ne fust qu'elle estoit immortelle elle en fust morte de courroux. Mais pour son soulas final elle transforma le corps de son amy en une fleur de couleur purpurine. Or mon chier espoux et amy se le cas semblable advenoit de toy (que les dieux ne vueillent) soyes seur et certain que je qui ne suis pas immortelle auroye tantost trouvé chemin à la mort, car après ton deffinement je ne quiers vivre une seule heure. Parquoy je te prie mon très doux cueur que tu nous reserves tous deux en vie tant que nature ayt fait son droit cours sans ce que mort violente face abreger les jours l'ung de l'autre. Aussi je t'admonneste par grant attention que tu ne frequentes en ces foretz presentes sans bonne compaignie de paour que d'aventure le hault dieu Jupiter ne te face ravir et emporter aux cieulx par ses aigles sacrées ainsi qu'il feit jadis le beau Ganymedes ton ancestre et parent. Car ainsi comme ainsi je ne vouldroye faire demoure en ce mortel monde après toy. Alors Paris en l'accollant amoureusement luy disoit qu'elle n'eust aucunement soucy de sa personne, car bien eviteroit tous ces dangiers. Les freres et compaignons de Paris qui veoient et entendoient une amour si parfaicte entre ces deux personnages en prisoient beaucoup l'affaire et leur attribuoient grant felicité.

Ainsi passoit le temps le gentil bergier Paris Alexandre avec la gracieuse brunette Pegasis Oenone son espouse en une haulte tranquillité, profonde paix et amour incredible content des simples metz de nature, en humble habitation et société pastoralle. Lequel estat seur et pacifique mieux luy eust valu tousjours entretenir que depuis par ambicieux appetit vouloir estre vestu de pourpre et servy de metz delicieux en palais royal et en communication de princes et ou meillieu du tumulte bellique où n'y a riens sinon grief soing, et inquietude insupportable. Lesquelles choses l'enveloppererent en griefve tribulation et finablement à la mort trop temprifve pour avoir aspiré à la beaulté de Helaine comme vous verrez ci après.

Or recite Boccace ou sixiesme livre de la genealogie des dieux que dedans aucune espace de temps le ventre arrondit et enfla à la gracieuse nymphe Pegasis Oenone pour la croissance du doulx fruict et semence qui dedans se vegetoit. Si se trouva enceincte d'enfant et moult bien luy seoit si que Paris en receut une merveilleuse lyesse. Le terme venu que par droit de Nature elle devoit descharger de sa portée, la nymphe accoucha d'ung beau filz qui fut nommé Daphnis. En laquelle petite creature par joyeux spectacle on pouvoit facilement recongnoistre la semblance et grant beaulté de Paris. Et consécutivement l'an revolu elle fut derechef grosse d'ung autre enfant qui fut appelé Ideus. Toutesfois comme j'estime ilz ne vesquirent point, car on ne treuve par escript riens de leurs gestes, ou s'ilz demeurerent aucun temps en vie si furent ilz nourris obscurement entre les pastoureaulx sans chose digne de memoire : car je n'ay veu acteur quelconque qui en escrive acune chose plus avant : sinon Ovide ou iiij de sa Metamorphose, qui en touche ung mot en passant, disant que Daphnis Ideus c'est à dire des montaignes Idées fut transmué en pierre, par la malveillance et jalousie d'une nymphe du pays, neantmoins je ne scay s'il entend d'iceluy Daphnis fils de Paris.

Boccace ne parlant desditz deux enfans peult sembler entendre qu'ilz ne fussent point conceuz legitimement : mais saulve sa grace, car Dictis de Crete très ancien historien et qui estoit du temps de Troye asseure du contraire, disant en son iij. livre en la personne de Priam qui parle à Achilles ces propres paroles : Quem (scilicet Alexandrum) conjugio deinde Oenone iunetum, etc. Et puis au iiij. livre : Alexandri funus per partem aliam portae ad Oenonem : quae ei ante raptum Helenae denupserat, etc. Pareillement Strabo très diligent investigateur de l'antiquité troyenne dit en son xiij. livre de sa Geographie ces motz exprès : In Vebrinia regione Alexandri et Oenones sepulturam ostendit : quam dicunt uxorem Alexandri fuisse priusquam Helenam raperet, etc. Parquoy appert qu'il ne fault aucunement doubter que la dicte nymphe ne fust sa propre femme et espouse legitime. Et aussi ne fault point mettre en dubitation qu'elle ne fust gentilfemme et de bonne maison, car à le prendre en bon sens selon ce que met Boccace ou xiii. chapitre du vii. livre la généalogie des dieux, nymphes sont dictes toutes nobles pucelles ou femmes tendres et delicates de bonne complexion fresche, sanguine et humide souefvement nourries en chambres et salles umbreuses loing de hasle. Et pour ce les appellent les poetes Nayades ou Napées comme deesses de fleuves et fontaines pour l'humidité succulente qui est en elles. Et au contraire, femmes agrestes seiches et consumées de labeur et de paine quotidienne, ne sont point dictes nymphes. Et autant que la nymphe Pegasis Oenone est tenue fille du fleuve Xanthus comme Ubertin commentateur des epistres d'Ovide, combien que Antoine Volse la dise estre fille du fleuve Yphrites, il faut supposer que son pere estoit quelque puissant homme ayant son tenement et possessions autour du rivage du dit fleuve, et de la fontaine Creusa pour laquelle raison elle est appelée Pegasis, c'est à dire nymphe ou Fée de fontaine. Car pege en Grec signifie fontaine en françoys (comme met le dit Ubertin) pour lesquelles raisons ladicte nymphe Napée, ou se vous voulez Nayade, selon que met Lucan en son ix. livre disant : quo vertice Nais, Luserit Oenone, Soy confiant de la grandeur de son origine reprouche en son epistre à Paris son ingratitude : disant que trop est mescongnoissant de la laisser pour une autre quand il est parvenu à meilleure fortune : Attendu que luy estant comme ung povre cerf et esclave entre les pastoureaulx elle qui estoit femme noble issue de hault lignaige le daigna bien prendre en mary. Et ses mots sont telz en la dicte epistre d'Ovide : Nondum tantus eras cum te contenta marito, Edita de Magno flumine : Nympha fui. Qui nunc Priamides, etc.

De toutes lesquelles choses amplement informée la Royne Hecuba fut très contente et luy pleut bien de tout. Si avoit incessamment l'oreille aux escouttes et l'œil au bois, pour trouver occasion de getter son chier enfant Paris hors de l'exil où il estoit, et le reduire près de sa personne. Et est vraysemblable qu'elle ne se passa point de l'aler veoir occultement en son nouveau mesnaige : paravanture d'aller à la chasse ou pour visiter les troupeaulx du roy, ou en quelque autre maniere. Neantmoins elle n'en feit encores aucun semblant, pource que trop craignoit d'offenser le roy. Or quant aux dessus ditz deux enfans de Paris il n'en sera plus faicte aucune mention doresenavant en ce present volume, car comme dèsjà est dit autre chose ne s'en treuve. Mais il fault mettre son entente à continuer heureusement nostre matiere à l'aide de Dieu.

Jacopo Sannazaro, L'Arcadie, 1485-1544.

Le texte extrait de l'Arcadie de Sannazaro que nous reproduisons ici illustre le principe de composition de l'œuvre entière. Chaque unité structurelle se referme autour d'une situation vécue ou exprimée par un des héros-bergers, ce qui constitue l'Eglogue, suivie d'un commentaire ou Prose où se manifestent les réactions de la collectivité pastorale.

Chaque membre de l'élite arcadienne doit être avant tout amoureux et poète. C'est dire que la femme, absente des jeux champêtres, demeure présente dans la totalité du discours. Elle assume la double fonction d'inspiratrice de la pratique poétique elle-même, et de référence esthétique autour de quoi s'organisa le nouveau code « rustique ».

A ces éléments thématiques et formels qui semblaient bien dignes de susciter la faveur des lecteurs du XVIᵉ siècle, s'ajoute l'attrait d'un catalogue de « clés » autobiographiques de l'œuvre que le traducteur dresse à la fin du recueil.

En fait, le succès de cette **Arcadie** *semble avoir été des plus médiocres. Malgré la réputation de son traducteur, la seule édition de 1544 n'a pu à elle seule assurer auprès du public français une diffusion importante des images de la « bergerie » de Sannazaro.*

L.H.H.

L'ARCADIE

de Messire Jacques SANNAZAR,
mise d'italien en françoys
par Jehan MARTIN,
secrétaire de Monseigneur
Révérendissime Cardinal de
Lenoncourt

Paris, Vascosan & Corrozet

1544

EGLOGUE I

Ergasto :

Menant un jour mes aigneaux en pasture
Le long d'une eau, par un cas d'adventure
Un clair soleil m'apparust en ses undes,
Qui me lya de des tresses bien blondes,
Et imprima sus mon cœur une face,
Dont le taint fraiz, Laict & Roses efface
Puis se plongea en mon ame de sorte
Qu'impossible est que jamais il en sorte.
De ce poix seul mon cœur estant grevé
Qu'esbahy suis comme il n'en est crevé
Veu que dehors fut mis soubs un joug tel
Que j'ay du mal plus qu'aultre homme mortel.
Dire le puy, Amy, l'experience
Me faict quasi perdre la patience.
Je vis premier luire l'un de ses yeux
Puis l'autre après en maintien gracieux.
Bien me souvient qu'elle estoit rebrassée
Jusqu'aux genoux, et que teste baissée
Au chault du jour un linge en l'eau lavoit,
Chantant si doux que tout ravy m'avoit :
Mais aussitost comm'elle m'entrevoit
Elle se teut, que pas un mot ne deit,
Dont j'eus grand deuil : & pour plus me fascher,
Elle s'en va sa robe delascher
Pour s'en couvrir : puis sans craindre advanture
En l'eau se met jusques à la ceincture :
Pourquoy de rage, à moins de dire ouy,
En terre cheus tout plat esvanouy.

Lors par pitié me voulant secourir,
Elle s'escrie & se prend à courir
Tout droict à moy, si que ses cris trenchans
Feirent venir tous les pasteurs des champs,
Qui des moyens plus de mille tenterent
Pour me resourdre : & tant en inventerent
Que mon esprit de sortir appresté,
Fust (pour adonc) en mon corps arresté,
Remédiant à ma vie doubteuse.
Cela voyant la pucelle honteuse
Se retira, monstrant se repentir
Du bon secours que m'avoit faict sentir.
Pourquoy mon cœur de sa beaulté surpris,
De désir fut plus vivement espris.
Je pense bien que cela feit la belle
Pour se monstrer gracieuse & rebelle.
Rebelle est bien d'user de ces façons,
Et froide plus que neige & que glassons :
Car nuyt & jour à mon secours la crye,
Mais ne luy chault de ce dont je la prye.
Ces bois icy sçavent assez combien
Je luy desire & d'honneur & de bien,
Si font ruysseaux, montagnes, gens & bestes
Car sans cesser jours ouvrables & festes,
En souspirant d'amour qui me provoque,
Je la supplie, & doucement invoque.
Tout mon bestail qui sans cesse m'escoute,
Soit qu'il rumine en l'umbre ou au bois broute,
Sçait quantesfois je la nomme en un jour
Piteusement, sans pause ne sejour.
Aussy parfois Echo qui me convoye
Me faict tourner quand elle me renvoye
Son joly nom jusques à mes oreilles
Sonnant en l'air si doux que c'est merveilles.
Ces arbres cy d'elle tiennent propos,
Soyent agits du vent ou de repos :
Et nostre bien chascun à son escorce
Comme elle y est gravée à fine force
Ce qui me faict, telle fois est, complaindre,
Et puis chanter gayement sans me faindre.
Pour son plaisir, mes Toreaux & Belliers
Font bien souvent des combats singuliers.

En escoutant la piteuse lamentation du dolent Ergasto, chascun de nous ne fust moins remply de pitié que d'esbahissement : car combien que sa voix debile & ses accents entrerompuz nous eussent desjà faict plusieurs fois grievement souspirer, si est ce qu'en se taisant, seulement l'obgect de son visaige défaict & mortifié, sa perruque herissée, & ses yeux tous meurdriz, à fine force de pleurer, nous eussent peu donner occasion de nouvelle amertume. Mais quand il eut mis fin à ses parolles et que semblablement les foretz resonnantes se feurent appaisées, il n'y eut aucun de la compaignie qui eust courage de l'abandonner pour retourner aux jeux entrepris ny qui se souciast d'achever les commencez : ainsi estoit chascun si marry de son infortune, que tous particulierement s'efforçoyent selon leur puissance ou sçavoir, le retirer de son erreur, luy enseignant aucuns remedes plus faciles à dire qu'à mettre en execution. Puis voyant que le soleil approchoit de l'occident & que les fascheux grillons jà commençoyent à criqueter dans les crevasses de la terre, sentans approcher les tenebres de la nuyt, nous ne voulans permettre que le povre desolé demourast là tout seul, quasi par contraincte le levasmes sur ses pieds ; & incontinent le petit pas, feismes rentrer noz bestes devers leur estable.

Jorge de Montemayor, La Diane. 1558-1582.

A l'origine en Espagne du courant de la « Novela Pastoril », los siete Libros de la Diana *de Jorge de Montemayor, paraissent en 1558. Ils ne s'appuient guère sur les souvenirs d'une tradition pastorale dont les manifestations, surtout poétiques, courent à travers la littérature espagnole. L'auteur, Portugais d'origine, enregistrait les apports et le succès tout récents de la combinaison chevaleresque et pastorale de* Menima e moça de Bernardim Ribeiro *mais travaillait aussi sur d'autres textes connus, en Italien ou en traduction : le* Ninfale fiesolano *de Boccace, et surtout l'*Arcadie *de Sannazaro, lu et admiré dans la péninsule bien avant sa traduction en Espagnol en 1549.*

L'artifice du déplacement bucolique, dont on connaît la fortune ultérieure, autorise la réutilisation des subtilités amoureuses et des théories idéales puisées aux sources de Leone Hebreo, dont les milieux de cour, à la recherche de lieux sur lesquels ne pèsent pas les contraintes du réel, se montreront particulièrement friands.

C'est en 1578 que paraît en France la première traduction de la Diane, *due à Nicolas Colin. Nous donnons ici la version qu'en tira Gabriel Chappuys en 1582. Une nouvelle traduction, de Pavillon, paraîtra en 1603. Ces dates tardives montrent que c'est comme une annonce des nouveaux courants du début du XVII*e *siècle qu'il convient de considérer ce texte : ce n'est qu'à ce moment en effet qu'il jouera un rôle réellement productif dans la littérature française ; la traduction de Pavillon paraît quatre ans avant les débuts de l'*Astrée.

*C'est pourquoi nous avons choisi deux courts extraits qui, en même temps qu'ils prolongent directement les polémiques sur la femme et les discussions sur la nature de l'amour du XVI*e *siècle, marquent le lien qui existe entre la littérature de cour de cette époque et la préciosité.*

L.G.

LES SEPT LIVRES
DE LA DIANE

de George de Montemayor,

traduits de l'espagnol en françois,
esquelz par plusieurs plaisantes histoires
sont décritz les variables et estranges
effects de l'honneste amour

Rheims, Jean de Foigny

1578

Le traducteur est Nicole Colin

Les interlocuteurs sont Sirene, berger, que Diane qu'il aimait et de qui il était aimé, vient pourtant de délaisser pour épouser Delio, et la bergère Selvage, qui deviendra à la fin du roman, sous l'effet de l'eau enchantée de Felicia, l'amie de Sirene.

Dites moy, pour quelle occasion estes vous si muables, qu'en un moment vous faites tomber un Pasteur du plus haut de sa félicité au plus profond de sa misere et calamité ? Sçavez vous à quoy j'attribue cela ? à ce que vous n'avez vraie et entiere cognoissance de ce qui est entre vos mains. Vous parlez, & vous meslez de traiter de l'amour, & n'estes pas capables de l'entendre : voicz comme vous pourriez le bien conduire & gouverner. Je te dis Sirene, (respondit Selvage) que la cause pour laquelle nous autres Bergeres sommes subjettes à oublier, n'est autre, sinon la mesme, d'autant que de vous autres nous sommes oubliées. Il y a des choses que l'amour fait & deffait : il y en a que les temps & les lieux font changer quelque-fois, ou les mettre souz silence : mais non pas pour defaut d'entendement qui soit aux femmes, y en ayant eu au monde infinies, qui eussent bien peu enseigner les hommes à vivre, & encores aussi bien à aymer, si l'amour eust esté chose, qui eust peu estre enseignée. Mais avec tout cela, je ne croy pas qu'il y ait en ce monde plus basse et infortunée condition, que celle des femmes. Car si elles parlent à vous, incontinent vous estimez qu'elles meurent d'amour : si elles ne vous dient rien, vous croiez qu'elles sont fantastiques, ou alterées : si le recueil qu'elles vous font, respondant à voz paroles, ne vient à vostre propos & intention, vous le tenez pour hypocrisie. Elles n'ont aucune privauté qui ne vous semble desmesurée. Si elles se taisent, vous dites qu'elles sont bestes : si elles parlent, qu'elles sont ennuyeuses & insupportables : si elles vous aiment autant comme il leur est possible, vous croiez qu'elles sont meschantes : si elles vous mettent en oubly, & s'esloingnent des occasions d'estre diffamées, vous dites qu'elles sont inconstantes & peu fermes en un propos. De façon, qu'il n'est en la puissance de la femme, de se faire paroistre en vostre endroit bonne ou mauvaise, sinon entant qu'elle se propose de ne sortir jamais de ce que requiert vostre inclination. Selvage m'amie (dit Sirene) si toutes avoient ceste entendement & vivacité d'esprit, je croy bien qu'elles ne nous donneroient jamais occasion de nous pouvoir plaindre du peu de cas qu'elles font de nous.

Dame Felicia, la plus sage des bergères reçoit tous les bergers malheureux en amour dans le palais des Nymphes. Elle leur offre danses, chants et musique, et le réconfort de sa sage parole, avant de leur faire boire l'eau enchantée qui les guérira de leurs passions malheureuses.

Il ne me semble hors de propos, Dame Felicia, m'enquerir d'une chose, dont je n'ay oncques peu attaindre la congnoissance. Tous ceux qui ont quelque entendement, asseurent que le vray amour naist de la raison. Et s'il est ainsi, d'où vient, qu'il n'y a chose plus effrenée au monde, ny qui moins se laisse gouverner par icelle ? Felicia lui respondit. Ainsi comme ceste demande est plus que de Pasteur, aussi estoit il necessaire que fut plus que femme celle qui avoit à y respondre : mais à ce peu que je puis comprendre, il ne m'est advis qu'on doive penser que l'amour, quoy qu'il ait la raison pour mere, se limite ne gouverne par icelle : ains faut presupposer, que depuis que la raison de la congnoissance l'a engendré, c'est lors que moins il en veut estre gouverné : & est desbridé de telle maniere, que le plus souvent il tourne au dommage & prejudice de l'amant, d'autant que la plus part de ceux, qui bien aiment, viennent à s'oublier, & ne plus aimer eux mesmes, qui est contre toute raison & droit de nature. Qui est la cause, pour laquelle les peintres le peindent aveugle, & privé de toute raison. Et comme Venus sa mere a les yeux beaux, aussi il desire tousjours le plus beau. Ils le peindent nud, par ce que le bon amour ne se peut dissimuler par la raison, ny couvrir par la prudence. Ilz luy donnent les aesles, par ce qu'il entre avec grande legereté en l'ame de l'amant : & tant plus il est parfait, tant plus avec grande vistesse & alienation de soy mesme, va il à chercher la personne aimée : au moien dequoy Euripide disoit, que l'amant vit au corps de l'aymé. Ilz le peindent encores tirant de l'arc, par ce qu'il tire droit au cœur, comme à son propre but : & aussi pour ce que la playe d'amour est comme celle que fait la sajette estroite à l'entrée, & profonde à l'interieur de celuy qui ayme. Ceste plaie est difficile à veoir, mauvaise à penser, & fort tardive à guerir. De façon (Sirene) que tu ne dois t'esmerveiller, si l'amour parfait, quoy qu'il soit enfant de raison, ne se gouverne par icelle, car il n'y a chose qui depuis sa naissance corresponde moins à son origine. Aucuns disent, qu'il n'y a autre difference entre l'amour vicieux, & celuy qui ne l'est, sinon que l'un se gouverne par raison, & l'autre n'endure son gouvernement. Mais ilz se trompent, par ce que cest excès & impetuosité n'est point plus familier de l'amour deshonneste, que de l'honneste, si n'est qu'en l'un il augmente la

vertu, & en l'autre il fait le vice plus grand. Qui peut nier qu'en l'amour
qui est bon & honneste, ne se trouvent des effects merveilleux & exces-
sifz ? Qu'on le demande à plusieurs, qui pour le seul amour de Dieu n'ont
fait compte de leurs personnes, ny difficulté de perdre la vie pour icelui
(quoi que bien consideré le guerdon qu'ilz en attendoient, ilz ne donnoient
pas beaucoup). Et combien d'autres ont ilz consumé leurs personnes, &
emploié leurs vies, enflammez de l'amour de la vertu, & desireux de gloire
& renommée perpetuelle, chose que la raison ordinaire ne permet, ains
guide toutes ses actions, en sorte que la vie puisse estre honnestement conservée ? Combien d'autres exemples te pourois je amener d'une infinité,
qui pour la seule affection de leurs amis ont perdu la vie, & tout le surplus
qui se perd avec icelle ? Laissons cest amour & venons à celuy de l'homme
à la femme. Tu dois entendre que si l'amour que l'amant porte à sa maistresse (quoy qu'il soit enflammé d'une effrenée affection) naist de la raison, & d'une vraye congnoissance & jugement, qui pour ses seules vertuz
la juge digne d'estre aimée, que cest amour, (à ce qu'il me semble, & ne
me trompe point) n'est illicite pour elle mesme, sans esperer autre praticque ny guerdon de ses amours. Et ainsi voila ce qu'il me semble se pouvoir
respondre à ce que sur ce point tu m'as demandé.

Battista Guarini, Le berger fidèle, 1589-1593.

Depuis Sannazaro le monde heureux de l'Arcadie avait inspiré des églogues et des fables pastorales dialoguées, mais c'est en 1573 seulement, avec L'Aminte *du Tasse, que le drame pastoral s'affirme avec succès. Traduit, en 1591,* L'Aminte *aura de nombreuses éditions françaises au début du* XVIIᵉ *siècle. Pour illustrer ce courant du théâtre pastoral nous avons plutôt retenu* Le Berger Fidèle, *« tragi-comédie », en raison du relief dont y sont dotés les personnages féminins.*

Dans cette Arcadie désormais traditionnelle, le péché d'une femme infidèle a brisé le bonheur que Diane accordait à ses sujets. Un moyen s'offre d'apaiser le courrroux de la déesse : unir en mariage les représentants de deux lignées divines, Silvio fils du grand prêtre Montano et Amarillis descendante de Pan. Mais Silvio n'aime que la chasse, et Amarillis aime Myrtil, qui l'aime. L'intrigue complexe se développe dans plusieurs directions : Silvio l'insensible est aimé de Dorinde et Myrtil de Corisque, femme expérimentée et retorse, elle même convoitée par le Satyre. Accumulant les ruses et les mensonges, Corisque va pousser Amarillis dans les bras de Myrtil et fait surprendre les amoureux dans l'espoir de provoquer la mort de sa rivale. Ces différentes intrigues, très habilement conduites par Guarini, aboutissent au IVᵉ acte à une situation désespérée. Amarillis est condamnée à mort en vertu de la loi quand Myrtil s'offre à mourir à sa place le sacrifice volontaire de ce « berger fidèle » pourra lui aussi effacer la punition divine. Mais on découvre au dernier moment que Myrtil est, comme Silvio, fils de Montano et que son union avec Amarillis redonnera aux Arcadiens le bonheur perdu. Silvio se laisse toucher par l'amour de Dorinde, et Corisque, repentie et pardonnée, se plie à l'universelle loi d'amour et de paix. C'est le triomphe de la fidélité sur l'inconstance, du bien sur le mal.

A l'intérieur d'un déroulement qui peut apparaître comme un raccourci allégorique de l'histoire de l'humanité chrétienne (l'état d'innocence, la faute, la punition divine, le rachat par un sacrifice volontaire), le thème dominant de l'œuvre, le principal moteur de l'action dramatique est l'amour : de la bestialité du satyre à la grâce des nymphes organisant entre elles un concours de baisers, en passant par l'asservissement désespéré de Dorinde et la duplicité avide de Corisque, l'invitation au plaisir court à travers tout le Berger Fidèle. *Face à cette sensualité difficilement contenue, à cette loi éternelle de nature, la loi de Diane dresse ses principes stricts, codifiés en un formalisme religieux qui n'est pas sans relation avec le développement des pompes et des rites à l'âge de la Contre-Réforme : les Arcadiens ne devraient, dit un chœur, n'aimer que ce qui est permis. Ils en viennent alors à rêver eux aussi d'une Arcadie au second degré, d'une simplicité idyllique qui leur est refusée, celle où la simple bergère aime et est aimée. Entre les deux impératifs juxtaposés de la sensualité et du moralisme, une seule conciliation est possible : le* mariage. La passion de Myrtil et Amarillis est acceptée par la société dès lors que leur union devient légalement possible, et l'œuvre s'achève sur la glorification de l'hyménée. Nous avons déjà signalé cette exaltation de l'union de l'amour et du mariage, caractéristique des efforts de moralisation de la Contre-Réforme.

En fait, les milieux mondains de la cour des Este, pour qui Guarini, gentilhomme ferrarais, écrivit sa pièce, retrouvaient dans ce pays fictif, sous le masque de la pastorale, leurs propres problèmes. Corisque offre une nouvelle version du personnage de la dame de cour, volage, insensible, sans scrupules. Sa beauté dangereuse a tous les raffinements artificiels que dénoncent les moralistes : c'est une perruque qu'elle laisse aux mains du satyre qui croit enfin tenir sa proie. Mais Corisque échoue, elle doit se repentir, évoluer et se conformer elle aussi à la loi de la respectabilité sociale, car elle est allée trop loin. Malgré l'atmosphère d'hédonisme diffus qui imprègne le Berger fidèle, lorsqu'une femme revendique pour son propre compte la morale du Carpe diem, elle apparaît comme perverse, avide, fausse, endossant ainsi tous les défauts que la satire anti-féministe lui attribuait tratidionnellement.

Le succès du Beger fidèle, supérieur à celui de L'Aminte, fut considérable en Italie comme en France où la traduction de Brisset (1593) que nous donnons ici, fut rééditée en 1609, 1610, 1625, d'autres traductions paraissant en 1623, 1637, 1648 et pendant tout le XVIIe siècle, parallèlement à la diffusion du roman pastoral. Le Berger fidèle, premier grand spectacle visuel accompagné de musique est d'autre part, comme L'Aminte, aux sources de l'opéra.

M.F.P

LE BERGER FIDELLE
pastorale, de l'italien du
SEIGNEUR BAPTISTE GUARINI

Tours, J. Mettayer

1593

ACTE PREMIER, SCENE III
Corisque, Nymphe amoureuse de Myrtil.

Qui vit jamais, qui entendit oncques une plus estrange, une plus folle, une plus importune passion d'amour ? amour & hayne en un mesme suject sont tellement temperez que l'un par l'autre, & ne sçay comment s'entretient, se deffait, naist & meurt tout ensemble. Si je contemple les beautez de Myrtil, si je considere des pieds jusqu'à la teste, son maintien & son port, ses meurs, ses actions, ses regards, ses discours, Amour m'assaut d'un feu estrange, je brusle toute, & me semble que toute autre passion d'amour est surmontée de ceste cy seullement. Mais quand je viens à penser après à l'amour obstiné qu'il porte à une autre que moy, & qu'à son occasion il ne faict compte de moy, & m'esprise, ouy je le diray librement, mon excellente beauté de tant d'autres recherchée & les graces desirées qui sont en moy, je le hay tellement, je l'abhorre si fort, & le fuy tant, qu'il me semble qu'il n'est pas possible que mon cœur puisse estre eschauffé d'amour pour luy. Aucunesfois je parle ainsi à part moy : ô s'il m'estoit possible de jouyr de mon beau Mytil, si qu'il fust tout à moy, & autre n'en eust la jouissance, que tu serois plus que nulle autre bien-heureuse Corisque, alors s'eleve en moy une affection envers luy si douce, si humaine, & si gracieuse que je me resoudz de le poursuivre & de luy descouvrir mon amour, voire mesme de le prier. Quoy plus ? le desir m'espoinçonne tellement que je l'adorerois lors volontiers. Mais d'autre part revenant à moymesme je viens à dire. Quoy ? un dedaigneux, un fascheux, un mespriseur, un qui se faict serviteur d'une autre, un qui m'ose bien regarder, & ne m'adore point, un qui se defend si bien de ma beauté qu'il ne meurt point pour moy : & luy que je devrois voir comme une infinité d'autres, suppliant & en larmes prosterné à mes piedz, auray-je bien le cœur si lasche, qu'en larmes & suppliante, je me prosterne aux siens ? Non, non, il n'en sera pas ainsi. En pensant à cela telle colère s'allume en moy, contre luy & contre moy-mesme, qui ay tourné mes pensers à le suivre & mes yeux à le contempler, que j'en abhorre le nom de Myrtil & mon amour mesme plus que la mort. Et luy je le voudrois voir le plus malheureux & miserable berger qui vive : & s'il se pouvoit faire alors, je le tu'rois de mes mains propres, tant le courroux & le desir, la haine & l'amour me font la guerre. Et moy qui ay tousjours esté jusques icy la flame & la peine de mille cœurs, le tourment de mille & mille ames, je brusle & languis maintenant, & ressens en mon mal la peine & les lan-

gueurs d'autruy. Moy qui l'espace de tant d'années, nourrie en compagnie
civile, recherchée d'une infinité de beaux & gentils serviteurs, suis demeu-
rée invicible, trompant leurs desirs & leurs esperances, maintenant je me
trouve prise & vaincüe de l'amour d'un pauvre berger ? O sur toutes
autres miserable Corisque ! que seroit ce de toy maintenant si tu te trou-
vois denuée de serviteurs ? Que ferois-tu pour adoucir ton amoureuse
rage ? aprenne aujourd'huy à mes despens toute Dame à faire bonne provision d'amans, si je n'avois autre esbat ny autre amour que celuy de
Myrtil, ne serois-je pas bien pourveuë de serviteurs ?

> Celle, ma foy, n'est pas fine à demy
> Qui se réduit à n'avoir qu'un amy.

Corisque jamais ne sera si sotte. Quelle fidelité ? Quelle constance ? Ce
sont fables imaginaires, & impressions de vieux jaloux pour abuser les
plus simples. La foy au cœur d'une femme (si foy se trouve en aucune
d'entre-elles, car je n'en sçay rien) n'est vertu ny bonté, ains une fascheuse
necessité d'amour, une loy miserable de beauté surannée, qui se contente
d'un seul pour ne pouvoir estre cherie de plusieurs.

> Celle vrayment qui trop mal-avisée
> De maint amant se voyant courtisée
> D'un se contente, elle n'a rien en soy
> Qui de son sexe au monde face foy,
> Ou pour le moins si sa face denote
> Qu'elle soit femme, elle est bien femme sotte.

Que sert une beauté qui n'est point veuë, ou si elle est veuë, qui n'est
point courtisée ? si courtisée, courtisée d'un seul ? plus elle en a & plus ils
sont galans, plus elle s'en doit tenir heureuse, ayant par ce moyen un gage
au monde plus certain & plus seur.

> Car c'est l'honneur des Dames qui sont belles
> D'avoir plusieurs qui soient amoureux d'elles.

Ainsi se font aux villes les dames qui sont les plus accortes. Et les plus
belles & les plus apparentes sont celles qui le font le mieux ; refuser un
amant est péché entre elles, ou bien plustost sottise. Ce qu'un ne peut
faire, plusieurs le font : les uns sont pour servir, les autres pour donner,
les autres à un autre usage. & advient souvent qu'en n'y pensant point
l'un chasse la jalousie que l'autre aura donnée, ou la resveille en tel qui ne
l'avoit point auparavant. Ainsi les Dames se gouvernent aux villes, où suivant l'humeur & l'exemple d'une grande Dame j'ay apprins en jeunesse
l'art de faire l'amour. Elle me disoit, Corisque m'amie il faut faire des serviteurs comme on fait des robbes, en avoir plusieurs, n'en porter qu'une
& en changer souvent : la trop longue conversation engendre l'ennuy,
l'ennuy le mespris, le mespris la hayne. Enfin femme ne sçauroit pis faire

que d'attendre qu'on la desdaigne. Fay que ton serviteur parte ennuyé de
toy, non toy de luy. J'en ay tousjours fait ainsi, j'ayme d'en avoir provision : je les entretiens tous. J'en tiens un par la main, l'autre par les yeux :
mais le meilleur & le plus commode je le tiens au sein ; toutesfois entant
que je puis nul d'iceux ne loge en mon cœur. Mais je ne sçay comment à ce
coup y est entré Myrtil qui me tourmente merveilleusement, tellement que
je souspire par force, & qui pis est je souspire pour moy, & n'abuse personne : & mesme desrobant le repos à mes membres, & le sommeil à mes
yeux je ne fay qu'attendre l'Aurore, heureux temps des amans qui n'ont
point de repos. Je vay par ces forests ombrageuses cherchant les pas de
mon doux ennemy. Que feras-tu donc Corisque ? le pri'ras-tu ? ma hayne
ne le permet pas, quand je voudrois le faire. Le fuiras-tu ? non : Amour
ne le veut pas, bien que je le deusse faire. Que feray-je doncques ?
J'essayeray premier par blandices & par humbles prieres, je luy descouvri-
ray l'amour non pas l'amante, & si cela n'est suffisant j'y adjousteray la
tromperie. Mais où cela ne serviroit encor, le courroux aigrissant mon
ame fera une vengeance memorable. Myrtil, puisque tu ne veux point
l'amour, tu sentiras la hayne, je feray repentir ton Amarillis d'estre ma
corrivale, & tant aymée de toy. Enfin vous sçaurez l'un & l'autre combien peut au cœur d'une amante la hayne & le courroux.

ACTE PREMIER — SCENE V
Le Satyre, vieillard cy-devant amoureux de Corisque

> Comme l'ardeur aux fleurs, comme aux plantes l'hyver
> Et la gresle aux espics, & aux graines le ver,
> Et la glus aux oiseaux, & aux biches les toilles,
> Tel est l'Amour à l'homme & ses vertus sont telles :
> Quiconque soit celuy qui l'ait appelé feu
> Son pervers naturel ne connoissoit pas peu.

Voyez le feu, y a-t-il rien plus beau ? mais si vous y touchez, il n'est rien
plus cruel. Le monde n'a monstre plus horrible. Comme une beste farous-
che il dévore, comme un glaive il transperce, comme le vent il vole, & où
il met son pied impérieux, il faut que toute force cede, & tout pouvoir luy
face place. Il est ainsi d'Amour, car si tu le contemples en deux beaux
yeux, en une tresse blonde, ô comme il alleche ! ô comme il plaist ! ô
comme il semble qu'il ne respire que joye, & ne promet que repos. Mais si
tu t'acostes trop de luy, si tu le recherches de trop près, en sorte qu'il commence à glisser & acquerir pouvoir sur toy, l'Hyrcanie n'a tygre, la Lybie
n'a lyon si cruel, ny serpent si venimeux qui le surmonte ou esgale en
cruauté : plus que l'enfer, plus que la mort il est cruel, c'est l'ennemy de
pitié, le ministre de colere : & bref amour n'a rien moins qu'amour. Mais
pourquoy parlé-je de luy ? mais pourquoy le blasmé-je ? Quoy est-il cause
de ce que le monde peche : je ne diray pas en aymant mais à perdre le
temps en vain ? O feminine desloyauté ! c'est à toy que se doit rapporter
toute l'infamie & les travaux d'amour, de toy seulle derive, & non de luy,
tout ce que l'amour a de cruel & de meschant. Car luy qui de sa nature est

doux & traitable, incontinent il perd sa naturelle bonté : tu luy fermes entierement les passages de penetrer au sein, & de gaigner le cœur. Seulement en apparence tu le caresses & le niches. Ton soin, ta pompe, & ton plaisir gist seulement en l'escorce d'un visage fardé, ce n'est ta coustume de cherir avec loyauté, la loyauté de celuy qui t'ayme, & combattre avec l'amant à qui mieux aymera, à qui enserrera mieux un cœur en deux seins, & deux vouloirs en une ame. Mais dorer seulement une perruque follastre, & d'une partie d'icelle reprise en mille nœuds s'en ombrager le front, & de l'autre tissuë en ret entortillée, & enlassée par les branches de l'autre, prendre le cœur de mille amans mal avisez. Que c'est chose deshonneste & honteuse de te voir avec un pinceau te peindre les jouës, & couvrir les defauts de nature & du temps, & de voir comme la couleur plombée tu fais paroistre vermeille, comme tu aplanis tes rides, tu blanchis le noir, & avec une defectuosité tu en ostes une autre : ains plustost tu l'accrois. Souvent tu croises un fil, & prenant l'un des bouts avec les dens, & soustenant l'autre de la main gauche tu fais d'un nœud courant avec la main droite un certain tour, qui l'ouvre & qui le serre comme des forces, & l'adaptant sur l'inegal de ton visage qui cotonne, tu en arraches le poil follet, & temeraire qui y croist malgré qu'on en ait, & ce avec telle douleur que la penitence suit de bien près le peché. Mais tout cela n'est rien, encores que les façons & les mœurs se rapportent du tout aux œuvres. Quelle chose as-tu qui ne soit toute feinte ? si tu ouvres la bouche, tu mens ; si tu souspires, tes souspirs sont mensongers ; si tu jettes ta veuë, tes regards sont desguisez ; en somme toutes tes actions, tout ton maintien, tout ce qui se void en toy, & mesme ce qui ne se voit pas, soit que tu parles, soit que tu penses, soit que tu voises, soit que tu regardes, soit que tu plaignes, soit que tu ries, soit que tu chantes, tout est mensonge & tromperie. Mais encor tout cela est peu, abuser le plus celuy qui plus se fie, & moins aymer celuy qui en est le plus digne, hair la foy plus que la mort : voilà les moyens qui rendent amour cruel & pervers. Ainsi de toutes ses fautes, la faute en est à toy, ou bien plustost à celuy qui te croit. La faute en est donc à moy qui t'ai creu, mauvaise & perfide Corisque, venuë (ce croy-je) des maudites contrées d'Argos, où la paillardise fait sa derniere espreuve, à mon dam & à mon malheur. Mais tu te contrefais si bien, tu es si fine & rusée à dissimuler tes façons & pensées, que tu vas aujourd'huy entre les plus pudiques, haussant la teste d'un nom d'honneur qui ne t'appartient pas. Combien de tourmens ay-je soustenus ? combien ay-je souffert d'indignitez pour ceste cruelle ! je m'en repens de tout mon cœur, ains j'en ay honte : appren de ma peine & dommage, peu advisé amant.

> Si tu me crois, ne sois point idolastre,
> De la beauté d'une Dame folastre.
> Femme adorée est Deesse vrayment,
> Mais c'est d'enfer à parler proprement :
> Qui de sa part presumant toute chose
> De sa beauté, superbement propose
> De t'asservir, & Deesse envers toy,
> Te dedaisgner comme mortel : Et quoy,

De sa valeur encor elle se vante
Qu'elle est pareille à cela que tu chantes,
Quand, pauvre sot, pour l'amadoüer mieux
Tu la depeins la plus belle des Cieux.

A quoy tant de services ? tant de prieres ? tant de plaintes ? tant de souspirs ? telles armes soient pour les femmes & les petits enfans. Il faut que nos ames soient fortes & magnanimes mesmes à aymer. J'ay esté un temps que je croyais qu'en souspirant, pleurant & lamentant, la flamme d'amour se pouvoit resveiller au cœur d'une Dame. Mais j'aperçoy bien que je me suis trop abusé : car si elle a le cœur de caillous, tu essayes bien en vain avec des larmes molles & des souspirs legers dont tu la mignardes, la faire brusler, ou jetter estincelles, si le fusil ne bat fermement. Laisse, laisse tes armes, & tes souspirs, si tu veux faire acquest de ta Dame, si tu brusles d'un feu inextinguible, recele ton affection au plus secret de ton cœur autant que tu pourras : & plus selon l'occasion fay ce qu'Amour & nature t'enseigne, pource que la modestie en apparence est seulement une vertu de femme, tellement que traitter de modestie avec elles c'est un abus : & elle-mesmes qui en use si bien envers les autres, abhorre qu'on la pratique vers elle. Elle veut que l'amant l'admire en elle, non pas qu'il la mette en usage : avec ceste regle naturelle & droite si m'en crois, tu aime-ras tousjours. Car quant à moy, Corisque ne me verra plus, Corisque ne m'esprouvera plus doux amant, ains au contraire fier ennemy : & se sen-tira desormais assaillie non d'armes feminines, mais d'homme viril & entier. J'ay desja attrapé deux fois ceste meschante, & par deux fois elle m'est je ne sçay comment eschappée des mains : mais si elle arrive pour la troisième-fois au passage, j'ay deliberé de l'enserrer si bien qu'elle ne s'enfuira plus de moy. A propos elle a coustume de venir souvent en ces bocages : & moy je vais comme un bon limier flairant par tout. O quelle vengeance j'ay volonté d'en faire si je l'attrape ! comme je la meneray ! je luy feray voir que tel qui a esté aveugle ouvre bien les yeux quelquefois. Et qu'une femme malicieuse & sans foy ne se peut pas vanter longtemps de ses perfidies & meschancetez.

ACTE SECOND — SCENE V
Amarillis

O heureuses forest aymées ! & vous solitaires demeures, que volontiers je vous viens voir ! en bonne foy si mon destin m'avoit donné en sort de passer mon âge à moy-mesme, & vivre selon mon plaisir, je changerois librement les beaux jardins Elysiens, sejour des demy-Dieux, à vostre ombre gentille & agreable. Car si je vois bien clair, tous les biens de ce monde ne sont que maux, l'homme qui plus en a, en a moins, & est plus possédé qu'il ne possede : ce ne sont pas vrayment des biens, ce sont des liens de nostre franchise. Que sert en nostre jeunesse un tiltre superbe de beauté ? une renommée d'honneur ? une celeste extraction ? tant de faveurs du Ciel & de la terre, des possessions, des seigneuries, des plaines couvertes de biens, des feconds paturages, plus fecond encor le troupeau, si au milieu de tant de biens nous n'avons pas le cœur content ? Que bien heureuse est la bergere qui couverte à grand peine d'un simple habit de toile, propre neantmoins & gentil, est riche seulement de soy-mesme ornée de ses graces naturelles. En sa pauvreté douce elle ne sent la pauvreté, ne les incommoditez des richesses : mais elle possede tout ce qu'il luy faut pour n'estre point travaillée d'un importun desir d'avoir. Elle est nue veritablement, mais contente. Avec le miel des abeilles elle confit le miel de ses naturelles douceurs, & la fontaine où elle boit c'est elle qui la mire, & où elle se conseille en s'habillant, elle contente, tout le monde l'est. En vain pour elle le Ciel tempeste, sa pauvreté ne craint rien : nue voirement, mais contente. Seulement elle a un soucy libre au surplus : le troupeau que luy est commis paist les vertes herbettes, & elle paist de ses beaux yeux son amant : non point amant choisi des hommes, ou que le Ciel ait destiné, mais tel qu'Amour le luy a donné. A l'ombrage d'une myrtaye, œilladée elle œillade, & ne ressent flamme d'amour qu'elle ne la luy descouvre, & n'en descouvre aussy aucune que luy ne la ressente, nue voirement, mais contente. O vraye vie qui ne sçait que c'est la mort paravant qu'elle soit venue ! à la mienne volonté que je peusse changer ma condition à la tienne.

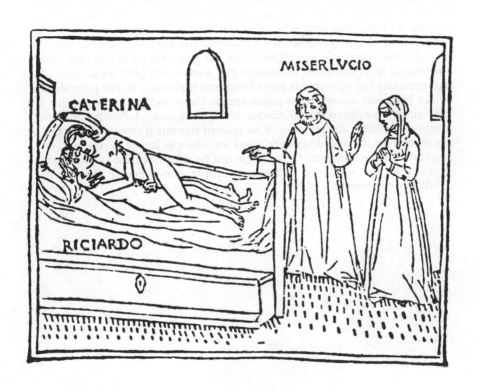

Trésor des contes

Giovanni Francesco Poggio Bracciolini, Les Facéties, 1438-1484.

Les Facéties *de Poge, secrétaire de la Curie Romaine et humaniste à qui l'on doit la redécouverte de nombreux manuscrits, dont le* De rerum Natura *de Lucrèce, furent rédigées en latin entre 1430 et 1452. Poge affirme rapporter les propos de ses confrères, clercs de la Curie, lors de leurs moments de détente. S'il a jugé bon de les transcrire c'est, dit-il dans son « Prothème », que « il est utile mesme aux gens contemplatifs & studieux, de recreer leurs entendemens par aulcune manière de jeux honnestes pour les ramener à hilarité & plaisance ». Facéties donc, et non nouvelles, chacun de ces récits, souvent très courts, vise à un effet comique, satirique ou obscène vers lequel converge toute la narration. Et l'on voit passer les victimes traditionnelles des plaisanteries médiévales : médecins, juges, prêtres, et femmes bien entendu, évoqués avec une vivacité et une liberté de langage qui, dès l'aube du* XVIᵉ *siècle, apparaîtra comme quelque peu choquante. En effet lorsque Guillaume Tardif dédie sa traduction à Charles VII et Anne de Bretagne il le fait en ces termes : « Et, pour vostre Royale Magesté entre ses grans affaires recreer, vous ay translaté, le plus pudiquement que j'ay peu, les Facecies de Poge » Transcrire pudiquement pour G. Tardif, c'était orienter les récits de Poge dans une perspective moralisante, dégager de chaque facétie son « sens moral » opposé à la « matière salle ». Parfois l'entreprise s'avère impossible, et il commente : « En ceste facecie n'y a riens moral, mais y est une responce orde ». Plus souvent, comme dans les exemples que nous donnons ci-dessous, il en tire une leçon de morale pratique visant à la bonne harmonie familiale. Cet effort de moralisation de l'œuvre de Poge se renforcera d'ailleurs dans la deuxième partie du* XVIᵉ *siècle, lorsque les éditions se feront de moins en moins correctes et de plus en plus incomplètes. La traduction de G. Tardif, qui dédia également à Charles VII un traité de fauconnerie et une traduction des* Apologues de Lorenzo Valla, *eut plusieurs éditions vers 1510 et fut constamment reproduite au* XVIᵉ *siècle. Parallèlement le texte latin fut très fréquemment édité à partir de 1470 environ, ceci dans toute l'Europe et jusqu'à Cracovie (1592).*

M.F.P.

LES FACETIES
DE POGE

translatées de latin en françoys
qui traitent de plusieurs choses moralles

Paris, Nicolas Bonfons

1549

*(Nous suivons le texte d'une édition de 1549
réédité par A. de Montaiglon en 1878)*

XLIII

De la femme obstinée qui appela son mary pouilleux,

Et commence au latin :
Colloquebamur aliquando, etc...

Si nous dit Poge : Quand nous estions en noz confabulations & joyeuses assemblées, nous parlions aulcunesfois de la pertinacité & obstination
d'une femme, disant qu'il est des femmes si persistentes en couraige
endurcy qu'elles aimeroyent mieulx mourir que se despartir de leur sentence ne faire aultrement que à leur opinion. Adonc l'ung des asistens,
pour approuver ceste chose par exemple, dit :

J'ay aultresfoys veu en noz cartiers une femme de cette condition,
laquelle tousjours estoit contraire à la voulenté de son mary, & speciale-
ment quand ilz tensoyent de parolles, elle vouloit tousjours avoir le dernier mot & ce qu'elle disoit soustenoit irrévocablement. Advint que une
foys, par une altercation qu'ilz prindrent, son mary & elle, de parolles,
elle l'appela pouilleux, ce qui despleut à l'homme tellement qu'il jura
qu'elle se desdiroit &, pour ce faire, la commença à battre de coups de
poing & de pied tant qu'il peult, mais tant plus la batoit & tant plus
pouilleux l'appeloit.

Adonc le mary, tout lassé de la battre, voyant la pertinacité de elle, se
obstina & jura par ses bons Dieux qu'elle retireroit la parolle & mettroit
fin à sa pertinacité, ou qu'il la getteroit en ung puis. Ceste femme obstinée
jura du contraire que au Dyable fust-elle se jà se desdiroit, mais tous les
jours par plus infestantes parolles pouilleux l'appeloit. Lors le mary print
une corde, lya sa femme par les espaulles & la plongea dedans le puis jusques au menton & jura que, se elle ne se abstenoit de l'appeler pouilleux,
qu'il la noyeroyt & suffocqueroit en l'eaue : mais nonobstant elle tous-

jours instantement sa parolle continuoit, & pour ce le mary, temptant & essayant luy oster sa pertinacité pour la mettre en dangier de mort, la devalla dedans l'eaue jusques par dessus la teste tant que plus ne pouvoit parler. Et lors la faulce & pertinace femme leva les mains en hault par dessus sa teste hors de l'eaue, & pour exprimer ce que de parolle ne pouvoit dire, commenca à serrer les pouces de ses deux mains l'ung sus l'autre, faignant de tuer des poux, pour monstrer que en son courage elle disoit & appeloit son mary pouilleux. Ainsi, devant qu'elle fust morte, ledit mary, voyant & pensant que c'estoit chose impossible de la convertir, tantost la retira hors de l'eau & lui laissa dire & faire du pis qu'elle peut.

En ceste Facétie est montrée la merveilleuse pertinacité & obstination de une maulvaise femme qui aymeroit mieux mourir que faire au contraire de son oppinion quelque chose que ce fust, ainsi que celle que, quant elle fut au puis & ne peut plus parler, pour montrer sa mauvaisetié, bouta les bras dessus l'eaue &, faignant à tuer des poulx, ainsi que femmes les tuent entre leurs doys, pour monstrer evidentement que en son couraige elle appeloit son mary pouilleux. Et est aussi monstré que c'est grant folie à ung homme cuyder convertir une maulvaise femme & obstinée : car mieulx aymeroyent mourir que se convertir, & pour tant dict Monseigneur Sainct Bernard, en en Epistole « De la chose familière » : Malam uxorem citius risu quam baculo castigabis : tu chastiras plus tost une maulvaise femme par toy rire, ne tenir compte de tout ce qu'elle dira ou fera, que tu ne feras par batre à coups de baston.

LIIII
D'ung chevalier Florentin qui cuidoit tenir sa chambriere et il tenoit sa femme.

   Et commence :
   Roffus, etc...

 Ung chevalier fut à Florence, nommé Roffus de Ricis, homme de belle stature, grand & puissant, fort hardy. Cestuy Roffus, non ayant revenu, se accointa de une vieille femme veufve, laquelle estoit à Florence, pour tant que celle vieille avoit force de ducatz & estoit puissamment riche : ainsi n'estoit pas amoureux Roffus de la vieille, mais de son argent, & est assez vraisemblable que, quand il avoit apétit de jouer du jeu d'amourettes, il queroit aultre pasture que sa vieille, qui n'avoit plus nulles dens.

 Advint que, pour servir en la maison de cestuy Roffus si fut admené une moult belle jeune jouvencelle, de quoy Roffus ne fut pas marry, car, tout aussi tost qu'il eust getté l'œil sur elle, il luy fut bien advis qu'il en feroit tout à son plaisir & que il s'en serviroit en lieu de la dame, qui estoit si vieille que n'avoit plus de dens. Pour tant commença Roffus à chascune heure instament prier ceste chambriere, luy promettre dons de diverses manieres, affin qu'elle fist à sa voulenté : toutes foys la fille, qui estoit moult saige, ne se vouloit point consentir ne faire ce deshonneur en la maison de sa maistresse, avecques ce qu'elle estoit toute entière & vouloit garder sa virginité, combien que son maistre la infestat merveilleusement , & ne sçavoit la dicte pouvre fille comment en eschapper, sinon qu'elle s'en alla devers sa maistresse & luy dist : Dame, telle chose est vostre mary ne cesse de courir à toutes heures après moy, & me presse fort de complaire à sa voulenté, tellement que je ne sçay que je face sinon que vous me donnés congié & que je m'en voyse, car je crains qu'en l'oppinion que dessus moy il a il ne me veuille user de rigueur & me prendre à force.

Quant la maistresse eut ouy ce que la jeune fille luy eust dict, elle fut bien contente & respondit : Ma fille, m'amye, je te sçay moult bon gré de vouloir garder ton honneur &, quelque chose que te die mon mary, garde toy bien de consentir à luy : nous trouverons bien moyen de le rappaiser sans que tu t'en voyses. Voicy qu'il faut que nous façons : la premiere fois qu'il t'en parlera, tu luy asségneras heure du soir en tel lieu secret. Lors adonc, quant l'heure sera venue, je m'en iray au lieu dessus dict et, pource qu'il ne verra goutte, il n'y mettra point de difference, car c'est tout ung quant il est nuyt. Ainsi quand il aura bien fait toute sa voulenté de moy, cuydant la faire de toy, je parleray à luy & adonc congnoistra il sa follie & jamais ne te requerra de deshonneur & vilennie, mais t'en aymera mieulx.

Tout ainsi que la dame devisa il fut fait, car, dès la première foys que Roffus pria sa chambriere, elle luy dict en ceste manière : Monseigneur, vous me faictes beaucoup d'ennuy, mais toutes foys, puisque c'est vostre plaisir que ne me voulez laissez en paix, je vous diray, pour garder vostre honneur & le mien, qu'il fault que nous façons, & aussi affin que madame vostre femme ne s'en appercoyve, à ce vespre que la nuyt approchera, en ung tel lieu secret de céans que vous sçavez, où personne ne va coustumièrement, je me rendray, & là me trouverez pour faire vostre plaisir, mais, je vous prie, gardons nostre honneur. — O, dist Roffus, qui moult fut joyeulx, m'amye, tu dis bien : je ne fauldray point à me trouver à l'heure que tu dis.

Ainsi s'en alla la fille vers la dame luy compter comment elle avoit assigné terme à son maistre & en quel lieu. Ainsi, quand vint l'heure, la dame s'en alla au lieu de l'assignation là où Roffus ne faillit pas que en ce lieu ténébreux, cuydant tenir sa chambriere, commence à patrouiller sa femme & luy faire cent petis atouchemens & baisiers pour cuyder esmouvoir nature, laquelle ne se peut oncques esmouvoir : il fut esbahy & honteux que son petit doy ne levoit. Lors la dame, ce appercevante ne peut plus attendre qu'elle ne parlast & dist : Va, merdeux chevalier : si tu eusses icy ta chambriere, tu eusses incontinent fait sa voulenté. — Ha, dist le chevalier, dea, ma femme, esse vous ? Par Dieu, je n'en sçavoye riens, mais mon petit compaignon est plus saige que moy, car à l'heure que par faulte de venir je t'ay prinse, estimant tenir ma Chambriere, il a bien sentu que tu estoys une maulvaise pièce de harnois : pour tant il a joué de retraicte & n'a oncque voulu lever la teste, pour baiser ne pour attouchement que j'ay fait sur toy. Ainsi fut Roffus deçeu qui cuydoit tenir sa Chambriere, laquelle demoura incorrompue, & luy en sçeut après bon gré.

En ceste facétie est réprouvé le vice de ceulx qui veullent honnir leur maison ainsi que Roffus, qui eust esté content d'avoir violée en sa maison une bonne preude fille, ce que jamais homme de bien ne doit faire, mais la doit deffendre & garder. D'aultre part y est monstré une belle condition que doyvent avoir tous loyaulx serviteurs, c'est de jamais vouloir faire deshonneur en la maison de leur maistre, non plus que la bonne Chambriere de Roffus qui, pour supplications, admonestemens de dons ou promesses, oncques ne voulut consentir à la voulenté de son maistre qui la requéroit de deshonneur.

Jean Boccace, Le décaméron, 1350-1545.

La présence du Décaméron ne saurait être ici satisfaisante. C'est le recueil entier qui serait pertinent de son Prologue à sa Conclusion finale, de la première nouvelle où est représentée « la mauvaistié d'un homme » à la centième, illustre s'il en est, en laquelle par l'exemple de Grisélidis, on apprend « aux riches hommes à se bien marier et aux femmes pauvres à estre patientes et obéissantes à leurs marys »... Telle est du moins la morale qui précède le récit de Dioneo dans la traduction française et qui marque bien, lors même que le recueil est tout entier proposé, la volonté sourde de le défaire, de le ramener à ce qu'on sait de toute antiquité dans l'oubli de ce que Dioneo lui-même énonce : que la conduite du marquis de Saluces est « folle bestialité » et péché. Dans l'ensemble du Décaméron, la fonction édifiante devient moins sûre et cette quasi sainteté de Grisélidis en contraste vif avec tout ce qui fait l'allégresse des contes et l'insolence, dont bien sûr Boccace s'excuse copieusement, de les vouer au service des Dames. Des dames qui rêvent d'amour s'entend, car pour les autres « il ne fault (...) que l'éguille, le fuzeau et le rouet ».

A la liberté utopique de l'assemblée galante qui se divertit de la peste qui fait rage à Florence correspond l'enfermement effectif des lectrices dont Boccace, détournant le code chevaleresque, se fait, par la plume, le libérateur. Il s'agit de délivrer du fantasme par l'imaginaire, telle est la tâche du livre. Il faut ruser avec l'enfermement qui est la loi, défaire ce qui s'engendre dans la clôture étouffante de l'ordre masculin : la versatilité et la mélancolie érotique des femmes. Tel est le nouveau combat de ce « champion des dames ». Le livre convoquera donc toutes les scènes possibles, tous les drames imaginables, toutes les plaisanteries y compris les moins convenables. Il s'en trouvera bien quelques-unes qui opéreront sur la lectrice, pourquoi pas l'histoire de Griselidis devenue moins édifiante que cathartique.

La lecture va permettre la décharge de ce qui autrement s'investit dans la rêverie amoureuse insatisfaite. Thérapie qui évidemment en son terme ne bouleverse pas l'ordre mais du moins celui-ci est-il explicité, exhibé : « Elles, comme honteuses et timides, tiennent le plus souvent dedans leurs cueurs delicatz les amoureuses flammes cachées, lesquelles combien plus de force elles ayent que les manifestes, ceux le sçavent qui l'ont eprouvé. Et oultre cecy, retirées de leurs voluntez et plaisirs par le vouloir des peres, des meres, des freres et des marys, le plus de temps demeurent enfermées dans le petit circuit de leurs chambres, voulant ores une chose et ores non, forgeant en une même heure en elles mesmes divers pensemens : lesquelz il n'est possible qu'ils soient tousjours plaisans... » Singulières facettes de l'œuvre de Boccace qui de la Flamette nous conduira au Corbaccio en passant par cette somme de possibles narratifs articulant l'utopie du désir et la réalité de Florence !

Le succès du livre fut immédiat et européen. En France, le texte fut traduit une quarantaine d'années après son écriture à partir d'une traduction latine, ceci en 1414 à la demande de Jean de Berry par Laurent de Premierfait. L'imprimerie rendit le livre à la bourgeoisie, d'abord dans la version de Premierfait, en 1485 Vérard l'édite remaniée, puis en 1545 dans la traduction qu'Antoine Le Maçon produisit à la demande de la Reine de Navarre. Admirable texte qui devrait faire oublier le fastidieux Heptaméron. *Parallèlement, l'histoire de Griselidis est passée des prestigieux manuscrits aux livrets de colportage (on se referera à l'étude de Elie Golinistcheff-Koutousoff et au catalogue de l'exposition* Boccace en France, *Bibliothèque Nationale, 1975). Le Décaméron se défait encore en de multiples recueils de contes dès le* XVᵉ *siècle : Philippe de Vigneulles, Nicolas de Troyes, Jeanne Flore, Jacques Yver, Chappuys...*

Que proposer ? Faut-il bien proposer puisqu'après tout il existe au moins une traduction moderne ? En dépit de l'arbitraire et au delà du problème des représentations féminines, c'est Antoine La Maçon qu'il nous a paru agréable et légitime de donner à lire. Un plaisir savoureux se prend à lire Boccace dans un texte dont on peut évidemment regretter infidélités, lacunes, contre-sens... mais tel qu'il est le texte de 1545 fait tomber des mains aussi bien telle traduction moderne que le pénible ouvrage de la reine de Navarre. Le choix très limité que nous proposons est centré sur l'aspect « compréhensif » d'un certain nombre de nouvelles à l'égard des désordres de la passion, aspect qui domine tout un courant de la théologie morale médiévale.

L'édition utilisée est l'édition originale légèrement corrigée de quelques fautes évidentes.

J.P.G

LE DECAMERON

de messire
JEHAN BOCCACE
florentin,
nouvellement traduict
d'italien en françoys
par maistre Anthoine
Le Maçon
Paris, Estienne Roffet

1545

CINQUIESME JOURNEE NOUVELLE QUATRIESME

Richard Menard trouvé par messire Litio de Valbonne couché avecques sa fille, l'espousa, & vesquirent depuis en bonne paix & amytié avecques le pere d'elle.

[...] J'ay esté tant de fois, & si fort picqué de vous (mes Dames) de ce que hier je vous meys en avant une matiere fascheuse à deviser, & pour vous faire plorer, qu'il me semble que si je veulx aucunement recompenser cest ennuy, je doy dire quelque chose qui vous face ung peu rire. Et par ainsi je suis deliberé de vous compter par une briefve nouvelle, une amytié où il n'y eut autre ennuy que de souspirs, & d'une courte peur, meslée de quelque honte, dont la fin fut néantmoins joyeuse.

Il n'y a encores guères de temps, que en la Romaigne y eut ung chevalier, fort honneste gentilhomme & bien condicionné, nommé messire Litio de Valbonne, lequel par fortune eut de sa femme nommée ma Dame Jaquemine, sur le commencement de sa vieillesse, une fille, qui devint (à mesure qu'elle croissoit) la plus belle & gracieuse de tout le pays. Et pource qu'ilz n'avoient que ceste-là, ilz l'aimoient & cherissoient grandement, & la gardoient fort songneusement : esperans de faire quelque grande alliance par elle. Semblablement y avoit lors, un beau jeune filz, ayant le tainct fraiz, nommé Richard, de la famille des Menards de Brettinore, qui frequentoit souvent en la maison de ce messire Litio, ne bougeant guères d'avec luy. Duquel messire Litio ne sa femme ne se doutoient non plus qu'ilz eussent faict de leur filz.

Cestuy-cy voyant à toute heure ceste fille qui estoit belle, gracieuse, plaine de bonnes mœurs, & desjà preste à marier, en devint desesperement amoureux : toutesfois qu'il mettoit toute la peine qu'il pouvoit à celer son amytié. Dequoy s'estant la fille apperceuë commença pareillement sans point fuir le coup, à l'aymer. Et ayant eu le jeune filz plusieurs fois grande voulonté de luy dire quelque parolle (ce qu'il avoit tousjours differé de craincte) à la fin il choysit ung jour son heure, & print hardiesse de luy dire : Catherine je te supplie que tu ne seuffres que je meure en t'aymant. La fille respondit soudainement : Pleust à Dieu que tu ne me feisses non plus mourir. Ceste responce augmanta beaucoup le plaisir & la hardiesse à Richard : dont il luy dist : Il ne tiendra jamais à moy que je ne face tout ce qu'il te plaira : mais il est en toy de trouver le moyen de nous rendre contens l'un de l'autre. La fille luy deit lors : Richard, tu voys comme je suis tenue de court, & par ainsi je ne puis penser comment tu sceusses venir à moy : mais si tu sçaiz inventer chose que je puisse faire sans recevoir honte, dy le moy, & je la feray. Richard, ayant pensé plusieurs moyens, deit soudainement : Catherine mamye je ne puis penser aucun moyen sinon que tu feisses tant, que tu peusses venir coucher sur la gallerie qui est près du jardin de ton père, là où si je te sçavoys la nuyct, je me parforceroys d'y venir sans faulte, encor qu'il soit fort hault. A qui Catherine respondit : Si tu te faiz fort d'y venir, je pense bien de faire tant que je y pourray coucher. Richard promeit qu'il le feroit, & cecy deit, s'entrebaisèrent seulement une paovre fois, à la desrobée, & puis s'enfuyrent.

Le jour ensuyvant, qui estoit vers la fin du moys de May, la fille commença devant sa mère à se plaindre de ce qu'elle n'avoit peu dormir la nuict precedente pour le grand chault qu'il avoit faict, la mere luy deit : Qu'est-ce que tu dys ma fille ? quel chault faict-il tant ? C'est bien tout au contraire : car il ne faict point de chault. A qui Catherine respondit : ma mère, vous le devriez dire à mon père, & par adventure que vous luy diriez verité, & davantaige, vous devriez considerer, combien les filles sont plus chaleureuses, que les femmes d'aage. La mere deit alors : Ma fille, la verité est ainsi : mais je ne puis pas faire chault & froid à mon plaisir, comme par adventure tu vouldroys : il fault endurer le temps comme la saison le donne, peult estre qu'il fera plus fraiz ceste autre nuict, & tu dormiras mieulx. Or Dieu le vueille deit Catherine : mais on n'a pas accoustumé de veoir, que quant on va plus avant en l'esté, les nuictz se voysent refroidissant. Que veulx-tu doncques qu'on face deit la mere ? Quand il plairoit à mon pere & à vous (respondst la fille), je feroys faire volontiers ung petit lict sur la gallerie près de sa chambre & sur le jardin, où je coucheroys, & oyant chanter le rossignol, estant le lieu fraiz, je seroye beaucoup mieulx que je ne suis en nostre chambre. La mere deit : Or sus, n'en parle plus, je le diray à ton père, & nous en ferons comme il luy plaira.

Lesquelles choses oyes par messire Litio de sa femme, pour ce qu'il estoit vieulx, & ung peu difficile en cecy, il deit : Quel rossignol est-cecy au chant duquel elle veut dormir ? Je la feray dormir au chant des cigalles. Ce que saichant Catherine, non seulement elle ne dormit point la nuict ensuyvant, plus de despit que de chault : mais aussi bien ne laissa jamais dormir sa mere, ne se plaignant que du chault. Parquoy, quand le matin fut venu, la mere s'en alla devers messire Litio & luy deit : Vous vous souciez bien peu de ceste fille : que vous importe il qu'elle couche en la gallerie ? elle n'a reposé toute la nuict en place de grand chault qu'elle avoit, & oultre ce vous esmerveillez vous si ce luy sera plaisir (elle qui n'est qu'un enfant) d'ouyr chanter le rossignol ? les enfans désirent tousjours les cho-

Iehan le Lorrain ouyt de nuict

HEVRTER A SON HVYS: PARQVOY

il esueilla sa femme: & elle luy faisant acroire que cestoit ung esperit, ilz sen allerent tous deux le coniurer auec une oraison, & depuis ne ouyrent heurter.

Nouuelle premiere.

Ire ce m'eust esté chose tresagreable que quelque autre que moy eust donné, s'il vous eust pleu, commencement à vne si belle matiere comme est celle dont nous deuons parler: Mais puis qu'il vous plaist que ie asseure toutes les autres, ie le feray voulétiers: & me parforceray (mes cheres dames) de dire chose qui vous puisse estre vtile à l'aduenir. Par ce que si les autres femmes sont aussi poureuses comme moy & mesmement des esperitz: desquelz toutes nous autres generalemét auons peur (combien que ie ne scay sur mon dieu que cest, & si ne

ses semblables à eux. Messire Litio, oyant cecy deit : Or allez en la bonne
heure : qu'on luy face faire un lict tel que vous vouldrez, & qu'on y mecte
quelques rideaulx de sarge : & qu'elle y dorme, & oye chanter le rossignol tout son saoul. Ce que ayant sceu Catherine, elle y feit dresser incontinent ung lict, & se promettant qu'elle y coucheroit celle nuict, feit tant
qu'elle veit Richard, auquel elle feit ung signe accordé entre eulx, par
lequel il entendit ce qu'il avoit à faire. Messire Litio, quand il sceut que sa
fille fut couchée, ferma ung huys qui alloit en la gallerie, & s'en alla
pareillement coucher.

Tout aussi tost que Richard sentit que tout le monde dormoit, il monta
avecques une eschelle qu'il avoit, sur ung mur, & de ce mur, se prenant à
certaines attentes d'ung autre mur (non sans grand peine & danger s'il
fust tumbé), gaigna la gallerie : où sans mener grand bruict, il fut receu de
la jeune fille avec très grande chère. Et après plusieurs baisers, ilz se cou-
cherent ensemble, & prindrent toute la nuict plaisir l'un de l'autre : fai-
sans chanter plusieurs fois le rossignol.

Or estanz en celle saison les nuictz courtes, & le plaisir grant (& desjà
approchant le jour, à quoy ilz ne pensoient), & avecques ce eux bruslans
de chault, tant pour la chaleur qu'il faisoit, que pour les folies qu'ilz
avoient faictes, ilz s'endormirent sans avoir aucune couverture sur eux :
tenant la fille son amy embrassé avec le bras droict : de la main gauche
par la chose que vous avez plus de honte de nommer, quand vous estes
entres les hommes : & eulx dormans en ceste maniere sans s'esveiller, le
jour survint : parquoy messire Litio se leva, lequel, se souvenant que sa
fille dormoit en la gallerie, ouvrit tout bellement l'huys, & se deit en soy-
mesmes : Que je voye comment le rossignol aura faict dormir ceste nuict
Catherine. Puis quand il fut plus oultre, il leva tout bellement les rideaulx
du lict, & veit Richart & elle couchez tous nudz : & embrassez de la sorte
cy-devant dicte. Parquoy congnoissant que c'estoit Richard, il sortit de là,
& s'en alla à la chambre de sa femme, & l'appela en luy disant : Sus, ma
femme, levez-vous tost, & venez voir que vostre fille a été si désireuse du
rossignol, & y a fait si bon guet, que elle l'a prins, elle tient en la main.
Comment est-il possible deit la femme ? Vous le verrez, deit messire Litio,
si vous vous depeschez de venir.

La Dame s'estant hastée de se vestir, suyvit tout bellement son mary, &
quand ilz furent arrivez au lict, & qu'ilz eurent levez les rideaulx, ma
Dame Jacquemine peut voir manifestement comment sa fille avoir prins,
& tenoit le rossignol, qu'elle desiroit tant ouyr chanter. Lors la Dame, se
tenant fort trompée de Richard, voulut cryer & luy dire injure. Mais messire Litio luy deit : Ma femme, sur tant que vous m'aymez, gardez vous
bien d'en sonner mot : car pour certain puisqu'elle l'a prins il sera sien.
Richard est gentil homme & riche enfant : nous ne sçaurions faire sinon
bonne alliance de luy, & s'il veut eschapper en marchant de là où il est, il
faudra premierement qu'il l'espouse, & lors il trouvera qu'il aura mis le
rossignol en sa propre caige, & non en celle d'autruy. Dequoy la mere se
rappaisa, voyant que son mary ne s'en courroissoit autrement. Et considerant que sa fille avoit eu bonne nuict, & qu'elle reposoit très bien, ayant
pris le rossignol, elle se teut.

Peu de temps après toutes ces parolles, Richard s'esveilla, & voyant qu'il estoit jour clair, se tint desjà pour tout mort : il appella Catherine, en luy disant Hélas, mamye comment ferons-nous ? Le jour est venu & il m'a surprins icy, ausquelles parolles messire Lition s'avança, & en tirant les rideaulx deit : Nous ferons très bien. Quant Richard le veit, il luy sembla qu'on luy arrachast le cueur du corps : & s'estant levé du lict deit : Monsieur je vous requiers pour Dieu mercy : je congnoys comme traistre & meschant, avoir merité la mort : parquoy faictes de moy ce qu'il vous plaira. Bien vous supplie-je, que vous ayez, s'il est possible, mercy de ma vie, & que je ne meure point. A qui messire Litio respondit : Richard, l'amour que je te portoye, & la fiance que j'avoye en toy, ne meritoyent point cecy : mais toutesfois, puisqu'il est ainsi, & que jeunesse t'a transporté à faire une si grande faute, affin que tu te ostes la mort, & à moy le deshonneur, je veulx avant que tu partes d'icy, que tu espouses Catherine pour ta legitime femme : à ce que tout ainsi qu'elle a esté tienne ceste nuict, elle le soit semblablement tant qu'elle vivra. Et en ceste maniere tu peulx acquerir mon amour & ta salvation : & où tu ne le vouldras faire, recommande hardiment ton ame à nostre Seigneur.

Cependant que ces parolles se dysoient la paovre Catherine lascha le rossignol, & s'estant recouverte commença à plourer bien fort, & à supplier son pere qu'il pardonnast à Richard : & d'autre part elle prioit Richard qu'il feist ce que son pere vouloit. Mais il ne falut trop grandes prieres en cecy : par ce que d'une part la honte de la faulte commise avec le desir de l'amender, & d'autre, la peur de mourir, & le desir de eschapper, & outre ce l'ardente amour & l'appetit de posseder la chose aymée, luy feirent dire liberallement sans point y songer, qu'il estoit tout prest de faire ce qu'il plaisoit au pere. Parquoy messire Litio empruncta de la mere ung de ses anneaux, & sans partir du lieu où ilz estoyent, Richard (en leur presence) espousa Catherine. Laquelle chose faicte, messire Litio & sa femme en les laissant deirent : Or reposez désormais : car vous en avez peut estre plus de besoing que de vous lever.

Quand ceulx-cy furent partiz les jeunes gens s'embrasserent ensemble : & n'ayans faict la nuict que six lieues, ilz en feirent encor deux avant que de se lever : & là ilz feirent fin à la premiere journée, puis quand ilz furent levez, & que Richard eut parlé plus à loysir à messire Litio, peu de jours après comme il faloit en la presence des parens & amys, il l'espousa derechef, & avecques grande feste la mena en sa maison, où il feit belles & honnorables nopces. Et longuement après il volla avecques elle, en paix & consolation pour rossignol de jour & de nuict, autant qu'il luy pleut.

SIXIESME JOURNEE NOUVELLE SEPTIESME

Ma dame Phelippe estant trouvée avec ung sien amy par son mary fut citée devant le juge, dont elle se delivra avec une prompte & plaisante responce & feit moderer le statut fait au paravant contre les femmes.

[...] Honnestes Dames c'est belle chose que de sçavoir bien parler à tous propos : mais je l'estime encores plus belle de le sçavoir faire quand la necessité le requiert, Ce que une gentilfemme dont je veulx parler sceut si bien faire, que non seulement elle en feit rire les auditeurs : mais aussi se desveloppa du danger de la mort, comme vous orrez.

En la ville de Prato y eut jadis ung edit non moins (à dire verité) blasmable que cruel, lequel commandoit sans faire aucune exception, que aussi tost fust bruslée la femme que son mary trouveroit en adultère avec quelque sien amy par amours, comme celle qui seroit abandonnée à quelque autre pour de l'argent. Et durant cest edict advint qu'une gentil femme belle & plus que nulle autre amoureuse, qui se nommoit madame Phelippe, fut trouvée en sa chambre une nuict par Regnault de Pugliesi son mary, entre les bras d'un beau jeune gentilhomme d'icelle ville, nommé Lazarin Quassagliotri, qu'elle aymoit comme soy-mesmes : Ce que voyant le mary, courroussé merveilleusement, à peine se sceut il retenir de courir sur eulx, & de les tuer. Et n'eust esté qu'il avoit peur de soy-mesmes, il l'eust fait en suyvant l'impetuosité de son courroux. S'estant doncques retenu de le faire, il ne se peut pourtant garder qu'il ne pour-chassast la rigueur de l'édit de Prato, chose qui ne luy estoit licite de faire (lui-même). C'est à sçavoir la mort de sa femme. Et par ainsi ayant tesmoignage assez suffisant, pour prouver la faulte de la dicte femme, aussi tost que le jour fut venu, sans en demander autre conseil l'alla accuser, & la feit adjourner. La dame qui estoit de grand cueur comme generalement ont accoustumé d'estre, celles qui ayment à bon escient, delibera contre le conseil & opinion de plusieurs de ses parens & amys, de comparoistre : & de vouloir plustost mourir virilement en confessant la verité que ne fuyant, vivre vilainement en exil par contumace : nyer qu'elle ne fust digne d'ung tel amy, comme estoit celuy entre les bras duquel elle avoit esté trouvée la nuict passée. Et s'en vint devant le Potestat fort bien accompagnée d'hommes & de femmes qui tous luy conseilloient de le nyer. Et luy demanda avec un visaige constant, & une voix ferme, qu'il luy demandoit. Le Potestat regardant ceste-cy, & la voyant belle de beau maintien, & selon que ses parolles tesmoignoient de grant cœur, commença d'avoir compassion d'elle, doubtant qu'elle ne confessast chose laquelle il fust contrainct pour faire son devoir de la faire mourir. Mais ne pouvant toutes fois delayer qu'il ne l'enquist de ce dont elle estoit accusée, il luy deit : Madame vostre mary (comme vous voyez) est icy qui se plainct de vous : disant qu'il vous a trouvée en adultere avec ung autre homme, & pource il demande que selon la rigueur d'ung edict que nous avons, je vous en face punir : & par consequent mourir : mais je ne puis le faire si vous ne le confessez. Et par ainsi regardez bien comment vous respondrez : & me dictes s'il est vray ce dont vostre mary vous accuse.

La Dame sans point s'estonner respondit plaisamment, Monsieur il est vray que Regnault est mon mary, & qu'il m'a trouvée ceste nuict passée entre les bras de Lazarin : où j'ai esté plusieurs autres fois par bonne & parfaicte amytié que je luy porte, & cecy je ne le nyeray jamais : mais vous sçavez bien & j'en suis certaine, que les loix qu'on faict en ung pays doivent estre communes, & faictes avec consentement de ceulx à qui elles touchent : ce qui n'est pas advenu de ceste-cy : Car elle n'est seulement rigoureuse que contre les paovres femmes, qui pourroient beaucoup mieulx satisfaire à plusieurs que les hommes. Et oultre ce, quand elle fut faicte, il n'y eut femme qui seulement y consentist : ne qui jamais y ait esté appellée, au moyen de quoy elle ne se peult appeler à bon droict que mauvaise, & si vous voulez estre executeur d'icelle au prejudice de ma personne & de vostre conscience, il est en vous de faire ce qui vous plaira : mais avant que vous procediez à donner aucune sentence, je vous supplie qu'il vous plaise me faire une petite grace : C'est à sçavoir que vous demandiez à mon mary, si toutes & quantes fois qu'il luy a pleu recevoir plaisir de moy je ne luy ay pas faict abandon de ma personne : A quoy Regnault sans attendre que le Potestat le luy demandast, respondit soudainement, que sans aucun doubte sa femme toutes les fois qu'il l'en avoit requise, ne luy avoit jamais reffusé aucun plaisir qu'il desirast prendre d'elle. Alors la dame continuant incontinent son propos deit : Je vous demande doncques monsieur le Potestat, s'il a tousjours pris de moy, ce que luy a pleu, & qui luy a esté besoing, que devois-je ou doy faire du demourant ? Le doy-je jetter aux chiens ? N'est-il pas plus raisonnable que j'en face plaisir à ung gentilhomme qui m'ayme plus que soy-mesme que le laisser perdre ou gaster ? Il y avoit là, à une telle examination & d'une grande & renommée dame comme ceste-cy estoit, presque tous ceulx de la ville de Prato, lesquelz oyant une si plaisante demande criyerent soudainement (après avoir ry leur saoul) tous d'une voix que la dame avoit raison & qu'elle disoit très bien. Tellement que avant qu'ilz partissent de là, l'on modifia par l'avis du Potestat, l'edit si cruel : & fut dit qu'il s'entendoit seulement de celles qui pour argent feroient tort à leur marys. Au moyen de quoy Regnault demourant confuz d'une si folle entreprise, se partit de l'auditoire : & la dame joyeuse & delivrée, estant quasi reschappée du feu, s'en retourna toute glorieuse à la maison.

L'un des moindres charmes du Décaméron *n'est pas que chaque journée s'achève sur une chanson. Celle qui suit, chantée par Dame Pampinée, clot la seconde journée. Contre-point rayonnant de l'élégie de Flamette, elle complète les textes narratifs cités ci-dessus, s'inscrivant comme eux dans la perspective tolérante à l'égard de la passion amoureuse qui caractérise tout un aspect de la littérature médiévale.*

Qui chantera doncques si je ne chante,
Moy qui me sens de tous desirs contente.
Vien doncq', amour, cause de tout mon heur,
De tout espoir, de tout effect joyeux.
Chantons ensemble ung peu : non de malheur,
Ny de souspirs, de peine, ou de douleur,
Qui tes plaisirs rendent plus doulcereulx :
Mais seulement de ton feu chaleureux,
Ouquel bruslant viz, en joye & doulceur,
En adorant ta deité puissante.

Au premier jour que senty ta chaleur,
De toy receu ung tel jeune amoureux,
Qu'il n'en est point de plus grand en valeur,
Ny de semblable en beauté & ardeur

Se peult trouver, ny mais tant vigoureux :
Si m'embrasay de luy & de ses yeulx,
Tant fermement & de telle fureur,
Qu'à toy chantant de joye je m'en vante.

Mais ce qui plus me donne de plaisir,
C'est que luy plaiz autant que luy à moy :
Et de ta grace, ô grand Dieu de desir.
Par quoy ne puys en ce monde choysir
Autre vouloir que celluy qu'en feroy :
Esperant paix en l'autre, par la foy
Que je luy porte : et Dieu qui à loysir
Voy tout cecy, m'en fera jouissante.

Gian Francesco Straparola, Les facétieuses nuits, 1550-1560.

La personnalité de l'auteur des Piacevoli Notti *n'est guère connue et s'efface derrière la présence d'un recueil dont la traduction connut un succès considérable.*

Selon la tradition du recueil italien de nouvelles, nous sommes dans un cadre raffiné où une société mi-fictive, mi-historique organise l'oubli du temps par la récitation du conte. Nous ne sommes pas à Fiesole mais dans un merveilleux palais de Murano, près de Venise. Le moment se prête à l'épicurisme, le Mardi gras est proche et la perspective du Carême rend plus impérieux l'appétit de plaisirs. Ceux-ci, comme à l'ordinaire, sont aussi une compensation à d'affreux malheurs, non pas il est vrai la peste, tout juste les troubles familiaux déchirant la famille milanaise des Sforza et condamnant Octavien Sforza, évêque de Lodi, et sa fille Lucrèce à l'exil vénitien. Si des nouvelles du recueil demeurent proches de la tradition boccacienne, d'autres, plus caractéristiques peut-être, font apparaître la tradition du conte merveilleux, qu'il appartienne à l'oralité européenne ou orientale.

La nouvelle que nous donnons est précisément de celles qui en dépit de tel détail qui semble récuser le il était une fois du conte (le roi Matthias de Hongrie par exemple, grand souverain humaniste du XVᵉ siècle), s'articule sur une tradition en même temps qu'elle apparaît comme l'une des versions que vont réécrire avec insistance le XVIIᵉ et le XVIIIᵉ siècle. Il s'agit de la Belle et la Bête dont Perrault donne une version lointaine dans son Riquet à la Houppe *et dont Mme de Beaumont donne la version la plus connue. On en oublie d'autres :* Marcassin et Serpentin vert *de Mme d'Aulnoy,* La Belle et la Bête *de Mme de Villeneuve, d'autres encore... Autant de textes qui vont travailler la transgression fascinante de l'amour pour une bête dans un sens moral plus ou moins édifiant. B. Bettelheim y trouve lui-même son juste compte, car après une telle histoire comment les jeunes filles ne croiraient-elles pas qu'il y a des raisons d'être confiantes dans l'avenir après les angoisses du premier moment !*

La version de Straparole est plus crue et la bienséance fort malmenée, le plaisir n'en est que plus grand. Cependant, ce qui est non moins évident c'est l'articulation du conte, ceux de Perrault et ceux de Bettelheim n'échapperaient pas à la règle, sur un solide tissu idéologique qu'on reconnaîtra sans peine si on a parcouru notre premier volume. Cela contribuait puissamment aux jeux du merveilleux, de l'interdit et des conformités vraisemblables qui caractérisent le conte « littéraire ».

Le recueil fut publié à Venise en 1550 pour sa première partie, en 1553 pour la seconde. Un traducteur connu pour sa traduction d'Apulée, au reste obscur, Jean Louveau, traduisit le premier livre en 1560. Sa traduction ne connut le succès que lorsque Larivey la reprit en 1573 en la complétant par celle du second livre. L'ensemble connut de multiples éditions. Nous avons d'ailleurs suivi ici une édition de 1726 précédée par une pré-

*face attribuée à B. de la Monnoye, grand spécialiste du XVIᵉ siècle et sou-
cieux de satisfaire « le goût que le siècle témoigne aujourd'huy pour l'antique ! »*

*Rappelons enfin que c'est encore chez Straparole qu'on peut trouver
l'origine du* Chat botté *de Perrault.*

J.P.G.

LES FACETIEUSES NUICTS
DU
SEIGNEUR STRAPAROLE

1726

LA SECONDE NUICT DES FABLES ET ENIGMES
du Seigneur Jean-François Straparole

Desjà Phebus avoit trempé ses roües dorées dedans les eaux salées de la mer Indienne, & ses luysans rayons ne donnoient plus de splendeur sur la terre : sa sœur cornüe pareillement dominoit desjà par tout les obscures tenebres avec sa claire & flamboyante lumiere : aussi les belles & esteincellantes estoilles avoient desjà par leur lueur donné la nayve peinture au Ciel, quand l'honneste & honorable Compagnie se retira au lieu acoustumé, pour continuer leurs plaisans propos. Et s'estant assis selon leur degré, Madame Lucrece commanda qu'on eust à poursuivre l'ordre tenu le soir précedent. Et pour autant qu'il restoit encore cinq Demoiselles pour raconter leurs nouvelles, la Dame enchargea au Trevisan qu'il eust à mettre en escrit leur nom, & le mettre en un vaisseau d'or : puis à l'extraire l'un après l'autre, comme on avoit desjà faict le soir precedent. Le Trevisan obeyssant au commandement de Madame, mit incontinent son vouloir en execution, & par fortune le premier qui saillit, ce fut le nom de la belle Isabelle ; le second de Fleurdiane ; le troisième d'Alienor ; la quatrième de Loyse ; le cinquième de Vincende : puis au son des fleutes ils commencerent à danser des branles que Moulin conduisoit, & Alienor, dont les Dames & les Gentilshommes en firent si grands ris, & en rient encore à present. Le branle rond finy, chacun s'assist. Alors les Damoiselles commencerent ceste chanson à la louange de Madame :

> Sans que jamais je change de propos :
> Quand vos vertus à tous j'annonceray,
> Quand tout honneur en vous prend son repos.

> Quelle beauté à vous compareray ?
> Quel cœur gentil, à bien du tout dispos ?
> Digne n'est pas du bien de l'autre vie,
> Si vostre los tousjours ne le convie.

La chanson amoureuse finie, Isabelle, à qui estoit escheu le premier lieu de la seconde nuict, commença joyeusement à raconter ce qui s'ensuit.

Galiot, Roy d'Angleterre, eut un fils nay porc, lequel se maria par trois fois, et ayant perdu sa peau de porc, devint un très beau jeune fils, qui depuis fut appelé le Roy porc.

Il n'y a au monde gracieuses dames langue tant eloquente et excellente en

bien dire, qui peust assez suffisamment exprimer combien l'homme est
tenu à son Createur, de l'avoir fait & formé homme en ce monde, & non
point beste brute. Et sur ceste matiere il me souvient d'un conte qu'on a
fait de nostre temps, d'un personnage qui nasquit porc, & depuis devint
un très beau jeune fils, appelé de tous le Roy porc.

Vous devez donc sçavoir, mes très chères dames, que Galiot fut roy
d'Angleterre, homme non moins riche aux biens de fortune, qu'en ceux de
l'esprit, & avoit pour sa femme la fille de Matthias, Roy de Hongrie,
nommée Hersile, qui en beauté, vertu & courtoisie, surmontoit toutes les
autres Princesses de son temps. Au reste, Galiot gouvernoit si bien son
royaume, qu'il ne se trouvoit aucun qui raisonnablement se peust plaindre
de luy. Ayans demeuré par longue espace de temps ensemble, fortune
voulut que jamais Hersile ne se peut engrossir ; ce qui deplaisoit grandement à l'un & à l'autre. Advint que Hersile se promenant une fois par son
jardin s'en alloit recueillant des fleurs, & se trouvant desjà un peu lasse,
apperceut un lieu plein de verdoyantes herbes, où elle s'assist, invitée du
sommeil, à cause des oyseaux qui chantoient sur la ramée, se vint à endor-
mir. Cependant voylà trois hautaines Fées qui vont passer en l'air, lesquelles voyans ceste jeune Dame endormie, s'arresterent, & ayant consideré la
beauté & bonne grace d'icelle, vont deliberer entr'elles de la faire inviolable et Fée. Elles furent donc en cela toutes trois d'accord. La premiere va
dire : Je veux qu'elle soit inviolable, & la premiere nuict qu'elle couchera
avec son mary qu'elle soit engrossie, & enfante le plus beau fils de ce
monde. La seconde dist : Je veux que personne ne la puisse offenser, &
que le fils qui naistra d'elle soit doüé de toutes les vertus & gentilesses qui
se peuvent imaginer. La troisième dit : Je veux qu'elle soit la plus sage &
la plus riche femme qui se puisse trouver ; mais que le fils qu'elle conce-
vra, naisse tout couvert de poil de porc, avec les contenances & maintien
d'un porc, & ne se puisse jamais changer de tel estat s'il ne prend premierement trois femmes. Ces trois Fées parties, Hersile s'esveille, & se leva
incontinent, & ayant prins ses fleurs qu'elle avoit recueilli, s'en retourna
au palais. Il ne se passa pas long-temps que Hersile s'engrossit, & quand
ce vint au temps d'enfanter, elle fit un fils qui n'avoit point membres
d'homme, mais plustost de porc. Ce qu'estant venu aux aureilles du Roy
& de la Royne, ils en conceurent une douleur merveilleuse : & afin que
tel enfantement ne redondast point au deshonneur de la Royne qui estoit
debonnaire, le Roy eut souventes fois fantaisie de le faire tuer & le jetter
en la mer. Mais considerant en son esprit, & pensant discrettement que le
fils, quel qu'il fust, estoit engendré de luy, & estoit de son sang, laissant
toute mauvaise intention qu'il pouvoit avoir en son cœur, ayant meslé la
pitié avec la douleur, voulut qu'il fust nourry & entretenu, non point
comme beste brute, mais comme animal raisonnable. Ce petit enfant
estant nourri en toute diligence, venoit souventes fois vers la Mere, & se
levant sur deux pattes, luy mettoit le petit groin en son giron, les petites
pattes sur ses genoux. Et la bonne mere ne laissoit pas de le caresser, en
luy mettant les mains sur sa peau peluë, & le baisoit & embrassoit tout
ainsi qu'une creature humaine. Cependant le petit fils se tourtilloit la
queuë, monstrant par signes evidens que les caresses maternelles luy
estoient fort agreables. Estant ce petit porc creu, commença à former la

parole humaine, & s'en alla par la ville, & se fourroit par les ordures &
immondices, comme font les autres porcs. Puis se trouvant ainsi ord &
sale, s'en retournoit en la maison, & en s'approchant du pere & de la
Mere, se frottoit à leurs beaux accoustremens, en les soüillant de fange &
puanteur : pour autant qu'ils n'avoient d'autre enfant que luy, ils portoient tout en patience. Un jour entre les autres, s'en venant au logis, ord
& sale, comme de coustume, se mit ainsi sur les vestemens de sa mere, &
luy dit en grondant : Ma mere, je me voudrois marier. Ce qu'entendant la
mere, luy respondit : Va fol que tu es, qui est celle qui te voudroit bien
prendre ? tu es puant & sale, & tu veux qu'un Baron ou un Chevalier te
donne la fille ? Il luy respondit en grondant, qu'il vouloit estre marié,
quoy qu'il en fut. La Royne ne sçachant comment s'y gouverner, s'en alla
trouver le Roy, en luy disant : Que ferons-nous ? vous voyez en quel estat
nous sommes, nostre fils veut à toutes forces estre marié, & n'y a aucune
qui le vueille prendre pour mary. Bien-tost après le petit Cochon retourna
vers sa mere, en grondant encore plus haut qu'il ne faisoit auparavant, &
disoit : Je veux estre marié, & ne cesseray jamais jusques à tant que j'aye
ceste jeune fille que j'ay aujourd'huy veu, car elle me plaist grandement.
C'estoit la fille d'une pauvre femme qui avoit trois filles, & chacune d'icelles estoit belle à merveille. Ce qu'entendant la Royne, envoya incontinent
querir ceste pauvre femme avec sa fille aisnée, & luy dit : Mere m'amie,
vous estes pauvre, & chargée de filles, si vous voulez consentir à ce que je
diray, vous deviendrez incontinent riche. J'ay ce fils que vous voyez lequel
je voudrois bien marier à vostre fille la plus grande. N'ayez point d'esgard
à luy qui est porc, mais au Roy & à moy : car à la fin elle demeurera
jouissante de ce Royaulme avec luy. La fille oyant ces paroles, se troubla
grandement & estant devenuë rouge comme la rose du matin, dit franchement qu'elle ne vouloit consentir par aucun moyen à telle chose. Toutesfois sa pauvre mere luy sceut si bien persuader avec plusieurs douces paroles, qu'elle en fut à la fin consentante. Le Cochon estant de retour au
logis, tout souillé, courut vers sa mere, qui luy dit : Mon fils, nous t'avons
trouvé une femme selon ton desir. Et ayant fait venir l'espousée, accous-
trée de riches vestemens, selon l'estat d'une Royne, se presenta devant le
Porc, lequel la voyant belle & gracieuse, s'en resjouissoit tout : & ainsi
puant l'environnoit, & avec le groin & les pattes luy faisoit les plus belles
caresses de ce monde, & pour qu'il luy souilloit tous ses accoustremens,
elle se repoussoit en arriere. Et le Porc luy disoit : Pourquoy me repous-
sez-vous ainsi ? ne vous ay-je pas fait faire ces acoustremens ? Et elle luy
respondit d'une voix hautaine : Ne toy, ni ton Royaume des Porcs ne me
les fis onc faire. Quand l'heure vut venuë de s'en aller reposer, la jeune
mariée dit : Que feray-je de ceste puante beste & infecte ? je le veux tuer
ceste nuict quand il sera sur le premier sommeil. Le Cochon, qui n'estoit
pas loing de là, entendant ce propos ne dit autre chose, mais s'en alla mettre en ce lict tant magnifique, estant tout couvert de fumier & de charo-
gne puante ; & avec son sale groin & ordes pattes, se mit à lever les lin-
ceulx deliez, & ayant tout soüillé de puantes infections, se coucha près de
l'espousée, laquelle ne demeura guères qu'elle ne s'endormist. Mais le
Porc feignant de dormir, luy vint à donner si grand coup en l'estomach
avec ses crochets, qu'elle demeura incontinant morte. Le Porc se levant le

matin assez tost s'en alla suivant sa coustume à paistre & se soüiller. Cependant la Royne s'en alla visiter sa belle fille, & l'ayant trouvée mise à mort par le Porc, en receut une très grande douleur. Estant le Porc de retour au logis, & estant rigoureusement reprins de sa Mere, il respondit qu'il luy avoit fait ce qu'elle luy avoit voulu faire : puis se partit tout courroucé.

Bien entendu, le Porc réclame une autre épouse, la Reine cède, lui donne la seconde fille de la pauvre femme qui connaît le même sort que son ainée. Après s'être fait grondé, le Porc exige la troisième fille, menace de mort la Reine qui résiste, puis cède.

La Royne fit venir la pauvre femme avec la troisième fille, nommée Meldine, & luy dit : Meldine, ma fille, je veux que tu prennes ce mien fils pour ton mary, & n'ayes point esgard à luy, mais à son pere & à moy ; car quand tu pourras temporiser avec luy, tu seras la plus heureuse & la plus contente fille de ce monde. Alors Meldine luy respondit d'un visage riant & gracieux, qu'elle en estoit fort contente, la remerciant humblement de ce que c'estoit son plaisir de la prendre pour sa fille. Et quand elle n'auroit jamais autre chose, celuy sembloit une grande faveur, que d'une pauvre fille qu'elle estoit, devenir en si peu de temps belle-fille d'un si puissant Roy. La Royne entendant une si gracieuse & amiable response, ne se peut tenir de plorer de la douceur qu'elle sentoit. Toutesfois elle craignoit qu'il ne luy en print autant comme aux deux autres. Or s'estant vestuë la nouvelle espouse de riches accoustremens, attendoit tousjours son cher espoux qu'il retournast au logis. Si tost que Monsieur le Porc fut venu, autant puant & souillé qu'il fut jamais, l'espouse le receut humainement, estendant sa precieuse robbe par terre, en le priant qu'il se couchast près d'elle. La Royne luy conseilloit de le faire reculer, ce qu'elle refusa [...] Monsieur le Porc qui ne dormait pas, mais entendoit clairement tout ce qu'on disoit, se levant sur ses pattes, luy léchoit le visage, la gorge, l'estomach & les espaules. Elle pareillement de son costé le caressoit & baisoit, en s'embrasant du tout d'amour. Quand l'heure fut venüe de s'aller reposer, l'espouse s'en alla coucher, attendant que son cher espoux y vint, lequel bien-tost ord & puant qu'il estoit, se vint coucher : elle commença à accoustrer la teste sur le chevet, en le couvrant fort bien, & fermant les courtines, afin qu'il n'endurast point de froid. Le jour venu, Monsieur le Porc ayant laissé sa place orde & puante, s'en alla paistre comme de coustume. Le matin la Royne s'en alla vers la chambre de l'espouse, & estimant voir ce qu'elle avoit veu des autres par le passé, trouva sa belle-fille toute joyeuse & contente, combien que le lict fust souillé d'ordures & d'infections, & remercia le bon Dieu d'un tel bien, de ce que son fils avoit trouvé une femme à son plaisir. Il ne se passa gueres de temps que Monsieur le Porc estant avec sa femme en propos joyeux, luy dit : Ma femme, m'amie Meldine, si je pensois que tu me manifestasses point mon secret, je te dirois à grand contentement & plaisir une chose que j'ay tenüe secrette jusques à present ; mais parce que je te cognois sage & discrette, & que tu m'aymes d'amour parfait, je t'en veux faire participante. Declarez-moy hardiment vostre secret, dit Meldine, car je vous promets de n'en dire jamais mot à personne sans vostre consentement. Estant Monsieur le Porc asseuré de sa femme, se vint oster sa puante & orde peau, & devint un beau jeune fils, & coucha toute la nuict estroictement entre les bras de sa chere Meldine.

Meldine accouche d'un fils parfaitement beau. Elle ne peut résister à l'envie de confier le secret à sa belle-mère. Le Roi et la Reine cachés observent comment leur fils étend sa peau de porc « par terre à costé de la chambre », le Roi ordonne qu'on la découpe. Très heureux le Roi abdique en faveur de son fils qui fut appelé le Roy Porc et, bien entendu, vécut avec sa Meldine « longuement en grande felicité ».

Matteo Bandello, Les Histoires tragiques, 1554-1568.

Avec ses 214 nouvelles, dont les trois premiers livres (176 nouvelles) furent publiés du vivant de l'auteur, Bandello affirmait son ambition de faire œuvre de chroniqueur de la société de son temps vue avec sa triple expérience d'ecclésiastique, de lettré et de courtisan. Son cadre favori : l'Italie du Nord ou la France (il fut évêque d'Agen). L'époque la plus souvent évoquée : la première moitié du XVIᵉ siècle qui suscita en Italie tant de bouleversements dont il fut le témoin direct (né en 1485 il mourut en 1561). Ses prétentions à « l'histoire véritable » s'appuient sur une organisation originale du recueil : rompant avec la tradition boccacesque d'une assemblée de conteurs située dans un cadre précis, il affirme transcrire des récits qu'il a entendu raconter tout au long de sa vie et feint de s'effacer derrière une multitude de narrateurs, personnages authentiques fréquentés par l'auteur et que sa plume seule réunit. De plus, chaque nouvelle est précédée d'une épître qui, précisant les circonstances du récit et le sens qu'on peut lui donner, fait apparaître un nouvel élément de l'art de Bandello : la volonté de donner à ses nouvelles une orientation utilisable du point du vue moral. Ces épîtres tissent autour des nouvelles un prestigieux réseau de dédicataires qui se superpose à celui des narrateurs pour relier plus étroitement Bandello au monde aristocratique de son temps.

La variété des sujets évoqués est à la mesure de la multiplicité des narrateurs et si la volonté de vérité est, comme dans L'Heptaméron, *assez illusoire, du moins le récit reste-t-il toujours vraisemblable : c'est la vie même des cours et des villes d'Italie que nous y trouvons, servant de toile de fond à des récits choisis pour leur aspect bouffon, exceptionnel ou sanglant. Dans cette évocation le plaisir de conter et d'étonner l'emporte bien souvent sur le but avoué d'édification morale et la nouvelle s'attarde complaisamment sur les ravages de la passion : trahisons, adultères, viols, incestes, crimes dont le dénouement souvent atroce témoigne moins d'une volonté de moralisme que d'une fascination certaine pour la violence.*

C'est précisément ce dernier aspect des Novelle *que devaient retenir les traducteurs français. Boaistuau d'abord, pour six nouvelles (dont l'histoire de Roméo et Juliette), puis Belleforest transformèrent les nouvelles de Bandello en sept volumes d'*Histoires Tragiques, *laissant de côté les exemples de vertu, les farces, les plaisanteries érotiques ou bouffonnes qui, dans le recueil italien, équilibraient les histoires d'amour et de mort. Belleforest sélectionna, bouleversa l'ordre des nouvelles et donna à chacune une orientation délibérément moralisatrice tant par ses préfaces que par ses digressions. Il prend d'ailleurs soin d'avertir loyalement le lecteur qu'il s'agit là d'un « embellissement donq (je ne l'appelleray plus traduction) », et qu'il ne s'est pas « asservi à la manière de parler dudit autheur : veu que je l'ay enrichi de sentences, d'adoption d'histoires, harangues & epistres, selon que j'ay veu que le cas le requeroit ». Pourquoi tant de modification ? Parce que Belleforest voit en Bandello un auteur « assez*

grossier » : *les nouvelles qu'il a triées sont « les perles d'emmy un fumier &*
ordure ». Et surtout Belleforest a des buts bien précis : il veut susciter
« *avec le plaisir, un appetit & honneste desir de suivre la vertu, & detester*
le vice », il espère par ses Histoires Tragiques « *faire voir à la jeunesse le*
degast, la ruine & malheur qui lui advient, si elle suit ses désirs volages &
lascifs ». *Le conteur s'est fait pédagogue et alourdit les narrations souvent*
vives de Bandelle d'enseignements pratiques : éducation des filles, choix
de leur époux, dangers de la danse, toutes réflexions qui n'existaient pas
dans le texte original. Cet effort de moralisation, déjà remarqué chez
Giraldi, est à relier à l'influence croissante (au moment où furent
publiées les traductions) de la Contre-Réforme : en Italie même le recueil
de Bandello ne reparaît qu'amputé, moralisé. Dans la nouvelle perspec-
tive qui était la leur, les Histoires Tragiques *eurent en France beaucoup*
de succès : constamment rééditées jusqu'à la fin du siècle (alors qu'il n'y
eut pendant la même période que trois éditions du texte italien), elles sus-
citèrent de nombreuses imitations : entre autres Le Printemps de Jacques
Yvet, *les* Nouvelles Histoires Tragiques *de Benigne Poissenot et en*
1614 les Histoires Tragiques de Nostre Temps *de Rosset.*

M.F.P.

LES HISTOIRES TRAGIQUES,
extraictes des œuvres italiennes de
BANDEL

et mises en langue françoise par
François de Belleforest
Tome II : Lyon, Rigaud
1616
Tome III Paris, Buon
1568

TOME II, NOUVELLE XXV

Mort piteuse de Julie de Gazole, laquelle se noya de despit, pour se voir violée.

Gazuolo, comme chacun sçait, est une ville, au duché de Mantoue, assise sur la rivière nommée l'Oglio, laquelle est vis à vis du père des fleuves, que les anciens ont appelé l'Eridant, et à present il porte le nom de Po, arrousant par ses embrassemens presque toute la terre d'Italie.

En celle ville il y a eu de nostre temps une fille nommée Julia, que le ciel devoit faire naistre Princesse ou grande Dame, à fin que le nom de sa vertu estant publié, eust servi de torche & flambeau à toute nostre jeunesse, le pere de laquelle estoit un povre homme, lequel pour toute richesse, n'avoit que ses bras à la peine desquels il s'essayoit de se substanter, & nourrir sa femme, & deux filles que Dieu lui avoit donné pour lustre de sa grande povreté : car quoy que la necessité induise souvent l'homme à faire choses, & contre l'honneur & vertu & reputation, si y a il des esprits si bien naiz, qu'au milieu de leur grande disette, monstrent les vrays effects de leur bonté, & la rare singularité de leur gentillesse : ce qui s'est assez declaré en ceste nostre Julia, laquelle comme elle fut plus gaillarde, courtoise, & bien apprise, que ne sont celles ordinairement qui sortent de pareille maison que la sienne, augmenta de tant plus sa louange par sa chasteté, qu'elle estoit abaissée de sang, & peu congneue par le nom de ses ancestres, lesquels elle a tous enrichis par la gloire de sa vie chaste & mort glorieuse. Et ce qui faisoit encor plus admirer ceste belle Contadine, c'estoit une singuliere & rare beauté, laquelle surpassoit toutes les filles de Gazuolo, non moins par sa bonne grace & lineament de corps, que la rose les moindres fleurs, durant la primevere. Et à dire le vray, quiconques la voyoit ou l'escoutoit parler, à grand peine l'eust-il prise pour fille de si bas lieu, tant elle estoit assurée en sa contenance, modeste en ses gestes, & courtoise en paroles, respondant si à propos à ce qu'on luy demandoit, que veu le peu d'age (elle n'ayant que quinze ou seize ans) elle eut fait honte aux plus accortes Damoiselles qui se nourrissoyent pour le temps d'adonc ès maisons des grands seigneur d'Italie, & l'eust prise en son service madame la Duchesse de Mantouë, si l'accident que j'espere vous compter ne luy fust si tost advenu. Or ceste fille estoit eslevée en travail, suyvant la vacation de son pere, & alloit ordinairement à journée, ores à sarcler, tantost à sarmenter : en somme, poursuyvant tous les exercices qu'usent continuellement les bonnes gens ès villages & petites villes, de sorte que jamais on ne la voyoit oysive, ni perdre une seule minute de temps qu'elle n'employast à faire quelque chose, sçachant fort bien que l'oysiveté est celle laquelle esbranle par la faineantise la chasteté des femmes les plus accortes qu'on sçache trouver & que les hommes qui sont sans occupation, tombent facilement ès laqs de folie, & meschanceté. C'est pourquoy le Poëte s'enquerant de la cause pour laquelle Egisthe estoit devenu adultere, respond tout soudain, disant :

La cause est prompte, il estoit paresseux.

Ceste belle Mantouäne, les jours des festes, suyvant la coustume du pays, s'en alloit avec ses compagnes s'esbattre & passer le temps avec telle honnesteté & modestie, que l'age & le sexe le requierent, sans que vilennie ni fols propos souillassent ni l'esprit, ni l'oreille de celles qui se posoyent en parade, pour manifester la liberté de leur vie, laquelle ne demandoit aucune retraitte pour parfaire les jeux. Et quand tout est dit, la pucelle qui cherche les coins de chambres, & les lieux égarez pour deviser, tant soit elle chaste ou modeste, si donne elle dequoy parler aux langues mesdisantes, qui occasionne un mauvais pensement à ceux mesmes qui ne soupçonnent pas trop à la legere. Qu'a affaire aussi la fille vertueuse, de se retirer loin des compagnies pour parler, puis que sa parole faut que se conforme à la vie, si elle vit comme elle doit, & parle comme elle passe sa vie ? Il n'est jà besoing que les lieux secrets soyent les seuls tesmoings de ces discours. Si plusieurs exemples de mauvaise digestion n'estoyent sortis de telle boutique, je ne feroys aucun arrest sur cecy, me contentant de loüer Julia, laquelle parloit comme elle vivoit, & estoyent ses mœurs conformes à sa parole. Passons toutesfois outre, contens que l'effect apprend les meres trop soigneuses, à ne laisser cacquetter leurs filles, sans contreroleur de leurs devis. Les cours des Princes & maisons des grands seigneurs ont empainte la chasteté sur le frontispice de leur palais, tant que ceste raisonnable captivité a tenues les filles en bride : mais depuis que, sans garde ni conduite, les damoiselles ont parlé en secret, & ont eu des cachettes pour faire & recevoir responses, Dieu sçait les beaux coups qui ont esté ruez, & combien de Dames ont esté prejudiciées en leur honneur & reputation. Mais continuons nostre propos, & suivons Julia qui, suivant les amorces d'amour, tomba ès laqs d'une pire peste, & fut enveloppée ès filets du desir d'un amoureux lascif, & plein de son vouloir, & paillard desordonné. En ce temps là estoit Evesque de Mantoüe le seigneur Loys Gonzague, frere du Marquis, lequel se tenant le plus souvent à Gazuolo, ne faut doubter que il n'y eust une belle & honneste suitte de gentils hommes & autres, qui estoyent de la maison de ce Prelat illustre, entre lesquels estoit un Ferrarois, qui servoit de valet de chambre, & qui, sans l'acte qu'il commit, ainsi que entendrez, pouvoit paroistre entre les plus gentils compagnons de ceux qui vivoient aux gages de l'Evesque : mais quoy ? une petite tache gaste souvent un fort beau accoustrement. Je vous ay desjà dit, que la coustume du pays porte que les feste l'on dresse le bal, où les jeunes filles peuvent se soulacer en veüe de toute le monde. En ces dances se trouva le Ferrarois, & voyant dancer autruy, apprint un bransle qui fut la fin pitoyable de celle sur qui il façonna ses mesures. Or à quoy qu'on veuille dire de l'art du dancer, si ne pense-je point qu'il soit sorty d'autre escole que de celle de Satan, veu les effects que de tous temps il a porté au monde. Laissant neantmoins les exemples qu'on peut colliger des histoires, tant divines que prophanes, sur la detestation de la dance, me contenteray de ce seul mot que le sage Romain a dit : Que jamais homme, ayant sain le cerveau, ne dança, tant les gestes des danceurs se rapportent aux contenances d'un fol moniacle. Ce valet de chambre episcopal, ayant regardé ententivement Julia, qui dançoit à l'envi, & sans mal penser, avec ses compagnes, estonné de sa galantise, & ravy pour ceste rare & exquise beauté, attiré à la voir plus, à cause de sa gaillardise & bonne grâce qu'elle avoit au bal, en devint en un moment si amoureux, que sans penser autre chose, il se delibera de la poursuyvre, & d'essayer d'en avoir la jouïssance.

A ceste cause, afin de sentir d'elle mesme si ce jeu luy viendroit à gré, il la vint prier d'un bransle, ce qu'elle ne refusa point, estant autant bien apprise, pour son calibre, comme elle estoit belle & vertueuse. Dès que le vallet de chambre sentit la douceur de ceste main delicate, quoy qu'elle travaillast tous les jours, si ne sentoit elle la rudesse de la peau d'une paysanne, il se veit encor brusler le cœur à petit feu, & experimentoit une guerre en soy, de laquelle il n'avoit encor fait jamais l'apprentissage. Durant ceste premiere dance, il ne fit que fantastiquer mille moyens pour oster ces apprehensions d'amour de sa cervelle, mais il falloit, en ce que la voyant, il sentoit amortir les flammes jà allumées en son cœur, c'estoit luy à sagement s'absenter de l'object de sa peine, & fuir le mal avant qu'il se fust vivement enraciné en ses entrailles, estant impossible d'approcher le feu des estouppes, sans que la vehemence ne les consume. Aussi un amant se voyant surpris, ne faut que penser d'estaindre l'ardeur de ceste rage qu'en s'esloignant de ce qu'il a trop après de soy, estant l'œil de la femme un vray attrait pour surprendre celuy qui de soy mesme se rend vaincu par son transport & affection mal bastie. Ainsi en advint il à ce beau amoureux, lequel à la seconde dance commença à s'emanciper & ayant fait le muet reprint cœur & parole, tenant quelques legers propos d'amour à sa nouvelle maistresse, luy disant qu'il ne sçavoit d'où est ce que pouvoit venir ce soudain changement en son esprit, que luy qui jamais n'avoit voulu assujettir sa liberté au service de femme du monde, maintenant void la chance tournée, & devint amoureux d'elle, avec transport, que si elle n'avoit pitié de luy, il estoit en grand danger de la vie : toutesfois estimoit-il son amour bien employé, s'estant addressé à une fille si belle qu'il esperoit qu'une beauté telle ne sçauroit estre sans la compagnie d'une grande douceur & courtoisie. La fille, qui estoit un vray miroir de chasteté, luy respondit sagement, & sans beaucoup s'esmouvoir, disant : Je ne sçay qui vous fait tenir ce langage en mon endroit, veu le peu de cognoissance que vous avez de moy qui ne sçay, & ne pretens guere sçavoir, que c'est que d'amour, n'estant guere bienseant à fille de mon estat de prester l'oreille à telles folies. Je suis d'avis que vous vous adressiez à vos pareilles, qui peut estre cognoissant vostre perfection vous escouteront, & satisferont à vos requestes : car à moy avez vous failly, qui vous declare dès à present que telle pauvre que je suis, j'aymeroye mieux souffrir la mort que donner la moindre attainte que soit à mon honneur, duquel je suis aussi jalouse, comme vous voulez par vos paroles m'en faire prodigue. Le Ferrarois, l'oyant ainsi parler, ne perdit cœur pourtant, revenant à ce proverbe, que pour un refus ne faut cesser de heurter à la porte. Ains estant le bal fini, luy dit tout bas : Mamie, pensez bien à ce que je vous ay dit, & ne soyez cause de la mort de celuy qui vous ayme si ardemment, à fin que ne vous en faille rendre honte devant Dieu. C'est le moindre de mes soucis, dit-elle, que ce conte, estant resolue que vous obeissant je serois plus coulpable que si vous mouriez par vostre folie. Pource, ne laissez de poursuyvre ailleurs, car je mourray plustost qu'endurer tel deshonneur, & donner diffame à la vertueuse pauvreté de mes parents. Il s'estonna de ceste responce, & congneut bien qu'il seroit bien difficile de faire bresche à muraille si forte, & si chastement cimentée. Mais ne laissa pourtant la suyvre, pour sçavoir le logis de Julia, laquelle allant & venant des champs, trouvoit souvent ce beau amoureux, lequel avec ses importunitéz ne cessoit de luy recommander sa cause, s'efforçant de reschauffer par ses prieres le cœur glacé de la chaste Contadine. Mais il gaignoit autant que s'il se fut occupé à compter le sablon menu qui couvre les deserts de l'Arabie deserte, d'autant qu'elle luy dit : C'est assez gazouillé pour perdre temps, je vous prie que ce soit la dernière fois, car tant que l'ame me battra au corps, ni vous ni autre vous venterez de mon amitié, seulement l'aura celuy à qui Dieu voudra que je sois conjointe par mariage. Et vrayement voilà une bien grande honnesteté, que les gens de nostre Evesque, au lieu de nous inciter à la vertu, soyent les ministres de toute ribaudise. Allez prescher celles qui sont de paste pareille à vos charnels pensemens, & ne courez plus par les champs après les filles, lesquelles aymant Dieu, & soigneuses de leur honneur, s'essayent de gaigner leur vie à la sueur de leur corps, & labeur continu de leurs mains. Vous ferez bien de me laisser en paix, & de donner repos à vostre esprit mesme, veu l'assurance que je vous donne derechef, que tant que je vivray, homme lascif ne se vantera d'avoir eu le dessus à mon vouloir de ma virginité, & chasteté jurée. L'amant qui n'estoit plus autre que l'esclave de folie, & le cœur duquel estoit incessamment rongé d'un fol desir de jouissance, tant plus Julia se monstroit fiere & restive, de tant s'enflammoit-il davantage, la poursuivant avec plus d'importunité que jamais [...]

Toutes ses prières et démarches s'avérant inutiles, le Ferrarais décide d'user de la force et, avec l'aide d'un ami, surprend Julia tandis qu'elle se rend seule aux champs. Une fois de plus elle repousse ses avances.

[...] Ces parolles dites, se doutant de quelque malheur, que la fière contenance du Ferrarois luy sembloit presager, & predire, & que le cœur la menaçant luy disoit, commença à s'en aller au petit pas lequel quelquefois elle redoubloit, comme advient à ceux qui n'osent courir où le plus ils desirent de s'esloigner. L'amant qui ne vouloit pas qu'un si bon morceau luy fust osté de la bouche, sans en rassasier son appetit, feignit avec toute douceur & courtoisie de la vouloir accompagner jusques à la ville. Or quelque escuse qu'elle sçeut amener, si fallut-il qu'elle passast par là, & qu'escoutant les plaintes de son amant elle print le chemin de son malheur, & telle peux-je bien dire. Car le meschant paillard, voyant qu'elle marchoit toujours, sans luy dire un seul mot, & taschoit par tous moyens de se sauver, sans luy faire bonne ny mauvaise responce, se voyant esloigné de toute compagnie, loing de la ville, & en lieu où la solitude le rendoit plus hardy, comme estant au milieu des bleds, qui estoient hauts & espais, tels que sont sur la fin de May, & pource luy dit : Et quoy ? la belle, pensez vous eschapper à si bon marché, & vous mocquer toujours de celuy qui vous aime plus que soy mesme ? Et par Dieu il ne sera pas ainsi, ains ferez ce que je veux, à quelque pris que ce soit. Ce disant, vous l'empogne & la baise, elle resiste de tout son pouvoir, & se met à crier au meurtre & à la force. Mais voicy le ministre d'iniquité, qui accompagnoit l'amant, lequel peut-être se fust adoucy aux douces requestes de la Julia, lequel vous l'empoigna, disant : toubeau, toubeau m'amie, c'est trop bravé pour une dame de vostre sorte, pensez vous qu'on soit icy venu pour s'amuser à vos doleances, & moins à vostre crierie ? Elle prie qu'on la face mourir, & que la mort luy sera plus aggreable que le faict qu'elle se voyoit desjà appresté, & par où il luy falloit passer. Mais le galand respond qu'il n'estoit point là venu pour user de saccagement ou massacre, mais seulement pour secourir son amy duquel la vie dependoit de ceste seule jouissance. C'estoit pitié d'ouyr les piteux regrets de la miserable pucelle, & les hauts cris qu'elle envoyoit en l'air, pour tesmoignage de son innocence ; & plus encor, qui eust veu sa triste contenance, lors que les paillards craignans qu'elle ne fut à la longue entendue, la baillonnerent autant cruellement, comme iniquement le Ferrarois ravit d'elle le pris & fleur de la virginité. Ce qu'ayant fait, s'essaye de l'apaiser, disant : Quoy ma mignonne, ne voulez vous pas laisser ces façons de faire tant farouches, desquelles jusques icy vous avez tourmenté ma vie ? Ne voulez vous point amoullir la durté de vostre courage, pour jouyr de l'aise d'une ferme amitié que je vous porteray tout le reste de mes jours ? Non, non, rejettez tout souci, & pensement, asseurez sur moy, qui suis deliberé si le trouvez bon, de vous entretenir desormais, & vous fournir toutes choses necessaires. Avez-vous faute d'argent ? En voicy, disoit-il, luy monstrant une bourse, ne pensez qu'à faire bonne chere, & vous donner du bon temps. Que s'il vous prend desir d'estre mariée, je vous y tiendray si bien la main, & vous y secourray de telle sorte, que vous aurez de quoy vous contenter. Elle estant desjà desbaillonnée, le regardant d'un œil tant felon, que peut celle qui se sent blessée jusques au plus sensible de son cœur, luy respondit : Ah chien infect, & boue infame, j'aurois un beau appuy sur un si meschant & detestable que tu es. Va avec ton argent, & ne pense que si meschamment & avec violence tu as eu de moy l'effect de tes lascifs desirs, que pour cela tu ayes corrompu le cœur, ni la chasteté de Julia : car chaste mourray-je pour m'aller plaindre de ta vilennie devant le Juge qui voit & cognoit toutes choses. Est-ce à toy à me contenter qui m'as osté ce que tout le monde ne sçauroit me restituer ? Non, non, c'est à Dieu qui me contentera, punissant les deux bourreaux de la virginité d'une fille malheureuse. Le Ferrarois s'essayoit encor de la consoler, & la rendre quoye par ses parolles & caresses, mais elle le rejettant, luy dit : Te suffise, homme brutal, d'avoir fait à ton plaisir, & avoir rassasié ton desordonné appetit, je te prie de grace que tu me laisses aller en paix, car te voyant le cœur me creve, & t'escoutant je pers toute patience. A quoy le galant obeit, craignant que quelqu'un ne survint, lequel oyant les plaintes de la fille, & oyant le discours de son ravissement n'en allast faire le recit à l'Evesque qui haissoit à mort ces vilennies. Allez que les galands s'en furent, la fille violée se commença prendre à ses beaux cheveux, & fondant toute en larmes se print à dire : Helas bon Dieu ! est-il possible que la rigueur de ta justice se feit tant aspre sur moy, que pour mes fautes passées, j'aye enduré une penitence si dure ? Ah pere eternel ! de quel œil regarder mes parens après avoir perdu ce qui me rendoit en toute compagnie ? Je ne sçaurois dissimuler ce que couvrir je ne pretens, feindre où la chose me touche de si près. Il faut effacer ceste tache par le moyen de ma mort, laquelle sera aussi soudaine, comme la trahison du meschant a esté cruelle pour massacrer ma chasteté & continence. Ainsi tout aussitost qu'elle eust dit ce mot, elle se recoiffe, & ayant essuyé ses yeux, s'en va à la ville, en la maison de son pere, lequel de malheur estoit encore absent. Là elle se vest de ses habits plus precieux, s'attiffe, & mignotte, comme si elle fust allée à la feste, & prenant sa sœur plus jeune qu'elle en sa compagnie, ayant fermé la porte de la maison, s'en alla chez une sienne tante, femme sage & discrette, laquelle gisoit au lict fort malade. A ceste cy avec souspirs, sanglots & larmes la povre fille compte tout le fait, & luy declare les points de son desastre. Ce fait, entrant en un'extase, & transport d'esprit à demi desesperée, cesse de plourer, gemir, & souspirer, disant ainsi : Et quoy ? est-ce maintenant qu'il se faut plaindre quand est besoin que le cœur monstre le plus de force ? Jà à Dieu ne plaise que celle là demeure en vie, laquelle a perdu l'honneur, lequel seul luy causoit le desir de vivre. Et quelle vie est celle où l'ame est assaillie de mort, & l'esprit affoibli par infamie ? Non, non, jamais homme ne monstrera au doigt celle Julia, que le paillard infame auroit corrompu sans qu'elle puinisse d'elle en soymesme la faute. Ma fin donnera à cognoistre à chacun, & fera foy à tout le monde, que c'a esté par force que le corps est pollu & violé, demeurant tousjours mon esprit entier, & sans aucune tache de consentement à ceste paillardise. C'est à vous, ma tante, à declarer à mes tristes parens ceste malheureuse desconvenue, & dire à chacun que Julia a perdu l'honneur en ce qui est apparoissant, mais que sa conscience s'en va tesmoigner au Ciel son integrité, & la cruauté barbaresque du malheureux, qui causant la perte d'une partie en moy, fait que volontairement je vay immoler ma vie aux ondes, pour laver les souilleures du corps, lesquelles j'ay receues en moy, par la paillardise du voleur de ma vie. Ayant dit cecy elle ne voulut attendre la responce, ni remonstrances de la sage dame, qui s'apprestoit de la desmouvoir de ceste fiere entreprise, ains s'en alla tout droit vers la riviere d'Oglio, & estant sur le bord d'icelle, elle s'escria disant ; Recoy, mon Dieu, en tes mains, celle qui ne peut vivre, ayant perdu la cause de sa vie, & soudain se lança en l'eau, la teste la premiere, là où ne fut gueres sans donner le signe de sa mort, estant absorbée & engloutie par les ondes. Sa sœur voyant cas si piteux, se mit à crier & lamenter, preste presque à la suivre à la trace, si le peuple ne fust survenu, lequel adverty du faict, le fit soudain entendre à l'Evesque. Dieu sçait en quel trouble fut toute la ville, pour la nouveauté du faict, & de quelle peine on eust estrené le galand, cause de ce desastre, s'il eust esté attrapé.

Tant y a que le seigneur Loys Gonzague fit pescher le corps, & le fit enter-
rer en la place commune de la ville, ne la voulant mettre en terre saincte, à
cause de son desespoir, esperant, avec le temps, d'y faire eslever en marbre ou bronze un tombeau digne de la louange & vertu d'une si vertueuse
fille, le corps de laquelle fut accompagné de larmes & pleurs de toutes les
dames de la ville, lesquelles honnoroyent la chasteté violée de celle qui fait
honte aux folles, lesquelles font plus de parade d'un masque d'integrité
que cestui de la mesme perfection requise aux plus accomplies que la terre
porte, & qui neantmoins ne peuvent resister à la simple apprehension des
assauts d'amour, tant s'en faut qu'il y faille user de force. Apprenez donc,
filles, non à vous noyer ni forfaire à vostre corps mais à resister aux charmes & piperies des amans & à ne donner occasion de poursuitte par les
signes attrayans & œillades peu discrettes desquelles la jeunesse ne fait
que trop son profit. La force de chasteté ne consiste point à respondre
doucement, à replicquer accortement, à rejetter les demandes inciviles des
poursuivans : ce sont des amorces que ce parlementer, ce sont des traicts
d'amour que ces hantises, & le feu de Cupidon que toutes ces delicatesses.
Fuyez, comme Julia, les approches & evitez la parole de celuy qui aime
plus en vous la beauté exterieure, que celle qui vous fait l'ame resplendissante, & qui paint l'honneur si vivement en vos faces, & l'engrave tellement en vos cœurs qu'à la mort et à la vie ce immortel renom fait vivre la
memoire de votre integrité.

TOME III, NOUVELLE I

*Deux Vénitiens, voisins et ennemis, ont courtisé la femme l'un de l'autre. Sur-
pris une nuit l'un chez l'autre par le guet, ils sont impliqués dans une affaire de
meurtre. Ils préfèrent se laisser condamner par la justice plutôt que de voir révé-
lée leur infortune conjugale réciproque. Leurs femmes viennent les défendre
devant le tribunal.*

[...] Or n'ont-ils occasion aucune de se douloir & plaindre de nous que
par un seul respect auquel nous avons & sentons véritablement plus
d'interest que piece de ceux qui se forgent des passions sans bien peser les
matieres : c'est entant qu'ils se sont trouvez surpris par le guet en la maison, en la chambre, & au lict l'un de l'autre. C'est icy que gist le nœud, &
tout le plus fort de ceste cause, c'est le vers qui ronge & tourmente le cœur
de nos fidelles espoux : & vous supplie, Prince tresdebonnaire, & vous
Magnifiques seigneurs, de leur faire dire si ce n'est la cause veritable de
leur desespoir, & l'occasion de la haine qu'ils nous portent. Le Duc, leur
gratifia en cecy, & ayant interrogé leurs marys, ouyt que sans rien dissimuler, ils appeloyent leurs femmes Putains impudiques, & ne faisoyent
conscience de publier leur honte devant une si noble, & honorable assemblée. Ce qu'oyant la damoiselle deffenderesse, tournant la parolle avec un
visage riant, mais qui ressentoit son amertume & mescontentement de se
voir ainsi injuriée, parla ainsi continuant sa harengue : C'est à nous, mon
cher espoux, de nous plaindre en telle infidelité qui avons souffert l'injure
par le moyen des plus desloyaux hommes que la terre porte. Et je voudroy

bien sçavoir de vous quels affaires vous aviez au logis de vostre ennemy, & qu'est ce qu'il cerchoit en vostre chambre, veu que je sçay ne luy avoir parlé de ma vie, & qu'aussi ma voisine cy presente ne vous favorisa onc d'une seule parolle. Mais avant que je parte d'icy, j'espere que ceste noble assemblée cognoistra nostre justice, & vous jugera pour infidelles & desloyaux en vostre mariage & pour vrais & injustes homicides de nostre honneur, qui ne fut onc violé que par vos desseins, & n'a eu atteinte que de vos pensées, nous estant telles qui jamais ne feismes faute qu'en vous aymant, & gardant loyauté veu la vie que nous sçavions estre menée par vous, & laquelle vous a guidez à la prison. Dressez, dressez vos plaintes contre vous, sans souiller ainsi l'honneur d'autruy, & soyez marris d'avoir cerché moyen de vous tromper l'un l'autre avec voz amours, estant saouls & dedaignans les viandes qui vous estoient ordinaires. Et quelle est la loy qui vous dispence plus de fausser la foy, & vous permette toute licence de tout faire, plutost qu'à celles qui vous sont jointes, & données, non pour esclaves, ains pour vous estre associées & compaignes ? Ne faut-il point que la foy soit esgalle au mariage, puis que la Loy lie l'homme & la femme sous un mesme serment & promesse ? Mais je laisseray à part ceste complainte afin que vous, Prince très illustre, & vous magnifiques seigneurs, entendiez pourquoi je tiens ce propos, & ayant ouy de fil en esguille notre droit, vous plaise de nous reconcilier nos marys & nous les rendre apaisez en nostre endroict selon que voz excellences verront que meritera nostre innocence : veu que nous sçavons bien que le dame qui se forfait en son honnesteté, & s'esgare en la loy de pudicité, ne merite point de jouyr de la lumiere plaisante de ceste vie. Il n'est jà besoing que je vous recite icy l'inimitié mortelle qui de longtemps a esté entre noz marys, comme asseurée qu'il n'y a si petit en ceste cité qui n'en aye la cognoissance. Mais je diray que ma voisine cy présente & moy, voyans la haine irreconciliable d'entre noz espoux, quoy que amies & fort familieres dès nostre enfance, comme ayant esté nourries ensemble, dissimulions nostre affection devant eux, mais quand ils estoient sortis du logis, il n'estoit jour que nous ne communicassions ensemble en nos jardins par le moyen d'une petite haie palissée simplement de roseaux. Or par succession de temps, nous prismes garde que noz marys, quittant le devoir d'Amitié à leurs espouses se mirent à œillader la femme de leur voisin, tellement que le mien faisoit service à ma compaigne, & le sien se montroit mon très affectionné serviteur. Les embassades trottoyent de toutes pars, les lettres ne manquoyent point, les rithmes n'y estoient pas oubliées, ainsi que nous montrerons, les ayant icy escrites & signées de mains de nos bons marys. Nous qui les aymons, & estimons plus qu'ils ne tiennent compte de noz honnestetez, dressames la partie telle que moy, par le moyen de Cassandre fille de chambre qui me sert, ayant donné assignation à Hieronyme, luy mettois son espouse entre les bras, & elle, sous la conduite de sa chambriere, faisoit venir Anselme avec lequel comme estant son espouse, je couchay sans reprehension : & qu'il soit vray, que l'un de vous, noz vaillants marys, die l'heure qu'il a veuë sa dame en veuë, & donne les signes de la chambre de son voisin. Loué soit Dieu, que sans l'offenser, nous avons contenté voz desordonnez apetis, & en vous trompant nous avons le ventre enflé par l'effait de telle tromperie. Que s'il n'y a autre forfait qui vous greve, ny autre crime qui

elance le ver de vostre conscience, je suis d'avis que vous teniez joyeux, &
allegres, & nous rendiez graces de la fourbe jouée. [...]

TOME III, NOUVELLE XLV.

Un gentilhomme Sienoys ayant trouvé sa femme estre adultere, la mena
hors de Siene, & la feit miserablement mourir, avec la servante qui estoit
consentante au malefice.

Siene (comme chacun sçait) a eu l'honneur de tout temps d'estre estimée
une des plus belles & riches citez entre les plus anciennes de Toscane, &
laquelle fut jadis bastie par les Gauloys Senonoys qui passerent en Italie
contre les Romains avec Brenne leur Capitaine, & depuis fut enrichie, &
augmentée par ce grand deffenseur de la Chrestienté, & l'honneur des
Françoys, Charles Martel, se plaisant en l'assiette de ceste belle, & magnifique cité. A Siene donc, y eut jadis (comme la ville de tout temps est
illustrée de fort belles dames) une damoiselle qui avoit attaint la perfection de beauté telle que l'homme sçauroit souhaiter en femme qui vive, &
autant gentille, accorte, & de bonne grace qu'on en sçeust pour lors en
Toscane, & de race ancienne, & fort riche maison, comme estant sortie
des Tolomei, lignée assez renommée, & illustre par toute celle contrée.
Ceste-cy venuë en l'age propice pour estre amourachée fut poursuyvie en
mariage par plusieurs jeunes & bragards gentilshommes, que si le choix
luy eust esté donné, elle ne se fust point ruée sur celuy que son pere luy
donna depuis en despit qu'en eust la fille. Or ce pere, qui comme tout
vieillard n'avoit point d'esgard aux desirs de la jeunesse, & ne se souvenant plus que l'aise d'une fille ne consiste point simplement à estre apariée
avecque quelque riche & puissant, maria Pie (ainsi s'appeloit ce miroir de
beauté) agée de quelque dixhuit à dixneuf ans, à un gentilhomme jeune de
cinquantecinq à soixante ans, & avec quel plaisir de la fille je vous le
laisse penser entre vous damoiselles qui estes en la fleur de vostre age, &
m'en rapporte à vous si Pie estant si mal pourveuë avoit grand occasion de
se contenter, vivant d'ordinaire comme une religieuse ou veufve reformée,
& ne sçachant presque pour quelle occasion est-ce qu'on l'avoit mariée.
Ce qui incita le pere avare à estre si cruel à ce sien enfant fut que le gentilhomme nommé Nello de la Pietra estoit le plus riche & aisé de Siene, & le
plus puissant qui fust en Maremme de Siene. Or Maremme est le païs qui
s'avoisine de la mer, estant du territoire & juridiction d'icelle cité, & qui
commence au fleuve Cornia par deça Sovretto, & s'estant jusqu'à la
riviere Pescie, ayant près de trente lieuës d'estendue. Ce messer Nello avec
toutes richesses estoit mal plaisant, chiche, hargneux, & soupçonneux au
possible, & pource se voyant avoir une chose si belle en sa puissance, &
congnoissant qu'il n'avoit dequoy pouvoir fournir à l'apointement,
comme celuy qui ayant la neige sur le mont ne pouvoit estre que froid aux
valées, se retira aux champs, ce qui donna un estrange mescontentement à
la damoiselle mal pourveuë, & plus encore, voyant la vilennie de son
espoux, qui lui faisoit faire plus de jeusnes qu'on ne sçauroit trouver en la
teste de la plus grande bigotte d'entre celles qui courent par les stations à
Rome. Il vouloit mortifier la chair de celle qui avec son extreme beauté

eust induit un jeusneur à prendre goust & appetit sur elle, & ce pendant il
se refroidissoit de luy mesme de telle sorte, qu'elle le voyant de tout sans
chaleur ny substance, fallut enfin que se pourveust d'autre pasture. Prenez
exemple peres & meres en ceste-ci, & ne soyez si convoiteux de la
richesse de voz filles, que vous oubliez pour cela de leur donner quelque
contentement, veu que comme dit le poëte, si tu veux bien marier une
femme il la faut joindre à son pareil. Or quelle egalité y a-il d'une jeune
fille, fresche, gaillarde, & bien disposée, avec un vieillard, have, grison,
cassé, & sans plaisir, & lequel ne sert que d'une statue de marbre froid
auprès de celle qui souhaite bien autre chose que les admonitions de continence par celuy qui ne peut parfaire ce qui est des appenages de mariage ?
Il voudroit mieux quelquefois pour vostre honneur que ces filles fussent
mortes sortant de la matrice, que les meurtrir ainsi en causant leur folie,
& vous repaissant d'un breuvage amer de courroux qui quelquefois vous
conduit au tombeau devant voz jour. Et aussi quelle loy permet-il la
tyrannie si grande sur voz enfans qu'à tout le moins un peu de liberté ne
leur soit donnée sur le choix de chose qui leur est de si grande consequence que le mariage ? Ne sçaves vous pas que ce qui est fait par con-
trainte en cest endroit mesmement, n'eut jamais bonne issue ? Je laisse
plusieurs exemples que je pourroy amener de nostre temps mesme, pour
poursuyvre nostre histoire, & voir quelle fin eut ce beau accouplement
d'une très-belle & jeune damoiselle, avec un vieillard cassé, jeusneur, &
sans force. [...]

Ses affaires amènent Messer Nello à s'installer à Siene pour quelque temps. Pie
noue une liaison avec un jeune gentilhomme, grâce à la complicité d'une de ses
servantes (Bandello emprunte à une autre aventure siennoise, l'Histoire
d'Eurial et de Lucrèce d'Aeneas Silvius Piccolomini, cf. plus haut, des éléments
romanesques pour étoffer son intrigue). Mais un vieux serviteur dénonce les
amants au mari.

[...] Nello qui se doutait desjà assez de son coquage, voyant sa femme
plus joyeuse que de coustume, ne requist grand serment de son homme
pour la foy de son rapport, joint qu'il sçavoit que ce n'estoit point de trop
longtemps que Pie familiarisoit ainsi sa servante, que ceste nouveauté de
courtoisie ne procedoit d'ailleurs sinon que la fille estoit celle qui moien-
noit les entrées & saillies de celuy qui l'envoioit en Cornouaille sans
bateau. A ceste cause, deffendant au vieillard de faire aucun semblant de
rien, se delibera de se venger & de sa femme & de la fille servante,
puisqu'il ne sçavoit qui estoit son lieutenant de couche ; & cognoissant
que sans grand peril de sa vie, il ne pourroit exploiter son dessein à Siene
où sa femme estoit fort apparentée, il prit complot de s'en aller. Par ainsi
ayant soudain mis ordre à ses affaires, il feit à l'improviste, & personne
n'y pensant point, trousser bagage, & prend la route de la Maremme avec
toute sa famille. Or quoy que Pie ignorast la cause d'un si soudain depart,
si eust-elle ne sçay quel elancement de cœur voyant qu'il luy fallust partir,
lequel estoit un vray prognostic de sa ruine ; mais surtout sa damoiselle se
douta du malheur sçachant que depuis le jour mesme qu'elle avoit mis

hors Augustin déguisé en femme, Nello n'avoit cessé de tenir propos au delateur, & l'avoit caressé deslors plus que de coustume. Elle se fust volontiers retirée en sa maison chez ses parens, mais le soudain depart de Nello luy boucha le chemin de l'effet de sa deliberation, qui fut cause qu'elle se prepara de tout souffrir, plustost que rien dire qui peut prejudicier à sa maistresse, laquelle elle voyoit en grand bransle de perdre la vie si Dieu ne luy faisoit quelque grace singuliere. La pauvre fille n'eust jamais pensé que le mary cruel, & jaloux, se fust acharné sur elle, qui n'avoit rien fait que pour obeïr à sa dame, comme si ès choses vicieuses, & vilaines on devoit obeïssance à quiconque soit ayant commandement & puissance, aussi fust elle trompée en ce sien discours d'esprit.

Car Nello ne fust pas si tost en Maremme qu'il vous fait mettre la main sur le collet de ceste pauvre fille, à fin de luy faire confesser tout ainsi qu'il s'estoit passé, & pour cognoistre d'elle celuy qui si subtilement visitoit le plus secret du logis de ce vaillant mary. On la tourmente, on la presse tant par flaterie que par menaces, mais jamais elle ne disoit rien qui touchast à ce qu'ils demandoient ; jusqu'à ce que Nello enragé de fureur y arrivant, dit : Baillez moy la torture à ceste petite paillarde, affin qu'elle apprenne d'estre une autre fois plus fidelle à ceux de qui elle deust avoir l'honneur en recommandation. La fille voyant le chevalet dressé s'esbahit de telle sorte que tout soudain elle confessa & les menées amoureuses & l'office qu'elle avoit fait, & la longueur du temps de la jouissance, & le nom de celuy qui avoit gaigné le cœur de Pie. Nello plus furieux qu'un Lyon commanda que sur le champ elle fust estranglée, ce qui fut fait & ce pendant Pie, oyant tout cecy, cognoissant que la mort luy estoit voisine se recommanda à Dieu luy suppliant de luy pardonner ses fautes & gemissant fort amerement pour sa vie passée, se repentant qu'elle n'avoit creu le conseil de ceste pauvre fille. Mais comme elle estoit en ces contemplations, voicy le mary qui entre, & la trouvant eplourée, & en oyant la raison, luy dit : Ha fauce & malheureuse femelle ne pense me gaigner ny adoucir par tes larmes traistresses, & trompeuses : ce n'est à present le temps de te plaindre pour chose que tu as choisie, & en as usé de ta franche volonté, mais c'estoit lors que ceste raison te devoit conduire, quand mechamment tu feis l'entreprise de me faucer la foy, & abuser de ma courtoisie. Pense seulement en Dieu, si tu as quelque soucy de ton ame, car la mort ne peux tu eschapper l'ayant si bien meritée que tu as, introduisant un adultere au lit legitime de ton espoux. Et ne pouvant plus parler, partie pressé de l'amour qu'il avoit porté à sa femme, partie de colère pour le tort receu, il commanda à ses gens qu'elle fust bien tost despechée.

Pie, voyant que ce seroit peine perdue que de demander pardon ou grace quelconque, tourna du tout son cœur à Dieu, faisant entière & longue confession de ses fautes, & ayant prié Dieu avecque telle devotion qu'on peut penser que prient ceux qui se voyent proches de leur jugement, elle suplia qu'avant qu'on luy donnast la mort qu'elle prenoit en gré, & confessoit l'avoir bien meritée, elle feust asseurée que son mary luy pardonnoit, affin (dit elle) qu'avecque ce contentement je m'en aille plus joyeuse en l'autre monde, & sans soucy de le laisser en sortant avec la grace de mon espoux que j'ay offencé, & auquel après Dieu, je fais à present ceste amende, & me recommande à ses devotes prieres & oraisons.

Cecy est rapporté au mary, lequel fondant en larmes leur dist : Allez, allez, je luy pardonne d'aussi bon cœur comme malgré moy je souffre de sa deffaite, & sans doute que s'il eust veu la belle & gentille Pie se representant constamment à la mort, & avecques quel desir elle requeroit le pardon de son mari avant mourir, il eust revoqué sa sentence. Ainsi pour amortir les chaleurs d'Amour mourut, & fut estranglée Pie de Tolomei de laquelle Dante parle au cinquieme chant de son Purgatoire disant :

> Souvienne toy de moy : car je suis celle Pie
> Qui a Sienne nasquis, & perdis la vie
> A Maremme, par cil qui d'un anneau ma foy
> Engagea m'espousant, puis m'esloigna de soy.

Le Nello n'osa de sa vie guere plus s'esloigner de ses terres tant craignant l'amy de la deffunte, que les parens liguez ensemble contre luy, veu que jamais homme ne conceut aucune mauvaise opinion de ceste damoiselle en Siene, qui faisoit croire à chascun que Nello y avoit plus procedé de meschanceté & soupçon que de justice qui fut en sa cause. Mais luy qui sçavoit la vraye blessure qui l'offençoit, se contentoit d'avoir osté & l'infamie & le soupçon d'icelle de sa maison ; ne se souciant de ce que les autres en pouvoyent penser, pourveu qu'il eust ce contentement en son âme, que puis qu'il n'avoit peu tuer celuy qui avoit corrompu sa femme, à tout le moins luy avoit esté loisible de se venger sur celle qui devoit le respecter, autrement que s'abandonner comme une femme folle au premier qui vint pour la poursuyvre. Et disoit que c'est à l'homme libre à chercher son adventure, & à la femme honneste de se deffendre : l'un estant surprins sur le fait, ne devoit estre espargné, & l'autre après encore ne pouvoit demeurer sans punition, veu que c'est un grand creve-cœur à l'homme de bon esprit de laisser jouïr de la communauté de sa table, & de son lit à celle qui, se faschant de ce qu'elle a, cherche ailleurs dequoy rassasier son incontinence. Mais d'autant que cest homme estoit aigry contre sa femme, & ne pouvoit se prévaloir de son adultere, nous le laisserons en ses fantasies & nous amuserons à chercher quelque autre subjet qui nous puisse donner autant de contentement, comme la diversité a coustume d'estre loüée par ceux qui comme la mousche à miel font leur proufit de diverses fleurs, & recueillent le miel de leur sçavoir de la lecture de plusieurs livres.

Le tombeau d'vne Paillarde.
DIALOGISME.

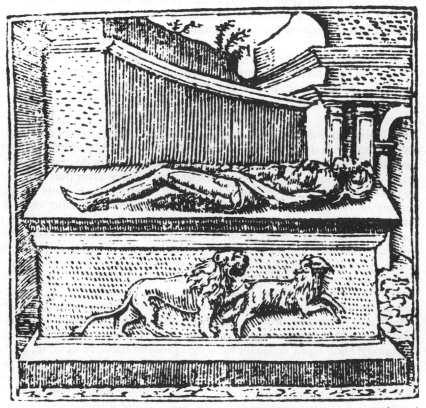

D. Quel sepulchre est (de Laï; de Corinthe)
    Cóment perit femme tát belle, & coincte?
R. (Laide estoit l'ors. Car ses vieux ans ve-
    nus
    Rendu auoit les armes à Venus)
D. Que signifie vng Belier escorché
    Par la Lyonne au derierre accroché
                   (Les

Autour de la Célestine

Fernando de Rojas, La Célestine, 1499-1578.

La Célestina, *dont la première édition espagnole connue date de 1499, est l'œuvre, au moins en majeure partie, de Fernando de Rojas, qui dut l'écrire quelques années auparavant.*

Très vite elle fut traduite en italien. Mais, contrairement à l'indication donnée par le titre de la première traduction en Français qui annonce : « Traduite de l'Italien en François », *c'est à partir du texte espagnol, et non de la traduction italienne, qu'elle fut établie. Elle parut en 1527 et connut plusieurs rééditions (1529, 1542...). Le recueil de Nicolas de Troyes :* Le Grand Parangon des Nouvelles Nouvelles, *témoigne du succès de l'œuvre puisque la première nouvelle du second volume, (le seul qui nous soit parvenu) comporte l'argument suivant :* « D'une maquerelle appelée Celestine, des filles qu'elle vendoit, puis refaisoit pucelles, des amours de deux compaignons et des grant finesses que font les femmes à d'aucuns amoureux qu'elles ont, avec plusieurs autres matieres bonnes et proufitables pour apprendre du bien et du mal ». *Ce texte, qui ne manque pas de qualités littéraires, date de 1535, et est une adaptation de la traduction de 1527.*

La venue de La Célestine *en France est donc précoce, mais c'est surtout dans le dernier quart du siècle qu'elle connut son véritable succès. 1578 voit paraître une nouvelle traduction qui coïncide avec une série d'œuvres qui d'une façon ou d'une autre constituent l'entour de* La Célestine *au sein de la production littéraire de cette époque : notons d'abord que l'une des éditions de 1578 la fait paraître accompagnée des textes sur les courtisanes de Du Bellay, parus dans les* Divers Jeux rustiques *en 1558 ; c'est autour de cette date de 1578 que paraissent le* Laberinthe d'Amour *de Boccace, les* Instructions pour les jeunes dames *de Piccolomini, les premières éditions du* Miroir des Courtisanes *de l'Aretin en attendant* les Contens *de Turnèbe, le théâtre de Larivey etc.*

La publication en 1560 du Lazarillo de Tormes *traduit en Français, celle en 1600 du* Guzman de Alfarache *situent également la traduction de la* Célestine *dans un puissant courant d'intérêt pour la picaresque espagnole. Cet aspect n'exclut pas pour autant le romanesque traditionnel qui retrouve à la même époque un nouvel élan.*

Avec les extraits du théâtre de Larivey, les fragments de La Célestine *que nous donnons ici constituent l'apport du théâtre à ce recueil ; il est évident que seule la présence d'une édition aisément accessible des* Contens *de Turnèbe nous a fait écarter cette œuvre : l'étude comparée du personnage de Françoise et de celui de Célestine serait en effet du plus grand intérêt.*

La traduction de 1578, par Jacques de Lavardin, que nous avons choisie, et qui se dit établie d'après la traduction italienne, a l'étonnant mérite en dépit d'erreurs de vocabulaire reproduites sans doute du texte italien, d'offrir un texte rapide, alerte, retrouvant avec aisance le langage

parlé, semé de proverbes et de maximes courantes, ainsi que le mouve-
ment souvent très théâtral du texte original espagnol. Même si Fernando
de Rojas, en écrivant sa Celestina *s'est adressé plus à des lecteurs qu'à des*
spectateurs, il reste qu'il l'a appelée « Comedia », et il s'agit bien de théâ-
tre ; ici les dialogues n'ont rien de commun avec les faux dialogues rassu-
rants d'Erasme, ils sont heurts de langage différents, générateurs de con-
flits qui ne se résoudront que par la violence, et la mise à mort du person-
nage dont le langage est le plus destructeur : Célestine.

L'œuvre est trop connue pour que nous ayons besoin d'en donner un
résumé, une édition bilingue moderne permettra de combler les vides lais-
sés par les coupures que nous avons dû pratiquer au sein du long premier
acte centré directement ou de biais sur la présentation de Célestine. Nous
y avons ajouté l'acte XVI, où l'on entend les parents de Mélibée parler de
son mariage sans se douter ni qu'elle les écoute, ni qu'elle a d'autres des-
seins.

L.G.

LA CELESTINE

tragicomédie,
Traduit d'Espagnol en
François
où se voyent les ruses et tromperies,
dont les maquerelles usent envers les fols
Amoureux
Rouen, Claude Le Villain

1598

ACTE PREMIER

Caliste déclare son amour à Mélibée qui, après avoir fait semblant de l'écouter avec bienveillance, l'éconduit durement. Désespéré, il s'enferme dans sa chambre. Un moment après, il appelle son valet Malican qui va lui servir de confident.

CAL.— Que te semble de mon mal

MAL.— Que vous aymez Melibée.

CAL.— Et rien que cela ?

MAL.— C'est faute assez grande de tenir sa volonté sujette à un seul lieu.

CAL.— Tu sçais bien peu de fermeté.

MAL.— Perseverance en mal n'est pas constance : ains endurcissement, ou opiniastreté s'appelle en nostre ville, vous autres Philosophes de Cupidon, nommez-là comme il vous plaira.

CAL.— Le mentir est mal seant à celuy qui remonstre à autruy. Pourquoy donc fais-tu gloire de loüer ton Elice ?

MAL.— Faites le bien que je vous dy, & non le mal que je fais.

CAL.— Que me reproches-tu donc ?

MAL.— Que me soumettez la dignité de l'homme à l'imperfection de la femme fragile.

CAL.— Femme ? ô grossier. Dieu, Dieu.

MAL.— Le croyez vous ainsi, ou si vous mocquez ?

CAL.— Que je me mocque ? Pour un Dieu je la croy, pour un Dieu, je la confesse : & ne croy qu'autre deité habite au ciel, quoy qu'elle demeure icy bas parmy nous.

MAL.— Ha, ha, ha, avez vous ouy blasphemer ?

CAL.— Dequoy ris tu ?

MAL.— Je me ris : parce qu'il m'estoit advis que pire invention de peché n'y eust au monde qu'en Sodome.

CAL.— Comment cela ?

MAL.— Pource que ceux-là pourchasserent un usage abominable avecque les Anges incogneus, & vous avecques Melibée que confessez un Dieu.

CAL.— En despit du fol qui m'a fait rire, ce que je n'esperois faire de l'an.

MAL.— Comment ? aviez vous donc à pleurer tout vostre vivant ?

CAL.— Ouy.

MAL.— Qui en est cause ?

CAL.— C'est que j'ayme celle, de laquelle si peu me sens digne, que je desespere de jamais en jouyr.

MAL.— O que jamais bonne mere ne te couva. Quel Nembroth ? quel Alexandre le Grand ? lesquels non seulement de l'Empire du monde universel, s'estimerent dignes, mais aussi de celuy du ciel.

CAL.— Je ne t'ay pas bien entendu, recommence, & ne te haste point.

MAL.— Je disois Monsieur, que vous, qui avez plus de cœur que Nembroth, ny Alexandre, vous deffiez d'avoir une femme, assez desquelles, & mesme qui sont colloquées en souveraineté se sont vilainement soumises à l'orde poitrine, & puante aleine de vils muletiers, & autres infames animaux.
N'avez vous leu de Pasiphaë avecques le Taureau, & de Minerve avecques le chien ?

CAL.— Je n'en croy rien. Ce sont toutes fables.

MAL.— Si le conte de ton aieule avecques le Singe est une fable, je n'en veux pour tesmoing que le cousteau de ton aieul qui le tua.

CAL.— Maudit soit le fol, quelles sourdes atteintes il donne.

MAL.— O je te grate, où il te demange. Lisez les histoires, estudiez les Philosophes, voyez les Poëtes, pleins sont leurs escrits, des ords, & deshonnestes exemples d'icelles & des ruines miserables qu'eurent ceux, qui comme vous se desmirent en elles de quelque chose que ce fust.
Escoutez Salomon, où il dit que les femmes, & le vin font l'homme apostater. Conseillez vous à Seneque, & verrez quelle estime il en fait. Entendez Aristote, regardez en S. Bernard : les Gentilz, les Juifz, les Crestiens, les Mores, tous sont de cest accord. Toutesfois de ce que d'elles j'ay dit, & ce que cy après j'en diray (afin que l'on ne s'abuse) prenez le au commun. Car maintes ont esté, & sont encores aujourd'huy saintes, nobles, vertueuses, desquelles les couronnes resplandissantes abolissent le général vitupere. Mais de ces autres, qui vous pourroit conter les mensonges, les legeretez, les ris, les feintes larmes, le soudain courroux : durant lequel, tout ce qu'elles s'imaginent faut qu'il soit fait sans dilation : Leurs dissimulations, & langues serpentines, leurs tromperies, maquerellages, charmes, moqueries, beau-semblans, & desamour : leur ingratitude, & inconstance, leur dit, leur desdit, leur presomption, & vaine gloire, leur folie, & despit, leur orgueil, & souspecçon, leur luxure, gourmandise, ordures & impudence. Considerez je vous supplie, quelle petite cervelle se cache sous ces voiles amples, & deliez, quelles pensées se couvent sous ces colliers, & carcans d'or sous ceste grande bobance, quelles imperfections couvrent ces pompeuses & magnifiques robbes. Vous diriez proprement de toutes, à les voir si parées, que ce sont autant d'images peintes de ces temples. C'est d'elles qu'il est dit, Armes du Diables, chef de peché, & destruction de Paradis. Avez vous point leu à la festivité de Saint Jean, où

l'on chante. Ceste-cy est la femme, l'antique malice, qui tira Adam des delices de Paradis. Ceste-cy jetta l'humain lignage en enfer, ceste-cy desprisa Helie le Prophete, & cetera.

CAL.— Dy moy, c'est Adam, ce Salomon, ce David, c'est Aristote, ce Virgile, ceux-ci en somme que tu dy, comment donc se laisserent ils aller jusques là d'estre commandez d'elles ? Suis-je suffisant plus qu'eux ?

MAL.— A ma volonté que je vous veisse esgaler à ceux qui les surmonterent, & non à ceux qui furent d'elles surmontez. Fuiez leurs deceptions : sçavez vous qu'elles font ? Choses difficiles à comprendre. Elles n'ont moyen ni raison. L'abandon qu'elles font d'elles, le commencement par rigueur. Elles vituperent par les ruës ceux qu'elles font entrer par les troux. Invitent, puis esconduisent, vous mandent que vous veniez à elles, puis vous disent nenny, se feignent enamourées, & passionnées jusque au mourir, legerement se despitent, & s'apaisent en mesme instant, veulent que l'on devine sur le champ leurs pensées. Elles sont fines, elles sont cautes : tellement que si par finesse s'acqueroit la victoire, les femmes commanderoient à l'univers. Il ne fut ne sera jamais rien pire que la femme entre les calamitez des hommes. O quelle playe ! O quel ennuy ! O quel tourment ! d'avoir à conferer avec elles, sauf durant ce bref moment qu'elles sont appareillées à ce doux deduit !

CAL.— Vois-tu mon Amy, plus m'en diras, plus d'inconveniens tu m'en ameineras, plus j'en suis ravy. Je ne sçay pas bonnement dont il procede.

MAL.— Jamais ne rempliray de sagesse cest esprit pertuisé. Cecy n'est pas conseil de jeunes gens (à ce que je voy) qui ne peuvent entendre raison, ni se gouverner. C'est un malheur quand celuy se pense maistre, qui ne fut oncques apprenty.

CAL.— Et toy qui t'en a tant appris ? qui t'a enseigné cecy ?

MAL.— Elles-mesmes, lesquelles depuis qu'elles se declarent, aussi tost perdent la honte : tellement que tout cecy, & pis encore, manifestent aux hommes. Parquoy Monsieur, mettez vous en la mesure d'honneur, & vous estimez davantage, à sçavoir, que vous estes plus digne que ne vous reputez, l'homme ne vaut que ce qu'il se prise. Et sans nulle doute l'extremité est pire se laisser dechoir de son grade, que de s'eslever plus haut qu'on ne doit.

CAL.— Mais que sera-il de moy d'avantage pour tout cecy ?

MAL.— Quoy ? En premier lieu vous estes homme d'esprit gentil, lequel avec cela nature a remply de ses meilleurs dons, comme beauté, grace, belle taille, & proportion de membres, force, & adresse, en après fortune vous a mediocrement departy de ses biens, & en telle quantité, que ceux que vous possedez au dedans joincts aux exterieurs, reluisent grandement & vous font paroistre. Car sans les biens temporels desquels fortune est la maistresse, il n'avient à personne en ceste vie d'estre bien heureux. Au demeurant, n'estes vous, par constellations benignes, bien voulu de tous ?

CAL.— Ouy, Mais non de Melibée. En tout ce que tu m'as haut loüé, Malican mon amy, elle emporte le prix, sans aucune proportion, soit que je considere sa noblesse, l'antiquité de sa race, son très ample patrimoine, son esprit très-divin, ses vertus excellentes, sa gravité, son maintien incomparable, ou soit que je contemple sa celeste beauté : de laquelle, je te prie, me laisser un peu discourir, afin d'alleger ma douleur : & sera mon propos de cela sans plus qui se descouvre à nos yeux. Car de ce qui leur est caché, si j'en sçavois parler, quel besoin seroit-il maintenant de contester sus ces tristes discours ?

MAL.— O quelles bourdes ! Quelles follies dira à ceste heure ce captif de mon maistre !

CAL.— Que dis-tu ?

MAL.— Je vous dy que parliez, & que j'auray grand plaisir de vous escouter. Autant te soit Dieu en aide, comme me sera aggreable ce sermon.

CAL.— Quoy ?

MAL.— Qu'ainsi Dieu me vueille aider, comme je seray aise de vous oüir.

CAL.— Pour l'amour de toy donc je les veux deduire par particularitez, & bien au long.

MAL.— Nous en sommes bien, c'est proprement ce que je cerche. Que Diable, jamais ne finira il son importunité ?

CAL.— Je viens premierement aux cheveux. As tu jamais veu ces riches bobines d'or si delié qui se file en Arabie ? Ils sont plus beaux encores, plus blons, & plus luisans, avecques leur longueur jusqu'aux talons, crespes, & mignonnement liez d'un subtil ruban. De la façon qu'elle se les tresse de bonne grace, il n'en faut pas plus, pour convertir les hommes en pierres.

MAL.— Mais plustost en Asnes.

CAL.— Qu'est-ce que tu as dit ? Dis le tout haut, que je l'entende.

MAL.— J'ay dit, Monsieur, que tels que ceux-là ne seroyent cheveux d'Asne.

CAL.— Hô la grosse beste ! Quelle sotte comparaison !

MAL.— Tu es bien plus sage ! Mais ainsi Dieu soit à ton aide, comme je le croy !

CAL.— Les yeux vers, & bien fendus, les paupieres longues, les sourcis deliez, le nez mediocre, la bouche petite, les dents blanches, & menuës, les levres grossettes, & vermeiles, la phisionomie du visage plus longue un peu que ronde, le sein relevé. La forme & rondeur de ses deux petits tetins, veu qu'on se perd en les regardans, qui te la pourroit exprimer ? le lustre de sa peau lisse tendrelette, & si blanche, qu'elle obscurcist la neige. Le teint naïf, & moyennement coloré, & tel, que nature le luy voulut donner.

MAL.— Ce fol est en la haute game.

CAL.— Les mains de juste grandeur, & douce charnure, & souëves à manier, les doigts longs, les ongles larges, & anellez, rouges, qu'ils semblent rubis entre des perles. La proportion que mes yeux envieux ne descouvrent, je la juge par l'exterieur indubitablement plus excellente, que celle que Paris jugea entre les trois Deesses.

MAL.— En aurez-vous tantost assez conté ?

CAL.— Le plus bref qu'il m'a esté possible selon la grandeur du sujet.

MAL.— Encore que tout cecy fust vray, si estes-vous plus digne estant homme.

CAL.— Raison ?

MAL.— Pource que la femme est imparfaite, au moyen duquel defaut, elle appete, & vous, & tout autre moindre que vous. N'avez vousleu cest endroit du Philosophe, où il dit ainsi : Comme la matiere affecte la forme, ainsi fait la femme l'homme.

CAL.— Hé mal'heureux que je suis ! hé quand verray-je cecy, entre moy & Melibée ?

MAL.— Cela est bien possible, voire, & que vous en serez aussi tost rassasié, qu'en devintes amoureux jouissant d'elle, & la voyant d'autres yeux libres, & exempts de l'erreur où vous estes à present.

CAL.— Je te respondrois volontiers ce que Nicomaque dist à un certain ignorant à qui n'avoit semblé belle l'Helene de Zeuzis, Pren mes yeux & tu la trouveras une Deesse. Et de quels yeux, sot, voudrois-tu que je la visse ?

MAL.— Avec yeux clair-voyans.

CAL.— Et à ceste heure de quels yeux la voy-je donc ?

MAL.— Avec yeux de miroër ardent, qui vous font prendre le peu pour le beaucoup, le moyen pour le grand. Mais afin, monsieur, que n'ayez à vous desesperer, je le veux entreprendre, & finir vostre desir.

Malican, qui va s'employer selon la tradition du valet, à servir les amours de son maître, connaît familièrement « une vieille barbuë appellée Celestine, caute et fine en toutes meschancetez », grande faiseuse de pucelage d'occasion. C'est elle qu'il conduit chez son maître alors que Corneille, autre valet de Caliste, les aperçoit frappant à la porte.

CORN.— Monsieur c'est une vieille putain deschirée, & Malican qui heurtoient si fort.

CAL.— Tay toy yvrogne, c'est ma tante, haste toy de leur ouvrir. Tousjours l'ay-je ainsi ouy dire, Que pour cuider fuir un peril, l'on se precipite en un plus dangereux. Pour avoir voulu celer cest affaire, à Corneille, auquel l'Amour, la loyauté, ou la crainte servent de bride, je seray tombé en la malveillance de celle-cy, qui n'a sur ma vie moindre pourvoir que Dieu.

CORN.— Pourquoy Monsieur vous tourmentez vous ? Qui vous meut de vous affliger ? Pensez-vous que soit reproché aux oreilles de ceste-cy comme je l'ay tantost appellée : Ne le croyez jà, non. Car moins elle ne s'en glorifie, que vous, quand on dict Caliste est adroit Cavalier : & puis c'est son vray surnom : & par tel tiltre est cognuë. Si elle se rencontre au milieu de cent femmes, & que quelqu'un luy die, vieille putain, elle tourne souvent la teste, & sans se fascher, y respond à face joyeuse. Es feste, & banquets, ès confrairies, ès nopces & compagnies, ès mortuailles, bref en tous lieux où le monde s'assemble, c'est tout leur devis, & entretien, que ceste vieille putain. Les chiens, par où elle passe, n'abbayent autre chose que son nom : toutes especes d'oiseaux, si tost qu'ils la voyent, c'est cela mesme que chante leur jargon. Si elle approche des oüailles ; elles le publient en beslant. Les Asnes, dès qu'elle est en prés, se prennent à braire vieille putain. Estant avecques les forgerons, autre bruit ne font leurs mar-

teaux. Rien que son nom ne coaccent les grenoüiles des marests. Charpen-
tiers, armuriers, chauderonniers, serreuriers, & toutes sortes d'artisans,
avecques leur outils ne forment en l'air que vieille putain. Conclusion tout
ce qui rend son, où qu'elle soit, represente un tel nom. Les faucheurs, &
moissonneurs travaillez au milieu des campaignes bruslantes, les laboureurs, & vignerons passent avecques ce nom, joyeusement leur tasche
journaliere. Les joüeurs du tablier s'ils viennent à perdre, recourent incontinent à ses louanges. O quel friand de bons rostis, ô quel avalleur de bons
morceaux estoit feu son mary ! Que voulez vous plus, veu que quand une
pierre vient contre l'autre à heurter, soudain elle resonne vieille putain.

CAL.— Comment le peux-tu sçavoir, ou la congnoistre ?

CORN.— Je le vous diray. Long temps a que feuë ma mere, bien pouvre femme, se tenoit en son cartier, laquelle à l'instance de celle-cy me
donna à elle pour servant, jaçoit qu'elle ne me recognoisse, pour le peu de
jours que je la servy, & le changement que l'aage m'a apporté.

CAL.— Que faisois-tu chez elle ?

CORN.— J'allois au marché, & luy apportois son vivre, je l'accompa-
gnois, & fournissois aux besoignes que mes tendres forces pouvoient suffire. Mais de ce peu de temps que j'y fus, je retins en ma fresche memoire,
ce que les ans n'ont peu oublier. La bonne Dame, au bout de ceste ruë le
long de la riviere tient une maison à l'escart des autres, demy fonduë, fort
mal reparée, & pirement meublée. Elle se mesle de demy-douzaine de
mestiers, qu'il vous convient entendre ? de lingerie, de parfumerie, de
maquerellage, de composer fars : s'aide un peu de charmes, & est maistresse de rabiller les virginitez perduës. L'art premiere servoit de couverture aux autres : sous ombre de laquelle, grand nombre de ces jeunes
chambrieres, pour s'en faire donner, entroyent chez elle, pour ouvrer che-
mises, collets, coëffes, & telles menuës hardes. Aucune n'y venoit desgar-
nie de provisions, comme jambons, grain, farine, bouteilles de vin, &
choses semblables, qu'à leurs maistresses elles pouvoyent desrobber : (je
ne parle des larcins de plus grande qualité) & leans se recelloyent toutes
marchandises. Elle estoit grand Amie d'escolliers, de Despensiers, de ceux
qui portent la clef de la cave & de vallets de gens d'Eglise : ausquels elle
exposoit en vente le sang des pauvres chetives : lesquelles hardiment
l'aventuroyent sous esperance de la nouvelle restitution qu'elle leur asseu-
roit. Tant avant passa ce negoce, que moyennant cela elle pratiquoit avec
les plus recluses : tellement qu'elle menoit à execution ses faux desseins :
& à celles-cy, à vostre avis, en quelle saison ? au sainct temps : comme
sont stations, pardons, processions de nuict, caresme, messes de la minuit
à Noël, du point du jour, & autres secrettes devotions. Maintes je vis
entrer chez elle desguisées, & après elles hommes pieds nuds, comme
penitens, & tous destachez : qui y venoyent pleurer leurs pechez. Quel
trafic, croyez vous que faisoit ceste cy ? Elle se disoit medecine d'enfans
en maillot : prenoit en un lieu du lin, & le bailloit en l'autre à filer : pour
excuse de hanter en toutes maison. Les unes l'appeloient mere decà, les
autres, mere delà, voilà la bonne femme, voicy venir la maistresse : au
reste fort cogneuë de toutes : & parmy tant d'occupations jamais ne per-
doit une Messe, ou unes Vespres, & l'eust on tousjours veuë ès couvens
de Moines, ou de Nonnains pour autant qu'elle y prenoit mieux ses assi-

gnations. Faisoit parfuns en sa maison, falsifioit le Storax, le benjoin, l'ambre, la civette, le Musc, la poudre de Cypre, & maintes autres senteurs. Elle tenoit une chambre pleine d'alambics, de fioles, & barillets de croye, d'airin, de voirre & d'estain : faits de mille façons. Composoit certaines eaux incorporées avec sublimé. Des fars cuits, lustres, clarifications, & un millier d'ointures infames, distilloit eaux tant & plus pour la face, de raspeures de Lupins, d'escorce d'escurée, de grande couleurée, de fiel d'infinis animaux, de verjust, & vin cuit distillez, & succrez. Subtilizoit la peau avec suc de limons & conturbin, moelle de Garza, ou moüettes, & autres confections innumerables. Tiroit eau de senteurs, de roses, de fleur d'orenges, de gessoumin, de chevre-fueil, & cloux de girogle incorporez avecque musc & civettes, & pulverisées avec du vin. Pour blondir les cheveux faisoit laissive de serment de vigne, de bois de chesne, de marrachemin blanc, de paille de spelte, avec salpestre, allum, mille feuille, & infinie drogues mixtionnées. Les graisses & beures qu'elle tenoit en reserve, seroit un ennuy à les denombrer, de vasche, de chamelle, d'ourse, de jument, de couleuvre, de connil, de Garza, de dain, de chat sauvage, de Taisson, de herisson, & de hybou. Des aprests qu'elle avoit pour faire bains de toutes sortes, c'est un miracle : comme aussi des herbes & racines qu'elle gardoit penduës en son grenier, au toict de sa maison, de camomille, de romarin, de guimauve, de fleur de pintartime, de fleur de feux, de cinabre, de spig, de laurier blanc, de torterose, de fleur sauvage, de pic d'or, & fueille teinte. Les huiles qu'elle vendoit pour le visage, il est incroyable, de Storax, de gessoumin, de lymons, de semence de mellons, de violettes de Mars, de benjoin, de fleur d'orenges, de pignons, de lupins, de zenzoles, & quelque peu de bausme dans une petite fiole qu'elle conservoit pour ceste balafre qui luy prend au travers du nez. L'art de r'abiller les virginitez perduës, aucunes d'icelles elle racoustroit avec vessies, les autres avec aiguilles de pelletier fort deliées, & fil de soye subtil, & ciré, qu'elle tenoit en une petite cassette peinturée, & bonne provision de racines propres à tel usage, sur une petite table comme, de fueille plasme, de fuste sanguin, d'oignons, d'esquille, ou oignon marin & Zeppecheval : & de cela faisoit merveilles, de maniere que passant par-cy l'Ambassadeur de France elle vendit par trois fois pour pucelle, une fille de sa nourriture qu'elle tenoit avec soy.

CAL.— Par ce moyen elle en auroit peu vendre une centaine.

CORN.— Ouy vray Dieu, & si remedioit par charité à maintes orphelines qui alloyent errantes, & se recommandoient à elle. En autre endroit on luy eust trouvé ses apprests pour donner remede à l'Amour, & pour faire aimer : c'estoyent os de cœur de cerf, langues de viperes, testes de cailles, cervelle d'asne, la toille qu'apportent à leur naissance les enfans, & de celle des poulains, & febves moresques, sablon de marine, cordeau de pendu, fleur de lierre, œil de loup, espine de herisson, pied de taisson, la pierre du nid de l'Aigle, graine de fougere, & autres matieres assez. Infinis hommes & femmes la venoient cercher. A aucuns demandoit le pain où ils mordoyent, à autres de leurs vestemens, à quelques uns de leurs cheveux : à plusieurs elle peignoit lettres de saffran és paulmes des mains : à ceux-cy donnoit certains cœurs de cire pleins d'aiguilles rompuës, à ceux-là certaines choses faictes en croye ou en plomb, fort espou-

ventables à voir. Figuroit images, prononçoit paroles en terre. Qui vous
pourroit raconter ce que faisoit ce vieil registre du putanisme ? Et ce pendant que cuidez vous que ce fust ? toutes baies, & belles impostures.

*Après divers échanges entre le valet et le maître, l'autre valet et Célestine,
Caliste donne l'ordre d'introduire la maquerelle.*

CAL.— Malican ?

MAL.— Monsieur ?

CAL.— Que fais-tu clef de ma vie ? ouvre leur, Corneille. Or l'ay-je
veuë : me voylà desjà guery, me voylà ressuscité. Voy quelle reverende
personne, & presence venerable ! le plus souvent à la phisionomie se
cognoist la vertu interieure. O vertueuse vieillesse ! ô glorieuse esperance
de mon dernier soulas ! ô fin de ma douce esperance ! ô salut de mes passions, vivification de ma vie ! ô remede de mes tourmens ! resurrection de
ma mort ! ô que j'ay grand envie de m'approcher de toy ! ô que je voudrois baiser la terre pressée de tes pieds benists, & la baise en ton honneur.

CEL.— C'est bien à propos de ce que je cerche. Les os que j'ay pieça
rongez, ce fat de ton maistre me les cuide donner à manger. Mais je luy
apreste autre sauce : au frire il la cognoistra. Di luy qu'il ferme la bouche,
& ouvre la bourse. Car me deffiant des effects, combien plus des parolles ? Qu'il baille des arres avant la main. Que te gratta, asne, sur la teste ?
De meilleure heure te falloit lever ce matin.

CORN.— En despit des oreilles qui tels propos escoutent ! Perdu est
qui après le perdu va, ô Caliste infortuné, abattu, & aveuglé ! Le voilà
veautré par terre qui adore la plus antique vieille putain qui jamais se
frotta les espaules par tous les bordeaux d'un pais, desconfit, vaincu, ter-
rassé. C'est fait de luy, il n'est plus capable de redemption, effort, ni conseil.

CAL.— Qu'est-ce Malican, qu'à dit nostre bonne mere ? Je croy qu'elle
pense que luy offre paroles pour remuneration.

MAL.— Me semble l'avoir ainsi entendu.

CAL.— Vien donc quant & moy, & m'apporte mes clefs. Car je luy
veux esclaircir ceste difficulté.

MAL.— Faictes donc monsieur, & allons tost : jamais ne faut laisser
croistre la mauvaise herbe parmy le bon grain, & moins le souspeçon
dedans le cœur des amis : ains soudain le nettoyer avecque l'espoussette
des bonnes œuvres.

CAL.— Tu as sagement parlé : suy moy, & ne tardons.

CEL.— Je suis joyeuse, Corneille de ceste opportunité, afin que tu
cognoisses le bien que je te veux, & la part que sans ton merite, tu as avec
moy, sans ton merite, dy-je, pour les propos qu'ay ouïs de ta bouche :
desquels je ne fais cas, d'autant que la vertu nous admoneste de monstrer
patience ès tentation, & ne rendre mal pour mal. Singulierement estans
tentez par les jeunes, & mal instruits ès affaires de ce monde : lesquels par
ignorance loyauté perdent eux & leurs maistres : comme tu fais à present
de Caliste. Je t'ay ouy, voire & ne pense pas que l'ouye avec les autres sens
exterieurs ne soit departie de moy, par la vieillesse. Car non seulement ce

que je voy, ouy, & cognoy : mais aussi le secret interieur je penetre avec les yeux intellectuels. Faut que tu saches, mon garçon, que Caliste brusle de l'amour de Melibée ; & ne le juges pour cela fol, ou insensé. Car le penetrant amour surmonte toutes choses. Ostez l'amour, & les voluptez de la vie, il n'y a plus rien en icelle que la triste mort : & veux bien t'apprendre, si jà tu ne le sçais, que ces deux maximes sont vrayes. Que l'homme est forcé d'aimer la femme, & la femme l'homme. La seconde, qu'à celuy qui bien aime est necessaire de se troubler en la douceur du souverain plaisir : lequel par le createur de toutes choses, a esté introduit pour perpetuer le genre humain : sans lequel il deviendroit à neant. Et non seulement des hommes : mais ès poissons, & bestes brutes, ès oiseaux, & reptiles qui se trainent sur le ventre : & mesme ès vegetatives, certaines plantes y a qui gardent cest ordre, si en peu de distance de terre elles sont situées l'une devant l'autre sans interpositions d'aucune chose. De là est venu que les herbolistes & laboureurs determinent y avoir entre les plantes masles, & femelles. Que diras-tu à cecy Corneille, petit follastre, petit Ange, petite perle de la vieille Celestine. Simple louveton, ô quel musequin friand ? Viença à moy paillardeau. Tu ne sçais que c'est de ce monde, ny de ses esbatememens. Mais la male rage me tuë, que si je te tiens une fois entre mes bras ! encore que je ne sois plus qu'une vieille ! Pource que tu es enroüé, & que le poil te commence à poindre, je croy que tu dois avoir mal reposé le bout du ventre.

CORN.— Comme queuë de scorpion.

CEL.— Et puis encore par aventure. Car celle là pique sans enflure, & la tienne fait enfler pour neuf mois.

CORN.— Hi, hi, hi.

CEL.— Le faux truandeau ! hé comme rit.

ACTE XVI

L'acte réunit le couple des parents, barbons chargés de réassumer les principes de la morale établie, et Mélibée qui plaide la morale des jeunes amants.

PLEB.— Alise ma femme, resveillons nos esprits, c'est assez dormy, contemplons icy comme s'enfuit nostre vie sans l'appercevoir. Le temps empané de nos années s'envole, les jours s'escoulent aussi viste que rivieres courantes, la mort nous suit, & nous tallonne : de laquelle nous sommes jà voisins, & comme tu vois, approchons fort de ses bannieres, selon le cours de nature. Nous le voyons par exemple, voulans arrester la pensée sur nos compagnons, freres, & gens de nostre temps qui s'en sont allez. Desjà les mange la terre, & sont pasture des vers. Tous ont rendu le tribut à Nature, & sont parvenus à leur dernier logis. Estans doncques incertains quand on nous appellera, & en voyans de si evidens signes, soyons ententifs à faire nostre paquet : afin qu'avec moins de crainte nous puissions cheminer dedans ce contraint et nécessité voyage. Ne nous laissons surprendre à despourveu, ni de prinsaut à celle mal-piteuse voix de la mort. Appareillons de bonne heure nos ames car mieux vaut prevenir qu'estre prevenus. Choisissons un bon successeur à nos biens : accompa-

gnons d'un bon mary nostre fille, selon nostre estat : afin qu'en tranquillité d'esprit, & sans regret nous departions de ce monde à quoy dès à present est requis d'entendre par bonne intelligence & conseil. Accomplis-
sons à ce coup cest affaire, par nous cy devant commencé que nostre non-
chalance ne laisse Melibée en mains de tuteurs, puis qu'elle est d'âge qui
reparera mieux sa maison que celle-cy. & ainsi l'asseureront des langues
mesdisantes. Car il n'y a vertu si parfaite qui n'ait des detracteurs. Puis
j'ay de tout temps ouy dire, qu'il n'y a or, ni argent, muraille, ni forteresses de si grande garde que la fille : il n'y a menuizier qui puisse faire porte,
par où le chat, & l'adultere ne passe. La fille est une penible et onereuse
possession. La marians, nous nous libererons de si laborieuse charge.
Rien ne conserve tant la bonne estime des vierges que de les pourveoir de
bonne heure. Qui seroit celuy en ceste ville qui desdaignast nostre
parenté ? Qui ne se tiendroit honoré d'un tel joyau en sa compagnie : veu
qu'en elle sont les quatre qualitez principalement requises ès mariage ? En
premier lieu sagesse, discretion, modestie, virginité. Secondement
beauté : pour le tiers il y a l'antiquité, & la noblesse de nostre race, &
pour le quatriesme, les grans biens : de tout cecy la doüa, & avantagea
nature. On la trouvera accomplie, en tout ce qu'on sçauroit desirer.

ALI.— Dieu la benie, Plebere mon Seigneur, & nous face la grace,
durant nostre vie d'en voir nos souhaits contentez. Je croy qu'il y aura
plustost faute de party digne de nostre fille, eu esgard à vos vertuz, & à la
noblesse de vostre sang, qu'il en vienne guere, qui la puissent meriter.
Mais estant cecy office de pere, & fort esloigné de celuy des femmes,
ordonnez-en comme il vous plaira, je le trouveray bon, & y obtemperera
vostre fille, selon son chaste maintien, sa modestie & humilité.

LUC.— Mais si tu sçavois tout, tu te d'espassionnerois. Ouy, ouy, c'est
bien parlé. Vous y estes, laissez-vous choir, le meilleur est desjà perdu,
vostre malheur s'appareille pour vos derniers ans. Caliste en a ceuilly la
fleur, il n'y à plus qui reface les virginitez, il n'est plus de Celestine au
monde. Vous vous esveillastes trop tard, plus matineux vous falloit estre.
Hola ma maistresse ! escoutez, escoutez.

MEL.— Que fais-tu cachée, folle ?

LUC.— Venez ici Mademoiselle, vous orrez vostre pere, & vostre
mere, comme ils ont haste de vous marier.

MEL.— Tay toy je te prie, ils t'orront. Laisse-les causer, laisse-les
ravasser. Un mois y a qu'ils n'ont autre chanson. Semble que le cœur leur
dit, l'ardent amour que je porte à Caliste : je ne sçay s'ils auroyent point
quelque souspeçon de nos amourettes. Je ne sçay que c'est, mais le soucy
les presse maintenant, plus que jamais. Or se travaillent en vain tant qu'il
leur plaira. La Cistre ne sert de rien au moulin. Qui sera celuy qui
m'ostera ma gloire ? qui me privera de mes plaisirs ? Caliste est mon ame,
ma vie, & mon tout : auquel j'ay fondé toutes mes esperances. je cognois
en luy que je ne vy abusée, & puis qu'il m'ayme dequoy le puis-je autrement payer ? Toutes dettes recoyvent compensation, en diverses manieres. Amour ne se paye, que de vray amour. Seulement à penser en luy, je
suis en liesse, le voyant je me resjoüis, le voyant je me glorifie. Avec luy je
veux aller, face de moy à son plaisir, veut-il passer la mer, je le suivray,
veut-il tournoyer la terre, me meine quant à luy, jamais ne l'abandonne-

ray, & me deust-il vendre pour esclave au païs des Turcs : rien ne me
departira de ses commandemens. Que mon pere me souffre jouyr de luy,
s'il veut jouyr de ma vie. Qu'ils n'entrent en ces follies, ni en ces resveries
de mariages. Mieux vaut vivre vraye amoureuse, que languir mal mariée.
Qu'ils me laissent esbattre ma fraische jeunesse, s'ils veulent jouyr de leur
foible vieillesse : autrement qu'ils m'apprestent bien tost ma ruine, & leur
tombeau. Autres douleurs ne me poinct, que le regret du temps perdu, &
de n'en avoir jouy, de ne l'avoir plustost cogneu, depuis que j'ay sçeu me
cognoistre. Fy de mary ! Je ne veux soüiller les liens de mariage, je ne
veux repestiferer les pestes matrimoniales des autres hommes, ainsi que
maintes en ont fait, plus sages, & plus grandes Dames que moy : desquelles, les unes furent tenües pour Deesses des Gentils, comme Venus, mere
d'Aenée, & de Cupidon, le Dieu d'Amour : laquelle ayant mary, viola la
foy maritale. Quelques unes embrasées de plus ardentes flammes comme-
morent de tres-horribles forfaits : Myrrhe avec son pere, Semiramis avecque son fils, Canace avecque son frere : & encore la violentée Thamar
fille du Roy David. Autres plus furieusement transgresserent les loix de
Nature, Pasiphaë avec un taureau, & estoyent celles-cy Roynes, & illustres Dames : sous l'offence desquelles la mienne tollerable pourra passer
sans reproche. Si mon cœur luy donnay n'en eust-je juste occasion ?
Estant requise, pourchassée, & esclavée de ses merites, sollicitée de si
astuce maistresse qu'estoit Celestine, & recherchée de si perilleuses visita-
tions premier que condescendre à son amour. Depuis cela, comme tu as
veu un mois durant, ne s'est une seule nuict passée, que nostre jardin,
ainsi qu'une forteresse, n'ay esté eschellé : & souvent y a perdu ses pas
tousjours le trouvant plus ferme, & constant. A mon occasion luy sont
morts deux serviteurs, son bien dissipé : Il dissimula son absence à toute
la ville, sur jour r'enfermé au logis, sous esperance de me voir la nuict.
Dehors, dehors ingratitude deslogez feintises, & tromperies envers si
loyal Amant. Je ne veux mary, pere, mere, ni parens : privée de Caliste,
me defaille la vie : laquelle ne m'agrée, que par ce qu'il en est joüissant.

LUC.— Paix, paix Madamoyselle, escoutez comme ils poursuivent.

PLEB.— Mais que t'en semble Alise ? en parlerons nous à notre fille ?
Ne luy ferons nous entendre de tant de gentils-hommes qui la demandent ? afin que franchement elle declare celuy qui est plus à son gré : puis
qu'en cecy les loix donnent liberté de choisir aux enfans, ores qu'ils soyent
sous la main des parens.

ALI.— Quels termes sont ce-cy Monsieur ? que sert à dire cela ? Aquoy
perdez vous temps. Qui portera si estranges nouvelles à Melibée, sans
l'espouvanter ? Pensez-vous qu'elle sçache que c'est que les hommes ? si
on se marie, ou que c'est de se marier ? Ni que de la conjonction de
l'homme, & de la femme s'engendrent les enfans ? Cuidez vous que sa
simplicité virginale luy peust amener quelque deshonneste desir de ce
qu'elle ne cognoist, & ne sçeut oncques que c'est ? Vous est-il advis que
elle peust pecher seulement de la pensée ? N'en croyez rien, non Monsieur. Si nous luy commandons d'en prendre un soit noble, soit vilain, soit
beau, soit laid, elle s'y accordera incontinent, & l'acceptera pour bon, je
m'en asseure. Je sçay bien comme j'ay nourry ma fille, bien gardée & bien
apprise.

MEL.— Lucresse ? Lucresse ? Cours, va viste, entre par la porte de la salle, & leur interromps leurs propos de quelque faux message qu'inventeras, si tu ne veux que je voise criant comme une folle. Car je desespere de l'erreur où je les voy, de me tenir si grossiere & ignorante.

LUC.— Bien Mademoyselle, je m'y en vois.

Pierre de Larivey, Comédies 1579-1611.

Publiées pour les six premières un an après la traduction de La Céles-tine, *les* Comédies *de Larivey indiquent que plus encore que le théâtre espagnol, la comédie italienne va être jusqu'au dix-huitième siècle l'objet privilégié des réécritures dramaturgiques françaises. Est-ce en fonction même de cet avenir qu'on ne chicana pas son statut d'écrivain français à Pierre de Larivey alors que ses* Comédies *auraient pu aussi bien rejoindre la tourbe anonyme des traductions « infidèles » ?*

Encore faut-il bien dire que la truculence du texte ne laisse pas oublier le scripteur français, une part qui demeurerait autrement largement inconnue du langage trivial vient s'inscrire dans ces « traductions ». C'est d'ailleurs cette verdeur que ne censurent pas encore les bienséances qui permet de faire lire ces textes dont la complexité « romanesque » stéréoty-pée lasserait, comme d'ailleurs, au delà du modèle italien, la dette à l'égard des comédies latines dont on retrouve tous les types obligés : vieil-lards libidineux, jeunes écervelés, maquerelles, ruffians...

Ce langage habite les personnages féminins, leur donnant une singu-lière présence, l'épouse elle-même, celle des Escholliers *par exemple, est une « forte en gueule » qui ouvre sur telle ou telle épouse moliéresque. Quant aux femmes d'amour, maquerelles et courtisanes, elles affichent, mais cette fois ce sera sans postérité, la puissance du désir. Si la vieille putain retirée qu'est la Guillemette de* La veuve *fantasme pour son compte en racontant les manèges d'une plus jeune, c'est bien que toute vieille qu'on la voie, elle « n'a pas l'estomac si cru » qu'elle ne digérât « bien encores une andouille ». La Méduse de la comédie* Le fidelle *va loin dans cette sorte de contre-culture féminine fascinante que représente la femme marginale. Larivey la fait passer des fards et onguents à la magie, à l'envoûtement et aux invocations sataniques (cf. II, 3). L'hori-zon est d'ailleurs assigné au delà du sexe même : c'est l'ordre social, l'appropriation privée que cette contre-culture féminine, mise en scène par des hommes pour un propos comique ne l'oublions pas, vise. La Clé-mence de* La veuve *proclame la mort de la conscience morale ainsi : « la nature a mis toutes choses en commun affin que chacun print ce qu'il pust : si les hommes ont amené pour loy ces séditieux mien et tien, qu'en avons nous affaire, d'autant que, quand ceste loy fut faicte, nous autres ne fusmes appelées au conseil ».*

Singulier espace que celui du texte comique qui exhibe et distancie les plus violentes interrogations. Comme d'ailleurs les plus sages résorptions morales... car les hommes, pourvu qu'ils soient d'âge mûr et de situation respectable, allient inévitablement à l'irrépressible concupiscence, la glace du discours établi, ressassant le savoir éternel. Fortuné, Fidelle, M. Josse font dans Le fidelle *une manière d'anthologie, Josse, le pédant, affirme avec « le tragique Sénèque : Dux malorum foemina, et scelerum artifex », Fortuné quant à lui récite les litanies : « elles sont de nature superbes, vai-*

nes, inconsistantes, légères, malignes, cruelles, ravissantes, meschantes, envieuses, incrédules, trompeuses, ambitieuses, frauduleuses, desloyalles, ingrattes, impétueuses, audacieuses et desréglées... » Langage de bois que la verdeur de la courtisane rompt, fard viril que la puanteur des corps interroge.

Nous citons Les escholliers et Les tromperies mais les lignes qui précèdent indiquent que d'autres textes auraient été possibles. Les escholliers appartiennent aux six comédies publiées en 1579, il s'agit d'une traduction « libre » de La Cecca de Razzi publiée en 1563 à Florence. On comprendra aisément en lisant la scène citée que les précautions d'Anastase seront inutiles et que sa fille épousera l'écolier, marginal fascinant et provisoire, avec lequel elle aura irrésistiblement couché. Quant aux Tromperies, elles appartiennent aux trois nouvelles comédies publiées en 1611, il s'agit d'une traduction des Inganni de Nicolas Sacchi, comédie jouée à Milan en 1547, imprimée à Florence en 1562. La date d'impression très proche de la précédente, le lieu identique, rappelant l'origine florentine de la famille de Larivey, donnent à penser que les traductions furent entreprises corrélativement même si les publications sont séparées par plus de trente ans. L'intrigue des Tromperies est extrêmement embrouillée, elle est fondée sur le travesti et les amours interdites qui peuvent en résulter. Nous avons retenu dans ce monde qui joue avec le tabou, la représentation d'une marginalité instituée dans laquelle la maquerelle va rejoindre le rôle du père-mari bourgeois de la comédie précédente.

J.P.G.

LES SIX PREMIERES COMEDIES FACECIEUSES
DE
PIERRE DE LARIVEY

champenois
A l'imitation des anciens Grecs, Latins
et modernes Italiens.
Paris, Abel l'Angelier

1579

LES ESCHOLLIERS

ACTE II, SCENE I
Anastase, vieillard, Lisette, sa femme.

Anastase.— Mon Dieu ! mon Dieu ! de quel ennuy pensé-je estre tourmenté un bon et pauvre pere de famille, qui, ayant (comme j'en cognois assez) deux ou trois filles, à marier, ne les peut pourveoir sans grandement s'incommoder. Le soin qu'il a d'amasser leur mariage ne l'afflige seulement, mais de leur trouver mary qui en moins de quatre mois ne mange tout. La jeunesse d'aujourd'huy est tant corrompue, depravée et mal conditionnée, que c'est merveilles. Les jeunes hommes, tant pauvres soient-ils, ne se soucient maintenant que de piaffer, suyvre les putains, le jeu, la taverne, et employer le plus beau et meilleur, non seulement de leur bien, mais de celuy des pauvres gens qu'ils rongent jusques à l'os, en accoustremens superflus, et qui ne leur servent que trois jours seulement : car, iceux passez, il les faut vendre à moitié de perte, pour à autre moitié de perte en faire de nouveaux, ou leur changer de façon. Et si quelque chose est pire, ils choisissent ce pire au lieu de la vertu, dont ils tiennent moins de compte qu'un pourceau d'un diamant. Et si de fortune il se rencontre aucun qui soit docile et de bonne nature, il est aussi tost corrompu par les autres. Ce qui advient aysement par ce que le nombre des meschans est infiny et le naturel des jeunes plus enclin à l'apparence du bien que les plaisirs nous presentent de premiere abordée, qu'au vray bien, qui de prime face se monstre laid et desplaisant. Il m'estoit advis avoir bien pourveu l'aisnée de mes deux filles : mais la fortune n'a voulu qu'entierement j'en aye eu le plaisir. Or maintenant, la voulant remarier, je trouve si peu de partis qui ne soient dangereux ou à craindre, que je ne sçay de quel costé me tourner : et jaçoit qu'il y ait eu desjà parolles de la bailler au filz de sire Gontran, je ne me puis resoudre, ayant oy dire que ce jeune homme ne bouge d'après les femmes, qui me faict douter, s'il espouse ceste-cy pour obeyr à son pere, qu'après il ne cesse de courtiser les unes et les autres, et qu'à cette occasion ma fille vive malcontente et desesperée. Je m'en vas jusques au Palais. Si j'y trouve le seigneur Gontran, je luy parleray encor de ceste affaire. Mais voicy ma femme qui vient deçà. Où diantre va-elle si tost ? car on ne dira vespre d'une bonne heure. Lisette ! Hé Lisette !, Lisette !

Lisette.— Qu'y a-il de nouveau ?

Anastase.— Qu'y a-il de nouveau ! Je ne sçay quelle femme vous estes : vous ne m'avez pas si tost veu les talons que vous vous estes parée comme une espousée pour aller faire vos monstres, et ne pensez pas que laissez ceste fille seule en la maison, dont mille inconveniens pourroient bien advenir, suffisans assez pour me vituperer à jamais, et vous faire vivre en un perpetuel deshonneur.

Lisette.— Mon Dieu ! donnez-moy patience.

Anastase.— Vous semble-il que ceste marchandise se doibve laisser ainsi seule ? Lisette ! Lisette ! si vous n'y avez l'œil, je crain voir nostre malencontre.

Lisette.— C'est à vous d'y prendre garde, et penser de la marier, sans entrer en ces soupsons. Et puis, pour vous en dire la verité, elle n'est née de mere qui donne occasion de penser à ces choses.

Anastase.— Je ne sçay de quelle mere elle est née, mais je sçay bien que je ne suis trop content qu'elle demeure seule. Que diable pensez-vous que ce soit ?

Lisette.— Je vous prie, ne m'en parlez point. Voudriez-vous que je fusse confinée en la maison sans aller à la messe ny matines ? J'aymerois aultant estre prisonniere. Dictes-moy, en conscience, voudriez vous qu'on vous fist ainsi ? Nenny, par mon âme. Aussi ne vous sçauriez-vous excuser que n'ayez le plus grand tort du monde. Non ! non ! je pense que, s'il n'estoit qu'incessamment je fais prieres à Dieu, eh ? eh ! hu ! hu ! hu ! pour le bien et santé de nous tous je ne sçay comme tout en iroit.

Anastase.— C'est assez, appaisez-vous et faictes à vostre fantaisie. Je vous dy seulement que l'office de l'homme est avoir soin des affaires de dehors, et le devoir de la femme est prendre garde à la maison, et à conserver ce que l'homme acquiert avec sueur et peine, et outre, d'avoir soucy des enfans, tant masles que femelles, autant qu'il est requis. Quant à moy, je m'efforceray de mon costé faire mon devoir, mais je veux aussi que faciez du vostre ce que vous devez, affin que je n'aye occasion de me plaindre, combien que, faisant autrement vous en recevriez plus grand blasme et vergogne que je ne ferois pas:

Lisette.— Et qu'en pourroit-il advenir ?

Anastase.— Je n'en sçay rien.

Lisette.— Il me l'est bien advis que vous n'en sçavez rien ! Mais laissez moy aller à mes devotions de peur qu'au lieu de bien faire vous ne me faciez perdre patience, ou dire quelque folie, si je demeure icy.

Anastase.— Pensez, pensez, Lisette, que je ne le dis pas sans cause. Je vous advise que ces escolliers sont gens endiablez, ausquels il ne se fault fier qu'à point. Aussi me semble-il qu'ils sont plus abonnez à toute postiquerie et meschanceté qu'à leurs livres.

Lisette.— Et quelle meschanceté font-ils ?

Anastase.— Toute leur estude est de desbaucher les filles, suborner les femmes mariées, decevoir les vefves, et engeoller les simples chambrieres.

Lisette.— Cela ne se faict sinon à celles qui le veullent bien.

Anastase.— Il me semble que Paris est conduict à telle misere par ces coureurs et batteurs de pavé, qu'il faut tenir les pouletz sous la cage, encore ne sont-ils trop asseurez. Je ne pense point que ce soient les escolliers, mais bien des hommes libres, vivans sans loy et à leur appetit.

Lisette.— Je ne vous entend pas ? Que voulez-vous dire par là ?

Anastase.— Je veux dire que je ne trouve bon que Susanne demeure seule au logis, par ce que escolliers ont tousjours la teste aux fenestres.

Lisette.— Et que diantre sçauroient-ils faire de leurs fenestres ?

Anastase.— Je sçay bien qu'ils ne sçauroient rien faire de là, mais je crain que tout en un coup ils n'entrent en la maison, et ne nous ruynent.

Lisette.— C'est autre chose. Et si nous n'avons point de pouletz !

Anastase. —Comme si cette generation ne faisoit autre mal que de desrobber des pouletz ! Vous ay-je pas dit qu'il n'y a mal, tant soit-il grand, qui ne leur semble très petit ? J'ay peur de nostre fille, m'entendez-vous à ceste heure ?

Lisette.— On n'entre pas ainsi à l'ayse aux maisons des gens de bien.

Anastase.— Vous estes mal informée. Ils ne seroient pas les premiers qui ont entré en la maison d'autruy par les fenestres, et monté jusques au feste d'un logis, avec des crochets et eschelles de cordes.

Lisette.— Je n'ay pas peur de cela : car, si entre tant d'escolliers on en trouve quelques uns de la sorte que vous dictes, et qui facent choses moins qu'honnestes, ce n'est à dire qu'ils soient tous meschans, parce qu'il y en a des bons et des mauvais. Toutes fois, ceux qui s'adonnent à telles meschancetés sont enfans de quelques pauvres gens mécaniques, issus de la lie du peuple, lesquels n'ont rien d'escolliers que le nom, au reste pires qu'advanturiers.

Anastase.— On trouve encore des meschans entre les nobles, et peut-estre plus qu'entre les roturiers et le menu peuple.

Lisette.— Tout ce que vous voudrez : si pensé-je que noz voisins sont les meilleurs jeunes hommes qui soient en Paris.

Anastase.— Or bien, faictes-en comme vous l'entendrez : je ne vous en parleray plus, ains regarderay seulement à l'oster de la maison, affin qu'à vostre plus grande commodité vous puissiez desormais aller à vos plaisirs.

Lisette.— Adieu ! Adieu ! je voy bien que vous me voulez mettre en colère.

Anastase.— Je sçay bien comme y remedier. Mon Dieu ? que ces femmes sont arrogantes et audacieuses ? Il leur est advis qu'elles sont plus sages que Salomon, et que personne ne les peut reprendre. Bref, si on a de la peine à trouver un jeune homme de bien, on ne travaille moins pour trouver une femme qui s'en contente. Si nous laissions courir les filles comme les garçons sans les tenir enfermées en la maison, il nous seroit autant mal-aisé en trouver une bonne et honneste qu'un jeune garçon vertueux et bien apris . Le diable ne dureroit pas avec elles quand elles ont leur chapperon coiffé de travers, tant elles sont de mauvaise nature. Il est advis à une femme qui se void un peu plus riche que son mary qu'elle doit tout manyer et que le gouvernement luy appartient de façon que le pauvret n'ose dire un mot qu'elle ne luy en responde mille, avec toutes les injures dont elle se pourra adviser comme : Que ferois-tu sans moy coquin ? les poux te mangeroient : il m'eust esté meilleur que mon pere m'eust coupé la gorge dès que je fus née que me marier avecques toy, pour eternellement endurer les peines que tu me donnes. Le mesme advient si un simple gentilhomme espouse une dame de grande maison, encores qu'il soit riche et homme de bien. Elle l'appellera belistre, pouilleux, relevé du fumier, hobereau, vilageois desguisé et semblables vilenyes. Mais à tels hommes qui endurent ces choses de leurs femmes, il seroit bon qu'elles leur fissent encores pis, puisqu'ils n'ont que le seul masque d'homme. Ha ! ha ! ha ! il me souvient d'un certain quidam, homme de qualité, que sa femme menoit par le nez comme un buffe : de mode qu'elle estoit monsieur le juge, ouvroit les lettres, rendoit response, oyoit les tesmoings, appointoit les partyes, bref eust volontiers jugé les procès, tant elle estoit rogue, voulant en tout et partout estre veuë maistresse. Voilà ! ceste breneuse de ma femme voudroit, ce croy-je, faire ainsi. Mais laissez-moy aller, que ceux icy ne sçachent rien de mes affaires.

TROIS NOUVELLES COMEDIES
DE
PIERRE DE LARIVEY

Champenois
A l'Imitation des anciens
Grecs, latins et modernes italiens
Troyes, Pierre Chevillot

1611

LES TROMPERIES

ACTE II, SCENE I.
Dorothée, courtisanne, le Médecin, Adrian.

Dorothée.— O chetive moy ! que je crain que ce pauvre Constant n'ayt prins en mauvaise part qu'on luy ait fermé l'huys, et que par desespoir il ne me laisse. Il ne se peut faire que le pauvret ne passe par icy. Je seroys ayse le veoir et le consoler. Que maudite soit ma trop fascheuse et mauvaise mere ! Je sçay bien qu'il en adviendra. Elle veut tant tirer à elle qu'elle me fera crever de jalousie. Mais voicy ce galant amoureux que la pitié maternelle m'a donné. O quel joly muguet ! ô quel tendre chevreau à qui la bouche sent encores le laict. Que la peste te vienne, vieil pourry, à qui les mains ne sentent que l'urine, ou ne puent que le clystere ! je veux mourir si je ne te pelle jusques aux os, sot puant que tu es. Par la croix que voilà, mon entretenement te coustera cher ! Tu refonderas les soixante escus pour le pauvre Consant. La belle happelourde ! il semble un homme de paille, un fantosme, un espouvantail de cheneviere. Je le veux un peu aborder. Dieu soit loué que l'on vous peut veoir ! il en est tantost temps.

Le Medecin.— Dieu vous contente, mon bien.

Dorothée.— Vous vous faictes bien attendre, beau sire ! il y a tantost une heure que je vous espie de pied coy. D'où venez vous si tard ? de veoir quelque belle fille ? Hé ! folastre, vous tenez grand compte d'une pauvre qui meurt après vous.

Le Médecin.— Ha ! ha ! ha ! Entrons en la maison, car je t'apporte quelque chose qui te sera agreable.

Adrian.— Quand il luy aura baillé la robbe, le martel cessera.

Dorothée.— Le mal vous mange avec vos presens, si vous pensez que je vous ayme pour cela ! Quoy que ce soit, reprenez les, je n'en veux point ; non, en bonne foy, je n'en veux point.

Adrian.— Elle n'en veut point : mais devant que nous partions, elle voudra quelque autre chose.

Dorothée.— O petit meschant ! le mal m'advienne si vous n'estes dur comme un chesne.

Le Medecin. Ha ! ha ! ha !

Dorothée.— Vous en riez, Peu d'amitié, peu de foy.

Le Medecin.— Entrons dedans, petite friande.

Dorothée.— O que si j'estois plus forte que vous, comme je me vengerois du martel que me mettez en teste ? O quelle rage vient de vous arracher ces poils d'argent ?

Le Medecin.— Ha ! ha ! ha ! Entrons Godinette, rondelette, doucelette : vien, ma toute belle, colombelle, tourterelle.

Dorothée.— Entrez devant, je vous suy. Entre, encores Adrian. La peste vienne à qui m'a amené ce vieil ranceux et poussif ! Faire caresse à ce glaireux et pourry n'est autre chose sinon embrasser les corps morts, baiser des cailloux, taster des vessies flasques et flestries, coucher avec des peaux d'un chat mort sans nerfs et sans os, succer un tetin qui n'a point de laict. Baveux, puant, recreu, qui es deux heures à t'affuster devant que ton marteau en puisse sonner une, va te pendre, je n'iray jà.

Le Medecin.— Dorothée, m'amour, venez.

Dorothée.— Ouy, ouy, crie tout ton saoul. Courez après ce beau muguet. Que la bosse te vienne, hume-urine ! ronge-estron ! Voicy le diable qui vient.

SCENE II
Dorothée, Gillette, maquerelle.

Gillette.— Que fais-tu sur ceste porte, affetée ? Atten-tu, que ton beau pigeon passe ? Que voilà qui est beau, se rendre ainsi serve d'un fraffrannier ! Est-ce là l'obeyssance que tu porte à ta mère ? Tu ne fais jamais ce que je te commande.

Dorothée.— Ains je ne fay que ce que vous m'avez apprins. N'ay-je pas le visage poly, la façon gentille, la contenance gracieuse, sous lesquels je cache une langue demanderesse, un esprit trompeur, un corps venal, un front hardy, une main ravissante, un entendement subtil ? Voilà le sommaire de vos enseignemens.

Gillette.— Adjouste-y le proverbe de Dame Liberée, que la courtisane doit avoir les yeux beaux, le courage faux, la face de miel, et le cœur de fiel, le visage rare et l'esprit avare, la bouche riante et la main trayante. Jadis, la bonne ame de ma mère avoit accoustumé de me dire que tes semblables devoient avoir le visage d'aymant pour attirer les cœurs de fer, la main de poix pour prendre toute chose, les parolles de succre pour amorcer et alaicter les personnes, l'estomac d'albastre, affin qu'il soit beau et sans pitié : et pour te le dire en un mot, elle devoit estre comme les gluaux, que jamais les oyseaux ne touchent qu'ils n'y laissent des plumes.

Dorothée.— Qui est celuy qui jamais m'a accostée à qui je n'aye rongé les biens, l'estomac et le cœur ?

Gillette.— Cela est vray. Mais combien de fois t'ay-je dit que tu n'entretiennes point Constant ? Comme m'as-tu obéy ? Que t'a-il donné ? que t'a-il fait porter en la maison ? O la belle chose ! tu cours après un je ne sçay qui, et te mocques du medecin, qui, s'il ne peut te donner, te ruë ! Par la mercy Dieu, s'il ne m'apporte de l'argent, il n'entrera point ceans.

Le Vieillard Amoureux.

Quãd Sophocles à ſoy(quoy qu'il fut vieux)
Archippe attraict par argent.Enuieux
Ieunes Gallans,à regret le porterent,
Et de telz vers,l'vn & l'autre noterent,
Comme vn chahuan ſier ſur vne charoigne,
Ainſi la garſe eſt cheʒ ce vieil yuroigne.

Trois choſes on dit eſtre deſplaiſantes à
Dieu,& au monde.Poure orgueilleux,Ieune
pareſſeux, & vieil luxurieux:car c'eſt contre
debuoir de Fortune,& Nature.

Les

Que je te voye plus parler à luy ny mesme lui faire signe !

Dorothée.— Vous me tueriez plustost, je vous le dy.

Gillette.— Je ne te defend point d'aymer ceux qui ne viennent jamais les mains vuydes, mais que tu laisses là ces damoiseaux et friquenelles où il n'y a rien à gaigner : fay caresses à ce capitaine qui revient de la guerre tout chargé d'escus. Entre, et vien embrasser le medecin, qui t'a apporté la plus belle robbe du monde. Fay-luy semblant que tu es amoureuse de luy : baise-le, mords-le, accole-le, car il te payera bien.

Dorothée.— Qui ? ce vieil pourry ? Que la peste l'estrangle !

Gillette.— O sotte ! bien heureuse est celle dont un vieil rassotté est amoureux ! Sçais-tu que dict une glose sur le chapitre troisieme du livre des *Quenouilles* :

> Au vieil rassotté fay caresses,
> Si en bref veux avoir richesses.

Et plus bas :

> Il fait cuisine sans lard
> Qui ne caresse le vieillard.

Escoute un peu : si tu voyois un anneau d'or en la bouë, ou quelque bague en du fumier, ne te baisserois-tu pas pour les prendre ?

Dorothée.— Pourquoi non ?

Gillette.— La bouë et le fumier, c'est le vieillard, et l'anneau et la bague sont les presens qu'il nous donne : par quoy, abaisse-toy un peu et ne sois desdaigneuse. Sçay-tu qu'on dit ? que :

> Le sot vieillard que l'amour picque
> Est une très bonne practique.

Dorothée.— Hé Dieu ! si d'autre je me rend amoureuse, si je mets mon cueur autre part,

> Mon Constant m'ouvre la poictrine
> Et un cruel martel me mine.

Gillette.—

> La courtisane enjalousée
> Quitte un chacun, et, abusée
> D'un tout seul, qui luy semble beau,
> Vit esclave et court au bordeau.

Aucune plus grande ruyne ne peut entrer en la maison d'une courtisane que celle-cy. Une garce comme toy devenir amoureuse ! hé !

Dorothée.— Si je ne puis faire autrement ? J'enten tous les jours chanter ces vers, faits de longue main :

> La dame qui n'est amoureuse
> Est une fontaine sans eau,
> Un corps sans ame et un anneau
> Sans une pierre precieuse.

Gillette.— Ouy mais tourne le feuillet, et tu trouveras escrit en grosses lettres :

> A l'hospital court ceste-là
> Qui rien ne grippe et faict cela.

Et en l'autre page :

> Pour un plaisir qui tant peu dure,
> Tout à beau loisir se repent

Celle qui se fait la monture
D'un chacun, et, qui rien n'en prent.
Dorothée.— C'est bien dit. Qui est l'amoureux qui se vante avoir rien gaigné avec moy ? Là où je m'attaque, je n'y laisse non plus que si la gresle avoit passé. Vous verrez comment je sçauray bien aujourd'huy plumer ce capitaine : laissez-moy faire, et si je lui feray pas bravement croire que j'ay un enfant de luy : permettez seulement que je jouysse de cestuy seul.

Gillette.— Tu as raison, envoye-luy encores des presens à l'hostel, friande, presomptueuse. Quelle outrecuydance est ceci ! Il luy est advis qu'elle en sçait plus que moy. Entre viste... A qui parlé-je ?

Jean Boccace, Le laberinthe d'Amour/Il Corbaccio, 1366-1571.

Dans Il Corbaccio, *l'auteur se met lui-même en scène : amoureux d'une belle veuve insensible à sa cour, il se desespère et envisage le suicide. Une nuit, un rêve étrange lui vient ; il est égaré dans une vallée hostile, dite « la vallée enchantée », ou « le labyrinthe d'amour », voire « la porcherie de Vénus ». Les mugissements qu'on y entend sont ceux des hommes que l'amour réduit à l'état de bêtes. C'est du moins ce que lui apprend un être venu à son secours : celui-ci est l'esprit du mari de la dame cruelle, condamné à ce purgatoire pour son avarice et une indulgence excessive envers les scélératesses de son épouse. Il entreprend, sur l'ordre de Dieu, de démontrer à Boccace combien celui-ci a tort d'être amoureux, tel un homme du commun, lui qui a étudié et fréquenté les Muses. Pour mieux le convaincre, le mari défunt dévoile alors toute la fausseté des charmes de son épouse, et des femmes en général, en une longue diatribe qui passe en revue les principaux défauts féminins. Lorsque Boccace se réveille, il est guéri et entreprend de conter son aventure pour rendre éventuellement le même service aux jeunes gens aveuglés par l'amour.*

Sous couvert d'un récit autobiographique (dont l'authenticité est discutée), Il Corbaccio *est un véritable traité anti-féministe. Boccace s'y inspire directement de l'*Epistula adversus jovinianum *de Saint Jérôme, de la VIe des* Satires *de Juvénal, et de la tradition médiévale antiféministe, recueils de proverbes, fabliaux, littérature de clercs. Une telle virulence peut surprendre de la part de l'auteur qui, quelques années plus tôt, avait dédié aux « graziosissime donne » son* Décaméron *fait pour leur plaire et les consoler, voire les célébrer (Introduction à la IVe journée). Cependant cet ouvrage n'est pas aveugle aux défauts féminins, certaines silhouettes sont celles de la tradition satirique et le recueil se clot sur l'exaltation de la soumission totale de la femme dans la nouvelle de Griselidis, conte médiéval dont la leçon ne contredit en rien celle du* Laberinthe. *Celui-ci atteste la vigueur au XIVe siècle d'une tradition antiféministe simplificatrice, qui ne conçoit pour la femme d'autres modèles qu'Eve ou Marie.*

Lorsque Belleforest publie sa traduction en 1571, il sent le besoin d'atténuer par son Épitre dédicatoire la violence de cette satire : il affirme s'y être intéressé « plus pour la diction que pour le sujet qui y est traité ». Il s'y est pourtant senti probablement assez à son aise, car sa traduction suit de fort près les invectives de Boccace, alors qu'il avait très librement « enrichi » les nouvelles de Bandello de longues digressions moralisatrices. La publication en 1571 du Laberinthe *(réimprimé en 1573) est l'un des derniers témoignages d'un antiféminisme qui, s'il apparait comme quelque peu suranné, peut cependant représenter encore un contrepoint utile. Cependant le texte peut aussi apparaître comme l'un des premiers élé-*

ments du renouveau polémique qui se manifeste à la fin du siècle (cf. Stances de Mme Liébaut). Ainsi se manifeste le piétinement du XVIᵉ siècle sur ce problème de la Femme, cette incapacité à dépasser les contradictions que Rabelais avait mises en scène dans son Tiers Livre.

M.F.P.

LE LABERINTHE D'AMOUR

de Messire Jean Boccace
autrement Invective contre une
mauvaise femme
Mis nouvellement d'Italien
en Françoys
par François de Belleforest

Paris, Jan Ruelle

1571

[...] Ces bestes de femmes n'aians onc default de malice, & qui en felonnie ne sentent aucun decroissement, consideranz leur vilté, & foiblesse, & combien est basse, & mesprisable leur condition, si est-ce qu'avec ceste leur naturelle petitesse, elles n'oublient moien aucun de s'agrandir. Or le premier point qu'elles ont pour ce faire, est de dresser des pieges à la liberté des hommes pour la surprendre, & leur oster : & n'y a ruse, ny effort plus grand pour y parvenir que celle grande beauté que nature leur a octroiée, & laquelle elles augmentent par artifice, & sans y espargner aucune sorte de fards, & drogueries, & mesmes des anellemens des cheveux sont de beaux filais pour contraindre les folz à se soumettre à la volonté de ces voleuses & cruelles. C'est icy que les dances & chansons servent d'amours pour surprendre ces pigeons à poil follet, & les assujettir pour ne les laisser désormais hors de servitude : & de ces façons de faire procedent les mariages : si que tantost les uns, ores les autres, ou espousent leurs dames, ou bien les ont pour amyes, lesquelles sont en plus grand nombre que les espouses legitimes. Dès aussi tost que ces alliances, & liaisons sont faites, elles s'estimans estre montées à quelque haut degré d'honneur, quoy que ne soyent si aveugles, qu'elles ne cognoissent bien que naturellement elles sont nées serves & esclaves, si que bastissans leur espoir sur des choses grandes, elles dressent leur desir, & aspirent à seigneurier, & commander sur l'homme. Mais en cecy fault que hipocrisie face son tour, & par ainsi elles taschent de gaigner païs en s'humiliant & usant toute douceur, & obeissance avec lesquelles ruses elles obtiennent de leurs trop simples marys les joyaux & parures, les abillemens de toutes sortes, que de jour à autre elles ayent pour se parer, & embellir, & les tirent de leurs marys plus que miserables, lesquelz ne se prennent point garde que tous ces amadouemens ne servent que pour leur oster la seigneurie, & puissance de commander d'entre les mainz, & la laisser à leurs femmes, qui emportent la victoire. Lesquelles dès que se voyent parées & leurs chambres enrichies, comme si c'estoit le cabinet d'une royne, & que elles cognoissent leurs maryz enlacez, pris, & qu'ils se sousmettent à leur volonté soudain elles laissant les tiltres de compagnie (quoy que serve de condition), ne font conscience d'usurper par tout moien & ruse la seigneurie sur ceux, à qui de droit appartient de commander. Regardez aux nouvelles façons d'habiz, aux galantises non accoustumées, & plustost lascives que bien seantes, & combien elles sont desireuses de pompes & superfluitez, tellement que pas une ne pense estre belle, sinon en tant qu'elle ressemble ès insolences d'habiz & folles eschancreures les publiques courtisanes, lesquelles ne sauroient tant inventer d'atours & nouveautez, que celles-cy, qui sont de leurs marys estimées pudiques, ne leur ravissent, & les imitent en leurs bobans, & superfluictez. Et ces pouvres maryz ayans ainsi despendu leurs deniers, afin qu'il ne semble point qu'ilz les ayent vainement emploiez, que c'est chose qui peut servir, ils souffrent qu'elles les dispensent en ces denrées, sans prendre esgard à quel but ou blanc doit fraper ceste saiette. Or combien elles deviennent fieres en leurs maisons par le moyen de ceste licence, les sotz, & miserables le sçavent, qui en font l'experience. Il y en a de telles qui, comme louves affamées, estans venues en la maison de leurs maris pour dissiper leurs substances, biens, & richesses, ne cessent nuit, & jour de quereller serviteurs & chambrieres, voire jusqu'aux parens, freres & enfans de leurs espoux, & se faignent estre soigneuses du bien duquel elles ne desirent que de faire les desgast & ruine. Sans que pour se monstrer avoir soucy de celuy, qu'elles n'aiment en sorte quelconque, il est impossible de reposer auprès d'elles, ains se passe toute la nuit en debatz & querelles, chacune disant au sien : je voy bien comme & combien tu m'aymes, & je seroy bien aveugle, si je ne m'apercevoy que tu en as de plus chere que je ne suis. Estime tu que j'ayes les yeux bendez, & que je ne sçache qui est celle après laquelle tu cours, & lui faiz poursuites & que je sois ignorante de tes tours, & à qui est ce que tu portes bon visage, & parles tous les jours plus que familierement. Hé miserable que je suis ! il y a si longtemps que je suis avec toy sans que jamais encor tu m'ayes dit, te couchant à mon costé, quelque parolle gracieuse. Ne suis-je pas aussi belle, que celle que tu poursuis ? Sçache donc que celuy qui deux bouches baise, faut que l'une luy semble puante, et luy vienne à contrecœur. Pense que tu ne m'as point trouvée en la boue : car dieu sçait combien de bons, & grands personnages y a, qui se fussent estimez heureux de m'avoir à femme sans douaire quelconque, & eusse esté dame, & d'eux, & de leurs biens & chevance. Hé ! que ce fut bien mon desastre, & infortune lorsque je vins avec parolle. Avec ce bon soir & parolles encore plus cuisantes, & aspres, sans raison, ou juste occasion quelconque, ces furies tourmentent sans cesse & toutes les nuitz leurs pauvres marys, lorsqu'ils pensent reposer, ayans travaillé tout le long de la journée. Et de ceux-ci, en a y plusieurs qui, sollicitez de ces alluméfeux, chassent leurs peres de leur compagnie, d'autres font chasser leurs enfans, les aucuns partagent avec leurs freres[1], avec lesquels ilz faisoient bon mesnage : & telz qui ne veulent voir ni mere, ny sœur en leur logis, afin que le camp demeure à leurs femmes, qui sur touz emportent la victoire. Mais le pis est qu'il y en a de telles, qui se voyant sans personne qui les esclaire, font largesse des biens du mary à leurs amys, & messageres

(1) se séparent de leurs frères.

d'amourettes : & sçache qu'il en y a plusieurs, que tu estimes fort chastes, & honnestes en ce nombre, lesquelles aymeroient mieux n'avoir qu'un œil qu'il leur fut reproché que elles se contentassent d'un seul homme. Quelle meschanceté y a il qu'elles ne s'enhardissent d'executer pour satisfaire à leurs apetiz desordonnez, & dereiglée fantasie ? Elles se faignent paoureuses, & craintives en ce qu'il ne faut point ; s'il est besoing de monter sur l'eau leur estomach delicat ne le sçauroit souffrir, de marcher la nuit n'y a ordre, car elles par trop craignent la rencontre des espritz, & lutins nocturnes, & si une Souris fait le moindre bruit, que le vent face remuer une fenestre, ou qu'une petite pierre tombe, elles en tressaillent toute de fraieur, & le sang leur fuyant au cœur les fait devenir froides, & tremblantes de crainte, comme si quelque peril de mort leur estoit représenté. Mais Dieu sçait, comme si elles sont hardies ès choses qui leur sont à gré, & lors qu'il est requis d'exploiter ce qu'elles ont en fantasie : car il n'y a aspreté de lieu, precipice de montaigne, hauteur de palais, ny crainte d'eau qui les empesche, & l'obscurité de la nuit est celle qui sert aux folles pour tromper le mary qui repose sur la fiance que il a de celle qui le trahit malheureusement.

[...]

En general, il n'y a guere femme, qui ne soit presomptueuse, & qui ne se face acroire que tout ce qu'elle fait luy est bien seant, qu'elle est digne de tout honneur & reverence, & que tous les hommes sans elles ne sont rien, & ne sçauroient vivre en ce monde : au reste fascheuses, orgueilleuses, desdaigneuses & desobeissantes, il n'est rien si difficile à supporter qu'une femme riche, ny qui plus vous cause de deplaisir que de voir s'enorgueillir celle qui de soy est povre. Ce qu'elles font, & ce qu'on leur encharge de faire n'est par elles exécuté sinon en tant que le gaing, ou le plaisir leur est représenté, car hors de là, elles n'ont devant les yeux que reproches, qu'on les veut tenir esclaves, & qu'elles sont par trop obeissantes, tellement que s'il ne leur vient à la fantasie, elles n'ont garde de rien faire de ce qui leur sera commandé. Outre ce (qui leur est un vice naturel & est empraint en elles, comme une tache sur une martre est perpetuelle), elles sont toutes non babillardes seulement ains fascheusement criardes. Les pauvres estudianz qui souffrent ordinairement froid, & chault, qui veillent, & jeusnent, & qui ayanz employé un long temz encor voyent ils que c'est peu ce qu'ilz ont appris : & neantmoins ces dames sont si presomptueuses qu'elles se font acroire, pour avoir ouy quelque discours le matin quelque peu de temps, qu'elles sçavent quel, & comme est causé le mouvement des cieux, combien il y a d'estoilles au ciel, & quelle est leur grandeur, comme se fait le cours du soleil & des autres Planettes, comme se causent le tonnerre, l'esclair, les gresles, l'arc céleste, & toutes les austres choses qui sont créées en l'air : sçavent aussi quel est le fluz, & le refluz de la mer, & d'où il procede, & où il retourne, & comme la terre produit ses fruiz, herbes, arbres, & plantes. N'ignorent point ce qui se fait aux Indes, & en Espaigne, & comme sont dressées les maisons des Ethiopiens, d'où prend sa source le Nil, & si le cristal s'engendre de glace ès parties septentrionales, ou si d'autre matiere il est produit. Mais encores sçavent elles mieux qui couche avec leur voisine, & du fait de qui ceste autre est enceinte, de combien de mois & en quel temps elle doit enfanter, & combien ceste

autre a de poursuivans, & lequel luy a donné l'anneau, & qui la ceinture
qu'elle porte : & combien d'œufz fait avau l'an la poulle de leur voisine,
& combien il faut de fusées de filet en une livre de lin : & pour faire court
tout ce que jamais les Troyens, les Grecs ou les Romains ont fait, celles-cy
vous en scauroient rendre compte : & sur tout sont informées estans à
l'Eglise, qu'est-ce que fait la chambriere, parlanz ores avec la fourniere,
tantost à la lavandiere, & puis aux revendeuses, ne cessant onc de babiller
& se faschant ne trouvans personne à qui rompre les oreilles avec leurs
importunitez & s'enfurianz si on leur fait quelque reproche. Il est vray
que de ceste soudaine & excellente saigesse, & sçavoir qu'elles appren-
nent en si peu d'heure, & de ceste inspiration saisissant leurs ames, on
sort un bien, qui est qu'elles adressent, & instruisent leurs filles à leur res-
sembler, & desrober, comme elles font, leurs maris, mais qu'elles en
ayent : avec quelles ruses elles doivent recevoir les lettres des amoureux
qui les prient, & comme il faut leur respondre, quelle voie il faut tenir à
les faire entrer secrètement en leur maison, & comme il faut contrefaire la
malade, afin que le lit leur demeure franc, le mary allant coucher ailleurs.
Aussy celuy est fol, qui pense qu'une mère impudique vueille avoir sa fille
plus sage qu'elle, plus chaste, plus pudique. Et ne faut jà qu'elles aillent à
leurs voisins, ayans quelque affaire, des mensonges, faux sermenz, parju-
remenz, forbes, inventions, souspirs infinis, & mille faintes larmes car
elles en ont à prester, & à revendre. Dieu sçait, que jamais je ne sceuz tant
penser, ny rechercher, que je peusse trouver, cognoistre, ny discerner, où
elles trouvent ces choses, les ayant si à propos, & à tout poinct ainsi que il
leur vient à la fantasie. Je te prie, voy, si jamais tu les sçaurois faire rendre, ny avouër une chose qu'un autre aura veuë de ses propres yeux : car
soudain tu auras d'une desinentie sur le nez, on te dira que tu as la berlue,
ou que tu as envoyé ta cervelle à rabiller, tu ne sçais point où tu es, tu es
frenetique, & ahannes en vain, & autres telles parolles poignantes. Que si
elles dient rien, voire meissent elles en avant qu'elles ont veu voler les
asnes, il les faut croire, car autrement ce sont querelles, inimitiez mortel-
les, embusches, & trahisons, & la haine qui toujours sera en campaigne.

Et sont si audacieuses, que si quelcun tasche tant soit peu de mespriser
leur peu de sens & la faiblesse de leur esprit, aussi tost leur responce est
preste, & diront, les Sibylles n'estoient elles pas femmes, comme si chascune de ce sexe devoit faire l'onziesme au nombre de ces dames excellentes. C'est cas merveilleux qu'en tant de milliers d'années qu'il y a que le
monde est fait, & en nombre tant infiny de femmes il y a eu, on en ait veu
qu'une douzaine choisie de Sibylles, qui fussent reputées & estimées sages
par les anciens, & ce avant la venue du filz de Dieu en ce monde : & toutes fois n'y a femme si vile ou abjette soit elle qui ne presume tant de soy,
& de sa perfection, qu'elle ne se pense estre assez sage, & suffisante pour
estre digne qu'on la mette au ranc de ces plus illustres. Mais entre toutes
leurs folies, & vanitez, ceste-cy est la plus forte & insupportable, lors
qu'elles se veulent monstrer plus excellentes, & leur sexe plus à priser que
les hommes, elles ne craignent de dire que tout ce qui est bon, est attribué
à leur sexe, & est honoré de leur tiltre, & nom de femelle : comme sont
les estoilles, les planettes, les muses, les graces, les vertuz, & les richesses ; auxquelles, n'estoit que la responce ne seroit pas honneste, il ne fau-

droit dire rien autre cas, sinon que pour vray ces choses sont en tout femelles, sauf qu'elles ne pissent point. Avec moins de consideration encor, & bien souvent, elles se glorifient, que celle très sainte, & très glorieuse royne, qui en ses flancz a porté le salut & rachapt de tout le monde, & qui est Vierge avant l'enfantement, Vierge en enfantant, & Vierge après avoir enfanté, & toujours entière : & que plusieurs autres qui pour leur singulière sainteté sont honorées en l'Eglise de Dieu, ont esté femmes, comme elles sont. Et pour ceste occasion, elles s'estiment dignes d'estre honorées & respectées : & concluent qu'on n'a raison quelconque d'accuser leur vilté, ny moyen ou argument de taxer leur imperfection, sans s'attaquer à ces dames glorieuses, qui jouissent de la felicité eternelle, & de là veulent elles dresser leur escu, bouclier, & deffence, & à celles-là mettent elles en main leur cause, auxquelles elles ne ressemblent aucunement sinon en tant que touche le sexe.

[...]

Pour ce retournant à propos & voulant deviser de ceste dame, laquelle possede de nouveau tes affections, je dis te voulant discourir des choses, qui ne pouvoient venir à ta congnoissance fut par veuë, ou de la seule imagination, car le sçachant tu l'eusses fuye, il me faut commencer par celle beauté, l'artifice de laquelle a esté, en si grande efficace, que non seulement toy, ains plusieurs autres, qui ne sont à estre parangonnez à tes valeurs, y ont esté pris, & senty esblouissement fort lourd à son encontre, touz estimanz grandement ceste frescheur de visage, laquelle estant fardée, & artificielle, & semblable aux roses matinales, plusieurs ne voyans point cler, ont estimé que fut naturelle. Laquelle, si & toy, & les autres folz, qui te ressembloient, eussent eu le moyen que j'avoy de la voir le matin quand elle se levoit, ains qu'elle eut adapté sur la face le fais toy belle, & fard abominable, sans tarder, & fort legerement ils se fussent aperceuz de leur faulte & folie. Or estoit la couleur de ceste-cy (& pense qu'encor l'est elle plus que jamais) lors que se levoit, blafarde, & entre verd, & jaune, mal painte comme rapportant à la tainture de la fumée d'une tuilerie, aussi sale, & mal en point qu'un oiseau qui est en muë, toute chargée de croustes, & tremblante de foiblesse : & si au contraire, & differente à ce qu'elle sembloit estre ayant eu loysir de s'attifer & parer, qu'à grand peine l'eut creu personne, sans l'avoir veuë mille fois ainsi que devant moy j'en voioy tous les jours les experiences. Et qui ignore que les paroitz noircies de fumée, je ne diray pas le visage des femmes, ne deviennent blanches, y ajoustant des couleurs de ceste parure, ainsi qu'il plaira au paintre d'en user ? Qui ne sçait aussi que pour demener la paste, qui est chose insensible, la mesme chair vive, quand bien elle seroit fletrie, se refait, & devient enflée, & plus pleine ? Elle se serroit tant, & se fardoit de telle sorte & se faisoit tellement relever la peau, qui s'avalloit durant le repos de la nuit, que moy qui l'avois veuë en sa propre figure, estois tout estonné, de la voir ainsi changée. Et si l'eusses veuë telle que tous les matins je la contemploy, avec son bonnet de nuit enfoncé dans la teste, & le couvre chef autour du col, le visage ainsi meurtri, comme j'ay dit, & ayant son manteau de nuit sur les espaules, se mettre auprès du feu, & y couvrer les cendres, assise sur les talons, & l'eut aperceuë, les yeux tout chassieux, enfoncez, & ternis, ne cesser de toussir, & cracher de grosses huistres hors d'ecaille, je ne doubte point que toutes les vertuz racomptées par ton amy, t'eussent peu induire à l'aimer, ains la voyant telle, eusses oublié cent mille de telles amours, & les eusses recommandées à tous les diables. Je suis asseuré que si tu l'eusses veuë en tel équipage, là où tu dis que l'oyant, les flammes d'Amour coururent tellement par ton cœur, & se saisirent de tes entrailles, comme elles font passant sur quelque chose ensoufrée et de matière combustible, que plustost il t'eust semblé de voir un sac de lie, ou un tas de fiens, & vilennie, & de laquelle tu t'en fusse fuy, ainsi qu'on evite les choses, qui nous desplaisent, & encor la fuiras, & dois fuir, te souvenant des choses telles que je te racompte, & lesquelles sont véritables. Mais il reste à poursuivre plus outre. Elle te sembla de belle stature, & ayant la chair ferme, & le sein poly, & pense estre aussi certain que je suis de la felicité par moy attendue, que tu estimois ce sein estre caillé, & pommelu, tel qu'il te paroissoit, sans que tu veisses ou peusses voir, les peaux & boyaux pendans qui se cachoient souz la blancheur de ses coletz, & guimpes, mais ton opinion estoit bien eslongnée de la verité : & jaçoit que plusieurs t'en puissent rendre tesmoignage, comme le sçachant, il faut que tu me croyes, qui ne pouvant faire autrement, en ay longuement à mon grand regret, senty l'experience. En celle enflure, & aboutissement que tu luy voyois serrer dessus la ceinture, sois asseuré que ce ne sont point estoupes, ni drapeaux, ains la seule chair de deux besaces pendantes, qui furent jadis deux pommes non encore meures, & agreables & à les voir, & à manier, tels je pense les porta dès le ventre de sa mere : mais laissons à part le reste : car d'où que l'occasion en vienne, ou que ce soit pour trop avoir esté par autre tiraillées, & maniées, ou par le trop de fardeau de celle qui les ainsi fait croistre, ses mamelles sont si demesurement accreuës & devenues longues, & comme retirées de leur place naturelle, que si elle les laissoit avaller, peut-estre lui iroient elles jusques par dessus le nombril tout ainsi vuides qu'on voit estre une vessie de porc desenflée. Et certainement si l'on s'aidoit aussi bien de chaperons à Florence, qu'on fait à Paris, elle pourroit se les getter aisement sur l'espaule tout ainsi qu'un bourlet d'advocat fait à la françoise. Et quoy plus ? Ainsi que les bendeaux estendent le cuir, & peau des joues, tout ainsi en fait elle du ventre lequel estant comme les rayons sillonnés d'un champ à plis, & enlassures, semble un sac pendant non autrement que celle panetière vuide qui pend aux Bœufs du col jusqu'à la poitrine :& peut estre fault-il qu'elle rehauce ces paneaux charnuz tout aussi bien que ses robes, & linge voulant descharger la vessie ou lors qu'on y veut enfourner la mauvaise guide. L'ordre et la suite de mon discours requiert à parler de choses, & nouvelles, & plus estranges que les precedentes, lesquelles tant moins je mettray en arriere, ou tant plus diligemment je reduiray en mon esprit, & memoire, tant plus de santé causeront à la maladie de ton ame. Et comme ainsi soit que je ne sçache au vray par quel costé commencer mon raisonnement, voulant parler du goulphe de Satalie en la valée d'Acheron, assis souz la mal-plaisante ombre des boys obscurs, & souvent aspres, & raboteux, & qui sont desagreables pour une gomme escumeuse qu'ilz jettent, & y repairant des animaux de nouvelle sorte, si est-ce pourtant que je t'en feray la description. L'entrée du goulphe est telle, & si grande, que quoy que ma frégate eut le mast assez grand, si ne fut-il jamais, tant fussent les eaux retirées, que je n'eusse eu le moyen d'y donner place à un mien compaignon, qui eut eu aussi bon arbre en son vaisseau que moy, sans que pour cela je me fusse incommodé en aucune sorte. Ah ! qu'ay je dit ? La plus grande armée que feit jamais le roy Robert toute ensemble enchaisnée & navigant à pleines voiles, sans tirer en haut le timon, y eut à son aise peu faire son entrée. Et est cas merveilleux, que jamais fuste ny navire n'y entra, lequel n'y perit, & qui las et rompu n'en fut tiré dehors, ainsi qu'on dit que font en Sicille, Scylle, & Charybde, l'un desquelz engloutit les naus, et l'autre puis après les removit ruinées. Ce goulphe est pour le vray un abisme d'enfer, lequel sera lors rassasié & plein, que la mer aura assez d'eau sans en prendre, ny attirer celle des rivières, & que le feu refusera de brusler le bois, qui luy sera présenté. Je tairy les rivieres sanglantes, les ruisseaux jaunissantz, et iceux chargez d'une escume blanche, & chancie, qui souvent est non moins puante au nez, que mal-plaisante à la veuë. Que veux-tu que je die du bourg de Maupertuys, posé entre deux montaignes relevées ? & duquel telle fois, soit avec le son furieux d'un très grand tonnerre, ou sans iceluy, sort une fumée ensoufrée & puante, tout ainsi qu'il en advient au Mongibele de Sycile, qu'il est impossible que personne puisse se tenir en la contrée tant est insupportable la puanteur. Je ne sçauroy que te dire autre cas, sinon que tandis que j'estois voisin de ce maudit lieu, où je demouray plus que je ne vouloy, je fus souvent si confuz, & mal-traité de ceste soufflée de vent pernicieux, que j'en pensay mourir miserablement. Autrement que de mesme sorte, ne te peux je parler de ceste saveur, & puanteur infectée sentant le bouquin, qui sortait de toute la masse de ce corps détestable, soit que le chauld, la lassitude & autres semblables mouvemens causent son gemissement, & le font respirer : car cest air est si fascheux, que joint avec les choses susdittes, on diroit que c'est l'haleine, & punaisie d'un Lyon eschauffé de colere : aussi durant l'ardeur de l'esté, il n'y a aucun qui ne fut plus content de l'esloigner que d'en faire approche. A ceste cause, si toy & autres, qui allez achetter chast en poche, vous trouvez deceuz, & trompez, ne vous en esbahissez en sorte quelconque.

Pietro Aretino, Histoire de Laïs et Lamia / I ragionamenti d'Amore, 1534-1595.

En 1534 l'Arétin, déjà scandaleusement célèbre pour les Sonnets Luxurieux, *fait imprimer à Venise (sous une fausse localisation parisienne) un volume de « Ragionamenti », c'est-à-dire d'entretiens, de discussions. Le prétexte de ceux-ci :* La Nanna *ne sait quelle carrière conseiller à sa fille* Pippa, *le cloître, le mariage ou le trottoir. Au cours de trois journées elle évoque pour son amie Antonia sa triple expérience de religieuse, d'épouse et de courtisane. La luxure est partout et les deux femmes finissent par conclure cyniquement qu'il vaut mieux faire de la Pippa une putain car celle-ci du moins ne trompe personne et n'a pas de prétentions à la vertu. Une seconde partie publiée en 1536 détaillera les conseils donnés à la jeune fille pour l'exercice de son art, évoquera les tours joués aux femmes par les hommes et traitera de la vie des entremetteuses.*

Le plus souvent les dialogues tournent au récit et le récit lui même se fragmente en nouvelles ou en scènes de comédie, tableaux multiples de la vie contemporaine tracés par la Nanna avec une complaisance marquée pour l'obscénité. Pourtant le scandale ne suffirait pas à expliquer le succès de l'œuvre. L'Arétin est un merveilleux conteur et ses Ragionamenti *témoignent d'un art ramassé de l'esquisse psychologique, d'un style désinvolte dont la vivacité excelle dans la transcription du langage parlé. La traduction que nous donnons ici a isolé de l'ensemble de l'œuvre la troisième journée de la première partie, c'est-à-dire la vie des courtisanes. C'est là le meilleur témoignage que nous ayions sur ce type social si important au XVI*ᵉ *siècle. Il s'agit de la courtisane dite « honnête », c'est-à-dire raffinée, cultivée, qui a, pour son pouvoir et son intelligence, fasciné de nombreux auteurs de l'époque. La Nanna, comme la courtisane évoquée par Du Bellay, joue de la musique et lit Pétrarque, et la très célèbre Tullia d'Aragona écrivit, avec sans doute l'aide d'un ami humaniste, un traité platonicien* Dialogue de l'infinité d'amour, *qui eut l'honneur de deux éditions vénitiennes. Le milieu du siècle vit leur apogée mais la réaction catholique les chargea de tous les maux et tenta, surtout à Rome, de les éliminer. C'est très certainement dans cette perspective prétenduement moralisatrice qu'il faut comprendre la publication isolée de cette journée : on veut, à l'époque ne voir dans les courtisanes que les scories d'une société par ailleurs sans ombres, alors que l'Arétin dressait avec une satisfaction implacable le constat d'amoralisme de toute son époque. Cette optique est confirmée par le sous-titre donné à l'œuvre et par l'adjonction en appendice de* La Vieille Courtisane de Du Bellay.

Signalons enfin que cette traduction n'est pas, contrairement à ce qu'annonce le titre, tirée de l'italien, mais de la version espagnole « Coloquio de las damas » qui dès 1549 isolait la troisième journée de la première partie l'accompagnant de commentaires édifiants. Ce double décalage linguistique alourdit fort la narration et fait perdre à la prose de

*l'Arétin une bonne partie de son charme. Nous avons pourtant voulu en
citer un fragment car, si l'on en croit Brantôme, l'Arétin était, malgré
l'absence de traduction française avant 1595, fort lu en France : « J'ai
connu un bon imprimeur vénitien à Paris, qui s'appelait messer Ber-
nardo, parent de ce grand Aldus Manutius de Venise, qui tenait sa boutique en la rue Saint-Jacques, qui me dit et jura une fois qu'en moins d'un
an il avait vendu plus de cinquante paires de livres de l'Arétin à force
gens mariés et non mariés, et à des femmes... ».*

M.F.P.

HISTOIRE DES AMOURS FAINTES & DISSIMULEES DE LAIS & LAMIA,

récitée par elles mesmes
mise en forme de Dialogue par P. Aretin,
où sont descouvertes les falaces & communes
tromperies dont usent les mieux affectées
courtisanes de ce temps à l'endroit de leurs amis
Traduit de l'Italien en Français & augmenté
de la vieille Courtisane de J. du Bellay

Paris, Anthoine du Brueil

1595

LAIS.— Ainsi que j'estois à Milan, advint que je couchay plusieurs nuicts avec un bragard [1], faiseur de boucliers, qui avoit longtemps esté en garnison à Siene, & suivy les compagnies de Gênes, voire s'estoit trouvé au sac de Rome, & en autres hazardeuses entreprises. Conclusion, il estoit tel homme, que quelque femme qui le voyait de demie lieüe loing, entendoit qu'il se falloit garder de luy comme du diable : si bien qu'en tout Milan ne se parloit d'autre chose. Et veux que tu saches que je n'ay acquis ce que j'ay de present, comme buissonniere, ains comme diablesse. Baste, laissons cela pour une autre saison. Tu dois sçavoir que se levant un matin d'auprès de moy, apperceus qu'il avoit dix ducats en sa bourse ; en sa bource dis-je, que la nuict ensuivant m'efforcay luy tirer de dessous l'aesle, ce qui ne me fut possible (ores que cauteleusement j'eusse laissé la chandelle allumée tout à propos à cet effet) : parquoy je differay m'en rendre contente à une autre fois. Quelque peu de temps après (me souvenant tousjours de cet affaire), comme il estoit en ma maison oysif & à repos, pensant qu'il me devoit toute sa vie tenir contente sans rien donner, feignis avoir acheté à un marchand quelque quantité de toille de Hollande & qu'il viendroit à certaine heure me demander dix escus que je luy devois pour autre toille qu'il m'avoit ja delivré à crédit : à quoy ne fit faute le supposé marchand, tellement que lors j'entendis qu'il estoit entré en la maison, me tiray près de mon bragard, & le feis chevalier de mon ordre, luy baillant l'accolée d'une main, & de l'autre applaudissois sa barbe tout doucement. Et le baisans à souhait, me prins à luy dire en ceste maniere : Me sçauriez vous à l'adventure (Amy) faire entendre qui est vostre amoureuse ? C'est vous, dit-il, de moy. Parquoy tant pour ceste response comme pour l'entretenir en contentement, je me mis d'avantage à le fes-

---

1. Soldat fanfaron, matamore.

toyer. Tandis que l'entretenois, & luy disois ces mots : Voulez vous que nous couchions ceste nuict ensemble ? La chambriere me dit : Madame, il y a assez longtemps que le marchand de toille est ceans. A ce propos je luy commanday qu'elle le feist entrer en la chambre où nous estions. Et lors mon bragard me demandant qui estoit cet homme & ce qu'il demandoit, je luy feis entendre qu'il venoit querir dix escus que je luy devois de reste des toilles qu'il m'avoit vendues, pour faire un pavillon [2]. Puis dis à ma servante : pren ceste clef, ouvre ce coffre & luy donne dix escus de l'argent que tu y trouveras. Cependant qu'elle alloit faire semblant d'ouvrir le coffre, je dorlotois & amadoüois mon mignon au possible. Mais pour autant que le marchand de toilles s'en vouloit aller, encores que j'eusse dit à ma servante qu'elle se despeschast luy compter argent, & qu'elle estoit toute troublée, je m'en allay droit à elle : laquelle empeschée à l'entour de la serrure de ce coffre ne le pouvoit ouvrir, & tout à propos, parce que comme l'argent n'estoit deu à celuy qui le demandoit, aussi n'avoit-elle la vraye clef qu'il falloit pour ouvrir le coffre. Ce que voulant dissimuler, feis mines qu'elle avoit efforcé la clef & meslé la serreure. Dequoy indignée (ce sembloit) me jettay sur elle, criant & frappant à coups de poing, disant : Ennemie mal'heureuse, tu m'as gasté mon coffre ! Puis la frappant tousjours, luy commanday qu'elle allast querir le serrurier, pour en faire ouverture. A quoy voulant optemperer s'y transporta, mais feit semblant de ne le trouver point, & retourna sans l'amener. Incontinent, monstrant plus de fascherie qu'auparavant, me tournay vers mon challand, & luy requis de grace, que s'il avoit dix escus sur soy, il m'en feist prest, afin que le marchand de toilles n'attendist d'avantage, pendant qu'on iroit cercher un homme pour lever la serrure, & que de l'argent qui y estoit il seroit rembourcé.

LAMIA.— Tu jouas (à mon advis) la plus grande & gracieuse trousse du monde, & n'ouy de ma vie la semblable.

LAIS.— La premiere chose qu'il fit ce fut de mettre la main à la bource, donnant dix escus à ce marchand, & lui dit : Tenez frere, & vous en allez à la grace de Dieu. Comme j'estois assaillant ce pauvre coffre, le frappant des pieds tant que je pouvois, puis non contente des grandes & petites offences que luy faisois, prins une pierre de laquelle je me voulois efforcer (ce sembloit) de l'ouvrir ; il me dit : Envoyez, Madame, querir un serrurier, vous le romprez plustost que l'ouvrir de ceste sorte. Desjà me disoit toy & vous [3] avec moindre respect qu'au precedent, sans plus user de Seigneurie, au moyen de la liberalité qu'il avoit usé envers moy, me prestant ces dix escus.

LAMIA.— Jesus que ton excellence faisoit belle incongruité.

LAIS.— Quand il m'eut retirée d'auprès ce coffre, qu'assiduement je traittois à coups de pied, il me mena vers le lict, en intention que nous coucherions ensemble à l'apresdinée : mais comme j'estois encores indeterminée si à ce je devois consentir ou non, on frappa à la porte. Et

---

2. Garniture de lit.
3. La traduction est quelque peu confuse. Dans le texte italien le bravache passe au tutoiement dès qu'il a déboursé les dix écus et la Nanna le remarque immédiatement.

comme je me voulois mettre à la fenestre pour voir qui c'estoit, il me retint
& pria que n'en feisse rien. En effet je me despestray de ses mains, &
regardant en bas, j'apperceuz un jeune Gentilhomme, monté sur une
mulle, qui desguisé, me presenta la crouppe : ce que j'acceptay, recevant
par même moyen la cappe d'un sien page, vestüe au surplus d'habits
d'homme, ainsi que soulois estre la plus-part du temps, & en cest equi-
page m'en allay avec luy. Dequoy indigné mon bragard (badaut qu'il
estoit) abbatit un portraict de ma personne representée en un tableau qui
pendoit à un tapis, & l'emporta (comme s'il eust voulu soy venger de
moy), & dèslors sort de ma maison, comme celuy qui quitte un jeu auquel
il a perdu son argent. Vray est que tost après il retourna avec un marteau
& tenailles, en deliberation d'enlever la serrure & prendre ses dix escus.
Mais ma chambriere qui estoit instruicte de ce qu'elle devoit faire, commença à crier à haute voix, & dit : On me desrobbe, on me desrobbe !
Aux larrons, aux larrons ? tellement que tout le voisinage fut tout à l'instant à ma porte. Ce qu'entendant, il se hasta le plus qu'il peut, & fit en
sorte qu'il enleva la serreure du coffre, où il trouva plusieurs petits vaisse-
lets pleins d'oignemens, qui servoient à ambellir la face & les mains, les
autres pour les cheveux, poudres & racines de mauves pour les dents,
empoix pour empeser les voiles & collets, un pot plein de pommade pour
adoucir l'aspreté du corps & des jambes, deux phiolles d'eau astringente
pour resserrer ce que tu sçais, & plusieurs autres menutez dont nous
usons à la conservation de nostre estat.

Textes féminins
de la fin du siècle

Textes féminins
de la fin du siècle

Œuvres de Mes Dames Des Roches, 1578 - « Epistre aux Dames »

Les textes réunis dans cette dernière subdivision ont tous été écrits par des auteurs féminins, et leurs parutions respectives se situent entre 1578 et 1595. Il s'agit des œuvres de Mesdames Des Roches, « mere et fille », et de Madame Liébaut, née Nicole Estienne. Si nous tenons compte, dans cette introduction, de quelques points de référence empruntés à l'œuvre de Marie de Romieu, nous avons écarté délibérément de ce dossier son Brief Discours que l'Excellence de la Femme surpasse celle de l'Homme, *(1581), dont l'intérêt informationnel et littéraire nous a semblé assez mince. Par ailleurs, le lecteur peut se reporter à une réédition fort accessible de 1878.*

A partir de ces caractéristiques externes, on peut dégager a priori un certain nombre d'éléments sur ces publications demeurées assez obscures : écrits et édités à la fin du siècle, ces textes de femmes sont-ils susceptibles d'apporter une réponse à la polémique féministe, ou tout au moins de dresser un bilan des éléments constitutifs de la question féminine ? C'est à ce seul titre qu'ils ont droit de figurer dans l'ensemble du recueil. En effet, leur retentissement limité, leur faible diffusion, ne leur permet guère, contrairement aux autres phénomènes littéraires étudiés précédemment, d'être considérés comme un point de départ, mais plutôt comme un aboutissement, une sorte d'illustration concrète, qui, dans sa discrétion, ne manque ni d'intérêt ni de richesse.

On peut au demeurant, s'élever contre le regroupement d'auteurs dont les registres d'expression sont aussi différents, selon leur appartenance au sexe féminin. Bien entendu, il n'est point question ici de se référer à un déterminisme biologique ou psychologique qui au départ donnerait la clé d'un certain nombre de généralités internes. C'est en tant que groupe social que la femme pose par l'acte d'écrire sa première affirmation de soi, au sein du contexte socio-économique qui l'entoure. Or cet « acte », que constitue l'écriture féminine, modifie pronfondément, et selon des données à peu près constantes, et son activité littéraire en tant que « pratique », et un noyau très important des données internes de l'œuvre qui se regroupent autour de cette fonction d'écrivain. Dès son origine, l'œuvre féminine se mue en réflexion sur son propre discours, et se fait selon les cas défense ou apologie.

La portée de cet « acte » d'écrire n'est cependant aucunement homogène. Le clivage le plus net entre les différents niveaux de signification qu'il peut offrir, se situe à la charnière entre « écriture » et « publication ». Marie de Romieu semble s'être désintéressée de la publication de ses œuvrettes mondaines qui furent éditées par les soins de son frère et précepteur Jacques de Romieu. De même, un certain Claude Le Villain, se charge, vers 1595, de présenter au public les « Stances » de Mme Liébaut, dont les autres œuvres sont restées à l'état manuscrit. C'est ici qu'apparaît la perspective bien différente dans laquelle les dames Des Roches vivent leur vocation littéraire. Non seulement leur activité plus régulière et soutenue se traduit par un nombre plus imp otant de publications, mais elles semblent être entrées dans le circuit économique de la production littéraire. C'est ce que prouve cette curieuse allusion de Madeleine Des Roches (la mère) aux pertes immobilières qu'avait subies son patrimoine pendant la Guerre Civile :

> *[...]J'apperceu deux maisons*
> *Que j'avois au faubour n'estre plus que tisons.*
> *[...]*
> *Ces deux maisons pouvoient valoir deux milles livres*
> *Plus que ne m'ont valu ma plume n'y mes livres.*
>   (œuvres de Mes Dames Des Roches. 1578.-
>   « Epistre au Roy »)

Cette distinction étant faite, revenons à un stade plus élémentaire encore de l'acte d'écrire. Celui-ci au moment de son accomplissement même se situe en porte à faux sur la conception traditionnelle de la production féminine : l'acte d'écrire en effet constitue une transgression de la tâche économique assignée à la femme dans le système patriarcal du XVIᵉ siècle.

Or ces bourgeoises éclairées de la Contre-Réforme sont, on le verra aisément, profondément pénétrées du respect de l'idéal « mesnager ». Elles célèbrent au besoin la participation indispensable, mais trop ignorée, de la mère de famille au profit public : Madame Liébaut est sensible au rôle de l'économie domestique dans la conservation du patrimoine, et l'image de la Femme Forte de Salomon garde, en cette fin de siècle tout son prestige. Ce n'est donc pas sans mauvaise conscience, nuancée parfois d'une ironie hésitante, que la fonction littéraire féminine essaye de s'affirmer au sein d'un conflit fondé essentiellement sur l'opposition travail/loisir. Marie de Romieu compare à ce sujet la production littéraire de son frère et la sienne :

> *« Prenez en bonne part, mon Frère, ce mien brief discours que je vous envoye, composé assez à la haste, n'ayant pas le loisir à cause de notre mesnage, de vacquer (comme vous dedié pour servir aux Muses) à chose si belle & si divine que les vers ».*
>   (Premières œuvres poétiques de Madamoiselle de Romieu,
>   Vivaroise, Paris, 1581)

La rhétorique assez banale de cette phrase se réfère en réalité à un jugement de valeur exactement inverse, mais symétrique de ce qui précède, ce qui nous fait déjà entrevoir l'univers de contradictions au sein de quoi se débat la conscience féminine. La vilenie du « mesnage » est implicitement opposée au « service des Muses », à cette « chose si belle et divine ». Nous entrons ici dans un système de classification hiérarchique, où la fonction que le groupe assigne à la femme est totalement accceptée *comme humiliante et « basse ». Nous empruntons à Madeleine des Roches la citation suivante :*

« Et si n'estant plus charitables, vous m'advisez que le silence ornement de la femme peut couvrir les fautes de la langue & de l'entendement : je respondray qu'il peut bien empescher la honte mais non pas accroistre l'honneur, aussi que le parler nous separe des animaux sans raison ».

(*œuvres de Mes Dames Des Roches, 1578,* -
« *Epistre aux Dames* »)

Nous voyons surgir ici deux axes différentiels qui se superposent à ceux qu'avait établis Marie de Romieu (travail matériel/travail cérébral) : le premier fondé sur l'opposition silence/raison s'étaye d'un second rapport antithétique implicite, animalité/humanité. Dans ce jeu de classification, on voit aisément que la nature immédiate de la femme est assimilée aux éléments « inférieurs ». Seule pourra la sauver la « Lettre », à qui ces dames attribuent, en bonnes humanistes, un pouvoir miraculeux et indiscuté. Une opposition hiérarchique apparaît encore ici, fondée sur l'axe nature/culture. C'est par le « debvoir » de l'étude que Madame Des Roches mère rappelle à sa fille la nécessité pour la femme de passer à un niveau d'être plus élaboré, où par un acte de totale sublimation doit se transfigurer son corps et son être social. Il est donc évident que le discours féminin s'appuie sur un système de valeurs entièrement conforme à celui qu'impose alors l'idéologie dominante, qui se fonde sur l'opposition hiérarchisée du « haut » et du « bas », de l'esprit sur le corps. Certes, Madame Liébaut proclame la nécessité de s'évader de la situation inférieure qu'assignent à la femme ces structures antithétiques, par un refus brutal de la condition matrimoniale, qui concrétise cette situation par l'humiliation physique et sociale :

Muses, qui chastement passez vostre bel age,
Sans vous assujetir aux lois de mariage...

Mais cette révolte ne va pas très loin : l'exemple traditionnel des Muses, et la condition religieuse que ce texte a servi à exalter sont des exutoires fort rassurants. Cette invocation ne sert qu'à corroborer docilement les structures hiérarchiques précédemment dénoncées, la chasteté, ornement du monde supérieur de l'intellect, s'opposant au « mariage », dont le lot semble être tout naturellement l'« assujetissement ». Ainsi Madame Liébaut approuve-t-elle le langage même de l'idéologie établie, source de ses « miseres et tourmens ».

De quoi pourra servir la description plus ou moins réaliste de l'« oppression » socio-économique subie par la femme qu'on trouvera dans ces pages ? Dans une perspective littéraire qui adopte, par son système rhétorique même, les valeurs qui fondent l'appareil hiérarchique de l'oppression, ces « thèmes », dont chez Mme Liébaut en particulier, on reconnaît l'inspiration peu personnelle, ne sont-ils autres choses que l'incidence anecdotique du discours ? La « clergie » féminine de la fin de ce siècle, si elle sait parfois exprimer, par la plume de Madeleine Des Roches en particulier, le paradoxe déchirant de son combat, ne fera rien pour remettre en question l'édifice social qui rend son existence si difficile et contradictoire. Son discours ne fera que le confirmer.

L.L.H.

LES ŒUVRES DE
MES DAMES DES ROCHES DE POETIERS

mere et fille

Paris, 1578

La Mere

EPISTRE A MA FILLE

Les anciens amateurs de sçavoir,
Disoient qu'à Dieu faut rendre le devoir,
Puis au pays, & le tiers au lignage,
Les induisant à force de courage,
Soit quelques fois pour souffrir passion,
Soit pour dompter la forte affection.
Au Seigneur Dieu je porte reverence,
Pour mon pays, je n'ay point de puissance,
Les hommes ont toute l'authorité,
Contre raison & contre l'équité :
Mais envers toy, fille qui m'es si proche,
Ce me seroit un grand blasme & reproche
De te conduire au sentier plus battu,
Veu que ton cœur est né à la vertu.
Il ne suffit pour tant d'estre bien née,
Le sens acquis nous rend morigenées
Et le flambeau dans nostre ame allumé
Sans le sçavoir est bientost consommé
La lettre sert d'une saincte racine,
Pour le regime, & pour la Medecine :
La lettre peut changer le vitieux,
La lettre accroist le cueur du vertueux,
La lettre est l'art qui prenant la matiere
Luy peut donner sa forme plus entiere.
Ce brief discours sur un tel argument
Soit bien receu de ton entendement,
Ma fille unique, & de moy cher tenue,
Non pour autant que tu en es venue
Et que dans toy je me voy un pourtraict
Du poil, du teint, de la taille & du traict
Façon, maintient parolle, contenance,
Et l'aage seul en faict la difference :
Ny pour nous voir tant semblables de corps,
Ny des espritz les gracieux accords,
Ni ceste douce aymable sympathie,
Qui faict aymer la semblable partie

N'ont point du tout causé l'entier effect
De mon amour envers toy si parfaict,
Ny les efforts mis en moy par nature,
Ny pour autant qu'es de ma nourriture.
Mais le penser, qu'entre tant de mal-heurs,
De maux, d'ennuis, de peines, de douleurs,
Sujection, tourment, travail, tristesse,
Qui puis treze ans ne m'ont point donné cesse,
Tu as, enfant, apporté un cueur fort,
Pour resister au violent effort
Qui m'accabloit, & m'offrit dès enfance
Amour, conseil, support, obéissance.
Le tout puissant à qui j'eu mon recours,
A faict de toy naistre mon seul secours :
Or je ne puis de plus grand benefices
Recompenser tes loüables offices,
Que te prier de faire ton devoir
Envers la Muse & le divin sçavoir.
« Mais le vray centre & globe de l'estude
« C'est de donner à vertu habitude,
« Et de vouloir en elle insinuer,
« L'abit se faict difficile à muer.
Tu es au temps pour apprendre bien née,
Et sembles estre aux Muses inclinée,
Le Ciel te face avoir tant de desir
Des sainctes mœurs, le seul juste plaisir,
Et le Daemon, qui l'œuvre a commencée
Guide si bien l'effect de ta pensée,
Que tesmoignant à la posterité
Combien d'honneur tu auras merité,
Tu sois un jour par vertu immortelle,
Je t'ay tousjours souhaitée estre telle.

ODE I

Si mes escris m'ont gravé sur la fasse
Le sacré nom de l'immortalité,
Je ne l'ay quis non plus que mérité,
Si je ne l'ay de faveur ou de grace.

Je ne descry Neptune en sa tourmente,
Je ne peins pas Jupiter irrité,
Le vase ouvert, la fuite d'equité,
Dont notre terre à bon droict se lamente.

L'enfant venu de Poros & Paenie,
Qu'on dist brusler le plus froid des glaçons
Se plaist d'ouyr les superbes chançons,

Et je me play d'une basse harmonie.

Mais qui pourroit chargé de tant de peines,
L'esprit geené de cent mille malheurs,
Veoir Apollon reverer les neufs seurs,
Et dignement puiser en leur fontaine.

Le Ciel a bien infuz dedans nostre Ame
Les petits feux principes de vertu :
Mais le chaud est par le froid combattu,
Si un beau bois n'alimente la flame.

Nature veut la lettre et l'exercice
Pour faire veoir un chef d'œuvre perfaict
Elle bien sage en toutes choses faict
Ses premiers traicts limer à l'artifice.

Nos parens ont de louäbles coustumes,
Pour nous tollir l'usage de raison,
De nous tenir closes dans la maison
Et nous donner le fuseau pour la plume.

Trassant nos paz selon la destinée
On nous promet liberté & plaisir :
Et nous payons l'obstiné desplaisir
Portant le dot sous les lois d'hymenée.

Bien tost après survient une misere
Qui naist en nous d'un desir mutuel
Accompagné d'un soing continuel
Qui suit tousjours l'entraille de la mere.

Il fault soubdain que nous changions l'office
Qui nous pouvoit quelque peu façonner
Où les marys ne nous feront sonner
Que l'obeir le soing, et l'avarice.

Quelc'un d'entr'eux, ayant fermé la porte
A la vertu nourrice du sçavoir,
En nous voyant craint de la recevoir
Pour ce qu'elle porte habit de nostre sorte.

L'autre reçoit l'esprit de jalousie,
Qui, possesseur d'une chaste beauté,
Au nid d'Amour loge la cruaulté,
En bourrellant sa propre fantasie.

Pyrrha choisist une claire semence
Pour repeupler le terrestre manoir

Et Deïcal sema le caillou noir,
Dont le ciel mesme a faict experience.

Mon Dieu, mon Dieu combien de tolerance,
Que je ne veux icy ramentevoir !
Il me suffit aux hommes faire veoir
Combien leurs loix nous font de violence.

Les plus beaux jours de noz vertes années,
Semblent les fleurs d'un printemps gracieux
Pressé d'orages et de vens pluvieux
Qui vont borner les courses terminées.

Aux temps heureux de ma saison passée
J'avoy bien l'aisle unie à mon costé,
Mais en perdant ma jeune liberté,
Avant le vol ma plume fut cassée.

Je voudroie bien m'arester sur le livre,
Et au papier mes peines souspirer :
Mais quelque soing m'en vient tousjours tirer,
Disant qu'il faut ma profession suivre

L'Agrigentin du sang de Stésichore
A dignement honoré le sçavoir,
Qui envers nous fit semblables devoirs,
Pareil miracle, on reverroit encore.

Dames, faisons ainsi que l'Amaranthe
Qui par l'hyver ne perd sa belle fleur :
L'esprit imbu de divine liqueur
Rend par labeur sa force plus duisante.

Pour supporter les maux de nostre vie,
Dieu nous fit part de l'intellect puissant
Pour le reduire à l'intellect agent
Maugré la mort, la fortune, et l'envie.

La Mère.

EPITAPHE DE FEU MAISTRE FRANCOIS ESBOISSARD SEIGNEUR DE LA VILLE, SON MARY

Contrairement à Madame Liébaut, Madeleine et Catherine Des Roches se sont plu à exalter les vertus du mariage. Elles en font volontiers un idéal de vie morale et religieuse : leurs réflexions, toutefois ne s'appuient pas uniquement sur des références bibliques ou littéraires. Voici, sous la plume de Madeleine Des Roches, l'expression lyrique de son amour pour son mari défunt. Ce n'est pas la seule évocation dans son œuvre d'une perte qui semble avoir assombri toute sa vie :

> O Espoux tant aymé qui me rendoit contente
> Que ta perte me donne un furieux remort

écrivait-elle treize ans après le début de son veuvage dans l'« Epistre au roy ». (Oeuvres, 1578)

Veux tu sçavoir passant, quel a esté mon estre,
Sçaches que la nature, & fortune, & les cieux,
Noble, riche & sçavant autrefois m'on fait naistre,
Me rendant possesseur de leurs dons precieux.

Apres avoir vescu d'une loüable vie,
Je fus pris d'un catere, & maintenant le sort
Des Parques me guerit de ceste maladie :
Je mourois en ma vie, & je vis en la mort,

Je fus trente ans Breton, vingt & huit ans mon espouse
Me retint dans Poëtiers, lié de chaste amour,
Mon ame devant Dieu maintenant se repose,
Et mon corps en ce lieu attand le dernier jour.

Mon corps n'est pas tout seul soubs ceste froide tombe,
Le cueur de ma compagne y gist avec le mien,
Jamais de son esprit nostre amytié ne tombe,
La mort ne trenche point ung si ferme lien ;

O Dieu, dont la vertu dedans le Ciel enclose
Enclost mesme le Ciel, vueillez que ma moitié
Toutes ses actions heureusement dispose,
Honorant pour jamais nostre saincte amytié.

La fille

EPISTRE A SA MERE
(extrait)

Beaucoup diront volontiers que je ne devoy point escrire de quelque subject que ce soit, mesme en ce temps que nous voyons tant de Poëtes en la France. Je ne veux faire autre responce à ce propos là, sinon qu'il y a bien assez d'hommes qui escrivent, mais peu de filles se meslent d'un tel exercice & j'ay tousjours desiré d'estre du nombre de peu : non pas que j'aye tant d'estime de moy que de me vouloir parangonner aux plus excellentes non plus qu'aux moindres : car je ne veux juger de moy ny par audace ny par vilité de cueur : au moins je ne me sentiray point coupable d'avoir perdu beaucoup de temps à composer un si petit ouvrage que cettuy-cy, pource que j'y ay jamais employé d'heures, fors celles que les autres filles mettent à visiter les compaignies pour estre veues de leurs plus gentilz serviteurs, desirans qu'ilz puissent devenir dignes chantres de leurs beautez, encores qu'elles ayent bien la puissance de se chanter elles-mesmes : toutesfois elles dedaignent de s'y prendre : approuvant (ce croi-je) l'opinion de Zinzime qui ne povoit estimer les Gentils-hommes Romains pour estre bien instruits en la Musique à saulter & voltiger, pour ce que les Seigneurs de Turquie faisoient faire tels exercices à leurs esclaves. Ainsi quelques unes des Damoiselles de ce temps, sans vouloir prendre la peine d'escrire se contentent de faire composer leurs serfs, attisant mille flammes amoureuses dans leurs cueurs, par la vertu desquelles ilz deviennent Poëtes mieux que s'ilz avoient beu toute l'onde sacrée de la fontaine des Muses. Mais quant à moy, qui n'ay jamais faict aveu d'aucun serviteur, & qui ne pense point meriter que les hommes se doivent asservir pour mon service : j'ay bien voulu suivre l'advis de la fille de Cleomenes qui reprenoit les Ambassadeurs Persans, dont ilz se faisoient accoustrer par des Gentils-hommes, comme s'ils n'eussent point eu de mains. Aussi je m'estimerois indigne de ce peu de graces que Dieu m'a donné par vostre moyen (ma mere) si de moymesme je n'essaïois de les faire paroistre : ce n'est pas que j'espere me tracer avec la plume une vie plus durable que celle que je tiens de Lachesis, aussy n'ay-je point quitté pour elle mes pelotons, ni laissé de mettre en œuvre la laine, la soye & l'or quand il a esté besoing, ou quand vous me l'avez commandé. J'ay seulement pensé de vous monstrer comment j'employe le temps de ma plus grande oisiveté, & vous supplie humblement (ma mere), de recevoir ces petits escrits qui vous en rendront tesmoignage : si vous en trouvez quelques uns qui soient assez bien nez, avoüez les s'il vous plaist pour vos nepveux, & ceux qui ne vous seront agreables, punissez-les à l'exemple de Jacob qui condemna la famille d'Isachar pour obeir à ses autres enfans.

La fille

A MA QUENOILLE

Quenoille mon soucy je vous promets et jure
De vous aimer tousjours et jamais ne changer
Vostre honneur domestic pour un bien estranger
Qui erre inconstamment et fort peu de temps dure.
Vous ayant au costé je suis beaucoup plus seure
Que si ancre et papier se venoient aranger
Tout à l'entour de moy, car pour me revanger
Vous pouvez bien plustost repousser une injure.
Mais Quenoille m'amie, il ne faut pas pourtant
Que pour vous estimer et pour vous aimer tant
Je delaisse du tout cette honneste coustume
D'escrire quelque fois en escrivant ainsi
L'escri de vos valeurs, Quenoille mon soucy,
Ayant dedans la main le fuseau et la plume.

La Fille

L'AGNODICE

[...]

L'envie regardant ceste dame piteuse
Dans soy-mesme sentit une ire serpenteuse
Roüant ses deux grans yeux pleins d'horreur & d'effroy,
Ah ! Je me vengeray (ce dit elle) de toy,
He, tu veux donc ayder, (sotte) tu veux deffendre
Phocion, dont je hay encor la morte cendre,
Saches qu'en peu de temps je te feray sentir
De ton hastif secours un tardif repentir :
Car en despit de toy j'animeray les ames
Des maris, qui seront les tyrans de leurs femmes,
Et qui leur deffendant le livre & le sçavoir,
Leur osteront aussi de vivre le pouvoir,
Aussi tost qu'elle eust dit, elle glisse aux mouëlles
Des hommes qui voyans leurs femmes doctes-belles,
Desirent effacer de leur entendement
Les lettres, des beautez le plus digne ornement :
Et ne voulant laisser chose qui leur agrée
Leur ostent le plaisir où l'ame se recrée.
Que ce fust à l'envie une grand cruauté
De martirer ainsi ceste douce beauté :
Les dames aussitost se trouverent suivies
De fiebvres, de langueurs, & d'autres maladies :
Mais sur tout la douleur de leurs enfantemens
Leurs faisoit supporter d'incroyables tourmens,
Aymant trop mieux mourir que d'estre peu honteuses
Contant aux Medecins leurs peines langoureuses.
Les femmes (ô pitié) n'osoient plus se mesler
De s'aider l'une l'autre, on les faisoit filler :
Leurs marys les voyans en ce cruel martyre,
Ne laissoient pas pourtant de gaucer & de rire,
Pour estre desirans deux nopces esprouver,
Ils n'avoient plus de soing de les vouloir sauver.
En ce temps, il y eut une Dame gentille,
Que le ciel avoit faict belle, sage & subtille,
Qui piteuse de voir ces visages si beaux,
Prontement engloutis des avares tombeaux,
Les voulant secourir couvrit sa double pomme
Afin d'estudier en accoustrement d'homme :
Pource qu'il estoit lors aux femmes interdit
De practiquer les arts, ou les voir par escrit.
Ceste Dame en cachant l'or de sa blonde tresse
Aprist la Medecine, & s'en feit grand maistresse,
Puis se resouvenant de son affection,
Voulut effectuer sa bonne intention,
Et guerir les douleurs de ses pauvres voisines

Par la vertu des fleurs, des feuilles & racines :
D'une herbe mesmement qui fut cueillie au lieu
Où Glauque la mengeant d'homme devint un Dieu
Ayant tout preparé la gentille Agnodice,
Se présente humblement pour leur faire service,
Mais les Dames pensant que ce fust un garçon,
Refusoient son secours d'une estrange façon.
L'on cognoissoit assez à leurs faces craintives
Qu'elles craignoient ses mains comme des mains lascives.
Agnodice voyant leur grande chasteté
Les estima beaucoup pour cette honnesteté,

Lors descouvrant du sein ses blanches pommes rondes,
Et de son chef doré les belles tresses blondes,
Monstre qu'elle estoit fille, & que son gentil cueur,
Les vouloit delivrer de leur triste langueur.
Les Dames admirant ceste honte naïfve,
Et de son teint douillet la blanche couleur vive,
Et de son sein poupin le petit mont jumeau,
Et de son chef sacré l'or crepelu si beau,
Et de ses yeux divins les flammes ravissantes,
Et de ses doux propos les graces attirantes
Baiserent mille fois & sa bouche & son sein,
Recevant le secours de son heureuse main.
On voit en peu de temps les femmes & pucelles
Reprendre leur teint frais, & devenir plus belles,
Mais l'envie presente à cest humain secours,
Proteste de bien tost en empescher le cours :
Elle mangeoit son cueur, miserable viande,
Digne repas de ceux où son pouvoir commande,
Et tenoit en la main un furieux serpent
Dont le cruel venin en tous lieux se respand.
Son autre main portoit une branche espineuse,
Son corps estoit plombé, sa face despiteuse,
Sa teste sans cheveux où faisoient plusieurs tours
Des viperes hideux qui la mordoient tousjours,
Trainant autour de soy ses furieuses rages,
Elle s'en va troubler les chastes mariages,
Car le repos d'autruy luy est propre malheur.
Aux hommes elle mist en soupçon la valeur
De la belle Agnodice & ses graces gentilles,
Disant que la beauté de leurs femmes & filles
Avoit plus de faveur que ne doivent penser
Celles qui voudroient leurs honneurs offenser.
Eux espris de fureur saisirent Agnodice
Pour en faire à l'envie un piteux sacrifice,
Helas ! sans la trouver coupable d'aucun tort,
Ils l'ont injustement condemnée à la mort :
La pauvrette voyant le mal heur qui s'appreste
Descouvrit prontement l'or de sa blonde teste

En monstrant son sein beau, aggreable sejour
Des Muses, des Vertus, des Graces, de l'amour.
Elle baissa les yeux pleins d'honneur & de honte,
Une vierge rougeur en la face luy monte,
Disant que le desir qui l'a faict desguiser,
N'est point de les tromper, mais pour authoriser
Les lettres, qu'elle apprist voulant servir leurs Dames
Que de la soupçonner des crimes tant infames,
C'est offencer nature & ses divines loix.
Depuis qu'elle eust parlé oncq une seulle voix
Ne s'esleva contre elle, ains toute l'assistance
Monstroit d'esmerveiller ceste rare excellence,
Ils estoient tous ravis, sans parler, ny mouvoir,
Ententifs seulement à l'ouyr & la voir,
Comme l'on voit parfois après un long orage
Rassenerer les vents, & calmer le rivage,
Quand les freres jumeaux qui regardoient sur mer,
Une piteuse nef en danger d'abismer,
La sauvant du peril des flots l'ont retirée
Pour luy faire aborder la rive desirée :
Les hommes tout ainsi vaincus par la pitié,
Rapaisent la fureur de leur inimitié,
Faisant à la pucelle une humble reverence,
Ils luy vont demander pardon de leur offence
Elle qui ressentit un plaisir singulier,
Les supplia bien fort de faire estudier
Les Dames du pays, sans envier la gloire
Que l'on a pour servir les filles de Memoire.
L'envie congnoissant ses efforts abbatus
Par les faicts d'Agnodice & ses rares vertus
A poursuivy depuis d'une haine immortelle
Les Dames qui estoient vertueuses comme elle.

LES ŒUVRES
DE
MESDAMES DES ROCHES

Mere et Fille
Seconde édition de la Tragi-comédie
de TOBIE et autres
œuvres poeticques

Paris, 1579

La Fille.

CHANSON DES AMAZONES

Nous faisons la guerre
Aux Rois de la terre
Bravant les plus glorieux,
Par nostre prudence
Et nostre vaillance,
Nous commandons en maints lieux,
Domptant les efforts
Des plus hardis & forts
D'un bras victorieux.

Nous chassons les vices
Par les exercices
Que la vertu nous apprend :
Fuyant comme peste
Le brandon moleste
Qui autour du cueur se prend :
Car la pureté
De nostre chasteté
Pour jamais le defend.

Nous tenons les hommes
Des lieux où nous sommes
Tous empeschez à filer :
Leur lasche courage
D'un plus bel ouvrage
N'est digne de se mesler :
Si quelqu'un de vous
S'en fasche contre nous
Qu'il vienne quereller.

La tragi-comedie de Tobie et Sarra

Le livre de Tobie est fort peu représenté parmi les références bibliques chères aux moralistes de la vie matrimoniale au XVIᵉ siècle. Cependant, l'histoire de Tobie et de Sara abonde en circonstances dont la valeur symbolique correspond aux idées les plus anciennes sur la femme et le mariage.

Le démon de Sara tout d'abord, incarnation maléfique de la physiologie féminine, s'oppose à la transgression de sa virginité, selon un thème mythique commun à de nombreuses sociétés humaines. L'homme ne pourra en surmonter le pouvoir magique que par un recours à la volonté divine, représentée ici par l'ange Raphaël, déguisé sous le nom d'Azarie.

Le personnage de Sara elle-même ensuite : nouvelle image de la damnation d'Eve, elle ne parvient à déjouer son destin par ses vertus qui font pourtant d'elle une digne héritière des grandes figures de la Genèse. Citons cette « prière de Sarra », exactement démarquée du texte biblique, Tobie, III, vv. 16-20 :

> Ayez doncques esgard à mon entiere foy,
> Desliez moy Seigneur, Seigneur desliez moy
> Du reproche honteux qui bourelle ma vie,
> Ou me l'ostez du tout. Las, je n'eus onc envie
> D'accointer aucun homme. Un si villain péché
> N'a jamais mon esprit ny mon corps entaché :
> Vous le sçavez mon Dieu que je suis chaste et pure,
> Que j'ay l'ame devote & le corps sans souillure.
> J'ay bien pris des maris, mais en me mariant
> Je craignois vostre nom, l'honorant & priant.

Ce terrible mystère du corps féminin, le mariage conforme aux volontés divines pourra l'exorciser. La « chasteté » en transfigurant le désir sexuel assurera au couple fécondité et survie spirituelle. La dernière partie du texte offre la représentation littéraire d'une cérémonie de mariage, se déroulant, conformément au texte biblique, en trois moments : le rite d'union symbolique des mains, l'engagement prononcé par les deux époux, la bénédiction formulée par les parents qui assument ici le rôle sacerdotal.

On pourra constater l'extrême fidélité de Catherine Des Roches à la démarche du récit biblique, à la réserve d'un retour en arrière légitimé par les nécessités dramatiques de son texte en se reportant pour la scène 2 au chapitre VI, vv. 10-22, pour la scène 5 au chapitre III, vv. 7-11, pour la scène 7 au chapitre VII, vv. 1-17.

L.L.H.

SCENE DEUXIEME
Azarie, Tobie

Azarie.—   Allons j'en suis content, je reconnais un homme
Yssu de tes parents, qui Ragüel se nomme
Demeurant icy près, il est riche de biens,
D'argent, terres, troupeaux, mais tout cela n'est rien
Au pris du beau thresor de sa grande famille :
C'est une belle, chaste, & gratieuse fille,
Unique de son pere & de sa mere aussi :
Elle est de chascun d'eux l'agreable souci
Et sera d'un mary bien tost accompaignée,
Car ils n'ont d'autre espoir de future lignée
Qu'en elle seulement, il te la faut donner,
Tu la pourras d'icy avec toy emmener
Demande la au pere ? Il te prendra en grace
Connoissant que tu es yssu de mesme race,
Connoissant que tu es honneste & vertueux
Il te la donnera, & s'en tiendra heureux.

Tobie.—   Je le voudrois fort, mais j'ay entendu dire
Qu'elle a eu sept marys que l'on a veu occire
Dès la premiere nuict qu'ils estoient retirez,
Avec elle en sa chambre, & si sont martirez
Par la force du Diable : Or moy j'ayme ma vie
Et ne veux point si tost qu'elle me soit ravie.
Les hommes ont souvent de femmes deux ou trois,
Mais leur vie jamais ils ne l'ont qu'une fois :
Je suis unique fils & de pere & de mere
Qui sentiroient Helas la vie plus amere
Que moymesmes la mort : je ne veux point mourir.

Azarie.—   Encontre ce danger je te veux secourir,
Tobie, assure-toy que ces mal-heureux Diables
Ne se prendront jamais à toy ni tes semblables,
Ils se prendront tousjours à l'homme deshonté :
Moque-Dieu, fauce-foy, lequel n'est surmonté
Sinon du fol desir de sa concupiscence,
Fol desir de Caval de qui l'ame ne pense
Qu'à trouver le moyen de chasser Dieu dehors :
Tels hommes sont-ils pas dignes de mille mors ?

Tobie.—   Ouy en verité : mais que faudroit-il faire
Pour fuir les efors de ce traiste adversaire ?
Les Diables sont meschans.

Azarie.—   Ah ne les crains jamais,
Dieu te defendra mieux, amy je te promets.
Escoute seulement. Quand tu auras ta femme

Montre toy plus aymant de la beauté de l'ame
Que de celle du corps, demeure chastement
Avec elle trois nuicts priant devotement
Sans jamais luy toucher, & fais brusler le foye
Du poisson que Tigris fit sortir en la voye
Pour aleger tes maux : le Diable s'enfuyra
Abhorrant ceste odeur que lors il sentira :
Dès la seconde nuict tu seras mis aux rooles
Des patriarches saincts, dont les sages parolles
Sont pour loy entre nous, & la troisieme nuict
Afin que de bon arbre il vienne de bon fruict,
Le Seigneur benira ton affection saincte :
En approchant Sarra ayez de Dieu la crainte,
Desire que ce soit pour avoir des enfans
Qui servent au Seigneur dès leurs plus jeunes ans
Et non pour accomplir un vouloir deshonneste :
La benediction qui couronna la teste
Du Sainct pere Abraham s'estendra sur les tiens,
Garde tous mes propos amy & t'en souviens.

. . . .

SCENE CINQUIESME
Sarra, la servante

La servante.—Je hayray pour jamais l'orgueil de ces maistresses,
          Qui soubz ombre d'avoir la faveur des richesses
          Mesprisent tout le monde, & ne pensent rien veoir
          Digne de leurs vertus & de leur grand pouvoir.

Sarra.—   Sus, sus, despeschez vous de faire vostre ouvrage,
          On vous prend seulement pour faire le mesnage
          Et non pour babiller & causer à chascun.

La servante.—Si vaut-il mieux user d'un entretien commun
          Que faire comme vous, qui ne parlez qu'au Diable.

Sarra.—   Meschante qui me tient que je ne vous accable
          De mille coups de poin ?

La servante.—   Hé ! quoy ? que ferez vous ?
          Me voulez vous tuer comme voz sept Espoux
          Ah malheureuse femme ! ah cruelle meurdriere !
          Voulez vous donc tuer maris & chambriere ?
          Jamais ne puissiez vous avoir aucuns enfans.
          Qui contentent voz yeux en leurs plus jeunes ans,
          Et dont le doux blandir de la voix Enfantine
          Vous chatouille le cueur au fond de la poitrine.

. . . .

SCENE SEPTIESME
Ragüel, Anne, Azaria, Tobie, Sarra

Ragüel.— Or voila que j'ay ouy ma femme, & je ne sçay
Si c'est un nouveau mal dont elle fait essay ?
Mais n'avez vous point veu la façon debonnaire
De mon neveu Tobie, en parlant de son pere ?

Anne.— Ouy, j'ay bien aperceu qu'il pleuroit tendrement.

Ragüel.— Que l'on doit esperer un humain traitement
De ce jeune garçon : Or pleust à Dieu m'amie
Que ma fille Sarra eust espousé Tobie,
Qu'il fust avecques nous pour nostre aide & secours,
Qu'il deust fermer nos yeux à la fin de nos jours.

Anne.— Mon Dieu que dites vous ! Ce seroit grand dommage
Que cest honneste fils mourust en si jeune age.
Vous sçavez bien (Monsieur) comment les sept maris
De la pauvre Sarra sont tous morts & peris.

Ragüel.— Peut estre cetuy-ci, qui est nostre plus proche
Vient pour nous delivrer de ce villain reproche :
Peut-estre le Seigneur l'a faict venir à nous,
Pour estre de Sarra perpetuel espoux.

Anne.— Et que vous me donez une douce esperance !

Ragüel.— Je voy dans ce jeune homme un humble contenance,
Un regard adouci, un geste gracieux :
Je connois bien aussi qu'il est devotieux,
Et qui le nom de Dieu parfaitement adore,
Cetuy là est vraymient très-digne qu'on l'honore

Anne.— Nostre fille avec luy seroit en grand repos.

Ragüel.— M'amie le voici, il faut changer propos.

Azarie.— L'excellente beauté de vostre fille unique,
Sa vertu, sa douceur & sa grace pudique
Ont si bien enlassé le cueur de cetuy-ci,
Que si vous ne prenez souci de son souci
Vous le verrez bien tost à la fin de sa vie :
Le lignage & sur tout la pitié vous convie
De le tenir pour vostre, il veut vous obeir.

Ragüel.— Je l'ayme comme un fils & ne le veux trahir,
Ma fille en esprouvant sept Nopces miserables
Me fait aussi grand peur d'en revoir de semblables.

Azarie.— Monsieur ne craignez point, les maris de Sarra
Sont tous mors l'ayant eüe & cet autre mourra
Si vous ne luy donnez. Vaut il pas mieux qu'il meure
Avec elle content, que mourir dès ceste heure,
Aussi bien vous est-il envoyé du Seigneur ?
Lequel n'a point voulu qu'un autre eust le bonheur
De jouir d'une femme & si chaste & si belle :
Car tous ceux qui l'avoient n'estoient pas dignes d'elle,
Mais cetuy-cy craint Dieu, il est predestiné
Pour espouser Sarra dès avant qu'il fust né.

Ragüel.— Je desire bien veoir un mary à ma fille
Mais je crains de le perdre et que la mort le pille.

Azarie.— Je puis vous assurer, qu'il vivra fort longtemps
Avec elle & sera pere de beaux enfans.

Tobie.— Si le doux souvenir de la premiere flame,
Qui jadis vous brula, vous tient encore en l'ame :
Au moins Monsieur pensez ce que je puis souffrir
Et recevez un fils que je viens vous offrir.
Si vous gardez aussi l'amour de vostre race
Ayez pitié de moy qui vous demande grace :
J'ayme tant vostre fille & avec tel devoir
Que de vivre sans elle, il n'est dans mon pouvoir.

Ragüel.— Tu l'auras (mon amy) si elle en est contente,
Qu'en dictes vous ma femme ?

Anne.—   Elle est obeissante,
Elle fera tousjours tout ce qui vous plaira.

Ragüel.— Allons parler à elle & voir qu'elle en dira.
Ma fille vous sçavez combien vous m'estes chere,
Vous congnoissez aussi l'amour de vostre mere,
Nous n'avons jamais eu autre plus grand desir
Que de vous procurer & profit & plaisir :
Nous vous donnons mari : un heureux mariage
Est plus digne de vous que ce piteux veufvage :
Vous avez tant pleuré la mort de vos maris,
Ores il faut changer vos tristes pleurs en ris,
Vous aurez un espoux de vostre parentage,
Beau, gracieux & doux, jeune, gaillard & sage :
Le voulez vous pas bien ?

Sarra.—   Je veux ce qui vous plaist
Mon pere, mais je crains.

Anne.—   Ha je sçay bien que c'est,

               Sarra ne craignez point, nous leur venons de dire :
               Mais pourtant mon Neveu vous ayme & vous desire,
               Et puis ce jeune fils qui est avecques luy
               Promet de le garder & de mal & d'ennuy.

Sarra.—   Dieu veuille qu'ainsi soit.

Ragüel.—   Approchez vous ma mie,
               Ça, donnez moy la main, venez que je vous lie
               D'un neu perpetuel.

Tobie.—   Hé je suis tant lié
               Mesmes auparavant que d'estre marié :
               De ses crepez cheveux une blonde cordelle
               Lie & serre mon cueur pour tout jamais à elle :
               Mais nonobstant cela, je luy jure la foy
               De l'honorer tousjours & l'aymer plus que moy.

Sarra.—   Je vous promets la foy que vos graces demandent
               Comme Dieu, les vertus & les loys le commandent

Ragüel.—   Le grand Dieu eternel vous face prosperer,
               Vous donnant tout le mieux que l'on puisse esperer.

Anne.—   Je requiers ses bontez que voz belles jeunesses
               Demeurent seur appuy de nos foibles vieillesses.

Chœur.—   Il n'est rien plus honorable
               Qu'une chaste affection :
               Il n'est rien plus agreable
               Qu'une douce passion.

               Il n'est rien qui plus attire
               Que de se veoir estimé :
               O que c'est un doux martyre
               Que d'aymer & d'estre aymé :

               Il n'est point de plus grand aise
               Qu'estre serré d'un beau Neu :
               Il n'est rien qui plus nous plaise
               Que de bruler d'un doux feu.

               Il faut d'une amour pudique
               Aymer les chastes beautez,
               Non pas d'un vouloir lubrique
               En chercher les privautez.

               Il faut avoir bonne veuë
               Premier qu'un tel feu toucher,

Et non pas à l'impourveuë
De ses flames approcher.

Voyez l'impudique flame
De sept amans que voicy,
Qui les prive de leur femme,
D'amour & vie aussy.

Et puis voyez ce Tobie
Que d'un cueur religieux,
Devotement sacrifié
Au souverain Dieu des dieux.

En aymant d'un amour sage
La fille de Ragüel,
Il gagne son mariage
Et rend grace à l'Eternel.

LES SECONDES ŒUVRES
DE MES DAMES DES ROCHES DE POICTIERS
MERE ET FILLE

La Fille

DIALOGUE DE PLACIDE ET DE SEVERE

Voici nostre voisin Severe, qui s'en vient ayant la face merveilleusement refrongnée : il a veu dans sa maison quelque personne qui luy fache, & s'en plaint tout à part luy.

SEV.— O la grant peine que c'est d'avoir Femmes, ou Filles à gouverner ! Vray'ment je ne m'estonne point, dont un renommé Philosophe, pense les devoir tenir au rang des Animaux sans raison. Et si jamais pauvre homme s'est trouvé affligé de leurs importunitez, je suis ce miserable. J'ay une femme rioteuse, facheuse, dedaigneuse ; j'ay une Fille eventée, affetée, efrontée : Ce-pendant il faut que je soufre en despit de moy, le chagrin de l'une, & la vanité de l'autre. Mais je voy le vieillard Placide venir en çà, lequel ayant en sa maison même charge inutile que moy, d'une Fille ennuyeuse, me pourra dire comment il se deporte envers elle, afin que je prenne son exemple, s'il me semble bon. Or je m'en vais le saluer, combien que ce ne soit pas ma coustume d'acoster gueres de peuple. Bonsoir Placide.

PLA.— Dieu vous contente, Seigneur Severe, vous & tout ce que vous aymez.

SEV.— Croyez que tel salut n'est pas universel : Car je n'ayme personne en ce monde que moy : aussy n'ay-je occasion d'aymer aucun.

PLA.— Hé dea ! n'avez vous point cause de tenir vostre Femme chere ?

SEV.— Ah ! qu'il vous est aisé à dire pour ce que vous n'en avez plus. Que je voudrois de bon cueur estre aussi heureux que vous ! La vostre est morte & la mienne seulement absente : qui par sa desplaisante vie me fait mourir à toute heure.

PLA.— Nous avons les opinions fort diverses de nos Femmes qui estoient peut estre encore plus diferentes entre elles.

SEV.— Je ne sçaurois penser qu'il y ait diference.
Car toutes sont des Hommes adversaires.

PLA.— *Mais toutes sont aux hommes necessaires.*
Et si ce n'estoit que je voi le desirable pourtraict de mon Espouse en la ace & aux coustumes de ma Fille, je languirois en cete penible vie.

SEV.— Oh le bon mari que vous aves esté ! Mais à propos de vostre Fille, dites moy comment elle se maintient.

PLA.— Comme je veux & qu'il me semble qu'elle doit.

SEV.— La mienne fait au contraire de son devoir & de ma volonté. Jamais, je n'ay vu si grand' trotiere : Elle voudroit voir en un jour l'un & l'autre my-ciel, comme les grues. Combien que je luy commande sur tout d'arrester au logis, d'avoir soing du mesnage : il n'est possible de la retenir. Je ne suis pas sorti plustost qu'elle est à la fenestre, à la porte, en la rüe, en visite, elle n'a point de repos, ny moy non plus. Or dites moy, que fait la vostre maintenant, où est elle ?

PLA.— En sa chambre.

SEV.— Seule ?

PLA.— Non, elle est avec des ames sans cors & des cors sans ames, faisant marcher les premiers dans un chariot ailé, donant aux autres espritz & mouvemens.

SEV.— Il semble que vous vouliez représenter quelque Medée.

PLA.— Non pas : mais bien une Fille aussi douce & debonnaire à son Pere, que Médée a voulu estre cruelle & mauvaise au sien.

SEV.— Quelz enigmes dictes vous donc ? je ne puis les entendre.

PLA.— Si ferez, ilz sont faciles. Ces cors animez par elle sont des Lutz & Violes que sa main fait ressonner : les Ames elevées dans un chariot ailé sont les belles sentences de Plutarque & de Seneque volantes sur les ailes de ses pensers & propos.

SEV.— Comment Placide ? luy permettez vous bien de lire telz Auteurs ? Et ne craignés vous point de les profaner, laissant passer leurs noms seulement par la bouche d'une Fille ?

PLA.— Ces philosophes avoient opinion que les personnes moins polues estoyent plus capables des disciplines. S'il est ainsi les Femmes & les Filles sont plus dignes des lettres que les Hommes pour estre plus sobres, chastes & paisibles.

SEV.— Vous me faites desesperer tenant ces propos : comme si l'imbecillité de ces petites bestioles devoit estre comparée à la grand sufisance qui journellement se connoist en nous. En outre cete preference leur permettant de lire, ce qu'il leur plaist, vous donnez licence de faire tout ce qu'elles veulent.

PLA.— Je l'entens ainsi. Mais estant guidées par les bonnes lettres, elles ne voudront rien faire qui ne soit raisonnable.

SEV.— Comme si la raison avoit place en elles.

PLA.— Ceux qui ont peu de raison
    L'accroissent bien par la Science,
    Mais elle quitte sa maison
    Aux maux que traine l'ignorance.

Soit que les Femmes vous semblent sottes, ou sages ; pourtant je serois d'advis qu'on leur permist tousjours de lire, afin que les unes se pussent diminuer la sottise, les autres acroistre la sagesse, par le moien des livres qui leur sont très necessaires, quand ce ne seroit que pour les retenir solitaires en la maison, sans estre oysives.

SEV.— O quel malheur de voir une Femme sçavante !

PLA.— Hé, quel est-il ? dites je vous prie.

SEV.— C'est un monstre.

PLA.— Si sont bien quelques fois les plus excellentes choses du Monde. Les monstres ne sont pas tousjours tesmoins de l'erreur de Nature, mais ilz demonstrent souvant combien sa puissance est grande. Les monstrueuses Beautez, Graces, Vertuz & Sciences d'Iocasie, la rendirent admirable entre les Hommes, & luy donnerent moien de se passer d'eux toute sa vie, demeurant en perpetuelle virginité.

SEV.— Ha ! vraiment je suis content, que toute les sçavantes demeurent encore ainsi, & jamais je ne conseilleray aux Hommes de les rechercher.

PLA.— Or dites moy Seigneur Severe, vous trouvez vous bien en mariage ?

SEV.— Autant mal qu'il est possible.

PLA.— Et vostre femme est-elle sçavante ?

SEV.— Ho, ce n'est qu'une grosse beste, qui ne sçait pas honorer son mary, ni ordonner son mesnage, ce que je veus qu'elle aprenne seulement, & non pas à frequenter les livres. Il ne luy faut autre Docteur que ma voix.

PLA.— Voire mais ainsi que vous dites, il y a long tans que vous prenez peine à la persuader, & n'y avez pas encore beaucoup advancé : de sorte que vos labeurs sont inutiles, ou vos plaintes fausses .

SEV.— Mes plaintes ne sont point fausses, mais ouy bien les femmes, comme j'en fais ordinaire preuve.

PLA.— Ce mal vous est justement deu, puisque la guerison estant en vostre puissance, vous ne voulez pas la recevoir. La Femme d'Isomache aprendroit à la vostre à faire son devoir, si vous luy commandiez de lire la Mesnagerie de Xenophon.

SEV.— Hen hen, si je l'avois trouvée en tel empéchement, je luy ferois sçavoir que sa main doit toucher la quenouille et non pas le livre.

PLA.— L'un de ces exercices aide l'autre. Pallas les avoit tous deux.

SEV.— Ce sont fables abusives. Les Femmes ne doivent jamais estudier.

PLA.— Pourquoy haïssez vous tant les innocentes Muses ? Et qui vous meut à les vouloir chasser de vostre chambre, de vostre table, de vostre feu, vu qu'elles n'y despendent rien, & profitent beaucoup ?

SEV.— Je sçay que les lettres sont entierement inutiles aux Femmes.

PLA.— Comme elles sont aux Hommes.

SEV.— Vous moquez. Aprendront elles la Theologie, pour se presanter en chaire, faire un sermon devant le peuple, aquerir des Benefices ?

PLA.— Non, mais elles aprendront la parole Divine, pour ce qu'elle commande aux Femmes d'obeïr à leurs maris, ainsi que l'on peut voir dans Genese ? Aiant des Enfans, il leur sera plus facile aussi de les maintenir en la crainte de Dieu, de leurs Peres, & d'elles mesmes. Davantage elles se guident heureusement par les preceptes de vertus, qui sont les plus riches benefices, que l'on puisse aquerir.

SEV.— J'aymerois mieux une Femme simple, qu'une qui voudroit subtiliser ses opinions. Aians apris ce que vous dites elles s'estiment trop fortes.

PLA.— Les Femmes simples & de foible entendement ressemblent ces rares nuées, qui craignant de fondre vont fuïant l'Astre journalier, ou s'il passe au travers d'elles, il n'y reste acune trace de ses raions, mais comme la nuë espaisse reçoit la clarté du Soleil, redoublant plusieurs fois en elle ceste belle face, qui la rend illustre : Ainsi la Femme prudente aiant rendu son Esprit fort par les discours de la philosophie morale, reçoit humblement tel image que luy veut donner son Mary, de qui le bien-aymé pourtrait paroist tousjours en ses pensées, en ses paroles, & en toutes ses actions.

SEV.— Vous dites merveilles : de sorte que je permetz à ma Femme &
à mes Filles de lire l'Escriture sainte, pourveu qu'elles ne passent point
outre.

PLA.— Je vous dis que toutes lettres leur sont necessaires, aussi bien
qu'à nous.

SEV.— Elles n'estudieront point aux Loix.

PLA.— Elles n'en doivent pas estre du tout ignorantes.

SEV.— Ha ! ha ! vous gastez tout Placide : vostre peu de jugement
sera cause que je revoqueray mon dernier propos, interdisant à leur sottise
ce que j'avois permis à vostre affection.

PLA.— Et voulez vous reprendre le peuple de Dieu pour s'estre laissé
juger à Debore ?

SEV.— Je ne parle point des Loix Hebrieues, mais du Droit Romain.

PLA.— Voire, mais une Femme s'obligeant pour son Mari, doit elle
renoncer au Droit Velleïen sans l'entendre ? Héé ! ceux qui ont Femmes
riches en ce pays, leur font bien sçavoir qu'elles peuvent donner leurs
meubles & acquetz avec le tiers de leurs heritages aux Maris sur-vivans :
pour ce que la loy de la coustume le permet.

SEV.— Les Hommes font profession de trois sortes de Sciences avec
lesquelles ilz pratiquent : de la Théologie, la Jurisprudence, & la Medecine. Je suis d'advis que vous apreniez aux Femmes encore le moien de
guerir les maladies, afin que de tous ars elles soyent en commun avecque
nous.

PLA.— Celle qui fut disciple du sçavant Hierophile, monstra bien
qu'elle apprenoit la Medecine pour le salut des autres. Il y en a encore
aujourd'huy, qui seules aident leurs petits enfans, allegent leurs voisines,
guerissent leurs servantes, usant de certains remedes domesticz, que
l'Experience fait connoistre.

SEV.— Celles qui sçavent tant de belles choses communement sont
glorieuses, & dedaignent leurs maris, faisant les suffisantes. Comme
j'apris l'autre jour d'une Tapisserie qui estoit devant la cheminée d'Acha-
riste, mon voisin. Il y avoit au milieu de la piece une Femme pompeuse,
assise en un Throne, tenant une plume en la main, un livre souz ses
piedz : autour de la Tapisserie estoit écrit :

> Quand une Femme sçait bien dire
> Et fait profession d'écrire,
> Elle dedaigne tous Auteurs
> Qui des ars furent inventeurs,
>
> Rien ne luy plaist, comme la fâche,
> Tousjours pensive elle remâche,
> Quelque parole de grand poix,
> Qui se doit merquer sur ses dois.
>
> Elle dit que sa Mere est folle,
> Son Pere n'a point de parole,
> Son Frere ne sçait aucun bien,
> Sa Sœur n'aprendra jamais rien.

Si la voisine est un peu belle
Ce n'est rien pour tant au pris d'elle,
De qui la grace & le sçavoir
Passent tout ce que l'on peut voir.

Quand elle sera en mariage,
L'on verra qu'une femme sage,
Gouverne beaucoup mieux les siens,
Que les Hommes plus anciens.

Fuyez donc la Femme sçavante,
Recherchez plustost l'ignorante.
L'une pourroit vous mespriser,
L'autre se laisse maistriser.

Voilà Placide ce que j'apris, & qui me semble bien digne d'estre noté.

PLA.— Ainsi vous recueillez soigneusement les enfumées authoritez des devants de cheminées ?

SEV.— Faut-il pas recevoir enseignement de tout ?

PLA.— Il faut rechercher la vérité de tout, mais ce que vous raportez est une erreur, que la raison & l'expérience font connoistre comme telle.

SEV.— L'experience monstre que les Femmes qui excedent la Commune, aiment peu leurs Maris.

PLA.— J'en appelle à tesmoins ces deux excellentes Romaines, Emponine & Arrie, qui en pouvant survivre leurs espoux les accompagnerent courageusement à la mort.

Ouy, pour ce que defendant les livres, vous dérobez à leurs yeux ces exemples, qui les pourroient emouvoir à sentir pour vous, cete extreme affection.

SEV.— Mais celles qui sont tant habiles veulent souvent parler, & je me fâche de tant de caquet.

Nicole Estienne, dame Liébaut, Les miseres de la femme mariée.

Plus connue en littérature sous le nom d'« Olimpe », Nicole Estienne, fiancée et inspiratrice du poète Jacques Grévin, cultivait volontiers les belles lettres, selon l'idéal humaniste en faveur dans son illustre famille. Le fond Dupuy à la Bibliothèque Nationale garde d'elle des sonnets manuscrits, qui, bien que non publiés, semblent avoir joui d'une certaine notoriété dans le milieu qui l'entourait.

Sans doute était-elle morte, lorsqu'un nommé Claude Le Villain publia ses étranges et pessimistes « Miseres de la Femme Mariée », que nous reproduisons ici intégralement. Ce très court recueil, dédicacé à « Madame de Medine, religieuses aux Ammurez de Rouen », contient, dès son texte de présentation, une opposition très nette entre vie matrimoniale et vie monacale, selon un jugement hiérarchique tout à fait conforme à la tradition patristique, et tel que le reprenait à son compte le Concile de Trente. L'autorité de St Paul en ces lignes est particulièrement révélatrice :

« Et ce vaisseau d'élection Monsieur S. Paul en parlant dans ses Epistres dit en ces termes : que qui se marie fait bien, mais qui ne se marie point fait encore mieux. Comme s'il vouloit entendre que l'on s'en abstint pour vouer à Dieu sa virginité : ce qui ne se peut toutesfois maintenir aisement, ni observer un tel vœu, sans y apporter pour aide & support la priere, le jeune, & la solitude, aussi que vous faictes, Madame, qui est un genre de vie qui excelle d'autant le mariage, que la contemplative excelle l'active ».

Il est curieux que cette condamnation de l'individu, et en particulier de l'individu féminin dans l'activité socio-économique du groupe, corresponde chronologiquement, en cette année 1595, à une nouvelle publication des 15 Joyes de Mariage, *tableau médiéval des « Miseres de l'homme marié »...*

Ce n'est pas là le seul élément de correspondance entre les deux œuvres. On remarquera chez Madame Liébaut, la reprise du procédé de présentation hypothétique de la situation familiale, qui constitue le fondement même de la démarche des 15 Joyes. *Les « Si » qui ouvrent les stances 23, 25, 27, présentent une vérité qui ne se veut pas empruntée à la réalité, mais qui se pose comme le postulat d'une démonstration quasi scientifique.*

Cette attitude « rhétorique » de Mme Liébaut, part en réalité d'une donnée encore plus détournée. Cet ouvrage, en effet, n'est autre qu'une réponse aux Stances de Mariage de Desportes, qui, dès 1578, revèlent la pérennité de l'héritage littéraire des 15 Joyes. *La même série de situations pitoyables est imaginée ici au détriment de l'homme :*

Si vous l'espousez riche il se peult preparer
De servir, de souffrir, de n'oser murmurer. (Stance XV)

> *Si vous la prenez pauvre, avec la pauvreté*
> *Vous espousez aussi mainte incommodité*
> *La charge des enfans, la peine, l'infortune. (Stance XVI)*

> *Si vous l'espousez belle, asseurez vous aussi*
> *De n'estre jamais franc de crainte & de soucy. (Stance XVIII)*

> *Si vous la prenez laide, adieu toute amytié. (Stance XIX)*

Il est permis de s'interroger sur les raisons qui ont amené les responsables de cette publication à choisir dans l'œuvre d'Olympe ce seul exercice littéraire : Pourquoy, par exemple n'a-t-on jamais imprimé les sonnets où elle répondait ainsi aux flammes pétrarquisantes de son admirateur :

> *Pour chanter mes beaultez point besoin de trompette,*
> *Le ciel m'a departi ses graces chichement.*

Si aucun vers des stances n'atteint le réalisme personnel de ce petit portrait, sans doute répondaient-elles davantage au goût du public et aux buts de la propagande idéologique du temps. En cette fin de siècle où la Contre-Réforme relance l'idéal de la vie contemplative, nous assistons à un exemple extrêmement frappant d'« utilisation » d'un texte.

L.L.H.

MADAME·LYEBAVLT

24

LES MISERES DE LA FEMME MARIEE

où se peuvent veoir les tourmens
qu'elle reçoit durant sa vie
mis en stances par

MADAME LIEBAUT

Paris,
s.d.

Muses, qui chastement passez vostre bel aage,
Sans vous assujetir aux loix de Mariage,
Sçachant combien la femme y endure de mal
Favorisez moy tant que je puisse descrire
Les travaux continus & le cruel martire
Qui sans fin nous talonne en ce sejour nuptial.

Du soleil tout voyant la lampe journaliere
Ne sçauroit remarquer en laissant sa carriere,
Rien de plus miserable & de plus tourmenté
Que la femme subiette à ces hommes iniques
Qui, despouveux d'amour par leurs loix tyranniques
Se font maistres du corps & de la volonté.

O grand Dieu tout puissant si la femme peu caute
Contre ton sainct vouloir avoit faict quelque faute
Tu la devois punir d'un moins aigre tourment.
Mais las ce n'est pas toy, Dieu rempli de clemence
Qui de tes serviteurs pourchasses la vengeance :
Tout ce mal'heur nous vient des hommes seulement.

Voyant que l'homme estoit triste & melancolique,
De soy-mesme ennemy, chagrin & fantastique,
Afin de corriger ce mauvais naturel :
Tu lui donnas la femme en beauté excellente,
Pour fidele compagne & non comme servante,
En chargeant à tous deux un amour mutuel.

O bienheureux accord, ô sacrée alliance,
Present digne des cieux, gracieuse accointance,
Plaine de tout plaisir, de grace & de douceur :
Si l'homme audacieux n'eust a sa fantasie
Changé les douces loix en dure tyrannie
Et l'on miel en amertume, & ta paix en rigueur.

A peine maintenant sommes nous hors d'enfance

LES MISERES DE LA FEMME MARIEE

où se peuvent veoir les tourmens
qu'elle reçoit durant sa vie,
mis en stances par

MADAME LIEBAUT

Paris,
s.d.

Muses, qui chastement passez vostre bel aage
Sans vous assujetir aux loix de Mariage,
Sçachant combien la femme y endure de mal
Favorisez moy tant que je puisse descrire
Les travaux continus & le cruel martire
Qui sans fin nous talonne en ce sejour nuptial.

Du soleil tout voyant la lampe journaliere
Ne sçauroit remarquer en faisant sa carriere,
Rien de plus miserable & de plus tourmenté
Que la femme subjette à ces hommes iniques
Qui, despouveuz d'amour, par leurs loix tiranicques
Se font maistres du corps & de la volonté.

O grand Dieu tout puissant si la femme peu caute
Contre ton sainct vouloir avoit faict quelque faute
Tu la devois punir d'un moins aigre tourment.
Mais las, ce n'est pas toy, Dieu rempli de clemence
Qui de tes serviteurs pourchasses la vengeance :
Tout ce mal'heur nous vient des hommes seulement.

Voyant que l'homme estoit triste & melancolique,
De soy mesme ennemy, chagrin & fantastique,
Afin de corriger ce mauvais naturel
Tu lui donnas la femme en beautez excellente,
Pour fidele compagne et non comme servante,
En chargeant à tous deux un amour mutuel.

O bienheureux accords, o sacrée alliance,
Present digne des cieux, gracieuse accointance,
Plaine de tout plaisir, de grace & de douceur :
Si l'homme audacieux n'eust à sa fantaisie
Changé tes douces loix en dure tirannie
Ton miel en amertume, & ta paix en rigueur.

A peine maintenant sommes nous hors d'enfance

Et n'avons pas encor du monde cognoissance
Que vous taschez desjà par dix mille moiens,
Par presens & discours, par des larmes contraintes
A nous embrasser dedans vos labirinthes,
Vos cruelles prisons, vos dangereux liens.

Et comme l'oiseleur pour les oiseaux attraire
En ses pipeuses rhetz sçait la voix contrefaire,
Ainsi par vos escritz cauteleux & rusez
Faictes semblant d'offrir vos bien humbles services,
A nous, qui ne sçachant vos fraudes & malices
Ne pensons que vos cueurs soient ainsi deguisez.

Nous sommes vostre cueur, nous sommes vos maistresses,
Ce ne sont que respectz, ce ne sont que caresses.
Le ciel, à vous ouir ne nous est rien au pris :
Puis vous sçavez donner quelque anneau quelque chaine,
Pour nous reduire après en immortelle gesne
Ainsi, par des appas, le poisson se sent pris.

Mais quelle deité ne seroit point surprise
En vous voyant user de si grande feintise ?
En voyant de vos yeux deux fontaines couler
Qui penseroit bon Dieu, qu'un si piteux visage
Avec la cruauté d'un desloyal courage
Couvassent le poison sous un brave parler.

Ainsi donc nous laissons la douceur de nos meres,
La maison paternelle & nos sœurs & nos freres,
Pour à vostre vouloir pauvreté consentir,
Et un seul petit mot promis à la legere
Nous fait vivre à jamais en peine & en misere,
En chagrin & tourment par un tard repentir.

Le jour des nopces vient tout plain de fascherie,
Bien qu'il soit desguisé de fraude & tromperie,
Borne de nos plaisirs, source de nos tourmens,
Si de bon jugement nos ames sont atteintes,
Nous descouvrons à l'œil que ces liesses feintes
Ne servent en nos maux que de desguisement.

Le son des instrumens, les chansons non pareilles
Qui d'accors mesurez ravissent les oreilles,
Les chemins tapissez, les habits somptueux,
Les banquets excessifs, la viande excellente
Semblent representer la boisson mal plaisante
Où l'on mesle parmy quelque miel gracieux.

Encore maintenant pour faire mariage,

On songe seulement aux biens & au lignage
Sans cognoistre les mœurs & les complexions :
Par ainsi ce lien trop rigoureux assemble
Deux contraires humeurs à tout jamais ensemble
Dont viennent puis après mille discensions.

On ne sçauroit penser combien la jeune femme
Endure de tourmens, & au corps & à l'ame,
Subjette à un vieillard remply de cruauté,
Qui jouit à son gré d'une jeunesse telle,
Pour ce qu'il la veut faire ou dame ou damoiselle,
Et pource qu'il est grand en bien & dignité.

Luy qui avoit coustume auparavent follastre
De diverses amours ses jeunes ans esbattre
Entretenant sa vie en toute oisiveté,
Se sent or'accablé de quelque mal funeste,
Qui malgré qu'il en ait en son lit le moleste,
Assez digne loyer de sa lubricité.

La femme prend le soin d'accomoder les viandes
Qui au goust du vieillard seront les plus friandes,
Sans prendre aucun repos ny la nuict ny le jour.
Et luy, se souvenant de sa folle jeunesse,
Si tant soit peu sa femme aucunesfois le laisse,
Pense qu'elle luy veut jouer un mauvais tour.

Et lors c'est grand pitié car l'aspre jalousie
Tourmente son esprit, le met en frenaisie
Et chasse loing de luy tout humain sentiment,
Les plus aspres tourmens des ames criminelles
Ne sont pour approcher des peines moins cruelles
Que ceste pauvre femme endure injustement.

Aussi voit on souvent qu'un homme malhabille
Indigne, espouzera quelque femme gentille,
Sage, de rare esprit & de bon jugement :
Mais luy ne faisant cas de toute sa science
(Comme la cruaulté suit tousjours l'ignorance)
L'en traitera plus mal & moins humainement.

Au lieu que si c'estoit un discret personnage
Qui avec le sçavoir eust de raison l'usage
Il rechercheroit & en feroit grand cas :
Se reputant heureux que la grace divine
D'un don si precieux l'auroit estimé digne,
Mais certes un tel homme est bien rare icy bas.

Si le cynique Grec au milieu d'une ville

N'en peut trouver un seul entre plus de dix mille,
Tenant en plain midy la lanterne en sa main,
Je pense qu'il faudroit une torche bien claire
En ce temps corrompu, & se porroit bien faire
Qu'on despendroit le temps & la lumiere en vain.

Car vrayement cet esprit & ceste ame divine
Rescognoissant au Ciel sa premiere origine,
Qui fait le vertueux du nom d'homme appeler
Et non pas celuy là qui seulement s'arreste,
Au corruptible corps commun à toute beste,
Qui vit dessous les eaux, sur la terre, ou en l'air ;

Il seroit donc besoin de grande prevoyance
Ains que faire un accord d'une telle importance,
Qui ne peut seulement que par mort prendre fin :
Attendu pour certain que ce n'est chose aisée
A quelque homme que soit une femme espouzée
De la voir sans ennuy, sans peine & sans chagrin.

S'elle en espouze un jeune en plaisir et liesse
En delices et jeux passera la jeunesse
Despendra son argent sans qu'il amasse rien.
Bien que la femme soit assez gentille et belle
Si aura-t-il toujours quelque amie nouvelle
Et sera réputé des plus hommes de bien.

Car c'est par ce moyen que l'humaine folie
A du grand Jupiter la puissance establie,
Parceque mesprisant sa Junon aux beaux yeux
Sans esclaver son cœur sous le joug d'Hymenée,
Suivant sa volonté lasche & desordonnée
Il sema ses amours en mille & mille lieux.

Si c'est quelque pauvre homme, helas qui pourrait dire
La honte, le mespris le chagrin le martyre
Qu'en son pauvre mesnage il lui faut endurer
Elle seule entretient la petite famille
Elleve les enfans, les nourrit, les habille
Contregardant son bien pour le faire durer.

Et toutes fois encore que l'homme se glorifie
Que c'est par son labeur que sa femme est nourrie
Et qu'il apporte seul le pain à la maison.
C'est beaucoup d'acquerir mais plus encore le prix
Quand l'on sait sagement garder la chose acquise
L'un despend de fortune et l'autre de raison.

S'elle espouse un riche, il faut qu'elle s'attende

D'obeir à l'instant à tout ce qu'il commande
Sans oser s'encquerir pourquoi c'est qu'il le fait,
Il veut faire le grand et superbe desdaigne
Celle qu'il a choisie pour espouze et compagne
En faisant moins de cas que d'un simple valet.

Mais que luy peut servir d'avoir un homme riche
S'il ne laisse pourtant d'estre villain et chiche ?
S'elle ne peut avoir ce qui est de besoin ?
Pour son petit mesnage : ou si vaincu de honte,
Il donne quelque argent, de luy en rendre compte
Comme une chambriere il faut qu'elle ait besoin.

Et cependant, Monsieur estant en compagnie
Alors prodiguement ses escus il manie,
Et hors de son logis se donne du bon temps
Puis quand il s'en revient fasché pour quelque affaire
Sur le seuil de son huis laisse la bonne chère
Sa femme a tous les cris, d'autres le passe-temps.

Il cherche occasion de prendre une querelle
Qui sera bien souvent pour un bout de chandelle,
Pour un morceau de bois, pour un voirre cassé ;
Elle qui n'en peut mais porte la folle enchere
Et sur elle à la fin retombe la colere
Et l'injuste courroux de ce fol insensé.

Ainsi de tous costez la femme est miserable.
Subjette à la merci de l'homme impitoyable
Qui luy fait plus de maux qu'on ne peut endurer,
Le captif est plus aise, et le pauvre forçaire
Encore en ses malheurs et l'un et l'autre espere
Mais elle doit sans plus à la mort esperer.

Ne s'en faut esbahir puisqu'eux, pleins de malices
N'ayant autre raison que leur seule injustice
Font et rompent les loix selon leur volonté
Et usurpant tous seuls à tort la seigneurie,
Qui de Dieu nous estoit en commun despartie
Nous ravissent, cruels, la chère liberté.

Je laisse maintenant l'incroyable tristesse
Que cette pauvre femme endure en sa grossesse
Le danger où elle est durant l'enfantement
La charge des enfans si penible et fascheuse
Combien pour son mary elle se rend soigneuse
Dont elle ne reçoit pour loyer que tourment.

Je n'aurois jamais fait si ne veux entreprendre

O Muses par mes vers de donner à entendre
Et nostre affliction, et leur grand cruauté ;
Puis en renouvellant tant de justes complaintes
J'ay peur que de pitié vos ames soient atteintes
Voyant que notre sexe est ainsi maltraicté.

Et quoy ? Voyons nous pas qu'ilz confessent eux mesmes
Si l'on se sent espris de quelque amour extreme,
Pour en estre delivre, il se faut marier,
Puis sans avoir esgard à serment ny promesse
Faire ensemble l'amour à divers maistresses
Et non en un endroict sa volonté fier.

TABLEAU CHRONOLOGIQUE 1530-1600

VOLUME I

VOLUME II

TEXTES CONTEMPORAINS	TEXTES DU VOLUME I		TEXTES DU VOLUME II	TEXTES CONTEMPORAINS
	BIBLE tr. Lefebvre d'Etaples	1530	AURELIO & ISABELLE J. de Florès/Anonyme	
	TRIUMPHES DE L'AMOUREUSE DAME J. Bouchet			
	L'ECONOMIC Xénophon/G. Tory	1531		
	LES ŒCONOMIQUES Aristote/S. Lowenborsch	1532	FLAMETTE Boccace/Anonyme	PANTAGRUEL Rabelais ADOLESCENCE CLEMENTINE Marot COMPTES AMOUREUX Jeanne Flore
	CONTROVERSES DES SEXE MASCULIN ET FEMININ G. du Pont de Drusac	1533		LA PRISON D'AMOUR Diego de San Pedro/Anon
	HECATOMPHILE Alberti/Anonyme	1534		GARGANTUA Rabelais
		1535	LA FIN DE FLAMETTE Juan de Florès/M. Scève	
INSTITUTIO CHRISTIANAE RELIGIONIS J. Calvin GOUVERNEMENT DE MARIAGE Plutarque/J. Lode JUGEMENT POETIQUE EN L'HONNEUR DES DAMES J. Bouchet		1536		BLASONS DU CORPS FEMININ

1537	DECLAMATION DE LA NOBLESSE ET EXCELLENCE DES DAMES — H.C. Agrippa/Anonyme		
1538	LE COURTISAN — Castiglione/J. Colin		LES ANGOISSES DOULOUREUSES — Hélisenne de Crenne
1539		ARNALTE ET LUCENDA — Diego de San Pedro/Herberay des Essars	
1540		AMADIS DE GAULE Ier livre — Montalvo/H. des Essars	
1541	LOUENGE ET HAULTESSE DU SEXE FEMININ — C. Agrippa/F. Habert; DIALOGUE MATRIMONIAL — Erasme/B. Aneau		
1542	LA PARFAICTE AMYE — Héroet; LE MESPRIS DE COURT — Guevara, A. Alaigre; L'AMYE DE COURT — La Borderie; L'INSTITUTION DE LA FEMME CHRESTIENNE — Vivès/P. de Changy	LE PHILOCOPE — Boccace/A. Sevin	
1543	LA CONTR'AMYE DE COURT — Ch. Fontaine	LE ROLAND FURIEUX — Arioste/Anonyme	
1544		L'ARCADIE — Sannazaro/J. Martin	LA DELIE — M. Scève
1545	LES AZOLAINS — Bembo/J. Martin	LE DECAMERON — Boccace/Le Maçon	RYMES — Pernette du Guillet
1546	DES VERTUS DES NOBLES DAMES — Plutarque : D. Sauvage; COMMENTAIRE SUR LE BANQUET — M. Ficin/Dubois		TIERS LIVRE — Rabelais; LE SONGE DE POLIPHILE — Colonna/J. Martin; LE PALMERIN D'OLIVE — Anonyme/J. de Voyer

1547	PROPOS RUSTIQUES N. du Fail THEAGENES & CHARICLEE Héliodore/H. Amyot		
1548	LAURE D'AVIGNON Pétrarque/V. Philieul		TRAITE DE LA DIGNITE DU MARIAGE Baduel/G. de la Garde
1549	AMADIS 8e LIVRE L'OLIVE Du Bellay LES ERREURS AMOUREUSES Pontus de Tyard		COLLOQUES Erasme/Cl. Marot
1550	ROLAND L'AMOUREUX Boiardo/J. Vincent PRIMALEON DE GRECE Anonyme/Vernassal		TRAITE DES SCANDALES Calvin UTOPIE Th. More/Le Blond DES DAMES DE RENOM Boccace/D. Sauvage
1551	EURIAL & LUCRESSE E.S. Piccolomini/Anon.		PHILOSOPHIE D'AMOUR Léon Hébreu/D. Sauvage
1552	LES AMOURS Ronsard - Baïf XIII sonnets de L'HONNESTE AMOUR Du Bellay QUART LIVRE Rabelais	LA PRISON D'AMOUR Diego de san Pedro/An.	
1553	PALMERIN D'ANGLETERRE Anonyme/J. Vincent AMADIS Xe LIVRE Gohorry		DISCOURS DES CHAMPS FAEZ Cl. de Taillemont
1554	FLORES & BLANCHEFLEUR A.N. de Reinoso/J. Vincent		ŒCONOMIQUES Aristote/G. Bounin
1555	ROLAND FURIEUX Arioste/Fournier ŒUVRES PROFANES Pétrarque/Philieul		LE FORT INEXPUGNABLE DE L'HONNEUR FEMININ F. De Billon

				ŒUVRES L. Labbé
1556				
1558	PRECEPTES NUPTIAUX Plutarque/La Tapie			DIVERS JEUX RUSTIQUES Du Bellay
1559			XVIII HISTOIRES TRAGI- QUES Bandello/Boaistuau	DAPHNIS & CHLOE Longus/Amyot
1560	SERMON DE CALVIN SUR LA MODESTIE DES FEMMES		CONTINUATIONS DES HIST TRAGIQUES Bandello/Belloforest FACETIEUSES NUICTS Straparole/Louveau	
1562	LE MESNAGIER Xénophon/F. de Ferris ?			LE MICROCOSME M. Scève
1563	DE LA BONTE ET MAUVAI- SETE DES FEMMES J. de Marconville	DECRETS DU CONCILE DE TRENTE /G. du Préau		
1564	L'ANTI-DRUSAC La Borie TRAITE DES DANSES Chesneau			
1565	LOIS CONNUBIALES Plutarque : J. de Marconville			
1566	SUR LA PARURE ET L'EDU- CATION DES FEMMES Terrullien/L. Daneau DOCTRINE ET INSTRUC- TION DES FILLES CHRES- TIENNES E. de Beaulieu			
1567		IMPOSTURES ET TROMPE- RIES DES DIABLES J. Wier/J. Grévin		
1571	LA MESNAGERIE - LES REGLES DE MARIAGE La Boétie Plutarque/			LE LABERINTHE D'AMOUR Boccace/Belleforest

	(col A)	(col B)	(col C)
1572	IMITATION DE QUELQUES CHANTS DE L'ARIOSTE Desportes		ŒUVRES MORALES Plutarque/Amyot
1573	CHANT XXVIII DU ROLAND FURIEUX Arioste/Rapin		INSTRUCTION POUR LES JEUNES DAMES A. Piccolomini/M. de Romieu (?)
1576	ROLAND FURIEUX Arioste/Chappuys POEMES Pierre de Brach LE NOUVEAU TRISTANT J. Maugin		
1578	LA PREMIERE SEPTMAINE Du Bartas	LA CELESTINE F. de Rojas/Lavardin LA DIANE Montemayor/N. Colin ŒUVRES de Mmes Des Roches	LA BEAUTE DES DAMES Firenzuola, J. Pallet L'EXCELLENCE DE LA FEMME Agrippa/L. Vivant
1579		SIX COMEDIES Larivey	INSTITUTION DE LA FEMME CHRESTIENNE Vivès/Turquet de Mayerne LA CIVILE CONVERSATION Guazzo/Chappuis TRAITE DES DANSES L. Daneau
1580	LES ESSAIS Montaigne L'ARIOSTE FRANCOYS Arioste/Boyssières	LE MIROIR DES COURTISANES Arétin/Anonyme	LE COURTISAN Castiglione/Chappuys LA DEMONOMANIE DES SORCIERS J. Bodin
1581	AMADIS DE GAULE XXIe LIVRE	ŒUVRES de Marie de Romieu	
1582	BRADAMANTE Robert Garnier		DIALOGUE ET DEVIS DES DEMOISELLES A. Piccolomini/F. d'Amboise

1583	DIALOGUES DE LA VIE CIVILE Giraldi Cinzio/Chappuys		
1584			LES CONTENTS Turnèbe ESSAI SUR LES SONNETS DU DIVIN PETRARQUE H. D'Avost
1585			LA FLAMETTE AMOUREUSE Boccace/G. Chappuys
1591			AMINTA T. Tasso/Le Loyer
1593		LE BERGER FIDELE Guarini/Brisset	
1595		MISERES DE LA FEMME MARIEE Dame Liébault HISTOIRE DES AMOURS FEINTES DE LAIS ET LAMIA Arétin/Anonyme	LA HIERUSALEM T. Tasso/Vigenere LA DELIVRANCE DE JERUSALEM T. Tasso/J. du Vigneau
1596			DIVINE COMEDIE Dante/B. Grancier
1600			LE GUZMAN D'ALFARACHE M. Aleman/Chappuys PETRARQUE EN RIME FRANCOISE Ph. de Maldeghem

DE LA NATURE D'AMOUR
M. Equicola/Chappuys

Table des matières

Table des illustrations

Achevé d'imprimer
sur les Presses de l'Université de Lille III

————

Façonné par
l'Imprimerie Centrale de l'Artois
rue Ste Marguerite à Arras

————

Dépôt légal — 4ème Trimestre 1984